Grandmaster Chess Move by Move

John Nunn

First published in the UK by Gambit Publications Ltd 2005
Reprinted 2006

Copyright © John Nunn 2005

ISBN 1 904600 34 4

DISTRIBUTION:
Worldwide (except USA): Central Books Ltd, 99 Wallis Rd, London E9 5LN.
Tel +44 (0)20 8986 4854 Fax +44 (0)20 8533 5821. E-mail: orders@Centralbooks.com
USA: Continental Enterprises Group, Inc., 302 West North 2nd Street, Seneca, SC 29678, USA.

For all other enquiries (including a full list of all Gambit chess titles) please contact the publishers, Gambit Publications Ltd, 6 Bradmore Park Rd, Hammersmith, London W6 0DS, England.
E-mail: info@gambitbooks.com
Or visit the GAMBIT web site at http://www.gambitbooks.com

Edited by Graham Burgess
Typeset by John Nunn
Cover image by Wolff Morrow
Printed in Great Britain by The Cromwell Press, Trowbridge, Wilts.

10 9 8 7 6 5 4 3 2

Gambit Publications Ltd
Managing Director: GM Murray Chandler
Chess Director: GM John Nunn
Editorial Director: FM Graham Burgess
German Editor: WFM Petra Nunn

Contents

Symbols

+	check
#	checkmate
!!	brilliant move
!	good move
!?	interesting move
?!	dubious move
?	bad move
??	blunder
Ch	championship
corr.	correspondence game
1-0	the game ends in a win for White
½-½	the game ends in a draw
0-1	the game ends in a win for Black
(D)	see next diagram

Introduction

I have published two previous collections of my best games. These were *Secrets of Grandmaster Play* (written jointly with Peter Griffiths, Batsford 1987) and *John Nunn's Best Games* (Batsford, 1995). The former book was reissued under my sole authorship by Batsford in 1997 with the title *Secrets of Grandmaster Chess*. This edition was entirely rewritten and contained a great deal of original and corrected analysis, plus a totally new section on my early career. *Secrets of Grandmaster Chess* covered my career up to 1985 and *John Nunn's Best Games* dealt with the period 1985-93. When I retired from tournament play in 2003, it was natural to produce a final volume on the last part of my career.

In writing this book I was mindful of the favourable reaction to my *Understanding Chess Move by Move* (Gambit, 2001); indeed, I have received several requests for a follow-up to this title. While *Grandmaster Chess Move by Move* is a traditional games collection, it has been written with the lessons of *Understanding Chess Move by Move* firmly in mind. The annotations are in a similar style to *Understanding Chess Move by Move*, although there are a few differences. The annotations are pitched at a slightly higher level than in *Understanding Chess Move by Move*, but the general principles are much the same. I have tried to comment on every significant moment in the game, keeping the explanations as general as possible and avoiding getting bogged down in too much analysis except where the position really demands it. A significant difference is that the games in *Understanding Chess Move by Move* were carefully chosen to illustrate various important themes, so although there were the messy details typical of any well-contested game, the various themes were clearly displayed. In practice few games are so clear-cut and most games involve a mixture of ideas as the players modify their plans in response to the development of the game. The games in this book show how various chess themes work out in real-world struggles. Before each game I mention a few key points to which the reader should devote particular attention, but the games in this book cannot be summarised in a few points.

Annotators often try to guess what was in a player's mind, but I generally try to avoid this when annotating third-party games because it is usually pure speculation. Even in those cases in which you have a chance to witness the post-mortem or discuss the game with the player, there is no guarantee that you will gain an accurate picture of the player's mental processes at the board. It is common for players to create retrospectively a logical structure for decisions that were actually made quite unsystematically. One of the advantages of annotating one's own games is that it is possible to speak from first-hand experience and in this book I have tried to be as honest as possible about subjective factors. This covers not only what I did or did not see at the board, but also such matters as the choice of openings.

Many readers of *Understanding Chess Move by Move* remarked that, despite my efforts, there was still too much analysis, so I think it is worth commenting on this point a little more. General principles can be very helpful in chess, as they can help you arrive at a list of 'candidate moves' without very much analysis. However, general principles also have severe limitations, not least because most of them have a large number of exceptions. Every move has pros and cons and is in accordance with some general principles but flouts others; how, then, do you decide which move to play? The answer is that you usually have to analyse. Annotators generally prefer to explain things in general terms and indeed this can be very helpful to readers since a good general principle can be worth pages of detailed analysis.

An excellent example may be quoted from Alekhine's notes in the New York 1927 tournament book. The following position arose in the game Vidmar-Nimzowitsch, New York 1927 (after the moves **1 d4 ♘f6 2 ♘f3 e6 3 c4 ♗b4+ 4 ♗d2 ♕e7 5 ♘c3 0-0 6 e3 d6 7 ♗e2 b6 8 0-0 ♗b7 9 ♕c2 ♘bd7 10 ♖ad1**).

Black continued **10...♗xc3 11 ♗xc3 ♘e4**, a manoeuvre which Alekhine approved of in the tournament book on the grounds that otherwise Black could only move a rook, whereas the position offers no clue as to where the rooks belong. This is an example of an annotation which is genuinely helpful in improving one's chess. In a position such as the above, one may easily start wondering about which rook to move, and whether to play the rook to d8 or e8. What Alekhine is saying is that if you start thinking like this, then it is a hint that you should try to find another plan which does not involve committing the rooks. Alekhine knew very well that all chess rules have exceptions, and his comment referred only to the specific position above, but the reader cannot fail to notice that his argument has much wider applicability. Note that Alekhine's remark is in direct contradiction to the advice found in many beginners' books, that you should castle and bring your rooks to d1 and e1 (or d8 and e8) as soon as possible.

Lesser annotators are often fond of propounding grand general principles, but these are often totally misleading. A typical example occurs in *Logical Chess Move by Move* (Simon & Schuster, 1957) by Irving Chernev (I have converted the descriptive notation to algebraic). His Game 3 goes **1 d4 d5 2 ♘f3 ♘f6 3 e3** and we read "Generally, it is dubious strategy to release one Bishop while shutting in the other". After **3...e6** he says "This deserves censure because it is a routine developing move which seems to take no thought of crossing White's plans". Yet a little later Game 8 went **1 d4 ♘f6 2 ♘f3 e6** ("...Black releases his King Bishop and does not commit himself to any specific line of defence.") **3 e3 d5** ("Black plants a Pawn firmly in the centre."). Now there is no censure for Black's play, only approval, but we have reached exactly the same position as the earlier game. What, then, can we make of Chernev's general principle on developing bishops? Basically, it's wrong. Many common openings flout it, such as the Queen's Gambit Declined, the Closed Ruy Lopez, the French and several lines of the Sicilian. Even in 1957 these openings were played by many World Champions.

If you are unlucky, the 'general principle' being put forward may not even apply to the specific position under discussion. Referring again to *Logical Chess Move by Move*, Game 12 goes **1 c4 e5 2 ♘c3 ♘f6 3 g3 d5! 4 cxd5 ♘xd5 5 ♗g2 ♘b6!** (his exclamation marks) and now we read "There is another bit of subtlety in the Knight's move, one that the modern master frequently utilizes. The Knight takes advantage of the Bishop's fianchetto development and bears down heavily on c4, *a square weakened by the bishop's absence*." The italics are Chernev's so he obviously considered this point important. However, it is absurd. White will inevitably play d3 (or possibly b3) to develop his c1-bishop, after which the knight cannot move to c4. Even if it could, it wouldn't attack anything and would be instantly driven away again. The game continued **6 ♘f3 ♘c6 7 0-0 ♗e7 8 d3 0-0**, reaching a standard position. The d3-pawn covers c4 and did so for the rest of the game, so this isn't even a case of annotation by hindsight. Chernev was trying to formulate a general principle, this time on the defects of the fianchetto development, but it's not one which has any contact with reality. Note also the "...modern master frequently utilizes", a typical attempt to give a nonsensical comment spurious validity. I had the awkward job of working on a new edition of this book issued by Batsford in 1998. It's always unpleasant to be an editor in this situation; there is a natural reluctance to alter the author's intention, but your primary duty is to the readers who are actually paying for the book, so if something is manifest nonsense then it has to be changed or removed. Thus you won't find the above excerpts in the Batsford edition. However, I was left with quite a headache and, indeed, I never again tackled the editing of such a book.

The main difference between Alekhine and Chernev is rather obvious: Alekhine was a world champion while Chernev only played in one high-class event, the 1942 US championship, in which he scored 6/15. Not all of Chernev's books are bad; he was clearly a chess enthusiast and when he stuck to elementary topics his effervescent writing style could be a benefit, but a player of his strength is unlikely to discover new general principles which somehow eluded great chess thinkers such as Tarrasch, Nimzowitsch and Réti. It is easy to be taken in by this type of annotation, which may appear to 'explain' a game, but which closer inspection reveals to be a tissue of superficiality. In the same way that pseudoscientific theories may appear convincing to those with little knowledge of science, 'pseudo-chess' books may appear convincing to their target audience. Unfortunately, such misleading chess books are distressingly common and whereas a belief in pseudoscience may not cost you rating points, a belief in pseudo-chess probably will.

General principles are often contradictory (rather like 'many hands make light work' and 'too many cooks spoil the broth') and you cannot follow all of them. Imagine you have the position after 1 e4 e5 2 ♘f3 ♘c6, but you don't know any opening theory. If you adhere to 'get castled quickly' then you will probably play 3 ♗c4 or 3 ♗b5; if you prefer to follow 'knights before bishops' then you will play 3 ♘c3; if you pay heed to 'control the centre' you might play 3 c3, hoping for 4 d4. In this case general principles might steer you away from 3 h3, for example, but they cannot help you decide between the many plausible options.

Another problem is that every move adheres to some general principles but contravenes others. Looking at a game in retrospect, it is easy to selectively quote general principles so that the winner's moves adhere to them, while the loser's moves flout them. This may give the impression that the game has followed a logical path from start to finish, but such annotations are totally misleading. Had the result of the game been reversed, the author would no doubt have chosen different general principles and criticized the moves he had earlier praised, and lauded those he had poured scorn on. Such 'annotation by result' is also regrettably common.

The conclusion is that, except for the most one-sided games, giving an accurate impression of a game requires a certain amount of concrete analysis. Where good and useful general comments are appropriate, I have made them (although I would not claim to equal Alekhine's insight), but if the correctness of a move depends on a tactical finesse deep in the analysis, I have given the analysis. I have gone to considerable effort to make my annotations in this book objective, so you will find quite a few question marks scattered around. I have used computer assistance in checking the analysis, mainly *Deep Fritz* and *Deep Junior* running on a computer with twin 2.8 GHz Xeon processors.

Opening annotations present a particular problem because giving a detailed theoretical coverage consumes a great deal of space and often only repeats material which may be found in specialized opening books. Therefore, in most cases I have restricted my opening remarks to a summary of the general ideas and the current theoretical conclusion. Some of the openings duplicate those found in *Understanding Chess Move by Move* and readers looking for a more detailed discussion of these openings may like to take a look in that book.

The bulk of the book consists of annotated games and game fragments interspersed with brief biographical snippets and tournament results. Near the end there are chapters featuring my study and problem compositions. The book concludes with two chapters on the state of the chess world and chess publishing, which would have broken up the main part of the book too much had they been included in their proper chronological places.

A compilation of games inevitably makes use of material which has appeared earlier in chess magazines and publications such as *Informator*, and this book is no exception. Some material has also appeared in other books by myself: Game 32 appeared in *Understanding Chess Move by Move* and parts of Games 19 and 30 appeared in *Secrets of Practical Chess* (Gambit, 1998). In all cases where notes have previously appeared, they have been rewritten and expanded for the present book. Studies 16-18 appeared in *Secrets of Pawnless Endings* (Gambit, 2002), study 19 in *Secrets of Rook Endings* (Gambit, 1999) and study 24 in *Endgame Challenge* (Gambit, 2002).

My previous games collection, *John Nunn's Best Games*, concluded with an extract from Bologan-Nunn, which was played in February 1993. Although I then briefly mentioned a couple of tournaments from the next few months, I was not able to give any games from these events, so I will start this book with the AEGON tournament in May 1993. The AEGON events were man vs computer tournaments held annually from 1986 to 1997. During the years I took part, the format was a Swiss system event in which an equal number of humans and computers took part, but with human vs human and computer vs computer pairings forbidden, so that each round was effectively a human vs computer match. The humans covered quite a wide range of playing strengths, and it was intended that the humans should have roughly the same average strength each year, so as to provide a benchmark by which the progress of the machines could be evaluated.

In 1993, man vs machine contests were something of a rarity, and the AEGON event attracted most of the leading chess programs. Looking back, it is interesting to see familiar names such as *Fritz* (which, however, often played under the name *Quest*). I competed at AEGON four times, from 1992 to 1995. In 1992 I scored 5/6, but in 1993, learning from my poor choice of openings the previous year, I managed 5½/6, tying for first with David Bronstein.

The following endgame is especially interesting as it includes many ideas typical of complex king and pawn endings: undermining the enemy pawn-structure, tempo-play, zugzwang and especially the prevention of counterplay (see White's 42nd move). It also shows how the calculation of such endings can be simplified by identifying key target positions.

Game 1
J. Nunn – *The King*
AEGON Man vs Machine, The Hague 1993

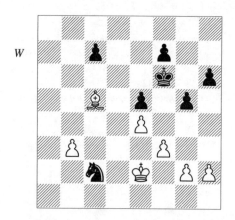

Material is equal, but Black's knight is badly placed. At any moment White can force a pawn ending by playing ♔d2, which obliges Black to reply ...♘d4. However, it is hard to say whether the resulting pawn ending is a win.

37 g3!

If White plays the immediate 37 ♔d2?, Black continues 37...♘d4 38 ♗xd4 exd4 39 b4 ♔e5 40 ♔d3 h5! (this is the key defence: Black pushes the pawn to h4, which stops White playing the undermining manoeuvre g3 and h4) 41

g3 h4 and is just in time to prevent h4 by White. Now White cannot make progress and the game is drawn.

It follows that White must improve his position before liquidating to a pawn ending. Advancing the g-pawn serves two purposes. Firstly, we have already seen that it is advantageous for both sides to occupy h4 with a pawn, and playing g3 gains a tempo towards that end. The second point is that after the exchange on d4 White might play f4, keeping Black's king out of e5 and depriving the d4-pawn of support.

37 ...   ♔e6

Essentially a waiting move. More active attempts also do not save the game:

1) 37...♘d4+ 38 ♗xd4 exd4 39 b4 and White wins as in the note to White's 40th move below.

2) 37...♘a1 (the knight cannot escape like this) 38 b4 ♘c2 (38...♘b3 loses to 39 ♗e3) 39 b5 *(D)* and now:

2a) 39...♔e6 40 ♔d2 (this leads to a forced win thanks to the advanced position of White's b-pawn) 40...♘d4 41 ♗xd4 exd4 42 ♔d3 ♔e5 43 f4+ (in this position White can dispense with

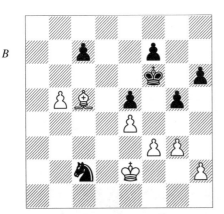

subtlety and head straight for the c7-pawn) 43...gxf4 44 gxf4+ ♔xf4 45 ♔xd4 h5 46 ♔d5 h4 47 ♔c6 and Black is too slow.

2b) 39...♘a1 40 ♔d3 (there is an alternative win by 40 b6 cxb6 41 ♗xb6 ♘c2 42 ♗c5 ♔e6 43 ♔d2 ♘d4 44 ♗xd4 exd4 45 f4 picking up the d4-pawn and winning; for example, 45...gxf4 46 gxf4 f5 47 e5 ♔d5 48 ♔d3 ♔c5 49 e6 ♔d6 50 ♔xd4 ♔xe6 51 ♔c5, etc.) 40...♘b3 41 ♔c4 ♘d2+ (41...♘a5+ 42 ♔d5 and White wins) 42 ♔d5 ♘xf3 43 ♗d6! cxd6 44 b6 and the b-pawn slips through.

3) 37...h5 is natural, again playing for the occupation of h4. However, White can now make use of the second point behind g3: 38 ♔d2 ♘d4 39 ♗xd4 exd4 40 f4! c5 (40...gxf4? 41 gxf4 is hopeless for Black because he no longer has the possibility of liquidating the h-pawns) 41 h4! (it is essential to prevent the exchange of h-pawns, since this would give Black's king a route to counterattack on the kingside; 41 ♔d3? h4 42 b4 cxb4 43 ♔xd4 hxg3 44 hxg3 gxf4 45 gxf4 ♔g6 46 ♔c4 ♘h5 47 ♔xb4 ♔g4 draws easily) 41...gxf4 42 gxf4 (now that the h5-square is blocked, Black's king cannot penetrate on the kingside) 42...♔e6 43 ♔d3 f5 (the only chance, or else White wins by ♔c4 followed by b4, picking up both Black's queenside pawns) 44 e5 ♔d5 (D).

We shall call this Position A, and it is a key position in the whole ending since it is a win for White whoever moves first. Clearly Black to play loses, since he must retreat his king, allowing ♔c4 followed by b4. The surprising feature is that White can win even if he is to move. It is true that both sides have protected passed pawns on the fifth rank, but the crucial difference is

that while White's e5-pawn is totally secure, Black's pawn-structure can still be undermined by a timely b4. However, putting this plan into action requires some finesse: 45 ♔d2! ♔c6 46 ♔c2 and now:

3a) 46...♔b5 47 ♔d3 ♔b6 48 ♔c4 ♔c6 49 b4 cxb4 50 ♔xd4 ♔b5 51 ♔d5 b3 (51...♔b6 52 ♔c4 wins for White) 52 e6 b2 53 e7 b1♕ 54 e8♕+ and White wins Black's queen.

3b) 46...♔b6 47 ♔d3 ♔b5 (White cannot win using only king manoeuvres, but in this position he can add an extra ingredient) 48 b4!! c4+ 49 ♔c2 (49 ♔d2 c3+ 50 ♔c1! also wins for White) 49...♔c6 50 ♔d2 ♔b5 51 e6 ♔c6 52 b5+ ♔d6 53 b6 and White will make a queen.

38   ♔d2

White has gained a vital tempo by playing g3 and this now wins.

38	...	♘d4
39	♗xd4	exd4 (D)

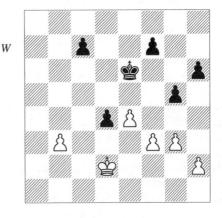

40   f4

40 b4 *(D)*, preventing ...c5, also wins:

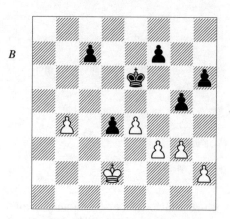

1) 40...♔d6 41 ♔d3 ♔e5 (41...c5 42 bxc5+ ♔xc5 43 h4 and White wins) 42 h4 c6 43 h5 f6 44 f4+ gxf4 45 gxf4+ ♔xf4 46 ♔xd4 ♔f3 47 e5 fxe5+ 48 ♔xe5 and the b-pawn promotes first.

2) 40...♔e5 41 ♔d3 h5 (41...f6 42 h4 h5 transposes) 42 h4! (here too White must prevent ...h4) 42...f6 (42...gxh4 43 f4+ ♔d6 44 gxh4 c5 45 b5 and White wins easily) 43 b5 (a position of reciprocal zugzwang) 43...gxh4 44 f4+ ♔d6 45 gxh4 ♔c5 46 f5! ♔xb5 47 e5 ♔c6 48 e6 ♔d6 49 ♔xd4 ♔c6 (49...♔e7 50 ♔d5 ♔e8 51 ♔c6 ♔d8 52 e7+ ♔xe7 53 ♔xc7 wins for White) 50 ♔c4 ♔d6 51 ♔b5 c5 52 ♔c4 ♔c6 53 e7 ♔d7 54 ♔xc5 ♔xe7 55 ♔c6 and Black will lose both his pawns.

40   ...   gxf4

40...c5 is met by 41 h4! (41 ♔d3? is wrong as it gives Black the chance to counterattack with his king: 41...gxf4 42 gxf4 ♔f6 43 b4 cxb4 44 ♔xd4 ♔g6 45 ♔c4 ♔h5 46 h3 ♔h4 47 e5 ♔h5! and draws) 41...gxf4 42 gxf4 ♔f6 transposes to the game.

41   gxf4   c5 *(D)*

Black must spend a tempo on this, otherwise his d4-pawn will be lost after b4, but now

White can seal the kingside. The alternative is 41...f5 (41...♔f6 loses to 42 b4) 42 e5 ♔d5 43 ♔d3 h5 (43...c5 44 h3 leads to Position A) 44 b4 h4 45 h3 c6 and now a simple triangulation does the trick: 46 ♔d2 ♔e6 47 ♔c2 ♔d5 48 ♔d3 c5 and White can win with either 49 b5 or 49 bxc5.

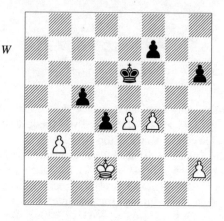

42   h4!

The winning move, preparing to meet ...♔f6 by h5. Thus Black's counterplay by ...♔f6-g6-h5 is prevented, and White has time to undermine Black's queenside pawns by b4. 42 ♔d3? only draws after 42...♔f6 43 b4 cxb4 44 ♔xd4 ♔g6 45 ♔c4 ♔h5 with a position which we saw in the note to Black's 40th move.

42   ...   ♔e7

42...f5 43 e5 is the same – White's king reaches c4 so he doesn't even need to use the White to play win from Position A.

43	♔d3	f5
44	e5	♔d7
45	b4	♔c6
46	bxc5	♔xc5
47	e6	1-0

The finish might be 47...♔d6 48 ♔xd4 ♔xe6 49 ♔c5 h5 50 ♔c6.

King and pawn endings which arise in over-the-board play are often quite simple to analyse, but if they are difficult, they tend to be very difficult. The above example shows how complex they can be and this poses serious problems when you have to play one with the limited time available over the board. If you can establish general principles then you may be able to reduce the amount of analysis substantially; in the above example, noting that each side would like to occupy h4 with a pawn is a big help.

You may also have to accept that you cannot analyse a king and pawn ending out to a definite result; in this case you have to make a general assessment. You may also have to be content with 'making progress' (for example, by gaining space) even if to begin with you cannot see a definite win. At home it may be possible to determine for sure if a position is winning, but aiming for perfection when you are actually at the board can be counterproductive.

After winning my first five games, I faced one of the leading programs in the last round. This game was a sign of things to come. Despite achieving a completely winning position, I learned for the first time how hard it can be to finish off a computer which finds the most resourceful defence at every turn.

Game 2
The King II – **J. Nunn**
AEGON Man vs Machine, The Hague 1993

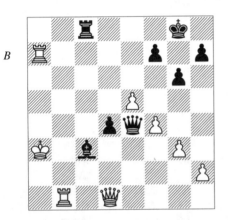

B

Despite White's extra material, he is in a losing position. His king is, of course, very exposed and most of his pieces are tied down to preventing a quick mate. This leaves him powerless to deal with the danger posed by the advancing d-pawn and Black's threats against White's kingside pawns. Yet it is in just such messy positions that it is hard to put the computer away. It was late in the evening, I was short of time and had already put in a huge effort to break down the computer's defences. Soon it all started to go wrong.

39 ... ♗d2!

There's nothing wrong with this very strong move. Black's main problem is that his bishop blocks the c-file and so prevents his rook from joining in the attack. The bishop move solves this problem and thus threatens the crushing 40...♖c2.

40 h3

This move totally confused me. I had been examining lines such as 40 ♖b3 ♗c1+ 41 ♔a2 d3! 42 ♕xd3 ♕g2+ 43 ♔a1 ♕g1 44 ♖a5 (44

♖a6 ♗xf4+ 45 ♔a2 ♗xe5 46 ♔a3 ♗g7 wins easily; with Black's bishop optimally placed on a diagonal leading to the white king, there is no hope of defending) 44...♕e1 45 ♖a6 ♗xf4+ 46 ♔a2 ♗xe5 47 ♔a3 ♗g7 and Black wins. Suddenly, the computer threw in the apparently irrelevant h3. In my confusion, I completely forgot my threat!

40 ... ♕d3+?

40...♖c2 wins at once. This careless check makes the win very difficult, if indeed possible at all.

41 ♔b2 (D)

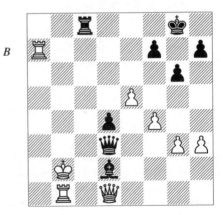

B

41 ... ♖b8+?

I thought I had seen a forced win, but it was not so. The best continuation is 41...♗c3+ 42 ♔a2 ♕xg3 43 e6! (the only try, playing to expose Black's king; 43 ♕g4? ♕f2+ 44 ♔a3 ♗b4+! 45 ♖xb4 ♕c2 46 ♕xc8+ ♕xc8 47 ♖bb7 d3 wins for Black; for example, 48 ♖xf7 d2 49 ♖g7+ ♔f8 50 ♖xh7 ♕c5+ 51 ♔b2 ♕xa7 52 ♖xa7 d1♕ and White's remaining pawns will fall) 43...♕f2+ (43...fxe6? 44 ♕b3 ♕g2+ 45 ♔a3 ♕c6 46 ♕b7 gives White enough counterplay to draw) 44 ♔b3 (44 ♔a3? d3 45 exf7+ ♔g7 46 f8♕+ ♔xf8 47 ♕a4 ♗d4 48 ♖xh7 ♕e3! and Black wins) 44...♗b2! (44...fxe6? 45 ♕f1 ♕e3 46 ♕a6 ♗b4+ 47 ♔a2 ♖c2+ 48 ♖b2 ♖xb2+ 49 ♔xb2 ♕xh3 50 ♕c8+ ♗f8 51 ♕c7 draws) 45 ♕d3 ♖c3+ 46 ♕xc3 dxc3 47 e7 ♕b6+ 48 ♔c2 ♕xa7 49 e8♕+ ♔g7 and Black has the advantage, although a win is far from certain.

| 42 | ♔a2 | ♕c4+ |
| 43 | ♖b3 | d3 |

Black threatens 44...♖xb3 45 ♕xb3 ♕c2+ and when I played my 40th and 41st moves I didn't see a defence.

44 ♖aa3!

The move I had overlooked. Now it is Black who has to fight for a draw.

| 44 | ... | ♖xb3 |

It would have been simpler to play 44...♗c3 45 ♔b1 ♖xb3+ 46 ♖xb3 (46 ♕xb3?? ♕e4 wins for Black) 46...d2 47 ♔c2 ♗a5+ 48 ♔b2 ♕d4+ and White cannot avoid the checks.

45	♕xb3	♕c2+
46	♕b2	♕c4+
47	♔b1	♗b4
48	♖a8+	♔g7
49	e6+	♔h6

49...f6 was also possible. After 50 ♖a7+ ♔h6 51 g4 ♕xf4 52 ♖d7 d2 53 ♕d4 d1♕+ 54 ♕xd1 ♕e4+ 55 ♔b2 ♕xe6 White has a nominal material advantage, but Black should have no trouble drawing. However, Black cannot play 49...♗c3? due to 50 exf7 and White wins.

| 50 | exf7 *(D)* | |

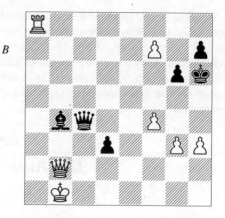

B

| 50 | ... | d2?! |

An inaccuracy. Black could have forced a clear draw by 50...♕e4 51 ♖d8 ♗c5! and there is no way to avoid perpetual check.

51 ♖d8

Now there is a forced sequence of checks leading to a queen ending with an extra pawn for White.

51	...	♕f1+
52	♔a2	♕a6+
53	♔b3	♕e6+
54	♔a4	♕a6+
55	♔xb4	♕b6+
56	♔c4	♕xd8
57	♕xd2	

Here the computer's operator offered a draw, which I accepted with some relief. After 57 ♕xd2 there are two possibilities: 57...♕c7+ 58 ♔d3 ♕xf7 59 g4 and 57...♕xd2 58 f8♕+ ♔h5 59 ♕e7 ♔h6. Both of these should lead to a draw, but Black would have to take care.

½-½

The following year's AEGON event saw a similar pattern. I won my first five games and achieved a completely winning position against *Zarkov 3.0* in the last round, only to slip up and allow the resourceful computer to snatch half a point. This led to a tie for first place between Larry Christiansen and myself. In 1995, the computers had become stronger and I lost two games to finish on 4/6. It seemed to me that the writing was on the wall and the computers would only become better and better. It is no fun to struggle more and more from year to year, and after AEGON 1995 I did not take part in any further man vs machine contests. Rather to my surprise, such events still occur from time to time. The two Kasparov vs *Deep Blue* matches are the most famous contests, but more recently there have been Kasparov vs *Junior* and Kramnik vs *Fritz* matches. In order to defeat Kasparov, IBM had to build a special-purpose machine and even then only succeeded with some degree of luck (Kasparov, of course, holds the view that the IBM team cheated, but there seems little evidence to support this), but the later events involved ordinary commercial programs running on powerful but off-the-shelf hardware. In late 2004, the humans tried their luck again with a team of Topalov, Ponomariov and Kariakin facing *Fritz*, *Hydra* (a special-purpose multiple-processor machine) and *Deep Junior*. The human team were by no means run-of-the-mill GMs; at the time of writing, Topalov is ranked third in the world while Ponomariov is an ex-FIDE world champion. Despite this, the machines crushed the humans by 8½-3½. Out of 12 games, the humans managed to win just one and, most embarrassing of all, *Fritz*, running on a 1.8 GHz notebook, managed to score 3½/4. We now have the situation in which a program you can buy in the local game shop, running on a standard notebook computer, can defeat almost any player in the world. The computers' dominance was only emphasized when, in 2005, Michael Adams lost 5½-½ in a match against Hydra. This event demonstrated that computers can play extremely well not only in wild, tactical struggles, but also in quiet positions.

Part of the reason for the computers' success is the inherently unfair nature of the competition. Computer programs have access to a vast openings library which is far larger than the equivalent human memory could ever be. Even if play should deviate from the computer's opening book, they can access a database of millions of practical games to determine which move has been most successful. Then, if you survive until the endgame, the computer is able to access its endgame databases. These allow it to play all 5-man and many 6-man endgames perfectly; moreover, if the computer sees a way to liquidate to a winning position from an endgame database, then it will take it. The computer's ability to access endgame databases within the analysis tree means that endgame databases affect a much wider range of positions than one might expect.

All these features have nothing to do with the basic chess-playing ability of the computer. What might be interesting is for the human 'chess engine' to face the computer 'chess engine', but that isn't what actually happens. The human has to face the machine's 'chess engine' plus several additional data access features, none of which correspond to any human ability. An additional point is that the computer's operator is able to modify the machine's behaviour from one game to the next. With just a couple of button presses, the computer can be switched from a positional style to an aggressive style, or its entire opening repertoire can be switched for another one. This makes it easy for the operator to customize the machine to exploit the weaknesses of each human opponent, while at the same time making it virtually impossible for the human to prepare for the computer.

All these factors make it hard to take any further interest in the increasingly one-sided man vs machine contests; the only way to render them interesting would be to limit the computer's data access in some way. However, quite apart from the obvious verification difficulties, even this would provide the humans with only a temporary stay of execution. The inexorable advance of computer hardware would eventually overcome the imposed limitations and then we would be back to square one.

Computers are very useful for chess preparation and analysis and, if used properly, for training. What you should not do is play games against them, since the result is bound to be demoralizing.

After the AEGON event, I spent two months devoted to writing, and then set off to Pardubice in the Czech Republic. This was a pleasant round-robin tournament, although when the wind was from a certain direction, an odd smell would drift over the town centre. When I asked about this, I was informed that the smell came from the explosives factory which was just down the road, This factory manufactured, amongst other things, Semtex, a favourite with terrorists. When the tournament started, I was concerned that I had not played against a human being for over five months, a fear which proved justified when I lost badly to Greenfeld in the first round. I spent the next few rounds trying to avoid a repeat of this disaster, but this run of draws came to an end in round 6.

The main themes in this game are White's space advantage and his grip on the dark squares resulting from the exchange of Black's dark-squared bishop at move 16. Black's only compensation is his actively-placed knight on e3. Although this knight allowed Black to set some traps (see move 26), his other pieces could not cooperate with it and White was able to reach a winning position. Although he then created unnecessary difficulties for himself, White eventually wrapped the game up.

Game 3
J. Nunn – I. Stohl
Pardubice 1993
Caro-Kann Defence, Advance Variation

1	e4	c6
2	d4	d5
3	e5	

Originally, this was played with the idea of meeting ...♗f5 with an aggressive plan involving g4 at some point. In the 1980s, some players, led by Nigel Short, introduced a more positional follow-up based on simple development. In this game White adopts the latter plan.

| 3 | ... | ♗f5 |

3...c5 is also quite a good reply. Black loses a tempo over the French, but has the advantage that his light-squared bishop may still be developed to f5 or g4.

4	♘f3	e6
5	♗e2	c5
6	0-0	

At the time this game was played, White normally preferred to support his centre with c3. Later on an alternative plan of playing ♗e3 rather than c3 became popular. This keeps open the option of playing c4 in one move and is currently thought more dangerous for Black.

| 6 | ... | ♘c6 *(D)* |

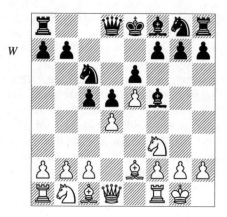

7   c3

I no longer believe that this naïve system promises White anything. In contrast to the French, the active position of his light-squared bishop relieves Black of many long-term positional worries. His only problem is how to develop his kingside pieces; if that is solved, he can look forward to instant equality.

| 7 | ... | cxd4 |

The safest route for Black. After the immediate 7...♘ge7 White has the interesting option 8 dxc5!?.

| 8 | cxd4 | ♘ge7 |
| 9 | b3 | |

White aims to complete the development of his minor pieces by ♗b2 and ♘bd2. The alternative is to play 9 ♗e3, but after 9...♗g4, followed by ...♘f5 and ...♗e7, Black finishes his kingside development without difficulty.

| 9 | ... | ♘c8 |

This is one way to solve the problem of Black's kingside development. It looks slightly artificial, but it is not bad. The knight will move to b6 where it might support queenside play by ...a5-a4, or it might move on to d7 to support ...f6. The most popular move here has been 9...♗e4, but to my mind the simplest line is 9...♖c8 10 ♗b2 ♘g6, taking advantage of the fact that f4 is no longer controlled. This continuation looks fine for Black.

| 10 | ♗b2 *(D)* | |

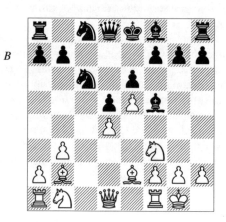

| 10 | ... | ♗e7 |
| 11 | ♘bd2 | |

11 ♘a3 followed by ♘c2-e3 is another possibility, but objectively speaking also promises White no advantage.

> **11 ... 0-0** *(D)*

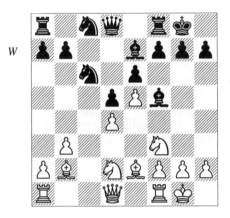

White has a slight space advantage, but given time Black will play ...f6 and gain more space for himself. White's most obvious problem is the knight on d2, which isn't doing anything active and currently has no decent square to move to. White could play ♖e1, followed by ♘f1-g3, but this is easily met by ...♗g6, when the knight isn't doing anything on g3. The alternative is to try to activate the knight on the queenside.

> **12 a3!?**

The only try for an advantage. 12 ♖c1?! ♘b4 and 12 ♘e1 ♕b6 are fine for Black.

> **12 ... h6?!**

Black aims to play ...f6, when ♘h4 is no longer dangerous due to ...♗h7, but this move is a definite inaccuracy. Black should not allow White to gain space on the queenside with b4 because then White can continue with ♘b3, aiming for c5. Black can hardly meet this by ...b6 because this would imprison his knight on c8. 12...f6? is even worse because of 13 ♘h4 fxe5 14 ♘xf5 ♖xf5 15 dxe5 (threatening 16 ♗g4) and now 15...♘xe5 just loses material to 16 g4.

12...a5! is simplest and best, just stopping White's plan dead in its tracks. In this case I think Black would have easy equality.

> **13 ♖c1?!**

Giving Black a second chance to play ...a5, but at the time neither player realized the importance of this. 13 b4 is more accurate.

> **13 ... f6?** *(D)*

This is the natural consequence of the previous move, but now White can gain the advantage. If Black allows White to execute his plan of queenside expansion, then he cannot equalize; for example, 13...♘b6 14 b4 a6 15 ♘b3 ♖c8 16 ♘c5 ♕c7 17 a4! (stronger than 17 ♕b3 ♘d7 or 17 ♕d2 ♘d7 18 ♕f4 ♖fd8) 17...♘d7 (Black must try to remove the c5-knight) 18 b5 ♘xc5 19 dxc5 ♘b4 20 ♕b3 ♗xc5 21 ♗d4 b6 22 a5 with an advantage for White. One line runs 22...♕b7 23 bxa6 ♘xa6 24 ♕b5 ♘c7 25 ♕b2 ♗xd4 26 ♘xd4 ♖b8 27 ♘xf5 (27 ♘c6 is met by 27...bxa5) 27...exf5 28 ♕c2 ♘e6 29 a6 and Black is under pressure. 13...a5 was still the right idea.

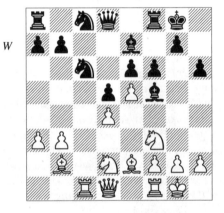

> **14 b4**

It cannot be wrong to continue with White's thematic plan, but there was even a second promising line: 14 ♗b5 ♘b6 (14...♕e8 15 ♖e1 is very uncomfortable for Black) 15 exf6 ♗xf6 16 ♗xc6 bxc6 17 ♖xc6 ♕e8 18 ♖c7 and Black does not have enough for the pawn. 14 exf6?! ♗xf6 15 ♘e5 might also be very slightly better for White, but after 15...♘8e7 Black has equalizing chances.

> **14 ... ♘b6**

Black cannot exchange on e5 first, because 14...fxe5 15 dxe5 ♘b6 16 b5 ♘a5 17 ♘d4 gives White a clear advantage.

> **15 exf6**

White must take account of Black's possible counterplay. Now that Black's knight is committed to b6, it can no longer move to e7 or d6, and so it is right to exchange on f6 and occupy e5. 15 ♘b3?! is wrong because after 15...♘c4! 16 ♗xc4 dxc4 17 ♖xc4 ♕d5 Black's strong pressure on the light squares gives him adequate compensation for the pawn.

| 15 | ... | &xf6 |
| 16 | &e5 (D) | |

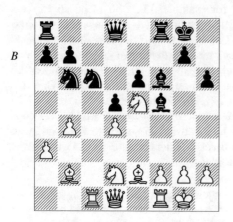

| 16 | ... | &xe5 |

It is understandable that Black does not want to allow White to take on c6, which would leave Black with a backward pawn on that square, but the exchange on e5 leaves him very weak on the dark squares. However, 16...&xe5 also gives White a very pleasant position after 17 dxe5 &e7 18 &b3 &c8 (18...&c4 just loses a pawn since after 19 &xc4 dxc4 20 &xc4, 20...&d3 fails to 21 &d4) 19 &d4, threatening &c5.

| 17 | dxe5 | a6 |

If White manages to establish control of d4 then his advantage will be indisputable, so Black has to prevent b5, driving the c6-knight away.

| 18 | &b3 | |

A good move. At some stage Black will have to play ...d4, or else White will surely blockade the d4-square. When this happens, the queen will both exert pressure on the e6-pawn and control the d3-square so that White can blockade the pawn with &d3.

| 18 | ... | &d7 |

The attack on e5 is no more than an inconvenience for White.

| 19 | &g3 | |

More accurate than 19 &e3, when 19...&b6 poses problems for White. The attempted tactical solution 20 &xb6 &xb6 21 &xa6 is dubious due to 21...&xa6 22 b5 &a4 23 bxc6 bxc6 24 &xc6 &b8 and White has no real winning chances in view of the opposite-coloured bishops and Black's active pieces. 19 f4 also gives

Black unnecessary chances after 19...&b6+ 20 &h1 a5 21 b5 &d4.

In the position after 19 &g3, the long-term prospects lie with White because of his two bishops and dark-square pressure. Therefore, White's priority is to limit Black's counterplay rather than advancing his own plans. Once Black has been reduced to passivity, White will not face any problems making progress. In practice, of course, matters are unlikely to be so simple. Black will probably realize that he is unlikely to survive by playing passively, and will at some stage make a break for activity, even if this means taking a risk. At this point the game is likely to become tactical, but if complications do arise, White will have a head start because of his positional assets. However, one should not be complacent in such situations. Just because right is on your side doesn't mean that the position will play itself; accuracy is still required.

| 19 | ... | d4 (D) |

Here is Black's attempt to break out. White was threatening to make progress by &b3, &fd1, and so on. Faced with the prospect of a lifeless position, Black decides to make use of his passed d-pawn. However, the risks involved in pushing the d-pawn are obvious: it has no pawn support, so it might easily be surrounded and lost. Also, in giving up control of c4 and e4, Black opens the door to the possibility of the d2-knight relocating to d6. After 19...&c8 or 19...&b6, White plays 20 &fd1 with a clear positional advantage, while 19...&g5 20 f4 &xg3 21 hxg3 is also unattractive for Black.

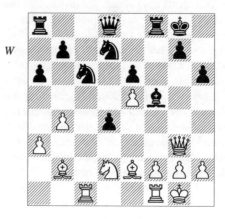

| 20 | f4 | |

First White must secure the e5-pawn.

20   ...   ♘b6

Covering c4, so for now White's knight cannot transfer to d6. Black also hopes to play ...♘d5-e3 at some stage. Note that 20...d3 21 ♗xd3 ♗xd3 22 ♕xd3 ♘dxe5 fails to 23 ♕c3 winning a piece.

21   ♗d3

21 ♗f3 followed by ♘e4 is also good, but I was happy to prevent Black's passed pawn from advancing any further.

21   ...   ♗xd3

21...♘d5 is no better, since after 22 ♘e4 ♘e3 23 ♖f2 ♖c8 24 ♖d2 White is ready to jump to c5 or d6 with his knight.

22   ♕xd3   ♘d5

23   g3

Defending f4 and threatening simply 24 ♘c4, which would both prevent ...♘e3 and take aim at the d6-square.

23   ...   ♘e3

Black has achieved his aim and brought his knight to the excellent square e3. Unfortunately, his other pieces are in no position to lend support to the knight.

24   ♖f2 (D)

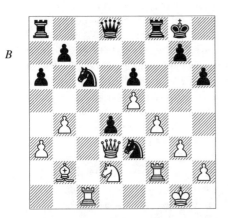

The plan is simply ♘e4 followed by ♖d2 and possibly ♘d6, cutting off support for the d4-pawn and winning it. There isn't much Black can do to prevent this.

24   ...   ♖c8

Or 24...♕d5 25 ♘f3 (25 ♘e4 ♘g4 26 ♖e2 ♘gxe5 27 fxe5 ♘xe5 28 ♕d1 may also be good for White, but there is no need to allow Black this degree of activity) 25...♘f5 26 ♖d2 ♖ad8 27 ♖c5 ♕d7 28 ♕e4 h5 29 ♘g5 and Black is under tremendous pressure. White

threatens both h3 followed by g4, and ♕e2 followed by ♕c4.

25   ♘e4

Heading for d6.

25   ...   ♖c7

25...♘f5 allows White strong pressure after 26 ♘c5 ♕e7 27 ♕e4 or 26 ♕b3 ♕e7 27 ♘c5 ♖fe8 28 h3, although there no immediate win. Black probably preferred the text-move because it sets a nasty trap.

26   ♕b3

At first sight 26 ♘d6? is simpler, winning the d4-pawn without any fuss. However, after the surprising reply 26...♘xe5! (I had overlooked this move during the game; instead I was worried about 26...♘f5 27 ♘xb7 ♘xb4, not noticing that 28 ♕xf5! wins a piece; perhaps I was lucky here, as if I had noticed 28 ♕xf5! I might have fallen into Black's trap) White must be content with a slight advantage after 27 ♕xd4, since 27 fxe5?! ♖xf2 28 ♔xf2 ♕f8+ 29 ♔e1 ♕f3 30 ♕e2 ♖xc1+ 31 ♗xc1 ♘g2+ 32 ♔d2 ♕c3+ 33 ♔d1 ♕b3+ 34 ♕c2 ♕f3+ only leads to a draw.

The move played, which takes aim at the exposed e6-pawn, should be sufficient for victory.

26   ...   d3 (D)

The alternatives are no better: 26...♕d5 27 ♕xd5 ♘xd5 28 ♘c5 ♖e8 29 ♘xb7 wins for White, 26...♖e7 27 ♘d6 ♕b6 28 ♖d2 will win the d-pawn within a few moves, and 26...♘d5 27 ♘d6 costs Black a pawn, as there is no real defence to the threats of 28 ♕d3 followed by ♗xd4 and 28 ♘xb7.

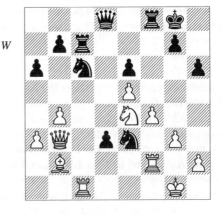

27   ♘d6!

White correctly refuses to be distracted by the e6-pawn and simply surrounds the dangerous d-pawn. After 27 ♕xe6+ ♔h8 28 ♕d6 (28 ♘d6?! runs into 28...♘d4!) 28...♖d7 29 ♕c5 ♘g4 30 ♖d2 ♖d5 Black has considerable compensation for the pawn.

     27   **...**   **♘d4**
     28   **♕xd3**

The pawn finally falls. Now Black is a pawn down with a bad position and the end should not be far off.

     28   **...**   **♖xc1+**
     29   **♗xc1**   **♘ef5** *(D)*

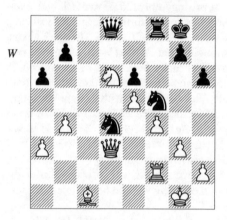

     30   **♗b2?!**

Although it does not change the result of the game, it would have been far simpler to play 30 ♘xb7 followed by ♘c5, with two extra pawns.

     30   **...**   **♘b5**
     31   **♖d2**   **♕b6+**
     32   **♔g2?!**

A further unnecessary complication, allowing Black to transfer his knight to d5 with gain of tempo. 32 ♔h1 would still have won without problems.

     32   **...**   **♖d8?**

After this there is no reprieve. 32...♘e3+ 33 ♔h3 ♘d5 was the only hope; White should still win, but it requires accurate play: 34 f5! ♘xd6 35 fxe6 ♘xb4 36 ♕xd6 ♘c6 37 e7 ♖e8 38 ♕e6+ ♔h8 39 ♗d4! ♕c7 (39...♕b5 40 ♖f2 ♘xe7 41 ♕f7 followed by e6 is winning for White) 40 ♗c5 ♘xe7 41 ♕f7 ♕c8+ 42 e6 ♘c6 43 ♖d7 ♖g8 44 ♕f5 with decisive pressure. One threat is 45 ♗e3 followed by ♗xh6.

     33   **♕b3** *(D)*

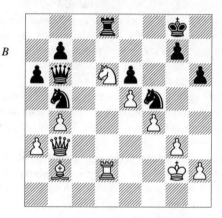

Once again the queen visits b3. This time the weakness of the e6-pawn dooms Black.

     33   **...**   **♕c6+**

33...♘c7 34 ♕c3 ♘b5 35 ♕c5 leads to an easily winning ending, while 33...♘fxd6 34 ♕xe6+ ♘f7 35 ♕xb6 ♖xd2+ 36 ♔h3 ♖xb2 37 e6 will leave White too far ahead on material.

     34   **♔h3**   **♕d7**

Or 34...♘fxd6 35 ♕xe6+ ♔f8 36 exd6 ♖xd6 37 ♕f5+ ♔g8 38 ♕g4! and White wins.

     35   **♘e4**   **1-0**

After 35...♘bd4 36 ♗xd4 ♘xd4 37 ♕e3 White will win a piece; for example, 37...♕d5 38 ♖d3! (even better than 38 ♘d6 ♘f5) 38...♖d7 39 ♘c5 ♖d8 40 ♘b3.

I had winning chances in each of the last three rounds, but unfortunately I wasn't able to convert any of these favourable positions into wins. Thus I ended on 50%, with just one win; not exactly a sparkling performance, but at least I had got back into the routine of playing chess without too much damage to my Elo rating.

My next event was the annual Lloyds Bank tournament in London. This year I was on good form and, apart from a loss to Tony Miles in round 6, I played reasonably well throughout. Of course, there were a couple of spots of luck, but it is practically impossible to do well in a large open tournament without having a bit of luck somewhere. My best two games came in the last two rounds.

In the following game, Black decided to leave his king in the centre. Many modern openings involve postponing or even abandoning castling, but this usually involves some risk. Here forceful play by White exposed Black's king, and although Black managed to create some last-ditch counterplay against White's queenside castled position, it was White's attack that struck first. It is also notable how both sides consistently played for the initiative without worrying too much about material.

Game 4
J. Nunn – M. Sadler
London (Lloyds Bank) 1993
Sicilian Defence, Najdorf Variation

1	e4	c5
2	♘f3	d6
3	d4	cxd4
4	♘xd4	♘f6
5	♘c3	a6
6	♗e3 *(D)*	

This line against the Najdorf has had an up-and-down history. Popular in the 1970s, it fell into a decline during the 1980s before regaining the limelight in the mid-1990s. Currently it, together with its close relative 6 f3, may be regarded as White's main continuation against the Najdorf.

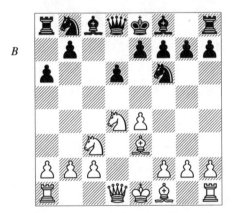

B

6	...	e5

True Najdorf players usually prefer to meet 6 ♗e3 by ...e5, because the whole point of 5...a6 is to prepare ...e5, and they will generally play ...e5 against any white 6th move which reasonably allows it. This also has the practical benefit that they need not study lines of the Scheveningen (which would arise after 6...e6). In addition to pushing the e-pawn, Black has a third important option in 6...♘g4, when there is a great deal of theory after the reply 7 ♗g5. However, some

players like to tease Black with 7 ♗c1, when there is nothing better than 7...♘f6; they then continue 8 f3, and only then ♗e3, a move-order which cuts out ...♘g4 at the cost of allowing Black some other possibilities.

7	♘b3	

7 ♘f3 was quite popular for a time in the early 1980s, but this move has now almost disappeared from practice.

7	...	♗e6

Covering the important d5-square. If White is careless, Black might be able to push his d-pawn under favourable circumstances.

8	f3	

White's basic strategy involves control of d5 coupled with a kingside pawn advance. Black must develop queenside counterplay quickly or he risks being crushed.

8	...	♘bd7

For detailed coverage of this opening, you should look in a theory book such as the excellent *The English Attack* by Tapani Sammalvuo (Gambit, 2004). One line which was undreamed of at the time this game was played is 8...h5. Although it looks odd, this prevents White's main plan of g4-g5; the drawback is that Black will find it harder to safeguard his king. 8...♗e7 is the other main continuation, aiming to castle before deciding how to develop queenside counterplay. However, many players dislike castling into White's coming attack and prefer to leave the king in the centre for the time being; such players generally prefer the text-move.

9	g4 *(D)*	

There are many finesses of move-order in this opening. If White tries to reach the game position by 9 ♕d2 b5 10 g4 (10 a4 is the most popular move, but at the time this game was played it was believed to give White no advantage; these days things are not so clear, and although theory extends well past move 20, no definite verdict can be given) then Black can play 10...♘b6, preparing to meet 11 g5 by 11...♘fd7 and thus avoiding having the knight sidelined at h5.

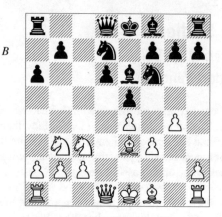

B

9 ... ♗e7

Black decides to transpose into an early ...♗e7 line. There are two other important continuations:

1) At the time this game was played, 9...♘b6 was held to be inaccurate based on the logic that ...♘c4 is only dangerous if Black can recapture on c4 with the b-pawn, and thus Black should play ...b5 before ...♘b6. However, 9...♘b6 has since been played by several strong players, including Garry Kasparov, so presumably this logic isn't as clear-cut as was once believed.

2) 9...b5 10 g5 b4 is a critical continuation which has been played frequently in recent years. Curiously, although this line appears perfectly natural, there isn't a single example of it in MegaBase 2004 dating from before 1998.

10 ♕d2

Having persuaded Black to forego playing an early ...b5, White transposes back to normal lines. There is nothing better since 10 g5 ♘h5 11 ♕d2 ♘f4! 12 ♗xf4 (12 h4 h6 is also awkward for White) 12...exf4 13 ♕xf4 ♗xg5 14 ♕xd6 ♗e7, followed by ...♗h4+ and ...0-0, gives Black fantastic compensation for the pawn.

10 ... b5?!

In his book *The English Attack* (mentioned above), Sammalvuo comments that this move "...was virtually refuted by John Nunn more than two decades ago, but still even grandmasters

play it occasionally. Even stranger is that some players seem to have forgotten about the refutation (11 a4!) and have opted for other lines." Very true. There are two alternatives:

1) 10...h6 aims to prevent White's g5 directly. The disadvantage is that it makes it harder for Black to castle kingside, since White would have an automatic breakthrough with h4 and g5. Although fairly popular in the mid-1990s, this line has now fallen into some theoretical disrepute and is played only rarely.

2) 10...0-0 is the soundest move, transposing to a standard position from the 8...♗e7 move-order.

11 a4!

This is the critical test of 10...b5. 11 g5 is less dangerous since 11...♘h5 (11...b4 12 ♘e2 ♘h5 13 ♘g3 gives White some advantage) 12 0-0-0 0-0 transposes into a line which offers Black fair equalizing chances.

11	...	b4
12	♘d5	♗xd5
13	exd5	(D)

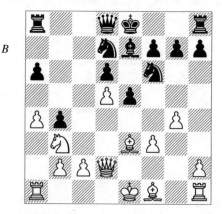

B

I believe that this position is favourable for White. The tactical justification for his play is that the obvious 13...♘b6 allows White to win a piece with the tricky tactical line 14 a5! ♘bxd5 15 g5 ♘xe3 16 gxf6 ♗xf6 17 ♕xe3 ♗h4+ 18 ♔d1. Then White has the advantage as Black doesn't have enough for the piece, although the technical task facing White is by no means easy.

13 ... ♕c7

Another possibility is 13...0-0 but then 14 g5 ♘h5 15 ♖g1 f5 16 ♕xb4 f4 17 ♗f2 ♖b8 18 ♕e4 ♗xg5 19 ♗d3 g6 20 0-0-0 ♘g7 21 ♕e1 ♘f5 22 ♗xf5 ♖xf5 23 ♘a5, heading for c6, was good for White in Nunn-Morris, Manchester 1980 (the game Sammalvuo referred to in which 11 a4! was introduced). Sadler tries a different idea.

14   g5   ♘h5 *(D)*

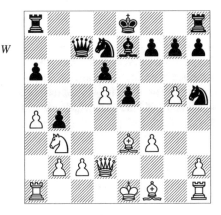

15   0-0-0

Strategically, White has a clear advantage. The b4-pawn is weak, and it is awkward to defend because ...♖b8 leaves a6 *en prise*, while ...a5 allows White to play ♗b5. Moreover, the h5-knight is out of play.

15   ...   ♘f4

Black offers a pawn in the hope of gaining some counterplay. 15...0-0 was perhaps a better attempt at a pawn sacrifice. If White is greedy and continues 16 ♕xb4 then Black develops a dangerous initiative after 16...♖fc8 (not, however, 16...♖ab8? allowing 17 ♕a5) 17 ♖d2 (17 ♗d3 ♖ab8 18 ♕e4 ♘hf6! 19 gxf6 ♘xf6 is fine for Black) 17...♖ab8 18 ♕a3 ♘b6 threatening 19...♘xd5. Therefore, White should prefer either 16 ♖g1, intending ♖g4, or simply 16 a5 blocking the queenside and fixing the weak pawns on b4 and a6. In both cases White retains a definite advantage.

16   h4

Better than 16 ♗xf4 exf4 17 ♕xf4 0-0, with ...♘e5 and possibly ...f6 to come, when Black has potential counterplay on the dark squares. If White could play ♗xf4 followed by ♘d4-c6 then Black would be in serious trouble, but the exchange on f4 frees the e5-square, so that ♘d4 may be met by ...♘e5.

16   ...   h6 *(D)*

Black seeks counterplay, but now his king is effectively committed to staying in the centre.

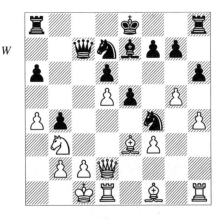

17   ♖g1

There were other tempting possibilities; for example, 17 ♗xf4 exf4 18 g6 0-0 (18...♗f6 19 gxf7+ ♔xf7 20 ♕xf4 is very good for White) 19 gxf7+ ♖xf7 20 ♗h3 ♔h8, when Black has weak squares on c6 and e6 and White can win a pawn on b4. However, it allows Black's bishop to become active on the long diagonal and I decided to maintain the pawn on g5 and thereby restrict the e7-bishop, even though this gives Black the h-file.

17   ...   hxg5
18   hxg5   ♖h4

Black must seek active play or he will lose a pawn at b4 or f4 without gaining any compensation.

19   ♔b1

The idea is that Black has no constructive moves, so White can afford to take his time; for example, White wins a piece in the event of 19...♘b6 20 ♕f2 ♘bxd5 21 ♗xf4. Even in very sharp positions, it is sometimes worthwhile taking time out for a consolidating move, although there is no excuse for laziness; one must check carefully to make sure that the extra tempo won't benefit the opponent.

19   ...   ♕d8

Black cannot sit back and wait while White gradually improves his position, so he decides to precipitate a crisis by attacking g5. It often happens that such an attempt by the defender triggers an eruption of tactics. White must find the right reply to maintain his advantage.

20   ♘d4!

With the deadly threat of 21 ♘c6. Black cannot reply 20...♘xd5 because of 21 ♘c6 ♘xe3 22 ♘xd8 ♘xd1 23 ♘c6 trapping the knight.

20...♗xg5 21 ♘f5 ♖h8 22 ♕xb4 followed by ♘xd6+ is equally hopeless for Black, so the reply is forced.

20   ...   exd4
21   ♗xf4   ♘b6

If White is permitted to consolidate with ♗g3, followed by f4, then the b4- and d4-pawns will inevitably fall, so Black must try to whip up a quick attack against White's relatively undefended king position. 21...♘e5 is bad due to 22 ♗g3 ♘xf3 23 ♕g2 ♘xg1 24 ♗xh4, trapping the knight.

22   ♗g3

After some sharp complications this turns out to be very good for White, but there was a second strong continuation in 22 ♕xd4 ♘xa4 (22...♘xd5? 23 ♕xd5 ♖xf4 24 ♖h1 is crushing) 23 ♕xg7! (not 23 ♕xb4? ♘xb2, however) with the point that 23...♖xf4 24 ♗h3! gives White a decisive attack.

22   ...   ♘xa4 (D)

The only chance. Passive moves are hopeless; for example, 22...♖h5 23 ♕xb4 ♘xd5 (23...♖xg5 24 ♖h1 ♖xg3 25 ♖h8+ ♗f8 26 ♖e1+ ♔d7 27 ♖xf8 ♕xf8 28 ♕xb6 wins for White) 24 ♕xd4 ♖xg5 25 ♖h1 ♔d7 26 ♗h4 and Black's position collapses.

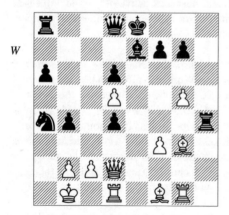

23   ♗c4!

The strongest move, deploying the bishop for the defence of White's king. 23 ♗xh4? is wrong and leads to a draw after 23...♘c3+ 24 ♔c1 (24 bxc3? bxc3 costs White his queen) 24...♘a2+ (after 24...♕a5? 25 ♕e1! White has winning chances) 25 ♔b1 ♘c3+ with perpetual check.

23 ♕xb4 was another possibility, but this is not entirely clear after 23...♘xb2 (23...♘c3+

24 bxc3 ♖b8 25 ♗xh4 dxc3 26 ♖d4 defends, since 26...a5 is met by 27 ♗b5+) 24 ♕xb2 (the only move) 24...♖b8 25 ♗xh4 ♖xb2+ 26 ♔xb2 and here the question is whether White is able to avoid perpetual check. The main line runs 26...♕b6+ 27 ♔c1 d3 (otherwise ♖d3 defends) 28 ♗xd3 (28 ♖g4 ♕e3+ 29 ♖d2 ♕xf3 is awkward for White) 28...♕e3+ 29 ♔b1 ♕b6+ 30 ♔a2 ♕a5+ 31 ♔b3 and, despite the apparently exposed position of White's king, Black cannot keep the checks going; for example, 31...♕b6+ 32 ♔c3 ♕c5+ (or 32...♕a5+ 33 ♔d4) 33 ♗c4 ♕e3+ 34 ♔b2. Therefore Black should try 31...♕xd5+ followed by ...♕xf3, recovering some material, although White has good winning chances once his pieces become coordinated. Not surprisingly, I disliked the idea of advancing my king to d4 and, in any case, the move played is objectively stronger.

23   ...   ♘c3+

Black cannot back out because 23...♖h5 24 f4 (24 ♕xd4 ♖xg5 25 f4 ♖xg3 26 ♖xg3 ♗f6 is less clear-cut; White's priority should be to keep Black's bishop out of f6) 24...♕b6 25 ♗b3 ♘c5 26 ♕xd4 ♔f8 27 ♖h1 gives White a winning attack.

24   bxc3 (D)

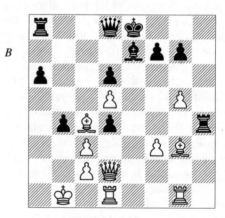

24   ...   dxc3

Once again Black doesn't have much choice, because 24...bxc3 25 ♕c1 ♖b8+ (25...♕b6+ 26 ♗b3 a5 27 ♔a1 a4 is no better, because after 28 ♕a3 Black must waste time moving the rook from h4, whereupon ♗c4 followed by ♖b1 repels the attack; 25...d3 is met by 26 ♗xh4 and Black has nothing dangerous) 26 ♗b3 a5 27 ♕a3 consolidates the extra piece. The move played not only attacks the queen, but also sets up the twin threats of 25...♖xc4 and 25...♕a5 followed by ...♕a3. However, with accurate play White has a forced win.

25   ♕e2!

The only move.

25   ...   ♕a5

At first sight White is in serious trouble, because both ♗xd6 and ♖d(or g)e1 are met by ...♖a7, and then there is no obvious way to prevent ...♕a3 followed by mate. In fact, there are two refutations of Black's play, the second of which I discovered only after the game. Since I had just 15 minutes left on my clock, I was content to check the win I had already discovered rather than search for a second one!

26   ♖de1   ♖a7 (D)

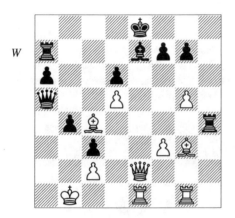

27   ♗f4!

This is the point of White's play. He is ready to meet ...♕a3 by ♗c1, and if Black plays 27...♖xf4 then 28 ♖h1 leaves Black totally helpless against the threat of ♖h8+. Without the possibility of ...♕a3, Black's attack is easily repulsed. I was very happy with this attractive combination, but when I got home I discovered that there was a 'cook', namely the equally attractive 27 ♗xa6!. At first sight it looks mad to open the a-file for Black's rook, but in fact there is no defence. The threat is 28 ♕b5+, and after 27...♕xa6 (27...♔f8 fails to 28 ♕b5) 28 ♕xa6 ♖xa6 29 ♗xh4 Black simply loses a rook, so he must play 27...♕a3 28 ♕b5+ ♖d7, when White has a choice of mates, either by 29 ♕b8+ ♖d8

30 ♗b5+ ♔f8 31 ♕xd8+ ♗xd8 32 ♖e8# or 29 ♖xe7+ ♔xe7 30 ♖e1+ ♔f8 31 ♕b8+.

27   ...   b3

The last fling, but now the attack is easily parried.

28   ♗xb3

Clearer than 28 cxb3 ♖xf4 29 ♖h1 c2+ (Black must deflect a piece from the e-file, or else ♖h8+ is crushing) 30 ♕xc2 (30 ♔b2 c1♕+ 31 ♖xc1 ♖d4 32 ♖c3 should also win) 30...♖h4 and Black fends off the immediate threats, although White can still win with accurate play: 31 ♕e2 ♖xh1 32 ♖xh1 ♔d7 33 ♖h8 (threatening g6) 33...g6 34 f4, followed by ♕g4+, with a decisive attack.

28   ...   ♖b7 (D)

A last chance, hoping for 29 ♖h1? ♖xh1 30 ♖xh1 ♕a3 31 ♗c1 ♖xb3+ 32 cxb3 ♕xb3+ 33 ♔a1? (33 ♗b2 should still win in the long run) 33...c2! and, rather surprisingly, White can only prevent mate by giving away a whole rook with 34 ♖h8+ and 35 ♖b8.

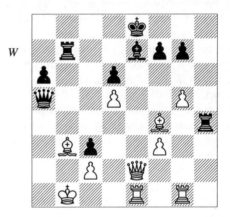

29   ♖g4

This move prevents the above line because White is threatening mate on e7 and so Black has no time for ...c2. 29 ♗xd6 ♖a4 30 ♕xe7+ ♖xe7 31 ♗xa4+ ♕xa4 32 ♖xe7+ ♔d8 33 ♖g4 also wins.

29   ...   ♖xg4

30   fxg4   ♕b4

31   ♕xa6   1-0

After 31...♔f8 the simplest win is by 32 ♖xe7 ♔xe7 33 ♗xd6+ ♕xd6 34 ♕xb7+.

In the next game, White played the opening passively, allowing Black not only to equalize but even to hope for an advantage. In the early middlegame Black offered an exchange sacrifice which

White accepted only reluctantly since it involved surrendering the fianchettoed bishop in front of his king. Such bishops often have a value greater than their nominal 3 points, and so it proves here. Black was able to attack along the weakened long diagonal, and with his queen and bishops operating in tandem, Black's threats soon proved overwhelming.

Game 5

S. Conquest – J. Nunn

London (Lloyds Bank) 1993
Sicilian Defence, 2 d3

1	e4	c5
2	d3	

This can lead to a normal Closed Sicilian, but Conquest adopts a passive opening strategy which gives him no real chance for an advantage. When confronted with something very unusual in the opening, the main trap you can fall into is to become too ambitious. Instead of simply continuing with 'normal' moves, you start to look for a 'refutation'. The result may only be to justify your opponent's play. It is usually best to stick to general opening principles; in this game Black is content simply to develop his pieces and occupy the centre. Nor does Black aim for too much; it requires truly bad play by White to give Black an opening advantage, and White's play is not really bad – it's just lacking in ambition. This means that although Black can reasonably hope to achieve comfortable equality, he should not expect to gain an advantage from the opening.

2	...	♘c6
3	g3	

3 ♘c3 is more likely to lead to a standard system.

3	...	d5

Taking advantage of White's omission of ♘c3 to stake a claim in the centre.

4	♘d2

The alternative is 4 exd5 ♕xd5 5 ♘f3 ♘d4 6 ♗g2 and now:

1) 6...♕e6+ 7 ♗e3 ♘f5 8 ♕e2 ♘xe3 9 fxe3 g6 10 ♘c3 ♗h6 11 e4 ♘f6 is unclear, Davies-Chandler, Blackpool Zonal 1990.

2) 6...♗h3 (this allows White a forced draw if he wants one) 7 ♗xh3 (7 0-0 ♗xg2 8 ♔xg2 is also equal) 7...♘xf3+ 8 ♔f1 ♘d2+ 9 ♔g1 ♘f3+, Davies-Renet, European Team Ch, Haifa 1989 and several other games.

4	...	♘f6
5	♗g2	e5 (D)

The most direct strategy. Black heads for a reversed King's Indian with a tempo less. Normally this would be a risky strategy, but here White is already committed to the slightly passive ♘d2, which prevents him from using his extra tempo effectively. In a number of games Black played 5...dxe4 6 dxe4 e5 7 ♘gf3 ♗e7 8 0-0 0-0 9 c3 ♕c7, but the early exchange on e4 is not necessary and only serves to improve White's position.

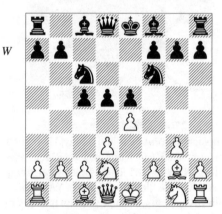

6	♘e2

In Arencibia-Kramnik, Biel Interzonal 1993, White continued 6 exd5 ♘xd5 7 ♘gf3 g6 8 0-0 ♗g7 9 ♘c4 0-0 10 ♖e1 ♖e8 11 ♘g5, whereupon Black played the curious 11...♖f8. This turned out well, because the continuation 12 c3 h6 13 ♘e4 b6 14 a4 ♗e6 15 h4 ♕e7 16 a5 f5 17 ♕a4 fxe4 18 ♕xc6 ♖ac8 19 ♕d6 ♕f6 20 ♖xe4 ♖cd8 21 ♕c6 ♘e7 22 ♕a4 ♕xf2+ 23 ♔h1 ♕xg3 24 ♗e3 ♘f5 25 ♖g1 ♘xh4 26 ♘xe5 b5 0-1 gave Kramnik a rapid victory. I expect that if White had repeated moves by 12 ♘f3, Black

B

fall) 43...♕f2+ (43...fxe6? 44 ♕b3 ♕g2+ 45 ♔a3 ♕c6 46 ♕b7 gives White enough counter-play to draw) 44 ♔b3 (44 ♔a3? d3 45 exf7+ ♔g7 46 f8♕+ ♔xf8 47 ♕a4 ♗d4 48 ♖xh7 ♕e3! and Black wins) 44...♗b2! (44...fxe6? 45 ♕f1 ♕e3 46 ♕a6 ♗b4+ 47 ♔a2 ♖c2+ 48 ♖b2 ♖xb2+ 49 ♔xb2 ♕xh3 50 ♕c8+ ♗f8 51 ♕c7 draws) 45 ♕d3 ♖c3+ 46 ♕xc3 47 e7 ♕b6+ 48 ♔c2 ♕xa7 49 e8♕+ ♔g7 and Black has the advantage, although a win is far from certain.

| 42 | ... | ♔a2 ♕c4+ |
| 43 | ♖b3 | d3 |

Black threatens 44...♖xb3 45 ♕xb3 ♕c2+ and when I played my 40th and 41st moves I didn't see a defence.

44 ♖aa3!

The move I had overlooked. Now it is Black who has to fight for a draw.

44 ... ♖xb3

It would have been simpler to play 44...♗c3 45 ♔b1 ♖xb3 46 ♕xb3?? ♕e4 wins for Black) 46...d2 47 ♔c2 ♗a5+ 48 ♔b2 ♕d4+ and White cannot avoid the checks.

45	♖xb3	♕c2+
46	♕b2	♕c4+
47	♗b1	♗b4
48	♖a8+	♔g7
49	e6+	♔h6

49...f6 51 g4 ♕xf4 52 ♖d7 d2 53 ♖d4 d1♕+ 54 ♔xd1 ♕e4+ 55 ♔b2 ♕xe6 White has a nominal material advantage, but Black should have no trouble drawing. However, Black cannot play 49...♔c3? due to 50 exf7 and White wins.

50 exf7 (D)

50 ... d2?!

An inaccuracy. Black could have forced a clear draw by 50...♕e4 51 ♖d8 ♗c5! and there is no way to avoid perpetual check.

51 ♖d8

Now there is a forced sequence of checks leading to a queen ending with an extra pawn for White.

51	...	♕f1+
52	♔a2	♕a6+
53	♔b3	♕e6+
54	♔a4	♕a6+
55	♔xb4	♕b6+
56	♔c4	♕xd8
57	♕xd2	

Here the computer's operator offered a draw, which I accepted with some relief. After 57 ♕xd2 there are two possibilities: 57...♕c7+ 58 ♔d3 ♕xf7 59 g4 and 57...♕xd2 58 f8♕+ ♔h5 59 ♕e7 ♔h6. Both of these should lead to a draw, but Black would have to take care.

½-½

The following year's AEGON event saw a similar pattern. I won my first five games and achieved a completely winning position against *Zarkov 3.0* in the last round, only to slip up and allow the resourceful computer to snatch half a point. This led to a tie for first place between Larry Christiansen and myself. In 1995, the computers had become stronger and I lost two games to finish on 4/6. It seemed to me that the writing was on the wall and the computers would only become better and better. It is no fun to struggle more and more from year to year, and after AEGON 1995 I did not take part in any further man *vs* machine contests. Rather to my surprise, such events still occur from time to time. The two Kasparov *vs Deep Blue* matches are the most famous contests, but more recently there have been Kasparov *vs Junior* and Kramnik *vs Fritz* matches. In order to defeat Kasparov, IBM had to build a special-purpose machine and even then only succeeded with some degree of luck (Kasparov, of course, holds the view that the IBM team cheated, but there seems little evidence to support this), but the later events involved ordinary commercial programs running on powerful but off-the-shelf hardware. In late 2004, the humans tried their luck again with a team of Topalov, Ponomariov and Karjakin facing *Fritz*, *Hydra* (a special-purpose multiple-processor win. At home it may be possible to determine for sure if a position is winning; but aiming for perfection when you are actually at the board can be counterproductive.

After winning my first five games, I faced one of the leading programs in the last round. This game was a sign of things to come. Despite achieving a completely winning position, I learned for the first time how hard it can be to finish off a computer which finds the most resourceful defence at every turn.

Game 2
The King II – J. Nunn
AEGON Man vs Machine, The Hague 1993

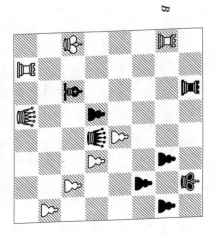

B

Despite White's extra material, he is in a losing position. His king is, of course, very exposed and most of his pieces are tied down to preventing a quick mate. This leaves him powerless to deal with the danger posed by the advancing d-pawn and Black's threats against White's kingside pawns. Yet it is in just such messy positions that it is hard to put the computer away. It was late in the evening, I was short of time and had already put in a huge effort to break down the computer's defences. Soon it all started to go wrong.

39 ... Bd2!

There's nothing wrong with this very strong move. Black's main problem is that his bishop blocks the c-file and so prevents his rook from joining in the attack. The bishop move solves this problem and thus threatens the crushing 40...Rc2.

40 h3

This move totally confused me. I had been examining lines such as 40 Rb3 Rc1+ 41 Ka2 d3! 42 Qxd3 Qg2+ 43 Ka1 Qg1 44 Ra5 (44 Ra6 Bxf4+ 45 Ka2 Bxe5 46 Ka3 Bg7 wins easily; with Black's bishop optimally placed on a diagonal leading to the white king, there is no hope of defending. 44...Qe1 45 Ra6 Bxf4+ 46 Ka2 Bxe5 47 Ka3 Bg7 and Black wins. Suddenly, the computer threw in the apparently irrelevant h3. In my confusion, I completely forgot my threat!

40 ... Qd3+?

40...Rc2 wins at once. This careless check makes the win very difficult, if indeed possible at all.

41 Kb2 (D)

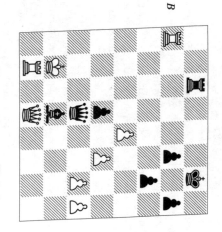

B

41 ... Rb8+?

I thought I had seen a forced win, but it was not so. The best continuation is 41...Bc3+ 42 Ka2 Qxg3 43 e6! (the only try, playing to expose Black's king; 43 Qg4? Qf2+ 44 Ka3 Bb4+! 45 Rxb4 Qc2 46 Qxc8+ Ka3 47 Qb7 d3 wins for Black; for example, 48 Rxf7 d2 49 Rg7+ Kf8 50 Rxh7 Qc5+ 51 Kb2 Qxa7 52 Rxa7 d1Q and White's remaining pawns will would have found a way to avoid the draw, for example by 12...♖e8 13 ♘g5 ♘b6!?.

Another idea is 6 ♘gf3, waiting for 6...♗e7 before playing 7 exd5 ♘xd5 8 0-0 0-0 9 ♖e1. In this case Black might be able to get away with 9...f6 10 c3 ♘c7, but his poor development would make me nervous. A safer option is 6...d4, leading to a kind of Petrosian System with a tempo less. In this blocked position the extra move has relatively little significance.

The move played in the game is again rather passive, and causes Black no problems.

| | 6 | ... | ♗e7 |
| | 7 | 0-0 | 0-0 *(D)* |

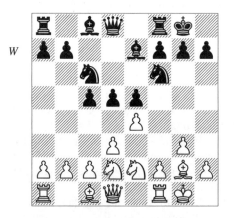

One often sees White adopting a reversed opening with an extra tempo, but it is surprising how often this strategy fails to give White any advantage. The problem is usually that black openings are designed mainly to achieve equality; having an extra tempo may make it easier to equalize, but does not change the fundamental strategy behind the opening. This game is a case in point. White is playing an insipid King's Indian with an extra tempo, but the general nature of his opening is the same – it is still insipid.

8   exd5

White cannot risk 8 f4 because 8...exf4 9 gxf4 dxe4 10 dxe4 ♗g4 gives Black a dangerous lead in development. I expected 8 h3 (preparing f4), although 8...dxe4 9 dxe4 b6 followed by ...♗a6 gives Black a pleasant position.

| | 8 | ... | ♘xd5 |
| | 9 | ♖e1?! | |

But now White is in danger of becoming worse. It would have been better to play 9 ♘c4

♗e6 10 f4 exf4 11 ♘xf4 ♘xf4 12 ♗xf4 ♗d5, with roughly equal chances.

| | 9 | ... | ♗e6 |

9...♗g4 was tempting, but I avoided it because 10 h3 ♗h5 (10...♗e6!? is interesting, however, as the additional h3 may favour Black) 11 ♗xd5 ♕xd5 12 ♘c3 ♗xd1 13 ♘xd5 ♗xc2 14 ♘xe7+ ♘xe7 15 ♖xe5 ♘c6 16 ♖xc5 more or less forces a draw. White's continuing timid play has raised Black's expectations to the extent that he is now avoiding lines leading to a forced draw. While it is right to be ambitious and hope to cause the opponent problems, ambition has to be related to the situation on the board. Good players are always looking for ways to trouble the opponent, even when they are slightly worse, but the best players are able to do this without compromising their position, so that even if their hopes fail to materialize, they are no worse off than before. Here the position is still objectively equal, but Black is right to be feeling positive because it is White who has to play accurately in order to maintain the balance.

| | 10 | ♘c4 | ♕c7 |

I played this only after some thought, because it involves an exchange sacrifice. However, it is a logical move because Black would prefer not to meet f4 by ...exf4, which solves White's development problems. By defending e5 with the queen, Black can meet f4 with a developing move.

| | 11 | f4 | ♖ad8 *(D)* |

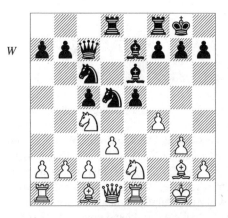

12   ♗d2?!

White decides to maintain the tension in the centre, while at the same time countering the threat of 12...♘xf4 followed by 13...♗xc4. However, this move is simply too slow and presents Black with a useful tempo. After the game Conquest revealed that he was already dissatisfied with his position but, as the analysis below demonstrates, this opinion was too pessimistic since White could still have maintained the balance with accurate play. The alternatives are:

1) 12 f5?! ♗xf5 13 ♗xd5 ♖xd5 14 ♘e3 and White will be the exchange for a pawn up, but at the cost of a horrible position after 14...♕d7 15 ♘xd5 ♕xd5 16 ♘c3 ♕d7, with ...♗g4 and ...f5-f4 to come.

2) 12 ♘xe5 ♘xe5 13 fxe5 ♕xe5 14 d4 (14 ♘f4?! ♕d4+ 15 ♔h1 ♘xf4 16 ♗xf4 ♗f6 leads to a slight advantage for Black) is a simple plan which leads to a roughly equal position. Play might continue 14...♕f5 (14...♕c7?! 15 c4 ♘b6 16 d5! ♘xc4 17 ♘c3 is clearly better for White and 14...♕h5 15 c4 ♘b6 16 d5 ♗g4 17 ♘f4!? is unclear) 15 c4 ♘b4 16 d5 ♕d3 and Black does not have more than a very faint edge.

3) 12 fxe5 (D) and now:

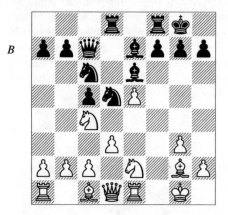

3a) 12...♘xe5 13 ♘f4 ♗g4 with a further branch:

3a1) 14 ♕d2 ♘xc4 and now White should avoid 15 ♘xd5? ♖xd5 which transposes to 15 ♕d2 in line '3a2' below. Instead 15 dxc4 is better, when 15...♘b6 (15...♘b4 16 ♕f2 is fine for White) is roughly equal.

3a2) 14 ♘xd5 ♖xd5 and now 15 ♕d2 is bad because of 15...♘xc4 16 ♕f4 ♖e5! 17 ♖e4 f5! winning material (as 18 ♖xc4 ♖e1+ 19 ♔f2 ♗d6 traps White's queen), while after 15 ♗xd5

♗xd1 16 ♖xd1 Black's material advantage gives him good winning chances. However, White has a third possibility: the incredible 15 ♖e2!!, a move which is practically impossible to see during a game. After this Black can only defend with precise play:

3a21) 15...♘f3+? 16 ♗xf3 ♗xf3 17 ♖xe7 wins for White.

3a22) 15...♗f3 16 ♗f4 with an awkward position for Black.

3a23) 15...♖d7 16 ♘xe5 ♕xe5 17 ♖xe5 ♗xd1 18 ♗h3 with an unpleasant ending for Black.

3a24) 15...♖d6! (one surprising turn deserves another; with this move Black can just about hold the balance) 16 ♘xe5 ♗xe2 17 ♕xe2 ♖e6 18 ♗f4 ♗f6 (18...♖d6? 19 ♗d5 ♖e7 20 ♖e1 ♖fe8 is tempting but allows the spectacular combination 21 ♘xf7! ♖xe2 22 ♘xd6+ ♔f8 23 ♖f1! ♖e1 24 ♘xe8 ♖xf1+ 25 ♔xf1 ♕b6 26 ♘c7 ♔e7 27 b3 and White is better) 19 ♗d5 ♖xe5 20 ♗xe5 ♕xe5 21 ♕xe5 ♗xe5 with a drawn ending.

3b) 12...b5 13 ♘d6 ♘xe5, but White can simply make off with a pawn by 14 ♘xb5 ♕b6 15 ♘bc3 and Black does not have enough compensation.

3c) 12...♕b8! is surprising but probably best. Black improves over line '3b' by defending the b5-pawn in advance, making use of the fact that 13 ♘f4 and 13 ♗f4 both lose a piece. White should play the natural 13 a4 (13 ♘e3 ♘xe3 14 ♗xe3 ♘xe5 15 ♗f4 ♗d6 gives Black an edge) 13...♘xe5 14 ♘f4 ♗g4 (D) and now:

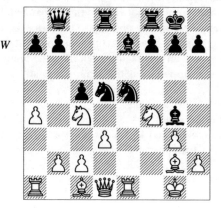

3c1) 15 ♘xd5?! ♖xd5 leads to a further branch:

3c11) 16 ♖e2 no longer works, as Black's queen is out of range in the line 16...♘f3+ 17 ♗xf3 (17 ♔f2 is met by 17...♘d4!) 17...♗xf3.

3c12) 16 ♕d2 ♘xc4 17 ♕c3 ♖e5 18 ♗f4 ♗d6 is slightly better for Black.

3c2) 15 ♕d2 (this is better) 15...♘xc4 16 dxc4 is level, which seems to be the correct evaluation of the position after 12 fxe5.

12   ...   ♗f6

The most obvious possibility; Black reinforces e5 and so stops all the tricky tactics in the previous note, and at the same time lines up against White's b-pawn. Of course, White could continue to play a waiting game with 13 ♕c1, but Black can do the same with 13...♖fe8, and Black's waiting moves have a more positive effect than White's. The only reason to hesitate about 12...♗f6 is that it allows White to win the exchange under more favourable circumstances than in line '1' of the previous note, but even so Black need not fear it.

13   f5

White thought a long time before reluctantly accepting the offered material.

13   ...   ♗xf5
14   ♗xd5   ♖xd5
15   ♘e3   ♕d7 (D)

Much better than 15...♗e6 16 ♘xd5 ♗xd5 17 ♘c3, when Black must quit the long diagonal.

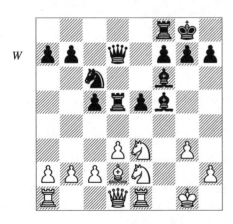

16   ♘xd5

White can also play 16 ♖f1, but Black then has a pleasant choice:

1) 16...e4!? 17 ♘xd5 (after 17 ♘f4 ♖e5 18 ♗c3 ♘d4 19 ♘xf5 ♕xf5 20 ♗xd4 cxd4 21 ♘d5 ♕g6 22 ♘xf6+ gxf6 23 dxe4 ♖xe4 Black retains some advantage) 17...♕xd5 when 18

dxe4?! ♕xe4 gives Black an enormous attack, but perhaps White can try to defend by 18 ♗c3.

2) 16...♗g4 17 ♘xd5 ♕xd5 is similar to the game.

3) 16...♗h3 17 ♘xd5 ♕xd5 18 ♖f2 ♗e7, followed by ...f5, is also not very different from the game.

16   ...   ♕xd5
17   ♘c3

Or else Black pins the knight by ...♗g4, which makes the situation even more unpleasant. Black has one pawn for the exchange, plus two active bishops, a lead in development and attacking chances against the exposed white king, all of which add up to more than enough compensation.

17   ...   ♕d7

Black's long-term plan involves switching the light-squared bishop to the long diagonal, clearing the way for ...f5 to dislodge any blockading piece White establishes on e4. Black's immediate threat is ...♗g4 followed by ...♘d4.

18   ♗e3

18 ♘e4 is most simply met by 18...♗e7.

18   ...   ♘d4

The simplest. The threat of ...♗g4 forces White to take, when Black obtains two mighty bishops against a knight, plus a strong attack.

19   ♗xd4   ♕xd4+
20   ♔g2   ♗d7! (D)

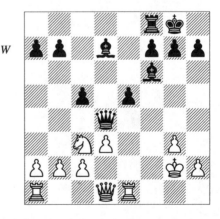

The bishop heads for the long diagonal.

21   ♕e2

White can close the diagonal temporarily by ♘e4, but sooner or later ...f5 will destroy the blockade. White would like to play h3 followed by ♔h2, when the immediate danger of a mate on the long diagonal would be over, but unfortunately 21 h3 &c6+ forces 22 ♘e4 when Black simply plays 22...♕xb2 adding a second pawn to his other assets.

| 21 | ... | &c6+ |
| 22 | ♔f1 | |

After 22 ♘e4 Black has a pleasant choice between the simple 22...♕xb2 and 22...&e7 23 c3 ♕d5 24 g4 g6 25 ♔g1 f5 26 gxf5 gxf5 27 ♘g3 &h4, with a winning position in either case.

| 22 | ... | ♕d7 |

The idea is to play ...&d8-c7, followed by ...f5. Note that White cannot take on e5 after ...&d8 because of the check on h3.

| 23 | ♔g1?! | |

This walks into Black's reply, but the position was very uncomfortable for White in any case. For example, 23 ♘e4 &e7 (threatening ...f5 followed by ...f4) 24 ♘f2 f6 (better than 24...♕d5 25 ♕e4!) 25 ♔g1 &d6 and now Black can force through ...f5.

| 23 | ... | e4! |

Thanks to White's inaccurate 23rd move, Black is able to activate his dark-squared bishop without wasting time on preparatory moves.

| 24 | dxe4 | |

Or 24 ♘xe4 &d4+ 25 ♔f1 ♕h3+ 26 ♕g2 ♕f5+ 27 ♔e2 ♕g4+ 28 ♔d2 f5, and Black wins.

| 24 | ... | &d4+ |
| 25 | ♔g2 | f5 (D) |

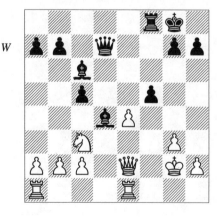

The last barrier is blown away and there is no shelter from the two bishops and the queen, which operate with lethal effect along three parallel diagonals. The threat is simply 26...fxe4.

| 26 | ♖f1 | |

Temporarily holding Black up.

| 26 | ... | ♖e8 |

Black would really like to take on e4 with the rook, so now ...b5-b4 is a strong threat.

| 27 | ♖ae1 | |

27 ♖ad1 ♕f7 (threatening ...&xc3 followed by ...♖xe4) 28 ♕d3 ♕e6 also wins for Black.

| 27 | ... | b5! |

Decisive. At the moment 27...&xc3 could have been met by 28 ♕c4+, but now 28...&xc3 29 bxc3 ♖xe4 is a threat. Black also intends ...b4 followed by either ...&xe4+ or ...♖xe4.

| 28 | ♕h5 | |

As good as anything else.

28	...	g6
29	♕g5	b4
30	♘d1	

30 ♘d5 ♖xe4 is crushing.

| 30 | ... | &xe4+ |
| 31 | ♔h3 | ♔g7 (D) |

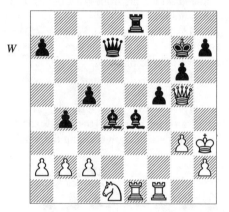

This modest king move is the clearest win. Black sets up a multitude of threats, including ...h6 followed by ...g5-g4+, or simply ....&f6 followed by ...f4+.

| 32 | c3 | |

The alternatives are no better: 32 ♘f2 &f3! (threatening 33...h6 and 33....&f6) 33 ♖xe8 (33 c3 &f6 34 ♕f4 ♕c6 wins for Black) 33...♕xe8 34 ♕d2 ♕c6 and Black wins, or 32 ♕d2 f4+ 33 g4 f3, with ...h5 to come.

| 32 | ... | &f6 |
| 33 | ♕c1 | |

Or 33 ♕f4 g5.

33	...	f4+
34	g4	♕d3+
	0-1	

White faces catastrophic loss of material.

These two wins lifted me into joint second place with Tony Miles on 8/10, half a point behind the winner Jon Speelman.

In the next few months I played only a few Bundesliga games and my next tournament was the traditional New Year event at Hastings. In the early 1990s, Hastings was a really strong tournament, with players such as Bareev and Judit Polgar taking part. However, by the end of 1993 a mild decline had set in. Gradually decreasing sponsorship meant that elite players could no longer be invited, and although the tournament was still very pleasant and beneficial to British chess, it no longer had any pretensions to grandeur. Unfortunately, the decline has continued up to the present day, and this once-proud event has now been reduced to a meagre existence huddling in a sports hall at the edge of a cold and windswept town.

I started with 2/3, and then began a run of three good wins which took me to the head of the table. All three of these games are given below. The first game features a very sharp line of the King's Indian. Accurate play is essential in such a double-edged opening, but here White played the opening with insufficient energy. Black was able to use his pawns to break up White's centre, and although the play was not entirely accurate, Black soon secured a clear advantage. White's king on c1 was prevented from reaching safety by Black's control of the f5-b1 diagonal, a typical ploy when the queenside castled position has been weakened by the advance of the c-pawn. When Black opened the c-file at move 25, White's king fell victim to a deadly attack.

Game 6
M. Sadler – J. Nunn
Hastings 1993/4
King's Indian Defence, Sämisch Variation

1	d4	♘f6
2	c4	g6
3	♘c3	♗g7
4	e4	d6
5	f3	0-0
6	♗g5	

The traditional Sämisch with 6 ♗e3 is one of the sharpest lines of the King's Indian. 6 ♗g5 is based on similar strategic ideas, but there are significant differences in detail. In one rather common case, however, these differences are irrelevant: if White later plays ♗h6, the two lines usually transpose into each other.

6	...	♘c6

Black's most common response to 6 ♗g5 is to transpose into a Benoni by 6...c5 7 d5 e6, followed by ...exd5. However, 6...♘c6 is a viable alternative.

7	♘ge2	a6
8	♕d2	♗d7
9	h4	h5

At one time a move such as this would have been inconceivable, as it flouts the general principle that you should not advance the pawns on the side where you are being attacked, especially if this is where your king is. However, meeting h4 by ...h5 has become more or less standard in this type of structure (the Sicilian Dragon is another example). Black's firm grip on g4 means that if White wants to break through on the kingside, he will have to do so sacrificially. However, Black must take care, since if he misjudges the situation then White's breakthrough will be devastating.

10	0-0-0	b5 *(D)*

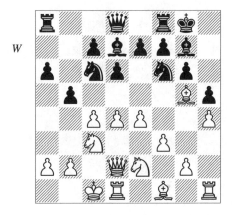

A critical moment. At Hastings the year before, Sadler had played 11 ♗h6 against me and scored a crushing victory. This time, perhaps fearing an improvement, he adopts a different and less critical line.

11   ♘d5

The previous game had continued 11 ♗h6 e5 12 ♘d5! (12 ♗xg7 ♔xg7 13 ♘d5 bxc4 is less dangerous) 12...♗xh6? 13 ♕xh6 bxc4 14 g4! (the active position of the queen on h6 justifies this move) 14...♘xd5 15 exd5 ♘b4 16 ♘g3! (correctly ignoring any material considerations, White plays directly for the attack) 16...c3 17 ♘xh5! gxh5 18 gxh5. Here there is no longer any defence and the game concluded 18...♗g4 19 ♖g1 f5 20 fxg4 f4 21 bxc3 ♘xa2+ 22 ♔c2 ♕xh4 23 ♕g6+ ♔h8 24 ♗d3 ♕e7 25 ♕h6+ ♔g8 26 ♕e6+ ♕xe6 27 dxe6 1-0 Sadler-Nunn, Hastings 1992/3. Naturally, I wasn't going to repeat the whole game, but in fact I had no absolutely terrifying innovation to hand.

Black's key mistake was to exchange bishops on h6 too early, which only served to draw White's queen into a dangerous attacking position. Black should have tried one of the following lines:

1) 12...♘xd4 13 ♘xd4 ♘xd5 (13...♗xh6? 14 ♕xh6 exd4 15 g4 is too dangerous) 14 ♗xg7 ♔xg7 15 cxd5 exd4 16 ♕xd4+ ♕f6 17 ♗e2 ♖ac8 with just an edge for White.

2) 12...exd4 13 ♗xg7 (13 ♘xd4 ♗xh6 14 ♕xh6 ♘xd4 15 ♖xd4 ♘xd5 16 cxd5 ♕f6 17 ♖d2 c5 18 dxc6 ♖ac8 is roughly equal; here the multiple exchanges have diluted White's attacking prospects) 13...♔xg7 14 ♘xd4 ♘e5 with unclear play.

11   ...   bxc4 *(D)*

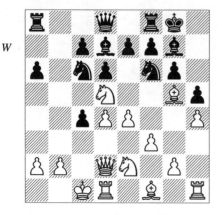

12   ♘xf6+?!

A definite inaccuracy; the early exchange on f6 diminishes White's attacking chances and gives Black the chance to break up White's centre. The critical line is definitely 12 g4!?, which Sadler himself preferred in a later game that he won quickly: 12...hxg4 13 h5 ♘xd5 14 exd5 gxf3 15 ♘f4 ♘xd4 16 hxg6 fxg6 17 ♘xg6 ♖e8 18 ♕h2 ♗f5 19 ♕h7+ ♔f7 20 ♖xd4 1-0 Sadler-Raisa, Gausdal 1994. Black's error was to exchange on d5. The greedy 13...♘xh5 is also bad; for example, 14 ♗h6 f6 (14...gxf3 15 ♗xg7 ♔xg7 16 ♖xh5 gxh5 17 ♕g5+ ♔h7 18 ♕xh5+ ♔g7 19 ♕g5+ ♔h7 20 ♗h3 forces mate, while 14...e5 15 ♘g3 is good for White) 15 ♘g3! (15 ♗xg7 ♔xg7 16 ♘g3 ♖h8 17 ♘xh5+ ♖xh5 18 ♖xh5 gxh5 19 ♗xc4 ♕h8 is unclear) 15...♘xg3 16 ♗xc4 ♗e6 17 ♗xg7 ♘xh1 18 ♖xh1 with a crushing attack. 13...♘h7! is the best defence, and now:

1) 14 hxg6 ♘xg5 15 ♕xg5 e6 16 ♕h5 fxg6 17 ♕xg6 exd5 18 ♕h7+ ♔f7 19 ♕h5+ and Black can either take a draw with 19...♔g8, or play for a win by 19...♔e7.

2) 14 fxg4 ♘xg5 15 ♕xg5 e6 favours Black.

3) 14 ♗h6 ♗xh6 15 ♕xh6 g5 16 f4 e6 17 ♘e3 ♔h8 is fine for Black.

4) 14 ♗e3 looks best, with a very unclear position.

12   ...   exf6
13   ♗h6   f5! *(D)*

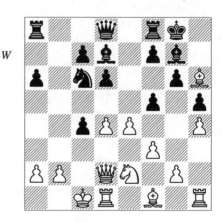

In the King's Indian, Black usually attacks the white centre on the dark squares by playing ...e5 or ...c5. It is quite unusual to see a light-squared attack such as this, but here it is very logical. If Black can exchange pawns on e4, then White will lose control over g4, which will bring his kingside attack to a dead halt. Moreover, Black will gain the g4-square for his light-squared bishop, which is normally a troublesome piece to develop in the Sämisch.

14 &xg7 &xg7
15 ᐠc3?

This is wrong because it allows Black to execute his plan without a fight. White's strategy is based on a kingside attack, and he should have continued with this plan, even at the cost of some material. Here are the alternatives:

1) 15 ₩c3? ₩f6 16 ₩xc4 fxe4 17 fxe4 ᖴab8 also favours Black.

2) 15 ᐠf4 fxe4 16 g4!? is unclear.

3) 15 exf5 &xf5 16 g4! hxg4 (16...&d3!? 17 gxh5 ₩f6 18 ᐠf4 &xf1 19 ᖴhxf1 ᖴab8 is also unclear) 17 ᐠg3 d5 (17...₩f6 18 ᐠxf5+ ₩xf5 19 fxg4 ₩xg4 20 h5 is dangerous for Black) 18 h5 ᖴh8 with a double-edged position.

15 ... fxe4
16 fxe4

There is nothing better. 16 ᐠxe4 d5 and 16 d5 ᐠe5 17 ᐠxe4 &f5 are also good for Black.

16 ... &g4 (D)

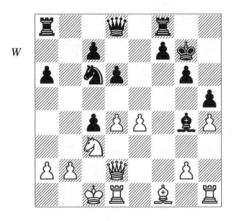

17 &e2

Not 17 ᖴe1 ₩f6 with an awkward attack on d4. After the text-move, Black has a clear advantage. He has almost completed his development, while White has yet to recover the pawn on c4. Moreover, White has no kingside attack left.

17 ... ₩d7

Not 17...ᐠb4 18 &xg4 ᐠd3+ 19 &b1 hxg4 20 h5 and White has revived his attack.

18 ᐠd5

Countering the threat of ...ᐠb4.

18 ... ᖴae8

If White had a chance to consolidate and regain the pawn on c4, then he might yet equalize. Therefore Black takes quick action, opening lines with the aim of launching a direct attack against the white king.

19 &f3

The only way to defend the e4-pawn.

19 ... f5!

The second ...f5 within a few moves contributes to the erosion of White's centre. With the e4-pawn gone, Black may gain control of the f5-b1 diagonal, preventing White's king from slipping away to safety.

20 exf5 (D)

20 &xg4 fxg4 is also very good for Black; for example, 21 ₩c2 (21 ᖴde1 ᐠe7 22 ᐠe3 d5 23 exd5 ᐠxd5 24 ᐠxc4 ₩c6 25 b3 ᐠb6 26 ₩c2 ᐠxc4 27 bxc4 ₩f6, attacking the d4- and h4-pawns, leaves White in serious trouble) 21...ᐠe7 22 ₩xc4 (22 ᐠe3 d5) 22...ᐠxd5 23 exd5 (23 ₩xd5 c6 wins the e4-pawn) 23...ᖴf2 with a clear advantage for Black.

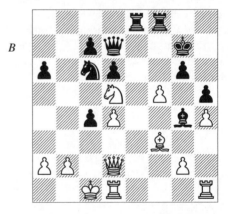

20 ... &xf5?

An error which jeopardizes Black's advantage. 20...&xf3? is also wrong, since after 21 f6+ (21 gxf3? ᖴxf5 22 ᐠf4 ₩f7 23 ᐠh3 ₩d5 is winning for Black) 21...&h7 22 gxf3 ₩f7 23 ₩g5 (23 ᐠb4? ᐠxb4 24 ₩xb4 ₩d5 will leave Black with a clear extra pawn) 23...ᐠxd4 24 ᖴxd4 ᖴe5 25 ₩f4 ᖴxd5 26 ᖴxd5 ₩xd5 27 ᖴe1 White's f-pawn suddenly becomes rather dangerous. The correct line is 20...₩xf5! 21 ᐠxc7 (21 ᐠe3 ᖴxe3 22 ₩xe3 ᐠb4 23 &e4

♘xa2+ 24 ♔b1 ♕a5 25 ♖df1 ♖b8 26 ♗b7
♗f5+ 27 ♖xf5 ♕xf5+ 28 ♔xa2 ♖xb7 leaves
Black two pawns up) 21...♖c8 22 ♗xg4 (22 d5
♖xc7 23 dxc6 ♗xf3 24 ♖hf1 ♕e5 25 ♖xf3
♖xf3 26 gxf3 ♖xc6 with a clear extra pawn for
Black) 22...♕xg4 (much better than 22...hxg4?
23 ♖hf1 ♕xf1 24 ♘e6+ ♔h7 25 ♖xf1 ♖xf1+
26 ♔c2 with advantage to White) 23 ♘d5
♕e4! 24 ♘c3 ♕f5 and the threat of ...♘b4 is
hard to meet; for example, 25 ♖hf1 ♕xf1 26
♖xf1 ♖xf1+ 27 ♘d1 ♖cf8 is clearly better for
Black.

This error was the result of poor judgement. I
wanted to transfer my bishop to the f5-b1 diagonal in the hope of attacking White's king, but
in fact there is no real attack while White's minor pieces are so active. In order to generate
threats against the white king, Black must drive
the knight away from d5; playing ...♕xf5 attacks d5 and at the same time prepares to exchange the bishop on f3, and was therefore the
correct choice.

21 ♕c3 ♘e7 (D)

Black belatedly realizes the importance of
eliminating the d5-knight. 21...♗d3 is well met
by 22 ♘f4! since 22...♖xf4 23 ♗xc6 costs
Black the exchange. Not, however, 22 ♘b6?,
which I was worried about during the game, because of the surprising reply 22...♘b4!, when
Black is much better. The alternative 21...♗e4
22 ♗xe4 ♖xe4 23 ♕xc4 is unclear.

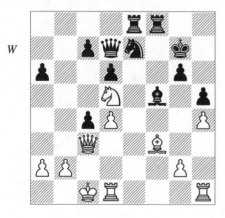

22 ♘xe7?

This allows Black to transfer his queen to a
more active position and once again tips the
scales in Black's favour. 22 ♖he1! was correct,
when White has every chance of equalizing.

Not, however, 22 ♕xc4? ♗e6 23 ♗e4 ♖b8 followed by ...c6 and Black wins a piece.

22 ... ♕xe7
23 ♖de1

White cannot play the other rook to e1 because his h4-pawn is hanging. Another idea is
23 ♕xc4 ♕e3+ 24 ♖d2 c6, and now:

1) 25 ♗d1 ♗e6 26 ♕d3 (26 ♕xa6 ♖f2 27
♕d3 ♕f4 is also very unpleasant for White)
26...♗d5 is very good for Black, since all his
pieces are more actively placed than their white
counterparts.

2) 25 ♖f1 a5 with strong pressure for Black;
e.g., 26 ♕e2 (26 d5 cxd5 27 ♕d4+ ♕xd4 28
♖xd4 ♖c8+ 29 ♔d1 ♖c2 30 ♖d2 ♖fc8 should
win for Black) 26...♕f4 27 ♕a6 ♕xh4 and
Black wins a pawn since 28 ♕xa5 ♖a8 is decisive.

23 ... ♕f6
24 ♖xe8 ♖xe8
25 ♕xc4

White finally gets his pawn back, but at the
cost of inactive pieces and an exposed king.

25 ... c5! (D)

Black strikes at once, opening the c-file.
White is now lost.

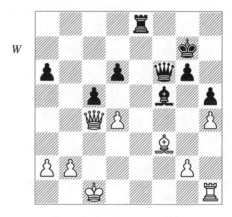

26 ♕xa6

26 dxc5 loses to 26...♖b8 27 ♕e2 (27 ♕c3
♕xc3+ 28 bxc3 ♖b1+ wins a rook) 27...♖b5 28
c6 (28 cxd6 ♖c5+ 29 ♔d1 ♕xd6+ 30 ♕d2
♗c2+ 31 ♔e1 ♖e5+ 32 ♗e2 ♗d3 is winning
for Black) 28...d5! 29 ♕f2 ♕xc6+ 30 ♔d1 ♕c4
with a decisive attack.

26 ... cxd4

26...♕xd4! is even simpler, since after 27
♕a5 (27 ♖d1 ♕f4+ 28 ♖d2 ♖e1+ 29 ♗d1 ♕e4

and Black wins) 27...♖e3 there is no real defence to the threat of 28...♕c4+.

    27 ♔d1

White's king is hopelessly exposed.

    27 ... ♖c8

Threatening to bring the queen into the attack by 28...♕e7, with the point that 29 ♖e1 ♖c1+ mates.

    28 ♖e1 ♗c2+
    29 ♔e2

29 ♔d2 ♕f4+ is even worse.

    29 ... d3+
    30 ♔f2 *(D)*

Or 30 ♔d2 ♕f4+ 31 ♖e3 ♕b4+ 32 ♔c1 d2#.

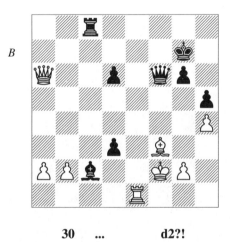

    30 ... d2?!

30...♕xh4+ 31 ♔f1 d2 wins at once.

    31 ♕b7+

31 ♕xc8 ♕xh4+ 32 g3 ♕h2+ 33 ♗g2 (or 33 ♔f1 ♗d3+) 33...dxe1♕+ 34 ♔xe1 ♕xg2 and Black wins.

    31 ... ♔h6
    32 ♖e7

32 ♕xc8 was the only chance, although 32...♕xh4+ 33 g3 dxe1♕+ (33...♕h2+ 34 ♗g2 dxe1♕+ 35 ♔xe1 ♕xg2?? is only a draw after 36 ♕f8+) 34 ♔xe1 ♕xg3+ 35 ♔e2 ♗d1+ 36 ♔xd1 ♕xf3+ 37 ♔e1 h4 is an easy enough win.

    32 ... ♕xh4+
    33 ♔g1 ♕e1+
    34 ♔h2 ♕h4+

A repetition to gain time on the clock.

    35 ♔g1 ♕e1+
    36 ♔h2 ♖c4!
    37 g3

37 ♖h7+ ♔g5 38 ♕d5+ ♕e5+ 39 ♕xe5+ dxe5 40 ♖d7 ♖d4 is winning for Black.

    37 ... ♕f2+
    38 ♗g2 d1♕

38...♖h4+ mates in five, but of course it makes no difference by this stage.

    39 ♖h7+ ♔g5
    40 ♕e7+ ♕f6
    41 ♕e3+ ♖f4
    42 ♖a7 ♕dd4

                     0-1

The next game features an ultra-sharp opening line, but after some complications a roughly equal position is reached. The key phase occurred round about move 26. Black has a well-placed knight on e5, whereas White's bishop on d3 looks rather passive. At first both players believed that Black should not exchange on d3, but in fact it is precisely this exchange which secures Black comfortable equality. It is often hard to overcome one's prejudices about matters which run contrary to intuition, and here it was White who first grasped the key idea of preserving the bishop from exchange. Black failed to react to the new situation and White was able to secure a clear endgame advantage, which he converted into a win by forceful play.

Game 7

J. Nunn – I. Rogers

Hastings 1993/4

Sicilian Defence, Najdorf/Scheveningen Variation

1	e4	c5	5	♘c3	a6
2	♘f3	d6	6	♗e3	e6
3	d4	cxd4			
4	♘xd4	♘f6			

In contrast to Game 4, Rogers prefers to adopt the Scheveningen pawn-structure. Play proceeds along one of the main lines of the English Attack.

7	**f3**	**b5**
8	**♕d2**	**♘bd7**
9	**g4**	**h6**
10	**0-0-0**	**♗b7**
11	**h4**	**b4**

It is essential for Black to take quick action to avoid being blown away by White's kingside attack. In keeping with traditional principles, this action takes the form of a counterattack in the centre.

12   ♘ce2

12 ♘ce2 was considered the main line at the time this game was played. Subsequent developments showed that 12 ♘a4! is the critical move; the precise assessment of this continuation is still being debated today.

12   ...   d5

13   ♘g3

For a long time, 13 ♗h3 was believed to be best, but after Black discovered the resource 13...dxe4 14 g5 hxg5 15 hxg5 exf3 16 ♘f4 ♘e4 17 ♕e1 ♖xh3!, the line with 13 ♗h3 fell into disrepute. For a time White switched to 13 ♘g3, but when that was also found wanting, the whole line with 12 ♘ce2 became obsolete, and attention switched to 12 ♘a4.

13   ...   ♗d6 *(D)*

13...dxe4! 14 g5 hxg5 15 hxg5 ♖xh1 16 ♘xh1 ♘d5 17 g6 ♕f6! was the continuation which sounded the death knell for 13 ♘g3.

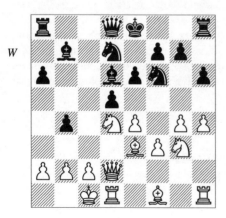

14   ♖g1!?

An interesting novelty, trying to improve over the previously played 14 ♘gf5. However, objectively speaking I don't think it gives White

any advantage. On the few occasions in which this line has arisen since 1993, White has invariably chosen 14 ♖g1. One of the main problems with 14 ♘gf5 is that after 14...♗f8 White doesn't have anything better than to repeat the position with 15 ♘g3. However, Black can also accept the sacrifice by 14...exf5 15 ♘xf5 ♗f8 16 e5 ♘xe5 (16...♘g8 is too passive and after 17 ♗d4 ♕a5 18 ♘d6+ ♗xd6 19 exd6 0-0-0 20 ♗xg7 ♖h7 21 ♗d4 White held a clear advantage in Thorhallsson-Arnason, Gardabaer 1991) 17 ♗d4 ♘c6 18 ♕e3+ ♔d7 *(D)* with an unclear position which is probably about equal. There are now two possibilities:

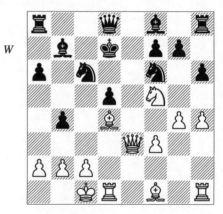

1) 19 ♗b6? ♕e8 20 ♕b3 ♔c8 21 ♗h3 g5 was good for Black in Ernst-Dževlan, Jönköping 1993.

2) 19 ♗xf6 ♕xf6 20 ♖xd5+ ♔c8 21 ♗c4 (21 ♕e8+ ♔c7 22 ♖d7+ ♔b6 23 ♕e3+ ♗c5 24 ♖xb7+ ♔xb7 25 ♕xc5 g6 is better for Black) 21...♘d8 (21...g6 22 ♖hd1 gxf5 23 ♕e8+ ♔c7 24 ♖d7+ ♔b6 25 ♖xb7+ ♔xb7 26 ♖d7+ ♔b6 27 ♕xa8 ♕xb2+ 28 ♔d1 ♕a1+ 29 ♔e2 ♕e5+ 30 ♔f1 ♕a1+ is perpetual check because 31 ♔g2?? is refuted by 31...♕g1+!) 22 ♖d3 ♗c6 23 ♖hd1 ♘b7 24 ♕f4 gives White enough compensation for the piece, but probably not more.

It follows that 14 ♘gf5 is not a realistic winning attempt, hence the attempted improvement in this game.

14   ...   ♕c7

The logical response, again taking aim at the insecure g3-knight.

15   g5?!

This move is rather risky. If White wants to play for an advantage perhaps he should try 15 f4!?, but the resulting complications are not especially convincing for him: 15...♘xg4 (not 15...♘xe4? 16 ♘xe4 dxe4 17 ♘xe6 with an excellent position for White) 16 ♘h5 ♘xe3 17 ♕xe3 (17 ♘xg7+ ♔e7 18 e5 ♘xd1 19 exd6+ ♔xd6 favours Black) 17...g6 18 ♘g7+ ♔e7 19 e5 ♗c5 20 ♘gxe6 fxe6 21 ♖xg6 ♗xd4 22 ♕xd4 ♖ag8 23 ♕xb4+ ♘c5 with a murky position, but it is hard to believe that White is better.

15 ♘h5 is safe but does not promise White an advantage: 15...g6 16 ♘xf6+ (only a very brave player would send his knight into enemy territory by 16 ♘g7+ ♔e7) 16...♘xf6 17 g5 hxg5 18 hxg5 ♘d7 19 f4 ♘c5 20 e5 (20 ♗g2 ♘xe4 21 ♗xe4 dxe4 22 ♘xe6 fxe6 23 ♕xd6 ♕xd6 24 ♖xd6 ♗d5 should be a draw) 20...♗e7 21 ♗d3 0-0-0 22 ♖h1 ♘e4 with equality, Winsnes-Svensson, Gothenburg 1994.

15 ... hxg5

This preliminary exchange is a good idea because it enables the h8-rook to enter play.

16 hxg5 ♗xg3
17 gxf6 ♘xf6
18 ♕xb4 *(D)*

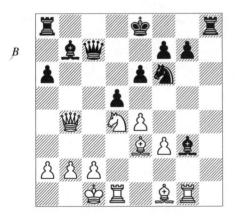

Material equality has been restored after a forced sequence of moves. It is true that Black's king is trapped in the centre, but his active pieces provide good compensation.

18 ... ♗d6

White was threatening 19 ♖xg3, hence the bishop returns to a useful square.

19 ♕a4+

19 ♕d2 ♖h2 is fine for Black.

19 ... ♔f8

Black has to move his king or he loses the g7-pawn, but on f8 the king is safe enough for

the moment since White's pieces are not active enough to launch an attack.

20 ♗d3

White completes his development. The position slightly favours Black, since his active pieces and extra central pawn are more important than his slightly insecure king.

20 ... ♘d7?!

Black mustn't get greedy since 20...dxe4 21 fxe4 ♗xe4? (21...♔g8 is still fine for Black) 22 ♗xe4 ♘xe4 23 ♘xe6+ fxe6 24 ♕xe4 wins for White. However, 20...e5! is a simple way to give Black an edge. After 21 ♘b3 (21 ♘f5? ♗c6 22 ♕b3 ♖b8 23 ♕c3 d4 24 ♘xd4 exd4 25 ♗xd4 ♗f4+ 26 ♔b1 ♗b5 leaves White with insufficient compensation for the piece) 21...dxe4 (21...d4? 22 ♗d2 is slightly better for White as Black no longer has pressure against the white centre) 22 ♗xe4 (22 fxe4? ♗c6 23 ♕c4 ♗xe4 and Black wins a pawn) 22...♘xe4 23 fxe4 ♖c8 24 c3 ♖h3 Black can claim a slight advantage thanks to his two bishops and active pieces.

The text-move threatens 21...♘c5.

21 ♘b3 *(D)*

A good move, intending to play 22 ♖h1. The immediate 21 ♖h1? is bad due to 21...♖xh1 22 ♖xh1 ♘c5 23 ♕a3 dxe4 and Black wins a pawn.

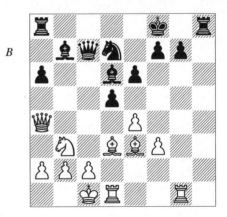

21 ... ♗c6?!

Not the best, because it practically forces White's strong reply. Moreover, on c6 the bishop is exposed to attack by White's knight (from a5 or d4). 21...♘e5 is sufficient to maintain the balance:

1) 22 ♔b1? ♘xf3 23 ♖h1 ♖xh1 24 ♖xh1 ♗c6 was better for Black in Ernst-Åström, Haparanda 1994.

2) 22 ♘a5?! ♘xf3 23 ♘xb7 (after 23 ♖h1 ♖xh1 24 ♖xh1 ♘e5 25 ♗e2 dxe4 it is not clear if White can justify his sacrifice) 23...♕xb7 24 ♖h1 ♖xh1 25 ♖xh1 ♘e5 and Black is slightly better.

3) 22 ♗e2 ♖h2 23 ♖d2 ♖xe2 24 ♖xe2 ♘xf3 25 ♖d1 ♖c8 26 exd5 ♗xd5 27 ♖xd5 exd5 is unclear.

4) 22 ♕d4 ♘xd3+ (22...♖g8?! 23 ♗e2 ♖c8 24 c3 favours White) 23 ♕xd3 ♖c8 leads to equality.

22   ♕a5

This severely restricts Black's options. He cannot play 22...dxe4 because 23 ♗xe4 wins material, while 22...♕xa5 23 ♘xa5 ♘e5 24 ♘xc6 ♘xc6 25 c3 gives White some advantage thanks to his two bishops. Meanwhile White threatens 23 ♖h1.

22   ...   ♘e5
23   ♗c5 (D)

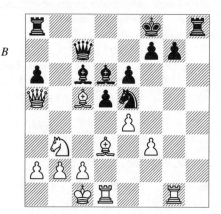

The exchange of dark-squared bishops favours White because Black's remaining bishop is passively placed.

23   ...   ♔g8

23...♘xd3+ 24 ♖xd3 ♔g8 25 ♗xd6 ♕xd6 26 ♕c3 ♖h7 27 e5 gives White a classic good knight vs bad bishop position.

24   ♗xd6   ♕xd6
25   ♘d4

The exchange of Black's best minor piece has tipped the balance in White's favour. His advantage is not great, but the weak pawn on a6 and the possibility of leaving Black with a bad bishop make life awkward for him.

25   ...   ♗b7 (D)
26   ♔b1?!

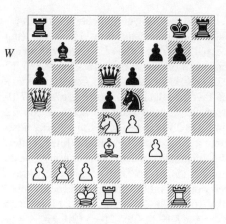

The immediate 26 ♗e2 is more accurate, depriving Black of the chance to swap on d3.

26   ...   ♖c8?!

Black should have taken the opportunity to exchange off the d3-bishop, and after 26...♘xd3 27 ♖xd3 ♖c8 the position would be roughly level. At first it looks odd to exchange the apparently well-placed knight on e5 for the passive d3-bishop, and for a time neither side appreciated the significance of this exchange.

27   ♗e2!

White is the first to grasp the essential feature of the position: if he can play f4 and e5 without allowing Black to exchange off his knight, then his own bishop will become 'good' while Black's will become 'bad'.

27   ...   g6?

Black fails to react to the new situation and allows White to force an ending in which he has a nearly decisive advantage. Other moves:

1) 27...dxe4? loses to 28 ♘f5!.

2) 27...♘g6 prevents the f4 and e5 plan, but after 28 exd5 ♗xd5 (28...♕xd5 loses to 29 ♕b6) 29 c4 White has a tremendous position; e.g., 29...♗b7 (29...♗xc4 30 ♗xc4 ♖xc4 31 ♘f5 ♕h2 32 ♕d8+ ♔h7 33 ♖h1 ♖xd8 34 ♖xh2+ ♖h4 35 ♖xh4+ ♘xh4 36 ♖xd8 wins for White) 30 ♘f5 ♕h2 31 ♘d6 ♕xe2 32 ♖ge1 ♕xf3 33 ♘xc8 ♗xc8 34 ♕d8+ ♘f8 35 ♕xc8 and White wins.

3) 27...♖h2! is best, with the point that 28 f4 can be met by 28...♘c6 29 ♕c3 ♘xd4 30 ♕xd4 ♕f8 with equality. White would have to find the hard-to-spot 28 ♕e1 (threatening 29 ♖xg7+ ♔xg7 30 ♕g3+) in order to maintain any advantage. The main line runs 28...♘g6 29 exd5 ♕xd5 (29...♗xd5 30 ♗d3 ♘e7 31

♕e3, intending ♕g5, maintains a slight plus for White) 30 ♗d3 ♕xd4 31 ♗xg6 ♕f2 32 ♖d7 ♕xe1+ 33 ♖xe1 fxg6 34 ♖xb7 ♖hxc2 35 a3 and Black has still not equalized; for example, 35...♖8c6 36 ♖e7 ♖f2 37 ♖1xe6 ♖xe6 38 ♖xe6 ♖xf3 39 ♖xa6 gives White some winning chances.

28	f4	♘c6

Forced, or else e5 gives White a massive positional advantage.

29	♕b6 *(D)*	

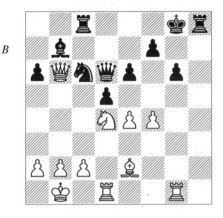

Pinning the knight and gaining time by attacking b7.

29	...	♕c7

The only other possibility is 29...♕b4, but then 30 ♕xb4 ♘xb4 31 a3 ♘c6 32 ♘xc6 ♖xc6 33 exd5 exd5 34 ♖xd5 leaves White a pawn up.

30	♕xc7	♖xc7

With the queens off, playing e5 is less attractive because Black's rook becomes active on h2. White can better use his initiative to damage Black's pawn-structure.

31	exd5	♘xd4

31...exd5 32 ♘xc6 wins a pawn, so Black must exchange on d4.

32	♖xd4	exd5

After 32...♗xd5 33 ♗xa6 ♖a7 34 c4 ♖xa6 35 cxd5 White remains a pawn up.

33	f5	

By exchanging on g6, White isolates all Black's pawns. With three weak pawns to defend and an inactive bishop, Black is sure to lose at least a pawn before very long. Since White retains his positional advantage, the loss of a pawn will probably prove decisive.

33	...	♔g7
34	fxg6	fxg6
35	♗d3	♖h6
36	♖b4	

Threatening to win the g-pawn with ♖b6. In this case all the remaining pawns would be on one side, but Black's split pawns and distant king would make the ending an almost certain win for White.

36	...	a5

The only defence.

37	♖a4!	

Much stronger than 37 ♖b6 ♗c6, when there is nothing clear.

37	...	♖c5
38	b4 *(D)*	

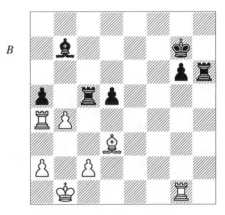

This is the point. Now 38...axb4 loses to 39 ♖a7 ♖c7 40 ♗a6 ♗xa6 41 ♖xc7+ ♔f8 42 ♖c6 and the g6-pawn falls.

38	...	♗c6
39	b5!	

Winning the exchange.

39	...	♗xb5

39...♖xb5+ 40 ♗xb5 ♗xb5 41 ♖xa5 ♗c4 42 ♖c5, followed by ♖c6, ties Black up and wins comfortably.

40	♖xa5	

In an echo of the note to White's 38th move, the bishop is pinned along a rank and Black must surrender material.

40	...	♗xd3
41	♖xc5	♗e4

Black has given up the exchange in relatively the best fashion, since on e4 the bishop secures his remaining pawns. However, White's passed a-pawn proves too strong.

42   a4

"Passed pawns must be pushed", the saying goes. Like most chess adages, there are almost as many exceptions as supporting cases. Pushing a passed pawn without due consideration may easily result in it being surrounded and lost. Here, however, the omens are favourable for pushing the a-pawn. Black's king is too distant to blockade it, which means that one of Black's other pieces must do the job, and in fact neither piece is well placed for holding up the a-pawn.

42   ...   ♖h8
43   ♔b2

White takes a little care. This move allows ♖a1 to support the a-pawn, and also introduces the idea of undermining the bishop by c4 at some stage.

43   ...   ♔f6 (D)

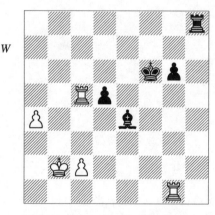

44   a5   ♖a8

Black has been forced to use his most powerful remaining piece for the humble duty of halting the a-pawn. The next step for White is to activate his king.

45   ♔c3   ♔e5
46   ♔b4

Threatening 47 c4.

46   ...   ♔d6

46...♖b8+ 47 ♔b5 ♖c8 48 a6 ♖c4+ 49 ♔a5 ♖xc2 50 a7 ♖a2+ 51 ♔b6 (threatening 52 ♖a5) 51...♔d6 52 ♖g4 ♗d3 53 ♖bb4 followed by ♖a4 is winning for White.

47   c4

Undermining the well-placed bishop is the simplest win.

47   ...   d4

47...dxc4 48 ♖d1+ ♔e6 49 ♖e1 and White wins the bishop.

48   ♖g4 (D)

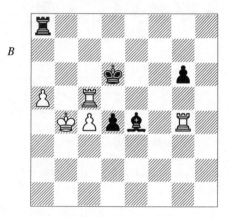

If the bishop moves, the d-pawn falls.

48   ...   ♖e8
49   ♖f4   ♖e6

After 49...d3 50 ♖f6+ ♔d7 51 ♔c3 White stops the d-pawn and wins easily.

50   ♖b5   1-0

Since 50...d3 51 ♖b6+ ♗c6 52 ♖d4+ costs Black the d-pawn.

The King's Gambit was once a very popular opening. Although it has a reputation for wild tactical play, it is actually founded on the sound strategic principle of exchanging White's non-central f-pawn for Black's central e-pawn. Unfortunately, 2 f4 has the defect of exposing White's king, and so the opening is not often played today, but the Queen's Gambit (1 d4 d5 2 c4), which is based on the same idea, remains extremely popular. In the following game some inaccurate opening play by Black allowed White to play f4 and gain the strategic benefits of the King's Gambit without the downside. White's solid centre and pressure along the half-open f-file caused Black problems, but his reaction of castling kingside only increased White's advantage. Black's kingside had been weakened by the advance ...h5, and White was able to steadily open lines on the kingside, first with g4, and then by exchanging the blockading knight on h5. Open lines are the key to many attacks, and here White's major pieces, operating on the open kingside files, created intolerable pressure against Black's king.

Game 8

J. Nunn – D. Barua

Hastings 1993/4

Four Knights Opening

1	e4	e5
2	♘f3	♘c6
3	♘c3	♘f6
4	♗b5	

The Four Knights Opening enjoyed a brief surge of popularity in the early 1990s after Nigel Short played it several times. His basic discovery was that the theoretical recipe for Black, 4...♘d4 5 ♗a4 ♗c5 6 ♘xe5 0-0 7 ♘d3 ♗b6 8 e5 ♘e8, offered White chances for an advantage based on 9 ♘d5!. The plan is to play the knight to the useful defensive square e3, while at the same time preparing c3 to push Black's knight away from d4. I also adopted the Four Knights for a time, but improvements were discovered for Black, and it soon became clear that White could not hope for an advantage. The Four Knights then returned to its former obscurity.

4	...	♘d4
5	♗a4	c6

This is indeed the best reply, and is far more reliable than 5...♗c5.

6	0-0 *(D)*	

The main problem for White is that 6 ♘xe5 d5! offers Black good compensation for the pawn. Black intends to develop his bishop to d6, not only forcing White to do something about the e5-knight but also bearing down on White's exposed kingside. At the same time the c6-d5 pawn-chain locks the a4-bishop out of play. The alternative 6 d3 b5 7 ♗b3 ♘xb3 8 axb3 d6 also promises White nothing.

6	...	♘xf3+?!

The move that killed off the Four Knights was 6...♕a5!. The idea is that at some point White will have to play ♗b3 (perhaps after ...b5 or ...♗b4 by Black) and then ...♘xb3 forces White to recapture with the c-pawn. The combination of capturing away from the centre and surrendering the two bishops is not very appealing for White, and the practical results have been very satisfactory for Black. However, at the time this game was played the strength of 6...♕a5 had not been appreciated.

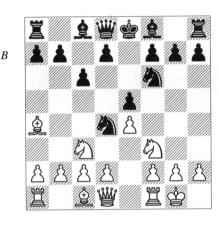

B

Exchanging on f3 is weaker, as the actively placed d4-knight is voluntarily exchanged. Moreover, Black surrenders the chance of acquiring the two bishops after a later ...b5. However, the general lack of tension in the position means that White will still have to work hard in order to secure an advantage.

7	♕xf3	d6
8	d3	h6

This move is rather slow and after this outing it was never repeated. However, if followed up correctly it is not bad. Other moves:

1) 8...♗g4 9 ♕g3 ♕d7 10 h3 ♗e6 11 ♘e2, with f4 to come, gave White a slight advantage in L.Paulsen-Schallopp, Berlin 1881(!).

2) 8...♗e7 is the most solid and safest move. White can gain the two bishops by 9 ♘d5 (another possibility is 9 ♕e2 0-0 10 f4 but it appears that Black can simply accept the pawn sacrifice by 10...exf4 11 ♗xf4 ♕b6+ 12 ♗e3 ♕xb2; for example, 13 ♕d2 ♕a3 14 ♖fb1?! ♗e6 15 ♖xb7 ♗d8! and White is in big trouble) and now:

2a) 9...♘xd5?! 10 exd5 b5 11 dxc6 is the tactical point justifying White's play. After 11...e4 (11...bxa4? loses to 12 c7) White has the choice between 12 c7 exf3 13 cxd8♕+ ♔xd8 14 ♗xb5 with a favourable ending, or 12 ♕xe4 d5 13 c7 ♕d7 14 ♕e5 bxa4 15 ♕xg7 ♖f8 16 ♗f4 with excellent compensation for the piece.

2b) 9...0-0 10 ♘xe7+ ♕xe7 11 ♗g5 and White has a faint edge thanks to the bishop-pair, but in this type of position, with all 16 pawns still on the board, it is unlikely to amount to anything significant.

9 ♕e2 *(D)*

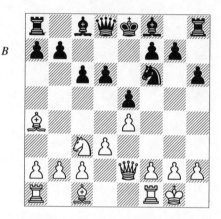

In order to have any chance of an advantage, White must create some tension in the centre. Playing d4 would involve the loss of a tempo, and in any case White's pieces are poorly placed to support this advance. Therefore White must aim for f4. This will probably lead to the exchange of Black's central e-pawn for White non-central f-pawn, and it will allow the f1-rook to enter play without loss of time.

9 ... ♗e6?!

After this White's advantage starts to become serious. 9...♗e7 10 f4 exf4 11 ♗xf4 0-0 (11...♕b6+ 12 ♔h1 ♕xb2? 13 ♘d5! is very good for White) 12 ♗b3 is also good for White, who has an extra central pawn and pressure against f7. Therefore, Black should have played 9...g5!, making use of his previous move to clamp down on White's most attractive plan. This drastic method of preventing f4 weakens the f5-square, but White's pieces are in no position to exploit this. After 10 ♘d1, followed by ♘e3 and c3, White has a slight advantage but no more than that.

10 ♗b3! *(D)*

The bishop wasn't doing anything on a4, so now it retreats to swap off Black's relatively active light-squared bishop. This simple positional move is much clearer than the pawn sacrifice 10 f4 exf4 11 ♗xf4 ♕b6+ 12 ♔h1 ♕xb2 13 ♘d5 0-0-0. Here it is tempting to continue

14 ♘xf6 ♕xf6 15 ♕e3, but after the surprising defence 15...♕c3! 16 ♕xa7 ♕c5 Black forces the exchange of queens and equalizes.

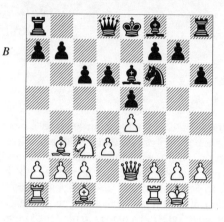

10 ... ♗xb3

This exchange improves White's pawn-structure further. Moreover, Black will sooner or later have to play ...a6, which costs him further time. He is still two moves from castling, and his lack of development is starting to look serious. However, the alternatives were also unappealing: 10...♗e7 11 f4 exf4 12 ♗xf4 0-0 13 ♗xe6 fxe6 14 e5 gives White a clear advantage, while 10...♕d7 11 f4 exf4 12 ♗xf4 ♗e7 13 ♖ae1 leaves Black far from equality.

11 axb3 g6

11...g5 is no longer acceptable, since Black has exchanged the light-squared bishop which could have been used to eliminate a white knight arriving on f5. After 11...♗e7 12 ♘d1 0-0 13 ♘e3, followed by ♘f5 and f4, White has an automatic attack on the kingside (note that 13...g6 loses a pawn after 14 ♘c4 ♔g7 15 ♕e3, attacking h6 and a7).

12 f4 ♗g7

12...exf4? 13 ♗xf4 ♗g7 is too slow as White can break through by 14 e5.

13 fxe5

13 ♕f3 is also good, keeping open the option of playing f5 at some stage.

13 ... dxe5

14 ♕f3 *(D)*

Stepping up the pressure along the half-open f-file.

14 ... ♕e7

14...0-0?! loses a pawn to 15 ♗xh6 although after 15...♗xh6 16 ♕xf6 ♗e3+ 17 ♔h1 ♕xf6

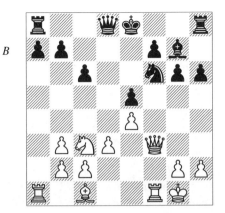

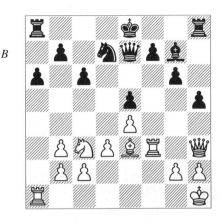

18 ℤxf6 ♔g7 19 ℤf3 ♗c5 White would have to work hard to exploit his advantage. Not surprisingly, Black does not want to surrender a pawn straight away and decides to defend f7 so as to play ...♘d7 and then ...0-0, which enables him to castle without the loss of a pawn.

| 15 | ♗e3 | a6 |
| 16 | ♔h1 | |

A useful preparatory move. Black will soon be ready to castle, and this move clears g1 for a rook to reinforce the coming kingside attack. 16 ♘a4 is less effective after 16...♘d7, followed by ...0-0, because the knight is not doing anything useful on a4 and will soon have to return.

| 16 | ... | ♘d7 |
| 17 | ♕h3 | |

White again prevents castling and forces a further concession from Black.

| 17 | ... | h5 |

After this Black can castle kingside without losing a pawn, but the protruding pawn at h5 gives White the leverage he needs to open up the kingside. 17...♕e6 avoids this particular problem, but the cost is a concession of a different type. After 18 ♕xe6+ fxe6 19 ♘a4 Black has a depressing position since he has no compensation for the pawn weaknesses. Of course this does not mean that White will necessarily win, but it is certain that Black will be in for a long and arduous defence.

| 18 | ℤf3 (D) | |
| 18 | ... | 0-0?! |

An error, since White's pieces are excellently placed to launch an immediate kingside attack. 18...♗h6! is best, planning to exchange his inactive bishop and eventually hide his king on the queenside. After 19 ℤaf1 f6 (not 19...♗xe3? 20 ℤxf7 ♕xf7 21 ℤxf7 ♔xf7 22 ♕xd7+ and White wins) White must play accurately to retain the advantage:

1) 20 ♘d1 ♗xe3 21 ♘xe3 ℤf8 followed by ...0-0-0 leaves White with no more than an edge.

2) 20 ♗xh6 ℤxh6 21 ♘d1 (21 ♘e2 ℤh8 22 d4 exd4 23 ♘xd4 0-0-0 is equal) 21...♔d8 22 ♘e3 ♔c7 and White has just a slight advantage.

3) 20 ♕g3! and now:

3a) 20...♕f7 21 ♗xh6 ℤxh6 22 ♕g5! fxg5 (22...♕g7 23 ℤxf6 ♘xf6 24 ℤxf6 0-0-0 25 ♕xe5 favours White) 23 ℤxf7 gives White a clear advantage.

3b) 20...♕g7 21 ♗xh6 ℤxh6 (21...♕xh6 22 ℤxf6) 22 ♘a4! and Black's position remains uncomfortable because the natural 22...0-0-0 runs into 23 ℤxf6! ♘xf6 24 ♕xe5 ♕c7 25 ♕xf6 with advantage to White.

| 19 | g4! | |

The most convincing move. White can of course also play 19 ℤaf1, but at the moment it is not clear whether the rook will be better placed on f1 or g1, so it makes sense to break open Black's kingside first.

| 19 | ... | hxg4 |

19...♘f6 20 gxh5 (20 ♗g5? hxg4 is tactically wrong since 21 ♗xf6? fails to 21...♕e6! and Black wins) 20...♘xh5 21 ℤg1, intending ♘e2-g3, is good for White. Note that 21...♘f4 22 ♗xf4 exf4 23 ℤxf4 ♗xc3 24 bxc3 ♕e5 loses to 25 ℤf5 ♕xc3 26 e5 with ℤh5 to come.

20	♕xg4	♘f6
21	♕h4 (D)	
21	...	♕e6

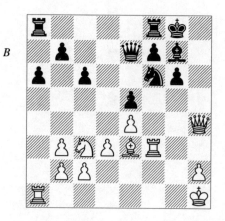

B

Black must unpin the knight, since 21...♖fd8, for example, loses to 22 ♗g5 ♖d6 23 ♖af1. 21...♘d5 is possible, but doesn't solve Black's problems since 22 ♗g5 f6 23 ♗d2 (23 ♖h3 ♘xc3 24 ♕h7+ ♔f7 25 ♗h6 ♔e6 26 bxc3 ♗xh6 27 ♕xh6 ♖g8 is less clear) 23...g5 24 ♕g4 ♘f4 25 ♖g1, followed by h4, keeps up the pressure.

22 ♗c5

A useful square for the bishop, cutting off the black king's escape-route.

22 ... ♖fe8

23 ♖g1

The other white rook slides into an attacking position. Only the c3-knight is not participating in the attack, and that defect can be remedied by the manoeuvre ♘e2-g3. Even though the build-up for White's attack is quite leisurely, there isn't much Black can do about it because there are no sources of counterplay. White's pawn-structure is very solid, and there are no pawn-levers which Black can use to disturb White. This is all in accordance with the general principle that a solid central pawn-structure helps justify a flank attack.

23 ... ♘h5

23...♘d7 24 ♗e3 drives White back temporarily, but after ♘e2-g3 White's knight will soon be jumping into f5 or h5.

24 ♘e2

If only the h5-knight could be removed, ♖h3 would give White a deadly attack along the h-file. White therefore sends his knight round to g3 to swap Black's defensive knight off.

24 ... ♖ab8

Black intends to push the bishop off the a3-f8 diagonal by ...b6. This move looks a bit

irrelevant but in fact Black has few constructive ideas.

25 ♘g3 ♘xg3+

Opening the h-file proves fatal, but Black was lost in any case:

1) 25...♗f6 26 ♕xh5 gxh5 27 ♘xh5+ ♔h8 28 ♖xf6 wins for White.

2) 25...♘f6 26 ♘f5! and White wins against any defence:

2a) 26...gxf5 27 ♖h3 leads to a quick win for White.

2b) 26...♘h7 27 ♖h3 ♘f8 (27...♘f6 28 ♘xg7 wins for White) 28 ♗xf8 ♔xf8 29 ♕h8+ ♗xh8 30 ♖xh8#.

2c) 26...♘h5 27 ♕xh5! gxh5 28 ♘xg7 with a decisive attack.

3) 25...♘f4 26 ♘f5! gxf5 (after 26...♕f6 27 ♘e7+ White wins the exchange) 27 ♖xf4 exf4 28 ♗d4 ♕g6 (28...f6 29 ♗xf6 wins for White) 29 ♗xg7 (29 exf5 ♕xg1+ 30 ♗xg1 f6 is less clear as Black's king is relatively secure) 29...♔xg7 30 exf5 ♕xg1+ 31 ♔xg1 ♖g8 32 ♔f2 should be winning for White. He will have ♕+2♗ vs 2♖, and in addition Black's king remains exposed.

26 ♖gxg3 (D)

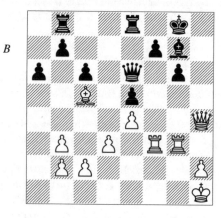

B

The deadly threat is 27 ♖h3. When I was younger, I would have quite happily sacrificed considerable material to reach an attacking position like this. As an older player, such a position seems much more attractive when it is reached with material equality!

26 ... b6

Forced. Black must free the f8-square for his king.

27 ♗e3

27 ♗a3 c5 only makes life harder for White.

27 ... ♕d7

There is no longer any hope of mounting a defence:

1) 27...♕e7 loses to 28 ♗g5 followed by ♖h3.

2) 27...f5 28 exf5 gxf5 29 ♖xg7+! ♔xg7 30 ♖g3+ ♔f8 31 ♗h6+ ♔f7 32 ♖g7+ ♔f8 33 ♖h7+ ♔g8 34 ♕g5+ and White mates next move.

3) 27...♖b7 28 ♗h6 ♕e7 29 ♗g5 ♕b4 30 ♖h3 ♖e6 31 ♕h7+ ♔f8 32 ♖f1, followed by ♖hf3, wins for White.

28 ♖h3 ♔f8
29 ♕h7 ♖b7

29...♖e6 30 ♗h6 ♗xh6 31 ♕xh6+ ♔e7 32 ♖xf7+ ♔xf7 33 ♕h7+ ♔e8 34 ♕h8+ ♔e7 35 ♖h7+ and White wins.

30 ♕xg6

30 ♗h6 ♗xh6 31 ♕h8+ ♔e7 32 ♕f6+ ♔f8 33 ♖xh6 is quicker, but it no longer matters.

30 ... ♖e6

30...♕xh3 31 ♕d6+ wins Black's queen, while 30...♕e6 loses to 31 ♕g2 followed by ♖h7.

31 ♖h8+! 1-0

After 31...♗xh8 32 ♗h6+ ♔e7 (32...♔e8 33 ♕g8+ ♔e7 34 ♕f8#) 33 ♖xf7+ ♔d8 (33...♔d6 34 ♗f8+ ♔c7 35 ♕xe6) 34 ♖xd7+ ♔xd7 35 ♕h7+ White wins easily.

A draw in round 7 and a win in round 8 left me half a point ahead of second-placed Krasenkow, and by coincidence we had to meet in the last round. I was Black, and although Krasenkow tried very hard to win, in the end I held the draw to take first prize outright with 7/9, a very high score for a round-robin event. Krasenkow's 6½ was also a good performance and indeed we were the only two players to finish above 50%!

In February, I travelled to Vejle in Denmark for a pleasant 10-player round-robin event. My start was far from auspicious, as after 4 rounds I had just 50%, including a win over local player P.Madsen who was destined to lose every game in the tournament. The culprit was a loss to Mortensen in which I unwisely attempted to play for a win in a level position.

In round 5 things took a turn for the better with the following game, in which White adopted the double-edged strategy of launching an attack before completing his development. The main theme of the game is the balance between material and development. White is willing to sacrifice a considerable amount of material (specifically, his a1-rook) in order to further his attack. Had Black accepted the rook, then White would have established a very dangerous lead in development. Black chose a different plan, based on the advance ...e5, but this involved two non-developing pawn moves, and by sacrificing a piece White was able to launch a deadly attack based on his better development and Black's insecure king. The correct path was later shown by Judit Polgar; Black could have secured an advantage by concentrating on development rather than material, and playing to eliminate White's important central d5-pawn. Fortunately for me, White's plan was good enough for a point in this game, before it was consigned to the rubbish heap of history.

Game 9

J. Nunn – M. Sher
Vejle 1994
Sicilian Defence, 2 c3

1 e4 c5
2 c3

What's this? The author of *Beating the Sicilian* dodging the critical lines? Well, yes, sometimes you just have to be practical. There is no doubt in my mind that if you really want to test the Sicilian then you have to play the main lines

of the Open Sicilian. The problem is that there are just so many of them: Najdorf, Sveshnikov, Dragon, Taimanov, Kan, Scheveningen, and many lesser lines. Each of these has its own huge body of theory and keeping up with developments in all of them is a substantial task. When you are young and have a large appetite for theory (and more time!) taking on such a burden is no problem. But as you become older, with other demands on your time (family, job, etc.) then it becomes more and more difficult to keep up with everything. At this stage it may make sense to reduce your theoretical overhead by adopting one of the 'lesser' lines against the Sicilian: 2 c3, or the Closed Sicilian, or lines with ♗b5. At this time I was toying with 2 c3, mixing it up with Open Sicilians. However, my results with 2 c3 were not especially good and later I started to play some lines with ♗b5 (see Games 42 and 43). However, I never gave up the Open Sicilian entirely (see Game 41) and this variety probably made it harder for opponents to prepare for me. Another reason for playing 2 c3 was that I had been helping Mickey Adams prepare for his Candidates match with Gelfand at the start of 1994, and we spent a long time looking at 2 c3 (although Mickey lost the match, he did win a good game, the fifth, with 2 c3).

2   ...   d5

The other major line is 2...♘f6, but the alternatives 2...d6, 2...e6 and 2...g6 are all perfectly playable.

3   exd5   ♕xd5
4   ♘f3 (D)

There aren't any major advantages to playing this rather than the immediate 4 d4. Perhaps the only possible point is that after 4 ♘f3 e5 White can try 5 ♘a3!? rather than the transpositional 5 d4.

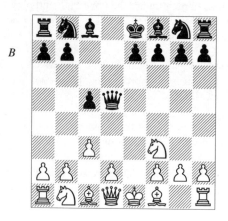

4   ...   ♘c6

Black has various systems available. The most common one these days is 4...♘f6 5 d4

♗g4, although the older 5...e6 is still often played. There are both pros and cons to playing 4...♘c6 rather than 4...♘f6. Black increases the pressure on d4, but at the same time exposes himself to a possible central push by c4 and d5. However, in many cases Black plays a later ...♘f6, and the two lines transpose.

5   d4   ♗g4

The combination of ...♘c6 and ...♗g4 is unusual, but perfectly playable.

6   ♗e2 (D)

6 dxc5!? is an interesting alternative which has become popular recently. It may offer White more chances of an advantage than the traditional 6 ♗e2.

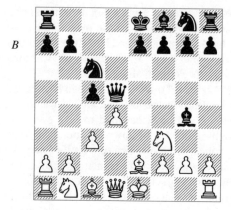

6   ...   e6

After this I was already on my own. Adams and I had looked at 6...cxd4 7 cxd4 e6, but we didn't examine the immediate 6...e6, perhaps being under the impression that allowing c4 and d5 couldn't be good. In fact, Black has two playable alternatives here:

1) 6...0-0-0!? is a very double-edged move. Black steps up the pressure against d4, but his king can be exposed on the queenside. To my mind this is taking one risk too many, but White has not managed to find a definite refutation: 7 ♗e3, 7 h3 and 7 0-0 are all possible replies, with the last perhaps the most dangerous.

2) 6...cxd4 7 cxd4 e6 8 h3 ♗h5 9 ♘c3 ♕a5 (in the lines with ...♘f6 rather than ...♘c6, it is normal to retreat the queen to d6 after ♘c3, but here 9...♕d6 is bad due to 10 d5 exd5 11 0-0! with a strong initiative) 10 0-0 ♘f6 with a standard type of position in which White has an edge.

The move played is probably less safe than 6...cxd4 7 cxd4 e6, but it is not really wrong.

7 h3

When Black develops his bishop to g4 in the c3 Sicilian, it is usually a good idea for White to push the bishop back to h5. This gives him the option of driving the bishop away by g4 at a moment's notice and in some lines it is important to prevent the bishop from returning to the queenside along the g4-c8 diagonal.

7 ... ♗h5

8 c4

This is White's only chance to demonstrate that 6...e6 is wrong. After 8 0-0 Black can exchange on d4 and we are back in standard lines.

8 ... ♕d6 (D)

Definitely the best square. 8...♕d8 9 g4 ♗g6 10 d5 really is good for White since in this position Black cannot yet castle, and 8...♕d7 9 g4 ♗g6 10 d5 exd5 11 cxd5 ♘b4 12 ♘e5 ♕xd5 13 ♗b5+ ♔d8 14 0-0 ♔c7 15 ♘c3 ♕xd1 16 ♖xd1 gave White fantastic play for the pawn in Adamski-L.Å.Schneider, Wroclaw 1981.

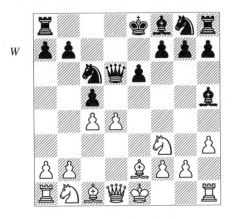

9 g4?

Despite its success in this game, I now have to admit that this move is wrong. Playing for a direct attack is a risky business so early in the game, when most of White's pieces are still at home. If the attack fails to break through, then White's self-inflicted weaknesses may well prove fatal. In such situations the result is often poised on a knife-edge, and a tactical resource several moves down the line may reverse the verdict on the whole continuation. That is the case here: White's initial success in this game led Nigel Short to repeat the idea, only for it to

be shot down in flames by Judit Polgar – more on that later. Suffice to say that if White sets his ambitions lower, then he should be able to secure a small advantage. The main line runs 9 d5 ♗xf3 10 ♗xf3 ♘d4 11 0-0 e5 12 ♗e3 ♘f6 13 ♘c3 ♗e7 14 ♗xd4 exd4 15 ♘b5 ♕d7 16 d6 ♗xd6 17 ♗xb7 ♖b8 18 ♖e1+ with a slight plus for White.

9 ... ♗g6

10 d5

Once started on the attacking path, there is no way back.

10 ... ♘b4

The only move. 10...exd5 11 cxd5 ♘b4 12 ♕a4+ ♔d8 (the preliminary exchange on d5 means that Black cannot play 12...♕d7 due to 13 ♗b5) 13 0-0 ♘f6 14 ♘c3 is dangerous for Black as his king is exposed in the centre of the board.

11 0-0 (D)

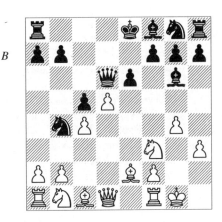

White offers the rook on a1, and during the game I spent most time on acceptance of the offer. However, the refutation of White's idea is based on simply ignoring the offered rook and playing for quick development.

11 ... f6?

The various possibilities are:

1) 11...♘c2?! (accepting the sacrifice gives White a very dangerous attack) 12 ♘a3! ♘xa1 (12...♘xa3 13 ♕a4+ favours White) 13 ♘b5 and now:

1a) 13...♕d7 14 ♘e5 only makes matters worse for Black.

1b) 13...♕b6 14 ♗f4 0-0-0 (14...♖c8 15 ♕a4 ♔d8 16 ♘xa7 is very good for White, while 14...♗c2 15 ♕d2 loses time for Black, since after White takes on a1 Black will have to move his bishop away) 15 ♗c7 ♕xb5 16 cxb5 ♔xc7 17 ♕xa1 exd5 18 b4! cxb4 19 ♕e5+ ♗d6 20 ♕xg7 with an advantage for White.

1c) 13...♕b8 (the critical try) 14 ♕a4 *(D)* (14 d6 ♗c2 15 ♕d2 f6 is unclear) and now:

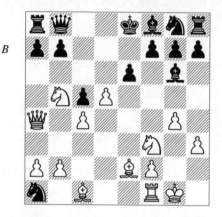

1c1) 14...♘f6 15 ♘c7+ ♔d8 16 ♗f4 ♗c2 17 ♕a5 ♔c8 18 ♖xa1 is winning for White.

1c2) 14...♗c2 15 ♘c7+ ♔d8 (15...♔e7 16 d6+ ♔xd6 17 ♗f4+ ♔e7 18 ♕b5 is winning for White) 16 ♕e8+ ♔xc7 17 ♗f4+ ♗d6 18 ♕xf7+ ♔b6 (18...♔d8 19 ♗xd6 ♕xd6 20 ♕xb7 ♖b8 21 ♕xg7 exd5 22 ♖xh8 ♔c7 23 ♖xa1 is very good for White) 19 ♕xe6 h5 (19...♘f6 20 ♗xd6 ♕c8 21 b4 wins for White) 20 ♗xd6 ♕e8 21 ♗e7+ ♔a5 22 ♗xc5 and White wins.

1c3) 14...♔d8 15 dxe6 fxe6 16 ♖d1+ ♔e7 17 ♘d6 ♕c7 (17...♘f6 18 ♗f4 ♗c2 19 ♕b5 ♗xd1 20 ♗xd1 a6 21 ♕xc5 and White wins) 18 ♗f4! ♗c2 19 ♕a3 ♗xd1 20 ♗xd1 ♕b6 21 ♕e3 (threatening 22 ♘g5) 21...h6 22 ♘e5 with a massive attack for White.

2) 11...exd5! 12 cxd5 0-0-0 (ignoring the a1-rook, Black seeks simply to win the d5-pawn) 13 ♘c3 *(D)* and now:

2a) 13...♘c2 14 ♘b5 with another branch:

2a1) 14...♖xd5? 15 ♗f4! b6 16 ♕xd5 (16 ♘c7?! ♕b7! 17 ♗a6 ♕xa6 18 ♘xa6 ♖xd1 19 ♖axd1 ♘e7 is unclear) 16...♖xd5 17 ♖ad1 and White's initiative is worth more than a pawn.

2a2) 14...♕b8! 15 ♗g5 ♘xa1 (15...f6? 16 ♗h4 ♘xa1 17 ♗g3 ♕a8 18 ♕a4 with a crushing attack) 16 ♗xd8 ♔xd8 17 ♖xa1 a6 18 ♘a3 ♕f4 19 ♘c4 is unclear.

2b) 13...♘xd5 14 ♘xd5 ♕xd5 15 ♕xd5 ♖xd5 16 ♗c4 ♖d8 17 ♘e5 f6 (17...♘f6? 18

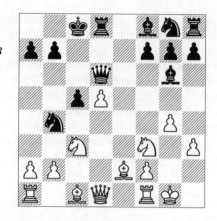

♗xf7 is very good for White, while 17...♗d6 18 ♘xf7 ♗xf7 19 ♗xf7 gives White an edge thanks to his two bishops) 18 ♘xg6 hxg6 19 ♗f4 ♗d6 20 ♗xd6 ♖xd6 21 ♖fe1 with good play for the pawn.

2c) 13...♘f6! was Judit Polgar's innovation. Black simply develops another piece and increases the pressure on d5; at the same time, Black reserves the option of playing ...♘c2 or ...♗c2 at some stage. White is now in trouble and the game Short-J.Polgar, Isle of Lewis (rapidplay) 1995 continued 14 ♕a4?! (probably not best, but in fact White doesn't have a good continuation) 14...a6 15 a3 ♗c2 16 b3 ♘bxd5 17 ♘xd5 ♕xd5 18 ♗f4 ♕xb3 with a winning position for Black.

The above analysis is very revealing and in many ways is typical for situations in which material is sacrificed in the opening. Sacrifices made later in the game, when the pieces are already developed, are normally made to expose the enemy king or to inflict serious positional weaknesses. Opening sacrifices are special in that the compensation often consists of a lead in development (which, it is true, may later be converted into a direct attack). Judging the balance between material and development is often quite difficult, but it is important not to underestimate the value of having more pieces in play. In the above analysis Black could win a rook, but this led to trouble. The correct course involved playing to win a mere pawn, because this could be achieved without interrupting Black's development.

The logic behind the move played is that Black was worried about White's bishop arriving on f4 after the queen is driven away by

♘c3-b5, so he anticipates this by preparing ...e5. At the same time he keeps White's other knight out of e5. Unfortunately, Black simply cannot afford a non-developing move in such a tense situation, and now White's attack breaks through by force.

12 ♘c3 ♘c2

Black goes for the rook on a1, but curiously he never gets a chance to take it! However, the alternatives were also good for White; for example, 12...e5 13 ♘h4 0-0-0 14 a3 ♘a6 15 ♗e3 followed by b4 gives White a strong attack without any sacrifice, while 12...exd5 is no longer effective after 13 a3! ♘c2 14 ♘xd5 ♘xa1 15 ♗f4 ♕c6 16 ♘c7+ ♔f7 17 ♘xa8 ♘c2 18 ♕d5+ ♕xd5 19 cxd5 with an excellent position for White, who has a large lead in development and a dangerous passed pawn.

13 ♘b5 ♕b6

Forced, as 13...♕b8 14 dxe6 is horrible for Black.

14 ♗f4 e5 (D)

Clearly the only move (and the point behind 12...f6?). 14...♖c8 loses to 15 dxe6 ♕xe6 16 ♗d3!.

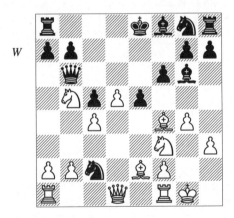

15 ♘xe5!

This is the refutation of Black's play. White not only ignores the a1-rook, but sacrifices an additional knight! The newly opened lines, coupled with Black's poor development, give White a tremendous attack.

15 ... fxe5

After 15...♘xa1 16 ♘xg6 hxg6 17 ♘c7+ White wins at once.

16 ♗xe5 0-0-0

There is no defence:

1) 16...♘xa1 17 ♘c7+ ♔f7 18 ♘xa8 ♕d8 19 f4 (19 d6 is also very strong) 19...♗c2 20 ♕xa1 ♕xa8 21 ♕c1 ♗e4 22 ♕e3 ♗c2 23 ♗b8! is a neat win.

2) 16...♖c8 17 d6 ♔d7 18 g5 ♖e8 19 ♗g4+ ♔d8 20 ♕f3 a6 21 d7 axb5 22 dxe8♕+ ♔xe8 23 ♗d7+ ♔xd7 24 ♕xf8 is also winning for White.

3) 16...♔f7 17 d6 ♕c6 (17...♘f6 18 ♗f3 ♘b4 19 g5 is also crushing) 18 ♖c1 ♘b4 19 a3 ♘a6 20 f4 with overwhelming threats.

17 g5!

The threat of ♗g4+ forces Black's reply.

17 ... h5

The lines 17...♘e7 18 ♗g4+ ♖d7 19 ♗c7, 17...♗f5 18 ♗g4! ♗xg4 19 ♕xg4+ ♖d7 20 ♕f5! (forking c2 and f8) and 17...♘xa1 18 ♗g4+ ♖d7 19 ♗xd7+ ♔xd7 20 ♕g4+ ♔d8 21 ♕f4 all win for White.

The interpolation of g5 and ...h5 greatly helps White, because Black can no longer meet ♗c7 by ...♕f6.

18 ♖c1 ♘b4

18...a6 loses to 19 ♗c7, while 18...♖d7 19 ♖xc2 a6 20 ♘c3 ♗xc2 21 ♕xc2 ♗d6 22 f4, with ♘e4 to come, will give White a crushing central pawn-mass. Therefore Black has to admit that the knight's mission to c2 has been a failure.

19 ♗c7

Black must give up his queen for three minor pieces, normally a reasonable trade but hopeless here thanks to White's two extra pawns and Black's poor development.

19 ... ♕xb5

Not 19...♕a6 20 ♗xd8 ♔xd8 21 a3 trapping the knight. 19...♕xc7 20 ♘xc7 ♔xc7 would have offered more resistance, but even here 21 a3 ♘a6 22 ♗d3 ♗xd3 23 ♕xd3 ♗d6 24 ♖ce1 ♘e7 25 ♖e6 will win for White in the end.

20 cxb5 ♔xc7

Black hopes that by giving up the queen on b5 he will be able to win the d5-pawn; however, he is never able to achieve this and in fact the white pawn on b5 only serves to trap the knight on b4.

21 ♗c4

Threatening 22 a3.

21 ... ♘e7
22 ♕f3 ♘c2

The knight hopes to escape to the excellent square d4. 22...♘bxd5 23 ♖fd1 is hopeless for

Black, while 22...♘f5 23 ♖fd1 ♔b8 24 a3 ♘d4 25 ♖xd4 cxd4 26 axb4 wins for White.

23   ♖fd1

White is quick to seal the escape-route.

23   ...   ♘d4 (D)

23...♔b8 loses to 24 d6.

24   ♖xd4

The simplest.

24   ...   cxd4
25   ♕f4+   ♔d7

25...♖d6 26 b6+ axb6 27 ♗b5+ and 25...♔b6 26 ♗d3 win for White.

26   b6

A curious echo of White's 17 g5: he pushes a pawn to free a square for the light-squared bishop.

1-0

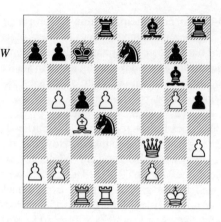

W

After 26...a6 (to prevent ♗b5+) 27 ♗b3 ♗d3 28 ♗a4+ ♗b5 29 ♗xb5+ axb5 30 ♕f7 White mates in a few moves.

I won two more games towards the end of the tournament to finish on 6/9, which was a respectable enough score, but insufficient to catch the Hansens (Curt and Lars Bo) who tied for first on 6½ points. Shortly afterwards, I travelled to Germany to play in the Bundesliga. I have played for quite a number of different clubs in the Bundesliga, but on this occasion I was representing Hamburg.

My game against Bologan started badly, and I soon found myself in a horrible position. The further course of the game shows that you should never give up hope. If you have a very bad position, one of the keys to a successful defence is to identify any possible assets in your position and then try to make the most of them. In the diagram below, Black's slightly exposed king and White's kingside pawn-majority provide a tiny glimmer of hope to offset the disaster on the rest of the board.

Game 10
J. Nunn – V. Bologan
Bundesliga 1993/4

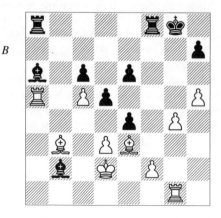

B

Luck undoubtedly plays a part in chess. In this position White is dead lost, and I seriously considered resigning. However, one thing stayed my hand. Bologan, although a very strong player, has a tendency to run short of time and remarkable things sometimes happen during time-trouble! Looking at the position, we can see few hopeful signs for White. Black, to move, has active pieces and a mobile central pawn-mass. White's pieces are scattered in ineffective and vulnerable positions and his king is exposed. White's kingside pawn-structure represents the remnants of his earlier futile attacking attempts; oddly, it is this apparently unimportant feature which eventually has a vital influence on the play.

| 26 | ... | **d4?** |

Even in a winning position, it is essential to look for the most accurate move. If you make a couple of inaccuracies, the chances of making a more serious error increase, so it is worth putting a little effort into finding a clean kill. The move played wins material, but it permits White to develop a few counterchances. Black had two straightforward wins:

1) 26...♖fb8 27 ♗c2 (27 ♗a2 ♗xd3 28 ♖xa8 ♖xa8 is also an easy win) 27...d4 and now Black wins the bishop without surrendering his e6-pawn.

2) 26...♗xd3 27 ♖xa8 ♖xa8 is even simpler. There is no defence to the threats of ...d4 and ...♖a3.

| 27 | **♗xe6+** |

This not only grabs a useful pawn but also drives Black's king onto the long diagonal, where it is exposed to various tactical possibilities. White is still lost, but at least now one can imagine Black going wrong.

| 27 | ... | **♔h8** |

Playing to win the a5-rook would backfire after 27...♔g7 28 dxe4 ♗c3+ 29 ♔c2 ♗xa5? (of course 29...dxe3 is still very good for Black, with play similar to the game) 30 ♗xd4+ ♔h6 31 ♗e3+ and White forces perpetual check.

| 28 | **dxe4** *(D)* |

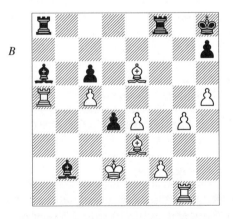

The only chance is to give up a piece.

| 28 | ... | **♗c3+!** |

Black finds the best way to gain material. After 28...dxe3+ 29 ♔xe3 ♗e5 30 f3 ♖fd8 31 ♖b1 ♖d3+ (31...♔g7 32 g5 is also unclear) 32 ♔f2 Black is caught in an uncomfortable pin on the a-file and it is doubtful whether he can win.

| 29 | **♔c2** | **dxe3** |

Not, of course, 29...♗xa5?? 30 ♗xd4+ and mate.

| 30 | **♖xa6** |

This is forced since 30 ♔xc3 exf2 costs White a whole rook.

| 30 | ... | **♖xa6** |
| 31 | **♔xc3** | **♖a3+** |

31...exf2 32 ♖f1 ♖a3+ is also good and would transpose to the note to Black's 32nd move.

| 32 | **♔d4** *(D)* |

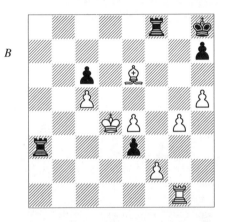

White goes up the board in the hope of using his king in an attack against Black's king. Also, when your opponent is in time-trouble it is usually a good idea to play actively.

| 32 | ... | **♖xf2?** |

This error throws the win into doubt. Black was probably worried that after 32...exf2 33 ♖f1 White would cut off the rook's support of the advanced pawn by ♗f5, but the solution to this was just to play the rook across the critical square by 33...♖ff3!. Then Black should win without too much trouble; for example, 34 ♔e5 ♖ae3 35 ♗c4 ♖e1 36 h6 (36 ♔d6 ♖xe4 37 ♗a6 ♖f6+ is even easier for Black) 36...♖xf1 37 ♗xf1 ♖e3 38 ♔d6 ♖xe4 39 ♔xc6 ♖xg4 40 ♔d7 ♖g1 41 ♗a6 f1♕ 42 ♗xf1 ♖xf1 43 c6 ♔g8 44 c7 ♖d1+ 45 ♔e7 ♖c1 46 ♔d8 ♔f7 and Black wins.

| 33 | **♖b1!** |

Threatening 34 ♖b8+ ♔g7 35 g5 ♖f8 36 ♖b7+ ♔h8 37 g6 followed by mate. One of the most unpleasant things which can happen in time-trouble is that your opponent suddenly develops counterplay from a situation in which you had been in total control. Such a shift often requires a fundamental reassessment of the position, but lack of time may force you to operate on a superficial move-by-move basis. 33 g5 is less effective, as 33...e2 34 Ξe1 Ξg2 35 ♗c4 Ξxg5 36 Ξxe2 Ξxh5 leaves Black with a decisive material advantage.

33   ...   Ξd2+?!

33...h6 probably offers more chances. However, even here 34 ♔e5 e2 35 Ξe1 Ξd3 36 ♗c4 Ξd2 37 ♗a6 ♔g7 38 ♗c4 Ξc2 (the only way for Black to make progress is to swap the e2-pawn for the c5-pawn) 39 ♗d3 Ξxc5+ 40 ♔d4 Ξa5 41 ♗xe2 ♔f6 42 ♔e3 Ξh2 43 ♔f4 leads to a position in which a win for Black is far from certain.

34   ♔e5 (D)

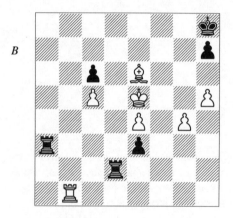

34   ...   e2?

The abrupt change of fortunes takes its toll on Black, since after this further error he is in danger of losing. However, by now there were no winning chances; for example:

1) 34...Ξa8 35 Ξe1 e2 36 g5 and White has sufficient counterplay.

2) 34...Ξad3 35 g5 Ξd1 36 Ξb7 e2 is an interesting line. White draws by 37 Ξe7! Ξd8

(37...Ξd5+ 38 exd5 e1♕+ 39 ♔d6 ♕g3+ 40 ♔xc6 ♕b8 41 g6 and it is time for Black to give perpetual check) 38 g6 hxg6 39 hxg6 Ξ8d5+ (the only move to avoid mate!) 40 ♔f6 Ξf1+ 41 ♗f5 Ξd8 (41...Ξdxf5+? loses: 42 exf5 e1♕ 43 Ξxe1 Ξxe1 44 ♔f7 Ξg1 45 f6 Ξg2 46 g7+ ♔h7 47 ♔f8 Ξg3 48 f7 Ξxg7 49 ♔e8 and White wins the pawn ending) 42 Ξh7+ ♔g8 43 Ξg7+ with perpetual check.

35   Ξb8+   ♔g7

36   g5 (D)

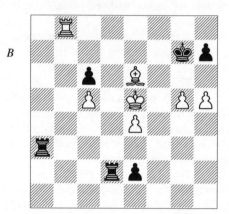

Suddenly Black is faced with a threat of mate in one. With only seconds left on his clock, he blunders, missing the draw that was still there with accurate play.

36   ...   h6??

The saving line was 36...Ξd5+! 37 ♗xd5 (37 exd5?? fails here because 37...e1♕+ 38 ♔d6 ♕g3+ picks up the rook) 37...cxd5 38 Ξb1 dxe4 39 ♔xe4 Ξc3! (the right idea, keeping the rook behind the dangerous c-pawn) 40 ♔d4 Ξc2 41 Ξe1 ♔f7 42 ♔d5 Ξd2+ 43 ♔c6 ♔e6 44 ♔c7 ♔f5 45 g6 hxg6 46 h6 ♔f6 47 c6 g5 48 h7 ♔g7 with a draw.

37   Ξg8+   1-0

It's mate next move.

In March I travelled to Monaco for an unusual chess event – the Amber tournament. The series of Amber tournaments started in 1992 and at the time of writing is still going strong. The event is sponsored by Mr and Mrs van Oosterom, and is named after their elder daughter, Melody Amber (the younger daughter's name is given to a billiards tournament). Joop van Oosterom was a founder of the Volmac software company, and when the company was finally sold, he became a wealthy man. He has sponsored a number of chess events since his retirement.

The format of the Amber tournament, a double-round event with one round of normal rapid chess and one round of blindfold rapid, has remained unchanged since the second Amber tournament. When the event started, some commentators poked fun at the unusual format, but these days the

Amber tournament has become an accepted part of the chess scene and the format does not seem at all out of place. In the intervening years, what one might call 'classical chess' tournaments, with slow time-limits and one game per day, have been in relative decline, while 'alternative chess' events such as rapid tournaments and the Amber tournament have increased enormously. I have attended all the Amber tournaments except the first. In 1993 I had the onerous duty of deciding where the diagrams should go in the bulletins, in 1994 and 1995 I participated myself and since then I have attended as a spectator. I had never played blindfold chess before and I realized that the event would be quite a challenge for me. Given the strength of the event I was quite satisfied with my result. I scored 4½/11 in the rapid event, and a pleasing 5/11 in the blindfold. My total of 9½/22, including 2-0 against both Ljubojević and Korchnoi, put me in a tie for 8th place with Yasser Seirawan.

An odd incident occurred against Anatoly Karpov. I had already won the rapid game with the aid of a considerable amount of luck and the following position arose in the blindfold game.

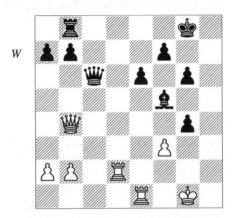

A. Karpov – J. Nunn
Monaco, Amber tournament (blindfold) 1994

I should explain that the players had to enter their moves into a computer (by mouse or key-board) and the only information given to them was the previous move played. In the above diagram, it was White to play and Karpov attempted to enter the move h3xg4 on the keyboard. Of course, this is illegal and the computer rejected the move. By the time he had realized what was wrong and tried to enter f3xg4, he had lost on time. One might think that a loss on time would be the end of the matter, but the struggle had only just begun. Karpov proceeded to make a considerable fuss, claim-ing that after he had entered the first, incorrect move, the computer had frozen and prevented him from correcting his move. All efforts to reproduce this 'fault' proved unsuccessful, and it seems likely that, in his haste, Karpov had forgotten to cancel the incorrect move before entering a new one. Karpov demanded that the game be replayed from the beginning, and to my astonishment one of the arbiters tended to agree with him. Seeing which way the wind was blowing, and having no wish to tire myself out playing an extra blindfold game, I made what I thought was the rather gener-ous offer to agree a draw. Karpov was at first disinclined to accept this, but I adamantly refused to replay the game and in the end he accepted. The position on the board is in fact winning for White, provided that after 37 fxg4 ♗c2 he finds the move 38 ♕d4! (the more obvious 38 ♖c1 lets Black off the hook after 38...♕e4); with only twenty seconds per move and playing blindfold, finding this would have been no easy task.

In June I competed in the King's Head weekend tournament in London, scoring 4½/5 to finish second behind Stuart Conquest. My next event was the annual Lloyds Bank tournament held in London during August. Sadly, this was to be the last Lloyds Bank tournament. The Lloyds Bank

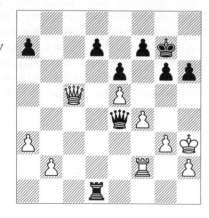

sponsorship was driven by the chess interest of the bank's chairman, Sir Jeremy Morse, who is a respected chess problemist (it is said that the famous fictional detective Inspector Morse is based partly on Sir Jeremy). Now Sir Jeremy was retiring and the bank's sponsorship was shifting to other areas. It is always unfortunate when a chess sponsor departs, but all sponsorship has a limited life and the chess world was very lucky to have such a long-running sponsor as Lloyds Bank. In fact I believe that Lloyds Bank got a very good deal with this sponsorship. The event attracted widespread publicity and in a successful piece of 'branding', it was always referred to as the 'Lloyds Bank tournament' and never as, for example, the 'London Open'. Sir Jeremy almost always presented the prizes at the Lloyds Bank tournament himself. Normally, when a representative of a sponsor gives a speech, it starts with something like "Well, I don't play chess myself, but...". However, Sir Jeremy once started his speech by telling his audience all about a selfmate in 342 moves, much to the bemusement of the foreign players.

I played in the first-ever Lloyds Bank tournament in 1977, scoring 7/10, and had competed several times during the intervening years. Over the years the tournament had become much stronger, and the 1994 tournament attracted a particularly wide range of grandmasters because it was a qualifier for the London leg of the Intel/PCA Speed Chess Grand Prix. Originally, there were going to be six qualifying places, but at the last moment somebody in the PCA decided to slip a computer into the speed chess event, thereby reducing the number of qualifying places available from the Lloyds Bank tournament from six to five.

This tournament was the first time I had seen digital chess clocks used on a large scale. Although these devices are entirely commonplace now, at the time they caused quite a lot of confusion. The switching of the display from hours and minutes to minutes and seconds when you reach the 20-minute mark caused some problems, as did the vexing question as to whether you have lost on time when the display shows 0:00 (the answer, by the way, is not necessarily). To add to the confusion, the arbiters seemed equally unprepared for the special problems posed by digital clocks. The upshot was that an extraordinary number of games ended in a loss on time as everybody struggled with the unfamiliar equipment. These days most events use digital clocks without problems, and it is hard to understand why they caused such difficulties on their introduction. However, progress is often like that: innovations are met with scepticism and hostility, which gradually shifts into acceptance and, in the end, they become regarded as essential.

I started with 1½/2 and my game in the third round had a neat finish.

Game 11
S. Björnsson – J. Nunn
London (Lloyds Bank) 1994

The position favours Black because his king is safer and his pieces more active. Given the relatively quiet position it doesn't appear very likely that Black will sacrifice his queen, but just watch what happens!

42   ♕e7?

It is understandable that White wants to set up a possible perpetual check, but taking his queen so far out of play is very risky. However, Black can also retain an advantage after other moves:

1) 42 ♕c3 g5 43 ♖d2 ♕e1 44 ♖xd1 ♕xd1 45 fxg5 hxg5 46 ♔g2 ♔g6 is clearly better for

Black because White's e5-pawn has lost its support and is very weak.

2) 42 b4 g5 43 ♕c2 ♕xc2 (43...♖d3 44 ♖d2 is just a draw) 44 ♖xc2 ♔g6 retains Black's advantage; for example, 45 ♔g4 (45 fxg5 hxg5 46 ♖c5 ♔f5 also favours Black) 45...h5+ 46 ♔f3 ♖d3+ 47 ♔e4 ♖xa3 48 fxg5 ♖b3 49 ♖c7 ♖xb4+ 50 ♔e3 ♖g4 and Black will be a pawn up in the rook ending.

42   ...   ♕f5+

Preventing the white check on f6 with gain of tempo.

43   ♔g2   d5!

Suddenly Black introduces a new element. If White doesn't take this pawn, then in addition to the above-mentioned advantages, Black will also have a dangerous passed pawn. Therefore White decides to capture.

44   exd6?!

Now, however, Black has a forced win. 44 ♕xa7 also loses, to 44...♕e4+ 45 ♔h3 ♖g1, followed by mate in a few moves.

44   ...   ♕e4+
45   ♔h3   ♖g1

The capture on d6 has removed the danger of a check on f6, so Black is free to pursue his attack against White's king. Of course, White has a dangerous d-pawn, but it turns out that Black's attack is irresistible.

46   d7

Resignation by White. The main line runs 46 f5 (46 ♕h4 ♕e1 47 ♖f3 ♕e2 mates quickly) 46...g5 and, amazingly, there is no defence to the threat of 47...♕h4+! (the queen sacrifice) 48 gxh4 g4#.

46   ...   ♕f5+
                    0-1

It's mate next move.

I also won in round 4, but then became bogged down in a run of three draws. This was particularly frustrating because in two of the games I missed a clear win. However, I moved ahead with a win in round 8, and in round 9 I arrived at the interesting position given below. The ensuing play shows that endings can be just as tactical and complicated as middlegame positions. This game features a curious mixture of chess and psychology. I hadn't seen White's 52nd move until he actually played it, and then I realized that I was losing a piece. Dropping a whole piece in an ending is usually the end of the game, but in this position there were some unusual features operating in Black's favour. I simply continued the game as if nothing had happened and, to the surprise of both players, it suddenly became clear that it was very difficult for White to exploit his extra piece. Petursson's disorientation must have been complete when Black turned down a repetition and started playing for a win. A final mistake on move 58 sealed White's fate.

Game 12

M. Petursson – J. Nunn

London (Lloyds Bank) 1994

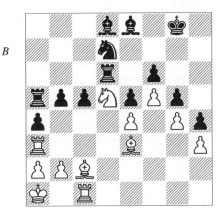

B

Considering that the first capture occurred on move 34, the players have done a good job of clearing some wood off the board. Black is a pawn up with menacing queenside pawns, but his passive bishops and White's active knight provide White with some compensation. I admit that during the game I seriously overestimated my position; I thought that if I exchanged the knight on d5, the queenside pawns would decide the issue.

42   ...   ♗f7?!

42...c4! was much simpler. After 43 ♖d1 (43 ♗d2 ♖a7 44 ♗b4 ♖da6, with ...♗b6 to come, is also very good for Black) 43...♖aa6 Black is ready to execute his plan of ...♗f7 and ...♗xd5, with excellent winning chances. The move played allows White to double rooks on the d-file, which not only solves the problem of the outlying rook on a3, but also creates threats along the d-file itself.

43   ♖d1   ♗xd5

It is too late for 43...c4, because White threatens 44 ♘xf6+.

44   ♖ad3! *(D)*

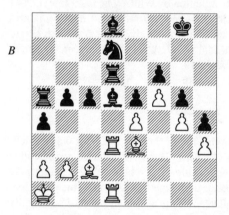

The only move, but a strong one. If White is left with a pawn on d5 then there will be no open files for his counterplay and the d5-pawn would soon become weak; in this case Black would indeed be winning.

44   ...   ♘b6?

It often happens that a small error is followed by a much more serious one. This is a result of failing to adapt to a new situation by lowering one's expectations. I still thought I was winning and clearly 44...♘b6, if it is tactically viable, will win by force. Since my position had been 'winning' a couple of moves ago, it seemed to be inevitable that the tactics would work, and I hardly bothered to check the details. As one might expect, a nasty surprise was waiting for me. The correct line was 44...♗e7 45 ♖xd5 ♖xd5 46 ♖xd5 ♘b6 47 ♖d1 ♖a6 (Black must defend the knight in order to meet ♗d3 by ...c4) 48 ♗d3 c4 49 ♗e2 and although Black still has winning chances, White's two bishops and active rook make Black's task significantly more complicated. The best plan is 49...♔f8 50 a3 ♔e8 51 ♔b1 ♘a8!, followed by ...♘c7, ...♖c6 and ...♗c5. Black should probably

win in the end, but this plan is not exactly obvious.

The move played not only throws away the win, but should even have given White an advantage.

45   ♗xc5

Of course, anything else is hopeless; for example, 45 exd5 c4 46 ♖3d2 ♘d7 followed by ...♗b6 leaves Black a pawn up with a positional advantage.

45   ...   ♖c6 *(D)*

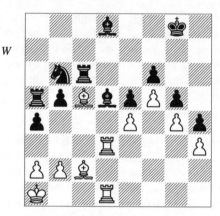

46   ♗b4?

This is enough to draw, but White had an even stronger continuation in 46 ♖c3! (46 ♗xb6? loses to 46...♗xb6), when Black has no good reply:

1) 46...♘d7 47 ♖xd5 ♘xc5 (after 47...♖xc5 48 ♖xd7 ♗b6 49 ♖d6 White wins the f6-pawn) 48 ♖xd8+ ♔f7 49 a3! is good for White.

2) 46...♗c4 47 ♖xd8+ ♔f7 48 ♗b4 ♖a7 (48...♖a8 49 ♖xa8 ♘xa8 50 ♗d3 also favours White) 49 ♔b1 ♖ac7 50 ♖d2! (the immediate 50 b3? is bad due to 50...axb3 51 axb3 ♗f1! targeting White's vulnerable kingside pawns) 50...♔g7 (Black has no useful moves) 51 b3 axb3 52 axb3 ♗f7 (now 52...♗f1? loses to 53 ♖f3) 53 ♖xc6 ♖xc6 54 ♖d8 and White's two active bishops coupled with Black's badly-placed knight give White a clear advantage.

46   ...   ♖a8

47   ♗b1!

This regains the piece and restores material equality.

47   ...   ♗xe4?!

A very risky move, which was not really the result of careful calculation but more a panicky response to the new situation. I realized that I had thrown away my winning position, and suddenly I couldn't even see a clear route to a draw! Had I been more composed, I would doubtless have realized that with accurate play Black is not really in danger. His safest line is 47...♖c4 48 a3 ♗xe4 (48...♖xe4 49 ♖xd5 ♘xd5 50 ♗xe4 ♘xb4 51 ♗xa8 ♘c2+ 52 ♔b1 ♘d4 53 ♖c1 favours White) 49 ♖xd8+ ♖xd8 50 ♖xd8+ and now:

1) 50...♔g7 51 ♗xe4 ♖xe4 52 ♖d6 ♘c4 (52...♘c8 53 ♖d7+ costs Black his knight) 53 ♖d7+ ♔g8 54 ♖e7 forces perpetual check by ♖e8+ and ♖e7+, since Black's king cannot escape to h6 due to mate.

2) 50...♔f7 51 ♗xe4 (the line 51 ♗a2 ♗g2 52 ♗xc4+ ♘xc4 will also lead to a draw since sooner or later White must give perpetual check) 51...♖xe4 52 ♗c5! (52 ♖d6 ♘c8 is less clear) 52...♘c4 53 ♖f8+ ♔g7 54 ♖e8 ♘a5 55 ♖e7+ and Black must acquiesce to perpetual check since 55...♔h6? 56 ♔a2 ♘b3 57 ♗b4 is winning for White, as the threat of moving the rook and then playing ♗f8# wins material.

The move played should probably also lead to a draw, but only after some hair-raising adventures.

48	♖xd8+	♖xd8
49	♖xd8+	♔f7
50	♗xe4 (D)	

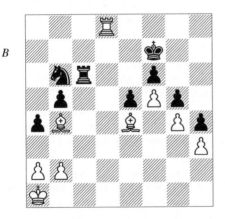

| 50 | ... | ♖c4 |

This was my idea. Black apparently wins the piece back and remains a pawn up. As Petursson immediately demonstrates, there is a flaw in Black's reasoning.

| 51 | ♗a5! |

White could force a draw by 51 a3 ♖xe4 52 ♗c5 transposing into the note to Black's 47th move, but the move played is more dangerous for Black since it wins a piece. What is odd is that, more or less by accident, winning the piece doesn't give White any real winning chances. In this respect Black, who had not yet realized that he is losing a piece, could count himself very lucky.

| 51 | ... | ♖xe4 |
| 52 | b3 (D) | |

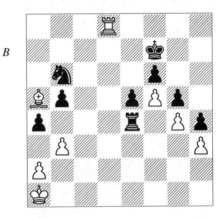

At one stroke White relieves his back rank and takes away the last flight-square from Black's knight, trapping it. I confess that I had overlooked this point when playing my 47th move. While White is taking the knight, Black will capture the h3-pawn. In the resulting position, White's bishop will be unable to help in the fight against Black's h-pawn because of the firmly defended pawn on e5, which completely blocks the b8-h2 diagonal. Thus White's rook has to remain on guard, ready to halt the h-pawn if Black should suddenly decide to push it. If Black could also win the g4-pawn, then the two connected passed pawns would be a formidable force. White, on the other hand, cannot easily make a passed pawn. His main chance lies in winning the f6-pawn, which breaks up the defence of e5 and allows his bishop to be deployed against the h-pawn. An important point is that it is very much in Black's favour for White's king to be confined, since Black can often gain a vital tempo by checking. During the game, neither player properly appreciated the significance of this factor. For example, here I could have played 52...a3 53 ♔b1 ♖e3 54 ♗xb6

♖xh3 which would have cut out the possibility in the following note. In this case White has no winning chances and must head for a draw by 55 ♗c5 ♖g3 56 ♖d7+, etc.

52	...	♖e3?!
53	♗xb6	♖xh3
54	bxa4?!	

This move should lead to a draw, but it would have been more accurate to play 54 ♔b2 axb3 55 a3!, which ensures that White's king will not be trapped on the first two ranks. After 55...♖g3 56 ♖d7+ ♔e8 57 ♖d6 ♖xg4 58 ♖xf6 h3 59 ♖h6 ♖g2+ 60 ♔xb3 g4 61 ♖h7 the most likely result is still a draw, but any advantage must lie with White.

| 54 | ... | bxa4 |
| 55 | ♖d7+ | ♔e8 (D) |

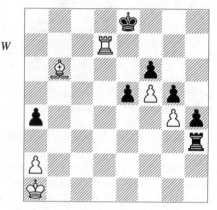

56   ♖d8+

White tries to gain time on the clock, but he is playing with fire because Black need not repeat the position. There were two satisfactory alternatives:

1) 56 ♖d6 should lead to a draw: 56...a3! (confining the king) 57 ♔b1 ♖h1+ 58 ♔c2 h3 (Black should only play ...h3 once he is sure that the pawn is truly dangerous, because otherwise the pawn has given up its secure position on h4 and will have to be defended by the rook) 59 ♖d8+ (59 ♖d2? h2 60 ♔d3 e4+ 61 ♔d4 e3 wins for Black, as does 59 ♖xf6? h2 60 ♖h6 ♖a1) 59...♔e7 (59...♔f7 60 ♖d7+ repeats) 60 ♖h8 ♔d6 (not 60...h2? 61 ♗c5+ ♔d7 62 ♗xa3 and wins) 61 ♗a5 h2 62 ♗d2! e4 63 ♔c3 ♔d5 and neither side can make progress.

2) 56 ♖d1 (playing to save the g-pawn) 56...♖c3 (56...♖g3 57 ♖g1 ♖f3 58 ♔b2 h3 59

♖h1 ♖g3 is also drawish) 57 ♔b2 ♖c4 58 ♗d8 ♔f7 59 ♖d7+ ♔e8 60 ♖d2 ♔f7 with a draw by repetition.

| 56 | ... | ♔e7 |

Playing for a win!

57   ♖h8

The idea is to play ♗d8+ to attack the f6-pawn. 57 ♖a8 was also possible; after 57...a3 58 ♔b1 (58 ♗c5+ ♔d7 59 ♗xa3 ♖g3 60 ♖a7+ ♔c6 61 ♗e7 h3 62 ♗xf6 h2 63 ♖h7 ♖g1+ 64 ♔b2 h1♕ 65 ♖xh1 ♖xh1 is slightly better for Black) 58...♔d6 the position is unclear, but I do not think Black can be worse.

| 57 | ... | a3 (D) |

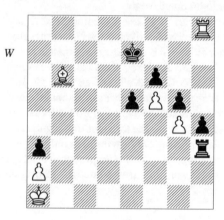

58   ♗d8+?

A serious error which results in White's pieces becoming totally tangled up. With correct play the position is still drawn, but White has to find a study-like resource: 58 ♔b1! ♖h1+ 59 ♔c2 ♖h2+ 60 ♔c3 ♖xa2 61 ♗d8+ ♔f7 62 ♖h7+ ♔g8 63 ♖d7 h3 64 ♗xf6 h2 65 ♗xg5 h1♕ 66 ♖d8+ with perpetual check.

| 58 | ... | ♔f7 |

Because of the mate threat White has to spend a tempo moving his king, and so has no time for ♖h6.

| 59 | ♔b1 | ♔g7 |

The rook's mission to h8 has been a failure; it has to turn around and come back again.

| 60 | ♖e8 | ♖d3! |

My best move of the game, found in the two minutes I had left to reach the move 60 time-control. The alternative was 60...♖h1+ 61 ♔c2 h3, but now 62 ♖e7+! (after 62 ♖e6 h2 63 ♗xf6+ ♔f7 64 ♗xe5 ♖c1+ 65 ♔xc1 h1♕+ 66 ♔c2 ♕f3! Black has fair winning chances)

62...♔f8 63 ♖h7 h2 64 ♗xf6 ♖a1 65 ♗xg5 h1♕ (65...♔g8 66 ♖d7 leads to perpetual check) 66 ♗e7+ ♔e8 67 ♖xh1 ♖xh1 68 ♗xa3 ♖h2+ 69 ♔c3 ♖h3+ 70 ♔b2 gives White good drawing chances.

The move played paralyses White's pieces because after 61 ♖e7+ ♔f8 he loses material, so in fact White cannot move his rook. Thus the bishop has to retreat, after which the rook can laboriously extract itself from e8, but the loss of time gives Black a winning position.

61 ♔c2 ♖d4

62 ♗b6

62 ♔b3 offers more resistance, but Black should win by 62...h3 63 ♖e7+ ♔f8 64 ♖h7 ♖d3+ 65 ♔c2 (65 ♔b4 loses to 65...♔g8!) 65...♔g8 66 ♖h5 ♖xd8 67 ♖xh3 ♖d4 68 ♖xa3 ♖xg4 69 ♖a8+ ♔g7 70 ♖a7+ ♔h6 71 ♖a6 (71 ♖f7 ♖c4+ 72 ♔d1 ♖c6 73 ♖e7 ♖a6 74 ♖e6 ♖xa2 75 ♖xf6+ ♔h5 76 ♖e6 g4 77 ♔e1 ♖a4! 78 ♖xe5 ♖f4 is decisive) 71...♖f4 72 ♖xf6+ ♔h5 73 ♔d3 g4 74 ♔e3 ♔g5 75 ♖f8 ♖xf5 76 ♖a8 g3 77 a4 ♔g4 78 ♖g8+ ♔h3 79 ♖h8+ ♔g2 80 a5 ♖f3+ 81 ♔e2 ♖a3 and White can resign.

62 ... ♖xg4 *(D)*

White has made no progress at all since move 55, while Black has removed an important pawn. White cannot even hope for perpetual check now, since Black's king can slip out via h5 and g4.

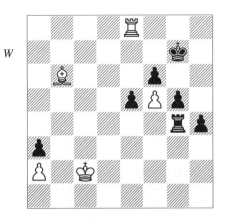

W

63 ♖e7+ ♔g8

64 ♖a7

After 64 ♖d7 h3 65 ♖d2 the simplest win is by 65...♖f4, preparing both ...g4 and ...♖xf5.

64 ... h3

The two connected passed pawns are too strong.

65 ♖a8+ ♔g7

66 ♖a7+ ♔h6

67 ♖a8 ♖g2+

68 ♔d3 ♔h5

69 ♖h8+ ♔g4

70 ♗d8 h2

0-1

After 71 ♔e4 ♖xa2 72 ♗xf6 ♖e2+, followed by ...a2, Black's pawns triumph.

In round 10 I drew to finish in a tie for third place on 7½/10, half a point more than I had achieved in the first Lloyds Bank tournament 17 years earlier. The multiple tie for third place was resolved by a blitz play-off amongst nine players to determine who should get the three remaining qualification places for the Intel/PCA speed chess event. Although I started the play-off well, a couple of losses near the end put me out of contention.

A few weeks later I travelled to the Isle of Man for an International Open. The Isle of Man is a small island in the Irish Sea which, although sharing much of British culture, is independent and has its own government and legal system. It is noted for tourism and financial services, the latter industry doubtless bolstered by the island's low tax rates. The Isle of Man tournament still exists and has steadily expanded over the intervening years; it is now an important fixture in the chess calendar and attracts many strong grandmasters from Europe. I played in solid style and went through the tournament without loss. With one round to go I had scored 5½/8 and in order to gain a major prize I had to win in the last round.

After a lacklustre opening, White was able to exploit a slip by Black to launch a dangerous kingside attack at the cost of a pawn or two. When things don't go according to plan, it is important not to be disheartened and resort to desperate measures too soon. In this game, Black decided that his position was bad and he lacked the motivation necessary to find the hidden defensive resource at move 21. This resource is based on two typical defensive motifs: returning the sacrificed material and utilizing control of the long diagonal for defensive purposes. The move played was followed by a second error (also a common occurrence) and the game was soon over.

Game 13
J. Nunn – J. Howell
Isle of Man 1994
Alekhine Defence

1	e4	♘f6
2	e5	♘d5
3	d4	d6
4	♘f3	g6
5	♗c4	♘b6
6	♗b3	♗g7
7	a4	a5

For a long time, this move was the automatic response to the advance of White's a-pawn. However, in 1990 Alburt introduced the line 7...dxe5 8 a5 ♘6d7, based on the point that the forcing 9 ♗xf7+ (in *Understanding Chess Move by Move*, I suggested 9 ♕e2 as an interesting alternative, but this doesn't seem to have caught on!) 9...♔xf7 10 ♘g5+ ♔g8 11 ♘e6 ♕e8 12 ♘xc7 ♕d8 13 ♘xa8 exd4 leads only to an unclear position. In fact, few players seem to have been tempted by 7...dxe5, and 7...a5 has remained by far the most popular move.

8	♕e2	0-0 *(D)*

Black cannot play 8...♗g4 at once since 9 ♗xf7+ wins.

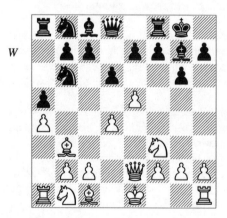

9	h3	

White must preserve the f3-knight from exchange or he will be unable to maintain his pawn on e5. This pawn is the key to White's strategy. If he can support it, then it will block out the g7-bishop and provide White with an enduring space advantage.

9	...	dxe5
10	dxe5	♘a6 *(D)*

A relatively new move. James Howell had faced 10...♘a6 himself in a game played shortly before this one, and had failed to gain any advantage with White. Now he was turning the tables. Black's idea is to bring the knight to the useful square c5. From here the knight attacks b3 and a4, although it exerts less pressure against e5 than if the knight were developed at c6. 10...♘c6 is the most common move, the usual continuation being 11 0-0 ♘d4 12 ♘xd4 ♕xd4 13 ♖e1 with a slight plus for White. The most famous example of this line is Short-Timman, Tilburg 1991 (the game in which Short advanced his king to g5; for detailed notes to this game, see *Understanding Chess Move by Move*).

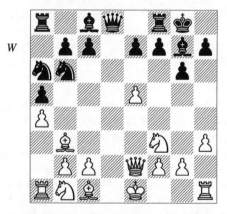

11	0-0?!	

White is more or less forced to allow one of his bishops to be exchanged, but he definitely chooses the wrong one. The best continuation is 11 ♗e3 ♘d5 12 0-0 (Howell played the dubious 12 ♗g5 in the aforementioned game in which he was White) 12...♘xe3 13 ♕xe3, when White's lead in development more than compensates for Black's two bishops. Black has an easy time after the text-move.

11	...	♘c5
12	♖d1	♕e8

13 ᐧc3 ᐧxb3

Black cannot play to win the a-pawn, since 13...Ꭰd7 14 ᐧd4! (14 Ꭰe3 is less precise, although even this gave White an edge after 14...ᐧxb3 15 cxb3 Ꭰc6 16 Ꭰxb6 cxb6 17 ᐧd5 in the later game Bosch-Zurmely, Groningen open 1997) 14...ᐧbxa4 15 ᐧxa4 ᐧxa4 (after 15...Ꭰxa4 16 Ꭰxa4 ᐧxa4 17 ᐧb5, White wins material) 16 e6 is winning for White.

14 cxb3 Ꭰe6
15 ᐧd4 Ꭰd5

15...ᐧc8 is a safe option, defending e6 and preparing the natural developing move ...ᐧd8. In this case I think White has no advantage.

16 ᐧxd5 ᐧxd5 (D)

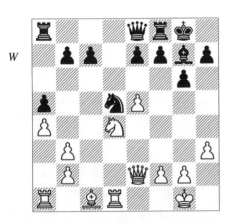

17 ᐧf5

The only try for an advantage. Black must either permit the exchange of his defensive bishop, or allow his kingside pawns to be broken up.

17 ... gxf5?!

I think this was the wrong decision. Black should have played 17...c6 18 ᐧxg7 ᐧxg7 19 ᐧd4 (19 ᐧd2 ᐧd7 20 ᐧh6+ ᐧg8 21 ᐧd4 f6 22 ᐧh4 ᐧf7 also doesn't lead anywhere for White) 19...ᐧd7 and now:

1) 20 ᐧh4 ᐧg8 (20...h5 21 Ꭰd2 ᐧfd8 22 ᐧe1 is similar) 21 Ꭰh6 ᐧfd8 22 ᐧe1 ᐧc7! aims to reposition the knight on the excellent defensive square e6. Although Black's kingside is slightly weak, it is hard to see how White can exploit this and, positionally speaking, Black is doing rather well.

2) 20 Ꭰd2 followed by ᐧd1 is safer, with a roughly balanced position. Black's strong knight balances his slightly weak kingside.

18 ᐧxd5

This line is more dangerous for Black as White has definite attacking chances.

18 ... ᐧc6

Black activates his queen and forces White to decide what he will do with his rook.

19 ᐧd3

The critical continuation. White is prepared to sacrifice his e-pawn in order to retain control of the d-file. After 19 ᐧb5 ᐧa6 Black is in no danger, while 19 ᐧd3 ᐧfd8 20 ᐧg3 ᐧe6 is totally harmless.

19 ... e6

Black is more or less forced to accept, since if he allows Ꭰf4 followed by ᐧc1, then he has a horrible position without any material compensation.

20 ᐧd7 Ꭰxe5
21 Ꭰh6 (D)

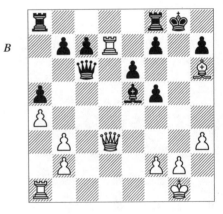

The first critical moment.

21 ... Ꭰxb2?

Black makes an error which proves fatal. Apparently Black believed that his position was bad in any case, so he decided simply to grab another pawn and hope for the best. He probably also reasoned that with two extra pawns, he need not fear the loss of the exchange. However, White does not take the exchange but plays for an attack instead. In fact, Black shouldn't have resorted to desperate measures so soon, since with correct defence he could still have held the game. The alternatives are:

1) 21...ᐧe4? 22 ᐧd2 Ꭰg7 23 Ꭰxg7 ᐧxg7 24 ᐧg5+ ᐧh8 25 ᐧf6+ ᐧg8 26 ᐧad1 with an overwhelming attack.

2) 21...Rfe8 (after this White can gain the advantage by accurate play) and now:

2a) 22 Qd1 (threatening 23 Rc1, forcing the queen away from the attack on d7, followed by Qh5) 22...Rxb2 (22...f4 23 Qh5 Qxd7 24 Qg5+ Kh8 25 Qxe5+ f6 26 Qxf6+ Kg8 27 Qg5+ Kh8 28 Qe5+ Kg8 29 Rc1 Re7 30 Qxf4 gives White a winning position) 23 Rb1 with a final branch:

2a1) 23...Bg7 24 Rc1 Qe4 (24...Rxd7 25 Qxd7 Red8 26 Qxc7 Bxh6 27 Rc2 gives White good winning chances) 25 Bxg7 Kxg7 26 Qh5 Rf8 27 Qg5+ Kh8 28 Qf6+ Kg8 29 Rcxc7 and White wins.

2a2) 23...Rf6! 24 Rc1 Qe4 25 Rc4 Qe5 and there is nothing clear for White; e.g., 26 Qh5 (26 Bf4 Qb2 27 Rcxc7 Rad8 28 Rxb7 Rxd7 29 Rxd7 Rc8 30 Qh5 Rf8 is approximately equal) 26...Re7 27 Rxe7 Bxe7 28 Rg4+ Kh8 29 Bg7+ Qxg7 30 Rxg7 Kxg7 31 Qf3 is slightly better for White, but a draw is the most likely result.

2b) 22 Qd2! f4 (D) (22...f6 23 Rc1 Qe4 24 Rg7+ Kh8 25 Qd7 f4 26 Rg4 forces mate, while 22...Bf6 23 Rc1 Qe4 24 Bg5 Bg7 25 f3 Qe5 26 Rcxc7 gives White a massive advantage) and now:

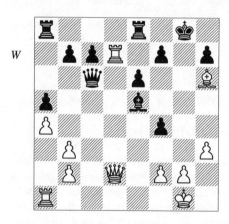

2b1) 23 Qd3 f5 (23...Bg7 24 Bxf4 e5 25 Qf5 Qf6 26 Qxf6 Bxf6 27 Be3 Re7 is slightly better for White) 24 Re1 Bd6 25 Rg7+ Kh8 and there is nothing clear for White; e.g., 26 Rg5 Re7 27 Rxe6!? Rxe6 28 Qd4+ Be5 29 Bg7+ Kg8 30 Bxe5+ Rg6 with a murky position.

2b2) 23 Rd1 and then:

2b21) 23...Bd6 24 Qe2 f3 (24...Kh8 25 Bg5 Kg8 26 Qh5 Qxd7 27 Bf6 mates) 25 Qe3 f6 26 Rg7+ Kh8 27 Qd3 f5 28 Qd4 e5 29 Qh4 Be7 (29...Re6 30 Qg5 with a quick mate to follow) 30 Qh5 e4 (30...fxg2 31 Rd3! with Rdg3 to come) 31 Rf7 Qg6 32 Qxg6 hxg6 33 Rd7 and White wins a piece.

2b22) 23...Qe4! 24 Re1 Qf5 25 Rxe5 Qxe5 26 Bxf4 Qf5 27 Bxc7 e5 is unclear.

2b3) 23 Re1! (the correct continuation of the attack; Black must decide at once which diagonal to keep his bishop on) 23...Bd6 (23...Bxb2 24 Qxb2 e5 25 Rxe5 Qxh6 26 Rf5 is very good for White) 24 Qd1! f3 (both 24...Kh8 25 Bg5 Kg8 26 Bf6 f3 27 Qd2 Qc5 28 Rxd6! and 24...f5 25 Rg7+ Kh8 26 Qh5 Re7 27 Rxe7 Bxe7 28 Bxf4 Kg8 29 Qh6 win for White) 25 Qd4 Bf8 26 Qg4+ Kh8 27 Bg5 Bg7 28 Rxf7 with material equality and a very strong attack for White.

3) 21...Bd6! (D) (it looks suicidal to move the bishop off the long diagonal, but the threat to the d7-rook forces White to act at once, and it turns out that without the participation of the a1-rook he can do no better than perpetual check) and now:

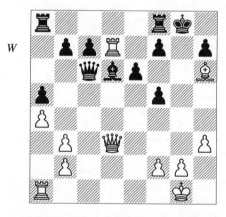

3a) 22 Qd4 f6 23 Rg7+ Kh8 24 Qh4 (24 Re1 Qe8 followed by ...Rf7 defends) 24...Qe4 25 Qh5 (25 f4 Bxf4) 25...f4! (during the game I thought that the threat of Rxh7+ would be decisive, but I had overlooked this defence) 26 Rg4 Rg8 27 Qf7 Rxg4 28 Qxf6+ Kg8 29 hxg4 Qg6 and by returning the material Black fends off the attack.

3b) 22 Qd2 f4 (but not 22...Kh8? 23 Qg5 Be5 24 Rad1 Rfe8 25 Rd8 Qc2 26 Rxe8+ Rxe8 27 Qd8 Qc6 28 Rd7, when White wins) 23 Qe2 Kh8 and it is time for White to force a draw by 24 ♗g5 f6 25 ♖xh7+ ♔xh7 26 ♕h5+ ♔g8 27 ♕g6+ with perpetual check.

3c) 22 ♕e3 f4 23 ♗xf4 ♕xd7 24 ♗xd6 ♕xd6 25 ♕g5+ ♔h8 26 ♕f6+ also leads to perpetual check.

3d) 22 f4 ♔h8 23 ♗xf8 *(D)* and now:

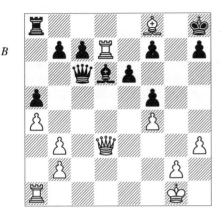

3d1) 23...♕xd7 24 ♕d4+ f6 25 ♕xf6+ ♔g8 26 ♗xd6 ♕xd6 (26...cxd6 27 ♖e1 ♖e8 28 ♖e3 also gives White a large advantage) 27 ♖e1 ♖a6 (27...♖e8 28 ♕g5+ ♔h8 29 ♔h2 favours White) 28 ♕g5+ ♔f7 29 ♕h6 ♔g8 30 ♔h2 and White has a definite advantage thanks to his safer king.

3d2) 23...♖xf8 24 ♕c3+ ♕xc3 25 bxc3 ♗xf4 represents White's best chance to play on. White can claim to be very slightly better thanks to his active rook on d7, but the result should be a draw.

It is easy to become despondent when the game has not gone as you had planned, and then there is a tendency just to 'go through the motions', look only at the most obvious lines, confirm that they are all bad and play one of them at random. In the above position, Black did not have the determination to go beyond the most obvious moves and find the rather counter-intuitive defence which would probably have saved half a point. Everybody knows players who are difficult to beat even when you have a favourable position. These are usually the players who have the tenacity to look for the best defence even when things have gone wrong.

22 ♖b1 *(D)*

The flashy 22 ♖c1? is met by 22...♕e4 23 ♕g3+ ♔h8 24 ♗xf8 ♖xf8 25 ♖cd1 ♗e5 and Black defends.

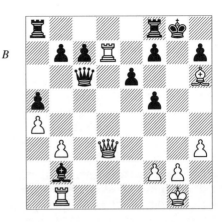

22 ... ♗g7?

By now Black was in time-trouble, and he collapses completely. However, White keeps a large advantage against any defence:

1) 22...f4 23 ♗xf4 e5 (23...♗g7 24 ♖c1 ♕a6 25 ♕g3 ♕e2 26 ♖cxc7 wins for White) 24 ♕g3+ ♕g6 25 ♖xb2 exf4 26 ♕xf4 and White will win a pawn while retaining a good position.

2) 22...♗e5 may be best, but after 23 ♖c1 Black is in big trouble: 23...♕b6 (23...♕e4 24 ♕xe4 fxe4 25 ♖c5 f6 26 ♗xf8 ♖xf8 27 ♖xa5 gives White a decisive material advantage) 24 ♕e2 ♗d6 (24...♗g7 25 ♗xg7 ♔xg7 26 ♕e5+ ♔g6 27 ♖c3 and mate soon follows, or 24...♗f6 25 ♖cxc7 ♖xb3 26 ♕h5 ♕b1+ 27 ♔h2 and f7 collapses) 25 ♕h5 ♕d4 (25...♔h8 26 ♗g5 ♗e5 27 ♖c4 followed by ♖h4 gives White a winning attack) 26 ♖cxc7 ♔h8 27 ♗g5! ♕a1+ 28 ♖c1 ♕g7 29 ♖d1 ♗e5 30 ♗h6 ♕f6 31 ♗xf8 ♖xf8 32 ♖xb7 and White is the exchange up.

23 ♕g3

Forcing material gain.

23 ... ♕c3

The only move to avoid mate.

24	♕xc3	♗xc3
25	♗xf8	♖xf8
26	♖xc7	♗b4
27	♖xb7	

White is a clear exchange up.

27	...	♖d8
28	g3	♔g7
29	♖c1	**1-0**

Doubling rooks on the seventh will tie Black down to the defence on f7 and leave him with no chance to save the game.

My score of 6½/9 was sufficient to reach a tie for second place, half a point behind the winner Bogdan Lalić. The Bundesliga season started a few weeks after this tournament, and this year I was playing for a new club – Duisburg. When I switch clubs my first weekend is usually a disaster, but two good wins made this occasion an exception. Both games are given below.

In the first game, I played a very sharp line of the Najdorf but was soon reduced to improvisation at the board. Needless to say, this isn't the way I recommend playing the openings, but in real life there will always be times when your preparation or memory fails you and you have to make it up. In these cases you should aim to find a move which is sensible on general principles and which does not have an obvious refutation. In the following game, White's improvisation could have landed him in trouble, but in practice an unexpected move often succeeds even if, as in this case, a refutation exists. Black decided to give up the exchange to reach an ending in which he had the two bishops and a dangerous passed pawn, but by returning the exchange White liquidated to a pure minor-piece ending in which his better pawn-structure gave him a large advantage. White's technique was not especially good, but he reeled in the full point in the end.

Game 14
J. Nunn – R. Kuczynski
Bundesliga 1994/5
Sicilian Defence, Najdorf Variation

1	e4	c5
2	♘f3	d6
3	d4	cxd4
4	♘xd4	♘f6
5	♘c3	a6

The problem of how to meet the Najdorf has troubled 1 e4 players for several decades. At different times during my career I have played 6 ♗g5, 6 ♗c4, 6 ♗e2, 6 ♗e3 and 6 f4. At the time of this game I was not regularly playing any of these moves, but rather hopping from one to another depending on my opponent's repertoire. In Games 4 and 7 we saw 6 ♗e3, but for this encounter I decided to switch to the old-fashioned 6 ♗g5. Although at one time this was the main line against the Najdorf, in recent years it has fallen into disuse in top-level chess, with far more attention being devoted to the 6 ♗e3/6 f3 system. Mickey Adams and I had spent quite a long time looking at various 6 ♗g5 lines while preparing for his Candidates match against Gelfand, and I decided to try putting this work to good use.

6	♗g5	e6
7	f4	♘bd7

Black has quite a range of 7th moves. In addition to the double-edged Polugaevsky (7...b5) and Poisoned Pawn (7...♕b6) lines, Black has several moves which simply develop pieces.

These moves are 7...♘c6, 7...♗e7, 7...♘bd7 and 7...♕c7. The first of these tends to lead to distinctive play, but the others can all lead to the key main-line position, which arises after 7...♗e7 8 ♕f3 ♕c7 9 0-0-0 ♘bd7. In this key position, White's main options are 10 ♗d3 and 10 g4, with the latter currently being considered more critical. In this game Black uses 7...♘bd7 as a move-order finesse designed to avoid the 10 g4 line.

8	♕f3	♕c7
9	0-0-0	b5 *(D)*

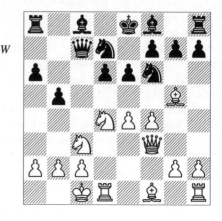

W

The first critical position of the 7...♘bd7 line. White has three main options: he can try to bash Black flat with 10 e5 or 10 ♗xb5, or he can simply develop his pieces with 10 ♗d3. Although theory in the first two lines has not exhausted the possibilities, there is little indication that White can gain the advantage; indeed, some of the lines after 10 e5 are forced draws. I therefore decided on the third option.

10 ♗d3 ♗b7
11 ♖he1 (D)

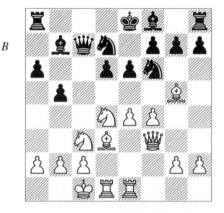

The second critical position of the 7...♘bd7 variation. Black must decide whether to transpose back into ...♗e7 lines or pursue an independent course.

11 ... ♗e7

Black decides to transpose into a position which is usually reached by the move-order 7...♗e7 8 ♕f3 ♕c7 9 0-0-0 ♘bd7 10 ♗d3 b5 11 ♖he1 ♗b7. As mentioned above, the move-order adopted in this game avoids the possibility of 10 g4, but it also rules out certain options for Black, especially the lines with ...h6 which theory regards as one of Black's best plans. If Black wishes to avoid such a transposition, then he has two main choices. The first is 11...♕b6 12 ♘d5!?, which is extremely complicated and probably a little better for White, while the second is 11...0-0-0, which is perfectly playable and leads to an unclear position. Note that 11...b4? is bad due to 12 ♘d5!, when White has a very strong attack.

12 ♕g3

The alternative is 12 ♘d5 which leads to vast complications after 12...♘xd5 or 12...exd5. According to theory, the latter line is fine for Black, with the result that this continuation has almost vanished. The move played improves

White's position by removing the queen from the long diagonal and setting up a latent threat to the g7-pawn.

12 ... b4

These days this is almost universally played. Black practically forces White to sacrifice with ♘d5, believing that this will not favour White even with the extra tempo ♕g3 thrown in. As for alternatives, 12...0-0-0 is bad due to 13 ♗xb5, while 12...h6 13 ♗xf6 ♗xf6 14 ♗xb5 also favours White.

13 ♘d5

White is committed now; any other move would be inconsistent.

13 ... exd5
14 e5

At the time this game was played, the alternative 14 exd5 was thought dubious for White after 14...♔d8. However, recently White has tried to revive this line with 15 ♘c6+ ♗xc6 16 dxc6 and indeed this looks like his most dangerous option. Whether this really offers White chances for an advantage only time will tell.

14 ... dxe5
15 fxe5 (D)

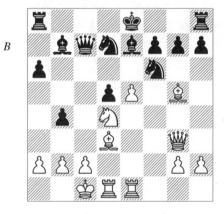

A key decision-point for Black.

15 ... 0-0-0

Perhaps fearful of an improvement, or possibly just aiming to avoid drawing lines, Black chooses a playable but slightly unusual alternative. 15...♘e4? is just bad in view of 16 ♗xe4 ♗xg5+ 17 ♕xg5 dxe4 18 ♘f5 ♕xe5 19 ♖f1! with a very strong attack, so the only real alternative is 15...♘h5. Then White has two options:
1) 16 ♕h4 (this move gives White at most equality) 16...♗xg5+ 17 ♕xg5 g6 18 e6 ♘c5

(18...♘df6 is also playable) 19 exf7+ ♔xf7 20 ♖f1+ ♔g8 21 ♘f5 ♖f8 (playing for the win; 21...♘e6 forces White to take an immediate perpetual check) 22 ♘e7+ ♔g7 23 ♗xg6 ♘e6 24 ♘f5+ ♖xf5 25 ♕xf5 ♘hf4 26 ♗h5 ♖f8 27 ♕g4+ ♔h8 28 g3 ♖c8 29 ♖f2 ♕c5 30 ♖fd2 ♘xh5 31 ♕xe6 leading to approximate equality.

2) 16 e6 (the queen sacrifice is thought to be the safest route to a draw) 16...♘xg3 17 exf7+ ♔xf7 18 ♖xe7+ ♔g8 19 hxg3 ♕xg3 20 ♘e6 ♕e5 21 ♖f1 ♘f8 (21...h6 is interesting but probably also equal) 22 ♗f5 g6 (22...♗c8 forces a draw by 23 ♖e8 ♔f7 24 ♖e7+) 23 ♘xf8 ♕xe7 24 ♗xe7 gxf5 25 ♖xf5 ♗c8 26 ♖f6 and White has enough for the exchange.

The move played also leads to a roughly level position, so objectively there is little to choose between the two moves. The fact that Black has two satisfactory lines reveals how harmless the whole 13 ♘d5 line is, at least in theory. In practice a firm grasp of the theoretical analysis is essential for both players.

16 ♘f5 (D)

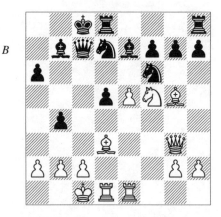

The only move.

16 ... ♗c5

16...♘xe5? loses to 17 ♘xe7+ ♕xe7 18 ♖xe5 ♕c7 19 ♗f4, with deadly threats along the h3-c8 and g3-b8 diagonals. 16...♗f8, however, is a reasonable alternative which avoids the game continuation. After 17 exf6 ♕xg3 18 hxg3 gxf6 (18...♘xf6 19 ♘h6! wins the exchange) 19 ♗h4 ♗c5 20 g4 White has compensation for the pawn, but I doubt whether he can claim any advantage.

17 ♘xg7!? (D)

This was an over-the-board improvisation. The alternative is 17 exf6 ♕xg3 18 hxg3 gxf6 19 ♗f4 ♘e5 20 ♗xe5 fxe5 21 ♖xe5 with a roughly level ending. At the time I believed that 17 ♘xg7 was a novelty, but I later discovered that it had been played earlier in an obscure correspondence game (of which more later). The move played is very double-edged and could have got White into trouble, but unexpected moves have a considerable impact in over-the-board play and succeed more often than one might expect.

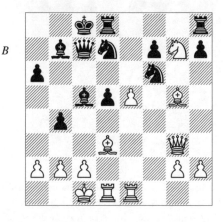

17 ... ♘e4

The alternatives are inferior:

1) 17...♘g8? is bad for two reasons:

1a) 18 e6 ♕xg3 19 exd7+ ♔xd7 (19...♖xd7 20 ♖e8+ ♔c7 21 hxg3 is very good for White) 20 hxg3 with a massive endgame advantage for White.

1b) 18 ♗xd8 ♔xd8 (18...♕xd8 loses to 19 e6) 19 ♘e6+ fxe6 20 ♕g7 ♔c8 21 ♕xh8 ♕d8 22 ♗xh7 should be winning for White.

2) 17...♘e8 (this is also inferior to the move played) 18 ♗xd8 (18 ♗f4? ♘xg7 19 e6 ♘h5! favours Black) 18...♔xd8 (18...♕xd8 19 e6 fxe6 20 ♘xe6 is also unclear) and now:

2a) 19 ♕g5+ ♗e7 20 ♕h6 ♗f8 forces a repetition.

2b) 19 ♗f5 ♖g8 (19...♗c8 20 ♘h5 is good for White) 20 ♘xe8 ♖xe8 21 ♕h4+ ♗e7 is unclear.

2c) 19 ♘h5! (intending ♗f5 and ♘f4) 19...f6 20 ♘f4 ♕b6 21 ♗f5 (21 e6 ♘e5 is fine for Black) 21...♗f2 22 ♕h3 ♘xe5 23 ♘xd5 ♗xd5 24 ♖xd5+ ♔c7 25 ♖ed1 with some advantage for White.

18 ♗xe4 dxe4

18...♖dg8? fails to 19 e6! ♖xg7 20 exd7+ ♕xd7 21 ♕e5 and White wins.

19 ♗xd8 ♖xd8

The only move, as both 19...♔xd8? 20 e6 and 19...♕xd8 20 e6 fxe6 21 ♘xe6 ♕b6 22 ♖xd7 ♔xd7 23 ♘xc5+ ♕xc5 24 ♕g7+ are winning for White.

20 e6 *(D)*

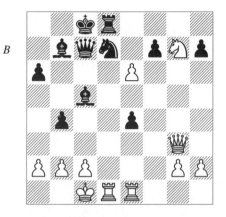

In general, two bishops are worth more than a rook and pawn, so White must keep up the momentum.

20 ... ♕xg3?

Black decides to sacrifice the exchange, relying on his two powerful bishops and dangerous e-pawn. However, this plan is a mistake because in many lines White can return the exchange to reach a favourable minor-piece ending. Had Black found the correct reply, then White would have had to take care to avoid falling into an inferior position. The analysis runs:

1) 20...♘e5? 21 ♖xd8+ ♔xd8 22 exf7 and White wins material.

2) 20...fxe6? 21 ♕xc7+ ♔xc7 22 ♘xe6+ ♔c8 23 ♖xd7 ♖xd7 (23...♗e3+ 24 ♖xe3 ♖xd7 25 ♘c5 is similar) 24 ♘xc5 ♖e7 25 ♔d2 must be winning for White as he is a clear pawn up and Black has a number of weak pawns.

3) 20...♘f8! is not just the only way for Black to maintain the balance – it even puts the burden of reaching a draw on White. Now:

3a) The correspondence game I mentioned above went 21 ♕xc7+ ♔xc7 22 exf7 ♖xd1+ 23 ♔xd1 ♗f2 24 ♘e8+ ♔d8 25 ♖f1 e3 26 ♔e2 and ended in a draw after 26...♗xg2 27 ♖d1+ ♔e7 28 ♘d6 ♗h3 29 ♖d4 h5 30 ♘c4 ♗g4+ 31

♔f1 ♗h3+ ½-½ Zrzavy-Hron, Czechoslovak corr. Ch. semi-final 1984. However, Black should have preferred 26...a5 27 ♖d1+ ♔e7 28 ♘c7 ♔xf7, when White has a difficult position.

3b) 21 ♖xd8+ (trying to keep the queens on is better, since Black's king is less safe than White's) 21...♔xd8 (21...♕xd8 22 exf7 ♕e7 23 ♕f4 ♗d5 24 ♖d1 ♗xf7 25 ♘f5 ♕c7 26 ♕xe4 is roughly equal) and now:

3b1) 22 ♕g5+ ♕e7 (22...♗e7 23 ♕h5 ♘xe6 24 ♖d1+ ♔c8 25 ♘xe6 fxe6 26 ♕e8+ ♗d8 27 ♕xe6+ ♔b8 28 ♕e8 repeats moves) 23 ♖d1+ (23 ♕f4 ♘xe6 24 ♕b8+ ♗c8 favours Black) 23...♔c7 (23...♔c8 24 ♕xe7 ♗xe7 25 exf7 is roughly equal) 24 ♕xe7+ ♗xe7 25 exf7 e3 26 ♘f5 ♗c5 27 ♖e1 ♗d5 28 ♘xe3 ♗xf7 with a likely draw.

3b2) 22 ♖d1+ ♔c8 23 ♕xc7+ ♔xc7 24 ♖f1 (24 exf7 e3 25 ♘e8+ ♔c6 26 ♘f6 ♗c8 gives Black some advantage) 24...♔d8 25 ♖xf7 ♗c8 26 ♖f5 ♗e3+ 27 ♔d1 ♘xe6 28 ♘xe6+ ♗xe6 29 ♖e5 ♔d7 30 ♖xe4 should also be a draw.

21 exd7+ ♖xd7

22 hxg3 ♖xd1+

22...♗f2 23 ♖xd7 ♔xd7 24 ♖d1+ ♔c6 25 ♖h1 is similar to the game.

23 ♔xd1 ♗f2 *(D)*

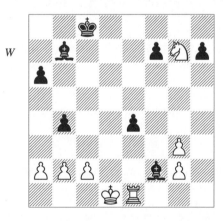

24 ♖h1!

The only move. After both 24 ♖e2 e3 and 24 ♖f1 e3 Black has enough compensation for the exchange.

24 ... e3

25 ♖xh7

The exchange of g2- and h7-pawns definitely favours White.

25   ...   ♗xg2
26   ♔e2   ♗c6

Threatening to force a draw by 27...♗b5+ 28 ♔f3 ♗c6+. After 26...♗d5 27 ♖h4 a5 28 ♖h5 ♗xa2 29 ♖xa5 White wins more easily.

27   ♖h5! *(D)*

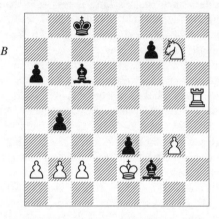

White plays to give up his rook for the light-squared bishop, thereby liquidating to a very favourable minor-piece ending.

27   ...   ♗b5+?!

Black makes life easy by falling in with White's plan. 27...♔d7 28 g4 ♗b5+ 29 ♖xb5 axb5 30 ♘f5 is similar to the game, so perhaps the best defence is 27...♔c7. After 28 ♖f5 ♔b6 29 g4 a5 (29...♗b5+ 30 ♖xb5+ ♔xb5 31 ♘f5 ♔c5 32 ♘xe3 is similar) 30 ♖f6 ♔c5 31 ♖xc6+ ♔xc6 32 ♘f5 ♔c5 33 ♘xe3 an ending similar to that in the game is reached, except that Black does not have doubled b-pawns. This increases Black's drawing chances, although it is hard to say whether it would have been enough to save the game.

28   ♖xb5   axb5
29   ♘f5

This ending is winning. Black will soon be a pawn down with a bad pawn-structure.

29   ...   ♔d7
30   ♔f3

Defending the g3-pawn so that White can safely take on e3. This is better than playing g4 followed by ♘xe3 as it keeps Black's bishop imprisoned for the moment.

30   ...   ♔c6

Black decides to keep his king near the weak queenside pawns. After 30...♔e6 31 ♘xe3 Black can try:

1) 31...♗g1 (passive defence loses in the long run) 32 ♔e4 ♗h2 33 g4 ♗e5 34 b3 (White has to take care once he has played b3 because some pawn endings are drawn) 34...f6 (34...♗b8 35 ♘f5 ♔f6 36 ♘d4 ♔g5 37 ♔f3 and White wins the b5-pawn) 35 ♘d5 ♗d6 36 c3 (36 ♘f4+ ♔f7 37 ♔f5?? ♗xf4 38 ♔xf4 ♔g6 is a draw) 36...bxc3 37 ♘xc3 b4 38 ♘d5 ♗c5 39 ♘f4+ ♔f7 40 ♔f5 followed by ♘d5 and White wins.

2) 31...♗xe3 32 ♔xe3 ♔f5 (this sets a nasty trap) 33 c3 bxc3 and now:

2a) 34 bxc3? ♔g4! draws; for example, 35 c4 (35 ♔f2 f5 36 a3 f4) 35...bxc4 36 a4 ♔xg3 37 a5 f5 38 a6 f4+ 39 ♔d2 f3 40 a7 c3+!.

2b) 34 b4! ♔g4 35 ♔d3 ♔xg3 36 a4 f5 37 axb5 and White promotes with check.

31   ♘h6

White decides to collect the f7-pawn and return for the e3-pawn later. 31 ♘xe3, followed by ♔e4, is a simpler win, with play similar to the previous note, although even more favourable for White as Black's king is offside.

31   ...   ♗e1

Black seizes the opportunity to play his bishop to d2, which makes it harder for White to manoeuvre his knight for fear of ...e2.

32   ♘xf7   ♔d5 *(D)*

Not 32...e2 33 ♘e5+ ♔d5 34 ♘d3 and White wins at once.

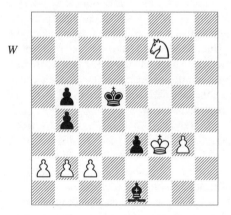

33   g4   ♗d2

Now White's knight cannot move to g5 or h6, so his only plan is to push the g-pawn.

34   g5   ♗c1

Forcing b3 is always a good idea as it cripples White's queenside pawns.

35	b3	♔e6
36	g6	♔f6
37	♘e5	

White manages to extract his knight. Now the idea is first to take one of Black's queenside pawns, and then to return for the e3-pawn.

37	...	♗d2
38	♔e2	♗c3

Or 38...♗c1 39 ♘g4+ ♔xg6 40 ♘xe3 ♗a3 (or else ♘d5 wins the b4-pawn) 41 ♔d3 and wins.

39	♘f3	♔xg6
40	♔xe3	

Now Black cannot prevent ♘d4, winning the b5-pawn.

40	...	♔f5
41	♘d4+	♔e5
42	♘xb5	♗b2 (D)

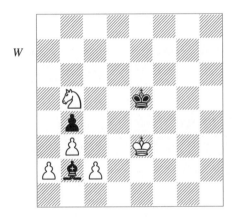

W

43 ♔d3?!

The position is a comfortable win for White, but now he starts to create problems for himself. There were two simple wins: 43 c3 bxc3 44 ♔d3 followed by ♘xc3, or 43 ♘c7 ♔d6 44 ♘a6 ♗c3 45 ♔d3 ♔d5 46 a3 and White wins a third pawn.

43	...	♔d5
44	c4+	

Again missing a simple win: 44 c3 ♔c5 45 ♔c2 ♗a1 46 ♔b1 forcing a won pawn ending.

44	...	♔c5

I suddenly realized that my last couple of moves had been wrong, and that I should now concentrate on finding a safe winning plan. After some thought I found a good and risk-free winning method; the first step is to extract the knight from the poor square b5.

45	♘c7	♔c6
46	♘d5	♔c5
47	♘f4	

The knight is heading for the d3-square, where it both attacks b4 and keeps Black's king out of c5.

47	...	♗e5
48	♔e4	♗c3
49	♘d3+	♔d6
50	♔e3	

The next step is to play the king round to c2, so as to threaten a3. Black's only defence is to play his king to a5.

50	...	♔c6
51	♔f3	

White first tries a little trick. If Black plays 51...♔d6, then White wins more easily by 52 ♔e2 ♔c6 (otherwise ♔d1-c2, etc.) 53 ♔d1 ♔b6 54 ♔c2 ♔a5 55 a3 and Black is too late. However, Black stays alert and puts up the best resistance.

51	...	♔b7
52	♔e2	♔b6
53	♔d1	♔a5
54	♘f4! (D)	

B

This is the key move. Just at this moment Black cannot play ...♔b6 due to ♘d5+, so White can imprison Black's king on the a-file.

54	...	♗g7
55	♘d5	♗f8

Black must defend the b4-pawn with his bishop in order to free his king. Having been driven off the c3-e1 diagonal by the formation of ♘d5 and ♔d1, the bishop is forced to settle on this inferior diagonal.

56	♔c2	♗c5

56...♗a6 57 ♔d3 ♗b7 58 c5 ♗xc5 59 ♔c4 followed by ♘xb4 is winning for White, so Black tries to block the c5-square.

57　♔d3　　　♗a6

This is now too slow to prevent White's king from arriving on d5.

58　♘f6　　　♗g1

58...♔b7 59 ♘e4 followed by c5 wins, as does 58...♗e7 59 ♘e4 ♔b6 60 ♔d4 ♔c6 61 c5.

59　♔e4　　　1-0

White plays ♔d5 and ♘e4, followed by c5, winning easily.

Every player has his or her own style. It is quite normal to like certain types of position and dislike others; within limits there is nothing wrong with this. However, if your tastes lead you to make objectively inferior moves, then something is wrong; flexibility is a key asset for a chess-player and once you have sacrificed this then you are at a disadvantage. In the following game, I tried to avoid a type of position in which I had faced problems before. Of course, a better attitude would have been to study the problematic type of position with the aim of handling it better. Bologan was not slow to exploit my prejudice and established a small but clear advantage. However, gaining an opening advantage is not necessarily the end of the game and the critical moment comes at move 23. In positions with a King's Indian pawn-structure, control of the e4-square is usually very important and an error by Black allowed White not only to secure e4, but also to stifle Black's counterplay. However, to achieve this White had to find the right move and Bologan, already running short of time, missed the crucial finesse. Curiously, then, Black's 23rd move, while objectively an error, actually turned out favourably by forcing White, who had previously been manoeuvring quietly, suddenly to find the one route to an advantage. When he failed to do this, White's control of e4 was undermined and, with the disappearance of his blockade, the potential energy of Black's position was released. After that it was all one-way traffic as White was driven steadily backwards.

Game 15
V. Bologan – J. Nunn
Bundesliga 1994/5
Pirc Defence

1　e4　　　d6

Although I played the Pirc quite frequently in my junior days, it had more or less vanished from my repertoire by the time of this game. However, I recalled a nice win against Bologan in the Pirc from 1993 (the finish of this game was given on page 317 of *John Nunn's Best Games*) and decided to repeat the opening.

2　d4　　　♘f6
3　♘c3　　　g6
4　g3

On the previous occasion Bologan had played the Austrian Attack (4 f4). This time he tries the Fianchetto Variation; quite a sensible choice, in fact, as I did not have a good record against this line. White plays mainly to restrict Black's counterplay and only then considers how to make progress himself.

4　...　　　♗g7
5　♗g2　　　0-0

6　♘ge2　　　e5
7　h3　　　♘c6

The key decision for Black against the Fianchetto Variation is where to develop his queen's knight. There are three possibilities: he can play ...♘c6, as in this game; ...♘bd7; or 7...c6 8 a4 a5, followed by ...♘a6. According to theory all these lines have roughly equal merit, and all offer Black good equalizing chances.

8　♗e3　　　♗d7

Once Black has committed his knight to c6, then he almost always has to play ...exd4 sooner or later. The reason is that there is a danger White might at some point close the centre by d5. It would not be particularly good to play 9 d5 right away because after 9...♘e7, followed by ...♘e8 and ...f5, Black would be able to generate King's Indian-style counterplay fairly quickly. White, on the other hand, will find his queenside play slower than in the King's Indian, because his c-pawn is still on c2. However, if Black continues to delay ...exd4, then d5 will become steadily more tempting for White. For example, the move ...♖e8 makes perfect sense if ...exd4 has been played, but if White plays d5 the rook is poorly placed on e8 and may have to return to f8 to support ...f5. I was not too keen on ...exd4, as this would lead to precisely the type of structure which I had found hard to handle in previous games. Thus I decided to play a waiting game, hoping to tempt d5 and thus arrive at a type of position in which I felt more at home.

9   0-0   ♖e8 (D)

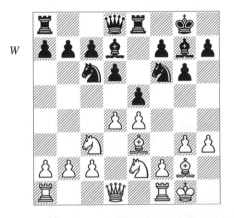

As mentioned above, this effectively costs Black two tempi if White now plays d5. However, even this wasn't enough to tempt White into pushing his d-pawn.

10   ♕d2!?

Perhaps guessing my reason for delaying ...exd4, Bologan plays an interesting and unusual move. The normal line is 10 ♖e1 a6 11 a4 and now Black has run out of sensible preparatory moves and is more or less forced to play 11...exd4. After 12 ♘xd4 we have a standard theoretical position in which Black has a range of options: 12...♘a5, 12...♖b8, 12...♕c8 and 12...♘b4. Bologan's 10 ♕d2 is designed to improve White's position after a possible d5 by aiming for kingside rather than queenside play.

10   ...   a6?

This is really going too far. Black should have realized that he is entering the danger zone and acquiesced to 10...exd4 11 ♘xd4 ♘a5, with good chances for equality.

11   d5!

Definitely the correct choice. The move ...a6 is now a total waste of time, and the extra tempo this gives White should allow him to secure an advantage.

11   ...   ♘e7
12   ♗g5?!

White's plan of playing f4 is the right idea, but the tempo spent on ♗g5 allows Black to organize his defence. The immediate 12 f4!, threatening 13 fxe5 dxe5 14 ♗g5, would have been much more unpleasant for Black. After 12...exf4 13 ♖xf4 (13 gxf4 ♘h5 gives White only a slight advantage, while 13 ♘xf4 ♗c8! 14 ♗d4 ♘d7 15 ♗xg7 ♔xg7 16 ♘d3 f6 is passive but fairly solid for Black) 13...♘h5 14 ♖f3 f5 15 exf5 ♘xf5 16 ♗f2 Black has an uncomfortable position since a later g4 will drive his pieces back.

12   ...   ♖f8!

The rook returns to a square which fits in better with the central pawn-structure, at the same time freeing e8 for the f6-knight.

13   f4   ♘e8
14   fxe5

White is unable to maintain the tension since after, for example, 14 ♖ae1 f6 15 ♗h4 h6, the h4-bishop is in trouble.

14   ...   dxe5

The exchange on e5 has relieved the pressure on Black's position. The e8-knight can move to d6, both blockading the d5-pawn and supporting eventual counterplay by ...f5.

15   ♘c1! (D)

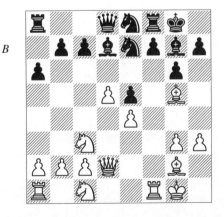

A good move. The knight has few active prospects on e2, so White redeploys it to the better square d3. There it presses on the e5-pawn, which is especially relevant if White plays ♗h6 to exchange dark-squared bishops. Moreover, the knight might jump to c5 if the opportunity arises.

15   ...   ♘d6

White retains a slight advantage. Black's long-term plan involves ...f5, while White will hope to move his c3-knight and push his c-pawn up the board. Black's problem is that ...f5 is not especially damaging, while the eventual arrival of White's pawn on c5 will break open Black's position. Therefore, the long-term chances will favour White.

16   b3

Both preventing ...f6 followed by ...♘c4 and supporting an eventual c-pawn advance.

16   ...   f6
17   ♗e3   ♕c8

Black's position is not yet solid enough for 17...f5?! because the e5-pawn is too weak, and White can exploit this by 18 ♘d3 b6 19 ♗h6 to secure a clear advantage. Black therefore plans to connect his rooks by playing ...b6 and ...♕b7; only when everything is ready will he play ...f5.

18   ♔h2   b6 (D)

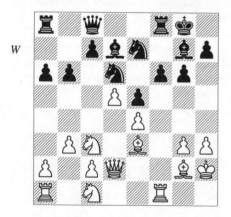

19   ♘d3   ♕b7

19...f5?! is still wrong as 20 ♗h6 ♗xh6 21 ♕xh6 fxe4 22 ♘xe5 ♘ef5 23 ♕f4 is much better for White.

20   ♘e2

Now White is ready to advance the c-pawn. After c4 and ♖ac1, he can either break Black's pawns apart by c5, or play for a pawn-roller by b4 and only then c5. It follows that Black must start some counter-action within the next few moves.

20   ...   f5

The problem with this move is that it is not easy to see where it leads. White simply defends the e4-square with ♘f2, and then Black runs out of ideas. Taking on e4 gives White control of e4, and Black is unlikely to be able to play ...f4. The alternative was to take steps to counter White's queenside play by 20...c5 but even this does not equalize. After 21 c4 (21 dxc6? ♗xc6 leaves the e4-pawn very weak) 21...♖ae8 22 ♖ac1 f5 23 ♘f2, followed by b4, White's queenside play starts to cause problems.

21   ♘f2! (D)

The correct choice. 21 ♗h6? is wrong in this position as Black can reply 21...♘xe4 22 ♗xe4 fxe4, and now:

1) 23 ♗xg7 ♖xf1 24 ♖xf1 exd3! 25 ♗f6 (25 ♕h6 dxe2 also wins for Black) 25...♘xd5 26 ♗xe5 (26 ♕xd3 ♖f8 and Black wins) 26...dxe2 27 ♕h6 exf1♘+ 28 ♔g1 ♔f7 wins for Black since the king runs away.

2) 23 ♖xf8+ ♗xf8 24 ♘xe5 ♗xh6 25 ♕xh6 ♕xd5 and Black is a pawn up.

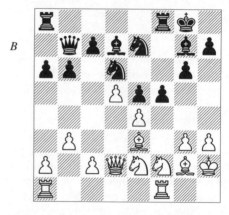

21   ...   ♖ae8

21...♖f7 22 c4 ♖af8 23 ♖ac1 leads to a situation similar to the game. Black has no immediate threats on the kingside while White is already on the verge of playing c5.

22   c4

Black finds it hard to develop any real counterplay to offset White's queenside advance.

22   ...   ♕c8

22...h5 is met by 23 ♗g5, preventing ...h4, and if then 23...♘f7 White plays 24 ♗xe7 ♖xe7 25 exf5, followed by d6, winning material.

23   Rac1   fxe4? *(D)*

Although objectively this is not the best move, as a result of it Black soon gains the advantage! 23...h5 would have been stronger; then 24 c5 (24 ♗g5 ♘f7 is not so clear now that Black's queen has left the long diagonal, while after 24 b4 fxe4 25 c5 bxc5 26 bxc5 ♘df5 Black has some counterplay) 24...bxc5 25 ♗xc5 ♕d8 followed by ...h4 will give Black some counterchances on the kingside.

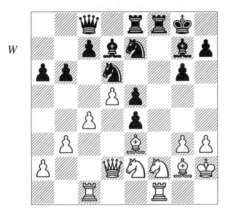

24   c5?

Bologan was starting to drift into his usual time-trouble, and at this critical moment failed to find the right move. 24 g4! is essential, keeping Black's pieces out of f5. Then Black has a very difficult position, as his pieces cannot develop any activity. After 24...h5 25 gxh5 gxh5 26 ♘g3 Black's king becomes seriously exposed.

24   ...   bxc5
25   ♗xc5   ♘ef5!

This move, which both defends d6 and prepares ...♗h6, gives Black sufficient counterplay. Indeed, White has to be careful to maintain the balance.

26   ♘xe4?!

It is well-known that when you are short of time it is hard to react correctly to an unexpected change in the position. White's anticipated strategic crush has dissolved into messy tactics, and now he makes a further slip. 26 ♕e1 is better, removing the queen from the exposed h6-c1 diagonal and preparing to lend additional support to the weak g3-pawn. After 26...♗h6 27 Rc3 or 26...e3 27 ♘g4 the position is very unclear.

26   ...   ♗h6

27   ♘g5

After 27 ♕c3 ♗xc1 28 Rxc1 ♘xe4 29 ♗xe4 ♘d6 White doesn't have enough for the exchange, so he is forced to pin his own knight.

27   ...   ♕d8

Removing the queen from the dangerous c-file with gain of tempo.

28   h4   e4 *(D)*

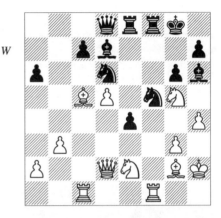

White has removed the first black e-pawn, but now the second one starts to look dangerous. Suddenly all Black's pieces, which had earlier appeared so passively placed, are playing an active part in the game. This comment applies especially to Black's rooks, which are well posted to support his growing initiative.

29   ♗e3

Allowing the exchange of White's dark-squared bishop is clearly a major concession, but there was no really satisfactory defence:

1) 29 a4 e3 30 ♕a5 ♗xg5 31 hxg5 ♕xg5 32 ♕xc7 Rf7! 33 ♗xd6 ♕h5+ 34 ♔g1 ♕xe2 35 ♗b4 gives Black a clear advantage due to his dangerous e-pawn.

2) 29 ♘d4 e3 30 ♕e2 ♗xg5 31 hxg5 ♕xg5 32 ♘xf5 ♘xf5 33 Rf3 (33 ♗xf8? loses to 33...♘xg3) 33...♘xg3 34 Rxf8+ Rxf8 35 ♕xe3 Rf4! gives Black a decisive attack.

29   ...   ♘xe3
30   Rxf8+

30 ♕xe3 ♘f5 31 ♕d2 e3, followed by either ...♗xg5 or ...♗b5, is excellent for Black.

30   ...   ♗xf8!

After the coming ...♘f5, Black will be able to transfer this bishop to d6, where it both attacks the weak g3-pawn and defends the vulnerable c7-pawn.

31   ♕xe3   ♘f5

White is given no chance to organize his defence.

32   ♕c3

Relatively best. After 32 ♕a7 ♗d6 33 ♕xa6 (33 ♘f4 h6 34 ♘xe4 ♘xg3 and Black wins) 33...h6 34 ♘h3 (34 ♘xe4 ♖xe4 35 ♗xe4 ♕xh4+ is also winning for Black) 34...♘xg3! 35 ♘xg3 ♕xh4 White can resign, while 32 ♕f2 e3 33 ♕f3 ♗d6 34 ♔g1 ♖f8 35 ♖c4 ♕e7, threatening ...♘xg3, gives Black a winning position.

32   ...   ♗d6
33   ♔g1

33 ♗xe4? loses after 33...♖xe4 34 ♘xe4 ♕xh4+.

33   ...   ♗e5 *(D)*

33...♗b5 is also tempting, but after 34 ♘f4 ♗e5 35 ♕e1 there is nothing clear-cut for Black.

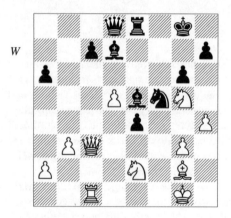

34   ♕e1

The best move, since 34 ♕c5 is met by 34...♗b5! (not 34...♘xg3? 35 ♘xg3 ♗xg3 36 d6! and suddenly White is better) 35 ♘e6 (35 ♕c2 ♗d3 36 ♕d2 ♘xg3 also wins for Black) 35...♖xe6 36 dxe6 ♘xg3 37 ♘xg3 ♗d4+ and Black wins.

34   ...   e3
35   a4

White seeks to prevent a possible ...♗b5, which would win the g3-pawn. The alternatives are no better, as 35 b4 ♕e7 followed by ...♗b5 is very good for Black, while interpolating 35 ♘f3 ♗d6 does not help White.

35   ...   ♕b8 *(D)*

Attacking the weak b3-pawn.

36   ♘f3?

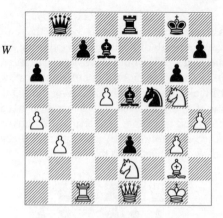

The strain of defending this unpleasant position in time-trouble finally tells; after this move White is definitely lost. The alternatives were:

1) 36 d6? cxd6 (36...♗xd6? 37 ♕c3 leaves Black's king too exposed) 37 ♕a5 ♔g7! 38 ♖c7 ♖e7 with a winning position for Black.

2) 36 ♘e4 ♘d6 37 ♘c5 ♗g4 and now:

2a) 38 ♘f4 e2! 39 ♔h2 ♘f5 with strong pressure.

2b) 38 ♘xa6 ♕xb3 39 ♘xc7 ♖c8 is very good for Black; e.g., 40 ♘e6 ♖xc1 41 ♘xc1 ♕b2 42 ♘d3 (42 ♕xe3 ♗xe6 wins for Black) 42...♕d2 43 ♕b1 ♗xe6 44 dxe6 e2 45 ♔h2 ♔g7! and Black wins.

2c) 38 b4! is relatively the best chance. After 38...♗xe2 39 ♘d7 ♕b7 40 ♕xe2 ♕xb4 41 ♘xe5 ♖xe5 42 ♖xc7 ♕xa4 Black is a pawn up, although the win may not be easy as Black's king is slightly exposed.

36   ...   ♗d6

White has no reasonable way to defend the b3-pawn.

37   ♘fd4

37 ♖b1 ♕b6 (threatening 38...♗b4) is also winning for Black; e.g., 38 a5 (if 38 ♔h1, then 38...♖e4, followed by ...♖g4) 38...♕b5 39 ♘g5 ♗b4 40 ♕d1 ♘xg3 41 ♘xg3 e2 42 ♘xe2 ♖xe2 43 ♕f1 ♗f5 44 ♖c1 ♕d3 gives Black a winning attack.

37   ...   ♘xd4
38   ♘xd4   ♕b6
39   ♖c4

39 ♘e2 ♕xb3 is hopeless for White.

39   ...   e2! *(D)*

Decisive. There is no viable defence to the threat of 40...♗xg3.

40   a5

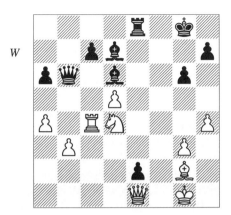

W

Or 40 &h2 罩e3.

40 ... 豐a7

40...豐xd4+ 41 罩xd4 皇c5 42 d6 皇xd4+ 43 &h2 cxd6 wins, but is unnecessarily complicated. However, 40...豐b8 was also very effective, with the neat point that 41 &h2 皇xg3+ 42 &xg3 c5+ is crushing.

41 &h2 皇b5

0-1

After 42 ②xb5 axb5 43 罩g4 (43 罩e4 罩xe4 44 皇xe4 豐e3, followed by taking on g3, wins for Black) 43...豐e3 44 a6 (44 b4 豐d3) 44...皇c5, followed by ...豐g1+, Black wins easily.

In November I started a period of hectic chess activity, although on the whole it was not very successful. First of all, I lost to Kramnik in the Bundesliga. Two weeks later I travelled to Torbay in the West of England for a weekend tournament. The reason for this was that I had a chance of winning the annual Grand Prix (at that time sponsored by Leigh) if I could increase my score by making 100% in a tournament, even a small one. Owing to my commitments in the last few weeks of the year, I had only one weekend free to achieve this, hence the trip to Torbay. Unfortunately, although I won my first four games, I was held to a draw in the last round by Aaron Summerscale and only tied for first place with him. This left Mark Hebden a clear run to win the Grand Prix and I had to be content with second place. At the following Bundesliga weekend I lost on Saturday and I was feeling pretty miserable for the Sunday game.

Under the circumstances, I was happy with a quiet opening without early complications. At move 16 White decided to liquidate the centre, leading to a position with open c-, d- and e-files. Positions with a totally open centre can be very deceptive. It is easy to suppose that all the rooks will be exchanged, with a quick handshake to follow, but this doesn't always happen. On the contrary, slight advantages (such as more active pieces or control of a key square) can prove remarkably persistent. The reason is that in most positions an advantage on one part of the board is often counterbalanced by a disadvantage somewhere else, and the defender can use this to generate counterplay. In symmetrical open positions there is usually no ready source of counterplay and so the defender is reduced to trying to neutralize the attacker's advantage rather than seeking active play himself. If the defender succeeds, then a draw can easily result, but it may not be so easy to achieve this. Black's key error in this game occurred on move 16, when he weakened his queenside light squares and undermined his own c6-knight. White went on to achieve a winning position, but then some very weak technique let Black back in the game, only for a final blunder to tip the balance in White's favour.

Game 16

J. Nunn – C. Lutz

Bundesliga 1994/5

Sicilian Defence, 2 c3

| 1 | e4 | c5 |
| 2 | c3 | |

Just as in Game 10, I decided to avoid the main lines of Sicilian theory.

| 2 | ... | d5 |

| 3 | exd5 | 豐xd5 |
| 4 | d4 | ②f6 |

Instead of Sher's early ...②c6, Lutz adopts the more standard plan of ...②f6 and ...皇g4.

| 5 | ②f3 | 皇g4 |

At one time, Black usually continued with
...e6 and ...♘c6 in this position, and while this
line has not been refuted, the modern preference is to develop the light-squared bishop before it is blocked in with ...e6.

6   ♗e2

Although this has always been White's most
popular move, there are several other ideas.
Perhaps the weakest is 6 ♕a4+, which is well
met by 6...♗d7. 6 ♘bd2, intending ♗c4, experienced a surge of popularity in the late 1990s,
but it was soon discovered that 6...♘c6 is a satisfactory reply. In recent years, the continuation
6 dxc5 has proved more of a test for Black, and
indeed this looks like White's best try for an advantage. At the time this game was played,
however, 6 ♗e2 was virtually the only move
played.

6   ...   e6 *(D)*

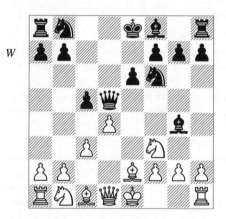

7   0-0

White will probably play h3 at some stage,
but it usually doesn't make any difference
whether it is now or later. However, there is one
line in which the insertion of h3 is important,
namely 7 h3 ♗h5 8 c4. The point is that 8...♕d7
can be met by 9 d5 exd5 10 g4 ♗g6 11 ♘e5,
which gives White a slight advantage, and so
Black usually prefers 8...♕d8. Then 9 ♘c3
cxd4 10 ♘xd4 ♗xe2 11 ♕a4+ leads to a position which Rozentalis and Harley analyse in
their book *Play the 2 c3 Sicilian* (Gambit, 2002).
They believe that White has a small advantage,
but it looks rather equal to me and indeed in
practice virtually every game following this
line has ended in a draw.

7   ...   ♘c6

8   ♗e3

White threatens to take on c5, so Black is virtually forced to exchange on d4, which allows
White to develop his queen's knight to c3.

8   ...   cxd4

9   cxd4   ♗e7

9...♗b4 was brought to the world's attention
by the game *Deep Blue*-Kasparov, Philadelphia
(3) 1996, although it had been played earlier a
few times. Black seeks to develop his bishop
more actively than on the traditional square e7.
If the bishop is chased by a3, it will move to a5
and then b6 to attack the d4-pawn. This continuation appears to offer Black safe equality and
is one of the reasons for the decline of the system White adopts in this game, and the ensuing
rise of 6 dxc5.

10   ♘c3   ♕d6 *(D)*

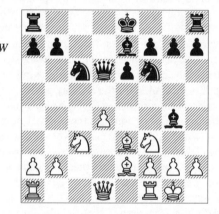

The best square for the queen, keeping her
majesty active and preparing ...0-0 followed by
...♖fd8, with pressure against d4. This is a key
position of the 6 ♗e2 system. At the time of this
game, Black was experiencing a few problems
in this line, but later developments showed
that White cannot really hope for an advantage
against accurate play.

11   h3

As mentioned above, this is almost always
played sooner or later. It is useful to have the
option of driving the bishop back with g4, and
in some lines in which White plays d5 and a series of exchanges takes place on that square, a
rook or queen arriving on d5 will attack the h5-
bishop.

11   ...   ♗h5

12   ♕b3

White's plan is to complete his development by bringing his rooks to c1 and d1, but he has to watch out for a possible ...♕b4 by Black. The exchange of queens favours Black because the attacking potential of the isolated d4-pawn can only be realized in a middlegame. Note that it is very rarely a good idea to chase Black's queen by ♘b5. Here, for example, 12 ♘b5 ♕b8 leads nowhere and the knight will soon have to return.

12 ... 0-0 (D)

12...♕b4 is premature here, since 13 g4 ♗g6 14 ♘e5! gives White the advantage.

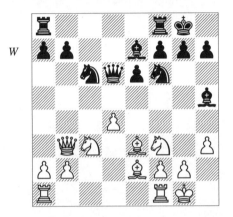

13 ♖fd1

The general characteristics of IQP (isolated queen's pawn) positions are well-known. The side with the IQP must avoid exchanges, play for an attack and look for a chance to push the pawn. His opponent must swap pieces off, restrain the pawn and either blockade it or attack it directly. However, this position is slightly different from a typical IQP position. In most IQP positions, White is able to play for direct threats on the kingside by ♗c2, ♕d3, etc., but here White's pieces are poorly placed for a direct attack. In any case, the fact that Black's light-squared bishop is outside the pawn-chain and can drop back to g6 makes any direct attack futile. Instead, White has to play more positionally, hoping to constrict Black while looking for a chance to play d5. However, the lack of any direct attacking chances for White means that, objectively speaking, he cannot hope for an advantage.

13 ... ♖fd8

Now 13...♕b4? is a real mistake because 14 d5! ♕xb3 15 axb3 exd5 16 ♘xd5 ♘xd5 17

♖xd5 (this line demonstrates the point made earlier about attacking the h5-bishop) 17...♗g6 18 ♖d7 gives White a large endgame advantage. However, with the rook on d8 Black is genuinely threatening ...♕b4, so now it is time for White to prevent it.

14 a3 (D)

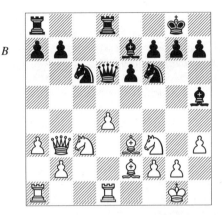

14 ... ♖ac8?!

Black has several possibilities at this point:

1) 14...♖ab8 is a solid move defending the b-pawn. The main line is 15 ♖ac1 ♘d5 and now 16 ♘xd5 exd5, 16 ♘b5 ♘a5! 17 ♕c2 ♗g6! and 16 ♘e4 ♕c7 are all fine for Black.

2) 14...♘d5 is another safe option. After 15 ♘xd5 ♕xd5 16 ♕xd5 (16 ♗c4 ♕d6 is fine for Black as 17 d5? loses to 17...♘a5) 16...♖xd5 17 g4 ♗g6 White cannot hope for an advantage.

3) 14...a6, preparing to expand on the queenside, is one of the most popular lines, but is more double-edged than the alternatives. After 15 ♖ac1 b5 16 d5 ♘a5 the position is very unclear.

My view is that the move played is inaccurate and makes it harder for Black to equalize. However, as there seem to be several satisfactory alternatives for Black, one can hardly put much faith in this line as White.

15 ♖ac1 ♕b8

This move allows White to achieve his central breakthrough, although with accurate defence this need not have caused Black too many problems. The theoretically recommended line is 15...♘d5 (15...b6 is also doubtful as after 16 ♕a4 White has awkward pressure) but here I think that White can retain an edge by 16 ♘xd5 (16 ♕xb7 ♖b8 17 ♕a6 ♘xe3 18 fxe3 ♗xf3 19

♗xf3 ♘xd4 20 ♕xd6 ♘xf3+ 21 gxf3 ♖xd6 is equal) 16...♕xd5 17 ♕xd5 (17 ♕xb7 ♘xd4 18 ♕xc8 ♘xe2+ 19 ♔f1 ♕xd1+ 20 ♖xd1 ♖xc8 21 ♔xe2 is equal) 17...exd5 (17...♖xd5 18 g4 ♗g6 19 ♘e5 favours White) 18 g4 ♗g6 19 ♘e5 ♗d6 and now both 20 ♘xc6 bxc6 21 b4 and 20 ♘xg6 hxg6 21 ♔g2 offer White a slight plus.

16   d5

White takes his chance. Playing the liquidating d5 in an IQP position is often a finely-balanced matter. In many positions it leads only to a series of exchanges with a dead-drawn position at the end. However, in other cases it can give White a persistent advantage. Here the signs are good for White: he will gain a tempo by attacking the h5-bishop and this same bishop will be left out of play on g6, where it does nothing to defend Black's queenside against White's coming attack. However, as we shall see, these advantages should not have been sufficient for a genuine advantage against accurate defence by Black.

16   ...   ♘xd5
17   ♘xd5   exd5
18   ♖xd5 *(D)*

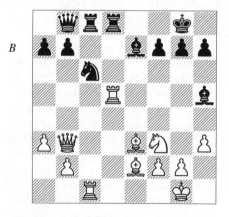

18   ...   ♗g6

Although this is not wrong, at this point Black had a chance to force immediate equality. The alternatives are:

1) 18...♖xd5 (exchanging rooks first fails to equalize) 19 ♕xd5 ♗g6 and now:

1a) 20 ♘d4 ♖d8 (20...♘xd4 21 ♖xc8+ ♕xc8 22 ♕xd4 a6 23 ♗f3 is very unpleasant for Black) 21 ♘xc6 bxc6 22 ♕a2 (Black must act quickly before White can exploit Black's weak pawns) 22...♕e5! 23 ♖xc6 ♗d6 24 g3

♕e8 threatens both ...♕xc6 and ...♗xg3 and gives Black adequate play for the pawn.

1b) 20 b4 ♖d8 21 ♕c4 is safer. White has a small but enduring advantage.

2) The correct defence is 18...♗xf3! 19 ♗xf3 (19 ♖xd8+ ♗xd8 20 ♗xf3 ♘d4 transposes) 19...♘d4! 20 ♖xd8+ (20 ♖xc8 ♘xf3+ 21 gxf3 ♕xc8 will also transpose) 20...♗xd8 (after 20...♖xd8? 21 ♗xd4 ♖xd4 22 ♗d5 White wins a pawn) 21 ♖xc8 ♘xf3+ 22 gxf3 ♕xc8 23 ♗xa7 ♕c1+! 24 ♔g2 ♕g5+ 25 ♔f1 (the only way to avoid perpetual check) 25...♕c1+ 26 ♔e2 ♗f6 27 ♕xb7 ♕c2+ 28 ♔f1 ♕c1+ with perpetual check in any case.

19   ♖b5 *(D)*

19 ♖cd1 ♖xd5 20 ♖xd5 ♖d8 gives White almost nothing.

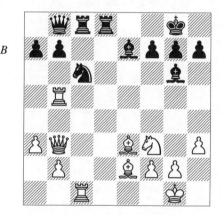

After the move played White has something to work with. His pieces are slightly more active than Black's and the g6-bishop is a little out of play. This move attempts to force a weakening of Black's queenside pawns.

19   ...   b6?

At last Black makes a significant mistake. This move weakens the queenside light squares and undermines the position of the c6-knight. Black could have kept White's advantage to a minimum by not touching his pawns:

1) 19...♖d7?! and now:

1a) 20 ♕a4 ♗f6 21 ♗f4 ♕a8 looks promising, but there is no follow-up for White.

1b) 20 ♗c4 ♗f6 (20...♗d6 21 ♗d5 gives White an edge) 21 ♗e6!? ♖d3! (not 21...fxe6? 22 ♕xe6+ ♔f7 23 ♖xc6, when White wins a pawn) 22 ♗xf7+ ♔h8 23 ♕e6 ♖d6 24 ♕a2 (trying to avoid a repetition, but playing for a win is risky) 24...b6 is unclear, as both 25 ♖bc5 b6 and 25 ♖b6 ♗d8 force White to give up the exchange.

1c) 20 ♖xc6! ♖xc6 21 ♘e5 ♖cc7 22 ♘xd7 ♖xd7 23 ♕a4 a6 24 ♕xa6 and White wins a pawn.

2) 19...♕a8 is solid, when White has no more than a faint edge. 20 ♖xb7?? is not possible due to 20...♘a5.

3) 19...♖c7! is the most logical move; Black defends b7 while preparing to double rooks if the opportunity arises. Then White cannot claim any advantage; for example, 20 ♗f4 (20 ♖d1 ♖cd7 21 ♖xd7 ♖xd7 22 ♕c4 ♕d8 is equal) 20...♗d6 21 ♗g5 (21 ♗xd6 ♖xd6 22 ♖bc5 ♕d8 is safe for Black) 21...♖e8 22 ♖d5 ♘e5 with equality.

20   ♖d5! *(D)*

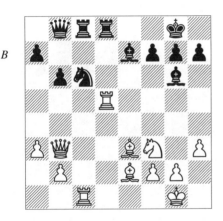

Having done its duty, the rook returns to the centre to allow the bishop to move to b5 or a6. Black is now in trouble.

20   ...   ♗f6

Or:

1) 20...♕b7 21 ♖xd8+ ♘xd8 (21...♖xd8 22 ♕a4 is very awkward for Black) 22 ♖xc8 ♖xc8 23 ♕a4 ♘c6 24 ♗b5 ♘a5 25 ♘e5 and White has continuing pressure.

2) 20...♖xd5 21 ♕xd5 ♕d6 22 ♕xd6 ♗xd6 23 ♗a6 ♖c7 24 ♖d1 ♗f8 25 ♗f4 ♖e7 26 ♗b5 is clearly better for White as Black's pieces are passively placed.

21   ♗a6? *(D)*

Tempting, but wrong. The simplest and best line is 21 ♖xd8+ ♘xd8 22 ♖xc8 ♕xc8 23 ♕a4, when the pressure against Black's queenside is hard to counter; for example, 23...♘c6 24 ♗b5

♘a5 (24...♘e5 25 ♘xe5 ♗xe5 26 ♕xa7 ♗xb2 27 a4 wins a pawn) 25 ♗a6! ♕c6 26 ♕f4 ♕a8 27 ♗d4 ♗e7 (27...♗xd4 loses to 28 ♘xd4 as there is no defence to the threat of b4) 28 ♕c7 ♗f8 29 ♘e5 with strong pressure for White. This line is a good example of how treacherous positions with an open centre can be. If one side has pressure, as White does here, then the lack of counterplay can make it difficult to nullify the pressure. Virtually the only defensive idea is liquidation, but if this doesn't work then the defender may be hard-pressed to prevent his position from gradually deteriorating.

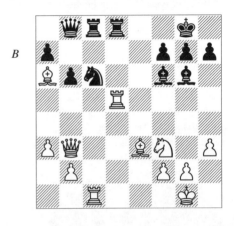

21   ...   ♘e7?

Black misses the chance which White's previous move presented to him. Black should have activated his offside bishop by 21...♗e4!, and now:

1) 22 ♖d2 ♘a5 (22...♗xf3 23 ♗xc8 ♖xd2 24 ♗xd2 ♘d4 fails to 25 ♕e3!, when White wins) 23 ♖xc8 ♖xc8 24 ♕d1 ♖e8 leaves White with very little.

2) 22 ♖xd8+ ♖xd8 23 ♘g5 ♗d5 (23...♗xg5 24 ♗xg5 gives White the safe advantage of the two bishops in an open position) 24 ♕c2 g6 (not 24...h6 25 ♕h7+ ♔f8 26 ♖e1! ♗e5 27 f4 and White wins) 25 ♘e4 ♗g7 (25...♗xb2? 26 ♕xb2 ♗xe4 27 ♖xc6! ♗xc6 28 ♗h6 wins for White, while 25...♗e5 26 ♗g5 ♖e8 transposes to line '2b' below) 26 ♗g5 and now:

2a) 26...♘d4 is tempting but dubious: 27 ♕d1 ♗b3 28 ♕d3 ♖e8 29 ♘f6+ ♗xf6 30 ♗xf6 and now:

2a1) 30...♕f4 31 ♕e3! ♕xe3 32 fxe3 ♘c2 (32...♘e6 33 ♗b5 ♖b8 34 e4 is also very unpleasant for Black) 33 ♔f2 is much better for

White thanks to the two bishops and Black's almost trapped knight.

2a2) 30...♘e2+ 31 ♕xe2! ♖xe2 32 ♗xe2 ♗a4 33 ♗g4 ♕f8 34 ♖c8 ♗e8 35 ♖d8 a5 (Black can only wait) 36 ♗d7 ♗xd7 37 ♖xd7 and Black loses his queen.

2b) 26...♖e8! 27 ♘f6+ ♗xf6 28 ♗xf6 ♕f4 (White's two bishops and Black's weakened kingside would normally give White a long-term advantage, but Black can exploit the temporary lack of coordination in White's army to force a draw) 29 ♗c3 ♘e5! 30 ♖d1 ♘f3+ 31 gxf3 ♕g5+ 32 ♔h2 ♕f4+ with perpetual check.

The move played is wrong because it allows White to occupy the seventh rank with a rook.

22   ♖xc8   ♖xc8

22...♘xc8 is even worse in view of 23 ♖xd8+ ♗xd8 24 ♕a4 ♘d6 25 ♗f4 ♗c7 (25...♕c7 26 ♕d4 ♗e7 27 ♘e5 is much better for White) 26 ♕d7 ♗f5 27 ♕e7 ♗e6 28 ♘d4 ♗d5 29 ♗e2, followed by ♗f3 (and if ...♗xf3, then gxf3), exposing the weak c6-square. White's advantage verges on the decisive.

23   ♖d7 *(D)*

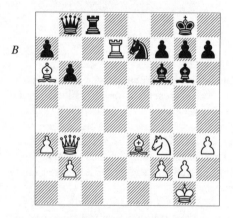

23   ...   ♖e8

The alternative 23...♖c2 24 ♘d4 ♗xd4 (or 24...♖c5 25 ♘e6! ♗c2 26 ♕a2 fxe6 27 ♗xc5 bxc5 28 ♕xe6+ ♔h8 29 ♖xe7 ♗xe7 30 ♕xe7 and White wins) 25 ♖xd4 ♘f5 26 ♕xc2 ♘xd4 27 ♕a4 ♘e6 28 ♕d7 is also very good for White.

24   ♕a4

The simplest; White's threats of ♗f4 or ♖b7 force Black to surrender the a7-pawn, which should be enough for a win in the long run. However, 24 ♕c4 ♗xb2 25 ♗f4 b5 26 ♗xb5 ♕a8 27 ♗e3 is also effective.

24   ...   ♗f5

Or 24...♗xb2 25 ♗f4 b5 (25...♕a8 26 ♗b7 traps the queen) 26 ♗xb5 ♕b6 27 ♖xa7 and White wins.

25   ♖b7?!

This only drives Black's queen to a better square. White should have played simply 25 ♖xa7, winning a pawn while retaining all his positional advantages. If then 25...♗c2, the reply 26 ♕b5 attacks the b6-pawn. An almost sure sign of bad form is an inability to convert winning positions convincingly into full points. My play during the last few months of 1994 was very poor, and even though I won this game you can see the signs of lack of confidence and inability to calculate accurately during this phase of the game.

25   ...   ♕d8

26   ♖xa7 *(D)*

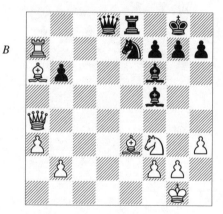

Even though White has missed a killing blow, his advantage should still be sufficient to win.

26   ...   ♘d5

26...♗xb2 loses to 27 ♗xb6, while 26...♘c8 27 ♖a8 ♖f8 28 ♘d4 ♗d7 29 ♕c4 is also winning for White.

27   ♗d4

Exchanging Black's most active minor piece.

27   ...   h6

27...♗xd4 28 ♕xd4 ♗e6 (28...♖e4 29 ♕d2 forces the rook back to e8) 29 ♗b5 ♖e7 30 ♖xe7 ♕xe7 31 ♗c4 will win for White in the end.

28   ♗xf6

Missing the decisive 28 ♗c4 ♖f8 29 ♗xf6 ♘xf6 30 ♗xf7+, winning a second pawn.

28   ...   ♘xf6

29	♗c4	♗g6

29...♖e7 30 ♖a8 ♗c8 31 ♗a6 ♖c7 32 ♕d4 ♕f8 33 ♘e5 is winning for White, while after 29...♗d7 30 ♕a6 ♕b8 31 ♕b7 ♕d6 32 ♕c7 ♕xc7 33 ♖xc7 ♗e6 34 ♘e5 White is a pawn up with an excellent position.

30	♕b3	

30 ♕c6 intending ♕c7 was more forceful.

30	...	♘d7
31	♕d1?	

Up to this point White has committed inaccuracies rather than errors, and none of his previous moves has really endangered the win. However, now the effect of time-trouble starts to be felt and White plays a move which lets Black back into the game. This further error is not a coincidence, but a clear consequence of the earlier slips. Had White played more convincingly earlier, he would not now be in time-trouble and the preconditions for an error would not be present.

31 ♕b5 would still have left White with a winning position.

31	...	♘e5! (D)

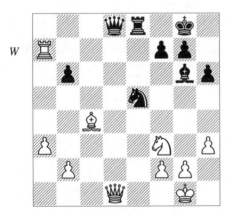

Oops! I hadn't seen that. It's the only move, but it is a good one which puts White's win in doubt.

32	♕xd8	♘xf3+
33	gxf3	♖xd8
34	♖b7	♖d6
35	b4?!	

It looks natural to push the pawns at once, but 35 ♔g2 ♖f6 36 ♔g3 was more accurate, taking time out to limit Black's counterplay. After this Black's rook lacks the active square f4, and White can safely advance his queenside pawns.

35	...	♖f6
36	a4	

36 ♔g2 ♗h5 37 ♖b8+ ♔h7 38 ♗d3+ ♗g6 39 ♗e4 is probably better, when Black can only activate his pieces by exchanging on e4, which improves White's pawn-structure.

36	...	♖f4! (D)

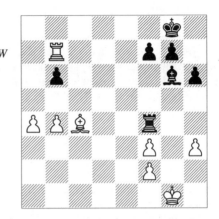

This is the point of Black's defence. White can choose between allowing the exchange of b-pawns, or moving his rook away from the attack on b6.

37	♖c7	

37 ♗b5 ♖xb4 38 ♖xb6 ♖b1+ 39 ♔g2 ♖a1 is of course favourable for White, but the win is not certain.

37	...	♖xf3
38	♖c6	♖f4??

With just seconds left on the clock, Black makes a terrible blunder. 38...♗e4! (38...♔f8? 39 ♖xb6 ♖xh3 40 ♗d5, occupying the long diagonal, should win for White) is best, occupying the important long diagonal. After 39 ♖xb6 ♔f8 (39...♖xh3 40 ♔f1 is similar) 40 a5 (40 ♗f1 ♖a3 41 a5 ♖a1 is an awkward pin) 40...♖xh3 41 ♔f1 ♔e7 (41...♖c3? 42 ♗a6 ♖a3 43 ♗b7 ♗xb7 44 ♖xb7 h5 45 ♖a7 ♖a1+ 46 ♔g2 and White wins, as his rook and pawns can advance without the help of the king) 42 ♗a6 (42 ♔e1 h5 43 a6 h4 44 ♖b8 ♖h1+ 45 ♔d2 ♔d6 gives Black fair drawing chances) 42...♖a3 43 ♗b7 ♗d3+ 44 ♔g2 ♔d7 the outcome is still not clear.

39	♖xg6	♖xc4
40	♖xb6	

The two connected passed pawns win easily.

40	...	♖c1+
41	♔g2	1-0

My next chess event was the Moscow Olympiad in December. This was the tenth consecutive Olympiad in which I had represented England, and as it turned out it was to be my last. It would have been nice to have finished with a good result, but unfortunately it was not to be.

Sometimes it is impossible to give a reason for a run of poor form, but quite often outside circumstances are clearly to blame. That was the case here, and unfortunately a number of factors combined to make it hard to concentrate on the chess. One factor was an unfortunate dispute which broke out prior to the Olympiad. I should explain that I was a member of the Selection Committee of the British Chess Federation. This small committee selected the English teams for the Olympiad and other important team events (although not junior events). Despite the name 'British Chess Federation', the BCF only has responsibility for English chess, and the separate teams for Scotland, Wales, Ireland and the Channel Islands are selected by their respective chess federations. Originally, the Olympiad had been scheduled to take place in Greece, and Nigel Short, one of our top players, had declined to participate (although, since he was living in Greece, it should have been rather convenient for him). Therefore, a team was selected omitting Nigel and naming Murray Chandler as captain. Then the Olympiad was switched, at short notice, to Moscow and suddenly Nigel wanted to play, but only on the condition that Murray was sacked as captain. The precise nature of his objection to Murray was not made entirely clear, but it seems that he disliked some items which had appeared in the *British Chess Magazine*, which at the time was owned by Murray. I regarded Nigel's condition as being obviously unacceptable, but apparently my view was not universally shared. I could not imagine the English football coach being sacked on the grounds that one of the players had an objection to him, and I did not see why it should be any different in chess. If all the players had a veto on the selection of captain, then it would very likely be impossible to select a captain at all. The result was a protracted and unpleasant dispute, which ended up consuming large amounts of my time just when I was very busy with other events and with preparing for the Olympiad. Moreover, some of those involved in this dispute did not make its resolution any easier by changing their positions virtually from day to day. The low point was reached when Nigel wrote to the sponsors of the team to complain about his 'treatment'. Dragging sponsors into a messy internal chess dispute can hardly be a good idea and is not conducive to maintaining good relations with them. To their credit, the British Chess Federation put in a good deal of effort to resolve this problem, and in the end Nigel agreed to play despite Murray's captaincy. However, this dispute, coupled with the long-running frigid relations between Nigel and Tony Miles, who was also in the team, led to a fairly chilly atmosphere in Moscow.

As a matter of fact, Tony was also not an easy character to accommodate. One of his longstanding requirements for participation in Olympiads was that he should not have to sit next to Jon Speelman. This wasn't because he disliked Jon, but because he found Jon's behaviour while sitting at the board to be so disturbing that he apparently could not bear to be in close proximity to him. Being captain of a chess team may seem an easy task, but I can assure you that it is not.

On top of this, the playing and hotel conditions at Moscow were, to put it politely, not ideal. The food provided was simply inedible and the boards were squeezed so closely together that walking around between moves was almost impossible. I won just a single game, in the first round, and lost twice. My remaining games were lacklustre draws. My overall score in the 10 Olympiads in which I participated was 48 wins, 37 draws and 14 losses for a total of 66½/99 or 67.2%.

The pre-event dispute left me with a sour taste in the mouth and soon after this I resigned from the selection committee. My experience is that, at least in the chess world, voluntary work results in far more unpleasantness than paid work. My time on the selection committee, which lasted for over a decade, was a case in point, and my work for the GMA, which was all totally unpaid, is another.

After Christmas, it was time to play at Hastings again; although my chess was still in poor shape, the final result was not too bad. I scored 5½/9 to finish in outright second place, the winner being the German grandmaster Thomas Luther, who scored 6½. I scored two wins and seven draws, and again my poor form was most clearly indicated by my failure to wrap up two technically winning positions.

A few days later I was in action in the Bundesliga and in one game a very interesting ending arose, in which Black, although a pawn down, held the advantage thanks to his active king and bishop. This example again shows how important tactics are in the endgame, even in a rather simplified position. White's error on move 41 left his rook tactically vulnerable on the long diagonal; see the note to White's 42nd move for the key variation exploiting this.

Game 17
D. Norwood – J. Nunn
Bundesliga 1994/5

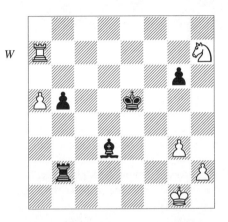

White is a pawn up in this endgame, but in virtually all other respects the position favours Black. His king is actively placed while White's is trapped on the back rank, and his bishop is far stronger than White's offside knight. Both sides have passed pawns and indeed White's is further advanced. However, Black can stop this pawn by using his bishop along the long diagonal, while Black's passed pawn may not be so easy to halt. We can summarize by saying that Black has the advantage, although it is not clear whether this will be sufficient to win in view of the limited number of pawns. It is interesting to note that both *Deep Junior 8* and *Deep Fritz 8* evaluate this position as 0.00 if you leave them on a long time. They are correct in assessing the position as drawn, but the fact that White has to play accurately to reach the half-point means that the practical chances lie with Black.

40   a6

This natural move is also the recommendation of the chess software.

40   ...   b4

For the moment Black need not take steps to counter the a-pawn; there will be time later.

41   Ra8?

In positions with advanced passed pawns, the dividing line between a draw and a loss is often quite fine, and with this move White crosses it. The correct defence is 41 Re7+! ♔d4 (41...♔d6 42 a7 Ra2 43 Rb7 ♔c5 44 ♘g5 is safe for White as his knight returns to active duty) 42 a7 Ra2 43 ♘f6! b3 44 Rb7 ♗c4 45 h4 ♔d3 (or 45...♔c3 46 ♘e4+ ♔d3 47 ♘c5+ ♔c2 48 ♘xb3 ♗xb3 49 g4 and White easily liquidates Black's last pawn) 46 Rd7+ (46 ♘d7 ♗d5 47 Rb5 also draws) 46...♔c2 47 ♘g4 ♗e2 48 ♘e3+ ♔c3 49 ♘d5+ ♔c4 50 ♘e3+ with a draw.

The move played is inaccurate for two reasons. The first is that White's rook remains in front of the pawn and it will take a further tempo to move it out of the way. The second is that White's rook is tactically vulnerable on the long diagonal.

41   ...   b3 *(D)*

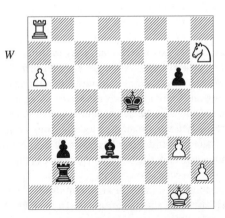

Of course Black uses the free tempo to push his pawn.

42   ♘g5

The line 42 ♖e8+ ♔d4 43 a7 ♖b1+ 44 ♔f2 ♖f1+ 45 ♔g2 ♖a1 shows how Black can often exploit the long-diagonal tactics to hold up White's pawn. There is now no defence; for example, 46 ♖b8 ♖xa7 47 ♖xb3 ♗e4+ wins a piece.

After 42 a7 ♖g2+! (the key tactical resource on which Black's play depends; 42...♖a2? 43 ♖e8+ only draws) 43 ♔h1 ♖a2 44 ♖b8 ♗e4+ 45 ♔g1 b2 Black wins the enemy rook.

The text-move attempts to bring the knight back into the battle, but it will arrive too late.

42	...	♖a2
43	a7	

Or 43 ♘f3+ ♔e4! 44 a7 (playing 44 ♘g5+ ♔d4 45 ♘f3+ ♔e3 only makes matters worse) 44...♔xf3 45 ♖f8+ ♔e3 46 a8♕ ♖xa8 47 ♖xa8 b2 and Black wins.

43	...	b2

This pawn will cost White his knight.

44	♘f3+	♔e4
45	♘d2+	♔e3
46	♖b8	

The only way for White to play on. He loses his knight but eliminates the b-pawn.

46	...	♖a1+
47	♔g2	♔xd2
48	♖xb2+	♔e3

Thanks to the preliminary check on a1, White cannot now defend his a-pawn with ♖b7. The piece-down ending is lost for White; admittedly, Black has only one pawn, but White has no chance of exchanging it and, more importantly, Black's very active pieces enable him to create direct threats against the white king.

49	g4 (D)

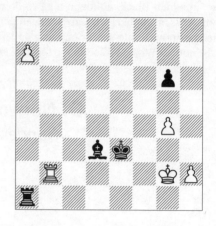

49	...	♔f4!

49...♖xa7 50 ♔g3 makes the win much harder for Black. This is an example of the type of small finesse which is very important when converting a winning position into a point.

50	h3

50 ♖f2+ ♔xg4 51 h3+ ♔g5 52 ♖f7 ♗f5 may save the a-pawn, but White will lose his h-pawn within a couple of moves.

50	...	♗e4+
51	♔f2	♖xa7

Intending 52...♖a3, attacking the h3-pawn.

52	♖b3	♖a2+
53	♔f1	♗f3

The idea is ...♔g3 with a mating attack.

54	♖b6	♔g3

0-1

Black wins after 55 ♖b1 ♖h2 or 55 ♔e1 ♖e2+ 56 ♔f1 ♖d2 57 ♖e6 ♖d1+.

Another factor which had weighed on my mind during the preceding months had been my mother's poor health. Although she had suffered from various problems for several years, by January 1995 it was obvious that the situation had become more serious. She went into hospital during January and at first there seemed to be some improvement, but then her condition suddenly deteriorated and towards the end of January it became obvious that nothing could be done. She died on 2nd February. My father had died long before, while I was still a teenager, and I suddenly felt alone. My chess career would never have got off the ground without the long-term support of my parents and without chess my life would have been poorer. Thanks, Mum and Dad, for chess and for everything else you gave me.

I had agreed to participate in a tournament in San Francisco later in February, and I was in two minds about whether to withdraw from it. However, I decided to play. My main motivation was a desire not to inconvenience the organizers, but in fact it turned out to be good for me. Swapping a cold grey London in February for sunny San Francisco could hardly fail to lift my spirits. In the first round an incident occurred which caused me to smile. I was playing Jonathan Tisdall and round about move 30 a dead-equal position had arisen on the board. Still feeling somewhat jet-lagged and depressed, I offered a draw and was quite surprised by his refusal. A few moves later he made an error and I won a long ending. After the game I asked why he had turned down the draw and it turned out that his habit of playing with his fingers pressed tightly in his ears had prevented him from hearing the offer at all.

I won a nice game in round 6. The basic theme of the Closed Ruy Lopez is White's attempt to maintain his central pawn duo on d4 and e4. Black has various ways to combat the enemy pawn-centre, such as ...c5, as in the Chigorin line, or pressure against e4, as in the Flohr-Zaitsev line. White should only resolve the tension in the centre by d5 or dxe5 under two circumstances: if he is forced to do so, or if he can gain a clear advantage by doing so. In the following game, Black's options were restricted by the fact that White was able to keep his centre intact and thereby retain a flexible position. In the end Black attempted to solve her problems tactically, but it is always a risky business to initiate tactics from a strategically inferior position. A neat combination by White picked up a pawn, and when Black tried to obtain compensation for the pawn, a rook sacrifice ripped open her kingside.

Game 18
J. Nunn – Xie Jun
San Francisco 1995
Ruy Lopez (Spanish), Closed

1	e4	e5
2	♘f3	♘c6
3	♗b5	a6
4	♗a4	♘f6
5	0-0	♗e7
6	♖e1	b5
7	♗b3	d6
8	a4	

Another of the openings that poses a problem as you get older is the Closed Ruy Lopez. If you play the main line 8 c3 0-0 9 h3 then you have to be able to cope with three major systems: the Flohr-Zaitsev (9...♗b7 10 d4 ♖e8), the Breyer (9...♘b8) and the Chigorin (9...♘a5), in addition to a number of less common variations. All these major systems have a large and constantly evolving body of theory; keeping up with them is a major task. Consequently, there is a temptation to explore some less well trodden paths, and the text-move is one of these. I had played it a few times in the mid-1980s, with mixed results, and after a ten-year gap I felt it was time to give it another try. To be honest, I don't think this move is likely to have Ruy Lopez players quaking with fear, since it commits White to a particular strategy uncomfortably early. However, as a surprise weapon it is not bad. Interestingly, it has quite a long pedigree. Alekhine and Rubinstein both played it,

and it was employed three times by Tarrasch in his 1911 match against Schlechter. The solid Schlechter tried three different replies, but only managed to scrape a single draw from the three games.

8	...	♗d7

This solid move is preferred by theory, although it is by no means forced. The most popular reply is 8...♗g4, but curiously enough the second most popular is 8...♗b7, which is one of the most dubious responses. The reason is that Black denies himself the possibility of ...♗g4, and then White need not play h3 and can head for a Flohr-Zaitsev system in which he has almost a free extra tempo.

9	c3	0-0 (D)
10	d3	

It is more common to play 10 d4. The move played leads to a strange hybrid system, the same as a normal d3 Ruy Lopez, except for the unusual extra moves a4 and ...♗d7. Probably this is slightly to Black's benefit, because ...♗d7 is a normal developing move, whereas it is far from clear that a4 will be a genuine asset for White.

10	...	♘a5

Playing for ...c5 is the most natural plan, although there is nothing wrong with 10...h6 followed by ...♖e8.

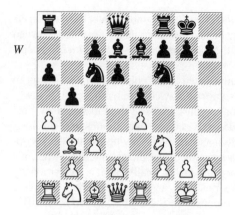

11   &c2   c5
12   ᐁbd2   ♕c7

Once again, 12...h6 13 ᐁf1 ♖e8 14 ᐁg3 &f8 would be a safe and solid plan, but as yet Black has done nothing wrong.

13   ᐁf1   b4?!

But this move strikes me as dubious. Now the situation on the queenside is resolved, which frees White's hands for play in the centre. 13...h6 would have been more flexible, keeping White guessing about Black's plans. 13...ᐁc6 14 ᐁe3 b4 is another idea, which at least prevents cxb4 (because Black can recapture with the knight), but then 15 ᐁd5 ᐁxd5 16 exd5 ᐁa5 17 d4 looks slightly better for White.

14   cxb4

White must not allow ...bxc3 followed by ...c4. My database contains two earlier games which had reached this position, but in both cases White had continued with the inferior 14 &g5.

14   ...   cxb4
15   ᐁe3 (D)

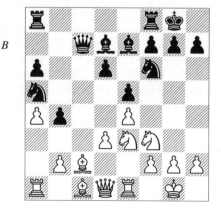

A flexible move. For the moment White is not sure whether he will continue with b3, followed by &b2 and d4, or more directly with d4 followed by &d2 and ♖c1. Therefore, he makes a move which is useful in either case, and waits to see Black's reply. At one time the f1-knight almost always went to g3 in the Closed Ruy Lopez, but these days there is more of a tendency to play it to e3 instead, where it controls d5. It all depends on the precise position, of course, but the additional option is worth bearing in mind.

15   ...   &e6?!

Aiming at the slightly weak b3-square, but the downside is that White will gain a tempo if he manages to play d4-d5. After the superior 15...♖fc8 I intended to continue with the alternative plan 16 b3; then 16...ᐁg4 (16...♕c3 17 ♖b1 doesn't help as the queen will be driven back) 17 ᐁc4 ᐁxc4 18 dxc4 gives White a faint edge because he has more possibilities of active play. One plan is &b2 and an eventual f4 to activate his bishops against the black king; another is ᐁd2-f1-e3, taking aim at d5; finally, White might consider a5 to isolate the b4-pawn.

16   d4 (D)

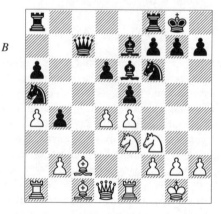

Now the dark side of the move ...&e6 is revealed, since White always has the option of closing the centre with gain of tempo.

16   ...   ♖fc8
17   h3!

I found this the hardest move of the game. White's queenside is still undeveloped, so my first instinct was to play 17 &d2, but this allows 17...ᐁg4! and Black frees her position; then the key line is 18 &xb4 ᐁc6 19 &c3 (19 &a3

②xd4 20 ②xd4 exd4 21 ②d5 ②xd5 22 exd5
♕xc2 23 ♕xg4 ②f6 favours Black) 19...②xd4
20 ②xd4 exd4 21 ♕xd4 ②f6, with equality.
Then I noticed that Black had no immediate
threat, so I decided to play the prophylactic h3,
intending ②d2 and ②c1. The basic rule in these
Closed Ruy Lopez positions is that if White can
maintain his d4-e4 pawn-centre without making too many concessions, then he will have at
least a slight advantage. Black's problem is that
she has to meet the pressure against e5, while
all the time having to worry about d4-d5. It is
the flexibility of White's centre which causes
Black problems, so White should only clear up
the centre by d4-d5 (or d4xe5) if he gains something concrete.

> **17 ... ②c4**

Neither black knight is especially well-placed,
but the one on a5 is in real danger of being
sidelined if White plays a later b3 (for example,
17...h6 would be met by 18 b3). Xie Jun decides to exchange it off, but now White can
complete his queenside development.

> **18 ②d3 ②xe3**
> **19 ②xe3 (D)**

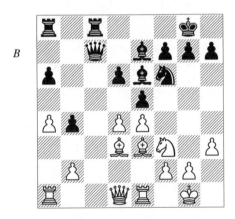

Now White has stabilized his d4-e4 pawn-
centre and can look forward to a safe advantage.

> **19 ... ♕b7?!**

Black attempts to find a tactical solution to
her problems, but there is a flaw in this scheme.
However, it must be admitted that the alternatives were also not very attractive; for example,
after 19...a5 White has the choice between:

1) 20 ②g5 ②d7 21 ♕b3 ②e8 22 ♖ac1 ♕b7
23 ②c4 ②d8 24 ②f3 gives White uncomfortable

pressure. If 24...♕xe4, then 25 dxe5 dxe5 26
②d4 with a large advantage for White.

2) 20 d5 ②d7 21 ②d2 is the safe choice.
White will continue with ♕e2 and ②c4, securing a positional advantage.

> **20 dxe5**

Not 20 d5?! ②xd5! 21 exd5 e4 with a fine
game for Black. White is willing to resolve the
central tension because he can see a concrete
route to an advantage. Indeed, the rest of the
game is virtually pure tactics.

> **20 ... dxe5**
> **21 ②xe5 ②xe4**

Or else Black remains a pawn down.

> **22 ②xe4**

Not 22 ♕f3? f5! and Black escapes.

> **22 ... ♕xe4**
> **23 ②g5 ♕b7 (D)**

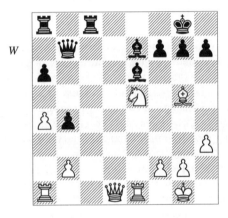

All this was forced. Now comes a tactical
blow.

> **24 ②xf7!**

White wins a pawn with this neat combination.

> **24 ... ♔xf7**

24...②xg5 25 ②xg5 ②d5 offers White a
pleasant choice: 26 ♖e7 ♕xe7 27 ♕xd5+ ♔h8
28 ②f7+ ♔g8 29 ②e5+ ♔h8 30 ♖e1! ♕f6 31
②f7+ ♔g8 32 ②d6+ ♔h8 33 ②xc8 leaves
White a clear pawn up, while 26 ♕d3 g6 27
♖e5 also allows White to consolidate an extra
pawn since 27...②xg2? loses to 28 f3!.

> **25 ♕h5+ ♔g8**
> **26 ♖xe6**

If Black now plays ordinary moves, then
White will consolidate his extra pawn with excellent winning chances. Therefore Xie Jun

tries to exploit the line-up of white pieces on
the fifth rank.

26   ...   ♖c5

The point of Black's defence.

27   h4

27 ♖xe7 ♕xe7 28 ♗xe7 ♖xh5 29 ♗xb4 is
just a draw, so White is obliged to defend his
bishop.

27   ...   h6 (D)

An understandable move, since otherwise
Black cannot regain the pawn. After 27...♖f8,
White wins by 28 ♖xe7 ♕xe7 29 ♕xh7+! ♔xh7
30 ♗xe7 with two extra pawns.

28   ♖xh6!

Once again Black's idea runs into a tactical
refutation.

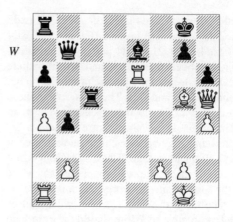

28	...	gxh6
29	♕g6+	♔h8
30	♕xh6+	♔g8
31	♕e6+	1-0

Black resigned because allowing White to
take on e7 gives White three pawns and an immense attack for the exchange. It follows that
31...♔f8 is forced, but then 32 ♗h6+ ♔e8 33
♖d1! leaves Black with no defence to the threats
of 34 ♕g6# and 34 ♕g8+.

In round 7 I played Walter Browne. We had met several times in the early 1980s, but I hadn't
seen him since. Walter was always famous for two things; his tendency to get into extreme time-
trouble, and the extraordinary facial and bodily contortions he would go through while in time-
trouble. Despite his addiction to time-trouble, he achieved a number of fine results and was several
times US champion. His ability to bang out moves while his flag was hanging verged on the unbe-
lievable and, as one would expect, he was a very fine blitz player. I had watched him play during the
earlier rounds of the tournament and noticed that these two characteristics had not changed at all in
the intervening decade. During my game against him he ran very short of time near move 40 and,
with two moves to make, his digital clock was showing precisely one second left. By now I had
much more experience with digital clocks, and I would have sworn that it was impossible to make
two moves in one second. Nevertheless, Browne managed it. I still feel that if I had done something
totally unexpected, such as putting my queen *en prise*, then the shock would have caused him to
lose on time, but of course I would have looked fairly silly if the idea had failed. While Browne
managed to survive the move 40 time-control, he did lose on time at move 60, in a position which
was by then drawn with correct defence.

In the end I tied for second place with Boris Gulko on 7½/11, half a point behind the winner
Viktor Korchnoi.

In March I participated for the second time in the Amber tournament. The 1995 event was even
stronger than the previous year, with such 'weak' players as Korchnoi, Seirawan and Zsuzsa Polgar
being replaced by Shirov, Nikolić and Lautier. Unfortunately, I was totally off-form and couldn't
recover from an abysmal start. My last place with 4/22 was pretty awful and it seemed clear that I
couldn't compete with the very top players at this type of chess.

In late April I returned to the AEGON man vs computer tournament, but as I have already mentioned I was rather unsuccessful and I did not take part in any further contests involving computers.
In June I once again played in the King's Head Open in London, this time scoring 4½/5 and tying
for first place with Stuart Conquest.

My international schedule continued in August with two events in the Netherlands. The first was
an Open tournament in Leeuwarden, in which the following attractive attacking game was played.
The fun started when White sacrificed a pawn at move 15. Black was more or less obliged to accept,
but in compensation White gained time and opened the h-file against Black's kingside. This type of

positional pawn sacrifice is quite common in modern play; there is no immediate attack, but the time gained allows a steady build-up of pressure which is hard to resist. Black castled kingside despite the open h-file, hoping that his secure bishop on g5 would enable him to fend off the attack. However, in a situation such as this, in which just one enemy piece stands between an attack and mate, violent measures to remove the last defender are often justified. Aided by a powerful pawn-wedge, which prevented Black from feeding any more defenders to the threatened sector, White managed to destroy the final barrier and the attack crashed through.

Game 19
J. Nunn – A. Vydeslaver
Leeuwarden 1995
Sicilian Defence, Richter-Rauzer

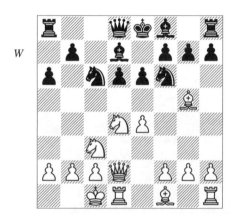

1	e4	c5
2	♘f3	d6
3	d4	cxd4
4	♘xd4	♘f6
5	♘c3	♘c6

Fashions in other Sicilian systems come and go, but the Classical Sicilian is perennially popular. At one time I played 6 ♗c4 here, but eventually I had to admit that against accurate defence the Velimirović Attack (the plan with ♗c4, ♗e3, ♕e2 and 0-0-0) doesn't give White any advantage. I therefore switched to 6 ♗g5, which has the best theoretical reputation. It is surprising that the Classical Sicilian isn't more popular, because if White wants to play for an advantage his options are rather limited, while Black has a range of reasonable systems.

6	♗g5	e6
7	♕d2	a6

There is little theoretically wrong with the 7...♗e7 and 8...0-0 line, but for some reason it is out of favour at the moment.

| 8 | 0-0-0 | ♗d7 *(D)* |

8...h6 is another major continuation. The fact that White has to be ready to meet several black systems makes it awkward to prepare for the Classical Sicilian if you intend to play 6 ♗g5.

| 9 | f3 | |

I have had quite good results with this move, which is a reasonable alternative to the more common 9 f4. The logic behind it is similar to that in other Sicilian systems involving f3, such as the Yugoslav Attack in the Dragon and the English Attack against the Najdorf. White reinforces his centre to make it harder for Black to generate counterplay, while at the same time

preparing a possible kingside pawn advance with g4 and h4.

| 9 | ... | ♗e7 |

The most popular reply.

| 10 | h4 | |

This flexible move is characteristic of the 9 f3 variation. White defends the g5-bishop to rule out any tactical tricks based on ...♘xe4 and at the same time gains space on the kingside. The h4-pawn might advance to h5 and then h6, or White might later play g4 with a traditional kingside pawn-storm.

| 10 | ... | ♖c8 |

Once again this has been the most common move, but it may not be the strongest. In the past few years the line 10...h6 11 ♗e3 h5 has attracted attention, the idea being to prevent any further kingside pawn advance by White. Although playing ...h5 makes it harder for Black to castle kingside, it turns out that depriving White of his main plan is a more important factor. This idea has achieved excellent results for

Black, and so far White has not found an effective antidote. We have already mentioned in Game 6 how these days Black is much more willing to stop a white kingside pawn advance by meeting h4 with ...h5. This example shows that a readiness to block White's h-pawn is not restricted to positions in which Black has a kingside fianchetto.

11   ♔b1

White continues his policy of playing flexible moves.

11   ...   h6 (D)

This perfectly reasonable move was played for the first time in this game. It then disappeared for some years before re-emerging. 11...b5 has been the most common move; then 12 ♘xc6 ♗xc6 13 ♘e2 followed by ♘d4 gives White a slight advantage. 11...h5 has also been played several times, with poor results. If Black wants to play ...h5, it appears more logical to drive the bishop back first with ...h6.

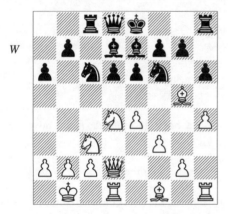

W

12   ♘xc6

It isn't clear if White needs to exchange on c6 so quickly. During the game I wanted to rule out the possibility of 12 ♗e3 ♘e5, but then White can simply continue 13 g4 with a version of the line 8...h6 9 ♗e3 ♗d7 10 f3 which favours White, since Black is committed to the rather passive moves ...♗e7 and ...♖c8.

12   ...   ♗xc6

After 12...bxc6 13 ♗xf6 gxf6 (13...♗xf6 14 ♕xd6 is very bad for Black; e.g., 14...♗xc3 15 bxc3 ♖b8+ 16 ♔a1 and not only is Black a pawn down, but his king is trapped in the centre and his bishop is inactive) 14 ♗xa6 ♖a8 15 ♗c4 Black certainly has some compensation

for the pawn, but it is probably insufficient since if necessary the c4-bishop can drop back to b3 to secure the queenside.

13   ♗e3 (D)

Here winning a pawn by 13 ♗xf6 ♗xf6 14 ♕xd6 is a bad idea, since 14...♕a5 (14...♕xd6 15 ♖xd6 ♔e7 is also fine for Black) gives Black excellent play for the pawn.

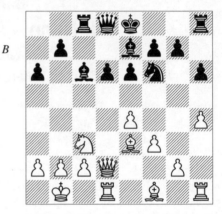

B

13   ...   d5?!

The traditional freeing move for Black in the Sicilian, but not very effective here as White can block the centre with e5. Other possibilities:

1) 13...0-0 is wrong. Once Black has played ...h6, it is often a mistake to castle early since the protruding h-pawn makes White's kingside pawn advance much more effective. Here, for example, 14 g4 gives White an automatic attack.

2) 13...b5 may be met by 14 ♘e2 or 14 ♗d3, with an edge for White in either case.

3) 13...h5 (the recent reappearance of 11...h6 has been based on this move, which is similar to the line mentioned in the note to Black's 10th move) 14 ♗g5 (the fact that this is probably White's best move emphasizes the point that Black should play ...h6 before ...h5, effectively gaining a tempo) 14...b5 15 ♗d3 and again White has a slight advantage.

After the move played it is hard to pinpoint any further error by Black and it seems that the pawn sacrifice White plays in this game is virtually a refutation of Black's strategy.

14   e5!

The only move to give White a chance for an advantage. 14 ♕e1 is bad because after 14...♕c7

White can no longer play e5, while 14 exd5 ♘xd5 15 ♘xd5 ♗xd5 16 c4 ♗c6 (certainly not 16...♗xc4? 17 ♕xd8+ ♗xd8 18 ♖c1 b5 19 b3 ♗xf1 20 ♖xc8 ♗xg2 21 ♖d1 ♔e7 22 ♗c5+ and White wins) leads only to equality.

14   ...   ♘d7

Attacking both e5 and h4.

15   f4!

The most forceful move; White is prepared to sacrifice the h4-pawn in order to gain time. He can avoid losing a pawn by 15 ♕e1, but this move wastes time and does not promise much for White. Black can reply:

1) 15...♘xe5? 16 ♗d4 f6 (16...♘g6 17 h5 is also very good for White) 17 f4 followed by ♕xe6, with a large advantage for White.

2) 15...♗b4 16 ♗d4 0-0 17 g4 ♗xc3? 18 ♗xc3 d4 19 ♖xd4 ♗xf3 20 ♖g1 is much better for White, H.Hunt-Madl, European Team Ch (women), Batumi 1999.

3) 15...b5! 16 ♕g3 ♕c7 is unclear.

15   ...   ♗xh4

Black is more or less forced to accept; otherwise White simply saves time over the previous note.

16   ♗d4 (D)

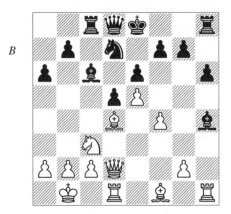

White does not have any immediate threats, but the extra time he gains from the pawn sacrifice enables him to build up a dangerous attacking position.

16   ...   ♗e7

Black would prefer not to play this move, since after a later f5 by White the bishop can settle on g5, and so playing it to e7 first loses a tempo. However, Black can't do much while his bishop is standing on the vulnerable square

h4 and so he reconciles himself to the possible loss of time. 16...b5 17 ♗d3 is similar to the game, while 16...0-0 looks suicidal, and sure enough 17 ♕e2! ♗e7 18 ♕g4 ♔h8 19 ♖d3 gives White a massive attack.

17   ♕f2

A good move. White denies Black's pieces the squares b6 and c5, while at the same time moving the queen out of the line of fire after a later ...♗g5.

17   ...   b5

Black intends ...b4 and ...♗b5, to activate his light-squared bishop and exchange at least one of White's attacking pieces. Other moves:

1) 17...g6 doesn't help as after 18 g4 White can force f5 in any case.

2) 17...♕a5 (aiming for ...♗c5 or ...♘c5, but White retains a very dangerous initiative) 18 f5 and now:

2a) 18...♘c5 19 ♕g3 ♗g5 20 a3 ♘d7 (after 20...b6 21 ♗d3 White has a clear advantage) 21 fxe6 fxe6 22 ♕xg5! hxg5 23 ♖xh8+ ♘f8 24 ♗d3 gives White a decisive attack.

2b) 18...♗c5 19 ♕g3! ♗xd4 20 ♖xd4 ♕c5 21 ♕xg7 ♕f8 22 ♕g3 is excellent for White.

18   f5 (D)

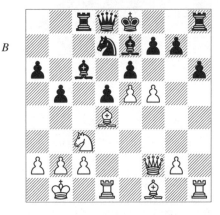

18   ...   ♗g5

It appears logical to occupy this secure outpost, but now White's attack gathers pace. However, the alternatives were also unappealing:

1) 18...b4 19 fxe6! (19 ♕g3 ♗g5 is less clear) 19...fxe6 20 ♗d3 ♕a5 21 ♗g6+ ♔d8 22 ♘e4 ♖f8 (22...dxe4 23 ♗b6+) 23 ♕e3 ♔c7 (23...♖c7 24 ♘d6, threatening 25 ♕h3 or 25 ♗f7, is very good for White) 24 ♘d6 ♖cd8 25

♗f7! ♘xe5 26 ♗xe5 ♗xd6 27 ♗xe6 with a clear advantage for White.

2) 18...exf5 is a tempting defence, aiming to transfer the knight to e6 and set up a solid blockade. Then:

2a) 19 ♕xf5 ♘f8 20 ♗xb5 (20 ♗d3 ♕d7 is also not very convincing) 20...axb5 21 ♖hf1 ♘e6 22 ♕xf7+ ♔d7 23 ♗b6 ♕xb6 24 ♘xd5 ♗xd5 25 ♖xd5+ ♔c7 26 ♕xe7+ ♔b8 and White's attack peters out. Note that 27 ♖d6? is refuted by 27...♕c7.

2b) 19 ♗d3! is the best reply as White keeps open the option of taking on f5 with either queen or bishop. Now:

2b1) 19...g6 20 g4! fxg4 21 ♖df1 ♖h7 22 e6 ♘f6 23 ♕f4! gives White a winning attack.

2b2) 19...♘f8 20 ♗xf5 ♘e6 21 ♘e4 ♘xd4 (21...dxe4 22 ♗b6 traps the queen) 22 ♖xd4 ♖b8 23 ♕g3 and Black is in serious trouble.

2b3) 19...b4 20 ♘e2 ♕c7 21 ♕xf5 ♘f8 22 ♘f4 with a very strong attack for White.

We now return to the position after 18...♗g5 (D):

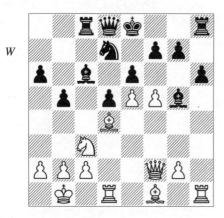

19 ♗d3

19 fxe6 fxe6 20 ♗d3 prevents castling and is also quite good for White, but is less incisive than the move played:

1) 20...♖f8?? 21 ♗g6+ ♔e7 22 ♗c5+ ♘xc5 23 ♕xc5+ ♔d7 24 ♕d6#.

2) 20...♕c7 and now:

2a) 21 ♗g6+ ♔d8 22 ♘e4 ♖f8 (22...♗e7 23 ♘d6 ♗xd6 24 exd6 ♕xd6 25 ♗xg7 ♖g8 26 ♕f7 ♔c7 27 ♖he1 should be winning for White) 23 ♘xg5 ♖xf2 (23...hxg5 loses to 24 ♕e3) 24 ♘xe6+ ♔e7 25 ♘xc7 ♖xg2 26 ♖hg1 ♖xg1 27 ♖xg1 ♖xc7 28 ♗f5 ♔f8 (28...g5 29 ♖h1 is

clearly better for White) 29 ♖g6 is good for White, but Black still has drawing chances.

2b) 21 ♖df1! ♔d8 (21...♖f8 22 ♗g6+ ♔d8 23 ♕xf8+ ♘xf8 24 ♖xf8+ ♔d7 25 ♖f7+ ♗e7 26 ♗c5 wins for White, while 21...♘xe5 22 ♕e1 ♗f6 23 ♖h5 picks up the e5-knight) 22 ♕f7 regains the pawn while keeping a strong attack.

3) 20...♕a5! 21 ♗g6+ ♔d8 22 ♘e4 ♖f8 23 ♕g1 ♗e7 24 ♘c5 ♗xc5 25 ♗xc5 ♘xc5 26 ♕xc5 ♔c7 27 ♕e7+ ♔b8 28 ♕xe6 favours White, but Black has defensive chances.

19 ... 0-0

This looks like castling into the fire, but Black hopes that the immovable bishop on g5 will be enough to fend off White's attack.

20 f6! (D)

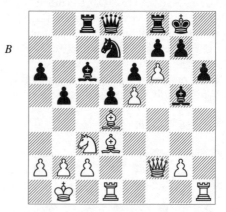

White drives a pawn wedge into Black's kingside, cutting off most of Black's pieces from the beleaguered sector. The one exception is the g5-bishop, but this last bastion will be demolished by force.

20 ... b4

The tactical justification for White's last move lies in the line 20...gxf6 21 exf6 ♕c7 (21...e5 22 ♖xh6! ♗xh6 23 ♕g3+ ♔h8 24 ♕h4 ♕xf6 25 ♗xe5 wins for White, while 21...♘xf6 22 ♖xh6 ♗xh6 23 ♗xf6 ♕c7 24 ♖h1 leads to mate) 22 ♕e2! (threatening 23 ♖xh6) 22...♖fd8 23 ♖xh6! ♗xh6 24 ♕g4+ ♔f8 25 ♖h1 ♔e8 26 ♕g8+ ♘f8 (26...♗f8 loses to 27 ♖h7) 27 ♗c5! ♗b7 28 ♗xf8 ♗xf8 29 ♖h7! (even stronger than 29 ♕xf8+) 29...♔d7 30 ♖xf7+ ♔c6 31 ♖xc7+ ♔xc7 32 ♕xe6 and the two connected passed pawns give White an easy win.

Since Black cannot remove the intruding pawn, he decides to continue on the queenside. Now White's task is to eliminate the g5-bishop, the only piece left defending Black's kingside.

21 ♜h5!

Getting rid of the bishop by the most direct means possible, regardless of the material cost involved. Not 21 ♞e2? ♝b5 and the exchange of the d3-bishop greatly weakens White's attack.

21 ... ♞xf6

Black decides to destroy the pawn-wedge at the cost of a piece. Other moves:

1) 21...bxc3 22 ♜xg5 hxg5 23 ♛g3 and Black will have to give up his queen to prevent mate within a few moves. If 23...♜b8, then 24 b3 and the end has only been delayed by one move.

2) 21...gxf6 22 exf6 bxc3 (or 22...♛c7 23 ♜xg5+ hxg5 24 g3! and White wins at once) 23 ♜xg5+ hxg5 24 ♛g3 mates in a few moves.

3) 21...♝xf6 22 exf6 ♞xf6 23 ♜xh6 bxc3 24 ♛h4 mates.

22 exf6 ♝xf6 (D)

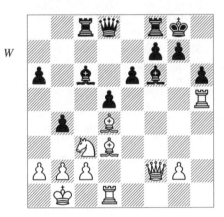

23 ♜xh6!

White should win in the end after 23 ♝xf6 ♛xf6 24 ♛xf6 gxf6 25 ♜h4! f5 (25...bxc3 26 ♜g4+ ♚h8 27 ♜h1 mates) 26 ♜xb4 but there might still be some work ahead. It is often better to put in a bit of effort to calculate a clear-cut finish in order to avoid having the game drag on unnecessarily. In this case continuing with the attack leads to a forced mate.

23 ... ♝xd4

24 ♝h7+ ♚h8
25 ♛xd4 e5 (D)

Forced, as 25...f6 26 ♜h5 and 25...bxc3 26 ♜dh1 both lead to a quick mate.

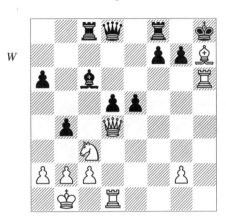

26 ♛xe5

26 ♛e3 gxh6 27 ♛xh6 also mates.

26 ... f6
27 ♛h2 gxh6
28 ♛xh6 ♛e7

Or 28...♜f7 29 ♝g6+ ♚g8 30 ♜h1, mating.

29 ♝f5+ ♚g8 (D)

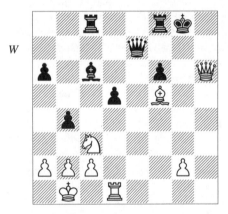

30 ♝e6+!

A neat finish.

30 ... ♜f7

30...♛xe6 31 ♛g6+ ♚h8 32 ♜h1+ mates.

31 ♜h1 1-0

It is mate next move.

The intriguing position below arose in round 6. I totally overlooked White's piece sacrifice at move 29 and my first reaction was that his passed c-pawn would prove decisive. When you have received a shock like this, it is essential to take the time necessary to calm down and look at the position objectively. It very often happens that you find a way to play on in a position which had at first sight appeared hopeless. That's what happened in this case: Black found a way to launch a surprising counterattack which saved the day despite the appearance of a second white queen.

Game 20
E. Gleizerov – J. Nunn
Leeuwarden 1995

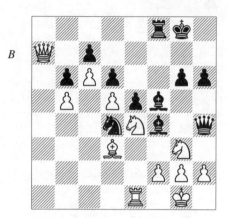

B

A typical King's Indian position. White has made considerable inroads on the queenside, but Black is restricted to a single weakness on that side of the board, namely the c7-pawn. On the kingside Black has developed some counterplay, and in particular he has managed to get his 'bad' bishop out to the active square f4 (much as in Game 22). However, in view of the number of white minor pieces on the kingside, Black is unlikely to be able to make any headway there directly. On balance, though, Black should have little trouble defending his one queenside weakness, so the kingside possibilities should give him slightly the better chances. One possibility for White is to sacrifice a piece on d6 in order to gain a passed pawn or two on the queenside. This is quite a dangerous idea which Black did not sufficiently take into account during the game.

27   ...   ♖f7?!

Unwisely allowing the sacrifice on d6. Even though a miraculous defence saves Black, he should certainly have chosen something else. 27...♗xg3 28 hxg3 ♕e7 is a safe continuation because White can't achieve anything on the queenside, while Black still has slight chances of generating real play on the kingside. However,

27...♕e7! would have been best of all, making no concessions. After 28 ♘xf5 gxf5 29 ♘g3 e4 30 ♗c4 ♗e5 Black has a slight advantage, so White would probably do better just to wait. However, even in this case Black has an edge.

28   ♕b8+   ♔g7
29   ♘xd6! (D)

A total shock for me. This bombshell dropped on the board just when I was counting on an advantage after 29 ♘xf5+ gxf5 30 ♘g3 e4 31 ♗f1 e3 (31...♗e5 is slightly better for Black, but pushing the pawn is even stronger) 32 ♖xe3 (32 fxe3 ♗xg3 33 hxg3 ♕xg3 and Black wins) 32...♗xe3 33 fxe3 f4 34 exf4 ♕e7 and White does not have enough for the exchange. However, after considerable thought I found a remarkable drawing line for Black.

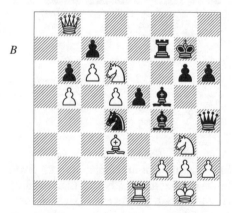

B

29   ...   cxd6

Forced, since 29...♗xd3 30 ♘xf7 ♔xf7 31 ♕xc7+ ♔f8 32 ♕b8+, followed by c7, wins for White.

30   ♗xf5 (D)

30 c7 ♗xg3 31 hxg3 ♕e7 32 c8♕ ♗xc8 33 ♕xc8 ♕f6 is roughly equal since Black has a strong knight but his b6-pawn is weak.

30   ...   ♗xg3

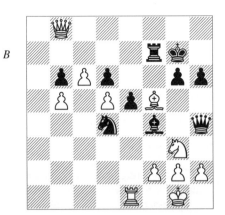

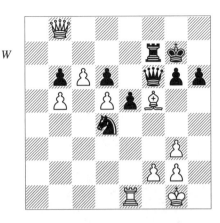

30...gxf5? loses to 31 c7. However, 30...♘xf5 may also lead to a draw with accurate play after 31 ♘xf5+ ♖xf5 32 g3:

1) 32...♗xg3 33 hxg3 ♕d4 34 ♖f1 ♕xd5 35 ♕c7+ (35 c7? ♖h5 leads to equality) 35...♔g8 36 ♕d8+ ♔g7 37 c7 ♖h5 38 ♕e7+ and White wins.

2) 32...♕g4! 33 ♕xd6 (after 33 c7 ♗xg3! 34 hxg3 ♕f3 35 ♖f1 ♖h5 it's time for White to force a draw by 36 ♕h8+) 33...♕f3 (Black must play for an attack or the connected passed pawns will prove too strong) 34 ♕c7+ ♖f7 35 ♕xb6 ♗d2 36 ♖a1 ♗b4! (not 36...♗a5? 37 ♕e3 and White wins) 37 c7 ♗a5! 38 ♖xa5 ♕d1+ with perpetual check.

31   hxg3

Or 31 fxg3 ♕g5 (31...♘e2+ 32 ♖xe2 ♕d4+ 33 ♖f2 ♖xf5 also leads to perpetual check) 32 ♗d3 ♕d2 33 ♖f1 ♕xd3 34 ♖xf7+ ♔xf7 35 ♕c7+ with a draw.

31   ...   ♕f6! (D)

This is the key move. Black will take on f5 with the queen, and then he is lined up for a drawing counterattack against f2.

32   c7

There is nothing better. 32 g4 gxf5 33 g5 is ingenious, but after 33...♕xg5 34 c7 ♘f3+ 35 ♔f1 ♘h2+ the result will be a draw in any case.

32	...	♕xf5
33	c8♕	♕xf2+
34	♔h2	

Or 34 ♔h1 ♕xe1+ 35 ♔h2 ♘f3+ 36 gxf3 ♕f2+ 37 ♔h3 (37 ♔h1? ♕xf3+ 38 ♔h2 ♕e2+ 39 ♔h3 ♕f1+ mates) 37...♕f1+ 38 ♔h2 (38 ♔h4? ♕h1+ 39 ♔h3 g5+ mates next move) 38...♕f2+, again with perpetual check.

34	...	♘f3+
35	♔h3	♘g5+
36	♔h2	

Certainly not 36 ♔h4? ♖f4+ 37 ♕g4 ♖xg4+ 38 ♔xg4 ♕d4+ and mate next move.

½-½

Unfortunately, I spoilt my chances by losing to Chuchelov in the penultimate round and even a win in the last round only left me in a tie for sixth place with 6/9. After Leeuwarden, I travelled directly to Amsterdam for the Donner Memorial tournament, a very pleasant and well-organized event consisting of a grandmaster round-robin tournament coupled with some large Swiss events. Unlike most of the participants, at least I was old enough to have actually played against Donner. My play was rather erratic in this event, but at least there was one game I could be proud of.

This game features a key battleground of the King's Indian, in which the main element is the traditional struggle of White's queenside play versus Black's kingside attack. It is tempting to regard the board as being separated into two halves, with each side ignoring the enemy attack until it finally touches down, but this view is rather naïve. Here Black pushed ahead with his pawns to such an extent that he was in danger of becoming overextended. Seizing his chance, White took action himself on the kingside; this is exactly what all the textbooks tell you **not** to do, but here it was justified as Black's development was somewhat lacking. The crucial moment came at move 21, with a position so complicated that it even confused Shirov. White had two playable continuations, but instead decided to sacrifice a piece for three pawns. However, this sacrifice allowed

Black to complete his development and seize the initiative himself; White's king came under direct attack and was chased up the board to its doom.

Game 21

A. Shirov – J. Nunn

Amsterdam (Donner Memorial) 1995

King's Indian Defence, Classical Variation

1	d4	♘f6
2	c4	g6
3	♘c3	♗g7
4	e4	d6
5	♗e2	0-0
6	♘f3	e5
7	0-0	♘c6
8	d5	♘e7 (D)

This variation of the King's Indian is often called the Mar del Plata Variation and it has been a key line for half a century. Here the traditional theme of White's queenside play versus Black's kingside attack is played out with particular clarity. Despite decades of analysis, the final verdict remains unclear, but today's leading players do not like the committal nature of Black's strategy and these days it is not often seen at the highest level.

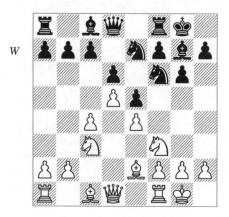

W

9	♘e1	♘e8

At one time 9...♘d7 was almost the only move played here, but 9...♘e8 became recognized as a valid continuation after Kasparov used it twice in 1992. These days 9...♘d7 is still regarded as the main line, but 9...♘e8 is an important alternative.

| 10 | ♗e3 | |

10 ♘d3 is the other main idea, when the likely continuation 10...f5 11 ♗d2 (11 f4 and 11 f3 are also possible) 11...♘f6 (if Black wants to avoid a transposition, then he should probably try 11...♔h8) transposes into the equivalent line with 9...♘d7.

10	...	f5
11	f3	f4
12	♗f2	h5

The logic behind this is that in most lines it doesn't make much difference whether Black plays ...g5 or ...h5 first, since both moves will usually be played sooner or later. However, after 12...g5 White has the additional possibility of playing 13 g4. In fact White hasn't taken advantage of this option very often, so it is hard to say whether it is to be feared, but Black risks little by cutting it out.

| 13 | c5 | |

The disadvantage of 9...♘e8 is that White can more easily achieve this advance. There are two counterbalancing advantages. First of all, if the exchange cxd6 cxd6 occurs, the knight on e8 defends White's entry square on c7. In the lines with 9...♘d7, Black often has to play his knight to f6 and then to e8 in order to achieve the same effect. The second advantage is revealed later in the game.

13	...	g5 (D)
14	a4	

White's most flexible and best move. The point is that exchanging on d6 doesn't achieve much by itself. Black's knight controls c7, so a plan involving ♖c1, ♕c2 and ♘b5 will be rather ineffective here. Therefore White instead aims for a4-a5, followed by cxd6 and ♘b5, attacking a7. Black will then be forced to play ...a6, after which the b6-square becomes available. This can be occupied either by White's bishop, or by his knight (after ♘b5-a3-c4).

| 14 | ... | ♖f6 |

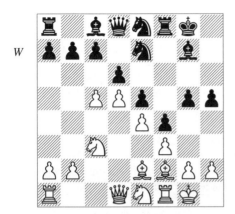

In the two games from 1992 mentioned above, Kasparov played ...♘g6, but this move is now rarely seen. The text-move is far more common, since after ...♖f6-g6 White will not find it easy to prevent ...g4.

15 a5?!

In my opinion this is inaccurate. As we shall see, Black often makes use of the knight on e8 by meeting cxd6 with ...♘xd6 and in this case the move a4-a5 is not especially useful. This suggests that White should play cxd6 sooner rather than later in order to discover as early as possible how Black is going to recapture on d6. The analysis runs 15 cxd6 (15 ♘b5 a6 16 cxd6 ♘xd6 17 ♘xd6 cxd6 transposes) 15...♘xd6 16 ♘b5 a6 17 ♘xd6 cxd6 18 ♘d3 (18 a5 is still inaccurate; if White is going to prepare ♗b6 he should do so with ♕b3, which is not only a useful developing move but also offers the alternative possibility of ♕b6) 18...♖g6 19 ♕b3 g4 20 ♕b6 and White has some advantage. The fact that this line is rather awkward for Black is one of the main arguments against 9...♘e8.

15 ... ♖g6
16 cxd6

16 ♘b5 has also been played a few times. Black should definitely reply 16...g4 since after 16...a6 17 cxd6 ♘xd6 18 ♘xd6 cxd6, Black's ...a6 is not only a wasted tempo, but even has the negative effect of weakening b6. After 16...g4, play might continue 17 cxd6 (17 ♔h1 ♗d7 18 cxd6 ♘xd6 19 ♕b3 g3 20 ♗g1 h4 21 ♘xd6 cxd6 22 ♗b5 h3 gave Black a strong attack in Kobylkin-Djukić, European Under-14 Ch, Rimavska Sobota 1996) 17...♘xd6 18 ♘xa7 g3 19 ♗c5 ♗d7 20 ♔h1 and now 20...♖xa7 21 ♗xa7 b6 22 axb6 cxb6 23 hxg3 fxg3 led to a

very unclear position in Nikitin-Yandarbiev, Samara 2002. However, 20...♘xd5!? is an interesting alternative; for example, 21 ♕xd5+ ♗e6 22 ♕d2 ♕h4 23 ♗g1 ♖xa7 24 ♖c1 ♘e8 with chances for both sides.

16 ... ♘xd6 (D)

Forced, as 16...cxd6 17 ♘b5 a6 18 ♗b6 ♕d7 19 ♘a7 is clearly good for White.

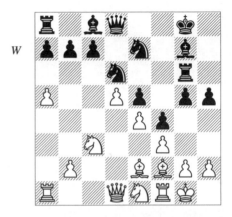

17 ♘d3

White has tried various other moves here, but none of them has led to any advantage for him. This bears out the point made in the note to White's 15th move about the inaccuracy of 15 a5. The main alternative is 17 ♘b5 (17 h3 ♔h8 18 ♘d3 ♘g8 followed by ...♘h6 and ...g4 gives Black reasonable play) 17...g4 18 ♘xd6 (18 ♘xa7 transposes into the note to White's 16th move) 18...cxd6 19 ♗h4 ♕f8 20 ♕a4 ♗f6 21 ♗xf6 ♖xf6 22 ♖c1 ♘g6, reaching a position of a familiar type except that one pair of knights has been exchanged. This exchange favours Black, because the main function of the knight on e8 is merely to defend c7, while White's knight on c3 can take an active part in the queenside attack by means of the typical manoeuvre ♘b5 (forcing ...a6) and then ♘a3-c4-b6. In other words, Black has exchanged a passive knight for an active one and the resulting position is roughly balanced. Two games continued 23 a6 ♖f7 24 ♗b5 ♕d8 25 axb7 ♗xb7 26 ♗c6 ♕b6+ 27 ♔h1 ♗a6 28 ♖g1 ♖c8?! (28...♖d8 is a better way to prevent the ♗d7-e6 transfer) 29 ♖c2?! (29 ♖c3!, threatening 30 ♖b3, is awkward for Black) 29...♖g7 30 ♗d7? ♖xc2 31 ♘xc2 and now 31...♗e2 32 ♘e1 ♔h7 33 ♗f5 ♔h6 was more or less equal in Ftačnik-Wojtkiewicz, Budapest Zonal Play-Off 1993, but in the later game Stiazhkin-Aga-maliev, Alushta 2002 Black significantly improved by 31...gxf3! 32 gxf3 ♕f2 and won after 33 ♗e6+? ♔h7 34 ♘e1 ♘h4 35 ♖xg7+ ♔xg7 0-1.

17   ...   g4 (D)

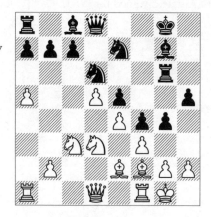

18   ♗h4

It is curious that White's best plan runs completely counter to the usual course of play in the Mar del Plata Variation. Here Black's kingside attack has developed much faster than usual, and indeed he is already threatening ...g3. Therefore, White's usual idea of playing along the c-file offers no hope. Instead, White must try to make use of the fact that Black's kingside advance has run ahead of his development – note that Black's queenside pieces are still on their original squares. Therefore White decides to open things up on the kingside by g3, but first he moves his bishop outside the pawn-chain. The immediate 18 g3 is bad due to 18...gxf3 19 ♗xf3 h4 20 g4 h3, when Black has awkward pressure on the kingside.

18   ...   ♕f8

18...g3 is wrong since 19 hxg3 fxg3 20 ♕e1 gives White a large advantage (G.Gutman-Varitsky, Rovno 2000).

19   g3

Van der Wiel gave 19 ♘c5 ♘ef5 20 exf5 ♘xf5 21 ♗f2 g3 22 ♘3e4 gxf2+ 23 ♖xf2 as better for White, but I do not agree with this as it seems to me that Black's outpost at e3 is more important than White's secure control of e4.

We have already seen in this book a number of cases in which the old adage of 'don't move

your pawns on the side where you are under attack' has been violated. All general chess principles have exceptions, but this one surely has more exceptions than most!

19   ...   ♗f6

Completely forced, or else Black is blown away by fxg4 followed by gxf4.

20   fxg4   hxg4 (D)

Better than 20...♗xg4 21 ♗xg4 ♖xg4 22 ♔h1, when Black's position is creaking. A particular worry is the weak e6-square, which can be occupied by ♘c5-e6.

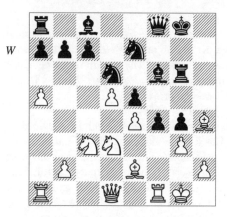

21   ♘xf4?

In some games, the advantage fluctuates from side to side and the game is only resolved after a long period of tension. In other games there is a single key moment which essentially decides the whole game. This game falls into the latter category. Shirov thought for a long time here, but gradually became more and more dissatisfied with his position and eventually decided on this dubious piece sacrifice. In this case psychological factors were probably at work, since a cool examination of the position reveals that White is not worse:

1) 21 ♗xf6 ♕xf6 (D) and now:

1a) 22 gxf4? ♕h4! (22...g3 23 ♗h5 ♕h4 24 ♕e2 is unclear) 23 ♕c2 (23 ♘xe5 g3 24 ♘f3 ♕h3 is winning for Black) 23...g3 24 ♗f3 exf4 and Black is much better.

1b) 22 ♖f2 looks best; White allows the pawn to advance to f3, but if this happens the kingside is more or less blocked and White does not have to worry about Black's attack. The game Kiriakov-Sotnikov, Russian Junior Ch, Moscow 1995 continued 22...f3?! 23 ♗f1

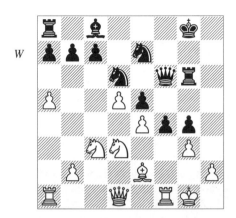

W

♗d7 24 ♘c5 ♖d8 25 ♕b3 a6 26 ♘d1 ♗c8 27 ♘e3 ♔g7 28 ♖c1 and White was slightly better. However, pushing the f-pawn straight away is too committal and makes life easy for White. Instead, 22...♕g7 23 ♗f1 (23 gxf4 g3 24 hxg3 ♖xg3+ 25 ♔h1 ♘xe4 26 ♘xe4 ♕h7+ is at least equal for Black) 23...♗d7 24 ♘c5 (24 gxf4 g3 25 hxg3 ♖xg3+ 26 ♗g2 ♗h3 27 ♕c2 ♖f8 gives Black a dangerous attack; if now 28 f5, then 28...♘exf5! 29 exf5 ♘xf5 leaves White in trouble) 24...♖d8 is a more flexible approach, and I think that Black can maintain the balance.

2) 21 gxf4!? ♗xh4 22 fxe5 is an interesting suggestion by Graham Burgess. After 22...♕h6 White can try:

2a) 23 exd6 g3 and now:

2a1) 24 dxe7? ♕e3+ 25 ♔g2 ♗h3+! (this leads to a forced mate) 26 ♔xh3 g2+ 27 ♖f3 (D) (27 ♗f3 ♗xe7 28 ♕d2 ♔g7 mates in two more moves).

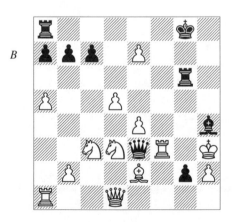

B

Now 27...♗e1!! is an absolutely stunning blow which mates in three more moves.

2a2) 24 ♗h5 ♗h3 25 ♖f4 ♖g5 26 dxe7 (26 ♖xh4? ♖xh5 27 hxg3 ♖xh4 28 gxh4 ♕xh4 29 ♕e2 ♔h8 30 ♕f2 ♖g8+ 31 ♔h2 ♕h6 gives Black a decisive attack) 26...♖xh5 27 ♖f8+ ♖xf8 28 exf8♕+ ♔xf8 29 ♕f3+ ♗f6! 30 hxg3 (not 30 ♘f4? ♗d4+ 31 ♔h1 ♗g4! 32 ♕xg3 ♗f3+ 33 ♘g2 ♗xg2+ 34 ♕xg2 ♗e5 35 ♖f1+ ♔e7 and Black wins) 30...♗g4 31 ♕xg4 ♗d4+ 32 ♔f1 ♖h1+ 33 ♔g2 ♖h2+ with a draw by perpetual check.

2b) 23 ♘f4 g3! (23...♘f7? 24 ♘xg6 ♕xg6 25 e6 ♘e5 26 ♔h1 is excellent for White) 24 ♘xg6 (24 exd6? ♗g5 is very good for Black) 24...♘xg6 (24...♘xe4 is ingenious, but after 25 ♘xe4! ♕e3+ 26 ♔h1 ♕xe4+ 27 ♗f3 ♕xg6 28 a6 White has the advantage) 25 exd6 ♗h3! (25...cxd6 26 ♗g4 ♕e3+ 27 ♔h1 ♕g5 28 ♗f3 favours White) 26 ♖f3 ♘e5 27 ♖xg3+ (27 dxc7? ♕g5! gives Black a crushing attack) 27...♗xg3 28 hxg3 ♖f8 and Black has sufficient compensation for the pawns.

21 ... exf4
22 ♖xf4

22 ♗xf6 ♕xf6 23 ♖xf4 ♕e5 is good for Black since 24 ♗xg4 may be met by 24...♕g5.

22 ... ♕h6! (D)

After 22...♕g7 23 ♗xf6! (23 ♖xf6 ♖xf6 24 e5 ♖f8 25 exd6 cxd6 is slightly better for Black) 23...♖xf6 24 e5 ♖xf4 25 gxf4 (not 25 exd6? ♖d4 and Black wins), with the idea of ♘e4-f6, only White can be better.

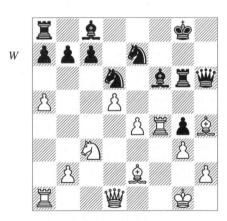

W

23 ♗xf6

Now 23 ♖xf6 ♖xf6 24 e5 fails totally after 24...♕e3+.

23 ... ♖xf6
24 ♖xf6

Shirov plays to gain a third pawn for the piece, but this allows Black to seize the initiative. However, there was nothing better:

1) 24 e5 ♖xf4 25 exd6 (25 gxf4 ♘df5 is now very good for Black because the attack on the f4-pawn gains a critical tempo) 25...♖f2! 26 ♔xf2 ♕xh2+ 27 ♔e1 (27 ♔f1 ♘f5 is much better for Black) 27...♕xg3+ 28 ♔d2 ♕xd6 with a clear advantage for Black.

2) 24 ♕f1 is an attempt to improve White's pawn-structure, but after 24...♖xf4 25 gxf4 (25 ♕xf4 ♕g7 followed by ...♘g6 is also very bad for White) 25...♘g6 26 f5 ♘e5 Black's knight arrives on e5 in any case.

24	...	♕xf6
25	♗xg4	♘g6

Heading for the excellent e5-square.

| 26 | ♗xc8 | ♖xc8 (D) |

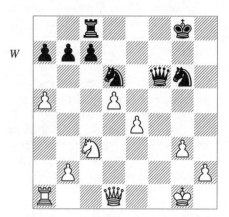

White has material equality, and the pawn cover in front of Black's king has entirely disappeared. Nevertheless, it is Black who has all the attacking chances because his knights are very active, while White's knight is tied passively to the defence of the weak e4-pawn. In the subsequent play it is usually better for Black to avoid the exchange of queens, as this would remove his attacking chances and increase the danger posed by White's kingside passed pawns.

| 27 | ♕g4 | ♖e8! |

Not 27...♖f8? 28 e5 ♕f5 29 ♕xf5 ♘xf5 with an unclear ending.

| 28 | ♖f1 | |

28 h4 ♕g7 29 h5 ♘e5 30 ♕xg7+ ♔xg7 is very good for Black because White's pawns are all blockaded and weak.

28	...	♕d4+
29	♔g2	♔g7

White has run out of threats and must face the unpleasant possibility of ...♘c4, taking aim at b2, e3 and e5.

| 30 | ♖f4? | |

Short of time, Shirov makes it easy. The critical line is 30 h4 ♘c4 31 ♖e1 but even here Black should win with accurate play; for example, 31...♖f8 32 h5 ♖f2+ 33 ♔h3 (33 ♔h1 ♕d2! 34 ♕xg6+ ♔f8 is winning for Black) 33...♘ce5 34 ♕g5 ♖h2+ 35 ♔xh2 ♘f3+ and Black wins White's queen.

30	...	♘c4
31	♕g5	

31 ♔h1 ♕d2 is also lost for White.

31	...	♕d2+
32	♔h3	

After 32 ♔g1 ♖f8 White's position collapses.

32	...	♖h8+
33	♔g4	♘ce5+
34	♔f5	

Shirov's king is not often chased around like this!

34	...	♖f8+
35	♔e6	♘d3! (D)

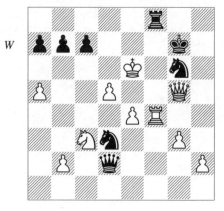

0-1

After 36 ♖f7+ ♖xf7 37 ♕xd2 Black has the choice between 37...♘c5# and 37...♘f8#.

In another game I had a remarkable stroke of luck. I won't say any more about it here, because I don't want to spoil the surprise.

Game 22
J. Piket – J. Nunn
Amsterdam (Donner Memorial) 1995

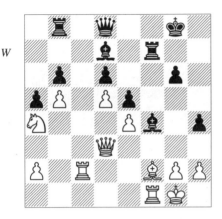

W

A typical King's Indian position. Black's queenside is disintegrating, but he has managed to get his 'bad' bishop to f4 and thereby gained some counterplay on the kingside. This counterplay certainly doesn't look all that impressive, but in fact it is rather hard for White to prove any advantage in this position.

31 Rc6!?

The most direct continuation, attacking b6 and d6, and provoking an immediate crisis. As usual in the King's Indian, Black's light-squared bishop is a key ingredient of his kingside play, and if he accepts the exchange sacrifice then his active possibilities vanish. However, White's move does have one negative feature – his rook was performing a useful defensive role on the second rank and removing it leaves White's kingside a little more vulnerable. The alternative 31 h3 ♗g3 32 ♗xg3 ♖xf1+ 33 ♔xf1 (33 ♕xf1 hxg3 34 ♖c3 ♕h4 is unclear) 33...hxg3 34 ♕xg3 ♗xb5+ 35 ♔g1 ♗e8 also doesn't give White much.

31 ... ♕g5

Black decides to abandon his queenside to its fate and stake everything on his kingside attack. 31...♗xc6? 32 dxc6 is very good for White; for example, 32...♔g7 33 ♕e2! ♕g5 (or else ♕g4, followed by ♘c3-d5, with a total grip on the position) 34 ♘xb6 ♖bf8 35 ♘d7 and the attack on the f8-rook squashes Black's counterplay.

32 ♘xb6

32 ♖xd6? ♖bf8 33 ♖xd7 is another attempt to give up the exchange, but this time Black keeps his attack. After 33...♖xd7 (33...♗xh2+ 34 ♔xh2 ♖xf2 35 ♖g1 ♖8f3 is similar to the game continuation and should lead to perpetual check, but Black need not acquiesce to a draw in this case) 34 ♗xb6 h3! 35 g3 (35 ♕xh3? loses to 35...♖h7) 35...♖f6 36 ♗f2 ♖df7 White has no real defence to the threats of 37...♗e3 and 37...♗xg3.

32 ... ♖bf8 *(D)*

This move is sufficient to force a draw, but in fact Black had a second playable continuation: 32...♗xc6 33 dxc6 ♖bf8 34 ♘d5 ♗g3! 35 hxg3 hxg3 36 ♕xg3 (or 36 ♗xg3 ♖xf1+ 37 ♕xf1 ♖xf1+ 38 ♔xf1 ♕c1+ 39 ♔f2 ♕c5+ 40 ♔f3 ♕xb5 41 c7 ♕d3+ 42 ♔g4 ♕xe4+ 43 ♔h3 and it is time for Black to give perpetual check) 36...♕xg3 37 ♗xg3 ♖xf1+ 38 ♔h2 with a very unclear position. One line runs 38...♔f7 39 ♗h4 ♖h8 40 ♔g3 ♔e6 41 b6 ♖c1 42 c7 ♖b1 with approximate equality.

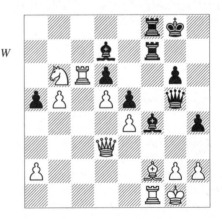

W

33 ♘xd7

33 ♖c2 was the only other possible move, but then 33...♗xb5! 34 ♕xb5 ♗e3 gives Black a deadly attack; for example, 35 ♘c8 (after 35 ♘d7 h3 36 g3 ♖f3! there is no real defence to the threat of 36...♖xg3+, while 35 ♕b2 h3 36 g3 ♕g4 leads to mate) 35...h3 36 g3 ♖f3 and Black wins.

| 33 | ... | ♗xh2+ |

The only move; Black has to keep up the momentum of the attack.

| 34 | ♔xh2 | ♖xf2 |
| 35 | ♖g1 | |

Forced, as 35 ♖xf2?? ♖xf2 36 ♕h3 ♕f4+ leads to mate.

| 35 | ... | ♖8f3 *(D)* |

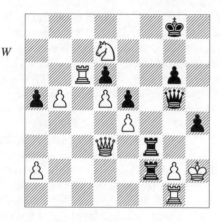

W

| 36 | ♕xf3 | |

Not 36 ♕d1?? ♖h3+ 37 ♔xh3 ♕g3#, so White has to surrender his queen.

| 36 | ... | ♖xf3 |
| 37 | gxf3 | |

Black can force perpetual check, but there is still some excitement to come.

37	...	♕f4+
38	♔h3	♕xf3+
39	♔xh4	

39 ♔h2 is an immediate draw, but the move played shouldn't risk anything.

| 39 | ... | ♕f2+ |

39...♕h5+ 40 ♔g3 ♕g5+ 41 ♔f2 ♕d2+ 42 ♔f3 ♕d3+ is also perpetual check.

| 40 | ♖g3 *(D)* | |

40 ♔g5 ♔g7! (40...♕xg1+? is wrong because after 41 ♔f6 ♕f1+ 42 ♔e6 ♕xb5 43 ♔xd6 the passed d-pawn becomes very dangerous) 41

♘xe5 ♕e3+ 42 ♔h4 ♕xg1 43 ♖c7+ ♔f8 also leads to a draw.

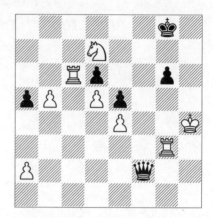

B

Both sides were in extreme time-trouble and had abandoned writing the moves down. At this point I thought that 40...♕h2+ forced mate, based on the lines 41 ♔g4 ♕h5#, 41 ♖h3 ♕f4# and 41 ♔g5 ♔g7 followed by 42...♕h5#. I therefore played...

| 40 | ... | ♕h2+ |

...with an air of tremendous confidence. Piket looked at this check for about a second and promptly resigned (**0-1**). In fact 40...♕f4+ would have been simpler, when 41 ♔h3 (41 ♖g4?? ♕h2+ 42 ♔g5 ♔g7 mates) 41...♕h6+ 42 ♔g2 ♕d2+ 43 ♔g1 ♕e1+ 44 ♔g2 ♕e2+ is an immediate perpetual check. The problem with 40...♕h2+ is that White can reply 41 ♔g5 ♔g7 (41...♕xg3+? 42 ♔f6 is winning for White since his king can hide amongst the black pawns while the b-pawn marches onward) 42 ♘xe5 and now it is Black who must play accurately to ensure the draw: 42...♕h6+ (42...♕xg3+ is inferior as after 43 ♘g4 there is no immediate perpetual check) 43 ♔g4 dxe5 44 ♖c7+ ♔g8 and White cannot coordinate his rooks sufficiently to prevent perpetual check. It is indeed unusual for a grandmaster to resign in a drawn position.

In October, the Bundesliga season started again and my first-round game was against the Dutch grandmaster Paul van der Sterren. As we are the same age, we often met in junior events during the 1970s. Years later, I had a critical game against him in the last round of the 1988 Thessaloniki Olympiad. The draw I saved from a dead lost position secured the silver medals for England, but deprived Paul of his final GM norm. Happily, he soon gained the GM title in any case. The current game is the last we played against each other and provided me with a nice positional win.

There are several openings in which Black ends up with an offside knight on a5. The most notorious of these is the King's Indian, and indeed many games have been lost by Black solely on account of this knight, which can easily be sidelined for the whole game. In the Closed Ruy Lopez, Black's knight may also venture to a5, but this is normally a temporary measure since the knight can usually return to the centre easily enough. However, it can happen that the game opens up while the knight is still on a5, and in this case Black may lack the time necessary to recentralize the knight. That is what happens in this game: a fierce battle rages in the centre of the board and when the dust settles Black is missing his a5-knight, which remains in limbo until the end of the game. A second important theme in this game is the idea of preventing the defender from escaping from his difficulties by means of a positional sacrifice (see White's 20th and 23rd moves).

Game 23
J. Nunn – P. van der Sterren
Bundesliga 1995/6
Ruy Lopez (Spanish), Closed

1	e4	e5
2	♘f3	♘c6
3	♗b5	a6
4	♗a4	♘f6
5	0-0	♗e7
6	♖e1	b5
7	♗b3	d6
8	c3	0-0 *(D)*

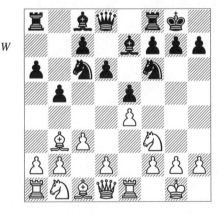

W

9   d3

I have already mentioned in Game 18 that keeping up with theory in all the main lines of the Closed Ruy Lopez is quite a burden. In that game, I played 8 a4 to steer the game along less well travelled paths. In this encounter I decided to follow a similar strategy, but using the 9 d3 system instead. These d3 lines are nothing new and have been played occasionally for decades. At the time this game was played, very few GMs were using 9 d3 except as a surprise weapon.

Fischer, for example, played it once in his 1992 rematch against Spassky, but the rest of the time he preferred the standard d4 variations. However, in the past decade a few players, such as Adams and Judit Polgar, have used it more regularly. Objectively speaking, it promises White less than the usual lines with d4, but it is not without some merits and can be effective, especially against an insufficiently prepared opponent. The basic idea behind 9 d3 may be seen if we consider the standard line of the Flohr-Zaitsev system, namely 9 h3 (if White wants to play d4, he usually plays this first, since 9 d4 ♗g4 is believed to cause Black few problems) 9...♗b7 10 d4 ♖e8 11 ♘bd2 ♗f8. Here White would like to play his d2-knight to f1 and g3, a standard manoeuvre in the Closed Ruy Lopez to free the queenside pieces. However, Black's pressure against e4 makes this impossible, because 12 ♘f1? runs into 12...exd4 13 cxd4 ♘a5 with a triple attack on e4. Thus, in this line (and in the Breyer Variation 9 h3 ♘b8) White has trouble moving his knight away from d2, and this blocks his queenside development. The 9 d3 system is based on the plan of transferring the knight to g3 while the e4-pawn is securely defended by the d3-pawn, and only then playing for d4. The plus side is that Black can't really prevent this plan, but the minus side is that White loses a tempo by playing d3 and then d4. However, under certain circumstances White can regain the tempo. This can happen, for example, if Black plays ...♗b7 too soon. Once Black has forfeited the chance to play

...♗g4, White may be able to manage without h3. This recovers the tempo lost by playing d3 and then d4.

9   ...   ♘a5

Playing for ...c5 is the most natural system, although there are other possibilities. However, although 9 d3 is a rather slow and positional system, Black shouldn't believe that he can get away with anything. For example, in Nunn-C.Richter, Bundesliga 2002/3 Black continued 9...♖e8 10 ♘bd2 ♗f8 11 ♘f1 ♘b8 12 ♘g3 ♗b7, attempting to play a kind of Breyer system. However, this particular move-order left f7 weak and White was able to strike by 13 ♘g5! d5 (13...♖e7 14 ♘f5 ♖d7 15 ♕f3 is also very unpleasant because 15...h6? loses to 16 ♘xf7! ♖xf7 17 ♕g3 g5 18 ♗xg5!) 14 d4 ♘bd7 15 exd5 exd4 (the key point is that 15...h6 fails to 16 ♘e6! fxe6 17 dxe6 and White regains the piece with a large advantage) 16 d6 ♖xe1+ 17 ♕xe1 ♘d5 18 dxc7 ♕xc7 19 cxd4. White has won a pawn, although Black's blockade on d5 offers some compensation. The conclusion was 19...♘7f6 20 ♗d2 ♖e8 21 ♕f1 ♕b6 22 ♕d3 a5? (after 22...h6 23 ♘f3 ♗d6 White would still have a long way to go to exploit his extra pawn) 23 ♘h5 1-0 as White wins further material.

10   ♗c2   c5
11   ♘bd2   ♖e8 *(D)*

The most flexible move, although of course there is also nothing wrong with 11...♘c6.

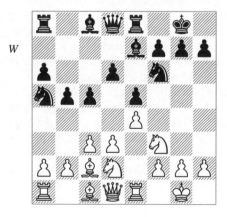

12   ♘f1

The main point of playing 9 d3 is to ensure that White can complete his knight transfer to g3, so this is the only logical move.

12   ...   h6

Whether to spend a tempo on ...h6 represents a key decision for Black. The alternative is 12...♗f8, when White is more or less forced to play 13 ♗g5 or else Black has simply gained a tempo by leaving his pawn on h7. After 13...h6 14 ♗h4 Black has quite a range of moves; 14...g5, 14...♗e7 and 14...g6 are all playable. Theory is rather vague on which line is best and on the assessment of the resulting positions. That is one of the nice things about 9 d3 – theory is less mature than in the main lines of the Closed Ruy Lopez, so players have to think rather than simply recite memorized lines.

13   ♘g3

White's knight has reached its destination.

13   ...   ♗f8 *(D)*

Note how Black delays ...♗b7, so that he still has the chance to meet d4 by ...♗g4.

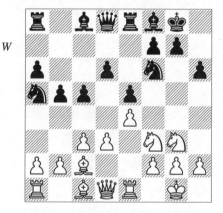

14   d4

Now it is White who faces an important decision regarding his h-pawn. He can either give in and play 14 h3, or he can try to play 14 d4 even though Black still has the option of ...♗g4. Even though 14 h3 has been played quite often, I believe that 14...g6 followed by ...♗g7 is comfortable for Black and so 14 d4 is the only way White can play for an advantage.

14   ...   cxd4

The alternative 14...♕c7 is also reasonable.

15   cxd4   exd4?!

This move looks wrong. Black surrenders the centre when he is not forced to do so, and draws the white knight into a more active position. It would only make sense if Black were able to force through a favourable ...d5, liquidating the centre completely, but it turns out that this is impossible. Black has three main alternatives:

1) 15...♞c6 16 d5 ♞b4 17 ♗b1 is similar to the standard line 9 h3 ♞a5 10 ♗c2 c5 11 d4 ♕c7 12 ♞bd2 cxd4 13 cxd4 ♞c6 14 d5 ♞b4 15 ♗b1. However, White's knight transfer to g3 looks more useful than Black's extra moves ...♖e8 and ...♗f8, so I would assess this as slightly better for White.

2) 15...♗g4 is perhaps also a little dubious. It is true that White is now forced to play d5, but the bishop is not especially well placed on g4 and will soon have to retreat or take on f3. Nunn-A.Marić, Hastings 1994/5 continued 16 d5 ♞h5 17 h3 ♗xf3 18 ♕xf3 ♞xg3 19 ♕xg3 ♔h8 20 ♗d3 ♖c8 21 ♗e2 ♗e7 22 a4 ♖b8 23 axb5 axb5 24 b3 b4 25 ♗d2 ♗g5 26 ♗xg5 hxg5 27 ♖ec1 ♞b7 28 ♖a7 ♔g8 29 ♖c6 with strong pressure for White.

3) 15...♕c7 is the soundest line for Black, simply keeping as many options open as possible. White may have nothing better than 16 h3, when 16...♗d7 gives Black every reason to hope for equality.

16 ♞xd4 *(D)*

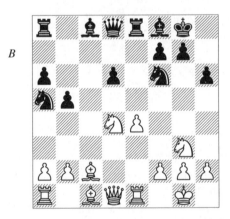

In addition to the problems posed by White's active pieces, Black also has trouble activating the offside knight on a5.

16 ... ♗b7

Black puts pressure on e4 and prepares to rescue his knight with ...♞c6. Other moves:

1) 16...♗d7 may be met by 17 ♗f4 or 17 b3. In the latter case, 17...♞c6 18 ♞xc6 ♗xc6 transposes into the note to Black's 17th move.

2) 16...g6 17 b3 ♗g7 18 ♗b2 h5 was played in B.Mortensen-L.Cooper, Hastings 1995/6 and

now 19 ♞f3 would have maintained a small but safe advantage for White.

17 b3

Preparing ♗b2, when the bishop will be actively placed on the long diagonal.

17 ... d5?! *(D)*

Too ambitious. Black wants to strike in the centre, but this gives White dangerous attacking chances against Black's king. Alternatives:

1) 17...♕c7 is wrong because it weakens the f6-knight. White won quickly in Mekhitarian-Lopez Silva, Botucatu 2003 after 18 ♗b2 d5 19 ♞df5 ♖e6 20 e5 ♞d7 21 ♖c1 ♕d8 22 ♞d6 ♗c6 23 ♗f5 ♖xe5 24 ♞xf7! 1-0.

2) 17...♖c8 18 ♗b2 g6 19 ♕d2 h5 20 ♞f3 ♞c6 was played in Hazai-Pavlović, Copenhagen 1987. White has a slight advantage.

3) 17...♞c6 18 ♞xc6 ♗xc6 19 ♗b2, Rybak-Ilczuk, Poland 1998, is also slightly better for White.

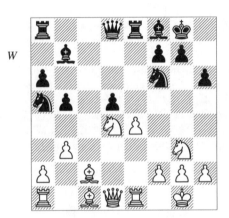

18 e5

The natural move since otherwise the centre is cleared of pawns and a draw can be expected. Positionally, the move e5 is right as the b7-bishop is now obstructed by the d5-pawn, while by driving the knight away from f6 White increases his kingside attacking chances. Now everything depends on whether the e5-pawn is strong or weak.

18 ... ♞e4

Forced, as 18...♞d7 loses to 19 ♕d3 g6 20 e6. With the text-move, Black hopes to force exchanges which would free his position.

19 ♗b2!

White refuses the pawn since after 19 ♞xe4 dxe4 20 ♗xe4 ♗xe4 21 ♖xe4 ♞c6 22 ♗b2

♖xe5 Black regains the pawn with an equal position. Instead White simply continues his development. In general, White would be quite happy for Black to exchange knights on g3, because then he would have an automatic attack by ♕d3 (meeting ...g6 by e6). However, I was not prepared to spend a move forcing it by playing 19 f3 which, quite apart from the lost tempo, weakens the a7-g1 diagonal. The analysis runs 19 f3 ♘xg3 20 hxg3 ♗c5 (20...♘c6 also gives Black enough counterplay) 21 ♔h2 ♕c7 22 ♕d3 ♗xd4 23 ♕h7+ ♔f8 and White has no more than a draw after 24 ♗a3+ ♗c5 25 ♕h8+ ♔e7 26 ♕xg7 ♗xa3 27 ♕f6+ ♔f8, etc.

The text-move threatens to win a pawn on e4, so Black is forced to take some action.

19 ... ♕b8 (D)

This unexpected move does not turn out well for Black, but the alternatives were also unattractive:

1) 19...♖xe5 20 f3 ♗b4 21 fxe4 ♗xe1 22 ♕xe1 ♕b6 23 ♔h1 gives White a large advantage, since an assault on g7 by ♘df5 is imminent.

2) 19...♗b4 20 ♖e3 ♖xe5 is also bad, but the reason is more complex: 21 ♘df5 ♖e6 22 ♗xg7 ♖g6 (22...♕g5 loses to 23 ♗b2) 23 ♘xh6+! ♔xg7 24 ♘gf5+ ♔h7 (24...♔f8 25 ♕d4 ♕f6 26 ♕xb4+ ♘d6 27 ♖ae1 is horrible for Black) 25 ♖h3 with a decisive attack.

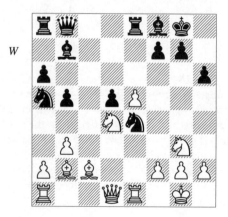

20 e6

A key moment, as White has a number of tempting continuations. However, I favoured the simple text-move as it gives White a substantial positional advantage with no risk attached. Here are the other possibilities:

1) 20 ♘xe4?! dxe4 21 ♗xe4 ♗xe4 22 ♖xe4 ♖xe5 allows Black to equalize.

2) 20 ♕g4?! ♕xe5 21 ♘df5 ♕xb2 22 ♘xh6+ ♔h7 23 ♘xf7 ♕xc2 (later analysis revealed that 23...♕f6 is even stronger, since then White may be struggling to reach a draw) 24 ♖xe4 was initially quite tempting, since 24...dxe4? loses to 25 ♘g5+ ♔g8 26 ♕f5. However, further thought showed that 24...♖xe4 25 ♘xe4 dxe4 26 ♕h5+ ♔g8 27 ♘g5 e3 forces White to take a draw by perpetual check.

3) 20 ♘gf5 ♖xe5 21 ♕g4 is another line that looks quite dangerous, but after 21...g6 22 f3 h5 the position is totally unclear.

4) 20 ♘df5 ♖xe5! 21 ♗xe5 ♕xe5 gives Black fair compensation for the exchange.

5) 20 ♖e3 (D) is an interesting attacking attempt which forces Black to play accurately:

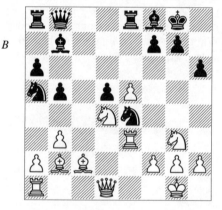

5a) 20...♕xe5 21 f3 ♘f2 (21...♕g5 loses to 22 ♗c1!) 22 ♖xe5 ♘xd1 23 ♖xe8 ♘xb2 24 ♖xf8+ ♔xf8 25 ♖b1 ♘bc4 26 bxc4 and, with a piece for two pawns, White has very good winning chances.

5b) 20...♘xg3 21 ♖xg3 ♕xe5 22 ♕d2 is much better for White.

5c) 20...♖xe5! 21 ♕e1 ♕c7 22 f3 ♘xg3 23 ♖xe5 ♘c6 24 ♘xc6 ♕xc6 25 ♕xg3 ♕xc2 and White's small material advantage may not be enough to win.

Lines '4' and '5' above feature a typical defensive ploy: giving up the exchange to defuse an attack. In the resulting positions, Black has fended off the attack and with a pawn and a solid position for the exchange he has excellent drawing chances. The attacker must always be on the lookout for ways in which the defender can surrender some material to 'buy off' the attack, in order to avoid them.

20 ... ♕f4

Best, as 20...fxe6 21 ♘xe4 dxe4 22 ♗xe4 gives White a large advantage based on the weak e-pawn, White's more active pieces and Black's badly placed a5-knight. Note that 22...♗b4? is wrong because of 23 ♘xe6! ♗xe1 24 ♕d7 mating.

21 ♘xe4 dxe4

22 g3 *(D)*

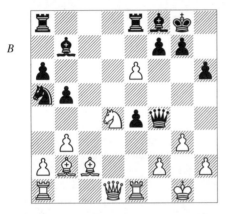

Now Black's queen must move onto the long diagonal or else White simply takes on e4. However, White then has various tactical ideas involving a discovered attack.

22 ... ♕e5

22...♕f6 is also dismal for Black. White can choose between:

1) 23 ♕d2 (this move aims simply to win a pawn) 23...fxe6! (the only chance for Black) 24 ♕xa5 e5 25 ♗xe4 (25 ♘e2?? e3 26 fxe3 ♕c6 wins for Black) 25...♗xe4 26 ♖xe4 exd4 27 ♗xd4 ♕c6 28 ♖xe8 ♖xe8 29 ♖e1 and White is a clear pawn up in the ending.

2) 23 ♗xe4!? (trying to win the pawn under more favourable circumstances) 23...fxe6 and now:

2a) 24 ♖c1 ♖ad8 25 ♕h5 e5 26 ♘f3 (26 ♗xb7 ♘xb7 and 26 ♘f5 ♗xe4 27 ♖xe4 ♘c6 also offer White nothing clear) 26...♗xe4 27 ♖xe4 g6 28 ♖g4 ♔h7 29 ♖c7+ ♖e7 30 ♖xe7+ ♗xe7 31 ♕xe5 ♕xe5 32 ♘xe5 ♖d2 gives Black more drawing chances.

2b) 24 ♕h5 ♖ad8 and now White has nothing better than 25 ♖ac1, transposing into line '2a'.

2c) 24 ♕g4! (probably White's best line) 24...♖ad8 (24...e5 25 ♘f3 ♗d6 26 ♖e2 ♖e7 27 ♖ae1 ♖ae8 28 ♘h4 is also very awkward for Black) 25 ♖ac1 e5 (25...♗a3 26 ♗xa3 ♖xd4 27 ♕h5 and White wins) 26 ♘f3 ♘c6 27 ♖ed1 with very strong pressure for White.

23 ♕g4! *(D)*

Even when one has the advantage, accuracy is essential to curtail defensive possibilities by the opponent. 23 ♕e2?! is wrong on account of 23...f5. Then the obvious 24 ♕h5 runs into 24...♖xe6! 25 ♘xe6 ♕xe6 and again we have a situation in which Black has surrendered a small amount of material in return for the elimination of White's pressure. Black's pieces, which were hitherto poorly placed, are now much more active; indeed, once he has played ...♘c6, all his pieces are on reasonable squares. There is also the psychological aspect to consider. If one has the initiative and is pressing hard, cashing it all in for a small material advantage (a pawn or the exchange for a pawn) may not be the best option. The sudden change in the type of play required is often difficult to accomplish, and the attacker may easily find himself 'losing the thread of the game'. Clearly, each position has to be judged on its merits, but the decision as to whether to cash in a positional advantage for extra material can be a difficult one, even for grandmasters.

23 ... h5

There is no good move:

1) 23...f5 can now be met by 24 ♕g6! ♖ac8 (24...♕f6 25 ♕xf6 gxf6 26 g4 fxg4 27 ♗xe4 wins for White) 25 ♖ac1 ♕f6 (25...♗b4 26 ♖ed1 ♗c5 27 ♗c3! b4 28 ♘xf5 ♖xe6 29

♘xh6+ ♔h8 30 ♕g4 and White wins) 26 ♕xf6 gxf6 27 ♘xf5 ♖xe6 28 f3 e3 29 ♘xe3 ♗c5 30 ♔f2 with a winning position for White; for example, 30...♗b6 31 ♗f5 or 30...♖ce8 31 ♗h7+.

2) 23...♗b4 is best met by 24 ♖xe4! ♗xe4 25 ♗xe4 ♖a7 26 exf7+ ♖xf7 27 ♗g6 and White will be a pawn up with an excellent position.

3) 23...fxe6 24 ♗xe4 ♗xe4 25 ♖xe4 ♕f6 26 ♖ae1 and White will win a pawn while retaining the initiative; clearly there can be no doubts about gaining material if the attack persists.

24　　♕e2　　　　fxe6

Now there is nothing better than this capture, since 24...f5 25 ♕xh5 costs Black a vital pawn.

25　　♗xe4

This leads to a general liquidation into an ending where Black has several weak pawns and his knight is still out of play on a5.

25　　...　　　　♕xe4
26　　♕xe4　　　♗xe4
27　　♖xe4

There is no saving the e6-pawn. Black could have put up much more resistance than he actually does, but this is clearly a depressing position for him. Even after the loss of the e-pawn, Black is troubled by his vulnerable h5- and a6-pawns.

27　　...　　　　♖ac8?! *(D)*

Black should have tried bringing his knight back into the game. After 27...♘b7 28 ♖xe6 ♘c5 29 ♖xe8 ♖xe8 30 ♖d1 White has a clear extra pawn, but Black could still fight on with slight chances of a draw.

W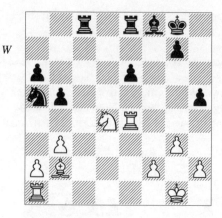

28　　♖ae1!

Now when White takes on e6 he can recapture with his rook, immediately targeting the weak a6-pawn. Moreover, the d4-knight stays where it is, covering c2. 28 ♖xe6? ♖xe6 29 ♘xe6 is wrong as 29...♖c2 gives Black counterplay. This is another example of a small finesse which turns a difficult technical win into a much easier one.

28　　...　　　　♗b4?!

Now it's all over since Black will lose two pawns. After 28...♘b7 29 ♖xe6 ♖xe6 30 ♖xe6 ♘c5 31 ♖e3 g6 32 ♘f3 White should win in the end with his extra pawn and active pieces, but it would still require some work.

29　　♖1e2　　　♗c3

There is nothing better.

30　　♗xc3　　　♖xc3
31　　♖xe6　　　1-0

Black will also lose the pawn on a6.

Shortly after this game, on 28th October 1995, I married the German woman player Petra Fink. We had met at a tournament held in Vienna during October 1991; I was playing in the grandmaster group and Petra in the open Swiss event. While I was wandering around the tournament hall, I noticed a woman playing the strong IM Rotshtein. Despite a rating difference of around 400 points, she had played sharply in the opening, sacrificed a pawn and had the IM under considerable pressure. Later on Rotshtein managed to liquidate to a rook ending with equal pawns, which he won with his superior endgame technique, but nevertheless I found the woman's attitude admirable and asked her out to dinner. Initially she turned me down, but I repeated the offer another day, this time successfully. From there the relationship developed and we travelled together to a number of chess events. In 1994 Petra moved to London and one year later we were exchanging marriage vows.

The routine of a professional chess-player is awkward to combine with family life. It involves being away from home for long periods, and unless you are one of the world's really top players, the erratic income it provides may prove awkward when it comes to regular demands such as mortgage payments. I doubt if many banks would be receptive to the explanation that this month's payment will be late because of an unfortunate accident on the back rank. I was now happy I had started a typesetting business, which provided a regular income to supplement chess-playing. Petra also became skilled at typesetting, and this side of the Nunn operations was rapidly becoming dominant. Most of the typesetting work was done for Batsford, but we also handled some work from other publishers. Times for professional chess-players were gradually becoming harder, especially in countries such as England with almost no indigenous professional chess life. The meagre rewards to be earned were now fought over tooth-and-nail by a host of hungry grandmasters, many from Eastern Europe and especially the former Soviet Union. Circumstances operated against Western GMs; 1000 Deutschmarks was a substantial prize for a Russian GM in 1995, but wouldn't keep you going for long if you lived in Western Europe. Under the pressure of circumstances, my chess activities gradually dwindled. Once such a process starts, it tends to be an accelerating process. As you spend more time on other things, there is less time to work on chess; this makes preparation more difficult, and leads to inferior results, which creates further pressure to switch time away from chess. 1995 was my last year with what one might describe as a full tournament schedule. From this point on, my chess activities started to decline, with fewer and fewer tournaments. However, I always found time to participate in the Bundesliga, which was better suited to part-time players. Having only two games in a weekend made it possible to prepare properly, and in this event I was able to maintain and even improve my results.

A week after the wedding I was back in action in the Bundesliga, with a tough fight against a fellow English grandmaster.

This is a tremendously complicated game in which White plays for a direct attack from an early stage. When facing an onslaught against your king, you must both stay calm and bear in mind the general principles for fending off attacks. Many of these can be seen in this game: a counter-action in the centre (move 19), returning sacrificed material and liquidation, especially the exchange of queens. White's attack is in fact objectively correct, in the sense that it is good enough for a draw. However, Hodgson's determination to press for a win eventually proved his undoing when he took one risk too many (move 26).

Game 24

J. Hodgson – J. Nunn

Bundesliga 1995/6

Trompowsky Opening

1	d4	♘f6
2	♗g5	

Not surprisingly, Julian Hodgson chooses the Trompowsky opening, which he has played virtually throughout his career. He has achieved excellent results with this opening, and thanks to his efforts the Trompowsky has been transformed from an eccentric sideline into a fully-fledged opening. True, some of his ideas, such as 2...♘e4 3 h4, seem unlikely to become established opening theory, but his many discoveries in the 2...♘e4 3 ♗f4 line assure him a lasting place in the history of the Trompowsky.

2	...	♘e4

This has always seemed to me the most natural reply, and the only genuine attempt to exploit White's second move.

3	♗f4	d5 *(D)*

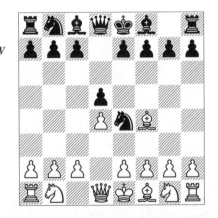

The second most popular move in this position, but I doubt if it is the best since Black will have to retreat his knight, losing two tempi, while White has only lost one tempo with his bishop. True, the extra move White gains (f3) cannot count as a full tempo gain, but it is certainly worth something. There is no doubt that 3...c5 is the critical continuation, for which see Game 45.

4   e3 *(D)*

In my view the most accurate move; White does not yet commit himself to f3 and keeps Black in the dark about his intentions. It is interesting to note that White has scored 62% from the position after 4 e3, which is better than most mainstream openings, so he can already count his opening strategy a success. The main alternative plan is 4 f3 ♘f6 5 e4 dxe4 6 ♘c3, the idea being that after 6...exf3 7 ♘xf3 White has a Blackmar-Diemer Gambit with an extra tempo (the normal Blackmar-Diemer runs 1 d4 d5 2 e4 dxe4 3 ♘c3 ♘f6 4 f3 exf3 5 ♘xf3). Whether that makes the gambit sound is hard to say, but in the hands of a strong attacking player it might well prove dangerous. One example is 7...g6 8 ♗c4 ♗g7 9 ♕e2 0-0 10 0-0-0 c6 11 d5 cxd5 12 ♘xd5 ♘xd5 13 ♖xd5 ♕b6 14 ♖b5 ♕c6 15 ♘e5 ♕e8 16 h4 ♘c6 17 h5 and White has strong kingside pressure, Hodgson-A.G.Panchenko, Bern 1994.

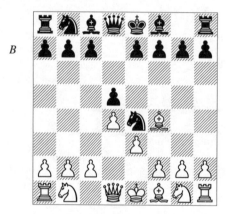

B

4   ...   ♗f5

4...c5 is met by 5 ♗d3 cxd4 6 ♗xe4 dxe4 7 exd4, when White's lead in development compensates for the two bishops. A sample line is 7...♘c6 8 ♘e2 ♗g4 9 ♘bc3 e6 10 h3 ♗h5 11 ♘xe4 ♗xe2 12 ♕xe2 ♘xd4 13 ♕d3 ♘c6 14 0-0-0 and White's more active pieces and better development gave him a clear endgame advantage in Hodgson-Wells, Oxford 1998.

Black instead prefers a natural developing move, but now White can use the tempo-gaining f3 to start a pawn advance on the kingside.

5   f3   ♘f6

5...♘d6 has also been played quite often; after 6 ♘d2 e6 7 c4 ♘xc4 8 ♘xc4 dxc4 9 ♗xc4 White has an edge thanks to his slight lead in development. Black can force White's king to move by 9...♗b4+, but after 10 ♔f2 the king is safe and the b4-bishop will have to retreat soon.

6   g4

I don't think this is White's best move. The problem is that it is too committal and gives White's hand away too soon. 6 c4 is more awkward, leaving Black in doubt about whether White will play g4. After the natural 6...e6, White continues in the same vein with 7 ♘c3, again reserving the option of g4 but also causing Black to worry about ♕b3. I suspect that this plan gives White the advantage, a feeling which is supported by White's excellent practical results after 6 c4.

6   ...   ♗g6
7   h4   h5

7...h6 is also possible, and after 8 ♗d3 ♗xd3 9 ♕xd3 c5 the position is roughly equal. However, I preferred to block the pawn-structure on the kingside in order to make that part of the board safer for my king.

8   g5   ♘fd7 *(D)*

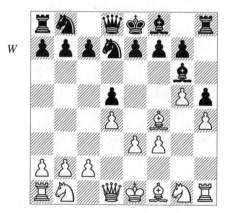

W

This position occurs nine times in my database with a score of one win for White, five wins for Black and three draws. I realize that this is only a small sample, but it does indicate that White has not found it easy to handle the position.

9   ♘c3

Alternatives:

1) 9 c4 dxc4 (9...c6 is also playable) 10 ♗xc4 ♘c6, aiming for a quick ...e5, looks fine for Black.

2) 9 ♗d3 ♗xd3 10 ♕xd3 ♘c6 (10...e6 followed by ...c5 is another plan) 11 g6 f6 12 ♘c3 ♘b6 13 ♕f5 ♕d7 14 ♕xd7+ ♔xd7 15 0-0-0 e6 was Miles-Van Wely, Linares Zonal 1995. Now Miles blundered with 16 e4? losing a pawn after 16...♘e7. After the correct 16 ♘ge2, the position would be roughly equal.

The move played aims for e4 rather than c4.

9   ...   c6

Ultra-solid but probably unnecessarily passive. 9...e6 10 ♗d3 ♗xd3 11 ♕xd3 g6 is more accurate, because in many lines Black will be able to play ...c5 in one move. During the game I was nervous about the possibility of 12 ♘b5 ♘a6 13 e4, since it seemed to me that it might be hard to drive the knight away from b5 (...c6 can be met by ♘d6+). However, after 13...♗e7 14 0-0-0 ♘b6 Black will eventually be able to play ...c6, so my fear was groundless.

10   ♗d3   ♗xd3
11   ♕xd3   g6 (D)

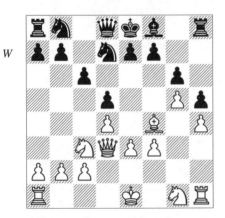

Again the cautious approach: Black rules out the possibility of g6 by White. Black's plan is quite simple – now that the light-squared bishops have disappeared, he will erect a solid pawn-chain on the light squares. His king will be relatively safe on the kingside, where the pawn-structure is blocked, and counterplay will come via an eventual ...c5. White must try to use his lead in development to launch a direct attack before Black can consolidate.

12   e4   e6
13   0-0-0

The open h2-b8 diagonal indicates that the black king will have to move to the kingside. Although the pawn-structure is blocked there, White might eventually be able to break through by means of a sacrifice.

13   ...   ♗e7
14   ♖e1! (D)

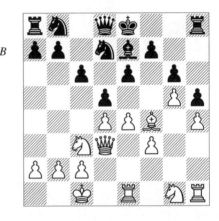

This may appear slightly artificial, but it is an ingenious move which sets up some dangerous tactical ideas. The threat is 15 exd5 cxd5 16 ♖xe6 fxe6 17 ♕xg6+ ♔f8 18 ♕xe6 and White will win at least one more pawn, leaving him with four pawns and a persistent attack for the rook. I would judge this to be favourable for White and therefore Black has to meet this threat. Moreover, as we shall see in the following note, Black cannot now castle. The alternative was simply to develop by 14 ♘ge2 or 14 ♘h3, but in my view the text-move causes Black more problems.

14   ...   ♘a6

Another point behind White's last move is that 14...0-0 is bad owing to 15 exd5 exd5 (15...cxd5 loses to 16 ♖xe6 fxe6 17 ♕xg6+ ♔h8 18 ♕h6+ ♔g8 19 ♕xe6+ ♔g7 20 ♕h6+ ♔g8 21 ♕g6+ ♔h8 22 ♕xh5+ ♔g7 23 ♕h6+ ♔g8 24 ♕g6+ ♔h8 25 ♘xd5 with five pawns and a tremendous attack for the rook) 16 ♖h2, followed by ♖he2, when White is ahead in development and has firm control of the only open file.

15   a3

Now 15 exd5 is answered by 15...♘b4! (not 15...cxd5 16 ♘xd5! ♕a5 17 ♘c3 ♘b4 18 ♕c4, when Black doesn't really have enough for the pawn) 16 ♕e2 cxd5 17 a3 ♘c6 and Black has significantly improved the position of his pieces. White therefore cuts out the ...♘b4 resource and renews the threat of exd5.

15   ...   ♘b6 *(D)*

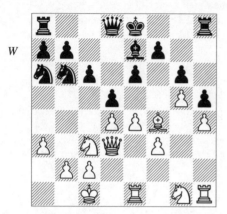

Overprotection of d5 is the key to stopping White's various tactical tricks on that square. Black still can't castle because of the exd5 and ♖xe6 idea, but he aims to improve his position gradually and castle later.

16   ♗e5!

White finds a bold and creative plan to open lines on the kingside. It is understandable that he should go for this idea because if he just plays normal developing moves, Black will improve his position with a plan such as ...♕d7 (defending e6), ...0-0, ...♖fd8 and ...♖ac8, ready for an eventual break with ...c5. If this break eventually comes, then it will be very powerful because Black's pieces are well-placed for a queenside attack. One sample line is 16 ♘h3 ♘c4 (it is hard to dislodge the knight from this excellent square, from which it not only menaces White's queenside but also prevents ♗e5) 17 ♘f2 ♕b6 18 ♘cd1 0-0 and Black has a good position, since now if White plays 19 exd5 cxd5 then the queen covers e6.

16   ...   0-0

Now that the e-file is blocked there is no sacrifice on e6, so Black can castle.

17   ♗f6

This is the point of White's play. Black is more or less forced to take since otherwise White will play e5, cementing the bishop in place. Then White would be able to break

through by means of ♘h3-f4 followed by a sacrifice such as ♘xh5 or ♘xg6. However, accepting the pawn has its risks since the g-file is opened and Black's minor pieces are far away on the queenside.

The alternative was to play 17 ♘h3, aiming for ♘f4 and a sacrificial breakthrough. This could lead to huge complications after 17...♘c4 18 exd5 cxd5 19 ♘f4 ♕a5 (not 19...♘xe5? 20 ♖xe5 and Black cannot prevent a sacrifice at e6 or g6) 20 ♘xg6 ♗xa3; for example, 21 ♘xd5 exd5 22 bxa3 ♖fe8 23 ♘f4 ♘b4 24 ♕b3 with a totally unclear position.

17   ...   ♗xf6
18   gxf6   ♕xf6
19   ♘h3 *(D)*

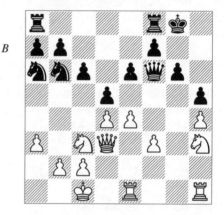

The danger on the kingside is clear – White will play ♖eg1 followed by e5 and a sacrifice on g6 (if Black meets e5 by ...♕f5, then White will move his own queen and trap Black's with ♖g5). Black must take immediate action to disrupt this plan.

19   ...   c5!

A necessary move, threatening ...♕xd4 and so forcing White to play e5 before he is fully prepared for it. It also provides Black with the means of breaking up White's pawn-chain with ...cxd4.

20   e5   ♕f5

So far both sides have conducted the game well and the position is roughly balanced. Now, however, the game dissolves into tactics and inaccuracies start to creep in.

21   ♕d2

White is tempted by the possibility of transferring his queen to h6 and indeed the position remains roughly equal after this move. However, White had an interesting alternative in 21 ♕xf5!? exf5 22 e6. Admittedly, he is a pawn down, but Black's kingside is full of holes and his g6-pawn will be weak. Black also still suffers from the fact that his knights are stuck on the queenside. Objectively the position is probably equal, but Black has to take considerable care: 22...cxd4 (22...♖fe8 23 exf7+ ♔xf7 24 ♘b5 ♔f6 25 ♘f4, threatening 26 ♘d6 and 26 ♖hg1, is unpleasant for Black) 23 ♘b5 ♘c5 (23...d3 24 ♘f4! appears more awkward for Black) 24 e7 (24 ♘f4 ♘xe6 25 ♘xe6 fxe6 26 ♖xe6 ♔g7 27 ♖he1 is unclear) 24...♖fe8 25 ♘f4 (25 ♘d6 ♘e6 gives Black enough for the exchange) 25...d3! 26 cxd3 (26 b4 ♘e6 27 ♘xe6 fxe6 28 ♘c7 ♖xe7 29 ♘xa8 d2+ 30 ♔xd2 ♘xa8 and again Black has enough play for the exchange) 26...♖ac8 27 ♔b1 ♖c6 28 d4 ♘e6 29 ♘xe6 fxe6 30 ♘xa7 ♖d6 31 ♘b5 ♖c6 and the result is a draw by repetition.

21 ... ♘c4

This is not a mistake, but Black could have restricted White's options by playing 21...cxd4 22 ♘b5 ♘c4, when the tactics lead to a more or less forced draw after 23 ♕h6 (not 23 ♘xd4? ♘xd2 24 ♔xd2 ♕xh3 25 ♖xh3 ♘c5 and Black consolidates his extra pawn) 23...d3! 24 ♘g5 d2+ 25 ♔b1 dxe1♕+ 26 ♖xe1 ♖fe8 (not 26...♖fc8? 27 ♕h7+ ♔f8 28 ♘d4 ♕f4? 29 ♘dxe6+ and White wins) 27 ♕h7+ ♔f8 28 ♘d4 ♕f4 29 ♘e2 ♕f5 repeating the position.

22 ♕h6 cxd4 (D)

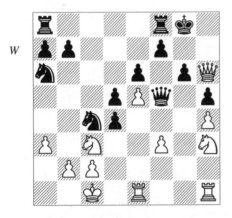

23 ♘xd5

The main alternative is 23 ♘g5 (23 ♘b5 transposes into the note to Black's 21st move,

which leads to a draw), which also leads to a draw, although Black must defend accurately (Black could have avoided this possibility by playing 21...cxd4):

1) 23...♖fc8? 24 ♘xd5 exd5 25 e6 wins for White.

2) 23...♖fd8?! 24 ♘b5 ♕f4+ 25 ♔b1 ♘c5 26 ♘xd4 gives White a strong attack for the sacrifice of just one pawn. One plausible line runs 26...♖d7 (after 26...♖ac8 27 ♖hg1 Black cannot prevent a sacrificial breakthrough on e6) 27 c3 ♖ad8 28 ♖e2 and Black is virtually paralysed by the need to defend against White's various tactical possibilities.

3) 23...♖fe8! 24 ♘b5 (24 ♘xd5 transposes into the game) 24...d3 (24...♘c5?! 25 ♘xd4 is similar to line '2') 25 cxd3 ♘c5! 26 ♘d4 ♘xd3+ 27 ♔b1 ♕f4 28 ♘dxe6! ♖xe6 (28...fxe6 29 ♕xg6+ ♔f8 30 ♕h6+ ♔g8 31 ♕h7+ ♔f8 32 ♕h8+ ♔e7 33 ♕g7+ ♔d8 34 ♕xb7 wins for White) 29 ♕h7+ ♔f8 30 ♘xe6+ fxe6 31 ♕h8+ ♔f7 32 ♕xa8 ♘xe1 33 ♕xb7+ ♔f8 34 ♖xe1 ♕xh4 and the position is roughly equal, since Black's active knight and passed h-pawn balance White's slight material advantage.

Thus 23 ♘b5 and 23 ♘g5 should both lead to a draw. Instead of these, White decides to play for a win with an unexpected piece sacrifice. As this also leads to a roughly equal position, there is no objective reason to prefer one line over another. Hodgson's fighting spirit is certainly admirable, although in this game he eventually oversteps the mark in his search for victory.

23 ... exd5 (D)

24 ♘g5 ♖fe8

This is forced because after, for example, 24...♖fc8?, Black is crushed by 25 e6!.

25   e6   fxe6 (D)

Again Black has no choice since 25...♖xe6 26 ♕h7+ ♔f8 27 ♕h8+ ♔e7 28 ♕xa8 favours White due to the continued exposure of Black's king.

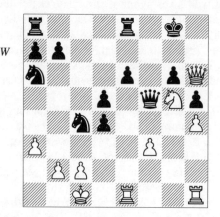

26   ♖hg1?

This is certainly one risk too many. White's best continuation is 26 ♕h7+ ♔f8, and now:

1) 27 ♕h8+ ♔e7 28 ♖xe6+ wins Black's queen but the resulting position is bad for White; for example, 28...♕xe6 29 ♕g7+ ♔d6 30 ♘xe6 ♖xe6 31 ♕xb7 ♘c7 32 b3 ♘b6 33 a4 d3 34 cxd3 (34 a5 ♘d7 35 ♕b4+ ♘c5 36 cxd3 ♘7a6 is very good for Black) 34...♔d7! (White's queen is in trouble; the immediate threat is 35...♖ee8 and 36...♖eb8) 35 ♖h2 (35 a5 ♖ee8 36 axb6 axb6 should win for Black) 35...♘c4! 36 ♕b4 ♘e5 with a clear advantage for Black. Once Black gets his pieces coordinated, the rooks and knight will make a dangerous attacking force.

2) 27 ♕h6+! ♔e7 (27...♔g8, repeating the position, is Black's safest option) 28 ♖xe6+ ♔d8 29 ♖xe8+ ♔xe8 30 ♕h8+ ♕f8 31 ♖e1+ (31 ♕xd4 ♘c7 looks inadequate for White) 31...♔d7 32 ♕h7+ ♔c6 33 ♖e6+ ♘d6 34 ♘f7 ♖d8 35 ♖xg6 ♕e7 36 ♘xd8+ ♕xd8 37 ♕xh5 with a roughly equal position.

26   ...   d3 (D)

After White's error on the previous move, Black even had a second promising continuation. The alternative is 26...e5 27 ♘h3 ♖e6 28 ♘f4! (the only chance) and the position looks as if it should be winning for Black, but it is

hard to prove anything more than a modest advantage:

1) 28...d3 29 ♘xe6 d2+ 30 ♔d1 dxe1♕+ 31 ♔xe1 ♔f7 32 ♕h7+ ♔xe6 33 ♖xg6+ ♕xg6 34 ♕xg6+ ♔d7 35 ♕xh5 ♘c5 36 ♕f7+ ♔c6 37 h5 and Black has no advantage in view of the strength of the h-pawn.

2) 28...♘e3 29 ♖xe3 ♖c8 30 ♔b1 is unclear.

3) 28...♘xa3 29 bxa3 ♖c8 30 ♖xg6+ (30 ♖g2 ♖ec6 31 ♖xg6+ ♖xg6 32 ♕xg6+ ♕xg6 33 ♘xg6 transposes) 30...♖xg6 31 ♕xg6+ ♕xg6 32 ♘xg6 ♔g7 33 ♘xe5 ♘c5 with an endgame advantage for Black. He is a pawn up but has doubled isolated pawns (although White cannot boast about his own pawn-structure).

4) 28...♘b4! seems to be relatively best. After 29 ♖g2 (29 axb4 ♖a6 30 ♖xg6+ ♕xg6 31 ♕xg6+ ♖xg6 32 ♘xg6 ♖e8 is winning for Black) 29...♘d2! 30 axb4 (or 30 ♖xd2 exf4 31 ♖xe6 ♕xe6 32 axb4 ♖e8 33 ♖e2! ♕f7 34 ♖g2 ♖e1+ 35 ♔d2 ♖e6 36 ♕xh5 ♔g7 37 ♕g5 and, although the position favours Black, he has nothing really clear) 30...♖c8 31 ♖xd2 exf4 32 ♖xe6 ♕xe6 33 ♖xd4 Black has a modest advantage.

Objectively speaking, there isn't much to choose between 26...e5 and the move played.

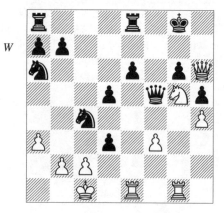

27   ♘e4!

White finds the best chance. He heads for an ending which, although better for Black, still offers White some hope of saving the game. The other possibilities are:

1) 27 ♕h7+ ♔f8 28 ♕h8+ (28 ♕h6+ ♔e7 29 ♖xe6+ ♔d8 30 ♖xe8+ ♔xe8 31 ♖e1+ ♔d7 32 ♕g7+ ♔c6 33 ♖e6+ ♘d6 34 ♕c3+ ♘c5 35 b4 ♕f4+ 36 ♔b2 b6 37 bxc5 bxc5 38 ♕xd3

Rb8+ 39 ♔a2 Rb6 is also much better for Black) 28...♔e7 29 Rxe6+ Qxe6 30 Qg7+ ♔d6 31 Nxe6 Re7 (31...d2+ 32 ♔d1 Rxe6 33 b3 is less clear) 32 Qh6 d2+ 33 ♔d1 Rxe6 34 Rxg6 Nxb2+ 35 ♔xd2 Nc4+ 36 ♔d1 Nc5 and Black has a clear advantage.

2) 27 cxd3 Nc5! 28 ♔b1 Re7 29 Ne4 (or 29 Nxe6 Rh7 30 Qxg6+ Qxg6 31 Rxg6+ ♔f7 32 dxc4 ♔xg6 33 Nxc5 dxc4 with a clear extra exchange for Black) 29...dxe4 30 fxe4 (30 Rxg6+ ♔f7 31 fxe4 Qf2! wins for Black) 30...Qe5 31 Rxg6+ Rg7 32 dxc4 Rxg6 33 Qxg6+ Qg7 and White's attack collapses.

| 27 | ... | Ne5 |

The only move. Not 27...♔f7? 28 Qh7+ ♔f8 29 Rxg6 Qf7 30 Qh6+ ♔e7 31 Qg5+ ♔d7 32 Rg7 and White wins.

| 28 | Nd6 | |

White has no choice but to allow an exchange of queens. After 28 Rg5 dxe4 29 Rxf5 exf5 30 fxe4 Rad8 Black has too much for the queen, while 28 Nd2 Re7 29 Rg5 Qf8 30 Qxf8+ Rxf8 31 Rgxe5 Rc7 32 c3 Nc5 leaves Black two pawns up.

| 28 | ... | Qf8 |

Forcing the reply.

| 29 | Qxf8+ | Rxf8 |
| 30 | Rxe5 | Rf6 (D) |

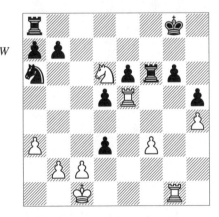

For the moment Black is two pawns up but White can regain one immediately. However, Black should be able to consolidate the other pawn and this gives him some winning prospects.

| 31 | cxd3 | |

The simplest and best move, as after the alternatives Black secures a larger advantage:

1) 31 Rxh5 Rd8 32 Nxb7 (32 Nb5 dxc2 33 ♔xc2 Rc8+ 34 ♔d2 Nc5 35 Nxa7 Nb3+ 36 ♔e3 d4+ 37 ♔e4 Ra8 38 Nb5 Nd2+ 39 ♔d3 Nxf3 40 Rg4 Rd8 wins for Black) 32...Rc8 33 c3 Rb8 34 Na5 (34 Nd6 Nc5 35 f4 Na4 36 ♔d2 Rxb2+ 37 ♔xd3 e5! 38 Nf5 Nc5+ 39 ♔e3 exf4+ 40 ♔d4 Nd7 is very good for Black) 34...d2+ 35 ♔c2 d1Q+ 36 ♔xd1 Rxb2 37 Rhg5 ♔h7 38 R1g3 Nc5 and Black is clearly better (the main threat is 39...Ne4).

2) 31 Reg5 ♔h7 32 cxd3 e5 33 Nb5 (33 Nxb7 Rb8 34 Na5 Nc5 35 b3 Nxb3+ 36 Nxb3 Rxb3 37 Rxe5 Rxa3 38 ♔d2 d4 and Black should win with his extra pawn and threats against White's weak pawns) 33...Nc5 34 d4 Nd3+ 35 ♔c2 (35 ♔d2 Nxb2 36 dxe5 Nc4+ 37 ♔c2 Rb6 38 Nd4 Rc8 with a large advantage for Black) 35...Rxf3 36 Nd6 (36 Rxg6 Rc8+ 37 ♔b1 Rc1+ leaves Black a pawn up) 36...Raf8 with a clear advantage for Black.

After the text-move, the complications have died down and we can assess the position. On Black's side he has an extra pawn and White has three isolated pawns. However, weighed against this White has active pieces and Black's backward g- and e-pawns are a handicap. On balance, Black has a definite advantage but the position is probably still within the bounds of a draw. However, the earlier complications had left both players (especially White) in time-trouble, and this soon exerts an influence on the play.

| 31 | ... | Nc5 |

Black gives priority to bringing his knight into play. The main alternative was 31...Rd8, but this is not especially clear; for example, 32 Nxb7 (32 Nb5 ♔f7 33 b4 is also possible, since 33...Rxf3 may be answered by 34 Rxe6) 32...Rb8 33 Na5 (33 Nd6? Nc5 34 ♔d2 ♔f8 leaves White's knight in difficulties) 33...Nc5 34 Reg5 ♔f7 35 Nc6 Nxd3+ 36 ♔d2 Rb6 37 Nd8+ ♔e7 38 Nxe6 and White has stirred up complications.

| 32 | ♔d2 | |

Again best, since 32 ♔c2 Rd8 33 d4 (33 Nb5 a6 34 Nd4 ♔f7 followed by ...Nd7 and ...e5 is very good for Black) 33...Rxd6 34 dxc5 Rc6 35 Rxh5 Rxc5+ 36 ♔d2 Rc4 is very bad for White.

| 32 | ... | ♔h7 |

With the white king on d2, the continuation 32...Rd8 33 Nb5 a6 34 Nd4 ♔f7 proves less effective due to a surprising defence by White: 35 ♔e3 ♘d7 36 f4! and if Black takes the e5-rook then his own rook is trapped. Black can arrange to free the f6-rook by 36...♖e8 37 b4 ♔f8, but surprisingly White can continue to offer it by 38 a4. Then 38...♘xe5 39 fxe5 ♖f7 40 ♖xg6 leads to a position which looks very difficult to win for Black because White's active pieces partially offset Black's extra material.

Black therefore prefers to defend his g6-pawn and thus genuinely attack White's f3-pawn.

33   b4
33 ♖eg5 is less accurate. Black can continue:

1) 33...♖d8 34 ♘b5 ♖xf3? 35 ♖xg6 ♖xd3+ 36 ♔e2 is drawn.

2) 33...e5 34 b4 ♘b3+ (34...♘xd3 35 ♔xd3 ♖xd6 36 ♖xe5 ♖f8 also only offers Black a modest advantage) 35 ♔c3 ♘d4 36 ♖xe5 ♘xf3 37 ♖f1 and White has drawing chances.

3) 33...a5 looks like the best chance. After 34 d4 ♘b3+ 35 ♔e3 ♖af8 36 ♖1g3 b6 Black has consolidated his extra pawn and can continue with ideas such as ...a4 followed by ...♘a5, or ...♘a1-c2+.

33   ...   ♘d7 (D)

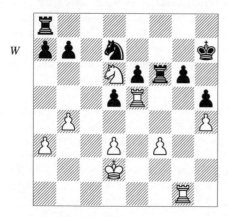

34   ♖ee1?!
After defending accurately for several moves, White starts to go astray. After 34 ♖eg5! b6 35 ♖c1 I think that White's active pieces should enable him to hold the game; for example, 35...e5 36 ♘b5 ♖af8 37 ♖c7 ♖8f7 38 d4 ♖xf3 39 ♘d6 ♖f2+ 40 ♔e1 with a draw.

34   ...   a5
35   ♖c1?
This is a more significant error. 35 ♘xb7?! is also doubtful as 35...axb4 36 axb4 ♖a2+ 37

♔c3 (37 ♔e3 ♘e5 38 ♖g3 ♖b2 is very promising for Black) 37...♖a3+ 38 ♔c2 ♖xf3 39 ♖xe6 ♖f2+ 40 ♔b1 ♖b3+ 41 ♔c1 ♘f8 42 ♖e7+ ♔g8 43 ♘c5 ♖xb4 gives Black good chances of a win.

35 bxa5! is best, and after 35...♖xa5 36 ♘e8 ♖f5 37 ♘d6 (37 ♖xe6? ♘e5 is very good for Black) 37...♘e5 38 ♖xe5! ♖xe5 39 f4 ♖f5 40 ♘xf5 gxf5 41 ♖b1 ♖xa3 42 ♖xb7+ ♔g6 we reach a rook ending with Black having an extra pawn. White still faces some problems but it is unlikely that Black's advantage is enough to guarantee a win.

The move played allows Black to activate his knight.

35   ...   ♘e5
Suddenly White suffers from the weakness of his f3-pawn.

36   ♖gf1
The only chance.

36   ...   axb4 (D)
36...♖xf3 37 ♖c7+ ♔g8 38 ♖xf3 ♘xf3+ 39 ♔e3 ♘xh4 40 ♔f4 is not totally clear despite Black's three extra pawns since White's pieces are extremely active.

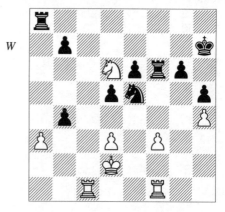

37   axb4?
After this further error the game finishes abruptly. White had to try 37 f4, but Black should still win with accurate play: 37...♖af8 38 ♖c7+ ♔h6 39 axb4 (39 d4 ♘c6 40 axb4 ♘xd4 41 ♖xb7 e5 looks winning for Black, although he will need to take care) 39...♖xf4 40 ♖xf4 ♖xf4 and Black should win despite the dangerous b-pawn; for example, 41 ♖xb7 ♖xh4 42 b5 ♔g5! (moving the king out from its current vulnerable position) 43 b6 ♖b4 44 ♔c3

♘c6 45 ♘c8 h4 with a decisive advantage for Black.

| 37 | ... | ♘xf3+ |
| 38 | ♔e3 | |

After 38 ♔d1 e5 Black also wins easily.

I also had an interesting game during the next Bundesliga weekend. The Poisoned Pawn is one of the sharpest opening lines around, and anyone who ventures into it must be very well prepared. Usually this opening results in complex middlegame positions, but the line I chose in this game leads instead to an endgame. The position seemed rather drawish, but on move 25 White sacrificed a pawn to activate his pieces. With accurate defence Black could have held on, but approaching time-trouble caused some inaccuracies and Black was soon in serious trouble.

Game 25

J. Nunn – I. Stohl

Bundesliga 1995/6

Sicilian Defence, Najdorf Variation

1	e4	c5
2	♘f3	d6
3	d4	cxd4
4	♘xd4	♘f6
5	♘c3	a6

Once again I faced the decision as to which line to play against the Najdorf. In two previous games against Stohl I had played 6 f4 and 6 ♗e3, winning with the former and losing with the latter. I decided it was time to try a third move in the hope of introducing a small element of surprise.

6   ♗g5

The same choice as in Game 14. Stohl's opening preparation is highly regarded and I was hoping to steer the game into paths with which I was familiar.

6	...	e6
7	f4	♕b6
8	♕d2	♕xb2
9	♘b3	(D)

Even if 6 ♗g5 wasn't a surprise, perhaps this move was, because I had only played it once before in serious tournament play. However, I had looked at this line while working with Mickey Adams before his Candidates match against Gelfand in 1994, and indeed the current game followed one of the games of that match for some time. If you have already played over the earlier games in this book, you will recall that this is not the first time I have

| 38 | ... | d4+ |
| | 0-1 | |

White loses yet more material after 39 ♔e4 (39 ♔e2 runs into 39...♖a2+ 40 ♔d1 ♖d2#) 39...♘d2+.

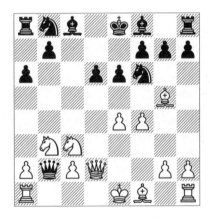

mentioned my work with Mickey. Perhaps by coincidence, quite a few of the lines we looked at later turned up in my games, and it is clear I gained a great deal from analysing with such a strong player.

9   ...   ♘c6

A key moment for Black. The move played allows a forced tactical sequence liquidating to an ending which is marginally better for White. The alternative 9...♕a3 is more ambitious; Black intends to hang on to the pawn but leaves the queen sidelined for some time. Here is not the place to go deeply into the extensive theory of the Poisoned Pawn – anyone interested can refer to my book *The Complete Najdorf: 6 ♗g5* (Batsford, 1996).

10   ♗xf6

If White does not want to play an ending he can try 10 ♗d3, although the theoretical verdict on this move is that it is unlikely to give White any advantage.

| | 10 | ... | gxf6 |
| | 11 | ♘a4 | |

White is now more or less committed to this forcing sequence, since 11 ♗e2 f5 12 exf5 ♗g7 gives Black a fine position.

	11	...	♛a3
	12	♘b6	♖b8
	13	♘c4	

White must continue along the narrow path since he has made so many concessions, both materially and positionally, that any respite would allow Black to consolidate.

| | 13 | ... | ♛a4 |
| | 14 | a3 | |

Other moves, such as 14 ♗e2 and 14 ♔f2, are playable, but they are unlikely to do more than equalize. 14 ♘xd6+? ♗xd6 15 ♛xd6 is wrong since after 15...♛xe4+ 16 ♔f2 ♛b4 Black keeps his extra pawn without making any concessions.

The text-move takes away some squares from Black's queen and threatens 15 ♗e2, followed by taking on d6 at a favourable moment.

| | 14 | ... | b5 |

It is best to force White's hand as quickly as possible, since White can improve his position by ♗e2 and 0-0, while Black's possible moves are less constructive.

	15	♘xd6+	♗xd6
	16	♛xd6	♛xe4+
	17	♗e2 (D)	

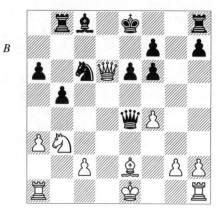

| | 17 | ... | ♛d5 |

The white queen is menacingly posted, and Black is well advised to exchange it straight away. The main problem with this line from Black's point of view is that while the ending is only very slightly better for White, it offers Black no winning chances at all. In view of this, some players have tried 17...♗b7 in order to keep the queens on, but this is very risky as we can see from the game Vouldis-Paunović, Kavala 1997, which continued 18 ♘c5 ♛d4 (18...♛d5 19 ♛xd5 exd5 20 0-0-0 is worse for Black than Nunn-Stohl, since his bishop belongs on e6 and not on b7) 19 ♖d1 ♛c3+ (19...♛xd6 20 ♖xd6 ♗a8 21 ♔f2 is very unpleasant for Black; White can build up his position with ♖hd1 and regain the pawn at will on the queenside) 20 ♔f2 ♖d8 21 ♘d7 ♖g8 (after 21...♗c8 22 ♖d3 ♖xd7 23 ♛xd7+ ♗xd7 24 ♖xc3 or 21...♘b8 22 ♖d3 ♖xd7 23 ♛xd7+ ♘xd7 24 ♖xc3 White has good winning chances with the extra exchange) 22 ♗f3? (missing 22 ♖d3! ♖xg2+ 23 ♔f1! and Black is lost; after 23...♖g8 the most convincing win is 24 ♖g1 ♖xg1+ 25 ♔xg1 ♛e1+ 26 ♗f1 and Black cannot defend f6) 22...♘a5? (22...♛xc2+ 23 ♔e3 ♖xd7 24 ♛xd7+ ♔f8 25 ♛xb7 ♘a5 would have put up more of a fight, although White would retain an advantage with correct play) 23 ♖he1 1-0 since there is no defence to the deadly threat of 24 ♖xe6+.

| | 18 | ♛xd5 | exd5 |
| | 19 | 0-0-0 (D) | |

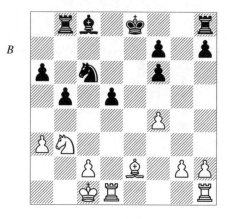

We can pause to assess the ending. First of all, Black is a pawn up. However, White can regain the pawn by a combination of ♗f3 and ♖he1, meeting ...♗e6 with either ♘c5 or g4

followed by f5. After the pawn is regained, there isn't much to choose between the two pawn-structures: Black has broken kingside pawns while White's queenside pawn-structure is damaged. White will usually have slightly more active pieces, since his rooks will already be on the central files, and this should suffice for an edge. Despite this, the strong drawish tendency in the position is obvious and indeed in MegaBase 2004 six out of seven games reaching this position ended in a draw. When I was analysing with Mickey, we felt that this line was not a bad try: White has chances to exert pressure and there is no risk involved at all. However, looking at it now I feel that against reasonable defence White's winning chances are very slight. The limited number of pawns and lack of tension severely curtail White's prospects. One further point is that White should not necessarily regain the pawn at the earliest possible opportunity; it is often better to step up the pressure first.

> **19 ... ♘e7** *(D)*

Although Stohl must have been familiar with this line, he was spending a great deal of time over his moves whereas I was playing very quickly. It may well be that he was worried about an improvement, although I had nothing devastating prepared. 19...♗e6 is likely to transpose to the game.

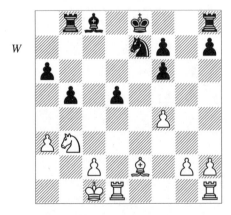

> **20 ♗f3**

White doesn't intend to play 21 ♗xd5 since he should not allow his bishop to be exchanged for Black's passive knight. Rather he intends 21 ♖he1, increasing the pressure and looking for a better chance to take on d5.

> **20 ... ♗e6**
> **21 ♖he1 0-0**

The best defence. 21...f5 is inferior, because after 22 ♗xd5 ♘xd5 23 ♖xd5 0-0 24 ♖d6 ♖fd8 25 ♖ed1 ♖xd6 26 ♖xd6 ♖c8 27 ♔b2 White has strong pressure and may well win a pawn soon. 21...♖g8 22 ♘d4 ♖b6 23 f5 ♗c8 was played in Lanc-Novikov, Camaguey 1987 and now the simplest line is 24 ♗xd5 ♔f8 25 ♗e4, when White's more active pieces give him the advantage.

> **22 g4**

The best try. 22 ♘c5 ♖b6 23 ♘d7 ♗xd7 24 ♖xe7 ♗e6 25 ♗xd5 ♗xd5 26 ♖xd5 ♖c8 causes Black no problems, while 22 ♘d4 ♖b6 23 g4 can be met by either 23...f5 or 23...♖e8.

> **22 ... f5**

22...♘g6 23 f5 ♘e5 24 ♗g2 ♗c8 25 ♗xd5 leaves White with an edge, so the move played is again best.

> **23 gxf5 ♘xf5** *(D)*

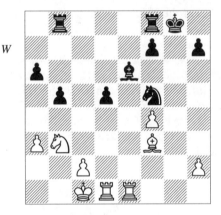

> **24 ♘c5**

The first new move of the game, deviating from 24 ♗xd5 as played in the earlier Adams-Gelfand game. Although 24 ♘c5 was played later, this does not necessarily mean that it is an improvement! In fact I now think that whatever winning chances White has in this ending lie in taking immediately on d5. After 24 ♗xd5 ♖be8 White may continue:

1) 25 ♘c5 ♗xd5 26 ♖xe8 ♖xe8 27 ♖xd5 ♘e3 is fine for Black.

2) 25 ♗xe6 ♖xe6 26 ♖xe6 fxe6 27 ♘c5 ♘e3 (27...♖f6 28 ♘xa6 e5 29 ♘c7 exf4 30 ♘xb5 f3 is also safe for Black, Kazoks-Silva, ICCF e-mail 1997) 28 ♘xe6 ♖c8 29 ♖g1+ ♔f7

30 ♘g5+ ♔f6 31 ♘e4+ ♔e6 32 ♖g5 ♖xc2+ 33 ♔b1 ♖c6 34 ♖e5+ ♔d7 35 ♘c5+ ♔d6 36 ♘b7+ ½-½ Adams-Gelfand, Candidates match (3), Wijk aan Zee 1994.

3) 25 ♗b7! (this looks like White's best try) 25...♗c8 (25...♖b8? 26 ♘c5! favours White, while 25...♗xb3 26 cxb3 ♖xe1 27 ♖xe1 ♘d6 28 ♗d5 gives White an edge) 26 ♗xc8 ♖xc8 27 ♖e5 ♘h4 28 ♖d6 ♘g6 (28...♘f3? 29 ♖e3 ♘xh2 30 ♖g3+ ♔h8 31 ♖h6 ♘f1 32 ♖f3 traps the knight) 29 ♖g5 h6 and now Lopez Murcia-Ollmann, corr. World Cup semi-final 1998 finished 30 ♖g2 ♔h7 31 f5 ♘f4 32 ♖gd2 ♖fe8 33 ♔b2 ♖e5 ½-½. However, 30 ♖g3! is much stronger, as the rook isn't attacked when the knight comes to f4; after 30...♔h7 31 f5 ♘f4 32 ♔b2 White still has annoying pressure.

24 ... ♘e7! (D)

An excellent defensive move. Black makes it hard for White to regain his pawn without allowing a further liquidation. 24...♖be8 is less accurate as after 25 ♖e5 (25 ♘xa6 ♖a8 26 ♘c7 ♖xa3 27 ♗xd5 ♗xd5 28 ♖xd5 ♖a1+ 29 ♔d2 ♖xe1 30 ♔xe1 ♘e3 is very drawish) White can keep an edge:

1) 25...♘h4 26 ♗xd5 ♗xd5 (26...♘g6? 27 ♘xe6! fxe6 28 ♖xe6 ♖xe6 29 f5! favours White) 27 ♖exd5 with continuing pressure for White.

2) 25...♔h8 26 ♗xd5 (26 ♘xa6 ♖a8 27 ♘c7 ♖xa3 28 ♗xd5 ♘e3 is equal) 26...♗xd5 27 ♖xf5 ♗c4 28 ♘xa6 ♖a8 29 ♖d6 and White retains a slight plus.

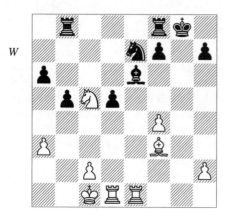

25 f5!?

25 ♘d7 ♗xd7 26 ♖xe7 ♗e6 27 ♗xd5 ♗xd5 28 ♖xd5 ♖fe8 is only a draw, so White tries to sharpen the game by sacrificing a pawn. In return for giving up the weak f-pawn, White increases the activity of his pieces.

25 ... ♘xf5

There is nothing wrong with this, but it would have been simpler to play 25...♖bc8 26 ♘xe6 fxe6 27 ♖xe6 ♖xf5 28 ♗g4 ♖f2 (28...♖f4 29 h3 ♖c7 30 ♖xa6 is slightly better for White) 29 ♖d2 (29 ♖xe7 ♖cxc2+ is perpetual check) 29...♖xd2 30 ♔xd2 ♘c6 31 ♖d6 ♖c7 with an inevitable draw.

26 ♗xd5 ♗c8!

Another good move. 26...♗xd5? loses to 27 ♖xd5 ♘g7 28 ♘d7 ♖bd8 (or 28...♖fd8 29 ♖ed1) 29 ♖dd1 ♖fe8 30 ♘f6+ winning the exchange. After 26...♖be8 27 ♗xe6 fxe6 28 ♘xa6 ♖e7 29 ♘b4 White retains an edge as the b5- and e6-pawns are both vulnerable, and Black must cope with the immediate threat of 30 ♘c6.

27 ♖e5!

A better try than 27 ♖g1+ ♔h8 28 ♗xf7 ♖b6, when Black is close to a draw. Now White threatens both 28 ♘xa6 and 28 ♖f1.

27 ... ♖b6

This final accurate defensive move should have been enough to secure a draw. Black defends the a6-pawn and prepares to activate his rook along the third rank.

28 ♖f1 ♘g7
29 ♖e7 (D)

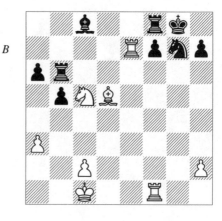

29 ... ♘e6?!

Having defended with great precision for several moves, Black makes a slip which gives White unnecessary chances. Either 29...♘f5 or 29...♗f5 would have left White with no more than a draw. The knight is poorly placed on e6 since it obstructs both the b6-rook and the c8-bishop, so White avoids exchanging it.

30   ♘e4!

This doesn't carry an immediate threat, although if Black does nothing White can step up the pressure by pushing his h-pawn. Playing 30 ♖f6?! at once is dubious because of 30...♖d6 31 ♗b3 (31 ♘xe6 ♗xe6 32 ♗xe6 fxe6 33 ♖fxe6 ♖f6 is dead drawn) 31...♔g7 32 ♘e4 (not 32 ♖fxe6? ♗xe6 33 ♘xe6+ ♔f6 34 ♘xf8 ♔xe7 35 ♘xh7 f6 with a clear advantage for Black) 32...♖d4 33 ♗xe6 ♖xe4 34 ♖fxf7+ ♖xf7 35 ♖xf7+ ♔g6 and White is certainly not better.

30   ...   ♘d8 (D)

Black decides to retreat the badly-placed knight, covering f7 and at the same time avoiding the annoying pin with ♖f6. Now Black's rook and bishop are once again free to move. The alternative 30...♔g7 31 ♖f6 is awkward for Black, who is virtually paralysed, although it must be admitted that White finds it hard to make progress. One line runs 31...a5 32 h4 h5 (32...b4 33 axb4 axb4 34 h5 ♖a6 35 h6+ ♔g8 36 ♖f2 gives White a clear advantage) 33 c3! (33 ♖f5 ♘d4 34 ♖xh5 ♗f5 doesn't offer White much) 33...b4 34 cxb4 axb4 35 a4 and White still has some advantage.

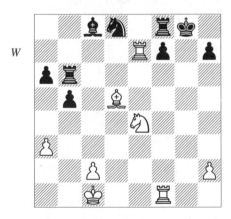

31   ♘g5

While Black has been transferring his knight from g7 to d8, White's has moved from c5 to a dangerous attacking position on g5. Black must take care.

31   ...   ♖d6?!

After this further slip Black is in real difficulties. 31...♖g6 is also dubious due to 32 h4 (32 ♘xf7 is inferior as 32...♗e6 33 ♗xe6 ♘xe6

dissipates White's pressure), but 31...♔g7! would have kept the balance.

32   ♗e4!

After 32 ♘xf7?! ♘xf7 33 ♗xf7+ ♔h8 White has regained the pawn, but given away any winning chances. It is the h-pawn White wants, as he can come back for the f-pawn later.

32   ...   ♖h6?

The danger with spending a long time on relatively insignificant nuances in the early middlegame is that later, when you face a really critical decision, you don't have enough time left to give it proper consideration. With this move Black tries to defend the h-pawn, but it turns out that White can take it in any case. 32...♖d7? is also bad since White wins by 33 ♖xd7 ♗xd7 34 ♘xh7. 32...♔g7 was still the best chance, although after 33 ♘xh7 ♔h8 34 ♖g1+ ♔h6 35 ♘g5 f6 36 ♘f3 f5 37 ♗d3 ♖g6 38 ♖ge1 White retains the advantage as Black's minor pieces are very poorly placed.

33   ♖g1   ♔h8 (D)

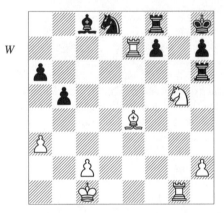

34   ♘xh7!

White makes off with an important pawn since 34...♖xh7 35 ♗xh7 ♔xh7 36 ♖e4 forces mate.

34   ...   ♘c6

Forced, since the f8-rook cannot move, but in any case Black is in a hopeless situation.

35   ♖c7   ♖d8

The only move, as 35...♖e8 loses to 36 ♖xc6 ♖xc6 37 ♗xc6 ♖e6 38 ♗e4! ♖xe4 39 ♘f6.

36   ♘g5

36 ♖xf7 is also very strong, when White is a pawn up with a good position. Black cannot reply 36...♖xh2 (36...♘e5 37 ♖e7 does not help

Black) because of 37 ♘f8 ♘d4 38 ♘g6+ ♔g8 39 ♘e5+ ♔h8 40 ♖gg7 and White has a decisive attack.

36   ...   ♘e5

Again forced.

37   ♖xf7

An unpleasant move to meet in time-trouble. White threatens the decisive 38 ♖e7.

37   ...   ♖e8

There is no hope of saving the game; for example, 37...♘c4 38 ♖c7 ♘d6 39 ♖d1 with crushing pressure.

38   ♖c7   ♖xh2 (D)

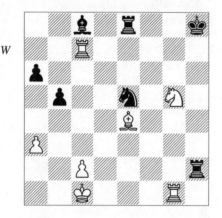

Grabbing this pawn should lead to tactical disaster, but if White is allowed to play h3 then he keeps an extra pawn in addition to all his other advantages.

39   ♖c5!

A difficult move to spot, as it is counter-intuitive to remove the rook from the seventh rank. However, Black has no reasonable reply to the threat of 40 ♖xe5 ♖xe5 41 ♘f7#.

39   ...   ♖f2

Forced, as everything else loses material immediately.

40   ♘f3?

With Black having only seconds left on his clock, White makes an unfortunate error. Had Black found the right reply then at the very least this move would have made the win far more difficult. 40 ♗c6! would have been decisive:

1) 40...♘xc6 41 ♖xc6 ♖h2 42 ♘f7+ ♔h7 43 ♖c7 wins at least a piece.

2) 40...♗d7 41 ♗xd7 ♘xd7 42 ♖c3 ♖ee2 43 ♘e6 ♖g2 44 ♖c8+ ♔h7 45 ♖h1+ ♖h2 46 ♖xh2+ ♖xh2 47 ♖c7 picks up the knight.

3) 40...♖e7 41 ♖h1+ ♔g7 42 ♖h7+ ♔f8 (42...♔f6 43 ♘e4+) 43 ♖xe7 and again White wins a piece.

1-0

Black lost on time while in the act of playing 40...♘g4?. After this move White can win a piece with a series of checks: 41 ♖h1+ ♔g7 42 ♖g5+ ♔f6 (42...♔f7 43 ♖h7+ is the same) 43 ♖g6+ ♔e7 44 ♖h7+ ♔f8 45 ♖h8+ ♔e7 46 ♖xe8+ ♔xe8 47 ♖g8+ and Black loses one of his minor pieces.

Black should have played 40...♗f5!, a move which provides a surprisingly resilient defence. Only deep analysis can determine if White can still win: 41 ♗c6 ♘xf3 (41...♖xc2+ 42 ♖xc2 ♗xc2 43 ♖h1+ ♗h7 44 ♗xe8 ♘xf3 45 ♗g6 ♘g5 46 ♗xh7 ♘xh7 47 ♖h6 a5 48 ♖h5 b4 49 a4 and White wins easily) 42 ♖h1+ and now:

1) 42...♔g7 43 ♗xe8 ♘d4 44 ♖c7+! ♔f6 (44...♔g8 45 ♗f7+ ♔g7 46 ♗e6+ ♔f6 47 ♗xf5 and White wins) 45 ♖h6+ ♔g5 46 ♖xa6 ♗xc2 47 ♗xb5 and, although it won't be easy, White should win in the end.

2) 42...♔g8 (D) puts up more of a fight.

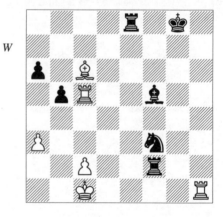

2a) 43 ♖xf5 ♖e3 leaves Black in a very awkward pin, but it is hard for White to make progress:

2a1) 44 ♖f4 ♖h2 (44...♖xa3 45 ♗d5+ ♔g7 46 ♖f7+ ♔g6 47 ♖h8 ♖e3 48 ♖g8+ ♔h6 49 ♖f6+ ♔h7 50 ♖gf8 and White wins) 45 ♗xf3 (45 ♖g4+ ♔f7 46 ♖xh2 ♘xh2 47 ♖h4 ♖e2 48 ♗b7 a5 49 ♗a6 ♖g2 50 ♗xb5 ♘g4 51 ♔b2 is certainly better for White, but unlikely to be a win) 45...♖xh1+ 46 ♗xh1 ♖e1+ 47 ♔b2 ♖xh1 48 ♖f6 ♖h4! 49 ♖xa6 ♔f7 50 ♖b6 ♔e7 51

♖xb5 ♔d7 and Black can draw according to the ♖+2♙ vs ♖ database.

2a2) 44 ♗d5+ ♔g7 45 ♖f7+ ♔g6 46 ♖h8 ♖f1+ 47 ♔b2 ♘d2 48 ♖g8+ ♔h6 49 ♖xf1 ♘xf1 50 ♖a8 ♖e5 51 ♖xa6+ ♔g5 52 ♗c6 ♘e3 and here White has fair winning chances since the b5-pawn is weak and Black's king is still quite far away. However, there seems to be no way to win the b5-pawn by force so it is impossible to claim a definite win.

2b) 43 ♗xe8 ♘d4 44 ♖d1! (this forcing continuation seems best) 44...♖xc2+ 45 ♖xc2 ♘xc2 *(D)* and now White faces a tough choice:

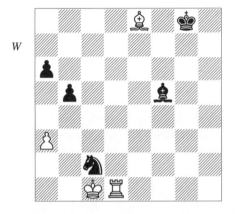

W

2b1) 46 ♖d5 and then:

2b11) 46...♗e4 47 ♗c6. This looks like the end for Black, as White emerges a piece up (and has the right bishop for the a-pawn), but there is a positional draw danger which White must take into account. In order to understand this ending we need to look at the following position first.

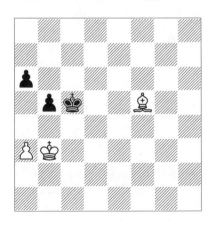

White to play wins, Black to play draws

Taking the Black-to-play case first, he can draw by 1...a5! (the only drawing move) 2 ♗g4 ♔d4 3 ♗d7 b4 4 a4 ♔c5 (this is a positional draw; White can only try to win by outflanking the black king, but as soon as White's king is far enough away, Black can draw by pushing his b-pawn) 5 ♗e6 ♔d4 6 ♔c2 ♔e3 7 ♗b3 ♔d4 8 ♔d2 ♔e4 9 ♗c2+ ♔d4 10 ♗d3 ♔c5 11 ♗f1 (11 ♔e3 b3 draws) 11...♔d4 and White cannot make progress.

When White is to play, he wins by keeping Black's king away from d4: 1 ♔c3 a5 2 ♔d3 b4 (2...♔d5 3 ♗d7 ♔c5 4 ♗e8 is similar) 3 a4 ♔d5 4 ♗g6 ♔c5 5 ♗f7 and Black's king has to retreat, after which White wins the enemy pawns.

This analysis makes the situation clear: Black draws if he can get his king to d4, but otherwise he loses.

Returning to the position after 47 ♗c6, we can now deduce that White wins after 47...♗xd5 (or 47...♔f7 48 ♖d7+ ♔e8 49 ♗xe4 ♔xd7 50 ♔xc2 ♔d6 51 ♔d3, which also wins for White) 48 ♗xd5+ ♔f8 (after 48...♔g7 49 ♔xc2 ♔f6 50 ♔d3 White covers d4 and wins) 49 ♔xc2 ♔e7 50 ♔d3 and again Black is too slow.

2b12) 46...♗h7! (an amazing move; after it I don't see a clear win) 47 ♔b2 (47 ♖d8 ♘xa3 48 ♗xb5+ ♔f7 49 ♗xa6 ♔e6 draws according to the 6-man tablebases) 47...♔f8 48 ♗h5 and while White still has good practical winning chances, again it is hard to claim a forced win.

2b2) 46 ♖d8! *(D)* is a subtle finesse leading to a forced win:

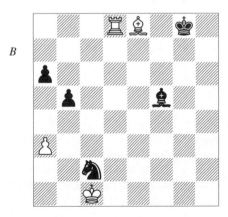

B

46...♔g7 (46...♔f8 47 ♗g6+ ♔e7 48 ♖e8+ ♔d7 49 ♗xf5+ ♔xe8 50 ♔xc2 wins easily) 47

♖d5 (now that the king is on g7, Black cannot play ...♗h7 due to ♖d7+ and ♖xh7, and so his bishop runs out of squares) 47...♗e4 (47...♔f6 48 ♖xf5+ ♔xf5 49 ♔xc2 and White wins) 48 ♖e5 ♗d3 49 ♔d2 and the diagonal proves too short for the bishop.

My chess activity was significantly reduced in 1996 and indeed I did not participate in a single international tournament (if one does not count the first half of the 1996/7 Hastings tournament). However, I did take part in some weekend tournaments, which I could more easily reconcile with a busy program of typesetting work. The first of these was at Hastings and was played just after the main tournament (in which I did not participate); I scored 4½/6. In February, Petra and I travelled to Bunratty in Ireland for a pleasant weekend event which I have since attended fairly regularly. On this occasion I scored 5½/6 and tied for first place with Daniel King. In March I played in an event in London, tying for first place with Julian Hodgson on 4½/5.

It is of course less likely that a really good game will be played in a weekend event. The variable quality of opposition, the fast time-limit and the fact that you may have to play three games in a day all reduce the chance of producing anything worthwhile. However, sometimes everything goes right and a genuinely interesting game is the result. The following game, played in a weekend tournament in London during June, is a case in point.

This is another complex Najdorf struggle. Early on, Black makes a positional sacrifice of a piece for two pawns. In doing so, he breaks up White's kingside pawn-mass and activates his bishops. At first, Black's compensation hardly looks adequate, but in situations with opposite-side castling, defusing or at least delaying the enemy attack may offer good value for a material investment. Analysis shows the position to be roughly balanced, but in such a double-edged position every tempo counts and there is no such thing as a 'small' mistake. On move 20 Black lost a vital tempo and, thanks to a spectacular move clearing the first rank, White's attack struck first.

Game 26

J. Nunn – B. Lalić

London 1996

Sicilian Defence, Najdorf Variation

1	e4	c5
2	♘f3	d6
3	d4	♘f6
4	♘c3	cxd4
5	♘xd4	a6
6	♗g5	e6
7	f4	♗e7
8	♕f3	♕c7
9	0-0-0	♘bd7
10	g4	b5 (D)

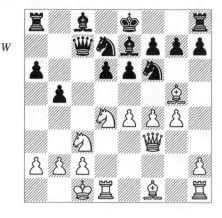

W

A familiar position in the Najdorf. In the late 1950s and 1960s, this position was one of the key battlegrounds of the Najdorf and featured in several important Fischer games. It arises less often these days because attention has switched to other white 6th moves, but the complexities of the position have never been fully resolved.

11   a3!?

Although this was not a rapid game, it was played in a weekend open tournament with a relatively fast time-limit, and in such a situation it is usually a good idea to play something a bit unexpected in the opening. The standard line is

11 ♗xf6 ♘xf6 12 g5 ♘d7 13 f5 (see Game 41 for more about this continuation), reaching a position which theory has investigated very deeply. The idea behind 11 a3 is to play 12 ♗xf6 ♘xf6 13 f5, putting immediate pressure on the e6-pawn. Then Black will be unable to meet a later g5 with ...♘d7 because this would lose the e6-pawn. For this plan to work, White needs a couple of moves of peace and quiet, hence the move a3, temporarily holding Black up on the queenside. The position White is aiming for is that arising after White's 13th move in the game, but there are two ways White can head for this; the first, as played here, is 11 a3 ♖b8 12 ♗xf6 ♘xf6 13 f5 and the second is 11 ♗xf6 ♘xf6 12 a3 ♖b8 13 f5. The defect of the first move-order is that Black may play 12...gxf6 (see the note to Black's 12th move in the game) and the rather more serious defect of the second is that Black may play 12...♘d7, which effectively nullifies White's whole plan because he does not now pin the knight down to f6. In fact, White has nothing better than 13 g5, transposing to a well-known line which is believed to be safe for Black. The move-order problem is already sufficient reason to dismiss this continuation for White, at least from the theoretical point of view, but it turns out that even if White reaches his target position he cannot hope for an advantage against accurate play. However, as we have noted several times in this book, unexpected opening ideas work relatively often even if their objective merits are rather doubtful; the pressure of finding the right reply over the board is often too great a task at tournament time-limits.

Now we return to 11 a3 *(D)*:

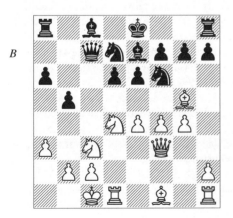

11 ... ♖b8

11...♗b7 is also played frequently. However, this appears less logical to me since the idea of ...♖b8 and ...b4 is surely the natural way to exploit White's a3. The best reply to 11...♗b7 is probably 12 h4, posing the problem of what Black is going to do with his king.

12 ♗xf6 ♘xf6 *(D)*

As noted above, with the move-order White employs in this game Black has the option of playing 12...gxf6. This reaches the standard position arising after 11 ♗xf6 gxf6, but with the moves a3 and ...♖b8 added. These additional moves operate in Black's favour. In the standard line, White's main plan is to increase the pressure on the sensitive e6-point by f5 and ♘ce2-f4. This takes quite a few moves, but during this period Black is unable to generate much queenside counterplay. However, the added a3 and ...♖b8 make a big difference because Black can immediately generate play with ...b4, and so White doesn't have enough time for his usual quiet manoeuvring. After 13 f5 ♘e5 14 ♕h3, Black has a choice. He can play the standard 14...0-0 with an improved version of the normal lines, or he can try the immediate 14...b4, when a draw by repetition might easily result after 15 axb4 ♖xb4 16 fxe6 fxe6 17 g5 ♕a5 18 ♘b3 ♕c7 19 ♘d4, etc. At any rate it does not seem that Black can be worse after 12...gxf6.

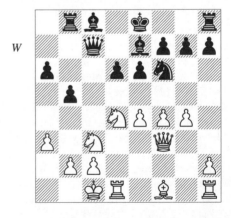

13 f5

Now White has reached his target position. Even this is insufficient for an advantage against accurate play by Black, but the position is rather complicated and there are many possibilities to go wrong.

13 ... e5

The main line and Black's soundest move. The alternative 13...0-0!? (13...b4 14 axb4 ♖xb4 15 g5 is awkward for Black) looks risky but is not necessarily bad. After 14 g5 Black can play:

1) 14...♘d7 15 f6 leads to an unclear position after both 15...♗d8 and 15...gxf6 16 gxf6 ♘xf6 17 e5 dxe5 18 ♘c6 ♔h8 19 ♘xb8 ♕xb8, the latter being Kavalek-Donner, Wijk aan Zee 1969.

2) 14...♘e8 15 ♖g1 b4 16 axb4 ♖xb4 17 ♖g3 looks dangerous for Black but is not really clear after 17...♕c5 18 ♘b3 ♕e5.

14 ♘de2 (D)

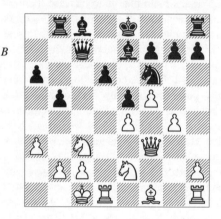

White's plan is obvious: to play g5 and seize control of d5.

14 ... ♗b7

This looks like a natural move because it contests control of d5, but it blocks the b-file and deprives Black of the possibility of ...b4. The critical alternative continuation is 14...b4 15 axb4 ♖xb4 16 g5 ♘xe4 17 ♘xe4 ♗b7 18 ♘2c3 (the interesting 18 ♘2g3!?, leading to a very unclear position, was tried in J.Howell-Mai, Hamburg 1995; the idea is that White leaves the third rank clear so as to use the queen for the defence of the queenside) 18...♗xg5+ 19 ♔b1 and now:

1) 19...♕b6 20 ♗b5+ (the line 20 b3 ♖xb3+ 21 cxb3 ♕xb3+ 22 ♔a1 ♗xe4 23 ♕xe4 ♕c3+ 24 ♔a2 0-0 is dangerous only for White, while 20 ♕d3 ♖xb2+ 21 ♔a1 0-0 22 ♕xd6 ♕xd6 23 ♘xd6 ♖xc2 is also fine for Black) 20...axb5 21 ♘xd6+ (21 ♘d5 ♗xd5 22 ♖xd5 ♖a4 is unclear) 21...♕xd6 22 ♕xb7 ♖xb2+ with perpetual check, Luk-Yuey, IECC e-mail 1998.

2) 19...0-0 20 ♖g1 (D) and now:

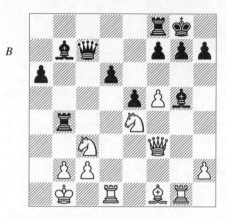

2a) 20...♖xb2+? 21 ♔xb2 ♕b6+ fails to 22 ♗b5.

2b) 20...♕b6? 21 ♖xg5 ♗xe4 22 ♘xe4 ♖xb2+ 23 ♔c1 and Black's attack is inadequate.

2c) 20...♖b8?! 21 b3 ♕b6 22 ♗c4! (22 ♗b5 h6 23 h4 ♗xh4 is roughly equal) 22...♖xc4 23 ♖xg5 ♖xc3 24 ♘f6+ ♔h8 25 ♕xc3 gxf6 26 ♖g4 is excellent for White.

2d) 20...♖c8! 21 ♕d3 ♖xb2+! (21...♕b6? 22 ♕xd6 ♖xb2+ 23 ♔a1 ♗e3? 24 ♖xg7+ ♔xg7 25 ♕xe5+ ♔f8 26 ♖d7 1-0 Pioch-Podzielny, corr. 1984) 22 ♔xb2 ♕b6+ 23 ♔a2 (23 ♘b5 ♗xe4 24 ♕xe4 ♕xg1 gives Black good play for the piece) 23...♕a5+ with perpetual check.

However, finding one's way through all this at a fast time-limit is very tricky. The move played is about equally good and gives Black sufficient compensation for the piece he is about to sacrifice.

15 g5 (D)

I think this is the most accurate continuation. The alternative 15 ♘g3 has been played a few times, and now:

1) 15...♗a8? 16 g5 ♘d7 17 f6 gxf6 18 ♘h5 was very good for White in Botterill-Mecking, Hastings 1971/2.

2) 15...d5!? 16 ♘xd5 (16 g5 ♘xe4 seems fine for Black) 16...♘xd5 17 exd5 0-0 18 ♘e4 ♖fd8 19 f6 ♗xf6 20 ♘xf6+ gxf6 21 ♕xf6 ♗xd5 and White probably has nothing better than perpetual check.

3) 15...♖c8 16 ♗d3 (16 g5 ♘xe4 17 ♘gxe4 d5 18 f6 dxe4 19 fxg7 ♖g8 looks roughly equal) 16...♘d7 is unclear.

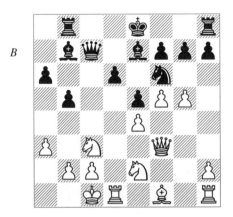

B

15   ...   ♘xe4!

Black is effectively committed to this sacrifice as the passive 15...♘d7 16 h4 ♕a5 17 ♘d5 ♗xd5 18 ♖xd5 gave White a safe positional advantage in Mrdja-Schumi, Verona 1998.

16   ♘xe4   d5

After 16...♖c8?! 17 c3 (17 ♕d3?? ♕xc2+ 18 ♕xc2 ♖xc2+ 19 ♔xc2 ♗xe4+ wins for Black) 17...d5 18 ♘f2 ♗xg5+ 19 ♔b1 0-0 20 ♖g1 Black does not have enough for the piece.

17   ♘4c3   d4

17...♗xg5+ 18 ♔b1 ♖c8 19 ♗g2 is bad for Black, as his d-pawn is now pinned.

18   ♘e4

White has lost some time moving his knight backwards and forwards, but Black is unable to make any immediate impression on White's relatively solid position.

18   ...   ♗xg5+
19   ♔b1   0-0 (D)

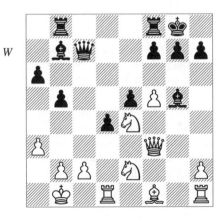

W

Now we can pause to assess the position. Black has two pawns for the piece and White is stuck in an awkward pin on the long diagonal. Black also has an active dark-squared bishop which might, for example, settle on e3. However, other factors work against Black. The open g-file means that White still has some attacking chances on the kingside, while Black is still a few moves away from creating a serious threat on the queenside. The key point is that White cannot simply rely on his slight material advantage to win the game. The formation of pawn on d4 and bishop on e3 will cut White's position in half, and an eventual breakthrough by ...b4 will be very strong because White will have trouble feeding pieces to the queenside. White has two possible plans: he can give priority to defending the queenside, or he can pursue an attack on the kingside.

20   ♘2g3 (D)

The e2-knight should move so as to defend c2 with ♗d3, but which way should it go? It is hard to decide which plan to adopt as Black obtains attacking chances after either continuation. 20 ♘c1 is met by 20...♖fc8 21 ♗d3 b4 (21...♗xc1 is inaccurate because after 22 ♔xc1 White can run with his king towards the kingside) 22 axb4 ♗xe4 23 ♗xe4 ♖xb4 and Black has sufficient play for the piece. One line is 24 ♘b3?! a5 25 ♖hg1 ♗f6 and now White is even in difficulties.

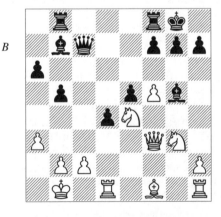

B

White therefore prefers to play his knight to the kingside to augment his attacking chances there.

20   ...   ♔h8?

Up to here both sides have played accurately and the position is roughly balanced. However, Black suddenly becomes nervous about the open g-file and wastes a tempo moving his king to a position in which it is no safer than it was on g8. This position is not one in which a tempo can be lightly thrown away and White now seizes the initiative. 20...♖fc8 21 ♗d3 b4! (D) was the correct continuation:

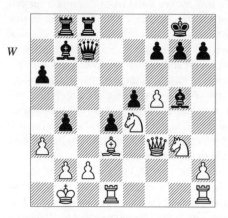

1) 22 a4 b3 23 cxb3 ♕b6 24 ♗c2 ♗e3 25 ♕e2 ♗d5 gives Black enough play for the piece.

2) 22 axb4 ♗xe4 23 ♘xe4 ♖xb4 24 b3 ♗e3 (24...♕b6 25 ♕g2 ♗e3 is also unclear) 25 f6 g6 and now:

2a) 26 h4 ♖cb8! 27 ♔b2 (27 ♖h2? ♖a4! wins for Black) 27...♕b6 28 ♔a1 a5 with a very dangerous attack for Black.

2b) 26 ♖he1 ♕b6 27 ♔a1 ♖b8 28 ♕h3 ♕a5+ 29 ♔b2 ♕d5! favours Black.

3) 22 ♕g4 with three options:

3a) 22...f6 23 ♘xg5 bxa3 (23...fxg5 24 f6! gxf6 25 ♖hf1 favours White) 24 ♘e6 ♗f3 25 ♘xc7 ♗xg4 26 ♘e6 ♖xb2+ 27 ♔a1 gives White a clear advantage.

3b) 22...♗h6 23 f6 ♗xe4 24 ♕xe4 g6 25 ♘f5 bxa3 26 ♘xh6+ ♔f8 27 ♔c1 (27 ♕d5 ♖b5 28 ♕xf7+ ♕xf7 29 ♘xf7 ♖xb2+ 30 ♔a1 ♔xf7 is a likely draw) 27...axb2+ 28 ♔d2 a5 29 h4 a4 30 h5 and White's attack is likely to be stronger than Black's queenside advance.

3c) 22...♗e3! is unclear; one line runs 23 ♘h5 f6 24 ♘hxf6+ ♔h8 25 ♘xh7 ♗xe4 and Black is at least equal.

In a way it is a little surprising that Black has such good compensation for the piece, but his slow-burning queenside attack is genuinely dangerous when it finally arrives.

Now we return to 20...♔h8? (D):

21   h4!

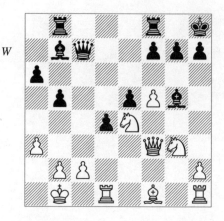

White at once hits on the weakness of Black's previous move. When White plays f6 Black has to reply ...g6, which gives White the possibility of opening up the h-file by pushing his h-pawn.

21   ...   ♗e3

21...♗f4 is the alternative, and this also requires accurate play by White in order to break through:

1) 22 ♘h5? ♗e3 (22...♗xe4 23 ♕xe4 ♗e3 24 ♖h3 ♖fc8 25 ♗d3 b4 26 ♖xe3 dxe3 27 axb4 is clearly better for White) 23 ♘xg7 b4! 24 axb4 ♗xe4 25 ♕xe4 ♖xb4 and Black's attack is stronger.

2) 22 f6 g6 23 ♗d3 (23 h5? drops a piece to 23...♗xg3) 23...b4 24 h5 bxa3 25 hxg6 fxg6 26 ♖xh7+! (the same basic theme as in the game) 26...♖xh7 (26...♔xh7 27 ♖h1+ ♔g8 28 ♕g4 ♗xe4 29 ♘xe4 ♖xb2+ 30 ♔a1 wins for White) 27 ♖h1 ♗h6 (after 27...♗xe4 28 ♖xh7+ ♔xh7 29 ♘xe4 White has a decisive attack) 28 b3 and, despite Black's extra material, he has no reasonable defence to the threats of 29 ♖h2 (followed by ♕h1) and 29 ♕g4 (followed by ♘g5); for example, 28...♗d5 29 ♕g4 ♖b7 30 ♘g5 ♗xh1 31 ♘xh7 ♖xh7 32 ♕xg6 e4 33 ♘xe4 and White wins.

22   f6   g6
23   h5

White's attack arrives more quickly than in the note to Black's 20th move and this extra time makes a huge difference.

23   ...   b4
24   hxg6   fxg6 (D)

The critical moment. White has made some progress on the kingside, but it is still hard to see how to break through. Meanwhile, Black is

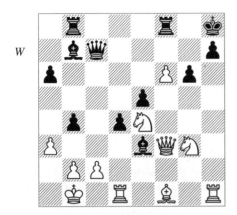

W

ready with his own threats on the other side of the board.

25 ♗c4!!

This spectacular move is the solution. Other moves allow Black to develop his queenside threats much as in the note to Black's 20th move. On c4, the bishop cuts off the escape-route of Black's king and threatens the deadly 26 f7, so Black has no time to push forward on the queenside. Moreover, in some lines the bishop can drop back to b3 to block the b-file. The final point is that White opens the first rank and so allows the d1-rook to move to h1 (after a sacrifice on h7).

25 ... ♗f4

There are several possibilities, but Black cannot save the game:

1) 25...♕xc4 26 ♖xh7+! ♔xh7 27 ♖h1+ ♔g8 28 ♕g4 ♗xe4 29 ♘xe4 ♖xf6 (29...♔f7 30 ♖h7+ ♔e8 31 ♕d7#) 30 ♘xf6+ ♔g7 (30...♔f7 31 ♘d7! wins for White) 31 ♘h5+ ♔f8 32 ♕xg6 and Black cannot defend.

2) 25...bxa3 26 f7 ♗f4 (26...♕b6 27 b3 doesn't help Black, while after 26...♕e7 27 ♘f5! gxf5 28 ♕h5 h6 29 ♖dg1 there is no defence to the threat of 30 ♕xh6+) 27 ♖xh7+ ♔xh7 28 ♖h1+ ♔g7 29 ♘f5+ gxf5 30 ♕g2+ leads to mate.

3) 25...♗xe4 26 ♘xe4 bxa3 (White also wins after the alternative 26...♕xc4 27 ♖xh7+ ♔xh7 28 ♖h1+ ♔g8 29 ♕h3 ♖b7 30 ♘d6) 27 f7 and now:

3a) 27...♗f4 28 ♖xh7+ ♔xh7 29 ♖h1+ ♔g7 30 ♕h3 ♖h8 31 ♕xh8+ ♖xh8 32 ♖xh8 ♕xf7 33 ♗xf7 ♔xh8 34 ♗xg6 and Black cannot save the ending because his pawns are firmly blockaded.

3b) 27...♖xb2+ 28 ♔a1 ♖b6 29 ♖xh7+ (29 ♗e6 also wins) 29...♔xh7 30 ♖h1+ ♔g7 31 ♕h3 ♖b1+ 32 ♔xb1 transposes to line '3c'.

3c) 27...♖b6 28 ♖xh7+ ♔xh7 29 ♕h3+ ♔g7 30 ♖h1 ♖xb2+ 31 ♔a1 ♖b1+ 32 ♔xb1 ♕b7+ 33 ♗b3 ♖xe4 34 ♕h8+ ♖xh8 35 ♖xh8 ♕f3 36 ♖g8+ ♔h6 37 f8♕+ ♕xf8 38 ♖xf8 wins for White as the four pawns are no match for the rook.

26 ♖xh7+!

Another shattering blow. This rook sacrifice gives White a decisive attack. The next few moves are forced.

26 ... ♕xh7
27 ♖h1 ♗h6
28 f7

Threatening 29 ♕f6+ followed by mate. The reply is forced.

28 ... ♕g7
29 ♖h2

White intends to play ♕h1, breaking through on h6. 29 ♕g4, threatening 30 ♕g5, is equally good.

29 ... ♗xe4

Forced, as Black's only hope is to defend the h6-bishop with his rook from b6.

30 ♘xe4 g5

If 30...♖b6, then 31 ♘g5 blocks the g-pawn, whereupon there is no way for Black to prevent 32 ♕h1.

31 ♘d6 (D)

By now there are several routes to victory. 31 ♕h1 ♖b6 32 ♘c5, followed by ♘d7, is perhaps even simpler.

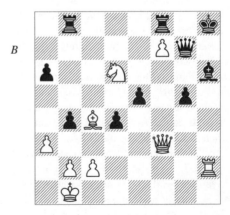

B

The move played renews the threat of 32 ♕h1, so again Black has no choice.

31	...	♖b6
32	♘f5	g4

White also wins after 32...♖xf7 33 ♗xf7 ♕xf7 34 ♕a8+ ♔h7 35 ♕e4 and 32...♖f6 33 ♕h1 ♔h7 34 ♗d3.

33	♕g3	♕g5
34	♕xe5+	♔h7
35	♗d3	1-0

After 35...♖g6 36 ♖xh6+ ♖xh6 37 ♘e7+ ♖g6 38 ♕xg5 White mates quickly.

I started with four wins and drew in the last round with Mickey Adams. My total of 4½/5 was enough to tie for first place with Mickey and Aaron Summerscale. After this I played no chess at all for four months, until it was time for the Bundesliga season to start again. My very first game of the season provided a good win.

In the Deferred Steinitz Variation of the Ruy Lopez with 5 ♗xc6+ bxc6 6 d4, Black's strategy revolves around supporting the e5-square (which is often occupied by a black pawn). Black usually leaves his king in the centre for some time. Securing the key e5-square provides Black's position with a firm foundation to resist White's attacking attempts but conversely, if White can undermine Black's control then he will suffer from his centralized king. The following game revolves around the battle for the e5-square. Black made a slip at move 13 which gave White the chance to focus his attacking efforts against e5. Every time Black brought a piece to support e5, White exchanged it off. Eventually White won the battle for e5, and his attack crashed through.

Game 27

J. Nunn – R. Slobodjan

Bundesliga 1996/7

Ruy Lopez (Spanish), Deferred Steinitz Variation

1	e4	e5
2	♘f3	♘c6
3	♗b5	a6
4	♗a4	d6

The Deferred Steinitz Variation of the Ruy Lopez has a reputation as a solid but slightly passive line.

5 ♗xc6+

The main continuations are 5 0-0 and 5 c3, but the move played is also quite popular. Objectively speaking, I must admit that White has fewer chances for the advantage after 5 ♗xc6+ than in the two main lines, but it can be very effective if Black is not completely sure of the theory. Taking on c6 apparently loses a tempo compared to the standard Exchange Variation (4 ♗xc6), because White has played ♗a4 and only then ♗xc6+, but the extra move ...d6 has the defect that Black must now recapture with the b-pawn. This is in contrast to 4 ♗xc6, when Black replies 4...dxc6. 'Capture towards the centre' is usually good advice, but 4...dxc6 is usually preferred since it frees Black's bishop and makes his development easier (similar reasoning applies in the line 1 e4 c5 2 ♘f3 ♘c6 3

♗b5 g6 4 ♗xc6, when Black usually plays 4...dxc6).

5	...	bxc6
6	d4	

The rapid attack on e5 forces Black either to exchange on d4, which is a slight concession, or to support the centre by ...f6, which is solid but leaves Black lagging in development.

6	...	f6 *(D)*

After 6...exd4 White can recapture with either queen or knight, keeping an edge in either case.

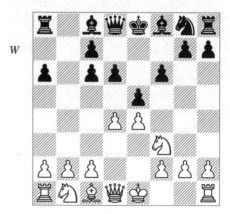

7   ᄊc3

Some players believe that it is important to prevent the manoeuvre ...g6 and ...ᄊh6-f7, which routes the knight to a square supporting Black's central strongpoint on e5, but others hold that it doesn't make much difference. Playing the knight to f7 takes an extra move compared to ...ᄊe7, but the knight is more comfortably placed on f7, where it does not obstruct Black's other pieces. In this game White gives Black the chance to play his knight to f7, but Black avoids this option and play immediately returns to normal lines.

7   ...   ᄊe7

After 7...g6 8 ₩d3 (if Black is allowed to complete his development in peace, then he can count the ...g6 plan a success) 8...ዿg7 9 ዿe3 ᄊh6 10 ₩c4!? the position is unclear.

8   ዿe3   ᄊg6 (D)

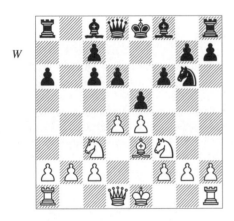

9   ₩e2

The main decision for White in this line is where to put his queen, since 9 ₩e2, 9 ₩d2 and 9 ₩d3 are all possible. Moreover, White may play h4 at virtually any moment, to which Black usually replies ...h5. The merits of the various queen moves are still being debated by theory, but I prefer 9 ₩e2. White will castle queenside, and this move clears the d-file for the action of his rook. Moreover, in some lines the white queen can emerge to c4 (possibly to prevent castling by Black).

9   ...   ዿe6

It doesn't matter whether Black plays ...ዿe6 or ...ዿe7 first, since both moves will probably be played within the next few moves and then the lines transpose. The long-term prospects in

this position tend to favour Black, who has the two bishops and a solid central pawn-mass. Therefore White must try to achieve something relatively quickly.

10   0-0-0   ዿe7
11   h4

The point of this move is to induce the reply ...h5. Then, after dxe5, Black will have an awkward choice as to whether to play ...ᄊxe5, when White has ᄊd4, possibly followed by f4, or ...fxe5, when White gains an outpost on g5.

11   ...   h5

An automatic response by Black, who cannot afford to allow h5 by White. Then ...ᄊf4 would be too risky, as after the exchange on f4 the f4-pawn would be too weak, while retreating with ...ᄊf8 looks very passive.

12   dxe5

White continues with his plan to secure g5.

12   ...   fxe5

12...ᄊxe5 13 ᄊd4 ዿc4 14 ₩e1 is slightly better for White.

13   ᄊg5 (D)

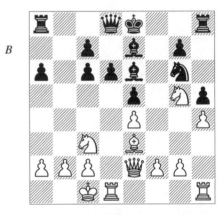

Now Black faces a key decision. Should he exchange White's knight?

13   ...   ዿg8?!

Up to here Black has played accurately, but I think this move is dubious. The knight is very strong on g5 and, although it creates no immediate threats, it exerts annoying pressure on Black's position. In particular, while the knight stays on g5, Black's h8-rook will remain imprisoned. In this game Black tries to ignore the knight and play with the two bishops, but his congested kingside and somewhat exposed king prove more important factors. After 13...ዿxg5

Black has every chance of equality; for example, 14 ♗xg5 ♕b8 15 g3 ♔d7 or 14 hxg5 h4 15 g3 hxg3 16 ♖xh8+ ♘xh8 17 ♕h5+ ♔d7 18 f4 exf4 19 ♗xf4 ♕e8 and in neither case can White prove an advantage.

14   g3

The strongest move. After f4 Black will have to worry about both f5 and fxe5. In the latter case the open f-file might lead to threats against the black king.

14   ...   ♗f6 (D)

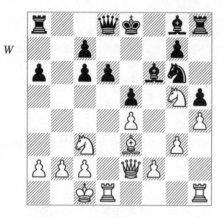

W

By positioning his bishop on the long diagonal, Black hopes to dissuade White from f4.

15   ♔b1

White decides to improve his position before playing f4, but in the two other games which have reached this position, White decided to strike immediately with 15 f4. Then:

1) 15...♕c8 16 f5 ♘f8 17 g4 hxg4 18 ♕xg4 ♖b8 19 h5 ♕b7 20 b3 ♕b4 21 ♗d2 was clearly better for White in F.Cuijpers-Kerkhoff, Netherlands Team Ch 1996/7.

2) 15...♕b8 16 ♘f3 ♕b4 17 a3 ♕c4 18 ♖d3 a5 19 ♕f2 ♖b8 20 fxe5 ♘xe5 21 ♘xe5 ♗xe5 22 ♗d4 (White adopts a strategy similar to that in the main game; by undermining Black's blockade on e5, White opens lines towards the enemy king) 22...♗xd4 23 ♖xd4 ♕c5 24 e5 and White has a dangerous initiative, Poluliakhov-Yandemirov, USSR Team Ch, Podolsk 1990.

3) 15...exf4 (this move was the reason I avoided 15 f4 in the game) 16 e5!? (16 gxf4 ♗xc3 17 bxc3 ♗xa2 is of course dangerous for Black, but I didn't see anything especially clear for White) and now:

3a) 16...♗xg5 17 exd6 cxd6 (17...fxe3 18 d7+ ♔f8 19 hxg5 ♗f7 20 ♖hf1 ♕e7 21 ♕d3 gives White a dangerous attack, while after 17...f3 18 ♕xf3 ♘e5 19 d7+ ♕xd7 20 ♕e4 ♗xe3+ 21 ♕xe3 ♕e6 22 ♖he1 White regains the piece with the better ending) 18 ♗xf4+ ♕e7 (18...♗e7 loses to 19 ♖xd6) 19 ♕g2! (after 19 ♗xg5 ♕xe2 20 ♘xe2 ♔d7 21 ♘f4 ♘xf4 22 ♗xf4 d5 23 ♗e5 ♖h6 24 ♗xg7 White is unlikely to win) 19...♗xf4+ 20 gxf4 0-0-0 (White wins after 20...♔f7 21 ♖hg1) 21 ♕xg6 ♕e3+ 22 ♔b1 ♕xf4 23 ♖he1 and White has excellent play for the pawn.

3b) 16...fxe3!? 17 exf6 gxf6 18 ♘ge4 (18 ♘f3 ♕e7 19 ♖de1 ♘e5 20 ♕xe3 is unclear) 18...f5 19 ♘g5 ♕e7 20 ♖hf1 gives White a considerable initiative, but Black is two pawns up.

I saw the 15 f4 and 16 e5 idea during the game, but after considering it for some time, I decided it was too risky and unclear, especially as White has a perfectly satisfactory alternative which involves no risk.

15   ...   ♕c8?! (D)

This is inaccurate, because it allows White to remove his knight from the vulnerable c3-square and then play f4. 15...♕b8 is better, since then White's play develops far more slowly: 16 ♔a1 (16 ♘a4 can be met by 16...♕b5, while 16 ♕d3 ♕b4 17 a3 ♕c4 is close to equality) 16...♕b4 17 a3 ♕b7 18 ♕d3 ♖b8 19 ♖b1 and only now is White ready to play f4.

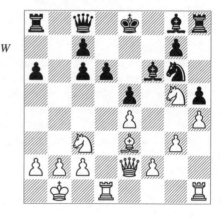

W

16   ♘a4!

A very strong move. White simply removes his knight from the potential attack of the f6-bishop and is ready for a quick f4.

16   ...   ♕b7

Threatening ...♕b5.

17   b3   ♘e7

With the knight on a4 blocking the ...a5-a4 plan, Black's main source of queenside play is the advance ...c5-c4. However, White has prepared to meet ...c5 by c4, nullifying Black's potential play. In anticipation of this, Black prepares to meet White's c4 with ...♘c6-d4, occupying the weakened d4-square.

Other ideas:

1) 17...♕b5 18 c4 ♕b4 19 f4 ♖b8 20 ♘b2 favours White as Black doesn't have any real queenside play, while White is making progress in the centre.

2) 17...c5 18 c4 ♘e7 19 ♕d3 makes life awkward for Black, since now 19...♘c6 fails to 20 ♘xc5. Therefore, Black would have to play 19...♕c8 first. However, even in this case White maintains some advantage by 20 f4 ♘c6 21 ♘c3 ♘d4 22 fxe5 ♗xe5 23 ♖hf1.

18   f4

Black's ...♘e7 has weakened his control of e5, so now White switches plans and launches a direct assault on the e5-square.

18   ...   c5 (D)

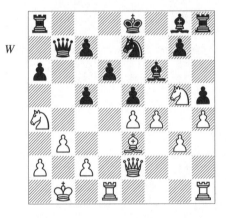

19   fxe5

White's plan is very simple – every time a black piece appears on e5, White will swap it off. If, as seems likely, Black ends up having to play ...dxe5, then there will be open d- and f-files pointing at Black's king.

19   ...   ♗xe5

20   ♘f3

First it is the bishop's turn to be eliminated. This move offers the e-pawn, but Black cannot get away with taking it.

20   ...   ♘g6

20...♕xe4 21 ♘xe5 ♕xe5 22 ♖he1 gives White a decisive attack; for example, 22...♔d7 23 ♕g2 ♗d5 24 ♕d2! and material loss is inevitable. Moreover, Black cannot retain his bishop with 20...♗f6 because 21 ♗xc5! dxc5 22 e5 regains the piece, while at the same time opening lines against Black's king. Therefore Black decides to reinforce the e5-square.

21   ♘xe5   ♘xe5

22   ♗f4 (D)

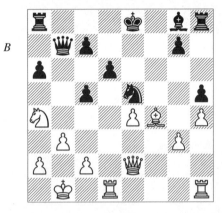

The bishop has been replaced by the knight, but now White gets set to eliminate the knight. None of Black's remaining pieces can defend e5, so Black will have to take with the pawn, opening the d-file and cutting out any hopes of queenside castling. Black's whole opening strategy was based on reinforcing the e5-square, so it is not surprising that the collapse of this strategy has serious consequences.

22   ...   c4

22...0-0-0 is of course impossible because 23 ♗xe5 dxe5 24 ♖xd8+ ♔xd8 25 ♘xc5 wins two pawns, so Black pushes his c-pawn to avoid losing it after the coming ♗xe5.

23   ♗xe5   dxe5

24   ♖hf1

Now White cruelly cuts out the possibility of castling kingside as well. Black is lost because his king will be defenceless against the coming storm.

24   ...   cxb3

25   axb3   ♗f7

The only chance, blocking the f-file so as to castle kingside, but Black is too late. 25...♖d8 loses to 26 ♖f8+ ♔xf8 27 ♖xd8+ ♔e7 28

♕f2! ♔xd8 29 ♕f8+ ♔d7 30 ♘c5+, while
25...♗xb3 26 cxb3 ♕xb3+ 27 ♘b2 is hopeless.

26   ♘c5

26 ♖xf7 ♔xf7 27 ♖d7+ ♔e8 (27...♔g8 28
♕c4+ ♔h7 29 ♕f7 and 27...♔g6 28 ♕e3 lead
to mate) 28 ♖xg7 wins easily enough as Black
can no longer castle, but the move played is also
very strong.

26   ...   ♕c6

Or 26...♕b5 27 ♕f3 0-0 28 ♘d7, winning
easily.

27   ♘d7 (D)

27 ♕f3 wins the exchange as in the previous
note and might have been simpler, but the move
played is also good.

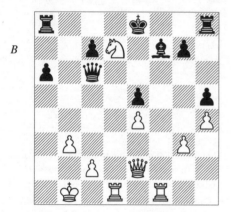

B

The knight cuts out kingside castling directly, while queenside castling is impossible
because the f7-bishop is hanging.

27   ...   ♕b5

After 27...♗e6 28 ♘xe5 ♕b5 29 ♕xb5+
axb5 30 ♘g6 ♖g8 31 ♘f4 ♔e7 32 ♘d5+ ♗xd5
33 ♖xd5, White forks b5 and h5 and will be two
pawns up for nothing.

28   ♕f2   ♗e6

28...0-0-0 is legal, but loses to 29 ♕a7 ♖xd7
30 ♕a8+ ♕b8 31 ♕xb8+ ♔xb8 32 ♖xd7.

29   ♘f6+

White's knight continues to cause havoc.

29   ...   ♔f7 (D)

29...gxf6 30 ♕xf6 is hopeless for Black, so
he must move his king. 29...♔e7 loses to 30
♖d5! (much stronger than 30 ♘d5+ ♗xd5 31
♖xd5 ♖af8 32 ♖xb5 ♖xf2 33 ♖xe5+ ♔f6
when, surprisingly, White only wins a pawn)
30...♗xd5 31 ♘xd5+ ♔d8 (31...♔d6 32 ♕f7
♖ac8 33 ♕g6+ ♔c5 34 ♖f3 and White wins) 32
♕f5 with decisive threats.

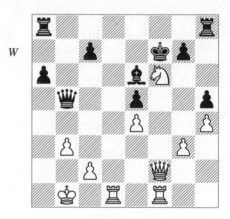

W

30   ♘d5+

One of many winning possibilities.

30   ...   ♔g6

31   ♘xc7

Picking up the exchange and a pawn.

31   ...   ♕c6

32   ♘xa8   ♖xa8

33   ♕e3

The situation is quite hopeless but Black,
who was in time-trouble, plays on to the bitter
end.

33   ...   ♔h7

34   ♕g5   ♗g4

35   ♖f7   ♖g8

36   ♖d5   ♕c3

37   ♕xe5

37 ♖d6 mates in a few moves, but of course it
doesn't matter now.

37   ...   ♕e1+

38   ♔b2   1-0

In late November, Petra and I travelled to another weekend event in Ireland, this time in Kilkenny. I scored 4½/6, sharing second place with Chris Ward, a point behind the winner Mickey Adams. A few weeks later it was once again time to venture to Hastings for the regular annual
appointments with chess, sea air and freezing cold restaurants. Mickey Adams was suffering from
a nasty cold at the start of the event and unexpectedly lost his first three games – indeed, he should
have lost the fourth as well, since Glenn Flear missed several forced mates in two. However, even a

virus-afflicted Mickey is no pushover, and I was happy with the result of the following game, played in round 2.

Positional exchange sacrifices are quite common these days, but it is still easy to misjudge them. Even such a strong player as Adams mistakenly allowed Black to give up the exchange on move 27. In return Black obtained one pawn, broke up White's pawn-structure and activated his bishops. This should have given Black the advantage, but my eagerness to regain the sacrificed material caused me to throw away my advantage. When you have a dangerous initiative, it is important not to cash it in for material too soon. A slip by White allowed Black to win a pawn, but in the resulting rook ending Black missed a chance (on move 41) to activate his rook. Of the three positions a rook can occupy with respect to a passed pawn, it is usually worst for the rook to be in front of the pawn and best for it to be behind the pawn. Defending the pawn from the side lies somewhere between these two extremes. Black could have switched his rook from the front position to the side position, which would have given him a likely win. Missing this chance gave White excellent drawing chances, but a serious error by Adams cost him the game.

Game 28

M. Adams – J. Nunn

Hastings 1996/7

Sicilian Defence, 2 ♘f3 e6 3 c3

1	e4	c5
2	♘f3	e6
3	c3	

At the time I was playing the Sveshnikov Variation and Adams decides to avoid tackling it. Although the lines 2 c3 and 2 ♘f3 e6 3 c3 may transpose into each other, the 3 c3 move-order restricts both sides' options to some extent.

| 3 | ... | d5 |

If Black plays 3...♘f6 then the different move-order doesn't have much impact, but in the ...d5 lines it makes a difference.

| 4 | exd5 | |

For 4 e5 see Game 35.

| 4 | ... | exd5 |

Here we see one of the key differences. These days the main line after 2 c3 d5 3 exd5 ♕xd5 4 d4 is 4...♘f6 5 ♘f3 ♗g4 (see Game 16), but this isn't possible if Black has already played ...e6. Black can still play the older lines with ...♘f6 and ...♘c6, since these don't depend on ...♗g4, but I preferred to take advantage of the additional move ...e6 to recapture on d5 with the pawn.

| 5 | d4 | ♘c6 |
| 6 | ♗e3 (D) | |

This line is designed to force Black to decide what he is going to do with his c5-pawn. The

main alternative is 6 ♗b5 ♗d6 7 dxc5 ♗xc5 8 0-0 ♘e7 9 ♘bd2 0-0 10 ♘b3 ♗d6 (10...♗b6 is also possible) 11 ♗d3, which transposes into a position which often arises from the French via a move-order such as 1 e4 e6 2 d4 d5 3 ♘d2 c5 4 exd5 exd5 5 ♘gf3 ♘c6 6 ♗b5 ♗d6 7 dxc5 ♗xc5 8 0-0 ♘e7 9 ♘b3 ♗d6 10 c3 0-0 11 ♗d3. In my view, this system offers White greater chances for an advantage than the one adopted by Adams in this game. However, such opinions are to a considerable extent matters of taste.

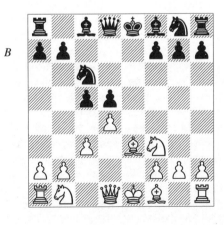

| 6 | ... | c4 |

6...cxd4 is also perfectly playable and offers good chances for equality.

7   b3

White must remove the cramping pawn, otherwise Black achieves a comfortable position straight away.

7   ...   cxb3

Almost universally played, since it is too risky to try to maintain the pawn-chain by 7...b5; for example, 8 a4 ♕a5 9 ♘bd2 b4 10 cxb4 ♘xb4 11 bxc4 ♗f5 12 ♖c1 ♖c8 13 c5 ♘d3+ 14 ♗xd3 ♗xd3 (Tereshkova-Zagorskaya, Minsk 1996) and now 15 ♕b3! ♗c4 16 ♖xc4 dxc4 17 ♕xc4 gives White a massive initiative.

8   axb3 *(D)*

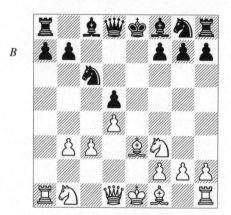

At first sight, the exchange of Black's c-pawn for White's a-pawn must favour White, on the general principle that a more central pawn is a greater asset than a less central one. However, in this case the exchange of pawns doesn't give White much. It is often the case that minor static advantages don't count for much unless they are coupled with additional dynamic assets, such as more active pieces or a lead in development. Here Black has no problems with his development, and once his pieces are in play White will have problems proving an advantage. Things would be different if White could exert pressure on the isolated d5-pawn, but his pieces are poorly placed for this. If White plays c4, Black just supports d5 and ignores the c4-pawn; he may even benefit from gaining access to the b4-square. Matters are rather different in the analogous line 1 e4 c5 2 c3 e6 3 d4 d5 4 exd5 exd5 5 ♗e3 c4 6 b3 cxb3 7 axb3 ♘c6. Here White can continue 8 ♗d3 ♗d6 9 ♕f3 ♘ge7 10 ♘e2 and from e2 the knight can move to f4 to target the d5-pawn, or

to g3 to aim at the sensitive f5-square. This line gives White more chances to gain the initiative than the one in the game (where, of course, White's knight was committed to f3 before he even played c3).

8   ...   ♗d6
9   ♗d3   ♘ge7

The best square for the knight as Black not only supports d5, but also prepares to exchange White's active light-squared bishop by ...♗f5.

10   ♕c2 *(D)*

The most accurate continuation, as the immediate 10 0-0 can be met by 10...♗f5. However, the position of the queen on c2 may cost White a tempo later, since after a subsequent ...♖c8 White will have to deal with the threat of ...♘b4.

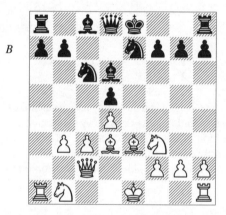

10   ...   h6

Black wants to castle before deciding how to develop his remaining pieces and for this plan a preliminary ...h6 is essential. However, the simplest continuation is probably 10...♗g4 11 ♘bd2 ♖c8 12 ♕b1 ♗h5, aiming for the exchange of bishops by ...♗g6. This plan avoids spending a tempo on ...h6 and should equalize; for example, 13 0-0 (13 ♗xh7?? g6 14 ♘g5 ♘f5 15 ♕d3 ♔f8! will cost White a piece within a few moves) 13...♗g6 14 ♘h4 ♕c7 15 ♘df3 ♗xd3 16 ♕xd3 0-0 and complete equality is not far off.

11   0-0   0-0
12   b4

This has been the most popular move but it seems to me that after it White cannot hope for an advantage. The alternatives are:

1) 12 h3 looks rather slow. After 12...♗e6 13 ♘bd2 ♖c8 14 ♕b1 ♕d7 Black again threatens ...♗f5, and if White seeks to prevent this by 15 ♘h4, then the piece sacrifice 15...♗xh3! 16 gxh3 ♕xh3 17 ♘df3 f5 gives Black a dangerous attack.

2) 12 ♘h4 is perhaps White's only hope for an advantage. He covers the f5-square again and prepares to advance his f-pawn. However, such a plan is rather double-edged and after 12...♕c7 13 f4 ♗d7 14 ♘d2 ♖fe8 15 ♖ae1 b5, for example, Black should have enough counterplay.

12   ...   ♗g4

The most natural reply. Now Black gains time to complete his development.

13   ♘bd2

The alternative 13 b5 (13 ♘h4 ♖c8 14 h3 ♗h5 is roughly equal, but not 14...♘xb4? 15 ♕d2 and Black is suddenly in trouble) 13...♗xf3 14 bxc6 is complicated, but does not give White any advantage against correct play:

1) 14...♕c8 15 ♘d2! (15 gxf3 ♕h3 16 f4 ♕g4+ is a draw) 15...♗xg2 (15...♗h5 16 cxb7 ♕xb7 17 c4 gives White an edge) 16 ♔xg2 ♕g4+ 17 ♔h1 ♕h3 18 f4 ♕xe3 19 ♖f3 ♕e6 20 cxb7 offers White some advantage.

2) 14...♘xc6! 15 gxf3 ♕h4 16 ♖e1 (16 f4 ♕g4+ draws, but this might be White's best continuation) 16...♖fe8 17 ♔f1 ♕xh2 with good compensation for the piece. Note that 18 ♔e2?? fails to 18...♖xe3+ 19 ♔xe3 ♖e8+ 20 ♔d2 ♕xf2+ 21 ♗e2 ♗g3 22 ♘a3 ♘xd4 23 cxd4 ♕e3+ 24 ♔d1 ♕xd4+ and White loses both his rooks.

13   ...   ♖c8
14   ♕b1 (D)

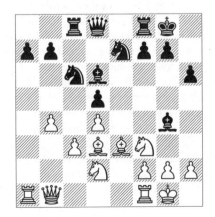

White must keep his queen on the b1-h7 diagonal in order to prevent ...♗f5.

14   ...   a6

A safety-first move. Black prevents b5 (see next note) and prepares ...♘a7-b5, which not only blocks White's b-pawn but also exerts pressure on the backward c3-pawn. If White exchanges on b5, then Black will have doubled isolated pawns but White will have surrendered his best minor piece.

The more dynamic 14...f5!? was the main alternative. This wins a pawn virtually by force, but weakens e5 and leaves Black's pieces misplaced. The main line runs 15 b5 ♘a5 16 ♘e5 ♖xc3 17 ♗f4 and in compensation for the pawn White can point to the g4-bishop and a5-knight. After 17...♕c7 18 ♖e1 ♗h5 19 h4 b6 20 ♕b2 or 17...g5 18 ♗g3 ♗h5 19 f4 the position can only be judged unclear.

15   h3

Here 15 b5 is definitely bad in view of 15...axb5 16 ♕xb5 f5 17 h3 ♗h5, when the threat of ...f4 is not easy to meet.

15   ...   ♗h5 (D)

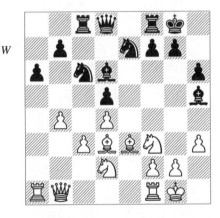

Now Black is genuinely threatening ...f5 since without the possibility of b5 White cannot gain control of the e5-square.

16   ♘h4

With one move White prevents both ...f5 and ...♗g6.

16   ...   ♘a7

Black replies with his own multi-purpose move. This prevents White's b5 and prepares ...♘b5, while at the same time attacking the c3-pawn directly.

17   ♖c1

White decides simply to defend the attacked pawn. He could have tried sacrificing the pawn by 17 ♘b3 ♖xc3 18 ♘c5, but after 18...♗xc5 19 dxc5 ♘ec6 20 ♘f5 ♖xd3! 21 ♕xd3 ♗g6 22 g4 ♘b5 Black has good play for his modest material investment.

17   ...   ♘b5
18   ♗xb5?!

White decides to damage Black's pawn-structure, but in my view the resulting light-square weaknesses are a more important factor than the broken pawns. 18 ♕b3 would have maintained the balance; for example, 18...f5 19 c4 (19 ♘df3? costs White material after 19...g5 20 ♘xf5 ♘xf5 21 ♕xd5+ ♔g7 since he cannot take on f5 due to ...♗h2+) 19...dxc4 (19...f4 20 cxb5 fxe3 21 fxe3 ♖xc1+ 22 ♖xc1 axb5 is also satisfactory for Black) 20 ♘xc4 ♔h8 21 ♘xd6 ♖xc1+ 22 ♖xc1 ♕xd6 with a roughly balanced position.

18   ...   axb5
19   ♘f5

White wisely exchanges his offside knight before ...♕d7 cuts out the possibility of ♘f5.

19   ...   ♗g6
20   ♘xe7+   ♕xe7
21   ♕b3 (D)

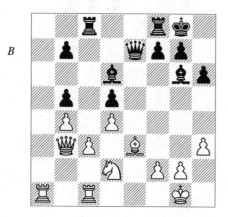

21   ...   ♖fd8?!

Black commits an inaccuracy. d8 cannot be the right square for this rook since all it is doing there is preventing White from taking on d5. It would have been much better to use the queen for this duty, leaving the rook to occupy the open e-file. After either 21...♕d7 22 ♘f1 ♖fe8 or 21...♕e6 22 ♘f1 ♗f5 Black would have a slight advantage.

22   ♘f1   ♕f6
23   ♕d1!

An excellent defensive move, intending ♕e2. Black's pieces are poorly placed to meet the attack on the b5-pawn.

23   ...   ♖c7

Black prepares a counterattack against the c3-pawn.

24   ♖a5

After 24 ♕e2 ♗f5! it is very dangerous to take the pawn:

1) 25 ♕xb5 ♕g6 (25...♗xh3 26 gxh3 ♕g6+ 27 ♔h1 ♕e4+ only leads to perpetual check) 26 ♔h1 ♗d3 transposes to line '2'.

2) 25 ♔h1 ♕g6 26 ♕xb5 ♗d3 27 ♕b6 (27 ♕xd5?? ♗e4 wins for Black) 27...♖e8 with a very dangerous initiative for Black.

24   ...   b6 (D)

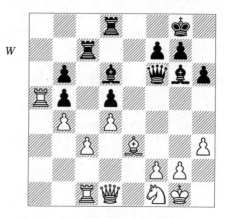

The best way to meet the attack on the b5-pawn.

25   ♖a6

White dare not play 25 ♖xb5? because after 25...♗f8 26 ♕e2 ♕c6 the rook is totally immobilized and is in danger of being lost after ...f6 and ...♗e8. However, Black would have preferred to avoid ...b6 since after ♖a6 his pieces have the additional duty of defending the b6-pawn. At the moment White cannot take it due to ...♗h2+, but later on one of Black's pieces may become tied down to covering b6.

25   ...   ♖dc8
26   ♗d2

White has met the attack on c3 and now plans ♘e3 and ♕e2, exerting pressure against d5 and b5 respectively.

26   ...   ♗e4

Aiming for counterplay on the kingside before White organizes his pieces to attack the weak pawns.

27   ♖ca1? *(D)*

A definite error since White should not have allowed the exchange sacrifice on c3. He should have played 27 ♘e3 (not 27 ♕e2? ♗xb4 28 f3 ♗f5 29 ♕xb5 ♗xc3, which favours Black) 27...♕e6 and now:

1) 28 ♕f1?! ♗f4 29 ♕xb5 ♗xe3 with another branch:

1a) 30 fxe3 ♕g6 31 ♕f1 ♖c6! (31...♗d3 32 ♖xb6 ♕xb6 33 ♕xd3 ♖a7 is only slightly better for Black) 32 ♖a7 ♖f6 33 ♕e2 ♗f3 34 ♕f2 ♕h5 with a decisive attack for Black.

1b) 30 ♗xe3 ♕g6 31 ♕f1 ♗d3 32 ♖xb6 ♗xf1 33 ♖xg6 fxg6 34 ♔xf1 ♖xc3 and Black has a clear endgame advantage.

2) 28 ♕e2 ♗xb4 29 ♕xb5 ♗xc3 30 ♖xb6 ♕e7 31 ♖b8 ♕d8 32 ♖xc8 ♕xc8 with equality.

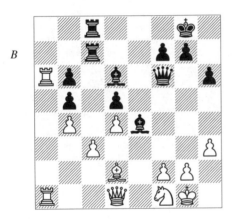

27   ...   ♖xc3!

Black seizes his chance. 27...♕g6 is well met by 28 ♕g4.

28   ♗xc3   ♖xc3

This is an awkward position for White since Black already has one pawn for the exchange and in addition White's b4- and d4-pawns are weak. If Black can consolidate a second pawn for the exchange, then he will have the advantage thanks to his active pieces and bishop-pair.

29   ♖xb6 *(D)*

White decides to return the exchange immediately. Attempting to hang on to the material is very risky:

1) 29 ♖6a3 ♖c4 wins the d4-pawn while maintaining the pressure.

2) 29 ♕d2 ♗xb4 doesn't help White at all.

3) 29 f3 ♗d3 again picks up the d4-pawn.

4) 29 ♘d2 and now:

4a) 29...♗f5 30 ♘f3 allows White to activate his knight.

4b) 29...♕xd4 30 ♘xe4 ♕xe4 31 ♖xb6 ♕f4 32 g3 ♖xg3+ 33 fxg3 ♕xg3+ 34 ♔f1 ♕xh3+ 35 ♔e2 ♕g2+ 36 ♔e3! and Black must be content with a draw.

4c) 29...♕f4 (this looks dangerous but it only leads to perpetual check) 30 ♘xe4 dxe4 (30...♕h2+ 31 ♔f1 dxe4 32 ♖a8+ ♔h7 33 ♕g4 favours White) 31 g3 (not 31 ♖xb6? ♕h2+ 32 ♔f1 ♗f4 and Black wins) 31...♖xg3+ (31...♕f5 32 ♕g4 is not dangerous for White) 32 fxg3 ♕xg3+ 33 ♔f1 ♕xh3+ 34 ♔f2 (34 ♔e2? ♕g2+ 35 ♔e3 f5 36 d5 ♗e5 wins for Black, while 34 ♔e1 ♗b4+ 35 ♔f2 ♗d6 will also lead to perpetual check) 34...♕h2+ 35 ♔f1 (35 ♔e3 f5 36 ♖a8+ ♔h7 37 ♕f1 ♕g3+ 38 ♔d2 ♗xb4+ 39 ♔c2 ♕c3+ 40 ♔b1 is another draw) 35...♕h1+ with a draw.

4d) 29...♖d3! 30 ♕e2 ♕xd4 31 ♘xe4 dxe4 with two pawns and a dangerous initiative for the exchange. After 32 ♕g4 ♕e5 33 ♖a7 h5 or 32 ♖6a2 ♕e5 33 g3 ♗xb4 White's position is very unpleasant.

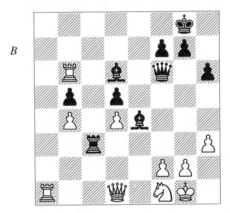

29   ...   ♗h2+?

Here the safety-first approach was definitely wrong. Black grabs at the chance to regain the exchange, but in doing so surrenders all his advantage. He should have played 29...♖c2!, and now:

1) 30 ♘d2 ♗h2+! 31 ♔xh2 ♕xf2 32 ♕g4 ♕xd2 33 ♖g1 ♕xb4 34 ♕g3 ♔h7 and Black has a large advantage.

2) 30 f3 ♕g5 31 ♕xc2 (31 g4 ♗h2+ 32 ♘xh2 ♕e3+ 33 ♔h1 ♖xh2+ 34 ♔xh2 ♕f2+ 35 ♔h1 ♗xf3+ wins for Black) 31...♗xc2 32 ♖xd6 ♗b3 is clearly better for Black as White suffers from his weak queenside pawns and poorly coordinated rooks.

3) 30 ♕e1 ♗h2+ 31 ♘xh2 ♕xb6 regains the exchange under much more favourable circumstances than in the game. Indeed, White is bound to lose a pawn within a few moves.

30   ♔xh2   ♕xb6
31   ♘g3

Now that White has activated his knight, Black cannot claim an advantage.

31   ...   ♔h7

Playing to win a pawn by either 31...♖d3 or 31...♖c4 is met by 32 ♕h5, threatening 33 ♖a8+, and White has sufficient counterplay. 31...♕b8 is another idea, preventing ♖a8+ and pinning the knight. However, in this case too White has no problems provided he plays actively by 32 ♕g4 ♖c4 33 ♕d7.

32   ♘xe4

This is enough to maintain the balance, but 32 ♕e1! would have been even simpler; for example, 32...♕c7 (not 32...♕xd4?, when 33 ♘e2 ♕e5+ 34 f4 wins a rook) 33 ♖a7! ♖xg3 34 ♖xc7 ♖xg2+ 35 ♔h1 with perpetual check to come.

32   ...   dxe4 (D)

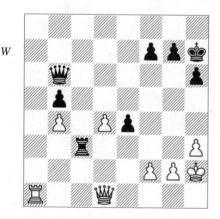

If Black is given a chance to consolidate then he would have the advantage since White has two weak pawns while Black only has one. However, by active play White can keep Black off balance.

33   ♕g4   ♕d6+

34   ♔g1   ♕d5

The best practical chance, covering e4 and f5. Now Black only needs one more tempo to play ...f5 and consolidate his position.

35   ♖e1?

Giving Black the crucial tempo he requires. 35 ♖a7! was correct, pinning the f-pawn against the mate at g7. In this case the position would be completely equal.

35   ...   f5

Now White is in difficulties since he cannot avoid losing a pawn.

36   ♕f4

The best chance. 36 ♕h5 ♖c2 followed by ...♖d2 is even worse for White.

36   ...   ♖c4
37   g4 (D)

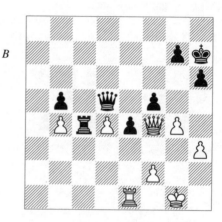

White finds the most resilient defence. Since he will inevitably lose a pawn, White tries to reduce the number of pawns as much as possible in the hope of holding a rook ending a pawn down.

37   ...   fxg4

Stronger than 37...♖xb4 38 gxf5 ♖xd4 39 f6 (39 ♕g4 ♕c6 40 ♖e3 also offers White defensive chances) 39...gxf6 40 ♕xf6 ♕g5+ 41 ♕xg5 hxg5, when it is not clear if Black can win; for example, 42 f3 exf3 43 ♔f2 b4 44 ♔xf3 b3 (after 44...♖f4+ 45 ♔g3 ♖f7 46 h4 White draws easily) 45 ♖e7+ ♔g6 46 ♖b7 ♖d3+ 47 ♔g4 ♔f6 48 ♖b5 ♔e6 49 ♖xg5 ♖d4+ 50 ♔f3 ♖b4 51 ♖g1 ♔d5 52 ♖b1! and the position is drawn. If Black could win White's rook while keeping the white king cut off on the third rank then he would win. However, Black faces the problem that as soon as he blocks his rook with ...♔c4 or ...♔d4, White plays ♔g4 and activates his king. Playing the king round the other side of the rook also doesn't work because ...♔a4 can be met by ♖a1+.

38 ♕xe4+

38 ♖xe4 gxh3 39 ♕e5 ♕f7 40 ♕g3 ♖xb4 41 ♕xh3 ♖b2 should win for Black in view of his extra pawn and White's unsafe king.

38	...	♕xe4
39	♖xe4	gxh3
40	♔h2	♖xb4
41	♔xh3	*(D)*

White has no time for 41 ♖e5 because 41...♖b3 retains the h3-pawn.

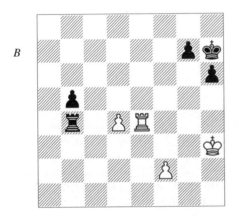

41 ... ♔g6?

This allows White to activate his rook and tie Black's rook down to the b-file. 41...♖c4! was correct, freeing the b-pawn as quickly as possible. In this case Black should win; for example, 42 ♖e5 (the only chance as 42 ♔g3 b4 43 ♔f3 b3 is an easy win for Black) 42...b4 and now:

1) 43 d5 ♖d4 44 ♔g2 b3 45 ♖e3 ♖b4 46 d6 b2 47 d7 b1♕ 48 d8♕ (Black wins because of his safer king) 48...♖g4+ 49 ♔f3 (49 ♖g3 ♕e4+ 50 ♔f1 ♖xg3 51 fxg3 ♕f3+ wins another pawn, while 49 ♔h3 ♖g6 leads to a quick mate) 49...♕f5+ 50 ♔e2 ♖a4 and Black has a winning attack.

2) 43 ♖d5 ♖c3+! (forcing White's king to decide whether to go up or down the board) 44 ♔g2 (44 ♔g4 ♖c8 threatens ...♖b8, and after 45 ♖b5 ♖c4 46 ♖d5 b3 Black wins easily because the d4-pawn is hanging with check) 44...b3 (the immediate 44...g5 is also promising) 45 ♖b5 g5! (an important move gaining space on the kingside) 46 ♖b6 (46 ♖b7+ ♔g6

47 ♖b6+ ♔f5 48 ♖xh6 ♔e4 and Black wins comfortably) 46...♔g7 47 d5 (after 47 ♔f1 h5 White's king cannot move to the queenside because this would allow the h-pawn through) 47...h5 48 d6 ♔f6 49 d7+ (49 ♖b5 ♖d3 50 d7 ♔e7 51 ♖xg5 h4 52 f3 ♔xd7 wins for Black) 49...♔e7 50 ♖b7 h4 51 ♔h2 g4 52 ♔g2 h3+ 53 ♔h2 ♖c2 54 ♖xb3 ♖xf2+ 55 ♔g1 ♖f3 and Black wins.

42 ♖e5!

White seizes his chance. Black's rook can now only move along the b-file since the exchange of b- and d-pawns would leave a theoretically drawn ending. Having the rook in front of the b-pawn is much less effective than having it on c4.

42	...	♔f6
43	♔g3	g5 *(D)*

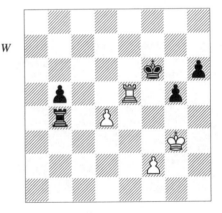

The best try. Black aims to gain space on the kingside and eventually to force White's king back.

44 f4??

An uncharacteristic blunder from Adams, probably occasioned by the severe cold he was suffering from. In attempting to exchange a pair of pawns, White loses a second pawn. Despite the reduced material, it is quite hard to say whether the position is won with correct play. However, my feeling is that it should be a draw, based on the following analysis:

1) 44 ♖c5 (an attempt to check Black's king from the side) 44...h5 45 ♖c6+ (45 f4? ♖b3+ 46 ♔f2 gxf4 47 ♖xh5 b4 48 ♖b5 ♔e6 49 ♖e5+ ♔d6 50 ♖b5 ♔c6 51 ♖c5+ ♔b6 52 ♖f5 f3 53 ♖f8 ♔b5 is winning for Black) 45...♔e7 and now:

1a) 46 Ἐh6?! Ἐxd4 (not 46...h4+? 47 ἄg4 Ἐxd4+ 48 ἄxg5 b4 49 f4 Ἐd5+ 50 f5 Ἐb5 51 Ἐxh4 b3 52 Ἐh1 with a draw) 47 Ἐxh5 Ἐd5 48 Ἐh6 ἄd7 49 ἄg4 (49 f4 gxf4+ 50 ἄxf4 Ἐd6! and Black wins according to the tablebases) 49...ἄc7 50 f3 reaches an interesting position in which precise play is needed to win:

1a1) 50...b4? is wrong and allows White to draw by 51 f4 gxf4 52 ἄxf4 Ἐd6 (after 52...b3 53 Ἐh1 ἄb6 54 ἄe4! White gains a key tempo) 53 Ἐxd6 ἄxd6 54 ἄe4 and this would be a win with the pawn on b5, but is drawn here.

1a2) 50...Ἐc5! (moving the rook out of range of White's king) 51 Ἐe6 (or 51 Ἐh1 ἄb6 52 Ἐb1 Ἐd5 53 ἄh5 ἄc5 54 Ἐc1+ ἄd4 55 Ἐb1 ἄc3 56 Ἐc1+ ἄb2 and Black wins) 51...b4 52 f4 gxf4 53 ἄxf4 b3 54 Ἐe1 ἄb6 55 Ἐb1 Ἐc3 56 ἄe4 ἄc5 and White's king cannot approach, so Black wins.

1b) 46 Ἐc5! Ἐb3+! (D) (46...h4+ 47 ἄg4 Ἐxd4+ 48 ἄxg5 b4 49 Ἐc7+ ἄe6 50 Ἐh7 Ἐd5+ 51 ἄxh4 Ἐb5 52 ἄg4 b3 53 Ἐh1 b2 54 Ἐb1 draws as White's king is able to support his pawn) and now:

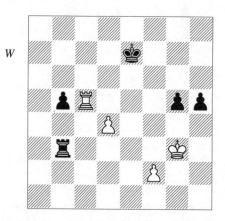

1b1) 47 f3 (this looks wrong as it exposes the white king to checks along the second rank) 47...Ἐb1 48 f4 (48 ἄf2 ἄf6 49 f4 gxf4 50 Ἐxh5 b4 and 48 ἄg2 ἄf6 49 d5 Ἐb2+ 50 ἄg1 g4 51 fxg4 hxg4 52 d6 ἄe6 53 Ἐd5 ἄd7 54 Ἐd3 b4 55 ἄf1 Ἐc2 56 Ἐb3 Ἐc4 57 Ἐd3 Ἐc6 both win for Black) 48...h4+ 49 ἄg4 gxf4 50 ἄxf4 (50 ἄxh4 b4 51 ἄg4 b3 52 Ἐe5+ ἄd6 53 Ἐe2 b2 54 ἄf5 ἄd5 wins for Black) 50...b4 51 Ἐb5 b3 52 ἄf3 ἄd6 53 ἄg2 ἄc6 54 Ἐb4 ἄd5 (D) reaches an interesting position which seems to be a win for Black.

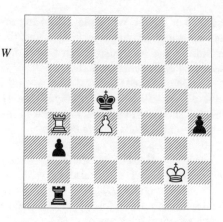

However, looking at the diagram one would hardly expect that the key winning idea is to play Black's rook to a7! The winning line runs 55 ἄh2 ἄe4 56 ἄg2 ἄd3 57 d5 ἄc3 58 Ἐb8 Ἐd1 59 Ἐc8+ ἄb2 60 Ἐd8 (60 Ἐc5 ἄa3 wins for Black) 60...ἄc2 61 Ἐc8+ ἄb1 62 Ἐd8 b2 63 d6 Ἐd2+ 64 ἄh3 (64 ἄh1 ἄc2 65 Ἐc8+ ἄd3 and Black wins because his pawn promotes with check) 64...Ἐd3+ (64...ἄc2? 65 Ἐc8+ ἄd3 66 d7 is a draw here) 65 ἄxh4 (65 ἄg2 Ἐa3 66 d7 Ἐa7 is winning for Black) 65...Ἐb3 66 d7 (66 Ἐc8 Ἐb7 67 Ἐc7 Ἐb8 68 d7 ἄa2 wins for Black) 66...Ἐb7 67 ἄg5 Ἐa7! (the key idea: Black shields his own king while keeping White's pawn under observation) 68 ἄf6 ἄa2 and Black wins by one tempo.

1b2) 47 ἄg2! ἄf6 48 d5 (48 f4? gxf4 49 Ἐxh5 b4 50 Ἐb5 ἄe6 51 ἄf2 ἄd6 52 Ἐf5 Ἐd3 and Black wins) 48...b4 49 Ἐb5 (49 d6? Ἐd3 50 Ἐb5 Ἐd4 51 d7 ἄe7 52 ἄh3 ἄxd7 53 Ἐxg5 Ἐf4 54 Ἐb5 ἄc6 55 Ἐb8 h4 is winning for Black) 49...ἄe5 50 d6+ ἄxd6 51 Ἐxg5 h4 52 Ἐb5 ἄc6 53 Ἐb8 ἄc5 54 Ἐc8+ ἄd4 55 Ἐd8+ ἄc4 56 Ἐc8+ ἄd3 57 Ἐb8 (White must keep Black's rook tied down; after 57 ἄh3? Ἐc3 58 Ἐb8 ἄc2+ 59 ἄxh4 b3 60 f4 b2 61 Ἐxb2+ ἄxb2 62 ἄg5 ἄb3 Black wins) 57...Ἐb1 (57...Ἐb2 58 ἄh3 ἄc3 59 Ἐc8+ ἄb3 60 f4 Ἐf2 61 Ἐf8 ἄc2 62 ἄxh4 b3 63 ἄg5 is also drawn) 58 Ἐb7! (58 f4? ἄe4 and 58 ἄh3? ἄe2 win for Black) 58...b3 and now:

1b21) 59 ἄh3? ἄc2 60 Ἐc7+ ἄb2 61 ἄxh4 Ἐc1 62 Ἐb7 Ἐf1 63 ἄg3 ἄc2 64 Ἐc7+ ἄb1 65 f4 (or 65 ἄf3 Ἐe1) 65...b2 66 ἄg4 ἄa2 wins for Black.

1b22) 59 f4! ἄc3 60 Ἐc7+ ἄb2 61 f5 Ἐd1 62 f6 Ἐd6 63 f7 Ἐf6 64 Ἐe7 ἄa2 65 ἄh3 Ἐf4

66 ♖a7+ ♔b1 67 ♖e7 b2 68 ♖c7 and White secures the draw.

2) 44 ♔f3! looks like a simpler path to a draw. White prepares to meet ...♖b3+ by ♔e4, keeping his king more active than in line '1'. Play might continue 44...h5 (44...♖b3+ 45 ♔e4 only helps White) 45 ♖d5 ♖b3+ (or 45...h4 46 ♖d6+ ♔e7 47 ♖d5 ♖b3+ 48 ♔e4 g4 49 ♖h5 g3 50 fxg3 hxg3 51 ♖g5 b4 52 d5 ♖c3 53 ♔d4 and Black cannot make progress) 46 ♔e4 h4 47 ♖d6+ ♔f7 48 ♔f5 h3 (48...♖f3+ 49 ♔xg5 h3 50 ♖h6 b4 51 ♔g4 ♔g7 52 ♖h5 ♔g6 53 ♖g5+ ♔f6 54 ♖h5 draws) 49 ♖d7+ ♔e8 50 ♖h7 b4

51 ♔g4 ♖d3 52 f3 ♖xd4+ 53 ♔xg5 b3 54 ♖xh3 ♖b4 55 ♖h1 and White draws.

44　　...　　　　♖xd4

Not 44...gxf4+? 45 ♔g4! with a draw since Black cannot make progress. If Black's rook moves along the b-file White takes on f4, while the exchange of d- and b-pawns leads to an ending of ♖+f♙+h♙ vs ♖, which is easily drawn in this case due to the weakness of the f4-pawn.

After the text-move, White cannot take on g5, but after 45 ♖xb5 ♖xf4 he is two pawns down in a theoretically lost ending.

0-1

This was an interesting game in all its phases, although marred by some inaccuracies. After another win in round 4 against Motwani I was in a promising position in the tournament. In round 5 I met Xie Jun and soon had a very dubious position. Readers may conclude from reading this book that escaping from difficult positions is a speciality of mine, but in fact most grandmasters have the ability to put up a stiff resistance when things have gone wrong. Once again we see a key defensive idea in action: the defender must focus on whatever assets his position possesses and try to make the most of them. In the position below, these assets are the weak d6-pawn and the possibility of making a passed pawn by pushing the c-pawn.

Game 29
J. Nunn – Xie Jun
Hastings 1996/7

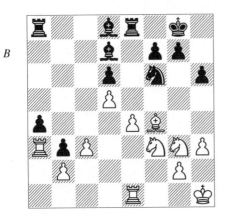

Material is equal, but positionally Black is on top. The position of the a3-rook needs no comment, but White's problem is that if this rook is repositioned to a1 and d1, then he will always have to worry about a breakthrough by ...a3. This is especially the case if all the rooks are exchanged. Additionally, Black has two active bishops. However, despite these advantages it

is not easy for Black to increase her advantage; apart from the a3-rook, White's pieces are all reasonably placed, and White is attacking the d6-pawn.

29　　...　　　　♗c7

This move looks slightly passive, but there is nothing wrong with it. Black intends simply to defend the d6-pawn while building up against the backward e4-pawn by ...♖e7 and ...♖ae8. Other ideas:

1) 29...♗b6 30 ♗xd6 ♗f2 is more active, but White can probably hold on with accurate defence: 31 ♖ea1 (31 ♖b1 ♘xe4 32 ♘xe4 ♖xe4 is very unpleasant for White, as the position is opening up nicely for Black's bishops, while 31 ♖e2 ♗xg3 32 ♗xg3 ♘xe4 33 ♔h2 ♘xg3 34 ♖xe8+ ♖xe8 35 ♔xg3 ♖e2 is winning for Black because the queenside passed pawns will be too strong) 31...♗xg3 (with the rook on a1, 31...♘xe4 32 ♘xe4 ♖xe4 fails to 33 ♖xb3) 32 ♗xg3 ♘xe4 33 ♔h2 and White has reasonable chances to save the game; for

example, 33...♖ac8 34 ♘e5 ♗b5 35 ♘c6 ♗xc6 36 dxc6 ♘xg3 37 ♔xg3 ♖xc6 38 ♖xa4 ♖e2 39 ♖a6 heads for a pawn-down rook ending which is probably drawn.

2) 29...♖a6 30 ♔h2 ♗a5 (30...♗b5 31 ♘d4 ♗c4 32 ♖ea1 is also not clear) looks promising, but again White may be able to hang on: 31 ♖aa1 ♗xc3!? 32 bxc3 b2 33 ♖a2 a3 34 ♗xd6 (34 ♖b1?! ♘xe4 35 ♘xe4 ♖xe4 36 ♗xd6 ♖xd6 37 ♖xa3 ♖b6 38 ♖a2 ♖e2 39 ♘d4 ♖d2 looks very promising for Black) 34...♖xd6 35 ♖xa3 ♘xd5 36 c4 ♘f4 37 ♖b3 with fair drawing chances.

30   ♖aa1 *(D)*

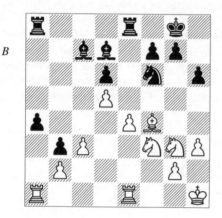

White scrambles to transfer his rook to a more normal position.

30   ...   ♖e7?!

Black continues with her plan, but now the position starts to become complicated. 30...♗b5 was probably the simplest way to step up the pressure, intending to transfer the bishop to d3. The critical line is 31 c4 (if White prevents ...♗d3 with 31 ♖ad1, then 31...a3 32 bxa3 ♖xa3 is very promising for Black because the b-pawn is a serious danger) 31...♗xc4 32 ♖ec1 (32 ♖ac1 ♗a5), but then 32...a3! 33 ♖xa3 ♖xa3 34 bxa3 ♘xe4 35 ♘xe4 ♖xe4 36 ♘d2 ♖xf4 37 ♘xc4 ♖f2 38 ♖b1 ♖c2 39 ♘e3 ♖c3 gives Black a near-decisive advantage.

31   c4

White makes a bid for counterplay. This not only cuts out ...♗b5, but also prepares to advance the pawn to c5.

31   ...   ♖ae8?

This appears consistent, but it is a mistake after which Black has no advantage and indeed

must play accurately to maintain the balance. 31...g5! was correct:

1) 32 ♘xg5 hxg5 (32...♖ae8? 33 ♘f3 ♘xe4 34 ♔h2 is safe for White) 33 ♗xg5 ♔g7 34 ♖f1 ♘xe4 35 ♘h5+ ♔g6! (35...♔f8 36 ♗xe7+ ♔xe7 37 ♖ae1 f5 is less clear) 36 ♗xe7 ♔xh5 37 ♖xf7 a3! 38 bxa3 ♔g6 39 ♖f4 ♘d2 40 ♖f6+ ♔h7 41 ♗xd6 b2 42 ♖g1 ♗xd6 43 ♖xd6 ♗f5 and White will soon have five pawns against two minor pieces. However, the pawns are insufficiently advanced to pose a real danger and so Black should win.

2) 32 ♗d2 ♖ae8 33 e5 dxe5 and now:

2a) 34 ♗c3 e4! 35 ♗xf6 (35 ♘f5 ♗xf5 36 ♗xf6 exf3 37 ♖xe7 ♖xe7 38 ♗xe7 f2 39 ♖f1 ♗g3 40 d6 ♔h7 should be winning for Black) 35...♗xg3 36 ♖e3 (36 c5 ♔f8 37 c6 exf3 38 ♗xe7+ ♖xe7 39 cxd7 ♖xd7 40 ♖e3 f2 looks winning for Black as 41 ♖xg3 ♖e7 costs White a rook) 36...exf3 37 ♖xe7 ♖xe7 38 ♗xe7 f2 39 ♗c5 ♗f5 40 d6 ♗xd6 41 ♗xd6 ♗d3 gives Black fair winning chances.

2b) 34 ♗b4 e4 35 ♘f1 exf3 36 ♖xe7 ♖xe7 37 ♗xe7 ♗e5 38 ♗a3 f2 gives Black good play for the exchange, but the position remains very complicated. One line runs 39 g4 h5 40 ♔g2 hxg4 41 hxg4 ♘xg4 42 c5 ♗f5 43 ♔f3 ♗d4 44 c6 ♘f6 and Black is better, but White still has chances to save the game.

32   c5 *(D)*

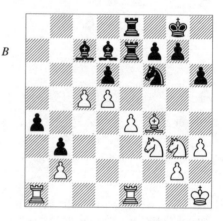

Now this pawn advances to c6, not only creating a protected passed pawn but also cutting off Black's support for the a4-pawn.

32   ...   ♘xe4?!

The best line is 32...♗a5 33 ♗xd6 (33 c6 ♗xe1 34 cxd7 ♖xd7 35 ♘xe1 ♘xe4 favours

Black, while 33 ♖ed1 dxc5 34 e5 ♗c3! 35 bxc3 ♘xd5 36 ♖xd5 b2 37 ♖b1 a3 38 ♖d2 ♖b8 is also unpleasant for White) 33...♗xe1 34 ♖xe1 ♖xe4 35 ♘xe4 ♘xe4 (35...♖xe4 36 ♖d1 ♖e2 37 c6 ♖xb2 38 ♗e5 ♖c2 is unclear and probably equal) 36 c6 ♘xd6 37 cxd7 ♖d8 38 ♖a1 ♖xd7 39 ♖xa4 with a draw in prospect.

33 c6

Not 33 ♘xe4 ♖xe4 34 ♖xe4 ♖xe4 35 cxd6 ♗b6 36 ♗e5 f6 37 ♗c3 ♗c5, when Black has a massive advantage thanks to her two bishops and queenside pawn-majority.

33 ... ♘xg3+

It is doubtful if Black can equalize now; for example, 33...♗c8 (not 33...♘f2+ 34 ♔h2 ♖xe1? 35 cxd7 and White wins) 34 ♘xe4! (34 ♖xa4 ♘f2+ 35 ♔g1 ♖xe1+ 36 ♘xe1 ♗b6 37 ♔f1 g5 38 ♗xd6 ♘d1 is at least equal for Black) 34...♖xe4 35 ♗d2 ♔f8 36 ♖xe4 ♖xe4 37 ♗c3 and White is better despite his minus pawn. Black's main problem is the threat of 38 ♘d2 ♖f4 39 ♘xb3 axb3 40 ♖a8, to which she doesn't have a good defence.

34 ♗xg3 ♖xe1+
35 ♗xe1!

I used up most of my remaining time on this move, which involves an exchange sacrifice. The alternative 35 ♘xe1 ♗f5 36 ♖xa4 ♗e4 37 ♖d4 (37 ♖a7 ♖c8 is very good for Black, since the d5-pawn cannot be defended) 37...f5 can only be better for Black.

35 ... ♗f5
36 ♖xa4 (D)

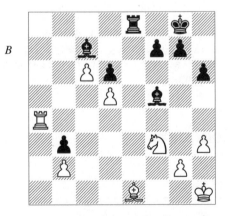

36 ... ♗e4

This is Black's idea; there are twin threats of 37...♗xf3, winning a piece, and 37...♗xd5,

demolishing White's pawn-chain. Thus White is forced to go in for tactics.

37 ♗a5! ♗xf3
38 gxf3 ♖a8

Black has no choice but to accept the material, since otherwise the protected passed pawn gives White a decisive advantage.

39 ♗xc7 ♖xa4
40 ♗xd6

A crucial moment.

40 ... ♖c4?!

This move loses instantly, but the position could not be saved in any case. The other possibility is 40...f6 41 ♗c5 (not 41 c7? ♖a8 and the pawns are blockaded, whereupon Black can expect to win) 41...♔f7 42 d6 ♔e6 43 d7 ♖a8. Here White can force a draw by 44 ♗b6 ♔e7 45 ♗c5+, but I could not see a clear-cut win during the game. Home analysis showed the way: 44 h4! h5 (there is no choice as 44...g5 and 44...g6 would be met by 45 ♗d4, when Black cannot prevent a deadly ♗xf6) 45 f4 (threatening 46 f5+) 45...f5 (or 45...g6 46 ♗d4) 46 ♔g2 and Black is totally paralysed, so White can just march his king to b7 (taking the b3-pawn along the way if he likes).

41 c7

White's next move cannot be prevented.

41 ... f6 (D)

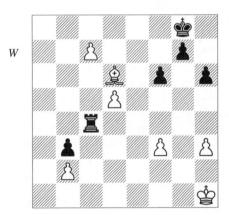

42 ♗c5!

By sacrificing his bishop, White gains time to push his d-pawn. I spotted this crucial idea while I was thinking about my 35th move. In this I was helped in two ways. Firstly, the variation is rather forced (what Robin Smith calls a 'box canyon' in his book *Modern Chess*

Analysis) and secondly, the following end-game study popped into my mind.

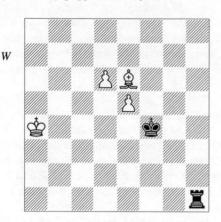

L. Prokeš
1st Prize, *Narodni Listy*, 1941
White to play and win

After **1 d7** White wins in three different variations using the same motif: a bishop sacrifice to clear the way for the e-pawn with gain of tempo:

1) 1...♖a1+ 2 ♗a2! ♖xa2+ 3 ♔b3 followed by e6.

2) 1...♖h8 2 ♗g8! ♖xg8 3 e6.

3) 1...♖d1 2 ♗d5! ♖xd5 3 e6.

Returning to the game, White can now promote a pawn by force.

42	...	♖xc5
43	d6	♔f7
44	d7	♖xc7
45	d8♕	♖c1+
46	♔g2	♖c2+
47	♔g3	♖xb2

It is sometimes possible to set up a fortress when you have rook vs queen with all the pawns on one side, but not here. White's f-pawn is able to drive away a rook settling on e5 or g5, and otherwise Black lacks stable squares for her rook.

| 48 | ♕d3 | |

The first task, easily enough accomplished, is to round up the b-pawn.

48	...	♔g8
49	♔f4	♔f8
50	♔f5	

Now Black must abandon the b-pawn, or else White's king penetrates at once.

50	...	♖c2
51	♕xb3	♖c5+
52	♔g6	♖g5+
53	♔h7	♔e7
54	f4	1-0

Black's rook cannot stay on the g-file in view of the forks by ♕b7+ or ♕e3+.

I scrambled a draw from a bad position against Sergei Movsesian in round 6, and in the next round I faced Stuart Conquest. After making some inaccuracies in the early middlegame, Black found himself in an awkward position, with a passive g6-bishop and weak dark squares. The critical moment came at move 17, when Black decided to offer a pawn to release his bishop. I saw that taking the pawn would temporarily leave White in an awkward pin. In such situations, it is easy to be lazy and refuse the pawn, knowing that White retains a considerable positional advantage in any case. But a pawn is worth some trouble and, after calculating the consequences carefully, I decided to take the pawn. White soon disentangled himself, when he was not only a pawn up but had also wrecked Black's pawn-structure. The end was not long in coming.

Game 30

J. Nunn – S. Conquest

Hastings 1996/7

Scandinavian Defence

1	e4	d5

When you play Stuart Conquest, there's little point preparing for the game, since he plays a huge range of openings. I hadn't expected the Scandinavian at all, so I just followed the normal lines.

2	exd5	♕xd5
3	♘c3	♕a5

4	d4	♘f6
5	♘f3	

There is quite a strong argument in favour of 5 ♗c4 c6 (the most common reply) 6 ♗d2, with play similar to that in Game 46. However, at the time of this game the subtleties of move-order in the Scandinavian were less well understood (at least by me!).

5	...	c6
6	♗d2	♗f5 (D)

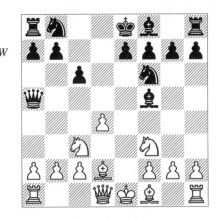

The 2...♕xd5 Scandinavian is built upon quite a simple strategic idea. Black will develop his light-squared bishop outside the pawn-chain, and then play ...c6 and ...e6. This enables him to set up a solid central pawn-structure without blocking in his bishop (as occurs in the French, for example). In many ways the opening is similar to the Caro-Kann, since both are based on a predominantly light-squared strategy. However, in the Caro-Kann White can adopt lines such as the Panov-Botvinnik Attack (1 e4 c6 2 d4 d5 3 exd5 cxd5 4 c4) or the Advance Variation (1 e4 c6 2 d4 d5 3 e5) which lead to strategically dissimilar positions. In the Scandinavian, White's options are more limited and Black is essentially forcing the pace from move one. Doubtless this is the reason that the opening is especially popular amongst club players. However, not everything about the Scandinavian is positive. If White takes care, Black's position can easily become rather passive, and in some of the sharper lines Black can get into trouble because his king remains in the centre for some time.

7	♗c4	e6
8	♘e4 (D)	

White has a wide range of options here, but it is not clear which line is the best:

1) 8 ♘d5 ♕d8 9 ♘xf6+ ♕xf6 is a straightforward line which has been played surprisingly often in practice. I do not think that this can cause Black any difficulties.

2) 8 0-0 ♘bd7 again looks too simple to trouble Black.

3) 8 ♕e2 is the most popular continuation and after 8...♗b4 9 0-0-0 ♘bd7 we reach a key position of Scandinavian theory. White may be able to gain an edge but not more than that.

The point behind the text-move is to reserve the option of playing either ♘xf6+ or ♘g3, depending on where Black moves his queen.

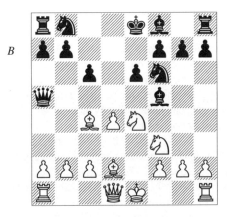

8	...	♕c7

There are three possible queen moves, but this natural retreat looks the safest. 8...♕d8 is playable, but perhaps slightly inferior to the other two moves since 9 ♘g3 ♗g4 (9...♗g6?! 10 h4 h6 11 ♘e5 ♗h7 12 ♕e2 ♘d5 13 0-0-0 ♘d7 14 f4 gives White a clear advantage) 10 c3 ♘bd7 11 h3 ♗xf3 12 ♕xf3 gives White an edge.

8...♕b6!? 9 ♘xf6+ gxf6 is an interesting idea. White has not been able to demonstrate any advantage in this line. After 10 ♗b3 (10 ♕e2 ♕xb2 11 0-0 ♕xc2 is not very convincing for White) 10...♘d7 Black has a solid position.

| 9 | ♘xf6+ | |

9 ♘g3 is also possible in this position; after 9...♗g4 (9...♗g6 10 h4 h6 11 ♘e5 looks slightly better for White) 10 h3 ♗xf3 11 ♕xf3 the position is similar to that arising after 8...♕d8 (Black's queen is on c7 instead of d8, but White has not been forced to play c3). Here, too, White probably has an edge.

9   ...   **gxf6** (D)

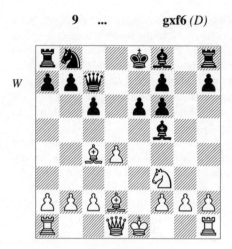

W

10   **℗e2!?**

This was an innovation, although the move is perfectly natural since it is obviously in White's interests to prepare queenside castling. In the years since this game was played, many players have gone down the same path, and the theoretical verdict seems to be that White can retain at most a faint edge. Alternatives:

1) 10 ♘h4 ♗g6 11 f4!? (11 ♘xg6 hxg6 12 ℗f3 ♘d7 gives White nothing) is an interesting possibility; after 11...f5 (11...♗e4 12 f5 is awkward for Black) 12 ℗f3 ♗e7 13 ℗h3 ♗f6 14 ♘f3 White recentralizes his knight while keeping the g6-bishop offside. This may offer White a slight advantage, but it is double-edged as the white queen remains out of play for the moment.

2) 10 c3 has been played a few times but seems to me to have little point. The d4-pawn is not attacked and so c3 may not be necessary; indeed, by opening the h7-b1 diagonal, it even exposes White's king after a later 0-0-0.

3) 10 ♗b3 is similar to the game in that White prepares ℗e2 followed by castling, but in this case White cautiously defends his c-pawn before moving the queen. This line can transpose into the game, but I think there is an advantage in leaving the bishop on c4 for the moment, as it may be that White will be able to save time by missing out ♗b3.

10   ...   **♘d7**

10...♗xc2 is too risky; after 11 d5! ♗g6 (or 11...cxd5 12 ♗b5+ ♘c6 13 ♘d4 ♗g6 14 ♖c1 and White crashes through on c6) 12 dxe6 fxe6 13 ♗xe6 White has an obvious advantage in view of Black's exposed king.

11   **0-0-0**

White again delays ♗b3; although in this game White does not make any real use of this delay, in some lines it may be important.

11   ...   **0-0-0**

Black can't exploit the position of the bishop on c4; for example, 11...♘b6 (11...b5 12 ♗d3 ♗xd3 13 ℗xd3 0-0-0 14 ♖he1 favours White as Black has weakened his queenside by pushing the b-pawn) and now:

1) 12 ♘h4!? ♘xc4 (12...♗g6 looks more sensible) 13 ℗xc4 ♗g6 14 d5! exd5 15 ♖he1+ ♗e4 16 ♖xe4+ dxe4 17 ℗xe4+ ℗e5 18 ℗g4 gave White excellent play for the exchange in S.Petrosian-Erenska, Bad Wörishofen 2000.

2) 12 ♗b3 a5 (12...c5 13 dxc5 ♗xc5 14 ♗c3 ♘d7 15 ♘d4 is dangerous for Black) 13 a3 a4 14 ♗a2 ♘d5 15 g3 gives White an edge.

12   **♘h4**

Sooner or later White will have to play ♗b3, since he cannot allow Black the tempo-gaining ...♘b6 for ever. After 12 ♗b3, play usually transposes to the game, but in Nunn-Hodgson, Reading 2000 Black tried to take advantage of White's move-order by 12...♗g4. However, this was not a particularly good idea and after 13 h3 ♗h5 14 g4 ♗g6 15 ♘h4 ♘b6 16 ℗f3 ♗e7 17 ♗f4 ℗d7 18 ♗g3 ♘d5 19 c4 ♘c7 20 ♘xg6 hxg6 21 ♔b1 ♘e8 White should have played 22 h4, with some advantage.

12   ...   **♗g6**

13   **♗b3** (D)

White cannot delay any longer since 13 g3 is met by 13...♘b6 attacking the d4-pawn.

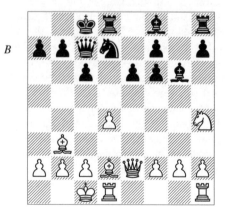

B

After the text-move White's plan is to improve his position with moves such as g3 and

Ihe1, leaving the option of ♘xg6 open for the moment.

13   ...   ♗d6?!

Black can safely steer the game towards equality by 13...c5! 14 d5 (14 ♗e3 ♘b6 15 dxc5 ♗xc5 is dead level) 14...♘b6 15 ♘xg6 (15 ♗a5?? loses material after 15...♕f4+) 15...hxg6 16 ♗a5 e5 17 c4 ♗d6, followed by ...f5, and Black has a satisfactory position. The immediate 13...♘b6 is wrong, however, since White can gain time by attacking the unde-fended f6-pawn: 14 ♕f3 ♗g7 15 ♗f4 ♕d7 16 Ihe1 ♘d5 17 ♗g3 and White is clearly better.

14   g3!

A very useful little move. White shields his h2-pawn, denies Black the f4-square and sets up a possible later idea of ♘g2 and ♗f4, should White want to exchange the dark-squared bish-ops.

14   ...   Ihe8 (D)

Black hasn't had a very comfortable time in this position. 14...♘b6 15 ♕f3 favours White, while 14...c5 is less effective now because 15 d5 ♘b6 (15...e5 16 c4 is similar) 16 ♗a5 (note that here White doesn't have to exchange on g6 first) 16...e5 17 c4, followed by ♗c2, gives White a strong grip on the light squares.

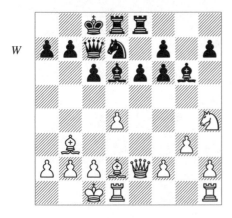

15   Ihe1   f5

The motivation behind this move is clear: Black wants to play ...♘f6 followed by either ...♗h5 or ...♘e4, depending on circumstances. Nevertheless, it is a considerable concession to block in the g6-bishop and White is quick to ex-ploit this. 15...♔b8 16 ♘g2 Ie7 was played in Ochsner-Danielsen, Danish Team Ch 1999/00 and now 17 ♘e3!, threatening ♘c4, is good for

White. If 17...c5, then 18 d5 and the knight is well-placed to control several important light squares.

16   ♘g2

White is no longer interested in exchanging the crippled bishop on g6. Instead, he aims to exchange off Black's dark-squared bishop with ♗f4 and then plant his knight on f4, with a strong bind.

16   ...   ♔b8?

Black does not appreciate the danger and al-lows White to proceed with his plan. 16...♘f6 is in keeping with Black's intended idea, but it fails for tactical reasons: 17 ♗g5 ♗e7 (17...♕e7 18 ♘f4 gives White a large advantage and 17...♗h5 18 f3 doesn't help) 18 ♗xe6+ fxe6 19 ♕xe6+ ♔b8 (after 19...♕d7 20 ♗xf6 ♗xf6 21 ♕xf6 ♕d5 22 Ixe8 Ixe8 23 ♘f4 ♕xa2 24 d5! White is much better, since not only is he a pawn up but in addition Black's bishop is virtually useless) 20 ♗xf6 Id6 21 ♕xe7 Ixe7 22 Ixe7 and White wins.

16...c5 is Black's best chance, but White can retain an advantage by 17 d5 (17 ♗f4 cxd4 18 Ixd4 ♘c5 19 Ic4 e5 20 ♗e3 is also slightly better for White) 17...e5 18 ♘e3!; for example, 18...♘f6 19 f3 ♔b8 20 ♗a4 Ie7 21 ♗c3 with awkward pressure (the immediate threat is 22 ♘c4).

17   ♗f4 (D)

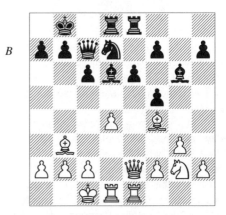

The exchange of bishops is greatly in White's favour since Black will be left with the inactive bishop on g6. White will follow up with ♘f4, which will increase the pressure on e6 to such an extent that ...f6 will never be possible. More-over, the knight on f4 will prevent Black from

activating his bishop by ...♘f6 and ...♗h5. In order to prevent White from establishing this total bind, Black decides to play ...f6 straight away.

17   ...   f6 *(D)*

Aiming for ...♗f7, which will at least be a step in the right direction for Black's bishop.

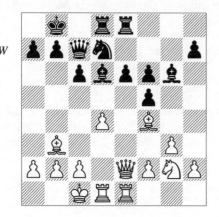

18   ♗xe6!

The correct decision, which I arrived at only after thinking for more than 20 minutes. Basically, White has three possible plans. The first is to win a pawn by 18 ♗xd6 ♕xd6 19 ♘f4 ♗f7 20 ♘xe6, and now:

1) 20...♗xe6? 21 ♗xe6 ♘f8 is wrong as White wins by 22 d5 cxd5 23 ♖xd5 ♕xd5 (23...♕c7 24 ♕d2 also wins for White) 24 ♗xd5 ♖xe2 25 ♖xe2 ♖xd5 26 ♖e8+.

2) 20...♘b6 (threatening ...♘d5) 21 g4 (more or less forced if White wants to have any hope of an advantage; 21 ♖d3 ♗xe6 22 ♗xe6 ♘d5 is fine for Black) 21...♗xe6 22 ♗xe6 fxg4 23 ♕xg4 ♕xh2 and White can only claim a small plus.

Secondly, White can ignore the e6-pawn altogether and continue to play positionally. In this case Black would be able to play ...♗f7, which would be a success for him. The final possibility is the move played in the game, which also wins a pawn but leaves White pinned along the e-file. In such situations it is easy to be lazy and, rather than carefully calculate the consequences of the more forcing moves, go for something safe but less ambitious. Such an attitude is dangerous and often leads to large advantages being gradually frittered away through lack of resolution. In this case I had enough

time to be able to calculate the consequences of the text-move and determine that the end result was very good for White. In this case an important factor is that the capture on e6 not only wins a pawn, but also leaves Black's kingside pawns very weak. Thus, even if White has to return the pawn at some stage, he can still look forward to a clear positional advantage.

18   ...   ♘f8

After 18...♗f7 19 ♕c4 ♘b6 20 ♕b3 White not only keeps his extra pawn, but can also look forward to a further harvest among Black's kingside pawns.

19   ♕c4

Forced.

19   ...   ♗h5

The main alternative is 19...♘xe6 20 ♖xe6 ♗xf4+ (20...♕f7 21 ♖xd6 and 20...♗f7 21 ♖xd6 ♖xd6 22 ♕b4 win for White) 21 ♘xf4 ♗f7, but White continues 22 d5 ♗xe6 23 ♘xe6 ♕d6 24 ♘xd8 ♖xd8 25 ♕h4 cxd5 26 ♕xh7 with an extra pawn and a positional advantage.

20   ♖d3! *(D)*

Not 20 ♗xd6? ♕xd6 21 ♗f7 ♖xe1 22 ♖xe1 ♗xf7 23 ♕xf7 ♕xd4 with equality for White at best.

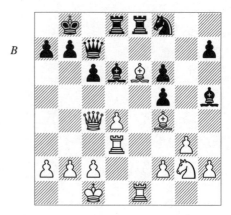

20   ...   ♘xe6

Black has nothing better; e.g., 20...b5 21 ♕b3 ♘xe6 22 ♖xe6 ♖xe6 23 ♕xe6 ♗xf4+ 24 ♘xf4 ♖e8 25 ♕b3 ♖e1+ 26 ♔d2 ♖d1+ (or 26...♗f7 27 ♕b4 ♖f1 28 ♖e3 ♖xf2+ 29 ♔e1 followed by ♕f8+ and White wins) 27 ♔c3 ♗f7 28 ♕b4 with a decisive advantage for White.

21   ♖xe6   ♖xe6?!

21...♗xf4+ 22 ♘xf4 ♗f7 offers more resistance, but after 23 d5 White should still win in the end:

1) 23...♗xe6 24 ♘xe6 ♕e5 25 ♘xd8 ♖xd8 26 d6 ♕e1+ 27 ♖d1 ♕xf2 28 ♕e6 and the powerful passed pawn is decisive.

2) 23...♕a5 24 b4 ♕b6 25 ♖xe8 ♖xe8 26 ♕d4 ♕xd4 27 ♖xd4 ♖e4 28 ♖xe4 fxe4 29 dxc6 bxc6 30 a3 with a winning minor-piece ending.

3) 23...♕b6 24 ♖xe8 ♖xe8 25 ♕d4 ♖e1+ 26 ♔d2 c5 27 ♕c4 ♖e4 28 ♕c3 and White consolidates his extra pawn.

22	♕xe6	♗xf4+
23	♘xf4	

White not only has an extra pawn, but can expect to win additional material in view of Black's very weak kingside pawns.

23	...	♖e8
24	♕xf5	

Taking the second pawn is simplest. Black gets a few checks but no significant counterplay.

24	...	♖e1+
25	♔d2	♖d1+
26	♔c3	♗g4 (D)

A last attempt to confuse the issue by deflecting White's queen away from f5.

27	♕c5	

27 ♕xg4 also wins after 27...♕a5+ 28 b4 ♕a3+ 29 ♔c4 ♕xa2+ (29...♕a6+ 30 ♔b3 ♖b1+ 31 ♔c3 and White wins) 30 ♔c5 ♕xc2+ 31 ♔d6 and the checks run out, but I decided to play the safe line. Note that here taking a safety-first approach is not wrong, since White clearly

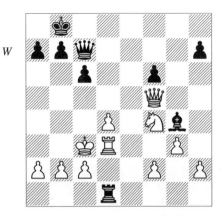

retains a decisive advantage even in the 'safe' line.

27	...	♖a1
28	♖e3	

Black's counterplay has dried up, and it is White's turn to go on the offensive.

28	...	♗c8
29	♖e7	

White is two pawns up with a strong initiative.

29	...	♕d8
30	♘e6	

Doubtless there were other ways to win, but this is simple and effective.

30	...	♗xe6
31	♖xe6	♖xa2
32	♕d6+	1-0

While Black is retrieving his rook from a2, White will make a meal of Black's kingside pawns.

With two rounds to go I was in sole lead, but then disaster struck when I lost to Mark Hebden. I was only able to draw against Glenn Flear in the last round, so the end result was a tie for first between Hebden, Rozentalis and myself.

Soon after Hastings I played my first ever game in the 4NCL (4 Nations Chess League), a team championship covering England, Wales, Scotland and Ireland. The history of this event is quite interesting. For many years the British Chess Federation (BCF) had organized a National Club Championship (NCC), which was a knock-out event for clubs. I was the Captain of the Oxford University NCC team for some years during the 1970s, and initially it was an enjoyable event to play in. However, at some stage the BCF decided to introduce rules designed to restrict teams to what they considered to be 'genuine' club members. This was a thinly-veiled attack on certain teams, especially the university teams, which had dominated the NCC during the 1970s (in the period 1970-1979, the NCC was won five times by Cambridge University and twice by Oxford University). The new rules, which were quite inappropriate for university teams, gave opposing teams plenty of scope to challenge the eligibility of university players. It may well be that some forces within the BCF, depressed at the dominance of the university teams and failing to see any way to counter this on the chessboard, had decided on a flank attack. As an example of the ludicrous situation that now arose, postal grandmaster Adrian Hollis, who had been a member of the Oxford University Chess Club for decades and had not played for any other team for 20 years, was now declared not to be a 'genuine' member of the club and was ruled ineligible to play in the NCC. All my appeals regarding this matter fell on deaf ears. My duties as Captain became more and more focused on disputes concerning the eligibility of players and I was soon happy to leave this job. Over the following years the NCC fell into a gradual decline, with fewer and fewer strong players taking part.

Then, in 1993, the 4NCL was founded (it was largely the brainchild of Chris Dunworth). In this event teams did not need to be associated with clubs, and there were essentially no restrictions on eligibility. The 4NCL quickly grew in popularity and was unquestionably one of the best chess developments in the UK during the 1990s.

One might have thought that the BCF which, under 'Objects of the Federation' on its website, gives 'To encourage the study and practice of chess in the Commonwealth', would have been pleased at the introduction of a new and popular chess event. Far from it. I attended a BCF meeting on a matter unrelated to the 4NCL and was astonished by a discussion which centred on how to destroy the upstart 4NCL, which was perceived as detracting from the BCF's own NCC. This discussion was particularly ironic in view of the fact that the BCF's own actions had so seriously undermined the prestige of the NCC, but thankfully nothing came of this discussion; in any case, there was little the BCF could do about the 4NCL. The BCF could at any stage in the preceding decades have established something similar to the 4NCL, but they did not; now that somebody else had done it, the BCF's reaction was entirely negative. The 4NCL has continued to expand up to the present day, and has remained independent from the BCF, while as for the NCC, I need only quote from the August 2005 issue of the *British Chess Magazine*, which reported that "The British Chess Federation's so-called National Club competition received only six entries this year...".

I played happily in the 4NCL for several years for what was basically the same team, although it changed its name several times. Three of the later games in this book are from the 4NCL.

My chess was now limited to team events with just a very occasional tournament. I didn't play any games in the period February to May 1997, but in June I ventured to Leon in Spain for a round-robin event of ten players. My lack of practice was soon revealed, since I lost in the first round against Granda Zuñiga, and continued with four rather uninspiring draws. However, I then started to played better and by scoring 3½ from my last four games I managed to achieve outright second place, a point behind the winner Granda.

This was followed by another gap of a few months until the World Team Championship in Lucerne in late October. This was in fact to be the last time I played for England (in over-the-board chess, at any rate) but I cannot count it a great success. Playing on bottom board, I was only chosen for two matches and both games ended in a draw.

My play for the rest of the year was indifferent. A poor 4/6 in the Kilkenny weekend tournament in Ireland was balanced by a couple of good wins in the 4NCL. After Christmas, it was Hastings time again, although this was to be my last appearance in the famous traditional tournament. I started with four solid draws, but then lost a topsy-turvy struggle to the French player Relange. In the following round I faced Chris Ward.

Chris Ward is a great fan of the Sicilian Dragon, and I decided to adopt a line involving liquidation to an ending. Dragon players love complicated middlegames and I hoped that the change of pace would disconcert him. It is hard to say how far to go in playing against your opponent's style. I would not go so far as to choose a clearly inferior variation, but where there is a choice between lines of roughly equal merit, it often pays to steer the game into territory uncomfortable for the opponent. Having a flexible style is an advantage when adopting this strategy. There is no benefit in making your opponent uncomfortable if you feel the same way, but if you are equally happy whatever the type of position, then you have a good chance of gaining a psychological advantage in your games.

Game 31

J. Nunn – C. Ward

Hastings 1997/8

Sicilian Defence, Dragon Variation

1	e4	c5
2	♘f3	d6
3	d4	cxd4
4	♘xd4	♘f6
5	♘c3	g6

Chris Ward has been a lifelong fan of the Dragon, and has written a great deal about it. Looking at his writings, one might conclude that I had found it tough to cope with his Dragon, and a couple of people commented to me to this effect. Perhaps this impression has arisen because a quickplay game I lost to Chris has featured on various occasions in his writings. However, the reality is that I have played four Dragon games against Chris at a normal time-limit and won all four.

6   ♗e3

If you don't have very much time for opening preparation, then it probably isn't a good idea to play the Yugoslav Attack and I have to admit that I adopted 6 g3 towards the end of my career. However, against Chris Ward I was generally willing to try the Yugoslav due to his tendency to play one particular line, which we will come to later. If your opponent shows a fixed preference for one variation, then your preparation becomes much simpler.

6	...	♗g7
7	f3	♘c6
8	♕d2	0-0 *(D)*

The line which Chris has been so fond of involves an early ...♕a5; for example, 9 ♗c4 ♗d7 10 0-0-0 ♕a5. It is curious that when the 'Dragon revival' started in the late 1960s, this was the line which Black almost always played. The logic is that the queen is actively placed on a5, and can easily take part in the attack against the white king. This applies especially if the traditional ...♖xc3 exchange sacrifice occurs. Moreover, playing the queen out allows the f8-rook to move to c8. This has two advantages: firstly the queen's rook remains available on the queenside (for example, to support a b-pawn push) and secondly, if White plays ♔b1 and then ♘d5, the sequence ...♕xd2 ♘xe7+ ♔f8 becomes available, attacking the knight. With all this logic behind ...♕a5, it is perhaps surprising that this line appears to be inferior, and has now virtually disappeared in favour of the ...♖c8 lines. There are in fact quite a few problems with ...♕a5, but the main one is that it is very committal. It is not at all clear that it will be a useful move in the subsequent play, and the modern trend is to play the more flexible moves (such as ...♖c8 and ...♘e5) first, leaving it until later to decide whether to develop the queen at a5.

9   ♗c4

9 g4 is a line which was popular in the 1980s but is now played infrequently. However, it is not a bad choice if you know that your opponent likes playing ...♗d7 and ...♕a5, because against this line Black's best is to put his bishop on e6! One example is Nunn-Ward, London (Lloyds Bank) 1984, which continued: **9...♘xd4?!** (this is inaccurate; 9...♗e6 is better, because then 10 h4 can be met by 10...d5) **10 ♗xd4 ♗e6 11 h4** (here White can miss out 0-0-0, which not only saves a tempo but also avoids giving Black a target to aim at) **11...♕a5 12 h5 ♖fc8 13 hxg6 hxg6 14 a3!** *(D)*.

A very unpleasant move. White shows his intention to improve his position as much as possible before deciding whether to castle. By

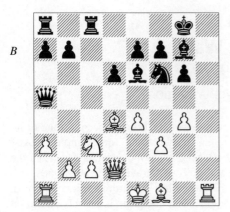

B

removing the a-pawn from attack, White ensures that he can castle at a moment's notice, but he will only do this when he is fully prepared. My database reveals that 14 a3 has scored 78% in practice, with Black failing to win a single game, which is strong evidence that Black is in trouble here. The game finished **14...Eab8** (14...b5 15 g5 ②h5 16 ②xb5 ♛xd2+ 17 ⌷xd2 and White wins a pawn) **15 ♗d3 ♗c4** (after 15...b5 16 b4 followed by ②xb5 White again wins a pawn for insufficient compensation; note how delaying castling allows White to play moves on the queenside which would be utterly impossible after 0-0-0) **16 ♛h2 e5?** (16...b5 is better; blocking the Dragon bishop is rarely good) **17 ♗e3 ♗e6** (17...♗xd3 18 cxd3 ♖xc3 19 ♗d2 favours White) **18 ♗h6 ♗h8** (D).

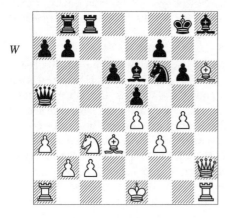

W

19 0-0-0 (now is the time for this move, when White's attack is already well-developed) **19...♛d8** (19...♖xc3 still fails to 20 ♗d2) **20 ②e2** (preventing the exchange sacrifice on c3 and switching the knight to help with the

kingside attack) **20...b5 21 ②g3** (with the deadly threat of 22 ②f5!) **21...♗xg4** (desperation) **22 ♗g5** (even stronger than just taking the piece) **22...♗h5 23 ②xh5 gxh5 24 ♗h6** (cutting off the king's escape-route) **24...⌷h7** (D).

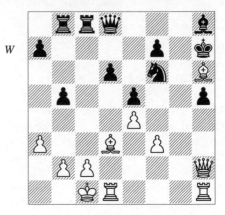

W

25 ♖dg1! ⌷xh6 (now White has a forced mate in 8) **26 ♛d2+ ⌷h7 27 ♛g5 ♛f8 28 ♛f5+ ⌷h6 29 ♖g5 1-0.** 30 ♛xf6+! will follow.

Now we return to the main game.

    9   ...   ♗d7 (D)

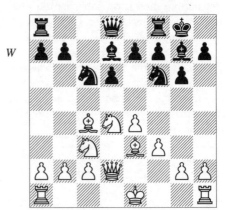

W

    10   0-0-0

10 h4 in most cases simply transposes back into the lines which arise after 10 0-0-0, but in a few situations it has independent significance. One of these arises if Black wants to play ...♛a5. The game Nunn-Ward, Islington Open 1990 continued: **10...♛a5 11 ②b3!?** (this is White's idea, at once trying to exploit the position of the queen on a5; in many lines White will again use the plan of delaying castling in order to avoid giving Black a target)

11...♕b4?! (11...♕c7 looks more solid; after
12 0-0-0 the position is unclear) **12 ♗d3** (now
White threatens to trap the queen with 13 a3, so
quick action is necessary) **12...♘a5** (the best
reply) **13 h5 ♖ac8** (13...♘xh5 14 g4 ♘f6 15
♗h6 ♗xh6 16 ♕xh6 ♘xb3 17 axb3 ♖fc8 looks
natural, but runs into 18 e5! dxe5 19 g5 ♘h5 20
♖xh5 and White wins) **14 ♗h6 ♘c4** (14...♘xb3
15 axb3 ♗xh6 16 ♕xh6 ♘xh5 17 ♖xh5 gxh5
18 ♕g5+ ♚h8 19 ♕xe7 ♗e6 20 ♕f6+ ♚g8 21
f4 favours White) **15 ♗xc4 ♗xh6 16 ♕xh6
♕xc4 17 g4** (White already has a dangerous attack, while Black hasn't got very far with his
counterplay) **17...♕e6 18 0-0-0 ♖xc3** (the traditional sacrifice, but ineffective in this position
because White's attack is too far advanced) **19
bxc3 a5?!** (19...♖c8 was the last chance) **20
♘d4 ♕e5** (20...♕xa2 21 hxg6 fxg6 22 g5 ♘h5
23 ♖xh5 gxh5 24 g6 and White wins) **21 hxg6
fxg6** (D).

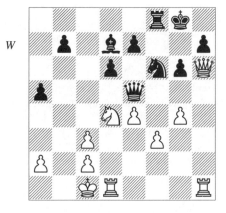

22 f4! ♕xe4 (22...♕c5 23 g5 ♘h5 24 ♖xh5
wins for White) **23 ♖de1** (the rest is forced)
**23...♕g2 24 g5 ♘h5 25 ♖xh5 gxh5 26 ♖xe7
♖f7 27 ♖xf7 ♚xf7 28 ♕xh7+ ♚e8 29 ♕h8+
♚e7 30 ♕f6+ ♚e8 31 g6 1-0.**

Now back to the main game:

10	**...**	**♕a5**

Chris decides to adopt his favourite line.
10...♖c8 11 ♗b3 ♘e5 is the standard continuation.

11	**h4**	**♘e5**
12	**♗b3**	**♖fc8** (D)

In this position White has four possible continuations.

13	**h5**

The alternatives are:

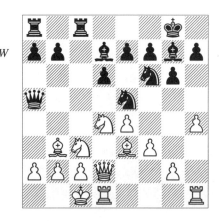

1) 13 ♗h6? is definitely wrong since after
13...♗xh6 14 ♕xh6 ♖xc3 15 bxc3 ♕xc3 Black
has excellent compensation for the exchange.

2) 13 ♚b1 is the most common move in
practice, but it may not be best since it is not
clear whether White really needs to tuck his
king away. Black may continue with either
13...♘c4 or 13...b5.

3) 13 g4 is the move that I now regard as
most accurate. See Game 32.

13	**... ♘xh5**

13...♖xc3!? is a critical continuation. Although it is logical and thematic, it has been
played surprisingly rarely. Accepting the exchange by 14 ♕xc3 ♕xc3 15 bxc3 ♘xh5 gives
Black excellent compensation, so the critical
continuation is 14 h6 ♖c5 15 ♕xa5 ♖xa5 16
hxg7 h5 (16...♚xg7 17 g4 will probably transpose after 17...h5) 17 g4 ♚xg7 18 gxh5 ♘xh5
19 ♖dg1 and White probably has sufficient play
for the pawn, but not more than that.

14	**♘d5!? (D)**

Not often played, but probably better than its
reputation. After a forced sequence, we reach
an ending in which White cannot be worse and
Black must take care. Statistics show that after
14 ♘d5 White has scored 70%, far higher than
any of the other moves in this position. The alternatives are 14 ♗h6 ♖xc3 (14...♘d3+ is also
possible), which gives Black good play for the
exchange, and 14 g4 ♘f6 15 ♗h6, when again
15...♖xc3 is fine for Black.

14	**... ♕xd2+**
15	**♖xd2**

It looks odd to give up a pawn and then immediately exchange queens, but White can regain the pawn by force.

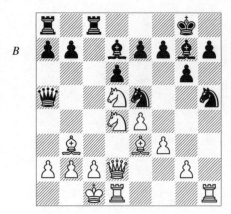

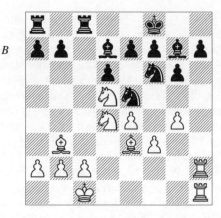

| 15 | ... | ♚f8 |
| 16 | g4 | ♘f6 |

This has been an almost automatic reply for Black. Alternatives are indeed inferior:

1) 16...♘g3 is suggested by the computer program *Junior*, but after 17 ♜g1 e6 18 ♘c3 a5 19 a4 ♘xf3 20 ♘xf3 ♗xc3 21 ♜xg3 ♗xd2+ 22 ♔xd2 White's strong initiative and dark-square pressure give him a clear advantage.

2) 16...♗xg4 17 fxg4 ♘xg4 18 ♗g5 e6 is effectively a trap which has caught three people: White wins by force after 19 ♘xe6+! fxe6 20 ♜f1+ ♔g8 21 ♘e7+ ♔h8 22 ♘xc8 ♜xc8 23 ♗xe6 ♜c5 24 ♜xd6 ♗f6 25 ♜d8+ and here Black resigned in Phillips-Boztas, Richmond rpd 1999 and Efimenko-Konguvel, Biel open 2001.

17   ♜dh2 (*D*)

The earlier game Nataf-Ward, Paris-London match 1994 had continued 17 ♘xf6 ♗xf6 18 ♜dh2 (18 ♜xh7 ♔g8 19 ♜h1 a5! is equal, Glek-Hodgson, Bundesliga 1994/5) 18...♘c4 19 ♗xc4 ♜xc4 20 ♜xh7 ♜ac8 with a satisfactory position for Black. The game eventually ended in a draw.

However, I regard the text-move as more accurate. White will inevitably win Black's h-pawn, leading to an ending in which White has an edge because of his more active rooks. Psychologically this line is a good choice since Dragon players usually revel in middlegame complications and do not like defending slightly worse endings; they feel especially uncomfortable when deprived of ...♜xc3. Moreover, the line is not at all harmless. Indeed, we shall see that in many variations White has dangerous attacking possibilities and if Black makes a

mistake, he can end up in trouble remarkably quickly.

| 17 | ... | ♘xd5 |

Black has four other main possibilities:

1) The key point behind White's previous move is that 17...♘c4? is now dubious on account of 18 ♗h6! ♗xh6+ 19 ♜xh6 ♘g8 20 ♜xh7 e6 21 ♘f4! ♘f6 (21...e5 22 ♘xg6+ fxg6 23 ♜xd7 exd4 24 ♜xb7 gives White fantastic compensation for the piece) 22 ♘dxe6+! ♗xe6 23 ♘xe6+ fxe6 24 ♜xb7 with some advantage for White since he will end up with three and more likely four pawns for the piece.

2) 17...♗xg4? (this is unsound) 18 ♘xf6 ♗xf6 19 fxg4 ♘xg4 20 ♜xh7 ♘xe3 21 ♜xf7+ ♔e8 22 ♜hh7! with a decisive attack for White, Pikula-Velimirović, Belgrade 2000.

3) 17...♘exg4 18 fxg4 ♘xg4 19 ♜xh7 ♘xe3 20 ♘xe3 ♗xd4 21 ♜xf7+ ♔e8 22 ♔b1 is very dangerous for Black; for example, 22...♗c6 23 ♗e6 ♗xe4 24 ♜hh7 ♗f6 25 ♘g4 gives White decisive threats.

4) 17...e6 18 ♘xf6 ♗xf6 19 ♜xh7 a5 (the alternative 19...♘d3+ 20 ♔b1 ♘c5 21 g5 ♗g7 is bad because of the tactical line 22 ♘f5! gxf5 23 exf5 exf5 24 ♜xg7 ♘xb3 25 ♜hh7 ♗e6 26 g6 ♔e7 27 ♗g5+ ♔d7 28 gxf7 ♜f8 29 axb3 with a winning ending for White, Murey-Ravisekhar, London 1986) is probably Black's best option. White can try:

4a) 20 a4 ♘d3+ 21 ♔b1 ♘c5 22 g5 ♗g7 23 ♘f5 only leads to a draw here: 23...exf5 24 ♜xg7 ♘xb3 25 ♜hh7 ♗e6 26 exf5 ♗xf5 27 ♜xf7+ ♔g8 28 ♜hg7+ ½-½ Dineley-Cueto Chajtur, Istanbul Olympiad 2000. The difference, of course, is that with ...a5 and a4 added, White is unable to play axb3.

4b) 20 g5 ♗g7 21 f4 (21 a3 a4 22 ♗a2 may give White an edge) 21...a4 (21...♘d3+ 22 ♔b1 ♘c5 23 f5 exf5 24 exf5 gxf5 25 g6! is unpleasant for Black) 22 ♗xe6 fxe6 23 fxe5 dxe5 with an unclear position, Guedon-Lehtinen, Budapest 2000.

Although 17...♘xd5 looks a perfectly natural continuation, it is worth noting that in my database White scored 8-0 after this move. Black's inability to manage even a single draw of course exaggerates White's prospects, but there is no doubt that the position is slightly uncomfortable for Black.

18 ♗xd5 (D)

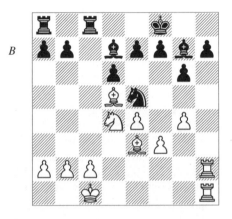

18 ... ♘c6?!

An innovation. Black has several options here:

1) 18...♗xg4 (this idea is ingenious but inadequate) 19 ♖xh7! (after 19 fxg4 ♘xg4 20 ♖xh7 ♘xe3 21 ♗xb7 ♔g8 22 ♗xa8 ♗xd4 Black has no problems) 19...♘xf3 20 ♘xf3 ♗xf3 21 ♗h6 ♗xh6+ 22 ♖1xh6 e6 23 ♗xb7 ♔e7 24 ♖h3 ♗h5 25 ♗xa8 ♖xa8 26 ♖c3 with a clear advantage for White.

2) 18...♖c7 (this has been the most common move in practice) 19 ♗h6 (19 ♖xh7 ♖ac8 20 c3 is also worth considering, avoiding an early exchange of dark-squared bishops; while it is sometimes good for White to swap these bishops, there are cases where it is better to leave them on the board since the attack on g7 prevents Black from extracting his king by ...e6 and ...♔e7) 19...♗xh6+ 20 ♖xh6 e6 21 ♗b3 a5 22 ♖xh7 ♖ac8 23 a3 b5 24 g5 ♘d3+ 25 ♔b1 ♘c5 26 ♗a2 b4 27 axb4 axb4 (F.Olafsson-Hort, Reykjavik 1972) and now 28 f4, threatening f5,

looks good for White since 28...♘xe4? fails to 29 ♗xe6! and White wins.

3) 18...♗c6!? (D) is untested, but is probably Black's best:

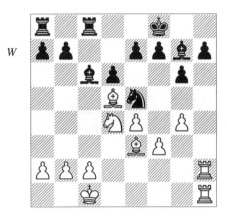

3a) 19 ♖xh7 ♗xd5 20 exd5 ♘c4 looks satisfactory for Black after 21 ♗f2 ♘b6 22 ♘b5 ♘xd5 23 ♘xa7 ♖cb8 or 21 ♗h6 ♗xh6+ 22 ♖1xh6 ♘e3 23 g5 ♔e8 24 ♖g7 ♘xd5.

3b) 19 ♗b3 ♗xe4 (this is the point of Black's previous move) 20 fxe4 ♘xg4 21 ♖f1! gives Black quite a range of things to take:

3b1) 21...♘xe3 22 ♖xf7+ ♔g8 23 ♖xe7+ ♘c4 24 ♘b5! ♗xb2+ 25 ♔d1 ♗e5 26 ♖hxh7 and White's initiative is worth more than a pawn.

3b2) 21...♘xh2 22 ♖xf7+ ♔g8 23 ♖f2+ ♔h8 24 ♖xh2 ♖f8 25 ♖h1 and the weakness of the e6-square is awkward for Black.

3b3) 21...♗f6 22 ♖xh7 ♘xe3 23 ♖xf7+ ♔e8 24 ♖1xf6 exf6 25 ♖xb7 is very good for White.

3b4) 21...♗xd4! 22 ♖xf7+ ♔e8 23 ♖xe7+ ♔xe7 24 ♖xh7+ ♔f6 25 ♖f7+ ♔e5 26 ♖e7+ ♔f6 27 ♖e6+ (of course White has a perpetual check if he wants it) 27...♔g7 28 ♗xd4+ ♔h6 29 ♗d5 ♖c7 30 ♖xd6 with an unclear position. White has just one pawn for the exchange, but his active centralized pieces are a significant factor.

19 ♘xc6!

Perhaps this move is slightly surprising, since it is normally a bad idea to exchange on c6 in the Sicilian and thereby strengthen Black's pawn-centre. Moreover, in this case the recapture ...bxc6 forces White to waste a tempo retreating his bishop. However, here Black's ...bxc6 doesn't really help him to set his central pawns in motion because a later ...e6 and ...d5 will imprison his light-squared bishop and leave him weak on the dark squares. Indeed, the closure of the c-file actually stifles Black's counterplay and gives White the time he needs to make progress on the kingside. Note that the tactical line 19 ♖xh7 ♘xd4 20 ♗xd4 ♗xd4 21 ♖xf7+ ♔e8 22 ♖hh7 ♗f6 23 ♗xb7 ♖ab8 24 ♗xc8 ♖xc8 fails since White's rooks have gone down a blind alley and he will lose material after a later ...♗e6.

19   ...   bxc6

After 19...♗xc6 20 ♗b3 White regains the pawn with an advantage thanks to his more active rooks.

20   ♗c4

Better than 20 ♗b3, which would expose the bishop to annoying attacks by ...a5-a4 or ...c5-c4.

20   ...   h6

Black believes that it is in his interests to swap dark-squared bishops. The alternative was to try exchanging the other bishops, but after 20...♗e6 21 ♗xe6 fxe6 22 ♖xh7 ♔g8 23 f4 White retains an advantage.

21   ♗xh6   ♗xh6+

22   ♖xh6 *(D)*

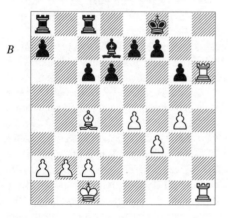

The threat is 23 ♖h8+ and 24 ♖1h7+, so Black must move his e-pawn.

22   ...   e6

The normal move, freeing e7 for the king while at the same time blocking the diagonal of White's bishop. However, it allows White to establish a dark-square grip so it was worth considering the alternative 22...e5 23 ♖h7 ♗e8. In this case White continues 24 f4! (24 g5 ♖d8 25

♖h8+ ♔e7 26 ♖1h7 is also good for White) 24...exf4 25 g5 ♖ab8 (25...♖d8 26 ♖f1 d5 27 exd5 cxd5 28 ♗d3 ♖d6 29 ♖xf4 gives White considerable pressure) 26 ♖f1 ♖b4 27 b3 d5 28 exd5 cxd5 29 ♗xd5 ♗b5 30 ♖d1, with ♖h4 to come, and Black is clearly worse.

23   f4

Gaining space. White might imprison Black's bishop by e5, or he might play f5 with a direct breakthrough.

23   ...   ♔e7

24   e5!

Playing for the dark-square bind is best. 24 f5 is less effective if Black finds the right reply:

1) 24...gxf5 25 gxf5 exf5 26 exf5 ♗xf5 27 ♖e1+ ♔f8 (27...♔d7 28 ♖f1 is crushing) 28 ♖f1 ♔g7 29 ♖xd6 ♗g6 30 ♖g1 with strong pressure for White.

2) 24...d5 25 ♗a6 ♖g8 26 fxg6 dxe4! (after 26...♖xg6? 27 ♖xg6 fxg6 28 ♖h7+ ♔d6 29 e5+ ♔c7 30 ♖g7 White is clearly better) 27 gxf7 ♖xg4 28 ♗e2 ♖f4 29 ♗h5 ♖f8 with only a minimal advantage for White.

24   ...   dxe5

After 24...d5 25 ♗d3 c5 (25...♖g8 26 ♖h7 is similar) 26 ♖h7 ♖g8 27 ♖1h6 g5 28 f5 exf5 29 gxf5 g4 30 e6 White has a dangerous attack.

25   fxe5 *(D)*

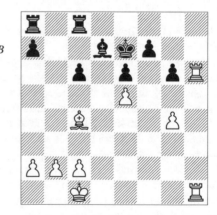

White's e5-pawn is isolated, but Black's rooks have no easy route to attack it. Thus White has time to build up against Black's kingside pawns by ♖h7 and either ♖f1-f6 or ♖1h6 and ♗d3.

25   ...   a5

Black hopes for ...a4 and ...♖a5, but this plan is too slow. However, passive defence by

25...♖g8 26 ♖h7 ♗e8 27 ♖f1 ♖b8 is no better. After 28 b3, followed by the activation of White's king, Black still has a very difficult position.

26	♖h7	a4
27	♖f1	♗e8?! *(D)*

This costs a pawn, but even after 27...♖f8 28 g5 (28 ♗d3?! ♖a5 29 ♗xg6 ♗e8 gives Black unnecessary counterplay) 28...♖a5 29 ♖e1, followed by advancing the white king (for example, by ♔d2-c3 and then b4), Black has an utterly miserable position.

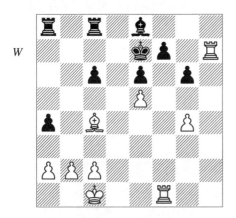

28   ♖f6!

This decisive move is stronger than 28 ♗d3 ♖a5 (28...♔d8? loses to 29 ♗xg6 fxg6 30 ♖d1+) 29 ♗xg6 ♖xe5 30 ♗xf7 ♗xf7 31 ♖hxf7+ ♔d6 and it is not clear if White can win.

28   ...   ♖a5

Black had intended 28...♔d8 but then noticed the deadly sacrifice 29 ♗xe6! fxe6 30 ♖xe6 ♗d7 (the alternative lines 30...♖cb8 31 ♖d6+ ♔c8 32 ♖e7 and 30...♖c7 31 ♖xe8+ are also hopeless) 31 ♖d6 ♖a7 32 e6 and White wins.

29   ♖xe6+

Losing this key pawn means the end is not far off.

29	...	♔d8
30	♖d6+	

This repetition was just to see if Black would make things easy by 30...♔c7 31 ♗xf7 ♖xe5 32 ♖e6!.

30	...	♔e7
31	♖e6+	♔d8
32	♖f6 *(D)*	

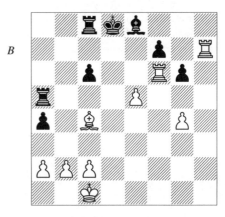

Best as White wins a pawn while retaining enormous pressure. In fact, Black can hardly avoid the loss of a second pawn.

32	...	♖xe5
33	♗xf7	♔e7

After 33...♗xf7 34 ♖fxf7 the doubled rooks on the seventh would be decisive, while 33...♖c7 34 ♗xg6 ♗xg6 35 ♖xc7 ♔xc7 36 ♖xg6 is an easy win thanks to the two extra pawns.

34   g5

Now Black loses more material.

34	...	♖xg5
35	♖e6+	♔f8
36	♗xe8	1-0

As 36...♖xe8 37 ♖h8+ picks up a rook.

Unfortunately this was to be the last bright spot in the tournament. I drew in rounds 7 and 8, and then committed a tactical oversight in the last round against Hebden to finish in joint sixth place on 4/9 – one of my worst-ever results at Hastings. The tournament was won by Sadler with the excellent score of 7/9. Why didn't I play again at Hastings? As usual, such decisions are based on a combination of factors. I still considered myself, at least to some extent, a professional player and when the tournament organizer starts off the invitation with something like "Well, we haven't got any money, but..." you can expect the worst. The sponsorship situation at Hastings had been deteriorating for some years, but nevertheless I still enjoyed playing. However, at some point the limit has to be reached beyond which there is little point in taking part. One thing I have learned in my many years of professional play is that if you are genuinely unhappy about some aspect of a tournament then it is better not to take part, because participating virtually guarantees a bad result. Of course, I realize that, especially these days, players are often unable to pick and choose and must take whatever is offered, but the same general principle holds – if you are looking forward to going to a tournament then you will probably play well; otherwise, stay away.

As it turned out, my battles with Chris Ward in the Dragon were not over, as we met soon afterwards in the 4NCL. This time I was more inclined to play a critical line, but over the board I realized that there was a huge hole in my rather hasty preparation. Fortunately, I was able to find a strong innovation over the board. This innovation was based on two factors: firstly, as White's king was still on c1, Black's attack along the b-file did not threaten immediate mate (as ...♕xb2+ could be met by ♔d2) and secondly, White could play to eliminate Black's Dragon bishop. White's 20th was the key move, offering a piece to remove Black's dark-squared bishop. Black declined the offer, but then he had to face a strong attack in a situation of material equality; White soon broke through to win material. An opening shock doesn't always have the happy ending of this game; preparation is crucial if you intend to play ultra-sharp opening lines.

Game 32

J. Nunn – C. Ward

British League (4NCL) 1997/8
Sicilian Defence, Dragon Variation

1	e4	c5
2	♘f3	d6
3	d4	cxd4
4	♘xd4	♘f6
5	♘c3	g6
6	♗e3	♗g7
7	f3	♘c6
8	♕d2	0-0
9	♗c4	♗d7
10	0-0-0	♕a5

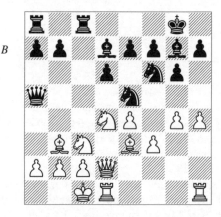

B

For comments on the moves up to here, see Game 31, which was played only three weeks before this one. Just as in that game, Chris Ward decides to use his favourite line, which these days is regarded as slightly unusual. I did not want to repeat precisely the same line as in the previous game, since no doubt he would have had an improvement prepared.

11	h4	♘e5
12	♗b3	♖fc8
13	g4 *(D)*	

Deviating from the previous game, in which I played 13 h5. For a summary of White's alternatives, see that game. My choice of this move was actually based on a conversation I had with Chris Ward after the previous game. Over breakfast, he commented that it was surprising 13 ♔b1 was so popular, as 13 g4 looked like a more useful move. This point came to mind

while I was preparing for the current game, and I decided to give his own recommendation a try! The move g4 aims primarily to play h5 without sacrificing a pawn, but it has some other good points: it allows the white queen to switch to h2, and in some lines in supports the piece sacrifice ♘f5.

13	...	b5

There are three possible plans here for Black:

1) The most obvious is 13...♘c4 14 ♗xc4 ♖xc4, but after 15 h5 ♖ac8 (15...♖xc3 16 ♕xc3 ♕xa2 17 hxg6 hxg6 18 ♕a3 doesn't really give Black enough for the exchange) 16 ♘b3 ♕a6 17 hxg6 fxg6 (17...hxg6 18 e5 is also bad for Black) White has a pleasant choice. The first

option is 18 e5, which gives White a dangerous attack, since 18...dxe5 loses a piece after 19 g5, while if the f6-knight moves White can reply 19 ♕h2. The second option is 18 ♔b1 followed by ♗d4, which gives White unpleasant threats without any risk at all.

2) Another idea is the surprising 13...♖c4!? *(D)*, and now:

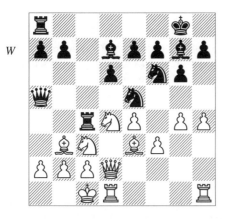

2a) 14 ♗xc4?! ♘xc4 15 ♕d3 ♕b4 16 ♘b3 ♘xe4! (an unexpected sacrifice on an apparently well-defended square, which gives Black at least equality) and now:

2a1) 17 ♕xe4? ♗xc3 18 ♗d4 ♘xb2 19 ♗xc3 ♕xc3 favours Black.

2a2) 17 ♘xe4 ♘xb2 18 ♕d5 ♘c4 19 ♗c5 dxc5 20 ♕xc5 ♕xc5 21 ♘bxc5 ♗c6 gives Black good compensation for the exchange.

2a3) 17 ♗d4 ♗xd4 18 ♕xd4 ♘xc3 19 ♕xc3 ♕xc3 20 bxc3 gives Black enough for the exchange.

2a4) 17 fxe4 ♗xc3 18 ♗d4 ♗xd4 19 ♕xd4 ♗xg4 is unclear.

2b) 14 g5! ♘h5 (after 14...♖xd4? 15 ♗xd4 ♘xf3 16 ♕f2! ♘xd4 17 ♖xd4 the weakness of f7 is fatal for Black) 15 f4 ♖xd4 (15...♘f3? 16 ♘xf3 ♖xc3 looks like another typical Dragon combination based on a dark-square break-through; however, they don't all work and in this case 17 e5! causes Black's position to collapse) 16 ♕xd4 ♘g4 17 e5! ♘g3 18 ♖he1 ♘f5 19 ♕d5 ♕xd5 20 ♘xd5 e6 21 ♗g1 exd5 22 ♗xd5 and White has the advantage as Black's queenside pawns are very weak, Rodriguez Guerrero-Guerra Bastida, Linares 2003.

The move played again aims for ...♘c4, but now with the idea of recapturing on c4 with the

pawn. This will give Black a ready-made attack against b2. The two problems with this plan are firstly that it is a little slow and secondly, thanks to White's omission of ♔b1, he may be able simply to ignore a black queen arriving on b2.

14   h5 *(D)*

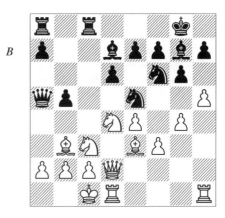

14   ...   ♘c4

On the evidence of Nunn-Ward and the accompanying analysis, this move is risky and if Black wants to play the ...♕a5 line, then he should try 14...b4! here. This move is tentatively recommended in *Play the Sicilian Dragon* by Edward Dearing (Gambit, 2004) and I agree that it seems to offer Black reasonable prospects. White can try:

1) 15 ♘d5 ♘xd5 16 exd5 ♘c4 17 ♕e2 (17 ♗xc4 ♖xc4 18 ♔b1 ♕xd5 19 ♕h2 is also unclear) 17...♘xe3 (17...♕xd5? 18 hxg6 hxg6 19 ♕h2 gives White a very dangerous attack) 18 ♕xe3 ♕b6 is unclear.

2) 15 ♘ce2 ♘c4 16 ♗xc4 ♖xc4 17 ♔b1 ♖ac8 (this position can arise by other move-orders) 18 hxg6 fxg6 19 ♖c1 ♕e5! and Dearing's assessment of unclear looks fair enough to me.

15   ♗xc4

After 15 ♕d3 ♘e5 White has nothing better than to repeat moves, since playing 16 ♕e2 positively invites Black to sacrifice on c3.

15   ...   bxc4

Now White has two free moves before Black lines up against b2.

16   ♗h6

A logical step. Either Black's bishop is exchanged, or White transfers his bishop to a more active square with gain of tempo. Note that White doesn't have to worry any more about ...♖xc3, so there is no problem about the white queen being drawn away if Black plays ...♗xh6.

16   ...   ♗h8

Forced, as Black cannot allow his defensive bishop to be exchanged; for example, 16...♖ab8 17 ♗xg7 ♔xg7 18 hxg6 fxg6 19 ♕h6+ ♔g8 20 ♘d5 and White wins.

17   ♘f5

A critical moment as White is now threatening mate in one on e7. This position arises 22 times in my database and White's score is overwhelming. However, closer analysis shows that Black has one playable continuation.

17   ...   ♖e8 *(D)*

This is the critical test. The only other try is 17...♗xf5 (17...gxf5 18 ♕g5+ leads to mate), but then 18 exf5! (after 18 gxf5? ♘xh5 it is doubtful whether White has anything better than a draw by 19 ♖xh5 ♗xc3 20 ♕xc3 ♕xc3 21 bxc3 gxh5 22 ♖g1+, etc.) 18...♖ab8 19 hxg6 fxg6 (19...hxg6 20 fxg6 ♕b4 21 ♕e3! ♕xb2+ 22 ♔d2 also gives White a large advantage) 20 ♕e3 (threatening mate in one) 20...e5 (after 20...♕e5 21 ♕xe5 dxe5 22 g5 ♘e8 23 ♖d7 Black has a terrible ending) 21 fxg6 hxg6 22 ♗g5 gives White a massive advantage.

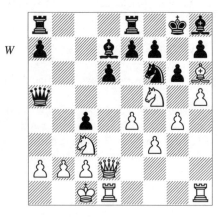

18   ♕g5!

Before the game, I looked at some recent copies of *Informator* to see if there had been any important games with the 10...♕a5 line. My eye was caught by the postal game V.Pavlov-Vaskin (*Informator 69*, Game 215; notes by Pavlov) which continued 18 ♗g7 ♗xf5 19

♗xh8 ♔xh8 20 exf5 ♖g8 21 ♖de1 ♖ae8 22 hxg6 fxg6 23 ♕h6 ♖g7 24 fxg6 ♖b8 and here White played 25 ♕f4 and won after a long, hard struggle. It didn't take long to spot that Black is just dead lost after 25 ♕h4!. This again threatens 26 ♖xe7 ♖xe7 27 ♕xf6+, against which Black has scant defence. If Black replies 25...♕b4 then White wins by 26 ♖xe7 ♕xb2+ 27 ♔d2 and, unlike the game, Black has no sacrifice on c3. I didn't have much time to prepare for the game, and in this team event there were several other possible opponents I could play, so I moved on without looking any further at this opening. When this position actually arrived on the board, I started mentally rubbing my hands with glee at the thought of springing 25 ♕h4! on Chris, when I thought that perhaps I should check the earlier moves in this line. I immediately received a dash of cold water, since it became obvious that after 18 ♗g7, Black could simply reply 18...gxf5 19 ♕g5 h6! 20 ♗xh6+ ♔h7, when Black is a piece up for very little. Clearly Chris had spotted this and was ready for any unwary victim following the *Informator* analysis. Obviously, I had to try something else. Fortunately for me, the position is in fact dangerous for Black, provided White finds the correct 18th move.

After the game I looked again at *Informator* and spotted a little note I hadn't noticed before, which gave 18...gxf5 as unclear after 19 ♕g5 h6 or 19 gxf5 ♗xg7 20 h6 ♗f8, with this last move being given the 'only move' symbol. As already noted, the first of these lines leaves Black a piece up for almost nothing, while the second is even more ludicrous. If Black plays 20...♗h8 21 ♖hg1+ ♔f8 instead of 20...♗f8, then he is two pieces up for nothing. White can only create a threat by tripling on the g-file, but even if he manages this, Black just plays ...e6 and the whole attack collapses. If anybody requires a stark warning that published analysis should always be checked carefully, then this is it.

We now return to 18 ♕g5! *(D)*:

Fortunately for me, my over-the-board search for an improvement quickly led me to the strong innovation 18 ♕g5. The threat of 19 ♘xe7+ forces Black to move his queen, but the net effect is that White has transferred his queen to a more aggressive position with gain of tempo.

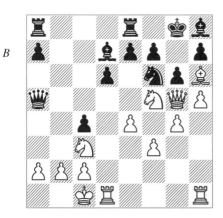

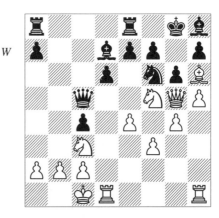

18 ... ♛b6?

Rather surprisingly, after 18 ♛g5 the six games in my database (including this one) gave White only a slight plus score (3 wins, 2 losses and 1 draw), all the more so in that only in one game did Black find the best reply. It is natural for Black to put his queen on the b-file so as to continue his attack against b2, but as noted above, ...♛xb2+ is not the end of the world for White and in many cases he can simply ignore it. The alternatives are:

1) 18...♛b4 19 hxg6 fxg6 20 ♗g7! is basically the same as the game.

2) 18...♛e5 19 ♛h4 ♖ab8 20 hxg6 fxg6 21 ♗e3 ♗xf5 22 gxf5 ♘h5 23 fxg6 hxg6 was played in J.Anderson-Tan, British Ch, Scarborough 2001, and now 24 ♖dg1 ♔f7 (White also wins after 24...♖xb2 25 ♖xg6+ ♔f7 26 ♖g5 ♖xc2+ 27 ♔d1) 25 ♖xg6! ♔xg6 26 f4 gives White a winning attack.

3) 18...♛c5! *(D)* is the only viable continuation. This move is purely defensive, and in such a sharp position it is normally better to play for a counter-attack rather than spend a tempo solely on defence. However, this case is an exception. Black defends his queen, and thus prevents ♘xe7+. At the same time he retains the pin on the f5-knight, which cuts out several attacking ideas for White. At first it seems that White must be able to blast his way through, but I have concluded that he can only hope for a slight advantage at best:

3a) 19 hxg6 fxg6 doesn't help White.

3b) 19 ♛h4 ♖ab8 20 hxg6 fxg6 and Black threatens 21...♛b4, while White has no obvious way through. The sacrificial attempt 21 ♘d5 ♘xd5 22 ♗g7 ♘f6 23 ♗xf6 ♗xf6 24

♛xh7+ ♔f8 25 ♛h6+ ♔f7 leads only to perpetual check.

3c) 19 e5 is the most direct attempt to smash Black. After 19...♗xf5 (not 19...dxe5? 20 ♘h4! and Black cannot prevent White from crashing through on g6) 20 gxf5 ♛xe5 21 ♖de1 (21 ♖h4 ♖ab8 22 hxg6 fxg6 23 fxg6 ♛xg5+ 24 ♗xg5 hxg6 25 ♖xc4 is equal) 21...♛c5 (21...♛a5 is also playable) 22 ♛f4 ♖ab8 (22...♘d5 23 ♘xd5 ♛xd5 24 fxg6 fxg6 25 hxg6 hxg6 26 ♖eg1 ♛e6 27 c3 gives White a dangerous attack in return for a pawn) 23 hxg6 hxg6 24 fxg6 fxg6 (24...♛b4? loses to 25 g7) the position is unclear.

3d) 19 ♖d5!? *(D)* and now:

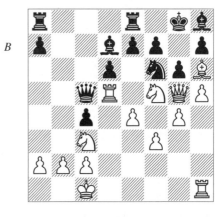

3d1) 19...♘xd5 20 hxg6 hxg6 (20...fxg6? 21 ♘xd5 ♗xf5 22 gxf5 ♖ab8 23 fxg6 ♗xb2+ 24 ♔d1 ♛d4+ 25 ♔e2 is very good for White) 21 ♘xd5 ♗xf5 22 ♗f8!? ♛d4 (22...♗xb2+? 23 ♔xb2 ♖ab8+ 24 ♔a1 and White wins) 23 c3 ♛e5 24 ♗xe7 ♗xg4 25 ♖xh8+ (25 fxg4 ♛xg5+ 26 ♗xg5 ♗g7 27 ♘f6+ ♔f8 is also a draw)

25...♛xh8 26 ♞f6+ ♚g7 27 ♞xe8+ ♛xe8 28 fxg4 ♚g8 29 ♝f6 ♛xe4 30 ♛h4 and Black must give perpetual check.

3d2) 19...♛b6 and now the fact that White's rook is on d5, preventing ♞d5, improves Black's defensive chances compared to the game; for example, 20 hxg6 fxg6 21 ♝g7 ♝xg7 22 ♞xg7 ♚xg7 23 ♛h6+ ♚g8 24 e5 dxe5 25 ♖xd7 ♖ab8 26 ♞e4 ♛xb2+ 27 ♚d1 with a likely draw.

3e) 19 ♞e3! is White's best chance to gain an advantage:

3e1) 19...♖ac8 20 e5! ♛xe5 (20...dxe5 21 hxg6 hxg6 22 ♝f8! ♖xf8 23 ♞e4 ♞xe4 24 ♛h6 wins Black's queen for two minor pieces) 21 hxg6 hxg6 22 ♛h4 looks promising for White.

3e2) 19...♛xg5 20 ♝xg5 ♝e6 gives White a slight endgame advantage.

After the move played, the f5-knight is unpinned and White's attack crashes through.

19 hxg6

The first step is to open the h-file.

19 ... fxg6 (D)

19...hxg6 20 ♝f8! is instantly decisive, so this is forced.

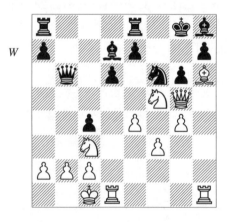

20 ♝g7!

This spectacular move provides a vivid demonstration of the importance of eliminating Black's defensive bishop. White is prepared to sacrifice a piece to get rid of it.

20 ... ♝xg7

Although Black has a range of moves, none of them provides a satisfactory defence:

1) 20...♖ab8 21 ♝xh8 ♛xb2+ 22 ♚d2 ♚xh8 loses to 23 ♖xh7+! ♞xh7 24 ♖h1, threatening 25 ♖xh7+, amongst other lines; e.g., 24...♝xf5

25 ♛h6 ♚g8 26 ♛xh7+ ♚f8 27 gxf5 with a quick mate to follow.

2) 20...♝xf5 21 ♝xh8 ♚xh8 22 gxf5 is also very unpleasant for Black; for example, 22...♖ab8 23 fxg6 ♛xb2+ 24 ♚d2 (threatening 25 ♖xh7+ ♞xh7 26 ♛h6) 24...♛b6 (24...♖g8 25 ♛xf6+! is a neat finish) 25 ♚e2! (stopping any annoying checks and renewing the threat) 25...♖b7 26 ♞d5 with a winning attack.

21 ♞xg7 (D)

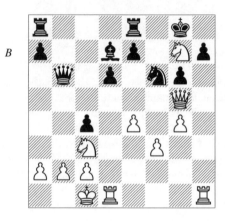

21 ... ♖eb8

Black decides to decline the offered piece. After 21...♚xg7 22 ♞d5! he has no good square for the queen:

1) 22...♛a5 23 ♛h6+ ♚f7 24 ♞xf6 ♚xf6 (24...exf6 25 ♖xd6 ♝e6 26 ♛xh7+ ♚f8 27 ♖xe6 ♖xe6 28 ♛b7! and White takes the a8-rook with check) 25 ♖d5 ♛b6 26 g5+ mating in a few moves.

2) 22...♛b7 23 ♞xf6 exf6 24 ♛h6+ ♚f7 25 ♛xh7+ ♚e6 26 f4 with a winning attack.

3) 22...♛c5 23 ♛h6+ ♚f7 24 g5! ♞h5 (after 24...♞xd5 25 ♛xh7+ White mates quickly, while 24...♞g8 25 ♛xh7+ ♚f8 26 ♛xg6 is crushing) 25 ♖xh5 gxh5 26 ♛xh7+ ♚f8 27 g6 ♝e6 28 ♛h8+ ♝g8 29 ♛h6#.

4) 22...♛b5 23 ♛h6+ ♚f7 24 g5 and White wins as after 22...♛c5.

22 ♞h5! (D)

White ignores the threat to b2 and concentrates on whittling away Black's kingside defenders. Once the f6-knight has gone, White's threats down the h-file will be decisive. Note that 22 ♞f5 is wrong, as Black can eliminate the knight with his bishop, which is not a vital defensive piece.

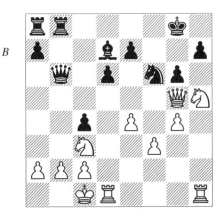

22 ... ♘xh5

22...♕xb2+ 23 ♔d2 doesn't help, since in some lines White can actually use the b-file for his attack:

1) 23...♖f8 24 ♘xf6+ exf6 (24...♖xf6 25 ♕d5+ ♔g7 26 ♕xa8 ♖xf3 and now White should play 27 ♖xh7+! otherwise he might even lose; the end might be 27...♔xh7 28 ♖h1+ ♔g7 29 ♕h8+ ♔f7 30 ♖h7+ ♔e6 31 ♖xe7+ ♔xe7 32 ♘d5+ winning the queen) 25 ♕d5+ ♔h8 26 ♖b1 ♕a3 27 ♖b7 ♖ad8 28 ♕e6! and wins, since 28...♗xe6 29 ♖hxh7+ ♔g8 30 ♖bg7# is mate.

2) 23...♘xh5 24 gxh5 gives White a decisive attack; for example, 24...♕b6 loses to 25 ♔e2! ♕b2 (25...♗e8 26 ♘d5 is no better) 26 ♘d5, while 24...♗e8 25 hxg6 ♗xg6 26 ♖xh7 ♔xh7 27 ♖h1+ ♔g7 28 ♕xe7+ ♔g8 29 ♕f6 mates.

3) 23...♕b6 24 ♘xf6+ exf6 25 ♕d5+ ♔g7 26 ♖xh7+! ♔xh7 27 ♕f7+ ♔h6 28 ♖h1+ ♔g5 29 f4+ ♔xg4 30 ♕xg6+ ♔f3 31 ♕h5+ ♗g4 32 ♖h3+ ♔xf4 33 ♘d5+ ♔e4 34 ♘xf6+ ♔f4 35 ♕xg4+ mates quickly.

Amazingly, the position after 22 ♘h5 arose again several years later with a GM playing Black. That game concluded 22...d5 23 ♘xf6+ exf6 24 ♕h6 ♗e6 25 ♕xh7+ ♔f8 26 ♕h8+ ♔e7 27 ♖h7+ ♔d6 28 ♕xf6 ♕e3+ 29 ♔b1 1-0 Lakos-Cebalo, Oberwart 2003. A painful loss and a warning not to play sharp openings if you are not prepared to keep up with the theory.

23 gxh5 ♗e8

23...♕xb2+ 24 ♔d2 transposes to line '2' of the previous note.

24 b3!

The simplest and most effective move. Now that Black's kingside minor pieces have gone,

White can afford to play this defensive move, which brings Black's queenside attack to a dead halt. White, on the other hand, retains a massive attack on the kingside – the immediate threat is 25 ♘d5. Note that 24 hxg6 ♗xg6 25 ♖xh7 ♔xh7 26 ♖h1+ ♔g7 27 ♕xe7+ ♔f7 only leads to a draw here, since Black's queen is controlling g1.

24 ... cxb3

25 axb3

There is no real defence to ♘d5.

25 ... ♕c5

25...e6 26 ♕f6 and 25...♗f7 26 hxg6 ♗xg6 27 ♘d5 are also hopeless for Black.

26 ♘d5 (D)

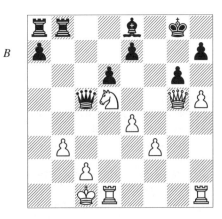

Now e7 falls.

26 ... ♖b7

26...♕a3+ 27 ♔d2 ♕a5+ 28 b4 brings the checks to an end, while after 28...♖xb4 we have an echo of the idea at move 18 since White can win Black's queen with a knight check.

27 ♘xe7+

Picking up the exchange.

27 ... ♖xe7

Both 27...♔f7 28 hxg6+ hxg6 29 ♖h7+ and 27...♔g7 28 ♘f5+ ♔g8 29 hxg6 ♗xg6 30 ♕f6 ♗xf5 31 ♖dg1+ ♗g6 32 ♖xg6+ hxg6 33 ♖h8# lead to mate.

28 ♕xe7

Black's material situation is hopeless.

28	...	♖c8
29	♖h2	gxh5
30	♖g2+	♗g6
31	♖xd6	♕e3+
32	♖gd2	♖f8
33	♖d8	♖xd8

34	♕xd8+	♔g7
35	♕d4+	

Perhaps White could have won more quickly another way, but there can't be anything wrong with this safe method.

35	...	♕xd4
36	♖xd4	h4
37	♔d2	h3
38	♔e3	♔h6
39	♔f4	1-0

Readers may have noticed that I haven't mentioned the Bundesliga much recently. The reason for this is that during the 1996/7 season Duisburg, the team I had played for since 1994, encountered some financial difficulties. The result was that I only played four games in that season and was forced to look for a new club for 1997/8. I didn't find anything satisfactory in the first division, and so I agreed to play for Andernach, a team which was currently in the second division but which was hoping to promote to the top league. I played one game for them in a match which they regarded as crucial for the promotion race, against Bad Godesburg. My game, against Kengis, was a draw but Andernach won the match and seemed set to reach the first division. Unfortunately, they then decided to save money by leaving out many of their top players for the rest of the season. Andernach fielded a team for one match (against Wattenscheid) which included my name on top board; however, they had deliberately not told me about the match and so they (or maybe 'I') lost this game by default. Apparently their idea was that by defaulting on board one against a relatively strong opponent (Peter Heine Nielsen) the rest of their players would get easier opponents and go on to win the match. I regarded the behaviour of Andernach as totally unacceptable, since it gave the appearance that I simply hadn't turned up for a match I was supposed to be playing in. It was also very unfair on Nielsen, who had to go to the trouble to turn up for a match and then not get a game. I had certainly never agreed that my name could used in this way, and to this day in MegaBase the game is given as a loss by default for me. Andernach's little scheme collapsed totally when, despite having a much stronger team (even without me!), they lost 6-2 to Wattenscheid and missed promotion.

Needless to say, after this episode I was on the search for another Bundesliga club and for the 1998/9 season I agreed to play for Lübeck, another ambitious second division club hoping for promotion. At the time there was a strong Scandinavian influence in the team, since Lars Bo Hansen and Jonny Hector were the other grandmasters. Lübeck turned out to be a friendly and well-organized team and I was happy to play for them for the next five years.

In February, I again travelled to Ireland for the Bunratty weekend event, coming joint first with the rising young star Luke McShane on 5/6.

A few months later there was a big change in my life: I became a father. Petra gave birth to our son Michael on the morning of 14th May. Michael was a month premature and weighed 2.2 kg (a little under 5 pounds). He looked very small at birth, but after a few days he started putting on weight and within a few years he was well above average height for his age.

In June I played in a small weekend tournament in nearby Reading, winning outright with 4½/5. After this I was again inactive, but in October the various leagues started and I was busy in both the German Bundesliga and the British 4NCL. The following game was played in November.

The opening of this game led to a central pawn-structure reminiscent of the French, although the positioning of the pieces was quite different. White's strategy was based on making it hard for Black to castle. Although Black was forced to keep his king in the centre for a long time, the blocked position meant that there was no immediate danger. However, as play developed, the position of Black's king started to become awkward, since possibilities for opening the position began to appear. Playing with the king in the centre requires considerable care and accuracy, and the critical moment arose at move 24. White had just played an inaccurate move, giving Black the chance to develop some counterplay on the queenside, which is what he had been playing for all along. Black backed away from this possibility because it would have opened some lines against his king, although analysis shows that White could not have exploited these. This lack of consistency doomed Black; White was able to switch his rook into a menacing position and the attack soon broke through.

Game 33
J. Nunn – M. Chandler
British League (4NCL) 1998/9
Modern Defence

1	e4	g6
2	d4	♝g7
3	♘c3	c6

This mixture of the Modern and Caro-Kann Defences is a solid but slightly passive opening for Black. As in the Caro-Kann, Black intends to challenge White's centre with ...d5.

4 ♝c4 (D)

The most radical reply to Black's opening: White tries to prevent ...d5, or at least to force a concession from Black along the way. 4 ♘f3 d5 5 h3 is White's most popular system, which suffices to give White a slight advantage, although it is hard to make progress against Black's solid set-up.

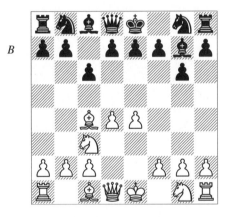

B

4	...	d6

Black gives up the idea of playing ...d5 and simply continues with his normal development. He hopes to show that White's bishop is not ideally posted on the rather exposed square c4. Black can in fact still play 4...d5 if he really wants to. After 5 exd5 b5 6 ♝b3 b4 (Black has to advance his queenside pawns in order to regain the pawn on d5, but this leaves them slightly weak) 7 ♘ce2 (7 ♘e4 cxd5 8 ♘c5 is also possible; later on the knight will drop back to d3) 7...cxd5 8 ♝d2 a5 9 a3 bxa3 10 ♖xa3 White has a slight advantage thanks to his lead in development and Black's weak a-pawn.

4...b5 5 ♝b3 a5 is another plan, but after 6 a3 it is not clear that Black has benefited from his queenside pawn push.

5 ♕f3

This is really the only critical continuation, since after 5 ♘f3 ♘f6, for example, we reach a harmless line of the Pirc in which the bishop is poorly placed on c4.

5 ... e6 (D)

The pawn sacrifice 5...♘f6 6 e5 dxe5 7 dxe5 ♘d5 8 ♘xd5 cxd5 9 ♝xd5 0-0 is a playable alternative. The main line runs 10 ♝xb7 ♕a5+ 11 c3 ♝xb7 12 ♕xb7 ♘a6 and Black has fair compensation for the pawn (although he is two pawns down at the moment, he will easily regain one).

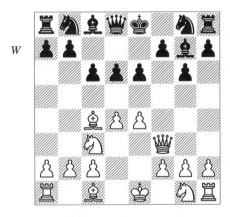

W

6 ♘ge2

This is a more flexible way to defend d4 than 6 ♝e3. The knight is unlikely to go anywhere apart from e2, but the dark-squared bishop might want to go to f4 or g5 later.

6	...	b5

Black has two basic plans in this position. He can either play to complete his development by ...♘d7, ...♘gf6 and ...0-0, or he can aim to chase the c4-bishop and gain space on the queenside. This latter plan had proved effective in an earlier game Nunn-Shirov, so Chandler repeats it here.

7	♝b3	a5

8   a3

Essentially forced, since 8 a4 b4 9 ♘d1 ♗a6 puts White's position under uncomfortable pressure.

8   ...   ♗a6

9   0-0

White prefers normal development to the sharper line 9 d5 cxd5 10 exd5 e5 11 ♘e4 h6 (not 11...♕c7? 12 c4 bxc4 13 ♗a4+ ♘d7 14 ♘2c3 ♔e7? 15 ♘xd6!, which led to a quick win for White in the famous game J.Polgar-Shirov, Amsterdam (Donner Memorial) 1995) 12 g4 ♘f6 which leads to unclear complications.

9   ...   ♘d7

10   ♗f4

White is able to develop quickly, since now 10...e5 loses a pawn after 11 ♗xe5!. Therefore Black must defend the d6-pawn with his queen.

10   ...   ♕e7

11   e5

This is much stronger than 11 ♖ad1 e5 12 ♗g5 ♘gf6 13 d5?! c5 14 a4 b4 15 ♘b5 ♘b6!? and Black already had a promising position in Nunn-Shirov, Bundesliga 1995/6. 11 e5 was suggested by Shirov after the game and appeared in his *Informator* notes. I adopted his idea and played it three times, winning all three games. Funnily enough, when Murray played it himself as White, he lost with it! More about this later.

11   ...   d5

12   ♕e3 (D)

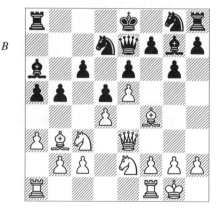

This is the point of the previous move. White tries to make it awkward for Black to develop his kingside since at the moment the g8-knight has nowhere to go.

12   ...   h6

Black has two basic plans for untangling his kingside pieces. He can either play ...♕d8, followed by ...♘e7, or he can try to break out straight away with 12...f6!?. In the latter case, the critical position arises after 13 ♖fe1 fxe5 14 dxe5 ♕f7 (D). If Black succeeds with his plan of playing ...♘e7, ...0-0 and advancing his queenside pawns then he will have an excellent game, so White must undertake immediate action. These are his options:

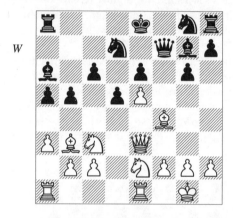

1) 15 ♘xd5? (this sacrifice appears incorrect) 15...cxd5 16 ♗xd5 exd5 17 e6 ♕e7 18 exd7+ ♔f7! 19 ♕h3 ♘f6 and White's attack was inadequate in Chandler-Hodgson, British Ch, Millfield 2000. Murray was certainly unfortunate to lose in this line with both colours.

2) 15 a4?! b4 16 ♘b5 cxb5 17 ♗xd5 is a better try, but again proves insufficient after 17...exd5 18 axb5 ♗b7! 19 e6 ♕e7 20 exd7+ ♔f7 with advantage to Black.

3) 15 ♘d4! (the best try, which should give White some advantage) 15...♘e7 16 ♕h3! (16 a4 b4 17 ♘e4 0-0 18 ♗g3 ♘f5 19 ♘xf5 gxf5 20 ♘d6 f4 is fine for Black, while 16 ♗h6 ♘f5 17 ♘xf5 gxf5 18 ♗xg7 ♕xg7 gives White nothing) 16...♘c5 17 ♗e3 (threatening 18 ♘dxb5) 17...♘xb3 18 ♘xb3 0-0 (18...♘f5 19 ♗c5 stops Black castling kingside) 19 ♗c5 a4 (19...♗c8 20 ♖e2 followed by ♘d4 also favours White) 20 ♘d4! ♕xf2+ 21 ♔h1 ♕f7 22 ♕xe6 with an advantage for White.

It is also possible to play 12...♕d8 straight away, without the preliminary ...h6, but this gives White the opportunity to play ♗h6 later on. Nunn-McFarland, London 1996 continued

13 ♘g3 ♘e7 14 ♘ce2 ♕c7 15 c3 (White prepares ♗c2 to bring the bishop back into play) 15...c5 16 ♗h6 0-0 17 ♖fe1 ♘c6 18 ♘h5! and now Black gave up the exchange by 18...♗h8 and lost in due course. Accepting the sacrifice was the critical line, but after 18...cxd4 (White wins after 18...♗xh6 19 ♕xh6 gxh5 20 ♘f4) 19 cxd4 ♗xh6 20 ♕xh6 gxh5 21 ♖ac1! (threatening 22 ♘f4) 21...♔h8 22 ♗xd5 exd5 23 ♖xc6 ♕b7 24 ♘g3 ♖g8 25 ♘f5 White wins, because there is no good defence to the threat of 26 ♕xh7+.

13   ♕d2! *(D)*

The bishop belongs on the c1-h6 diagonal, so White must make room for it in the event of ...g5. 13 ♖fe1 is inferior as 13...g5 14 ♗g3 (14 ♕g3 a4 15 ♗a2 b4 also gives Black counterplay) 14...h5, followed by ...♘h6, allows Black to solve his development problems.

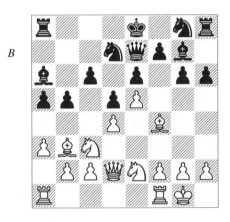

13   ...   ♕d8

Black tried a slightly different tack in the later game Nunn-R.Pert, British League (4NCL) 1999/00, which continued 13...♘b6 (13...g5 is risky, as after 14 ♗e3 White can quickly play f4) 14 ♖fe1 ♕c7 15 ♘g3 ♘e7 16 ♖ad1 ♖b8 17 ♕c1 (there are slight differences, but the general structure of the position is the same as in Nunn-Chandler; as soon as White rescues his light-squared bishop he should have an advantage) 17...♗f8 18 ♗d2 ♘d7 19 ♘ce2 ♕b6 20 c3 ♖c8 21 ♗c2 (Black faces problems similar to those in the main game; if he remains passive, White will eventually make progress on the kingside, for example by h4-h5, but if he aims for counterplay he may weaken himself) 21...c5 22 dxc5 ♘xc5 23 ♗e3 ♕c7 24 ♘d4

♗g7 25 ♗f4 with a modest but safe advantage for White, who eventually won.

14   ♖fe1   ♘e7
15   ♘g3

The same general plan as in the note to Black's 13th move. The knight on g3 dissuades Black from playing ...♘f5, and e2 is cleared for the manoeuvre ♘ce2, c3 and ♗c2, by which White activates his light-squared bishop.

15   ...   c5 *(D)*

I think Black is correct to take immediate action on the queenside, since if he waits then White will gradually improve his position as in Nunn-R.Pert. The alternative 15...♘f5 16 ♘xf5 gxf5 17 ♗e3 followed by ♖h3 is unpleasant for Black.

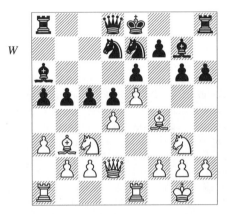

16   ♘ce2   cxd4?!

Opening the position looks wrong. Black cannot castle due to the pressure against his h6-pawn and although he now gets some play against White's weak e5-pawn, it doesn't compensate for the defects in his position. Other moves offered better equalizing chances:

1) 16...♘c6 17 c3 ♕h4 18 ♗c2 0-0 enables Black to get castled. It takes White some time to reorganize his position to make progress on the kingside; one plan is ♘f1, followed by ♘e3, ♗g3 and h4-h5.

2) 16...c4 17 ♗a2 ♘c6 18 b4 a4 19 c3 followed by ♖ad1 and ♗b1 gives White a slight advantage, although whether he can make any progress in such a blocked position is rather doubtful.

17   ♘xd4   ♕c7

Black is playing for pressure against e5, but it turns out that he can never take this pawn, so

White has time to activate the b3-bishop. Note the typical point that Black cannot win the e-pawn with 17...g5 because of 18 ♘h5!.

18 c3 *(D)*

Ignoring the attack on e5.

18 ... ♘b6

Now Black changes plan and abandons the attack on e5 in the hope of generating some play on the queenside. However, the fact that he still cannot castle proves a serious problem. Trying to win the e-pawn backfires:

1) 18...♗xe5? loses to 19 ♗xe5 ♘xe5 20 ♕f4.

2) 18...♘xe5? 19 ♕e3 also wins for White.

3) 18...g5? 19 ♘h5 0-0 (19...♗xe5 20 ♘g7+ ♔d8 21 ♗xe5 ♘xe5 22 ♘gxe6+ and White wins) 20 ♗xg5! hxg5 21 ♕xg5 ♘g6 22 ♘xe6 fxe6 23 ♕xg6 ♘c5 24 ♗c2 gives White a decisive attack.

19 ♖ad1

White wants to keep his queen on the c1-h6 diagonal in order to prevent castling, so it is a good idea to develop this rook now; otherwise it will be blocked in after ♕c1.

19 ... ♘c4

20 ♕c1 ♘c6

Black still can't grab the pawn, since after 20...♘xe5? 21 ♕e3 or 20...♗xe5? 21 ♗xe5 ♘xe5 22 ♕f4 he loses just as before. 20...g5 fails to 21 ♘h5 ♗xe5 22 ♘f6+ ♔d8 (22...♔f8 23 ♗xe5 ♘xe5 24 ♖xe5 wins for White) 23 ♗xe5 ♘xe5 24 ♕e3 ♘5g6 25 ♘xe6+ fxe6 26 ♗xd5 and White's attack crashes through; for example, 26...exd5 27 ♘xd5 ♘xd5 28 ♖xd5+ ♔c8 29 ♖c5 with an easy win.

21 ♘xc6 ♕xc6

22 ♘e2

Black has managed to exchange the powerful knight on d4, but now the other one comes across to take its place.

22 ... ♕b7

23 ♘d4

White has various ways to make progress. He might play on the queenside with ♗c2-d3 and b3, hoping to win the b5-pawn, or he might play for a kingside attack by ♖d3-g3 and ♗c2, with an eventual sacrifice on e6 or g6 in mind.

23 ... ♖c8 *(D)*

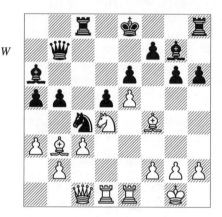

24 ♖d3?!

The rook is well placed on d3, since it can not only swing over to the kingside but can also lend support to a prospective weak pawn on c3 after ...b4 and ...bxc3 by Black. However, this move gives Black a tactical opportunity to exploit the undefended rook. I was reluctant to play 24 ♗c2, because Black appeared to be aiming for ...b4, and then White benefits from having a check on a4. I didn't want to waste a tempo by playing the bishop to c2 and then to a4. However, concrete calculation always prevails over general considerations and 24 ♗c2 was correct, with just a slight advantage for White.

24 ... ♘b6?

Black doesn't like the look of the check on a4 and decides to rule it out before proceeding with ...b4. However, he should have played 24...b4, not fearing the check because after 25 ♗a4+ ♔f8 Black can run with his king to h7. The key point is that 25 axb4 can be met by 25...♘xb2!, heading for d3. White therefore has little choice but to allow ...bxa3, when the weak a3-pawn provides Black with enough counterplay to hold the balance.

After the move played, White's plan is justified, since he can swing his rook into an active position on the kingside.

	25	♖g3	b4
	26	axb4	axb4
	27	♗c2	

Lining up for a sacrifice on g6.

| | 27 | ... | g5 |

Normal moves do not prevent the sacrifice; for example, 27...bxc3 28 bxc3 ♘c4 (28...♕c7 29 ♗xg6 fxg6 30 ♕b1 gives White a decisive attack, while 28...♗c4 29 ♗xg6 fxg6 30 ♖xg6 is also crushing for White) 29 ♗xg6 fxg6 30 ♖xg6 ♖c7 (30...♔f7 31 ♕c2 wins for White) 31 ♘xe6 ♖f7 32 ♕a1! ♗b5 33 ♘xg7+ ♖xg7 34 ♖xg7 ♕xg7 35 ♕a8+ ♔e7 36 ♕b7+ and White wins. Therefore, Black decides to take radical measures to prevent the sacrifice. However, pushing the pawn allows White to break through by an alternative method.

| | 28 | h4! (D) |

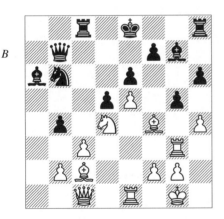

B

Forcing Black's hand. Now White's rook reaches the seventh rank.

	28	...	bxc3
	29	bxc3	gxf4

Or 29...♕c7 30 ♕e3! (an unexpected move threatening simply 31 hxg5 hxg5 32 ♗xg5) 30...gxf4 31 ♕xf4 ♖g8 (31...♗f8 32 ♕f6) 32 ♗h7 and White wins.

	30	♖xg7	♖xc3
	31	♕xf4	

Material is still equal but the deadly threats to e6 and f7, coupled with Black's exposed king, give White a winning position.

	31	...	♕e7
	32	♗g6	♖f8
	33	♕xh6	

When I was younger I might have been tempted to look for a knock-out blow, but these days I am happy to take a pawn and keep all my advantages. In fact 33 ♖a1 would have wrapped the game up at once; for example, 33...♗c8 34 ♘b5 or 33...♗d3 34 ♗xd3 ♖xd3 35 ♘b5.

| | 33 | ... | ♗c8 |

33...♖c4 34 ♘f3, followed by ♘g5, wins easily.

	34	♘b5	♖c6
	35	♘d6+	

35 ♖a1 followed by ♖a7 is also very effective.

	35	...	♖xd6
	36	exd6	♕f6

36...♕xd6 37 ♗h5 leads to a quick win for White.

| | 37 | ♖b1 | ♘c4 (D) |

37...fxg6 38 ♖xb6 ♕xf2+ 39 ♔h2 is hopeless for Black as 39...♕xb6 allows 40 ♖e7+ ♔d8 41 ♕xf8#.

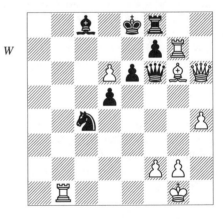

W

| | 38 | ♗xf7+ | |

The simplest.

	38	...	♖xf7
	39	♕xf6	♖xf6
	40	d7+	1-0

White mates after 40...♗xd7 41 ♖b8+, while 40...♔d8 41 ♖b8 wins a rook.

In December there was to be a small grandmaster tournament in Oxford, and I was happy to revisit the city where I spent so many years as a student and, later, as a lecturer. In the first round I drew with Julian Hodgson, while in round 2 I faced one of my new team-mates from Lübeck. Jonny Hector is a creative attacking player with a very sharp style. I was hoping to keep things quiet, but when he made a provocative move in the early middlegame (14...d5?!) I decided to try to exploit it, even though this meant stirring up complications. This is another situation in which a flexible style is important. If you are so scared of your opponent's tactical ability that you avoid all complications, then you risk letting him get away with things for which he should really be punished. It is a mistake to think like this; if you believe your opponent has gone wrong, you should never be scared of playing what you consider to be the best move, regardless of the resulting position. During the complications I missed the strongest line, but still emerged with enough advantage to win.

Game 34

J. Nunn – J. Hector

Oxford 1998

Ruy Lopez (Spanish), Møller Defence

1	e4	e5
2	♘f3	♘c6
3	♗b5	a6
4	♗a4	♘f6
5	0-0	♗c5

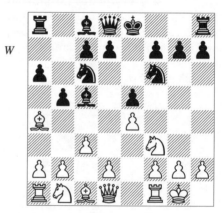

W

Lines with an early ...♗c5 have become an increasingly popular method of meeting the Ruy Lopez. In some ways these Møller lines are similar to the Arkhangelsk variation (5...b5 6 ♗b3 ♗b7), but they have the advantage of leaving the bishop on c8 for the moment, thereby retaining the option of developing it at either g4 or b7. There are two possible move-orders for Black. One is 5...b5 6 ♗b3 ♗c5, and the other is the immediate 5...♗c5. The latter, as played by Hector, has the advantage that White cannot play lines with an immediate a4, but the disadvantage is that White might play c3 and then drop his bishop back to c2 rather than b3, which might be a more useful square. In practice, the 5...b5 move-order is considerably more popular, but time will tell which is more accurate.

6	c3	b5 *(D)*
7	♗c2	

This is the only way to try to exploit Black's delay in playing ...b5, although it has the defect of giving Black the option of playing 7...d5. Apart from 7 ♗b3, transposing into other lines, the only other possibility is 7 d4. However, after 7...bxa4 8 dxc5 ♕e7 this line leads only to equality.

| 7 | ... | d6 |

In my opinion, which I know is not universally shared, this method of development does not fit in well with the delayed ...b5. It seems to me that when Black develops 'normally' by ...d6, ...0-0 and ...♖e8, the bishop is better placed on c2 than b3, since it supports the e4-pawn and makes it easier for White to maintain his d4-e4 pawn-centre. If one accepts this logic, then 7...d5 8 d4 dxe4 must be the critical test of 7 ♗c2, exploiting the fact that the bishop is not on b3. Then White has various possibilities, such as 9 ♘xe5, 9 dxc5 and even 9 ♘bd2!?. I had specially prepared this last move for the current game, but as Hector played 7...d6 it remained unused. I eventually employed it to win a blitz game against Agdestein! All these lines are rather complicated, and it would take us too far afield to explore the theory of the variation, but I will summarize it by saying that White has not managed to prove a convincing advantage after 7...d5.

8	**d4**	**♗b6**
9	**h3** *(D)*	

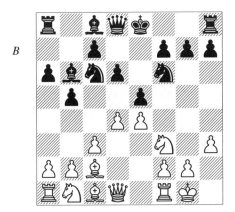

The advantage of the Møller as opposed to the Arkhangelsk is that Black can still play ...♗g4, so White more often has to spend a tempo on this move in order to maintain his pawn-centre. Although some players have preferred 9 a4, allowing 9...♗g4, it seems to me that White's best chance for an advantage is to maintain the d4-e4 pawn-centre, at least for the time being.

9	...	**0-0**
10	**♗e3**	

This seems the most logical – White simply supports his pawn-centre. There are two alternatives:

1) 10 ♗g5 h6 11 ♗h4 ♕e7 has been played a couple of times, but here White's dark-squared bishop appears less usefully posted, since the pin on the f6-knight is not really annoying for Black.

2) 10 a4 ♗b7 also does not appear very effective for White. The pressure on b5 is not genuinely serious (because even after 11 ♘a3 White is not threatening to win a pawn at b5) and Black is presented with a useful developing move.

10	...	**♗b7**

Now that ...♗g4 has been ruled out, this is the most natural square for the bishop.

11	**♘bd2**	**♖e8** *(D)*

Both sides continue with normal developing moves. In the seven games in my database reaching this position, White scored 4 wins and

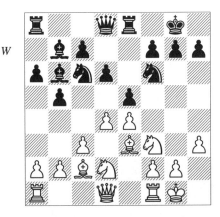

3 draws. Of course, this is only a small sample, but it backs up my claim that ♗c2 should not be met by ...d6.

12	**♖e1**	

12 d5 has also been played, but this move is illogical. One of the basic themes of the whole Ruy Lopez is White's attempt to maintain the d4-e4 pawn-centre. If he succeeds, then he is likely to have an advantage. Black, of course, can try all sorts of methods to disrupt White's centre, but the most usual is to play ...c5. Here this thrust is unusually difficult to arrange, as Black does not have a tempo-gaining ...♘a5. Voluntarily pushing the pawn to d5 surrenders this advantage and makes life easier for Black. After 12 d5 ♘e7 (12...♘a5 13 b4 ♘c4 14 ♘xc4 bxc4 15 ♘d2 favoured White in Ulybin-Hector, Gothenburg 1999) 13 ♗xb6 cxb6 both 14 ♘h4 ♗c8 15 c4 bxc4 16 ♘xc4 ♘g6 17 ♘xg6 hxg6 18 ♕d2 b5, Chandler-Stefansson, Reykjavik 2001 and 14 c4 bxc4 15 ♘xc4 b5 16 ♘e3 ♘g6, Morović-Christiansen, New York 1997, lead to equality.

12	...	**♖b8?!** *(D)*

In some lines White will play d5 followed by ♗xb6, establishing a central space advantage without the usual problem of having his centre undermined by a later ...c6. However, White should only push his d-pawn when he has improved his position to the utmost first. The slightly odd-looking 12...♖b8 intends to meet a later d5 by ...♗xe3, since after the sequence dxc6 ♗xd2 cxb7 White does not attack the a8-rook. However, Black's rook move does look slightly artificial and in the game the move ...♖b8 does not prove of any value to Black. Alternatives:

1) 12...h6 is the most reliable continuation, ruling out any possibilities of ♗g5 or ♘g5. It is interesting to note that this position can also arise with Black to move (when White plays ♗b3 and then ♗c2). After 13 a3 Black has tried four different moves, 13...♘b8, 13...♘a7, 13...♕d7 and 13...♗a7. In every case White has good chances to retain a slight advantage, but no more than that.

2) 12...exd4!? 13 cxd4 ♘b4 is a critical test of White's play:

2a) 14 ♗b1 (a tempting pawn sacrifice, but it doesn't quite work) 14...♗xe4 (not 14...♘xe4? 15 ♘xe4 ♗xe4 16 ♗g5 f6 17 ♖xe4 ♖xe4 18 ♗xe4 d5 19 ♕b3 fxg5 20 a3 ♔h8 21 ♗b1 ♘c6 22 ♕c2 and White wins) 15 ♘xe4 ♘xe4 with a further branch:

2a1) 16 ♗xe4 ♖xe4 17 ♘g5 ♖e7 and Black defends (but not 17...♖xe3?! 18 ♖xe3 ♕xg5 19 ♕e1, winning the b4-knight).

2a2) 16 ♕b3 c5 (16...♘c6 17 ♗xe4 ♖xe4 18 ♘g5 ♖e7 19 ♕c2 wins for White) 17 ♗xe4 ♖xe4 18 ♘g5 (18 a3? runs into 18...c4! 19 ♕xb4 ♗a5, a tactical point which recurs in several lines) 18...♖e7 19 dxc5 (19 a3? c4!) 19...dxc5 20 ♖ad1 ♕e8 and Black defends.

2b) 14 ♗g5! ♘xc2 15 ♕xc2 is the correct method. Black has, it is true, gained the two bishops, but he has given up the centre and faces a nasty pin on the kingside. After 15...h6 16 ♗h4 g5 17 ♗g3 ♘h5 18 ♗h2 ♘f4 19 ♗xf4 gxf4 20 e5 dxe5 21 dxe5 Black had serious problems in Jansa-Martinovsky, Wrexham 1998.

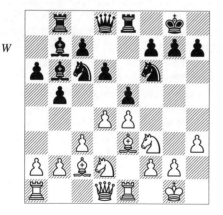

13 a3

White faces no immediate threat, so he spends a tempo ruling out ...exd4 followed by

...♘b4. Not, of course, 13 d5 ♗xe3 14 dxc6?, when 14...♗xd2 wins a pawn for Black – this was, after all, the point of ...♖b8.

13 ... h6
14 ♕e2 (D)

White's minor pieces are all well-placed, so the time has come to develop the queen. 14 ♕b1 is less effective since the queen is offside and Black can exploit this by 14...d5! 15 ♘xe5 ♘xe5 16 dxe5 ♗xe3 17 ♖xe3 ♖xe5 18 f4 ♖e8 19 e5 d4 with good counterplay; for example, 20 ♖d3 ♘d5 21 ♖xd4 c5 22 ♖d3 ♕h4 with advantage to Black.

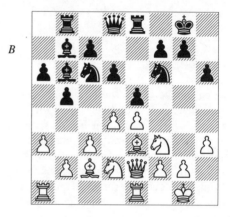

14 ... d5?!

Hector, true to his style, tries to break out tactically and hopes that the opposition of the e8-rook and White's queen will justify this move. 14...♕d7 (14...exd4 15 cxd4 ♘a5 16 e5 is dangerous for Black) is a more cautious approach, but White has a slight advantage after 15 ♕d3 (15 d5?! ♘e7 16 a4 ♗xe3 17 ♕xe3 c6 18 axb5 axb5 gives White nothing). Black's problem is that he soon runs out of constructive moves, while White finds it relatively easy to improve his position, for example by ♖ad1 and b4.

15 ♘xe5

Not 15 exd5? exd4 and Black wins, but 15 dxe5 also leads to a good position for White:

1) 15...♘xe5 16 ♘xe5 ♖xe5 (16...♗xe3 loses a pawn after 17 ♘xf7) 17 ♗xb6 cxb6 18 f4 ♖e8 19 e5 d4 20 cxd4 ♕xd4+ 21 ♕f2 ♕xf2+ 22 ♔xf2 ♘d5 23 g3 is very good for White as ♘e4-d6 is coming.

2) 15...dxe4 16 ♘xe4 ♘xe5 17 ♘xe5 ♖xe5 (17...♗xe4 18 ♗xb6 ♗xc2 19 ♗a7 and White wins material) 18 ♗xb6 and now:

2a) 18...cxb6 19 ♘xf6+ (19 ♖ad1 ♘d5 20 f4 also promises White an advantage) 19...gxf6 20 ♖ad1 ♖xe2 21 ♖xd8+ ♖xd8 22 ♖xe2 is clearly unpleasant for Black.

2b) 18...♘xe4 19 ♗d4 ♖e6 20 ♕g4 ♘f6 21 ♕f4 ♕d5 22 f3 and White's powerful bishop-pair gives him a definite advantage.

15   ...   dxe4

There is nothing better: 15...♘xe5 16 dxe5 ♗xe3 (16...♖xe5 transposes to line '1' of the previous note) 17 ♕xe3 ♖xe5 18 f4 ♖e8 19 e5, followed by ♘b3, gives White a firm grip on the dark squares, while 15...♘xe4 16 ♘xe4 dxe4 17 ♗xe4 ♘xe5 18 ♗xb7 ♖xb7 19 ♗f4 wins a pawn for White.

16   ♘g4 (D)

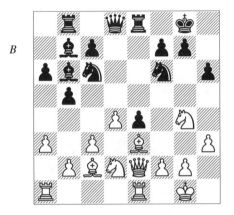

Aiming for the exchange of the f6-knight, which will put Black's e4-pawn in trouble.

16   ...   ♘h7

Black tries to muddy the waters. The other possibilities were not very tempting:

1) 16...♘a7 17 a4 (or 17 ♘xf6+ ♕xf6 18 ♕g4 ♕e6 19 ♗f4 with strong positional pressure for White) 17...bxa4 (17...c6 18 ♘xf6+ and White wins) 18 ♗xa4 ♖e6 (18...♘b5 19 ♘c4 is also awkward for Black) 19 ♗b3 and White has a large positional advantage.

2) 16...♘d5 might have been a better practical chance, because although White has a number of tempting continuations, there is no knock-out blow:

2a) 17 ♗xe4 h5 18 ♘h2 ♘xe3 19 fxe3 ♘xd4! 20 exd4 f5 is only slightly better for White.

2b) 17 ♘xe4!? (I intended to play this move during the game, but it seems that Black can

hold on with perfect defence) 17...f5 (17...h5 18 ♘h2 f5 19 ♘g5 g6 20 ♘hf3 is excellent for White; note that 20...f4 is met by 21 ♕d3) 18 ♘xh6+ gxh6 19 ♕h5 fxe4 (19...♖xe4 20 ♗xe4 fxe4 21 ♗xh6 ♕d7 22 ♖xe4 and 19...♕d7 20 ♘g3 ♘xe3 21 ♖xe3 ♖xe3 22 fxe3 ♕f7 23 ♕xh6 ♘e7 24 ♘h5 both give White a winning attack) 20 ♗xh6 (D) and now:

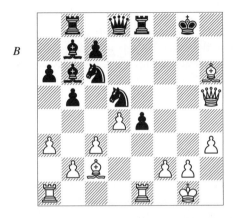

2b1) 20...♕d7? 21 ♗xe4 ♘xd4 (21...♖xe4 22 ♖xe4 and White wins) 22 cxd4 ♗xd4 23 ♗h7+! ♔h8 (23...♔xh7 24 ♗e3+ is also winning for White) 24 ♗f5 wins for White.

2b2) 20...♕f6! 21 ♗xe4 (21 ♖xe4 ♖xe4 22 ♗xe4 ♘ce7 is not clear since after 23 ♗h7+ ♔xh7 24 ♗g5+ ♔g7 25 ♗xf6+ ♘xf6 the very unusual material balance of queen and four pawns against four minor pieces arises; I suspect that Black is better) 21...♘ce7 (21...♘e5 22 dxe5 ♗xf2+ 23 ♔h1 ♖xe5 24 ♗h7+ ♔xh7 25 ♖xe5 ♕g6 26 ♗f4+! ♕xh5 27 ♖xh5+ ♔g6 28 ♖g5+ ♔h7 29 ♖f1 gives White a large endgame advantage) 22 ♗d3! ♕f7 23 ♕g5+ ♔h8 24 ♖e6! (forcing precise defence from Black) 24...♗c8 (the only move as 24...♖bd8 25 ♖ae1 ♗c8 26 ♖1e4! gives White a winning attack) with a final branch:

2b21) 25 ♖e5 ♖g8 26 ♖xe7 ♕xe7 27 ♕h5 ♕e8 28 ♕h4 ♖g6 is unclear.

2b22) 25 ♗g7+ ♕xg7 26 ♕h5+ ♔g8 27 ♕xe8+ ♕f8 28 ♕h5 ♕f7 (not 28...♕g7? 29 ♖e5) 29 ♖g6+ ♘xg6 30 ♗xg6 ♕e6 and again there is nothing clear for White.

2b23) 25 ♕e5+ ♔g8 26 ♕g3+, giving perpetual check, may be the most sensible option.

2c) 17 ♘xh6+! (the safest line) 17...gxh6 18 ♕g4+ ♔h8 19 ♗xh6 ♖g8 (19...♕f6 20 ♗g5

♕g7 21 ♗xe4 is excellent for White, who has three pawns and a dangerous attack for the piece) 20 ♕h5 ♘f6 21 ♕h4 ♘h7 (21...♘xd4 loses to 22 ♗g5+) 22 ♕xe4 ♖xg2+ (the best chance as 22...♘g6 23 ♕f4 ♕d6 24 ♗xg6 ♕xg6 25 ♘f3 is very good for White; for example, 25...♘xd4 26 ♘h4 ♘f3+ 27 ♘xf3 ♗xf3 28 ♕xf3 ♖xh6 29 ♕xf7 and White has too many pawns) 23 ♕xg2 ♕f6 24 ♗g7+ ♕xg7 25 ♕xg7+ ♔xg7 26 ♖e3 with a very promising ending for White. He has a rook and two pawns for a bishop and a knight, but in addition Black's king is exposed and his b6-bishop is locked out of play.

17   ♗xe4!

17 ♘xe4 f5 18 ♘xh6+ gxh6 19 ♘g3 ♘e7 may be better for White, but is less clear than the move played.

17   ...   ♖xe4

Black hopes to gain two pieces in return for a rook and a couple of pawns, which might not be so clear if there are few possibilities for White's rooks to become active.

18   ♘xe4   f5 (D)

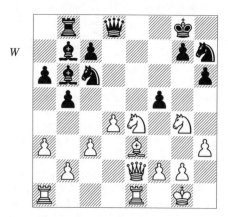

19   d5!

The most forceful line – White is prepared to offer a pawn to open the d-file for his other rook. However, the simple 19 ♘xh6+ gxh6 20 ♘g3! ♕d5 21 ♕h5 ♘e7 (21...♘xd4 loses to 22 ♕g6+ ♔h8 23 ♗xd4+ ♗xd4 24 ♖e8+ ♖xe8 25 ♕xe8+ ♘f8 26 ♕xf8+ ♔h7 27 ♕xf5+) 22 f3 is also very good for White, since the weakened kingside causes Black continuing problems.

19   ...   ♕xd5

Black must accept the pawn since 19...♘a5 20 ♗xb6 cxb6 21 ♖ad1 fxg4 22 ♕xg4 leaves

White material up with a massive positional advantage.

20   ♗xb6   cxb6 (D)

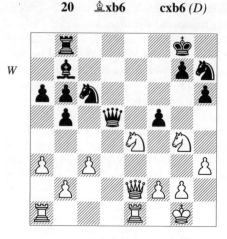

21   ♘xh6+?!

During the game, I was reminded of Lilienthal-Najdorf, Saltsjöbaden Interzonal 1948. This game appeared in *The Art of Attack in Chess* by Vuković, a book which I had recently edited. Here is the relevant position:

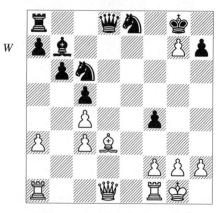

Lilienthal had just played a combination leading to the material balance of a rook and two pawns for two knights. That is nothing special in itself, but the point of White's play is that he was now able to offer a piece to allow his rooks to reach the central files with gain of time. The game continued 17 ♗xh7+! ♔xh7 18 ♕h5+ ♔xg7 19 ♖ad1 (although Black is way ahead on material, the attacking power of the major pieces against an exposed king is too much; it is particularly important that Black's knights are badly placed and have no footholds in the centre) 19...♕f6 (unsuccessfully attempting to stem the attack by returning some material; 19...♕c8 20 ♖fe1 ♔g8 21 ♕d5+ ♔h7 22 ♕f7+ ♘g7 23 ♖d7 ♕f8 24 ♕h5+ ♔g8 25 ♕d5+ ♔h8 26 ♖e6 also wins for White) 20 ♖d7+ ♔f8 21 ♖xb7 (now Black is down on material and in addition his king remains exposed; the game didn't last long) 21...♘d8 22 ♖d7 ♘f7 23 ♕d5 ♖b8 24 ♖e1 f3 25 ♖e3 1-0.

In this game, the key features were that White had a rook against three minor pieces, his rooks were on open d- and e-files and Black's king was very exposed. Had I pursued this analogy to its logical conclusion, then I might have discovered the following forced win: 21 ♖ad1! ♕xe4 (21...♕c4 22 ♘xh6+ gxh6 23 ♕xc4+ bxc4 24 ♘d6, picking up another pawn, is winning for White) 22 ♘xh6+ gxh6 (22...♔h8 23 ♕h5 ♘f6 24 ♘f7+ ♔g8 25 ♕g5 ♕c4 26 ♘d6 wins for White) 23 ♕h5 (here we see the close resemblance to Lilienthal-Najdorf; Black is defenceless) 23...♕c4 24 ♖d7 (24 ♕g6+ ♔h8 25 ♖d7 ♕g8 26 ♕xf5 also wins, as Black cannot meet the threat of ♖e3-g3) 24...♘f8 (24...♔h8 25 ♕xf5 ♕g8 26 ♖e3 gives White a winning attack – he is even a tempo up on the 24 ♕g6+ line) and during the game I stopped my analysis here since White's threats seemed too slow, but after 25 ♖c7 Black actually has no defence to the threats of 26 ♕xh6 and 26 ♖e3. After the move played, White retains a large advantage but Black can still put up a considerable resistance.

21 ... gxh6 *(D)*

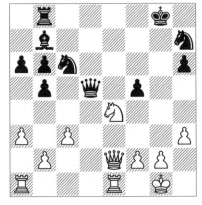

22 ♕h5

White's queen's rook can come to d1, and with both rooks operating on the central files, it is likely that one of them will penetrate and cause havoc in Black's position.

22 ... ♘e5

22...♘d4 loses to 23 ♘f6+ ♘xf6 24 ♕g6+ ♔h8 25 ♕xf6+ ♔g8 26 ♕g6+ ♔h8 27 cxd4, while 22...♕f7 23 ♕xf7+ ♔xf7 24 ♘d6+ ♔f6 25 ♖ad1 ♘e7 (or 25...♗a8 26 ♘e8+ ♔f7 27 ♖d7+ ♔g8 28 ♖g7+ ♔h8 29 ♖g6 and White wins) 26 ♘xb7 ♖xb7 27 ♖d6+ ♔g7 28 ♖ee6 gives White a winning ending.

23 ♖ad1 ♕f7

Not 23...♘d3 24 ♖xd3 ♕xd3 25 ♘f6+ ♘xf6 26 ♕g6+ ♔h8 27 ♕xf6+ ♔g8 28 ♖e7 mating.

24 ♘g3

This move is not bad, but it would have been simpler to continue 24 ♕xf7+ ♘xf7 (24...♔xf7 25 ♘d6+ ♔f6 26 ♘xb7 ♖xb7 27 ♖d6+ ♔e7 28 ♖xh6 and White wins) 25 ♘d6 ♘xd6 26 ♖xd6 with a terrible ending for Black. White wins another pawn straight away, and his rooks are far more active than Black's minor pieces.

24 ... ♕xh5
25 ♘xh5 *(D)*

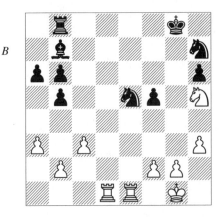

25 ... ♗e4

Or 25...♘f3+ (25...♗f3 is strongly met by 26 ♖d6) 26 gxf3 ♗xf3 27 ♘g3 (27 ♘f4? ♗xd1 28 ♖xd1 ♘f6 29 ♘d5 ♘xd5 30 ♖xd5 ♔g7 31 ♖xf5 ♖d8 gives Black good drawing chances) 27...♗xd1 28 ♖xd1 f4 29 ♘f5 h5 30 ♖d7 with a very large advantage for White, since Black will be unable to hang on to all his weak pawns.

26 ♖e3!

A strong move. Once the bishop is driven away by f3, Black will be unable to block either of the two central files and White's rooks will sweep into his position.

26 ... ♔f7

Black cannot prevent at least one rook from penetrating, after which his position becomes very difficult:

1) 26...♘c4 27 ♖g3+ ♔h8 28 ♖d7 ♘xb2 29 ♖g6 f4 30 ♖xh6 ♖f8 31 ♖d4 ♗f5 32 ♖xf4 is winning for White.

2) 26...♔h8 27 f3 ♘c4 28 ♖e2 ♗c6 29 b3 ♖g8 30 ♔f2 ♘xa3 31 ♖e7 ♗e8 32 ♘f4, followed by ♖d6, with a decisive attack.

3) 26...♔f8 27 f3 ♗c2 (27...♘c4 28 ♖e2 ♗c6 29 b3 ♘xa3 30 ♖e6 ♗e8 31 ♖xh6 is also very good for White) 28 ♖d4 ♘f7 (28...♘c4 29 ♖e2 ♗a4 30 ♖d5 ♔g8 31 ♖d7 looks like a win for White) 29 ♖e2 ♗b1 30 ♖e1 ♗c2 31 ♖d2 ♗b3 32 ♘g3 f4 33 ♘h5 picks up the f4-pawn, when White should win in the end.

27 f3 ♘c4
28 ♖e2 ♗c6
29 b3!

Driving the knight away from c4 and making the d6-square available for the rook.

29 ... ♘xa3

Or 29...♘a5 30 ♖d6 ♖e8 31 ♖xe8 ♗xe8 32 ♖xb6 ♘xb3 33 ♖xa6 and Black's pawns are dropping off.

30 ♖d6 *(D)*

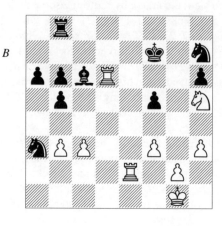

B

30 ... ♖c8?

Losing material, but even after the best defence 30...♗e8, the continuation 31 ♖xh6 ♔g8 32 ♘g3 f4 33 ♘f5 ♗f7 34 ♖e7 ♖f8 35 ♖xb6 ♗xb3 36 ♘d4 ♗d5 37 ♖xa6 wins for White without difficulty.

31 ♖xh6 ♘f8

31...♖e8 32 ♖a2 and White wins a piece.

32 ♖f6+ ♔g8
33 ♖e7 ♘h7
34 ♖g7+ 1-0

After 34...♔h8 35 ♖h6 it is mate next move.

This was followed by three quiet draws, but then I was struck down by a fairly nasty case of food poisoning, apparently resulting from a dodgy meal in an Oxford pub. Fortunately, Peter Wells agreed to postpone his game against me, and I limped to the finish line with a few more draws and a win in the last round. Under the circumstances, I was not unhappy with my third place, half a point behind joint winners Hodgson and Hector.

Since I was not participating at Hastings, I was able to spend the New Year at home for the first time in several years. With limited time available for playing chess, national leagues offered the most tempting possibilities for chess activity since they involved relatively short trips abroad. The French League was especially attractive in this respect, since it was played over three long weekends in the first half of the year. This compares favourably with the Bundesliga, which involves eight trips if you play in every round. When an opportunity arose to play for Monaco in the French League I was happy to accept. Everything went quite well until I faced the young French grandmaster Igor-Alexandre Nataf, who beat me brilliantly. After the game I was depressed not so much by the game itself, but by the realization that I would be seeing a lot more of this game in years to come. Indeed, it won the prize for the best game in *Informator 75* and has since been reproduced many times. At least I hope to avoid the fate of players such as von Bardeleben, who are remembered today only for games they lost. The day after I played Nataf, I faced another grandmaster, and the game served to improve my mood considerably.

The opening line White adopted in this game involves delaying the development of the queenside, often for a considerable time. Black decided to exploit this by taking quick action, and so the game dissolved into tactics with both players' pieces mostly on their original squares. Black's early activity netted him a pawn, but at the cost of weakening his position and having his king stuck in the centre. Such a situation is fraught with danger and any error is likely to be severely punished. The crucial mistake came at move 13, and White's unexpected reply was effectively a knock-out blow.

Game 35
J. Nunn – N. Miezis
French League 1999
Sicilian Defence, 2 ♘f3 e6 3 c3

1	e4	c5
2	♘f3	e6
3	c3	

Miezis is an expert on the Kan System (3 d4 cxd4 4 ♘xd4 a6) and has achieved excellent practical results with it, so I decided to shift the battleground to something which I hoped he would be less familiar with. Unfortunately, I was also unfamiliar with it since I had never played the 3 c3 d5 4 e5 system before in my life. However, I preferred to fight on territory which was unknown to both of us rather than on my opponent's home ground.

3	...	d5

3...♘f6 4 e5 ♘d5 is of course also playable, transposing into a position normally reached via 2 c3 ♘f6 3 e5 ♘d5 4 ♘f3 e6. However, I had noticed that Miezis invariably meets 2 c3 by 2...d5, so it seemed unlikely that he would go in for this line.

4	e5	

For 4 exd5 see Game 28.

4	...	d4 *(D)*

If Black plays 4...♘c6, White will reply 5 d4 transposing into the Advance Variation of the French (normally reached after 1 e4 e6 2 d4 d5 3 e5 c5 4 c3 ♘c6 5 ♘f3). However, many Sicilian players dislike this option, which leads to a type of position unfamiliar to them. The text-move is therefore a popular choice, cutting out d4 by White.

The position after 4...d4 is strategically quite interesting. The d4-pawn exerts a cramping influence on White's queenside and the fundamental question is whether White can solve the problem of developing his queenside pieces. Black has fewer development problems, but in the long run White's e5-pawn could form the basis of an attack by White if Black castles kingside.

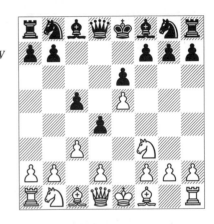

5	♗d3	

This move may appear rather odd, because blocking the d3-pawn is not going to help White get his dark-squared bishop into play. The trouble is that White is more or less forced to block in one bishop or the other, since releasing the c1-bishop by d3 only obstructs the other bishop. Therefore, White aims to castle quickly, which at least gives him the chance to support his e5-pawn by ♖e1 and, if necessary, ♕e2.

5 cxd4 cxd4 6 ♕a4+ ♘c6 7 ♗b5 ♗d7 is wrong as White cannot now win a pawn (8 ♗xc6 ♗xc6 9 ♕xd4 ♕xd4 10 ♘xd4 ♗xg2 is obviously good for Black), while otherwise White's queen and bishop are exposed to attack.

5	...	♘c6

The most natural move. Note that Black should never play ...dxc3, because after the reply dxc3 White can easily develop his queenside pieces, and then the cramping e5-pawn gives him the advantage.

6	0-0	g5!? *(D)*

6...♘ge7 is the most common continuation, when White replies either 7 ♖e1 or 7 ♗e4.

The text-move was unexpected and I was now on my own. Black's plan is rather clear:

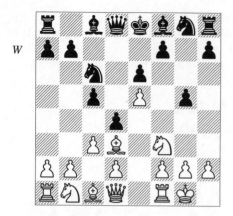

W

he simply intends to win the e5-pawn with a combination of ...g4 and ...♗g7. White cannot even reply 7 ♖e1?, because then 7...g4 traps the knight. At first I was at a loss as to how to proceed, but then I saw that by sacrificing the e5-pawn White could obtain a dangerous initiative.

7   ♗e4

Essentially the only move. White threatens to take on c6, not only relieving the pressure against e5 but also seriously damaging Black's queenside pawn-structure.

7   ...   ♗d7

7...g4 8 ♗xc6+ bxc6 9 ♘e1 h5 10 d3 is slightly better for White, as there are tempting squares for the b1-knight at c4 and e4, while White can support his e5-pawn by playing f4. Therefore Black decides to spend a tempo countering the threat of ♗xc6+.

8   d3

Opening the line of the c1-bishop so that the f3-knight can jump to the active square g5.

8   ...   g4

9   ♘g5!

This position has arisen four times in practice, with White winning all four games. Two of these encounters occurred before the present game, but I only became aware of this when I checked my database after the game. 9 ♗xc6 ♗xc6 10 ♘g5 avoids losing a pawn, but after 10...♕d5 11 ♕xg4 ♕xe5 the position is starting to open up, and this favours the side with the two bishops.

9   ...   ♘xe5

9...h6 is also possible:

1) 10 ♘h7 ♗g7 (10...♘xe5 11 ♘xf8 ♔xf8 12 ♖e1 ♕f6 13 ♗xb7 ♖b8 14 ♗e4 and White regains the sacrificed pawn with a clear advantage

in view of Black's misplaced king and weakened dark squares) 11 ♕xg4 ♗xe5 12 f4 ♗f6 13 ♗d2 ♕e7 14 ♘a3 0-0-0 with a very sharp and unclear position.

2) 10 ♘xf7!? ♔xf7 11 ♕xg4 is a positional piece sacrifice. Currently White has just two pawns for the piece, but he has long-term attacking chances because the black king lacks a safe spot. After 11...♘ge7 (11...♘xe5? loses to 12 ♕h5+ ♔f6 13 ♗f4) 12 ♘a3 h5 13 ♕f3+ ♘f5 14 ♗f4 ♖c8 15 ♖ae1 White had sufficient compensation in Sanduleac-Rajković, Pančevo 2002, a game which White eventually won.

Accepting the pawn is double-edged, since Black's early g-pawn advance has left him with several weaknesses, especially along the f-file.

10   f4 (D)

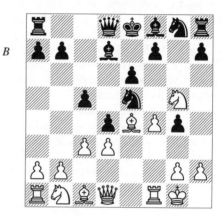

B

This allows the f1-rook to join in the attack from its original square.

10   ...   ♘g6

Black has various alternatives, but in every case White either regains the pawn or secures a dangerous initiative:

1) 10...h6 11 fxe5 hxg5 12 ♕xg4 ♗e7 was played in Tempone-Spangenberg, Buenos Aires 1992 and now 13 ♗xb7 ♖b8 14 ♗e4 ♕c7 15 ♕g3 ♘h6 16 ♘a3 would have been very good for White.

2) 10...♘c6 11 f5! exf5 and now:

2a) 12 ♗d5 ♘h6 13 ♕b3 with another branch:

2a1) 13...♕e7 14 ♗f4! (14 ♕xb7 ♖b8 15 ♕c7 ♕e5 is unclear) 14...0-0-0 15 ♘a3 with a strong initiative in return for the two pawns.

2a2) 13...♕f6 14 ♖e1+ ♗e7 15 ♕xb7 ♖b8 16 ♕c7 ♖c8 17 ♕g3 0-0 18 ♗f4 gives White fair compensation for the pawn, but he may not have any advantage.

2b) 12 ♗xf5 (this simple continuation is best) 12...♗xf5 13 ♖xf5 ♘f6 (D) and now:

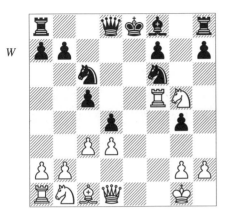

2b1) 14 ♘xf7? (a tempting but unsound sacrifice) 14...♔xf7 15 ♕b3+ ♔e8 (15...c4? 16 ♕xc4+ ♔e8 17 ♗g5 ♗e7 18 ♘d2 gives White a very dangerous attack) 16 ♕xb7 ♕d7! 17 ♕xa8+ ♔f7 and White will lose his queen.

2b2) 14 ♘d2! ♗g7 15 ♘de4 dxc3 16 bxc3 and Black is in difficulties:

2b21) 16...h6 17 ♘xf6+ ♗xf6 18 ♘e4 ♗d4+ (18...♗xc3? loses to 19 ♘xc3 ♕d4+ 20 ♔h1 ♕xc3 21 ♕e2+ followed by ♗b2) 19 ♔h1 ♘e7 20 ♖h5 ♗g7 21 ♗f4 with a large advantage for White.

2b22) 16...♘xe4 17 ♘xe4 0-0 18 ♕xg4 ♔h8 19 ♕h3, threatening 20 ♖h5, with an enormous attack.

3) 10...gxf3 11 ♘xf3 ♘g4 (11...♘c6? 12 ♘g5 ♘h6 13 ♕h5 ♕e7 14 ♘h3 is winning for White, while 11...♘g6 12 ♗xb7 ♖b8 13 ♗a6 gives White some advantage) 12 h3 ♘4f6 13 ♗xb7 ♖b8 14 ♗a6 ♗d6 15 ♘bd2 is better for White. It is very risky for Black to accept the pawn by 15...dxc3 16 bxc3 ♕a5 17 ♗c4 ♕xc3, since 18 ♘b3 followed by ♖b1 and ♗b2 gives White a dangerous attack.

11   f5

Opening up lines and taking aim at the weak f7-square.

11   ...   exf5
12   ♗xf5

12 ♕b3 ♘h6 13 ♗d5 looks dangerous, but after 13...♕e7 14 ♕xb7 ♖d8 15 ♗d2 ♗g7 there is nothing clear for White.

12   ...   ♗xf5

Or 12...♘e5 13 ♕b3 (threatening both 14 ♖e1 and the neat 14 ♘xf7 ♘xf7 15 ♗g6!) 13...♘h6 14 ♗e4 (stronger than 14 ♗xd7+ ♕xd7 15 ♘e4 0-0-0 16 ♗g5 ♘xd3, which isn't totally clear) 14...♕b6 (after 14...♗g7 15 ♕xb7 ♖c8 16 ♕xa7 White is a pawn up) 15 ♗xb7 ♖d8 16 ♖e1 ♗g7 17 ♗f4 f6 18 ♗d5 with very unpleasant pressure for White.

13   ♖xf5 (D)

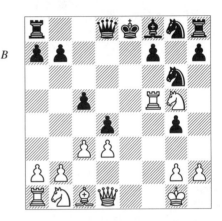

13   ...   ♘h6?

Up to here, Black has not made a significant error, but this natural move turns out to be a serious mistake. Black hopes to force the rook back and thereby gain time to develop his pieces, but after White's reply this scheme collapses and it turns out that Black has fatally weakened the f6-square. Alternatives:

1) 13...♘f6 14 ♘d2 (simple development is best) 14...dxc3 15 ♕b3! (15 bxc3 ♗g7 16 ♘de4 0-0 is fine for Black) 15...♕d7 16 ♖xf6 cxd2 17 ♗xd2 gives White a strong attack.

2) 13...♕d7! is the right way to attack the rook and keeps White's advantage to a minimum:

2a) 14 ♕e2+?! ♘8e7 (not 14...♗e7 15 ♘e4 ♕e6 16 ♗g5 ♗e7 17 ♘bd2 0-0-0 18 ♗xe7 ♘8xe7 19 ♖f6 ♕d5 20 ♕xg4+ ♔b8 21 c4 with a massive advantage for White) 15 ♖xf7 h6 (not 15...♘h6 16 ♘e4 ♔xf7 17 ♗xh6 ♘f5 18 ♕xg4 with excellent compensation for White) 16 ♖f6 hxg5 17 ♖xg6 g3 gives Black the initiative.

2b) 14 ♖f1 f6 15 ♕e2+ ♗e7 16 ♘e6 ♔f7 leads to a likely draw after 17 ♘g5+.

2c) 14 ♖xf7! ♗e7 15 ♖f1 (15 ♕b3 ♘f6 is unclear) 15...h6 16 ♘e4 0-0-0 17 c4 gives White an excellent knight on e4, but he has still to complete his queenside development. On balance, I think White should be slightly better here.

14   ♘e4! *(D)*

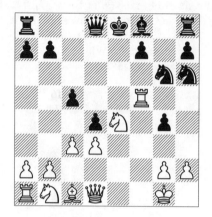

B

For a moment my opponent looked stunned as I played this move, so I suppose it was a complete surprise for him. White clears the g5-square for ♗g5, while at the same time the f6-square beckons to the knight. The crucial point is that taking the rook by 14...♘xf5 costs Black his queen after 15 ♕a4+ ♚e7 (or 15...♕d7 16 ♘f6+) 16 ♗g5+.

14   ...   ♗g7

There is nothing else. It is unusual for a player to be able to launch such a vicious attack with most of his pieces still on their original squares.

15   ♗g5   ♘e7

This move surprisingly costs Black a piece, but the position was lost in any case; for example, 15...♕b6 16 ♘f6+ ♗xf6 17 ♖xf6 ♕xb2 18 ♘d2 and the threats of ♘c4, ♖b1, ♕a4+ and ♗xh6 are too much, or 15...dxc3 16 bxc3 ♕c7 17 ♖xc5 ♕b6 18 ♕a4+ ♚f8 19 ♘bd2 followed by ♘c4 and Black's position is a total wreck.

16   ♖f6! *(D)*

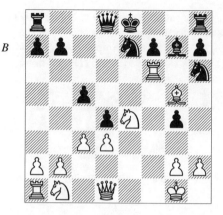

B

Threatening to take on h6, or to play 17 ♘d6+.

16   ...   dxc3

16...♗xf6 17 ♘xf6+ ♚f8 18 ♗xh6# is a nice mate.

17	bxc3	♕d5
18	♖d6	♕f5
19	♗xh6	

White cashes in his attack to win a piece.

19	...	♗xh6
20	♖xh6	0-0-0

Setting a neat trap.

21   ♘bd2

Now that White has avoided 21 ♘d6+?? ♖xd6 22 ♖xd6 ♕f4 trapping the rook, Black could well resign, but he limps on for several moves.

21   ...   ♘g6

If 21...♖xd3, then 22 ♘d6+.

22	♕b3	♕d5
23	♕xd5	♖xd5
24	♖f1	♖f8
25	♖xh7	f5
26	♖h5	♚c7
27	♘c4	♘e7
28	♖h7	♚d7
29	♘e3	1-0

Of the three leagues I played in during 1998/9, the French League proved the most troublesome for me. I scored just 4½/8, compared to 3/4 in the (second) Bundesliga and an excellent 5/6 in the 4NCL. In fact, after this season I only played one further game in the French League, since although I had agreed with the Monaco team captain to play in certain matches during the 2000 season, when the matches actually arrived I was left out of the team.

Since my chess was by now largely confined to national leagues, the summer period was inevitably one of little chess activity. In September I travelled to Reykjavik to play for my 4NCL club, Invicta Knights, in a qualification group for the European Clubs Cup. My experience is that if you have a long period away from chess, the first part of your chess ability that you lose is your common sense and it can take a few games before it returns. My first game in Reykjavik should serve as a warning about the type of error you are likely to commit.

Game 36

J. Nunn – D. McMahon

European Clubs Cup, Reykjavik 1999

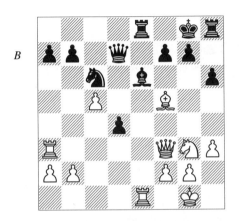

I was rated 370 points higher than my opponent and, not surprisingly, I was expecting to win. White does in fact have a slight advantage in the diagram due to Black's poor king position. Indeed, were it not for the potential danger posed by the passed d-pawn, Black would be in trouble.

27   ...   g6

Seeking to play ...♔g7 and thereby connect the rooks. At this point a sensible choice would be to exchange twice on e6 and then play ♖b3. Coupled with the idea of ♘e4-d6, this gives White an edge. However, I suddenly saw a combination to exploit the weak f6-square. An accurate calculation showed that in the main line White wins both black rooks for a bishop and a knight. Two exchanges up sounded like good news, and so I went for it. This is where the common sense deficiency comes into play. Yes, White wins quite a lot of material, but the whole idea has a major defect: it takes White's pieces totally out of play and leaves Black's forces ideally posted for pushing the d-pawn. When you are reasonably in form, such a point is obvious, but when you are out of practice you think 'with all that extra material, there's bound to be some way to stop the d-pawn' and just play it. Retribution wasn't long in coming.

28	♘e4?	♔g7
29	♘f6	♗xf5
30	♖xe8	♔xf6
31	♖xh8	♔g7 (D)

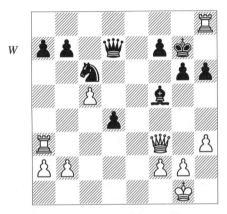

Here I suddenly realized White might well be dead lost. The only safe square for the rook is a8, and one can fairly say that the rooks on a3 and a8 are just about as badly placed as one could imagine for fighting against the d-pawn. Both sides were very short of time (running short of time is another typical symptom of lack of practice) so rather than passively retreat to the edges of the board I tried to mix the position up.

32   g4?

Computer analysis shows that White might just about defend the position by 32 ♖a8 d3 33 ♕d1 d2 34 ♖c3 ♘d4 35 ♔h2.

32   ...   ♗c2!

This move should have been the last nail in White's coffin.

33   ♖c3

There is little point commenting on White's desperate attempts to confuse Black.

33	...	d3
34	♖xd3	♗xd3
35	♖a8	♕d4

36	♖e8	♗c4
37	b4	♕a1+
38	♔h2	♕xa2

| 39 | ♕f4 | 1-0 |

Black, with a totally winning position, overstepped the time limit, much to my relief.

In my second game I was again in trouble, this time against the Danish grandmaster Henrik Danielsen. I had just about scrambled to an ending which I might have been able to draw when he lost on time. In my third and final game I ran into difficulties against Pigusov and was soon a pawn down in a rook ending. In fact Pigusov came within a few seconds of making it a clean sweep of wins on time, but a few quick moves brought him safely to the time-control and the game eventually ended in a draw.

My play in the 1999/00 winter league season was poor. I scored 3½/7 in the 4NCL, and 7½/15 for Lübeck in the Bundesliga (playing in every match!). Lübeck was now in the first division, and the team had been strengthened by the inclusion of players such as Shirov, Bareev and Speelman. However, a team is more than a collection of talented individuals – that indefinable characteristic called 'team spirit' is also an important factor, and as yet the Lübeck team had not developed this crucial ingredient. A further problem was that there were too many matches in which the leading players did not take part, which resulted in losses to teams that Lübeck should really have beaten. Despite having the third strongest Bundesliga team on paper, Lübeck were at one stage in danger of relegation and ended up in lowly eleventh place. The following game was one of my few bright spots from this season.

The Sveshnikov Variation of the Sicilian can result in bizarre positions in which normal chess intuition doesn't work very well. The particular line played in this game leads to a position in which all the major pieces are on the board, plus a pair of opposite-coloured bishops. It is well-known that opposite-coloured bishops tend to enhance any attacking possibilities in the middlegame, and since both kings had lost the right to castle there was no shortage of attacking possibilities. An inaccuracy by White left Black with slightly the better chances due to his more active bishop, but White should have been able to hold the game. The initiative is very important in this type of position, and White was wrong to allow Black's pieces to become active by grabbing a stray pawn on move 24. White immediately came under heavy pressure and soon a further error sealed his fate.

Game 37

H. Teske – J. Nunn

Bundesliga 1999/00

Sicilian Defence, Sveshnikov Variation

| 1 | e4 | |

Already a surprise for me. I had always thought of Teske as a quiet positional player, and so this choice of first move was unexpected.

1	...	c5
2	♘f3	e6
3	d4	cxd4
4	♘xd4	♘f6
5	♘c3	♘c6

Black's move-order aims to reach the Sveshnikov Variation without allowing various annoying sidelines, such as 1 e4 c5 2 ♘f3 ♘c6 3 ♗b5, or 1 e4 c5 2 ♘f3 ♘c6 3 d4 cxd4 4 ♘xd4 ♘f6 5 ♘c3 e5 6 ♘db5 d6 7 a4 (or 7 ♘d5). Its

main defect is that it allows the line 6 ♘xc6 bxc6 7 e5 ♘d5 8 ♘e4 which, at the time of writing, appears rather promising for White.

| 6 | ♘db5 | |

White decides to enter the Sveshnikov.

6	...	d6
7	♗f4	e5
8	♗g5	

Now we have reached the same position as after 1 e4 c5 2 ♘f3 ♘c6 3 d4 cxd4 4 ♘xd4 ♘f6 5 ♘c3 e5 6 ♘db5 d6 7 ♗g5, except that the move number is one higher – a fact that is one of the main problems when writing about the Sveshnikov!

8	...	a6
9	♗xf6	gxf6
10	♘a3	b5
11	♘d5	f5

The line 11...♗g7, followed by ...♘e7, is also very popular but in this game Black prefers to follow the traditional path.

12   ♗d3

At one time variations involving exf5 dominated theory in this position (either 12 exf5 or 12 c3 ♗g7 13 exf5), but in recent years many players have switched back to 12 ♗d3.

12   ...   ♗e6 (D)

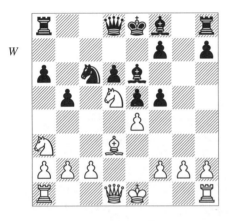

13   c4?!

A rather unusual continuation, which had me scratching my head trying to remember the theory. In the 1980s, 13 ♕h5 was the most popular move, but the success of the reply 13...♖g8! has led to the rise of 13 0-0 as White's main continuation. Then Black has two main replies, 13...♗g7 and 13...♗xd5 14 exd5 ♘e7, with the latter being the continuation of choice for most leading Sveshnikov practitioners. 13 c4 was played several times in the early days of the Sveshnikov and it has appeared occasionally ever since. Quite honestly, it is hard to see why it is still played since it is utterly harmless. Spending time on a pawn move which opens up the position when White's king is still in the centre is clearly a risky proposition. Black has at least two perfectly satisfactory responses, and indeed it is often White who ends up playing for equality. This raises the question as to why Teske chose the line. Apparently, it was intended as a kind of surprise weapon; in fact, I was surprised, but pleasantly so!

13   ...   ♗xd5

Black can also play 13...♕a5+, and now:

1) 14 ♕d2 ♕xd2+ 15 ♔xd2 ♗h6+ 16 ♔e1 has been played a few times, but Black has a powerful reply:

1a) 16...♗xd5 17 exd5 ♘d4 18 cxb5 e4 has been Black's choice in the practical examples. After 19 ♗c4 axb5 20 ♘xb5 ♘c2+ 21 ♔e2 ♘xa1 22 ♘c7+ ♔e7 23 ♘xa8 ♘c2 24 ♘b6 ♖b8 the position is roughly equal since Black's active pieces give him enough play for the pawn.

1b) 16...bxc4! 17 ♘xc4 fxe4 18 ♗xe4 0-0-0! 19 ♘ce3 (trying to stop ...f5) 19...♗xe3 20 fxe3 (20 ♘xe3 d5 favours Black) 20...f5 21 ♘b6+ ♔b7 22 ♗d5 ♔xb6 23 ♗xe6 f4! and Black is better.

2) 14 ♔f1 fxe4 (14...♗xd5 15 exd5 transposes to the game, which is also fine for Black) 15 ♗xe4 ♗g7 16 cxb5 (16 ♘f6+ ♗xf6 17 ♗xc6+ ♔e7 18 ♗xa8 ♖xa8 gives Black fantastic play for the exchange, while 16 ♘f4 exf4 17 ♗xc6+ ♔e7 18 ♗xa8 ♖xa8 is also awkward for White) 16...axb5 17 ♖c1 ♖a6 and Black can be happy with his position. If White does not try something immediately then Black consolidates, when his central pawn-mass and White's misplaced king give Black a clear advantage. On the other hand, immediate tactical blows fail to achieve anything for White; for example, 18 b4 ♕xa3 19 ♘c7+ ♔d7 20 ♘xa6 ♘d4 21 ♗b7 ♔e7! and Black has a clear advantage.

14   exd5 (D)

14 cxd5 is playable, although it cannot cause Black any problems after 14...♕a5+ 15 ♔f1 fxe4 16 ♗xe4 ♘e7 17 ♘c2 ♖c8.

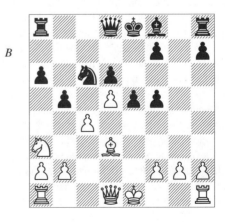

14   ...   ♕a5+

Of course White cannot hope for any advantage if the queens are exchanged, but the alternative is to misplace his king.

15   ♔f1

15 ♕d2 ♕xd2+ 16 ♔xd2 ♗h6+ 17 ♔e1 transposes to line '1a' in the note to Black's 13th move, with an assessment of approximate equality.

15   ...   ♘d4

16   cxb5

The main continuation. 16 ♘c2 ♘xc2 17 ♕xc2 e4 18 cxb5 ♗g7 gives Black no problems at all; for example, 19 ♕c6+?! ♔e7 20 b6 ♖ac8 21 ♕b7+ ♔f6 22 ♕xa6 ♕d2! with a strong attack for Black.

16   ...   axb5

17   ♘c2 (D)

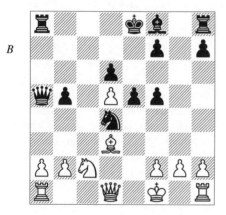

This is White's plan. He exchanges off the well-placed knight on d4 to leave a position with just major pieces and opposite-coloured bishops. He hopes that the weak black pawns on f5 and b5, coupled with Black's uncastled king, will give him the advantage. However, White's king is in many ways worse placed than Black's, since Black can restore communication between his rooks with ...♔e7, while White's king has no easy way out. In unbalanced positions, opposite-coloured bishops enhance the attacking prospects of whoever holds the initiative and provided Black is prepared to offer a pawn or two, he has chances of developing a dangerous attack. I believe that in this position White should be aiming to reach a draw (which he should achieve with accurate play).

17   ...   ♘xc2

18   ♗xc2?!

White is not satisfied with the positions arising after the usual 18 ♕xc2 and improvises an alternative. He plans to attack the f5-pawn and, if Black plays ...e4, to undermine Black's pawns with g4. Recapturing with the bishop also avoids a loss of tempo after ...e4 by Black. In principle this is a sound strategic idea, but it is not very effective here because it gives Black time to build up an initiative. I feel that this move is slightly worse than the usual 18 ♕xc2 in that Black has more prospects of an advantage, whereas the normal line 18 ♕xc2 e4 19 ♕c6+ ♔e7 20 ♗xb5 ♖a7 (D) is very close to equality:

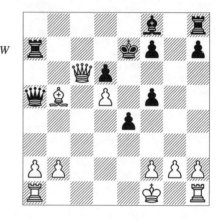

1) 21 ♕e8+?! ♔f6 (Black's dark-square control ensures that his king will not be in real danger) 22 g4 ♖e7 23 ♕b8 ♔e5! (a remarkable move) 24 f4+? (24 ♗c6 makes more sense, preparing to bring the queen back, but after 24...♕a6+ 25 ♔g2 ♕d3 Black has plenty of counterplay) 24...♔xf4 25 ♔e2 (25 ♕xd6+ ♖e5 also favours Black) 25...♔e5 26 ♖hf1 fxg4 and Black has a large advantage. The game Ivanović-Sveshnikov, Yugoslavia vs USSR, Krk 1976 concluded 27 b4 ♗g7! (not 27...♕xb4? 28 ♖f5+! ♔xf5 29 ♗d7+) 28 bxa5 ♖xb8 29 ♖ab1 f5 30 a6 f4 31 ♗c6 f3+ 32 ♔f2 ♖xb1 33 ♖xb1 ♔f4 34 ♖b4 ♗c3 35 ♖c4 ♔a5 36 ♔f1 ♗b6 37 ♗b7 h5 38 ♖c6 e3 39 ♖c4+ ♔g5 0-1. This was one of the great classic Sveshnikov games and, at least in part, was responsible for bringing the variation to wider attention.

2) 21 a4 (more sensible than sending White's queen off on a wild-goose chase) 21...♗g7 22 ♕c1 ♖b8 (threatening 23...♖xb5) 23 ♖b1 ♖xb5 24 axb5 ♕xb5+ 25 ♔g1 ♕xd5 (Black has a

pawn for the exchange, while White has still to activate his h1-rook; the position is roughly equal) 26 h4 ♕c5 (26...♕a5 27 ♖h3 ♖c7 is also level) 27 ♕xc5 dxc5 28 ♖h3 ♖b7 29 ♔f1 ♔e6 was safe for Black in Van der Wiel-Dolmatov, European Junior Ch, Groningen 1978/9 and the game was soon agreed drawn.

These lines show in a microcosm why the Sveshnikov is so enduringly popular at grandmaster level. Even if White plays accurately, Black still has a sound position while, as the course of Teske-Nunn shows, if White goes wrong then the punishment can be brutal.

18 ... e4

Black shields the f5-pawn and opens the diagonal for his bishop after a future ...♗g7. Black cannot hope to keep his f5-e4 pawn-chain intact indefinitely; his aim is rather to force White to spend time breaking it up, and to use that time to activate his pieces.

19 g4 (D)

White cannot attack the f5-pawn by 19 ♕h5 due to 19...♕b4 threatening 20...♕xb2. Then 20 ♕xf5? would lose a piece after 20...♕c4+. 19 ♕d4 is also dubious, since after 19...♖g8 followed by ...♗g7 White will only lose time.

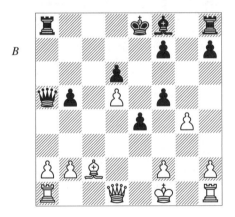

19 ... ♗g7

This natural move, targeting White's exposed queenside pawns, is the strongest. In the later game Schuermans-Goossens, Belgian Team Ch 2000/1 Black continued 19...♕b4 20 gxf5 ♖c8 21 ♗b3 ♗h6 22 ♕g4 ♔f8 23 f6 ♖e8 and now 24 ♖g1!, preventing Black from developing his h8-rook, would have given White a promising position. However, he played 24 ♖d1? and lost quickly: 24...♖g8 25 ♕h4 ♖g6 (threatening

26...♗g5) 26 ♖g1? e3! 27 f4 (27 ♕xb4 e2+ 28 ♔e1 ♖xg1#) 27...e2+ 28 ♔f2 ♕c5+ 0-1.

20 gxf5

There isn't anything sensible White can do about the attack on b2, so he proceeds with his own demolition plan.

20 ... ♗xb2

Black is not averse to grabbing White's queenside pawns, which not only improves the material situation but also gives Black a way to penetrate with his pieces along the a-file. The bishop's natural square is e5 and it does no harm to take a pawn on the way to this destination.

21 ♖b1 ♕xa2 (D)

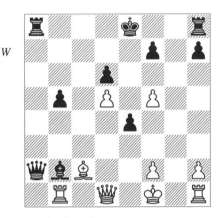

Black is temporarily a pawn up but this state of affairs will not last for long as White can easily win a pawn on e4 or b5 (maybe even both!). Black has two slight advantages. The first is that his king is safer than White's. With his bishop on e5 he will be able to play ...♔e7, connecting his rooks and removing the king from a vulnerable light square. He may later move the king to f6, for example in response to a check on the seventh rank. The second slight advantage is that his bishop is more active than White's, which is obstructed by the pawns on f5 and d5. However, the reduced number of pawns limits Black's winning possibilities and the opposite-coloured bishops mean a very likely draw if the queens are exchanged. Thus at this stage the position should still be within the bounds of a draw.

22 ♕e2

It looks risky for White to try to take both black pawns, but of course if he can get away with it without a disaster then he will virtually guarantee a draw in the event of a queen exchange. The main alternatives are:

1) 22 ♗xe4 ♗e5 (D) (22...♖g8 23 ♖g1 gives Black nothing) and now:

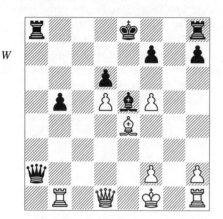

W

1a) 23 ♖xb5?! (this greedy move leads to serious trouble) 23...♖g8 24 ♕c2 (24 ♖g1 ♕c4+ 25 ♗d3 ♖xg1+ 26 ♔xg1 ♕h4 favours Black) 24...♔e7 25 ♖b7+ ♔f6 26 ♕c7 ♕a1+ 27 ♗b1 (27 ♔e2 ♖a2+ 28 ♗c2 ♖xc2+ 29 ♕xc2 ♕xh1 leaves Black a piece up) 27...♕a6+ 28 ♔e1 ♖ge8 29 ♕xf7+ (29 ♗e4 ♕a1+ 30 ♗b1 ♗f4+ leads to a forced mate after 31 ♔f1 ♕a6+ 32 ♔g2 ♖g8+ 33 ♔f3 ♕a3+ 34 ♔xf4 ♖a4+ 35 ♗e4 ♖g4+! 36 ♔xg4 ♖xe4+ 37 f4 h5+) 29...♔g5 30 ♖g1+ (30 h4+ ♔f4 wins for Black) 30...♔f4 31 ♔d2 ♗c3+! 32 ♔xc3 ♖ac8+ 33 ♖c7 ♕a5+ and Black wins.

1b) 23 ♖g1 is better, but Black can still retain an edge by 23...♔e7!:

1b1) 24 f6+ ♔xf6 25 ♕f3+ (25 ♖xb5 ♕c4+ 26 ♗d3 ♖a1 27 ♖b1 ♖xb1 28 ♕xb1 ♕xd5 gives Black an extra pawn) 25...♔e7 26 ♗d3 (26 ♖g4 h5 27 ♖g5 ♕c4+ favours Black) 26...♕d2 27 ♗xb5 ♖hc8! (27...♖hb8 28 ♔g2 gives Black nothing) 28 ♗c6 ♖cb8 29 ♔g2 ♕g5+ 30 ♔h1 ♕h4 31 ♕g2 ♖xb1 32 ♖xb1 ♖a3 and Black retains significant pressure.

1b2) 24 ♖xb5 ♕c4+ 25 ♗d3 ♖a1 26 ♖b1 ♖xb1 27 ♕xb1 ♕xd5 is slightly better for Black, although the result should be a draw.

2) 22 ♖g1 and now:

2a) 22...♕c4+ 23 ♕e2 ♖a2 (23...♕xe2+ 24 ♔xe2 ♗c3 25 ♖xb5 ♖a2 26 ♖b8+ ♔e7 27 f6+ ♗xf6 28 ♖b7+ ♔e8 29 ♔d2 is also safe for White) 24 ♕xc4 bxc4 25 ♖g4 ♔e7 26 ♖xe4+ ♔f6 27 ♖xc4 with an inevitable draw.

2b) 22...♗e5! is best, since White doesn't really have anything better than 23 ♗xe4 transposing into line '1b'.

| 22 | ... | ♗e5 |
| 23 | ♕xb5+ | ♔e7 (D) |

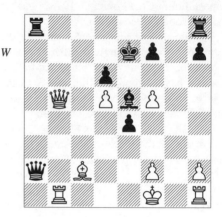

W

Up to here White has played well, but it is not easy to defend accurately when under sustained pressure and now White starts to go wrong.

24 ♗xe4?

A definite error, as now Black can gain time by chasing White's queen. The best defence is 24 ♕e2, since White can always take the e4-pawn later on. The main lines are:

1) 24...e3 25 fxe3 ♖hc8 26 ♗e4 ♖a4 27 ♕xa2 ♖xa2 28 ♖g1 and White should be able to draw.

2) 24...♖hb8 25 ♕xe4 ♖xb1+ 26 ♗xb1 and White defends.

3) 24...♖hc8 25 ♗xe4 ♕a3 26 ♗d3 ♖c1+ 27 ♔g2 ♖g8+ 28 ♔h3 ♖xh1 29 ♖xh1 and, rather surprisingly, Black seems unable to exploit the awkward position of White's king. Black retains slight pressure in these lines, but he cannot obtain serious winning chances.

| 24 | ... | ♖hb8 |
| 25 | ♕d3 | |

White cannot play 25 ♕xb8 ♖xb8 26 ♖xb8 due to 26...♗d4, so he is forced to retreat.

| 25 | ... | ♖a3 (D) |
| 26 | ♕c2? | |

It often happens that one error is immediately followed by another, and that is the case here. Other moves:

1) 26 f6+ is tempting, but not really effective. After 26...♔xf6 27 ♕d1 (27 ♕c2 ♖xb1+

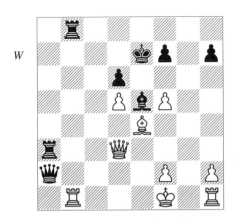

W

28 ♕xb1 ♕d2 wins as in the game) 27...♖c3!
28 ♖xb8 ♕c4+ 29 ♔g1 (29 ♔g2 ♕xe4+ 30
♔g1 ♖a3 31 ♖b1 ♖a8! is a neat win, switching
the rook round to g8) 29...♖c1! (29...♕xe4 30
♖b3 ♕a4 31 ♖b1 ♕h4 gives Black strong pressure, but there doesn't seem to be a clear win)
30 ♕xc1 ♕xc1+ 31 ♔g2 ♕g5+ 32 ♔f1 ♕f4 33
f3 ♕d2 (White is doomed by his bad king position and dark-square weaknesses) 34 ♖c8 (hoping to bring the rook back to c2) 34...♗c3! 35
h4 (35 ♖g1 loses at once to 35...♗d4, while 35
♖c7 ♔e5 36 ♖xf7 ♔d4 37 ♖c7 ♔e3 38 ♖xc3+
♕xc3 39 ♔g2 ♕g7+ 40 ♔h3 ♔f2 wins for
Black) 35...♔e5! 36 ♖g1 ♔f4 Black's king penetrates to e3 with decisive effect.

2) 26 ♕d1! was the only chance:

2a) 26...♖xb1 27 ♗xb1 ♕c4+ 28 ♔g2 ♕h4
29 h3 h5 30 ♕d2 and I do not see how Black
can make progress.

2b) 26...♕c4+ 27 ♕e2 ♖xb1+ 28 ♗xb1 is
tempting, but again it is hard to pinpoint a win
for Black:

2b1) 28...♕xd5 29 ♕e4 makes life easier
for White, as the ending offers minimal winning prospects, while 29...♕b3 30 f6+ ♔xf6 31
♕f5+ ♔e7 32 ♔g2 is safe for White.

2b2) 28...♕c1+ 29 ♕e1 ♕h6 30 h3 ♖c3 31
♕e4 gives White defensive chances.

2b3) 28...♕b3 29 ♕e4 ♕h3+ 30 ♔e2 (30
♔e1? ♖f3 is very dangerous) 30...♕h5+ 31 f3
♕g5 32 f4 ♕g4+ 33 ♔f2 ♕xf4+ 34 ♕xf4 ♗xf4
35 ♔g2 ♔f6 and the ending is slightly unpleasant for White, since his bishop is bad and all his
pawns are weak. However, in view of the reduced material it is not clear how many winning chances Black has.

2c) 26...♖g8! looks like the most dangerous
line. After 27 ♕c2 (not 27 ♖g1?? ♕c4+, while 27
♕h5 ♕c4+ 28 ♕e2 ♕c3 29 ♖g1 ♕h3+ 30 ♗g2
♕h4 gives Black strong pressure) 27...♕xc2 28
♗xc2 ♖a2 29 ♗b3 ♖d2 30 ♖g1 ♖b8 Black retains considerable pressure in the ending.

After the text-move, Black has a forced win.

| 26 | ... | ♖xb1+ |
| 27 | ♕xb1 | ♕d2! (D) |

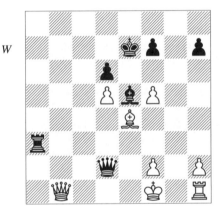

W

0-1

White has no real defence to the threat of
28...♖a1; for example, 28 ♕b7+ (28 ♔g2 ♕g5+)
28...♔f6 (threatening 29...♗d4) 29 ♕b6 ♕d1+
30 ♔g2 ♕g4+ 31 ♔f1 ♕xe4 32 ♕d8+ ♔xf5 33
♕c8+ ♔g6 34 ♖g1+ ♔h5 and Black wins.

In February 2000 I returned to Bunratty in Ireland, sharing first place with Mark Hebden on 5/6.
The summer was again fairly idle for me, but in September I took part in the Golombek Memorial
tournament held in Paignton, which was to be my last international tournament. Over the preceding
years I had become used to being the oldest player in the tournament, but I thought that perhaps this
tournament might include some players from my generation who had actually known Harry Golombek. However, I saw that once again I was the senior player and indeed many of the players were too
young to have ever met Golombek. The tournament was in fact very pleasant, with excellent playing
conditions. I played quite well and had a number of interesting games. The following was the best.

Tiger Hillarp Persson is an exceptionally dangerous attacking player, so a cautious attitude was
indicated for this game. Indeed, my rather timid opening play gave Black the chance to force a draw

on move 20, but he preferred to play on. However, the resulting rather quiet position evidently did not suit the Tiger, and White soon developed some awkward dark-squared pressure. My advantage increased until I had the position under almost complete control. Then I fell victim to one of the chess-player's worst enemies – impatience. Instead of quietly improving my position and making sure that Black could not develop any counterplay, I went for the kill straight away. The resulting sequence of moves still causes me embarrassment when I think about it today. Fortunately for me, Black was rather short of time and made a mistake just when the draw was within his grasp. White's attack was suddenly revived and Black's position crumbled.

Game 38
J. Nunn – T. Hillarp Persson
Paignton (Golombek Memorial) 2000
French Defence, Winawer (Nimzowitsch) Variation

| | 1 | e4 | e6 |

I felt somewhat nervous before this game as it was my first encounter with the Tiger and I was concerned about becoming one of the victims of his famous attacking style. However, the choice of opening somewhat relieved me – it didn't seem likely that I would be mated quickly on the white side of a French!

2	d4	d5
3	♘c3	♗b4
4	e5	c5
5	a3	♗xc3+
6	bxc3	♘e7
7	a4	♕a5
8	♗d2	♘bc6
9	♘f3	♗d7 *(D)*

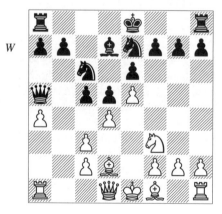

W

10   ♗b5!?

I have played this line fairly regularly for many years. Curiously, when I first adopted it, 10 ♗b5 was considered an unimportant sideline

compared to the standard 10 ♗e2. However, White's efforts to prove an advantage with 10 ♗e2 came to nothing, and so 10 ♗b5 has steadily increased in popularity. The result is that in MegaBase 2004 there are slightly more games with 10 ♗b5 than with 10 ♗e2 – the sideline has become the main line. I have to admit that objectively White cannot hope for much of an advantage with 10 ♗b5, but this reflects the fact that the Winawer French is one of Black's soundest openings from the theoretical point of view.

10   ...   f6

It is hard to say which line is Black's main continuation at this point, since in addition to the text-move, 10...♕c7, 10...a6 and 10...c4 have all been played quite often. All these moves are playable and theory doesn't give a clear preference for any of them. To my eye, the text-move, immediately challenging White's centre, looks the most logical, but this is just a subjective opinion.

11   ♕e2

11 0-0 and the rather harmless 11 exf6 have also been played frequently. However, the text-move, which allows White to maintain his central pawn on e5 for the moment, has always been my preference. To the best of my knowledge, it was first played in the game Nunn-Brenninkmeijer, Groningen 1988/9. In that game Black fell into the tactical trap that justifies the move (see the following note).

11   ...   ♕c7

This is Black's soundest move, stepping up the pressure against the e5-pawn. The trap is that after 11...fxe5? 12 ♘xe5 ♘xe5 White can afford to leave his b5-bishop *en prise* by 13 ♕xe5! because he can regain it with c4. After 13...♗xb5 14 c4 ♕b6 15 cxb5 (15 axb5 also favours White, but taking with the c-pawn is clearer) 15...0-0 16 dxc5 ♕xc5 17 ♕xe6+ Black has a miserable position and will soon be a pawn down. The extra pawn doesn't necessarily guarantee a win for White (and indeed in practice Black has scraped a couple of draws) but I don't think anyone would knowingly head for such a position as Black.

| | **12** | **0-0** | **a6** |

If Black wants to keep some tension in the position, this move is a good choice. However, I suspect that it is objectively inferior to the safe line 12...fxe5 13 ♗xc6 ♘xc6 14 ♘xe5 0-0 (14...♘xe5 15 ♗f4 0-0 16 ♗xe5 gave White some advantage in Chandler-Levitt, London (Lloyds Bank) 1994). Here White has tried both 15 ♘xc6 and 15 ♘xd7, but without demonstrating any advantage.

| | **13** | **♗xc6** | **♘xc6 (D)** |

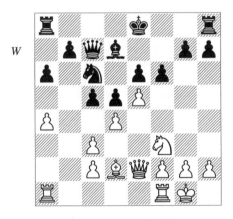

I had reached this position in an earlier game, Nunn-Kindermann, Vienna 1991. On that occasion I played 14 ♗c1 and won, and the question was whether to repeat the move in the current game. This type of decision is always awkward: should one allow the opponent to show off his 'improvement', or duck the challenge? In this case there didn't seem too much of a risk, as the quiet nature of the position meant that any improvement was likely to be equalizing rather than giving Black the advantage, so the downside was limited.

| | **14** | **♗c1?! (D)** |

Repeating the earlier game, but now I am not at all sure that this move is best. Other possibilities:

1) 14 ♗f4?! is wrong; after 14...cxd4 15 cxd4 ♘a5 Black has pressure down the c-file for which White has no real compensation. If 16 ♗g3 then simply 16...f5 and the bishop is out of play.

2) 14 ♖fe1 0-0-0 15 dxc5 fxe5 16 ♘xe5 ♕xe5 17 ♕xe5 ♘xe5 18 ♖xe5 gave White an edge but no genuine winning chances in Čabrilo-Draško, Budva 1996.

3) 14 exf6 gxf6 15 c4! looks like the most promising line for White:

3a) 15...0-0 16 cxd5 exd5 17 dxc5 gives White an edge.

3b) 15...dxc4 gives White an advantage after either 16 d5 ♘e7 17 dxe6 ♗c6 18 ♗c3 or the simple 16 dxc5.

3c) 15...♕d6 16 dxc5 ♕xc5 17 cxd5 ♕xd5 18 ♖ab1 is awkward as there is no really convenient way to defend the b7-pawn. If 18...0-0-0, then 19 c4 ♕h5 20 ♗f4 followed by ♕b2 is unpleasant.

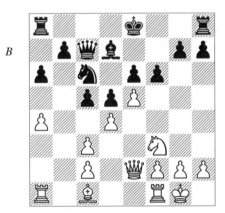

| | **14** | **...** | **cxd4** |

This can't be a bad move because it more or less forces White to exchange on f6. The alternatives are:

1) 14...fxe5 15 ♘xe5 0-0 (15...♘xe5 16 ♗f4 0-0 17 ♗xe5 ♕c8 18 ♖fd1 c4 19 ♕g4 ♖f7 20 ♖e1 ♕f8 21 a5 ♖f5 22 ♖e3 gives White a clear advantage thanks to his dominating bishop, Hellsten-Luodonpaa, Helsinki 1993) 16 ♘xd7 ♕xd7 17 ♗a3 and White is slightly better. Compared to the note to Black's 12th move, here the moves ♗c1 and ...a6 have been added,

which certainly favours White as his bishop can immediately move to the active square a3.

2) 14...0-0 is a good alternative; for example, 15 exf6 (15 ♗a3? fxe5 16 ♗xc5 e4! 17 ♘e5 ♘xe5 18 ♗xf8 ♖xf8 19 dxe5 ♕xc3 gives Black excellent compensation for the exchange, while 15 ♖e1? fxe5 16 ♘xe5 ♘xe5 17 ♕xe5 ♕xe5 18 ♖xe5 cxd4 19 cxd4 ♖fc8 will cost White a pawn) 15...♖xf6 16 ♗g5 ♖f7 17 ♗h4 cxd4 18 ♗g3 (18 cxd4 e5! favours Black since 19 dxe5? ♗g4 is very unpleasant for White) 18...♕b6 19 ♖fb1 ♕a7 and although White has some play for the pawn, he cannot have the advantage.

15   exf6

White has little choice, since 15 cxd4?! fxe5 16 ♘xe5 0-0 gives Black a comfortable position straight away.

15   ...   gxf6 (D)

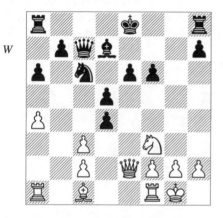

16   ♘xd4

Perhaps 16 cxd4 is better, when White has chances of an advantage. The threat is to open the position up with c4, but if Black plays 16...♘a5 then 17 ♗h6 (17 ♗a3 is poor here since the bishop cannot be maintained on the a3-f8 diagonal after 17...♘c4) 17...♖g8 18 ♘h4 0-0-0 19 ♕f3 is rather awkward for Black.

16   ...   ♕e5

Best, since 16...0-0-0 17 ♘xe6 ♖he8 18 ♘xc7 ♖xe2 19 ♘xd5 is good for White. 16...♘xd4 is playable, although after 17 cxd4 (17 ♕h5+ ♔d8 18 cxd4 is a double-edged idea which gives White enough play for the pawn after 18...♕xc2 19 ♗f4) 17...0-0 18 ♗h6 ♖f7 19 ♖a3 White has chances of an advantage.

17   ♕d2 (D)

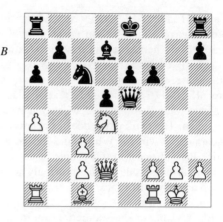

The only reasonable move. Black has the better pawn-structure, so White must place his faith in the attacking chances provided by the opposite-coloured bishops and Black's (temporarily) centralized king. It follows that White must keep queens on.

17   ...   ♖g8!?

This was suggested in my *Informator* notes to the earlier Nunn-Kindermann game and it was intriguing to see it suddenly appear on the board after an interval of nine years. It is worth giving the earlier game in full because it closely echoes the themes of the current game: 17...♘xd4 18 cxd4 ♕f5 19 ♕b4 ♖g8 (threatening to draw by sacrificing on g2) 20 ♖a3 (20 ♖e1!? would transpose into Nunn-Hillarp Persson) 20...♗c6 21 ♖g3 (we shall also see this idea in the Hillarp Persson game; White would like Black to exchange on g3, as this would provide support for the bishop on f4) 21...0-0-0?! (21...♔f7! 22 ♗a3 ♖ae8 23 c3 is better, with a roughly equal position) 22 ♕e7! (this carries the nasty threat of 23 ♗f4! ♕xf4 24 ♖xg8 ♖xg8 25 ♕xe6+) 22...e5 (as we shall see in the main game, playing ...e5 doesn't necessarily solve Black's problems since if he cannot maintain the pawn on e5, then pushing the e-pawn will only have weakened his pawn-structure; 22...♖de8 23 ♖xg8 ♖xg8 24 ♗f4 and 22...♖ge8 23 ♕c5 ♔b8 24 ♗a3 are clearly better for White, but perhaps Black could have tried 22...♔b8) 23 a5 ♗b5 (not 23...exd4 24 ♗f4!) 24 ♖e1 ♖xg3?! (relieving White of any worries along the g-file and giving him the f4-square should Black eventually be forced to move the e5-pawn) 25 hxg3 ♖e8 26 ♕c5+ ♗c6 27 ♗a3 (threatening to open things up by 28 c4) 27...♕d7 28 ♗b2 exd4

(28...♕c7 might be better, but 29 ♖e3 followed, if necessary, by ♕c3-e1, will force Black to move his e5-pawn; 28...e4 29 ♗c1 leads to the same type of problems as in Nunn-Hillarp Persson) 29 ♖xe8+ ♕xe8 30 ♗xd4 *(D)*.

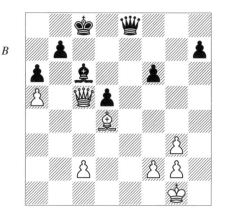

This is the type of position White is aiming for: his king is safe, while Black's is exposed; Black's pawn-majority is crippled while White's is not, and finally Black's kingside pawns are very weak. In summary, despite the opposite-coloured bishops, this position can be considered as almost lost for Black. The game ended: 30...f5 31 c3 (blocking the e1-a5 diagonal so that White can play ♕d6 without losing the a5-pawn to a check on e1) 31...♔d7 (trying to prevent ♕d6) 32 ♗e3 (White responds by transferring the bishop to f4) 32...♕e4 33 f3 ♕e5 (33...♕c4 34 ♕f8 ♕xc3 35 ♕xf5+ ♔d6 36 ♕f4+ ♔e6 37 ♗d4 ♕xa5 38 ♕h6+ ♔d7 39 ♕xh7+ ♔c8 40 g4 is very good for White) 34 ♗f4 ♕e1+ 35 ♔h2 ♕e7 (still trying to prevent White's queen from penetrating, but there are too many ways in) 36 ♕d4 ♔e8 37 ♕h8+ ♔d7 38 ♕g8 (threatening 39 ♗g5) 38...h5 39 ♗g5 ♕e8 40 ♕h7+ ♔e6 41 ♕h6+ ♔d7 42 ♕f6 (the first pawn falls) 42...♔c8 43 ♗f4 (playing for mate is even stronger than taking the f5-pawn) 43...♗d7 44 ♕d6 ♔d8 45 ♕b6+ ♔e7 46 ♕xb7 ♕c8 47 ♕xd5 ♕c6 48 ♗g5+ ♔f8 49 ♕e5 1-0 Nunn-Kindermann, Vienna 1991.

Now we return to 17...♖g8!? *(D)*:

18   ♖e1

Carelessly given a question mark in my 1991 notes on account of 18...♘xd4. Instead I recommended 18 f4, a fact which fortunately I had forgotten, since Black is certainly better after

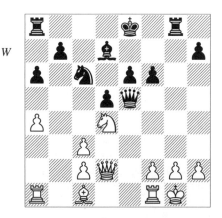

this move: 18...♕e4 (even 18...♕h5 19 f5 e5 20 ♘e6 ♗xe6 21 fxe6 0-0-0 22 ♖xf6 ♖g6 23 ♖xg6 ♕xg6 is not very pleasant for White) 19 f5 e5! (19...♘xd4 20 cxd4 ♖c8 21 ♖a2 is OK for White) 20 ♗a3 (20 ♘e6 ♗xe6 21 fxe6 ♖g6 is also good for Black) 20...♘a5! and now White is in serious trouble; for example, 21 ♖ae1 ♘c4 22 ♕f2 ♕g4 23 ♗c1 0-0-0 with a massive advantage for Black, or 21 ♘e6 ♘c4 22 ♕f2 ♗xe6 23 fxe6 ♕g4 and again White is in difficulties.

18   ...   ♘xd4

After 18...♕h5 19 ♘xe6 ♖xg2+ 20 ♔xg2 ♕g4+ 21 ♔f1 ♕h3+ 22 ♔e2 ♗xe6 23 ♕f4 Black probably doesn't have enough compensation for the exchange.

19   cxd4

For some reason this simple move wasn't mentioned in my 1991 notes. Not, of course, 19 ♖xe5? ♘f3+ and Black wins.

19   ...   ♕f5 *(D)*

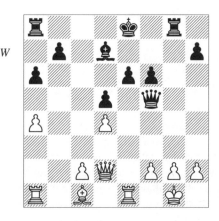

Now we have the same type of structure as in Nunn-Kindermann.

20 ♕b4!?

If White is going to make anything of the position, he has to exploit the weak dark squares, so this is a natural move.

20 ... 0-0-0

If Black is satisfied with a draw, then 20...♖c8 is a good move. The only reasonable reply is 21 ♗a3 but then 21...♖xg2+ 22 ♔xg2 ♕g4+ 23 ♔f1 ♕h3+ forces a draw, since 24 ♔e2?? loses to 24...♖xc2+. However, Black is perfectly justified in avoiding this, since he is by no means worse in this position.

21 ♖a3

Not so much an attacking move as a defensive one. White transfers the rook to g3 to block the dangerous g-file.

21 ... ♗c6

Black hopes that one day he will be able to break open the diagonal from c6 to g2 with a timely ...e5, meeting dxe5 by ...d4. The defect of this plan is that it is almost impossible to force White to take on e5.

22 ♖g3 (D)

Motivated in part by the Tiger's fearsome tactical reputation, White continues his safety-first strategy. 22 ♖ae3?! e5! 23 ♗b2 ♕xc2 leads to unnecessary complications.

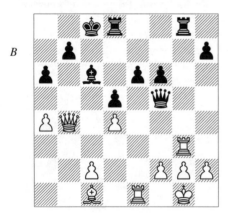

22 ... e5?!

Up to here, Black has played very well and has achieved equality, but now he starts to go astray. It is of course tempting to try to break open the c6-g2 diagonal with this move, but we have already seen in Nunn-Kindermann what can go wrong with this plan. The pawn on e5 can easily come under pressure, and if Black is forced to move it (by ...e4 or ...exd4) then his

dark squares becomes weaker and his kingside pawns subject to attack. The key feature of the position is Black's play along the g-file, and therefore Black should have tried to dislodge White's defensive rook by 22...h5 (accepting the pawn by 22...♕xc2 is very risky since 23 ♗f4 e5 24 ♖c3 ♕g6 25 ♗g3 gives White a dangerous attack) and now:

1) 23 h4 is dubious here because Black can simply grab a pawn by 23...♖xg3 24 fxg3 ♕xc2; for example, 25 ♗f4 e5 26 dxe5 d4 and Black is better.

2) 23 ♖xg8 ♖xg8 24 ♕e7 e5! and without the defensive rook on g3, Black's play along the half-open file enables him to hold the balance.

3) 23 ♕b6 h4 24 ♖c3 ♔d7 25 ♖xc6 bxc6 26 ♕b7+ ♔e8 27 ♗a3 ♖d7 28 ♕xc6 e5 and again Black can defend. One line is 29 dxe5 fxe5 30 c4 e4 31 cxd5 ♖xg2+ with perpetual check.

23 ♗b2 (D)

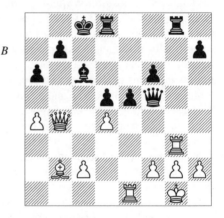

At once stepping up the pressure against the e5-pawn in the hope of forcing it to move.

23 ... e4?!

Black caves in rather easily and cuts out the possibility of ...♕xc2, while at the same time giving up any hope of opening the c6-g2 diagonal. 23...♖de8 would have restricted White to a slight advantage; after 24 ♕c5 (24 ♕d6 ♖xg3 25 hxg3 ♕xc2 26 ♖c1 ♕xb2 27 ♖xc6+ bxc6 28 ♕xc6+ ♔d8 29 ♕d6+ is a draw) 24...h5 25 h4 ♖xg3 26 fxg3 ♕g4 27 ♔h2 the position is unclear, but I would prefer to be White. One line is 27...♖g8 28 ♕a3 e4 29 ♗c1 ♔b8 30 ♗f4+ ♔a8 31 a5 and White has more active possibilities than Black.

24 ♗c1!

White at once switches the bishop back to c1, which virtually forces Black to keep a permanent watch on the f4-square to prevent White's bishop from arriving there.

24   ...   h5

The right idea, but a little too late as now White can safely play h4.

25   h4   ♖g4 (D)

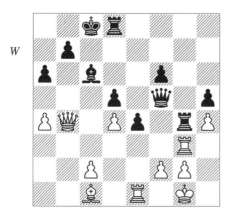

Black avoids Kindermann's mistake of exchanging on g3, but the position is still unpleasant for him. If Black leaves his rook on g8, then White can play a5 followed by ♕e7, with the tactical threat of ♗f4 as in the earlier game.

26   ♖xg4!

The centre is so blocked that there is little chance of Black activating his light-squared bishop, hence White can afford the drastic step of playing g3 in order to obtain f4 for the bishop. White's threats against the black king will not give Black a chance to exploit the weakened light squares on the kingside.

26   ...   ♕xg4

26...hxg4 27 g3 is even worse for Black, as then White has a protected passed pawn on the kingside.

27   ♕e7

Various motifs from the Kindermann game recur in the current encounter. The penetration by White's queen puts Black's position under stress.

27   ...   ♕f5

Simply defending the f6-pawn. The alternative is 27...♕xh4 (27...♗xa4 28 ♕xf6, with ♗f4 or ♗g5 to come, is clearly good for White) 28 g3 ♕h3 29 ♗f4 ♕d7 30 ♕xf6 and now:

1) 30...b6 31 a5 b5 32 ♕e5 ♔b7 33 ♕xh5 and White wins a pawn.

2) 30...♗xa4 31 c4! dxc4 32 ♕e5 ♕c6 33 ♖xe4 gives White a winning attack.

3) 30...♖e8 31 a5 and White has continuing pressure as Black's king is permanently trapped in an awkward position.

28   g3

Now White's bishop can at last reach the key square.

28   ...   ♖d7?!

This proves to be a waste of time, but Black is under pressure whatever he plays: 28...♗xa4 29 ♗f4 ♕d7 30 ♕xf6 ♖e8 31 ♖e3 is very bad for Black, and even 28...♖e8 29 ♕d6 ♕d7 30 ♕xf6 ♗xa4 31 ♗f4, which gives Black an extra tempo, is good for White since Black will certainly lose the h5-pawn in the next few moves. It is very hard to play accurately in positions such as this, where there is only the prospect of a long and arduous defence with no hint of active counterplay.

29   ♕c5 (D)

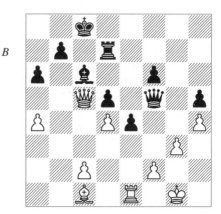

Threatening ♗f4 followed by ♕a7, so Black must waste more time giving his king an escape-route. Black decides simply to return with his rook, in order to allow his king to flee to d7 if necessary.

29   ...   ♖d8

29...♔b8? loses at once: 30 ♕f8+ ♔a7 31 ♗f4.

30   ♗f4

Although the position is very bad for Black, it is not easy for White to break through.

30   ...   ♕e6

31   f3

White seizes the opportunity to make further progress. The threat is simply 32 fxe4 dxe4 33 c4, followed by d5, so Black is forced to push his f-pawn. This was the only black pawn left defending the dark squares, and its advance gives White even more squares to play with.

31 ... f5 (D)

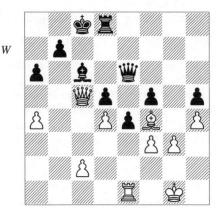

32 fxe4?

Up to this point White has played simply and forcefully and has achieved a dominating position. Over the next few moves, however, he loses the thread and allows Black unnecessary defensive chances. At the time, it seemed to me that the win was simple: exchange pawns on e4 to open the f-file, play ♗e5 and then penetrate along the f-file with the rook. However, it turns out to be not so simple to put this plan into action. It would have been better to proceed more slowly, since White could easily have improved his position with moves such as a5 and ♔h2 before undertaking any irrevocable action. In this case Black would have had scarcely any hope of saving the game. In my book *Secrets of Practical Chess*, I wrote "You may not be able to see a concrete reason why a particular 'tidying-up' move might be useful, but you lose nothing by playing it." Here my failure to take my own advice might have cost me half a point. Of course, when you are actually sitting at the board, it is quite easy to have a rush of blood to the head and to start thinking in terms of 'finishing off' the game, when in reality a more considered approach would offer better chances.

32 ... fxe4

Not 32...dxe4?, losing at once to 33 c4. The exchange on e4 has had the unfortunate effect

that if White plays, for example, ♖e3-c3, then Black can aim for perpetual check by ...♕g4. This restricts White's attacking possibilities.

33 ♗e5

Clearing the f-file ready for the invasion of White's rook, but an open file can be occupied by either player!

33 ... ♖d7

I had overlooked this move and I suddenly realized that after ...♖f7 Black and not White would be the one to benefit from the opening of the f-file. 33...♔d7 34 ♖f1 ♖g8 was a second reasonable line for Black, when again things would not be easy for White; for example, 35 ♔h2 ♕e7 aiming for ...♖f8.

34 ♕f8+?

As so often happens, one error is followed by a second. I was determined to prevent Black from occupying the f-file with his rook, and to achieve this aim I was willing to move my queen from its attacking position on c5 to the relative obscurity of the kingside. This wasn't a good idea, especially as after 34 ♕a7 ♖f7 35 ♕b8+ ♔d7 36 ♗f4 White would still have had a clear advantage. However, in this line White has been forced to abandon any hope of penetrating with his rook along the f-file.

34 ... ♖d8
35 ♕g7 ♕d7

35...♗d7 is also quite good; after 36 ♖e3 ♕c6 or 36 ♖f1 ♕c6 Black has reasonable counterplay.

36 ♕g6 (D)

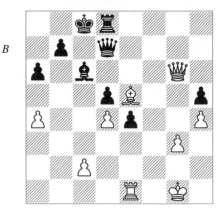

36 ... ♕e8?!

Black was short of time and this inaccuracy allows White to achieve his plan of occupying the f-file with his rook after all. Black, it is true, wins the a4-pawn, but White's threats easily compensate for the lost pawn. The correct continuation was 36...罩f8! 37 豐xh5 (37 a5 豐f5 forces the queens off) 37...奧xa4 and although White still has an edge due to his more active bishop, his advantage is just a pale shadow of its former glory.

37   豐h6!

At last a good move by White.

37   ...   奧xa4

Black cannot keep offering the exchange of queens by 37...豐f8 because of 38 豐e6+ 罩d7 39 罩b1 (threatening 40 豐xc6+) 39...奧xa4 40 豐xa6! and wins. Therefore Black has nothing better than to grab the a-pawn.

38   罩f1 (D)

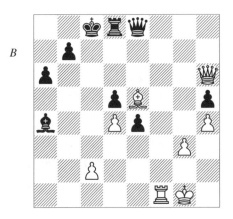

White has now achieved the position he was aiming for, albeit at the cost of his a-pawn (something he didn't intend!). In time-trouble, it is very hard to defend against White's threats.

38   ...   奧c6?

Black at once makes a mistake which gives White a decisive attack. The only defensive chance was 38...奧b5 39 罩f6 and now:

1) 39...豐d7 40 豐xh5 e3 41 罩f7 e2 42 奧f2 豐h3 43 豐f5+ 豐xf5+ 44 罩xf5 a5 45 h5 a4 46 罩f3 and White's two connected passed pawns should suffice for victory.

2) 39...奧e2 40 c4! 奧xc4 (40...dxc4 41 罩xa6 wins for White) 41 豐h7 罩d7 42 豐f5 and White wins, since the preliminary c4 has deprived Black of the defence ...奧g4.

3) 39...豐e7! is the key move. Black intends to penetrate via b4 or a3 and give perpetual check. After this he has excellent drawing

chances; for example, 40 奧d6 豐e8 41 奧f4 豐e7 or 40 豐f4 豐a3 41 奧b8 豐a1+ 42 含h2 豐c3 43 奧a7 豐xc2+ 44 含g1 豐b1+ with perpetual check.

39   罩f6 (D)

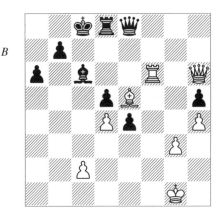

Not only is the bishop less actively placed on c6 than on b5, but it also prevents Black from activating his queen since it must guard c6 to stop 罩xc6+ by White.

39   ...   a5

Giving up hope, but by now there was no real defence:

1) 39...豐d7 40 豐xh5 (threatening 41 罩f7) 40...罩e8 (40...罩g8 41 奧f4 threatens 42 豐e5 and White wins after 41...罩e8 42 罩f7 豐d8 43 豐f5+) 41 罩f7 豐d8 offers White a choice of wins:

1a) 42 豐h6 a5 43 h5 a4 44 豐g7 奧d7 45 h6 e3 46 h7 a3 47 罩xd7 豐xd7 48 h8豐 罩xh8 49 豐xh8+ 豐d8 50 豐h3+ 豐d7 51 豐f1 and White wins easily; for example, 51...a2 52 豐f8+ 豐d8 53 豐c5+ 含d7 54 豐xd5+ and the pawns fall.

1b) 42 罩c7+ 豐xc7 43 奧xc7 含xc7 44 豐f7+ 含b6 45 含f2 e3+ 46 含e1 a5 47 豐g6 a4 48 豐d6 (stopping the pawns) 48...罩a8 49 豐a3 罩g8 50 豐c5+ 含c7 51 c4! 罩d8 52 h5 dxc4 53 h6 and Black cannot defend.

2) 39...e3 40 豐xe3 豐e7 41 豐c3 罩f8 42 罩xc6+! bxc6 43 豐xc6+ 含d8 44 豐a8+ 含d7 45 豐xd5+ 含e8 46 c4 should win for White. One line is 46...豐a3 47 含g2 豐a2+ 48 含h3 罩f2 49 豐c6+ 含e7 50 奧d6+ 含f7 51 豐d5+ 含f6 52 豐e5+ and White wins the h5-pawn with check.

40   豐f4

40 豐h7 also wins after 40...奧d7 (or 40...罩d7 41 豐f5) 41 c4! dxc4 42 罩b6 a4 43 罩b5! but,

even if I had seen this line, I would have preferred the simpler text-move.

40   ...   a4

Or 40...e3 41 ♖f7 e2 42 ♔f2 ♗d7 43 ♕f3 (threatening 44 ♕c3+) 43...♕e6 44 ♖f6 ♕e8 45 ♕c3+ ♗c6 46 ♕c5 followed by ♕b6 with a mating attack.

41   ♖f7

Threatening simply 42 ♖c7+.

41   ...   ♗d7 (D)

41...a3 42 ♖c7+ ♔b8 43 ♖xc6+ ♔a8 44 ♖c3 ♕a4 45 ♕c1 a2 46 ♖a3 is also winning for White.

After the text-move White has a forced mate in three.

42   ♗b8!   1-0

Black cannot prevent mate on c7. I think problemists call this type of move a Bristol

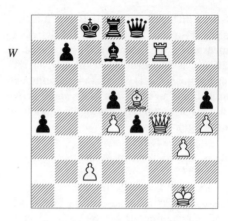

clearance. It occurs occasionally in over-the-board play, but usually on the long diagonal (for example, ...♗b7-h1 threatening ...♕a8-g2#).

The final result was a tie for first place with Klaus Bischoff on 5½/9. A few weeks after this game, a false rumour started circulating that I had died in a car crash. Such rumours can spread amazingly quickly via e-mail and online chess forums, and soon some concerned people started contacting me. Mark Crowther, the editor of TWIC, was subtle about it: he sent an e-mail asking if my e-mail address was still valid. When I replied that it was, he explained the real purpose behind his enquiry. The captain of the Lübeck Bundesliga team, with typical German directness, simply sent an e-mail asking if I was still alive. A couple of years later a similar false rumour was started about Peter Leko, but this time it was adorned with highly implausible details, for example that a pocket chess set had been found by his body with a position from one of his games on it. Despite its farfetched nature, this story took in a few people before being debunked. Such stories can be very upsetting for relatives and unfortunately the chess world appears to contain at least one warped person who enjoys causing distress. A few days later I had an opportunity to prove that I was still playing chess.

Games are very rarely decided by a single mistake, but that is the case with this game. Textbooks will tell you that a flank attack is best answered by a counter-action in the centre, and Sicilian players dream about smashing open the centre with ...d5 in response to a kingside pawn-storm by White. But it doesn't always work. In this game Black lashes out with ...d5, but his pieces aren't active enough to back it up, with the result that White can simply ignore Black's central play and press ahead with his own attack. Far from creating counterplay, ...d5 turns out to waste an important tempo; White's attack is soon so strong that he can afford to ignore material and just play for mate.

Game 39

J. Nunn – M. Borriss

Bundesliga 2000/1

Sicilian Defence, Keres Attack

1	e4	c5
2	♘f3	d6
3	d4	cxd4
4	♘xd4	♘f6

5	♘c3	e6
6	g4	

The Keres Attack has been a favourite of mine since my youth. Although its theoretical status is still uncertain, it is generally regarded as a dangerous system. Therefore, many players who like to reach Scheveningen-type positions as Black employ move-orders designed to avoid the Keres Attack. These include 2...e6 3 d4 cxd4 4 ♘xd4 ♘c6 5 ♘c3 d6 and the Najdorf (with 6 ♗e2 e6). Of course, each of these options requires that Black be able to cope with alternative white systems, but a lot of players seem to think that avoiding the Keres Attack makes it all worthwhile.

6 ... ♘c6

Black has several alternative lines against the Keres Attack, including 6...h6, 6...♗e7, 6...a6 and even 6...e5. Of these, 6...h6 has perhaps the best theoretical reputation, but the text-move is also not bad.

7 g5 ♘d7
8 h4

This is White's most flexible move-order. He will have to play h4 sooner or later and he does so straight away so as to keep as many options open as possible.

8 ... ♗e7
9 ♗e3 0-0 (D)

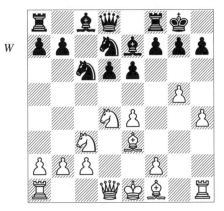

10 ♕h5

The big decision for White in this line is where to develop his queen. In addition to 10 ♕h5, the moves 10 ♕d2 and 10 ♕e2 are also very popular. Theory doesn't give a clear preference here, so the choice is largely a matter of taste. In an earlier game (see Nunn-Thorsteins from *John Nunn's Best Games*) I played 10 ♗c4, while in a later game I preferred 10 ♕d2. Mixing up lines like this can make it harder for an opponent to prepare for you, but in this case

my choice depended more on my mood on the day than a desire to confuse my opponents.

10 ... d5?

In *Beating the Sicilian 3* (Batsford, 1995) the section dealing with this line was written by Joe Gallagher and his comment on 10...d5 was "A central strike is the recommended reaction to a wing attack, but here it just emphasizes how active the white pieces are in comparison with their counterparts." This is a fair comment; indeed, the situation is even worse for Black than Gallagher suggests and after this mistake there is no satisfactory continuation for Black. The main line for Black is 10...a6 11 0-0-0 ♘xd4 (11...♖e8 is less common, but is certainly a playable move) 12 ♗xd4 b5 and now Joe recommended 13 e5!? in *BtS3*.

11 0-0-0 (D)

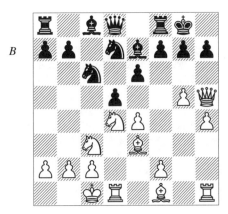

The thrust ...d5 did not create any genuine threats, so White simply continues with his development.

11 ... ♘b6

On b6 the knight doesn't exert any pressure against White's centre, giving him a free hand to proceed with his kingside attack. However, the alternatives are also very bad:

1) 11...dxe4 12 ♘xe4 ♕a5 13 ♘xc6 bxc6 14 ♗d4! gave White a very dangerous attack in Sax-Ehlvest, Reggio Emilia 1988/9. The game concluded 14...e5 15 ♗c3 ♕xa2 16 ♖xd7! ♗xd7 17 ♘f6+! ♗xf6 18 gxf6 ♕a1+ (18...♖fd8 19 ♗d3! h6 20 b4 gives White a decisive attack, while after 18...♕e6 19 ♗h3 ♕xf6 20 ♗xd7 White has a nearly decisive advantage) 19 ♔d2 ♕a4 20 b4! ♖fd8 21 ♗d3 gxf6 22 ♖a1 ♕b5 23 ♕xh7+ ♔f8 24 ♕h6+! ♔e7 25 ♗xb5 cxb5 26

♕e3 1-0. This game is a good example of how inaccurate play can easily lead to White's attack just rolling over Black.

2) 11...♘xd4 12 ♖xd4 (12 ♗xd4?? loses material after 12...e5 13 ♗e3 d4) 12...♗c5 is generally given as the best line, following Sax's annotations to his game against Ehlvest. However, White has an almost forced win: 13 exd5! (White overlooked this move in the two games in my database which reached this point) 13...♗xd4 14 ♗xd4 e5 (there is nothing better) 15 ♗d3 g6 (15...f5 16 gxf6 ♘xf6 17 ♕xe5, followed by ♖g1, gives White two pawns and a strong attack for the exchange) 16 ♕h6 exd4 17 h5 ♕e7 18 d6! and White wins.

12   f4

This is a useful move, taking away the e5-square from Black's c6-knight and increasing the danger posed by White's kingside pawn-mass. Black now must worry about how to deal with the threat of 13 exd5 (the simple 13 e5 is also a threat) 13...♘xd5 14 ♘xd5 exd5 16 ♗d3 g6 17 ♕f3, followed by h5, with a massive attack for White. The immediate 12 ♗d3 is weaker as Black may reply 12...♘e5.

12   ...   ♗b4

12...♗c5 is no better as after 13 ♔b1 Black must counter the threat of 14 ♘xc6.

13   ♗d3

The attack is now so strong that White can afford to ignore the doubling of his c-pawns.

13   ...   ♗xc3
14   bxc3 (D)

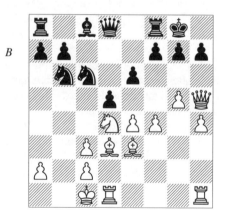

The main threat is 15 exd5 g6 16 ♕h6, followed by h5, with a crushing attack.

14   ...   e5

Now White wins by force, although there is no real defence:

1) 14...♕e7 15 e5 g6 16 ♕h6 ♘a5 (after 16...♕a3+ 17 ♔d2 ♘a4 18 h5 ♕xc3+ 19 ♔e2 the attack crashes through) 17 h5 ♘ac4 18 ♖de1 ♕a3+ (18...♘a4 19 ♘b5 is also winning for White) 19 ♔d1 ♘a4 20 ♘b5 wins for White.

2) 14...♘e7 15 exd5 g6 (15...♘g6 16 dxe6 ♕e7 17 f5 ♕a3+ 18 ♔d2 ♘d5 19 ♘b5 and White wins) 16 ♕h6 ♘exd5 17 h5 ♕e7 18 hxg6 fxg6 19 ♘b5! (not 19 ♗xg6?? ♕a3+, forcing mate) and now Black cannot meet the various threats such as 20 ♗xg6 and 20 ♗c5.

15   exd5!

15 ♘xc6 bxc6 16 exd5 g6 17 ♕h6 is also good, but there cannot be anything better than a forced mate!

15   ...   g6
16   ♕h6 (D)

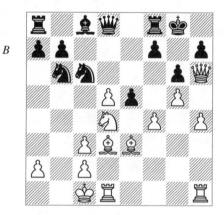

Threatening 17 h5.

16   ...   ♘xd4

Or 16...exd4 (16...♘xd5 17 h5 ♕e7 18 hxg6 fxg6 19 ♗c4 is also decisive) 17 h5 ♕e7 18 d6! ♕d7 (18...♕xe3+ 19 ♔b1 ♕xd3 20 ♖xd3 ♗f5 21 hxg6 ♗xg6 22 ♖g3 and White wins as Black cannot meet the threat of 23 f5 ♗xf5 24 g6) 19 f5 gxf5 20 g6 fxg6 21 hxg6 ♕g7 22 gxh7+ ♔h8 23 ♖dg1 ♕xh6 24 ♗xh6 ♖f7 25 ♖g8+! ♔xh7 26 ♖gg1 followed by mate.

17   h5

Mate is not far off so White can afford to ignore the knight.

17   ...   ♘f5

The only move, but now there is a nice finish.

18   ♗xf5   ♗xf5

18...gxf5 19 g6 fxg6 20 hxg6 ♕e7 21 ♗c5 and White mates.

19	hxg6	♗xg6 (D)
20	f5!	

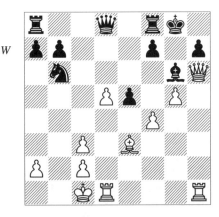

W

This is the point behind White's combination. By giving away two pawns, he opens the g-file in order to pin Black's bishop.

20	...	♗xf5
21	g6	♗xg6
22	♖dg1	1-0

It's mate in a few more moves; for example, 22...♖e8 23 ♖xg6+ fxg6 24 ♕xh7+ ♔f8 25 ♗h6#. It's rare for a single opening mistake to be punished so severely.

The 2000/1 league season was a great success for me. I scored 10/13 in the Bundesliga and 5½/7 in the 4NCL. It isn't often that you win a piece against a grandmaster in 11 moves, but that is what happened in one Bundesliga game.

Game 40

J. Nunn – M. Stangl

Bundesliga 2000/1

Sicilian Defence, Najdorf Variation

1 e4 c5 2 ♘f3 d6 3 d4 cxd4 4 ♘xd4 ♘f6 5 ♘c3 a6 6 ♗g5 e6 7 f4 ♘c6

This double-edged line was popular in the late 1990s but is now less frequently played.

8 e5 h6 9 ♗h4 g5 10 ♗g3!? *(D)*

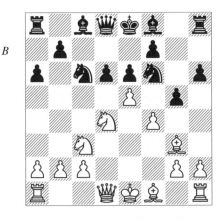

B

I had noticed that Stangl sometimes played the 7...♘c6 line and so had prepared this unusual move especially for him. Black's best continuation is 10...♘d5 and I had spent a long time analysing some very complicated lines

which might arise. While I doubted that White was objectively better, Black would certainly have a tough time finding his way through the complications over the board, so I was happy to try it. I was surprised when after some thought Stangl replied with a move losing a piece.

10 ... gxf4??

Judging by the frequency with which players make this blunder against me in Internet blitz games, it must be a very plausible mistake.

11 ♘xc6

The key point is that 11...bxc6 12 ♗h4! wins the pinned knight, since 12...dxe5 13 ♕xd8+ ♔xd8 14 ♗xf6+ wins a rook and a piece. In my book *Secrets of Practical Chess*, I mentioned how easy it is to overlook *switchback* moves and the manoeuvre ♗h4-g3-h4 is a good example of this.

11	...	♕b6
12	♗f2	♕xc6

Stangl is not the only player to have fallen into this trap. In a later game Grabarczyk-Tazbir, Stare Mesto 2003, Black lost even more quickly after 12...♕xb2 13 ♗d4 ♕a3 14 exd6 bxc6 15 ♗xf6 ♖g8 16 ♕d4 ♗d7 17 ♖d1 1-0.

13   exf6

Black is simply a piece down and could well have resigned here, but he plays on to the bitter end. The rest presents White with no difficulties.

13...♖g8 14 ♗e2 ♖g6 15 ♗f3 d5 16 ♕d4 ♗d6 17 0-0-0 ♗d7 18 ♘xd5 exd5 19 ♗xd5 ♕a4 20 ♖he1+ ♔f8 21 ♗b3 ♕xd4 22 ♖xd4 ♗c5 23 ♖xd7 ♗xf2 24 ♖xf7+ ♔g8 25 ♖g7+ ♔h8 26 ♖xg6 1-0

The 2000/1 season was a success not only for me personally, but also for the teams I was playing for. My English team, Beeson Gregory (this was really the same team as Invicta Knights, which I mentioned earlier, but it had undergone a name change to reflect a new sponsorship arrangement), won the 4NCL and Lübeck won the Bundesliga.

In 2001 I was totally inactive during the summer and only started playing again in September. Unfortunately, in early November I fell ill with bronchitis, which put me totally out of action for two months. During this period I was shocked to hear of the death of Tony Miles, who became the first British grandmaster in 1976. Tony was just two days older than me and so we often met in junior tournaments, starting in 1967 at the British Under-14 Championship. Our encounters continued at the adult level and we took part in many tournaments together, the last occasion being at Bunratty in early 2000.

Tony made a tremendous contribution to British chess. In the mid-1960s, the top British players were far below the strength of the East European grandmasters. Only Jonathan Penrose could make it a real contest but, despite some isolated successes in individual games, he never really broke through to the grandmaster level. The next generation, led by Keene and Hartston, were more successful, but expectations were still low. It was considered a success to draw against a Soviet grandmaster, and the quicker the better. Tony Miles was the first British player to take the battle to the Soviet grandmasters and his attitude infected the next generation of players. Tony's tournament record was exceptional, and only the very top players, such as Karpov and Kasparov, were able to exploit his uncompromising style and (usually) punish his impetuousness.

Tony also brought about a sea-change in British chess life. His view was that chess was a profession and, like any professional, he expected to be paid for his efforts. Up to the mid-1970s it was assumed that players would be happy to have the honour of playing for the English team in events such as Olympiads, and such participation was invariably on an expenses-only basis. Tony, however, insisted on remuneration and the crunch came when he refused to play for England in the 1977 European Team Championship Finals in Moscow. There was outrage in the British chess press and Tony was accused of disloyalty. However, he stuck to his principles and it is no coincidence that at the next team event, the 1978 Olympiad in Buenos Aires, appearance fees were paid to the players for the very first time. Small to begin with, these appearance fees gradually increased and in time put the team on a sound professional basis, thus setting the stage for the three Olympiad silver medals in the period 1984-8. For many years the English team was sponsored by bankers Duncan Lawrie, but since this arrangement finished, the sponsorship of the English team has become far more erratic and for some events it has been back to the bad old days of amateur participation and substandard teams.

On a personal level Tony was a difficult person to get on with. His main weakness was his almost total inability to see the viewpoint of another person. Despite his apparent self-confidence, he was actually quite vulnerable and did not take reverses well. Later in life he fell victim to mental illness. After Tony's death, Nigel Short wrote a good deal on Tony's psychiatric problems, even ascribing them to his own ascendancy to the No. 1 spot in England. However, I doubt this theory and have not seen any objective evidence to support Short's view. In my own conversations with Tony in his later years, he mentioned various things he found disturbing, but Nigel's Elo rating wasn't one of them.

My first game after returning from illness, in January 2002, was rather embarrassing. Playing White against IM Graeme Buckley, I blundered away a piece as early as move 16. I then cheekily offered a draw, which unsurprisingly was turned down. However, the position then became very tactical, and as I have noted earlier, calculating ability generally stays with you even after a long absence from chess. In the complications, I managed to regain the piece and eventually win the game. Despite this initial scare, I was soon playing reasonably again. The schedule of games for the Bundesliga had operated in my favour and I had only missed three games; in February I was back in action again.

I was studying opening theory much less now than in my peak years, so it was quite a surprise to score a win based largely on opening preparation. The line played doesn't actually lead to an opposite-coloured bishop position, but it shares many of the features of such positions. White has surrendered his dark-squared bishop, so Black's assets are his dark-squared control and his powerful knight on e5. White can take comfort in his light-squared pressure and agile knights which might hop into Black's position. In such a double-edged situation, small finesses can be very important and 16 h4! is one of these. Sooner or later Black will have to expel the white queen with ...g6 and then the h-pawn is ideally posted to advance to h5 and break open Black's kingside. This idea caused Black to lose the thread of the game and when Black's main asset, the e5-knight, was exchanged off on move 25, the end was not far away.

Game 41
J. Nunn – T. Heinemann
Bundesliga 2001/2
Sicilian Defence, Najdorf Variation

1	e4	c5
2	♘f3	d6
3	d4	cxd4
4	♘xd4	♘f6
5	♘c3	a6
6	♗g5	

Just as in Games 14, 25 and 26, I decided to go for the 6 ♗g5 line.

6	...	e6
7	f4	♗e7
8	♕f3	♕c7
9	0-0-0	♘bd7

We have reached one of the key positions of the 6 ♗g5 Najdorf. White has to decide between several systems, the most common of which are 10 ♗d3 and 10 g4. At one time 10 ♗d3 was the more popular system, but now it is believed that 10...h6 is a satisfactory reply (not that there is anything really wrong with 10...b5 – see Game 14 for more on this line).

10   g4

This move is one of the most venerable lines of the 6 ♗g5 Najdorf; it was popular in the 1960s and it is still played today. These days, the switch to other sixth moves by White has left these traditional lines slightly out in the cold, but this is only a relative matter – MegaBase 2004 gives roughly 90 games with

10 g4 from 2003 alone, including many grandmaster clashes.

10   ...   b5 (D)

11   ♗xf6

Clearing the path for the g4-pawn with gain of tempo. For 11 a3, see Game 26.

11   ...   ♘xf6

Fischer played 11...gxf6 a few times in his early career, but this move looks suspect and it is rarely seen these days. White's practical results in the critical line 12 f5 ♘e5 13 ♕h3 0-0 14 ♖g1 ♔h8 15 ♖g3! have been excellent and there is little incentive for Black to adopt this variation.

11...♗xf6 is a reasonable move and it is surprising that it is not played more often. In some places you will find this move dismissed on account of 12 ♗xb5, but after 12...♖b8! 13 ♗xd7+ ♗xd7 Black's two bishops and attacking chances on the queenside give him reasonable compensation for the pawn. Therefore White might do better to play 12 g5 but, in addition to 12...♗e7, transposing to the game, Black can also try 12...♗xd4 13 ♖xd4 ♗b7 and White has no more than an edge.

12   g5   ♘d7
13   f5 (D)

White has tried quite a range of moves here, but these days you hardly see anything apart from 13 f5. The alternatives, such as 13 a3 and 13 h4, are considered too slow for such a double-edged position.

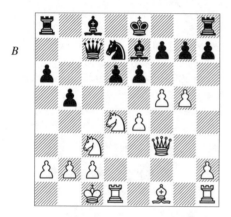

B

13   ...   ♗xg5+

This is a key decision for Black, as he can choose to take the game along either of two very different paths. The alternative is 13...♘c5 and after 14 f6 gxf6 15 gxf6 ♗f8 we reach a position in which there is a large body of theory. The critical continuation 16 ♖g1 leads to particularly sharp play, in which the slightest misstep by either side can be fatal.

Taking the pawn tends to lead to less double-edged positions, at least by Najdorf standards. Black is forced to return the pawn within a few moves, and everything depends on the assessment of the resulting position. My inclination to enter this variation was partly due to the fact that I had recently spent some time analysing it and had arrived at some rather interesting conclusions – but more of that later.

14   ♔b1   ♘e5

This is by far the most common move, the only real alternative being 14...0-0 15 fxe6 ♘b6. However, in this case 16 ♘d5 ♘xd5 17 exd5 gives White the advantage.

15   ♕h5

The attack on the bishop and threat to capture on e6 regains the pawn.

15   ...   ♕d8 (D)

A critical decision for Black. The move played has been most popular, but 15...♕e7 is a major alternative (15...♗f6 has also been tried, but in this case White should retain an advantage). As a result of my analysis, I had concluded that 15...♕d8 is inferior, and that 15...♕e7 gives Black better equalizing chances. Indeed, after 15...♕e7 16 ♘xe6 ♗xe6 17 fxe6 g6 18 exf7+ ♔xf7 19 ♕h3 ♔g7 20 ♘d5 White has just an edge.

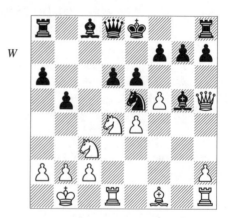

W

16   h4!

There is quite a range of moves for White here, but in my 1996 book *The Complete Najdorf: 6 ♗g5* I had commented (referring to 16 h4) that "it is surprising that this move is not more popular". My 2000 analysis of this line had built on the earlier hint and had shown that this relatively uncommon move was indeed White's best. The main alternatives are 16 ♘xe6, 16 ♖g1 and 16 fxe6. There isn't space here to go into the advantages and disadvantages of each move; interested readers should refer to my Najdorf book mentioned above.

16   ...   ♗f6

Retreating the bishop is an automatic response, but 16...b4 is worth considering. This response doesn't seem to have been tried in practice, but one possible line is 17 hxg5 bxc3 18 ♘xe6 ♗xe6 19 fxe6 g6 20 ♕h6 ♕b6 21 b3 fxe6 22 ♕h3!, followed by ♕xc3. Here I think White is better because Black's permanently weak h-pawn is more significant than his well-placed knight.

| 17 | fxe6 | 0-0 |
| 18 | ♗h3 *(D)* | |

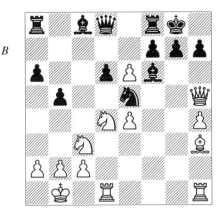

This is the key position of the 16 h4 line. Having the pawn on h4 is a huge advantage for White because sooner or later Black will have to play ...g6 to get rid of White's queen, but then the h4-pawn is perfectly placed to advance and break up Black's kingside. Note that the exchange of light-squared bishops is almost inevitable, which gives White's knights chances to hop in to d5 and possibly c6 or e6.

| 18 | ... | g6?! |

This does rather fall in with White's plan and is probably not the best. However, White retains some advantage in any case. The main line is 18...♔h8 (18...fxe6 19 ♗xe6+ ♔h8 20 ♘d5 transposes) 19 ♘d5 fxe6 20 ♗xe6 and now:

1) 20...♘c4 21 ♘c6! ♕e8 22 ♕xe8 ♖xe8 23 ♘xf6 ♖xe6 (23...gxf6 24 ♗xc4 bxc4 25 ♖xd6 ♖xe4 26 ♖xf6 leaves White a pawn up) 24 ♘d5 and Black cannot avoid losing the exchange. After 24...♗b7 25 ♘c7 ♖xe4 26 ♘xa8 ♗xa8 (26...♗xc6 27 b3 is also very good for White) 27 ♘b4 Black has some compensation, but certainly not enough.

2) 20...♗b7 looks like a better chance, but Black's position remains uncomfortable. The continuation 21 ♖df1 ♕e8 22 ♕d1 ♗xd5 23 ♗xd5 ♖c8 24 ♘e6 ♗f7 25 ♖f5 favoured White in Ilyes-Irzhanov, ICCF e-mail 2000.

| 19 | ♕e2 *(D)* |

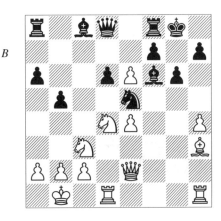

The fact that White won all seven of the games in my database reaching this position speaks for itself. Black is in trouble.

| 19 | ... | ♖e8?! |

Black has been disorientated by White's opening play and puts up little resistance. However, other moves also fail to solve Black's problems:

1) 19...♗xh4 20 ♕h2! g5 21 e7 ♕xe7 22 ♗xc8 ♖axc8 23 ♘f5 ♕a7 24 ♘d5 is winning for White, Shmuter-M.Löffler, Ostrava 1992.

2) 19...♔h8 20 h5 g5 21 ♘d5 fxe6 22 ♗xe6 ♘c4 23 ♘xf6 ♗xe6 (Stripunsky-Jaworski, Ceske Budejovice 1995) and now 24 ♘xh7! is the simplest win.

3) 19...fxe6 20 ♗xe6+ ♔h8 21 h5 gives White a large advantage.

4) 19...h5 20 ♘d5 ♗xh4 21 exf7+ ♖xf7 22 ♘e6 ♕e8 23 ♘ec7 and White wins material, Brkić-Krkljes, Croatian Team Ch, Rabac 2004.

| 20 | exf7+ | ♔xf7 |

20...♖xf7 loses material after 21 ♘c6 ♕b6 22 ♘d5 so Black has to allow his king to be displaced.

| 21 | h5 | |

Now White's h-pawn threatens to rip open the kingside, so Black makes an effort to avoid the opening of further lines.

| 21 | ... | g5 |

The problem is that this weakens the light squares even more, and f5 is added to the list of tempting destinations for White's knights.

| 22 | ♘d5 *(D)* | |

Threatening to win material with an f-file pin.

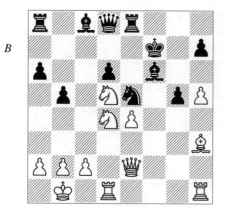

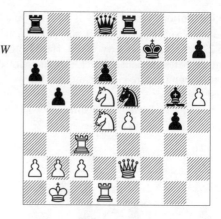

22 ... ♗xh3

Black strives to activate his dark-squared bishop at g5, but his position has so many defects (weak lights squares, exposed king, dominant white knights) that there is no salvation. However, after 22...♔g8 23 ♖hf1 ♗h8 (23...♗g7 24 ♗xc8 ♖xc8 25 h6 is even worse) 24 ♗xc8 ♖xc8 25 ♘f5 ♘f7 26 h6, followed by ♕f3 or ♕h5, Black's position will soon collapse in any case.

23 ♖xh3 g4

23...♔g8 24 ♖f1 ♗h8 25 ♘f5 is similar to the previous note.

24 ♖c3!

The only thing standing between Black and total destruction is the knight on e5, so White aims to swap it off.

24 ... ♗g5 (D)

Black has no time to prevent ♘c6 because he must first counter the threat of ♖f1.

25 ♘c6!

White could have won the exchange by 25 ♘c7 but it is much stronger to play for the attack.

25 ... ♘xc6
26 ♖xc6

The various threats of 27 ♕xg4, 27 ♖c7+ and 27 ♖f1+ are too much for Black.

26 ... ♖e5
27 ♕xg4

The rest is slaughter.

27 ... ♖a7
28 ♖c8 ♕d7
29 ♕f3+ ♔e6
30 ♖f8 1-0

It's mate in a few moves.

My traditional trip to Bunratty ended with sole second place on 5/6, half a point behind the winner Brian Kelly. The following Bundesliga weekend featured a game which could not have been a greater contrast to the previous one, at least as regards opening preparation, since this time I was on my own at move four!

There are two main points of interest in this game. The first is White's pawn sacrifice at move 12. Objectively speaking, Black should probably have accepted it, but I was not surprised when it was declined. Bönsch is a player with an attacking style, and the prospect of a long period of careful defence probably did not appeal to him. However, an error at move 16 soon cost Black a pawn, and before long the game reached a four-rook ending with White having two extra pawns. The game was far from over, because White's extra pawns were isolated and weak, while Black's rooks were tying White's pieces down to their defence. White made persistent efforts to give up one pawn to reach a single-rook ending with his rook behind an outside passed a-pawn, a situation believed to be winning ever since the famous game Alekhine-Capablanca, World Ch (34), Buenos Aires 1927. However, Black frustrated all White's efforts, and the draw was within sight when Black made an error allowing White to switch plans and launch a direct attack on Black's king. This attack, combined with the advanced c-pawn, proved sufficient for victory. It is easy to overlook such a sudden change of plan; for a long time the play had been dominated by the idea of giving up the c-pawn, which made it harder for Black to spot a totally different plan.

Game 42
J. Nunn – U. Bönsch
Bundesliga 2001/2
Sicilian Defence, Rossolimo

1	e4	c5
2	♘f3	♘c6
3	♗b5	

This was one of the first games in which I played 3 ♗b5. My motivation was to avoid my opponent's favourite Kalashnikov Variation (3 d4 cxd4 4 ♘xd4 e5 5 ♘b5 d6), which leads to rather boring positions and against which I do not have a good score.

3	...	d6

This move gave me a nasty shock, not because there is anything unusual about it but because I had failed to prepare for it. I had looked at 3 ♗b5 for a couple of days and had taken some care with the 3...e6 and 3...g6 lines which are most often played in practice. Although I was aware of 3...d6, for some reason I had totally forgotten to examine it. When I looked after the game, I realized that the book I had been working from considered 3...d6 under the move-order 2...d6 3 ♗b5+ ♘c6 and I had failed to spot the well-concealed note indicating the transposition. So now I was on my own ...

4	0-0	

I reasoned that if I played normal developing moves, then nothing too terrible could happen, so castling appeared a natural option.

4	...	♗d7

The most common move by far. 4...♗g4 5 h3 ♗h5 6 c3 is a sharper line, when Black's pin on the knight is slightly awkward, but the bishop may be missed on the queenside.

5	♖e1	

5 c3 is also popular, but this usually transposes to ♖e1 lines after 5...♘f6 6 ♖e1.

5	...	a6

5...♘f6 is the main alternative, waiting for White to commit himself to c3 before pushing the bishop away with ...a6. However, this gives White the option of 6 h3 which prevents the pin ...♗g4.

6	♗f1	

6 ♗xc6 ♗xc6, followed by either 7 c3 or 7 d4, is perhaps more critical, but as I knew nothing whatsoever about these lines, I decided to opt for the safe retreat to f1.

6	...	♗g4

The logical follow-up to the previous move, denying White the chance to play h3.

7	d3 *(D)*	

7 h3 looks wrong. After 7...♗xf3 8 ♕xf3 g6, followed by ...♗g7, Black obtains a firm grip on the d4-square and the white queen is misplaced on f3. If White wants to play h3, he should first play his queen's knight to d2, so as to recapture on f3 with a knight.

7 c3 is playable, but is really only logical if White is prepared to follow it up with d4; for example, 7...g6 8 d4 cxd4 9 cxd4 ♗xf3 10 gxf3. If White intends to meet ...g6 with d3, then it is more logical to play 7 d3, as this gives him more options.

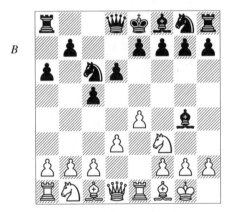

The move played introduces the simple plan of ♘bd2 followed by h3. If Black plays ...♗xf3, then after ♘xf3 White will be well placed to expand in the centre with c3 and d4. Black can retreat his bishop to h5, but he cannot both do this and develop his other bishop to the natural square g7 (because then g4 traps the h5-bishop). Black's third option, and the one he goes for in the game, is to play ...g6 but then retreat his bishop to d7. However, the manoeuvre ...♗d7-g4-d7 involves a certain loss of time.

7   ...   g6

If Black wants to play ...♗h5, then he should continue 7...♘f6 8 ♘bd2 e6 9 h3 ♗h5, but it is not clear that the bishop will be very happy when it is eventually driven back to g6. 10 b3 is one reasonable continuation for White.

8   ♘bd2   ♗g7

8...♗h6 is an interesting idea, planning the exchange of an extra pair of minor pieces. However, in this position it does not equalize because after 9 h3 ♗xf3 10 ♘xf3 ♗xc1 11 ♕xc1 ♘f6 12 ♕h6 White can prevent kingside castling and follow up with c3 and d4.

9   h3   ♗d7

Once Black has played ...g6, this is the only logical move. After 9...♗xf3 10 ♘xf3 ♘f6 11 c3 0-0 12 d4, White's two bishops and central control give him a clear and safe advantage. Wells-Porfiriadis, European Clubs Cup, Iraklion 1997 continued 12...e5 13 dxe5 dxe5 14 ♕c2 ♕e7 15 ♗e3 ♖fd8 16 ♘d2, when Black had a bad bishop and unpleasant weaknesses on the light squares.

10   c3

Now that White has expelled the bishop from g4, his control of d4 increases and he can again think about a central push with c3 and d4. Even though White is not currently threatening d4, he is ready to play it in case Black continues ...♘f6.

10   ...   b5 (D)

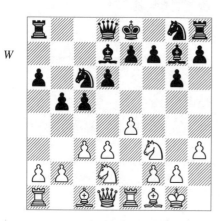

Black observes that White doesn't have very many useful moves, and tries to improve his position while delaying ...♘f6.

11   e5!

I was getting slightly fed up with normal developing moves and was looking for a way to

sharpen the position. Taking account of the fact that Black's last move weakened the c5-pawn (by ruling out the possibility of ...b6) I decided on this surprising thrust, which involves a pawn sacrifice. It might seem odd that White, who has so far played quietly and positionally, should now be justified in initiating tactics, but there are certain factors which encourage direct action. First of all, Black is still two moves from castling; secondly, there is the fact that Black has wasted time with ...♗d7-g4-d7 and thirdly, there is the aforementioned weakness of c5.

11   ...   ♘xe5

Practically forced, as the alternatives are definitely good for White:

1) 11...♗xe5 12 ♘e4 ♕b6 13 ♘xe5 ♘xe5 14 d4 cxd4 15 cxd4 ♘c4 16 b3 ♘a5 17 d5 gives White an immense attack for the pawn. Black's pieces are scattered uselessly around the edges on the board and he also suffers from serious weaknesses on the dark squares.

2) 11...dxe5 12 ♘e4 (this is where the weakness of c5 enters the picture) 12...♘f6 13 ♘xc5 ♘d5 14 ♕b3 with a positional advantage for White in view of the dominant c5-knight.

12   ♘xe5 (D)

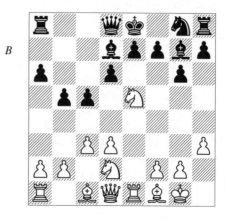

12   ...   dxe5?!

This must have been a difficult decision for Black. He could have kept the extra pawn by 12...♗xe5 13 ♘e4 (threatening both 14 ♘xc5 and 14 d4) 13...♕c7 14 d4 cxd4 15 cxd4 ♗g7 16 ♗f4 ♔f8 with a double-edged position. In return for the pawn, White has a lead in development and Black has been forced to play ...♔f8, but on the other hand there are no real weaknesses in Black's position. If White attacks f7 by ♕b3 and ♘g5, Black can defend by ...♗e8 and then expel the knight with ...h6. It is hard to evaluate such a position and a confident defensive player might well have been tempted to go in for this line. In retrospect, I think this was objectively Black's best option since the line adopted by Bönsch, which involves returning the pawn, gives White a slight positional advantage.

13 ♘b3

Black cannot defend the c5-pawn forever.

13 ... ♕c7

13...♖c8 14 ♗e3 ♕b6 is the only attempt to defend the c5-pawn, but it fails to 15 ♘xc5 ♖xc5 16 b4 winning material. Therefore Black plays to get castled while White is winning the pawn back. Note that the immediate 13...♘f6 is bad because after 14 ♖xe5 Black loses both pawns. Therefore Black defends the e5-pawn before playing ...♘f6.

14 ♗e3 ♘f6
15 ♗xc5 (D)

15 ♘xc5 ♗c6 16 d4 is inferior because Black can solve his problems with 16...♘d5.

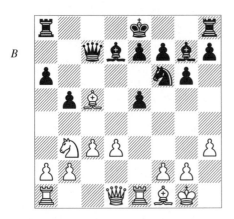

15 ... ♗e6

15...♗c6 is the alternative. This sometimes allows Black to meet d4 by ...e4, but on the other hand it blocks Black's attack on the c5-bishop. After 16 ♕e2 (16 d4 e4 is not dangerous for Black) 16...♘d5 (16...♘d7 17 ♗a3 is unpleasant for Black as he has to resort to artificial measures such as ...♗f6 in order to castle) 17 d4 exd4 18 ♗xd4 0-0 19 ♗xg7 ♔xg7 White can maintain a slight advantage by either 20 ♘d4 or 20 ♖ac1 followed by c4.

The text-move threatens to win a piece with ...♗xb3 and so forces White's hand.

16 d4 (D)

16 ♗a3 0-0 17 ♕e2 ♘d5 offers White nothing since 18 ♘c5 can be comfortably met by 18...♗f5.

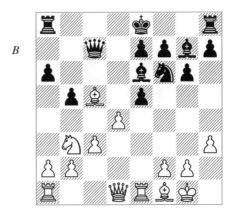

16 ... exd4?

This is a serious error which gives White the tempo he needs to increase the pressure on Black's position. 16...0-0 was correct:

1) 17 ♖xe5 ♘g4 18 hxg4 ♗xe5 19 dxe5 ♗xb3 20 ♕d4 ♗e6 21 ♗e2 gives White a pawn and some positional pressure for the exchange. While White should have enough for his small sacrifice, it is hard to believe that he has an advantage.

2) 17 dxe5 ♗xb3 18 ♕xb3 ♕xc5 19 exf6 ♗xf6 20 a4 bxa4 21 ♖xa4 a5 is equal.

3) 17 ♕e2 exd4 (17...e4 18 ♘d2 ♗d5 19 b3, with c4 to come, also looks a little better for White) 18 ♗xd4 ♖fe8 and, although I think that White still has an edge, this is clearly much better for Black than the game.

17 ♗xd4

The premature exchange on d4 means that White's ♘c5 will come at a moment when the e6-bishop doesn't have a good square to move to.

17 ... 0-0

There is nothing better since 17...♗xb3 18 ♕xb3 0-0 19 a4 gives White strong pressure against Black's queenside. Black will almost certainly lose a pawn within a few moves.

18 ♘c5 ♗c4

Black decides to give up a pawn to reach a position in which he can place considerable technical difficulties in White's path. The alternatives are worse:

1) 18...♗d5? 19 ♗xf6 exf6 20 ♕xd5 ♖fd8 (20...♖ad8 loses at once to 21 ♘xa6) 21 ♘xa6 ♖xa6 22 ♕xb5 leaves White two pawns up.

2) 18...♗f5 19 ♕f3 is much better for White. Now that he is attacking the a8-rook, 20 g4 is a major threat, and Black must also cope with the possibility of a4, which will very likely win a pawn on the queenside. If White needs to secure his c5-knight, he can simply play b4.

19   ♗xc4   bxc4
20   ♕e2

Attacking c4 and e7 and so winning a pawn.

20   ...   ♖fc8

Making life as hard as possible for White. If instead 20...♖fe8, then 21 ♕xc4 e5 22 ♗e3 ♘d7 23 ♖ad1 ♖ac8 24 b4 ♘xc5 25 ♗xc5 ♗f8 26 ♖d5 and Black has no compensation for the pawn.

21   ♕xc4 (D)

It wasn't easy deciding which pawn to take. After 21 ♕xe7 ♕xe7 22 ♖xe7 ♗f8 23 ♖e5! (after 23 ♖e2 ♖xc5 24 ♗xf6 ♗g7 the exchange of bishops will leave White with considerable technical problems, since for the moment his extra queenside pawn is not very useful) 23...♗d6 (23...♗xc5 24 ♖xc5 ♖xc5 25 ♗xc5 ♖b8 26 b4 is excellent for White) 24 ♖e2 ♖xc5 25 ♗xf6 it is to White's advantage that Black cannot immediately exchange bishops. However, this still doesn't look too easy to win, so on balance I think the move played was the better choice.

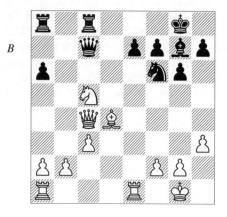

21   ...   e5

Having landed himself in a very difficult position, Black now puts up a fierce resistance.

22   ♗e3

I can't imagine many players wanting to go in for 22 ♖xe5 ♘g4 23 ♖ee1 ♕h2+ 24 ♔f1 ♕h1+ (24...♖ab8 25 b4 only helps White) 25 ♔e2 ♖e8+ 26 ♔f3 ♖xe1 27 ♖xe1 ♕xe1 28 hxg4 ♖d8 when, although White may not be worse, he has clearly made things harder for himself.

22   ...   ♘d7
23   b4

23 ♖ad1 ♘xc5 24 ♗xc5 ♗f8 (not 24...♕xc5? 25 ♖d8+) 25 b4 transposes.

23   ...   ♗f8
24   ♖ad1 (D)

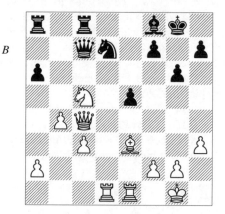

Threatening 25 ♖xd7 ♕xd7 26 ♘xd7 ♖xc4 27 ♘b6, consolidating White's extra pawn. If there is a general liquidation, then White's 3 to 1 queenside majority should be enough to win, provided he can avoid a serious pawn weakness.

24   ...   ♘xc5
25   ♗xc5

The other recapture 25 bxc5 is also very good. The idea is to play ♖d5 and ♖ed1, followed by penetrating to d7 or d8 with a rook. Note that Black cannot reply 25...♗xc5 due to 26 ♗xc5 ♕xc5 27 ♖d8+ winning.

25   ...   a5

25...♗xc5 26 bxc5 followed by ♖d5 makes things easier for White. Even though White has doubled c-pawns, the active position of White's pieces and the danger posed by the c5-pawn should be enough to win. Black therefore tries to make life harder for White by breaking up his queenside pawns, at the same time activating the a8-rook.

26 $\Box$d5

Defending c5 and threatening the e5-pawn.

26   ...   axb4

27   cxb4 (D)

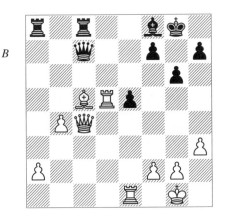

27   ... $\mathbb{W}$a7!

An excellent defensive move (which I had in fact overlooked), taking aim at the a2-pawn.

28 $\Box$e2

The simplest line is 28 $\Box$dxe5 $\mathbb{W}$xa2, but the exchange of e-pawn for a-pawn leaves White with just a single passed pawn, and it can be difficult to win such positions, especially if there are still many pieces on the board. If White goes for a general liquidation leaving just a pair of rooks, then he must ensure that he can put his rook behind the passed pawn, otherwise the game will probably be a draw.

The move played aims to retain both White's queenside pawns.

28   ... $\triangle$xc5

After 28...$\mathbb{W}$a4 29 $\mathbb{W}$d3 $\triangle$xc5 30 bxc5 f6 White's queenside pawns are broken, but 31 $\Box$d2 should lead to a win since with all the heavy pieces on the board he has good chances of launching a direct attack against Black's king.

29   bxc5 $\mathbb{W}$a4

Once again Black makes life hard for White. He is prepared to offer a second pawn in order to exchange queens and activate his rooks.

30 $\mathbb{W}$xa4?!

It was hard to resist taking the second pawn, but it would have been better to keep the queens on by 30 $\mathbb{W}$c3 e4 (30...f6 opens up the second rank and so gives White more attacking chances against Black's king; after 31 $\Box$ed2, for example, White should win) 31 $\Box$ed2, with excellent

winning chances. With the twin dangers of a weak back rank and a dangerous c-pawn, Black faces a very difficult defensive task.

30   ... $\Box$xa4

31 $\Box$dxe5

White's idea is that although Black will have no trouble winning one pawn back, White will then be able to reach a single rook ending with an outside passed pawn and his rook behind the pawn. All other things being equal, such endings are usually winning. However, Black finds a way to make life difficult for White – he refuses to take the pawn straight away and simply maintains the active position of his rooks.

31   ... $\Box$c4 (D)

The only move, as 31...$\Box$ca8 32 $\Box$e8+ $\Box$xe8 33 $\Box$xe8+ $\dot{\Xi}$g7 34 c6 $\Box$c4 35 a4 $\Box$xc6 36 $\Box$e1 followed by $\Box$a1 leads to the type of position White is aiming for.

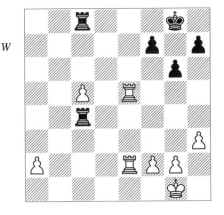

32   a3!

The best, clearing a2 and preparing to meet 32...$\Box$4xc5 33 $\Box$xc5 $\Box$xc5 by 34 $\Box$a2 followed by a4, when White again achieves his goal. Black therefore refuses to be tempted by the c-pawn and instead plays to activate his king.

32   ... $\dot{\Xi}$g7

33   f3

White also intends to bring his king out. The plan is $\dot{\Xi}$f2, followed by $\Box$d2 and $\dot{\Xi}$e2-d3, eventually forcing Black to take on c5 at a moment when White's rook can move to a2. In order to obstruct this plan, Black decides to transfer his c8-rook to a more active position.

Note that 33 $\Box$a2 is bad due to 33...$\dot{\Xi}$f6 34 $\Box$d5 $\Box$c1+ 35 $\dot{\Xi}$h2 $\Box$8xc5 36 $\Box$xc5 $\Box$xc5. Although this has the general structure White is aiming for, it is probably a draw since Black's king is actively placed while White's has been driven onto the h-file.

33 ... ♖a8

34 ♖2e3

Not 34 ♖a2 ♔f6 35 ♖d5 ♔e6 36 ♖d6+ ♔e7 37 ♖e2+ ♔f8 and White will lose a pawn under unfavourable circumstances.

34 ... ♖a5

Now Black's rooks are optimally placed for exerting pressure against both white queenside pawns. White's basic plan is to improve his position on the kingside by ♔f2, g4 and ♔g3. He can then play ♖d5 and switch to an attack on f7 by ♖d7 and ♖ee7. Then it doesn't matter if Black takes the queenside pawns because White's rooks and advanced pawns will create a mating attack on the kingside.

35 ♔f2

Unfortunately, White cannot play 35 g4 at once because after 35...♖axc5 36 ♖xc5 ♖xc5 37 ♖e1 (37 a4 ♖c1+ followed by ...♖a1 should draw) 37...♖c3 White's f-pawn is hanging.

35 ... ♖c2+! *(D)*

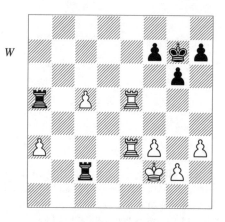

Black continues to defend accurately; now he seeks to obstruct White's plan of g4 and ♔g3. Other moves are inferior:

1) 35...♖axc5 36 ♖xc5 ♖xc5 37 ♖e2 ♔f6 38 a4 ♖a5 39 ♖a2 should win for White.

2) 35...h6 36 g4 ♖c2+ 37 ♔g3 ♖c4 38 ♖d5 ♖c2 39 ♖d7 ♖cxc5 40 ♖ee7 ♔f6 41 ♖xf7+ ♔e6 42 ♖de7+ ♔d5 43 ♖f6 and White wins.

36 ♔g3

White is obliged to block his g-pawn because 36 ♖e2 ♖c3 37 ♖a2 ♔f6 38 ♖d5 ♖axa3 is only a draw.

36 ... h5

This might be considered slightly inaccurate, since Black had two more direct defensive plans:

1) 36...♖b5 37 ♖e2 (37 a4 ♖bb2 is not clear) 37...♖c3 38 a4 ♖a5 39 ♖2e3 ♖c2 40 ♖3e4 ♔f6 and Black's king is becoming active. Next move he can take on c5 with drawing chances.

2) 36...♔f6 is the simplest. After 37 ♖d5 ♖axc5 38 ♖xc5 ♖xc5 39 a4 ♖a5 40 ♖e4 (also after 40 ♖a3 ♔e5 the active king gives Black good drawing chances) 40...♖c5 White can still play for a win, but I suspect that this should be a draw with accurate defence.

37 h4

Preventing the possibility of ...h4+. The partial fixing of the kingside pawn-structure does not make much difference to the position.

37 ... ♔f6

38 ♖d5 *(D)*

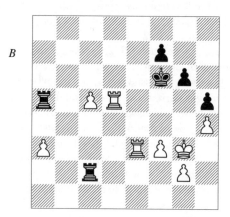

Threatening to launch an attack against f7 by doubling rooks on the seventh rank.

38 ... ♖b5?

Up to here Black has defended with amazing resourcefulness in a very difficult position, but this move definitely loses. He cannot ignore White's threat to attack f7, so now was the moment to regain one pawn. After 38...♖axc5 39 ♖xc5 ♖xc5 40 a4 ♖a5 Black retains drawing chances:

1) 41 ♖a3 ♔e5 offers White few winning prospects; for example, 42 ♔f2 ♔d4 43 ♔e2 ♖e5+ 44 ♔d2 ♖a5 45 ♔c2 (45 ♖e3 is answered by 45...f5) 45...♔c4 46 ♖a1 f6, followed by ...g5, and Black starts reducing the number of pawns.

2) 41 罩e4 is the best chance; for example, 41...罩c5 (threatening ...罩c2-a2) 42 ♔f2! (42 ♔f4 罩c2 43 g3 罩a2 should be a draw, while 42 罩e2 罩a5 repeats) and now:

2a) 42...罩c2+ 43 罩e2 罩c4 (43...罩c5 44 罩a2 罩a5 45 ♔e3 is fine for White as he has prevented Black's king from occupying a dominant position) 44 罩a2 罩xh4 45 a5 罩c4 46 a6 罩c8 47 a7 罩a8 48 ♔e3 should be a win for White.

2b) 42...♔f5 43 ♔e3 and White will make a run for the a-pawn even at the cost of losing the g-pawn. The position is still finely balanced between a draw and a win.

39   罩d6+

The direct 39 罩d7 罩bxc5 40 罩ee7 is also very promising.

39   ...   ♔g7

40   c6!

The immediate attack on f7 by 40 罩d7 罩bxc5 41 罩ee7 leads nowhere after 41...罩f5 but by combining the advance of the c-pawn with the possibility of doubling rooks on the seventh, White creates insuperable difficulties for Black.

40   ...   罩bb2

Black goes for a counterattack since other defences fail:

1) 40...罩bc5 41 a4 罩xc6 42 罩xc6 罩xc6 43 罩a3 with a clear win as White's a-pawn is further up the board and his king can occupy the fourth rank.

2) 40...罩b6 41 a4 罩a6 42 罩e4 ♔f8 43 ♔f4 ♔g7 44 罩b4 and the white king is free to move to the queenside.

41   罩e7   罩xg2+

42   ♔f4 (D)

The loss of the g-pawn isn't too important. The attack on f7, the advanced c-pawn and White's active king are sufficient to win.

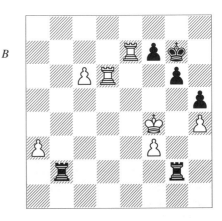

42   ...   罩h2

Or 42...罩bc2 43 c7 罩c4+ 44 ♔e3 罩gc2 45 罩dd7 罩2c3+ 46 ♔f2 ♔f6 47 罩xf7+ ♔e5 48 罩de7+ ♔d6 49 罩h7 (threatening 50 罩eg7) 49...罩xh4 50 罩eg7 ♔e5 51 罩xg6 with an easy win.

43   罩dd7   ♔h6

The only move, since 43...罩xh4+ 44 ♔g5 罩c4 45 罩xf7+ ♔g8 46 罩g7+ ♔f8 47 罩h7 ♔g8 48 ♔h6 leads to mate.

44   罩xf7   罩xh4+

45   ♔e5

Now the king goes up to support the c-pawn.

45   ...   罩e2+

After 45...罩c4 46 f4 White wins a rook due to the mate threat on h7.

46   ♔d6   罩d4+

46...♔g5 47 f4+ 罩xf4 48 罩xf4 ♔xf4 49 c7 罩c2 50 罩d8 h4 51 c8♕ 罩xc8 52 罩xc8 and White wins easily.

47   ♔c7   1-0

The situation is hopeless; e.g., 47...罩a4 48 f4 罩a7+ 49 ♔b6 罩xd7 50 cxd7 罩d2 51 ♔c7 罩c2+ 52 ♔d6 罩d2+ 53 ♔e7 罩e2+ 54 ♔f8 罩d2 55 ♔g8, followed by mate.

The Bundesliga was not the only team competition in which I played for Lübeck. The German Team Cup is a knock-out event for teams of four players and although it is far less prestigious than the Bundesliga, some quite strong teams are fielded, at least in later stages of the competition. In previous years my contribution to Lübeck's Cup success had been limited, but on this occasion I was able to play in the final against Baden Oos. The following win helped Lübeck to a 2½-1½ victory.

The whole of the game is dominated by White's efforts to prevent Black from castling. Tactics rage in the centre of the board, but still Black's king remains stuck on e8. Even when the queens are exchanged, the king remains awkwardly placed, not only subject to attack but also blocking the exit route of the h8-rook. Sometimes it is better to have the king in the centre in the endgame, but here White still has enough pieces to create serious threats. Finally White finds a way to liquidate to a winning ending with two extra pawns.

Game 43
J. Nunn – M. Krasenkow
German Team Cup Final, Baden-Baden 2002
Sicilian Defence, Rossolimo

1	e4	c5
2	♘f3	♞c6
3	♗b5	

I had no wish to challenge Krasenkow in the Sveshnikov Variation, since he is a renowned expert on that line, so it didn't take long for me to decide on ♗b5.

3	...	e6
4	0-0	♞ge7 (D)

This is a logical system for Black. His idea is to defend c6 with a piece, so as to avoid doubled pawns if White should exchange on that square. Then he will chase the bishop away with ...a6.

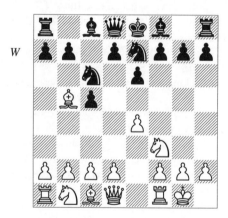

5	c3

White has several possibilities here. The most common move is 5 ♖e1, preparing to retreat the bishop to f1 after ...a6. The move played occurs only slightly less often, while 5 b3 and 5 ♘c3, although somewhat less popular, also have substantial followings.

5	...	a6

Here White cannot retreat the bishop to f1, so it has to go back to a4, rather as in the Ruy Lopez.

6	♗a4	b5
7	♗c2	

White's plan is quite obvious. He intends to form a central pawn duo by playing d4, and then continue his development. As in the Ruy Lopez, if White can maintain his central pawns on d4 and e4 without making any concession, then he will have a safe advantage. Therefore Black must take action to prevent this.

7	...	♗b7 (D)

The most accurate move. After 7...d5 8 e5 d4 (or else White plays d4) 9 ♗e4 White has good chances of retaining an advantage.

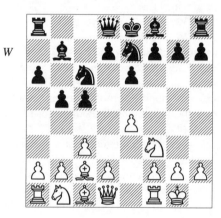

8	♕e2

Here again White has several possibilities:

1) 8 d4 is the most direct move. After 8...cxd4 9 ♘xd4 (9 cxd4 is inferior because 9...♞b4 forces the exchange of the light-squared bishop) 9...♞g6 10 f4 a position resembling the Open Sicilian arises. However, this line doesn't appear especially dangerous for Black since White's queenside development has yet to begin.

2) 8 a4 has been played quite frequently, but Black has the simple reply 8...♞g6 available so I doubt if White can count on any advantage.

3) 8 ♖e1 is the most common move, supporting the e4-pawn. The main line runs 8...d5 (8...♖c8 9 a4 followed by ♘a3 makes good sense for White, since now that Black's rook has left a8 White is actually threatening to win a pawn on b5; I doubt if Black can equalize in this line) 9 exd5 ♞xd5 10 d4 cxd4 11 cxd4 with a double-edged IQP position.

8 ♕e2 has the advantage that it both supports the e4-pawn and lends force to an attack on the b5-pawn by a4. White can decide later whether to develop his rook to e1 or d1.

8   ...   d5 *(D)*

The most popular move. The main alternatives are:

1) 8...♘g6 has been played many times, but I doubt if it is good since White can now play d4 with impunity. After 9 d4 cxd4 10 cxd4 ♘h4 (10...♗c8 may be a better chance, but 11 ♖d1 gives White a slight advantage) 11 ♘bd2 White consolidates his centre. Black's practical results have been very poor from this position, bearing out the point made above about White's central pawn duo.

2) 8...c4!? is a little-played but interesting possibility. After 9 b3 d5 10 exd5 ♘xd5 11 bxc4 ♘f4 12 ♕e3 ♗d6 Black offers a pawn in return for a lead in development.

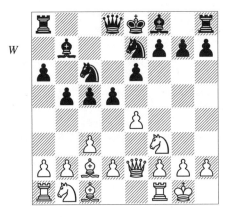

9   a4!?

This move was made up over the board. Objectively speaking, it doesn't really promise White any advantage, but it is always good to present novel problems to an opponent. Although 9 a4 has never been played before in this position, it leads by transposition to a position which has occurred twice before via other move-orders (although both games are rather obscure). Despite White's success in the current game, it doesn't appear to have been repeated since! The main line runs 9 e5 d4 10 ♗e4 ♘d5 with an unclear position; if White is happy with an IQP position, then he could try 9 d4 cxd4 10 exd5 ♘xd5 11 cxd4, as in W.Richter-Kosten, 2nd Bundesliga 1997/8.

9   ...   b4

9...dxe4 10 ♗xe4 b4 11 d4 cxd4 is also satisfactory:

1) 12 cxd4 ♘d5 is roughly equal.

2) 12 cxb4 is best met by 12...♘g6 with equality, rather than 12...d3 13 ♗xd3 ♘xb4 14 ♗e4 ♗xe4 15 ♕xe4 ♘ed5 16 ♘c3, which gives White some initiative.

3) 12 ♖d1 ♘d5! (12...♕c7 13 cxd4 gives White a favourable IQP position, while after 12...♘g6 13 ♘xd4 White has a clear advantage) and Black equalizes after 13 c4 ♘f6 14 ♗xc6+ ♗xc6 15 ♘xd4 ♕c7 or 13 ♘xd4 ♘xd4 14 ♖xd4 ♗c5.

10   d4 *(D)*

With this move we enter uncharted territory. In previous games White has tried other ideas, but it seems to me that only by taking direct action in the centre can White hope for any advantage. The analysis runs:

1) 10 d3 ♘g6 11 ♗g5 ♗e7 12 ♗xe7 ♕xe7 13 ♘bd2 0-0 14 ♕e3 ♖ac8 was fine for Black in the game Lhagva-Pritchett, Nice Olympiad 1974.

2) 10 ♖e1 and now 10...d4 11 cxd4 ♘xd4 12 ♘xd4 ♕xd4 13 d3 ♘c6 14 ♘d2 ♕f6 15 ♘f3 ♘d4 16 ♘xd4 cxd4 17 a5 ♗c5 18 ♗a4+ ♔e7?? 19 ♕h5 1-0 was the abrupt finish of Blocker-Castañeda, Philadelphia 1996, but it is not hard to find improvements for Black. For example, 10...b3! 11 ♗xb3 dxe4 is dangerous for White since both 12 ♕xe4 ♘a5 13 ♕c2 ♗xf3 14 gxf3 ♘g6 and 12 ♘g5 ♘e5 13 ♘xe4 ♘d3 14 ♖f1 ♘g6 give Black excellent play for the pawn.

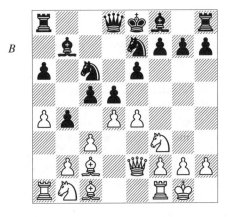

10   ...   bxc3

The various combinations of pawn captures result in a confusingly wide range of possibilities for Black. The main alternatives are:

1) 10...cxd4 (the soundest line) 11 cxd4 dxe4 (11...b3?! 12 ♗xb3 dxe4 13 ♕xe4 ♘a5 14 ♕d3 may be good for White) 12 ♗xe4 ♘d5 transposes to line '1' of the note to Black's 9th move, with an equal position.

2) 10...b3 11 ♗xb3 dxe4 12 ♘g5 cxd4 13 ♘d2!? is very unclear.

The move played is not really a mistake, but it does give White the chance to complicate the game.

11   dxc5!

White takes the opportunity to unbalance the position. The pawn on c5 appears weak, but it takes time to win it and this time allows White to establish a lead in development. 11 bxc3 cxd4 12 cxd4 ♘b4 is fine for Black.

11   ...   cxb2
12   ♗xb2 (D)

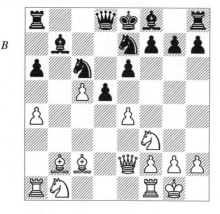

12   ...   d4?

However, this is doubtful. Black wants to shut out the b2-bishop by playing ...e5, and then round up the c5-pawn at his leisure. However, after White's reply this plan is no longer possible. Although it is not a serious issue at this stage, it is worth bearing in mind that Black is three moves away from castling, and so he cannot allow the position to be opened up too much. 12...dxe4 13 ♗xe4 ♘g6 14 ♕e3 is bad for Black, as the pressure against g7 makes it hard for him to develop his pieces, while White's can all come into play easily. The best move was 12...♘b4. After 13 ♘c3 d4 14 ♖fd1 ♘ec6 15 ♖ac1 ♗xc5 16 e5 a very complicated and

unclear position arises; one line is 16...♘xc2 17 ♘e4 ♗e7 18 ♖xc2 with a roughly level position.

13   e5?!

There were two other interesting continuations, which might well have offered better chances than this modest move:

1) 13 ♕c4 (D) has the aim of winning the d4-pawn while retaining the pawn on c5. Black may reply:

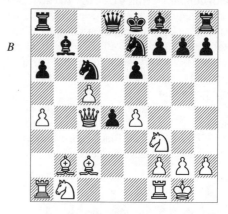

1a) 13...♘a5 14 ♕xd4 ♕xd4 15 ♘xd4 ♖c8 16 ♘d2 ♖xc5 17 ♖fc1 and White's better development gives him some advantage in the endgame.

1b) 13...♕c7 14 ♘xd4 ♘xd4 15 ♕xd4 ♘c6 16 ♕c3 e5 17 ♕g3 is awkward for Black, who still has to complete his development.

1c) 13...♘g6 14 ♘xd4 ♘ge5 15 ♕b3 ♘xd4 16 ♗xd4 ♕xd4 17 ♕xb7 ♕d8 with just a slight advantage for White.

2) 13 ♖d1!? e5 14 ♘xe5! ♘xe5 15 ♗xd4 was an idea which occupied quite a bit of my time during the game. In the end I decided it was just too risky, although home analysis shows that White has enough compensation for the piece: 15...♘d7 (15...♘5c6 16 ♗e3 ♕c8 17 ♘c3 followed by ♘d5 is unclear, while 15...♕b8 16 ♘c3 ♘7c6 17 ♗e3 ♗e7 18 ♘d5 0-0 19 f4 ♘g6 20 ♖ab1 ♖e8 21 e5 gives White strong pressure) 16 ♘c3 ♘c6 17 ♗e3 ♗e7 18 ♖ab1 ♕c8 19 ♘d5 and White has enough activity for the piece.

The move played prevents ...e5, and gives the b1-knight the tempting square e4 to aim for. However, it has the defects of opening the long diagonal for the b7-bishop and giving Black the d5-square for his e7-knight.

13   ...   ♘d5

Now Black can complete his kingside development, which should enable him to equalize.

14   ♘bd2   ♗xc5

There is nothing wrong with this simple capture, but it was also possible to play 14...♘db4 15 ♗d3 (15 ♗e4 d3 is unclear) 15...♗xc5 16 ♘e4 (16 ♘b3 ♘xd3 17 ♕xd3 ♗e7 is, if anything, slightly better for Black) 16...♗e7 17 ♖ad1 ♘xd3 18 ♖xd3 0-0 with an equal position.

15   ♘e4

Gaining time by attacking the bishop, and taking aim at both the weak d6-square and Black's poorly defended kingside.

15   ...   ♗e7

16   ♖fd1 *(D)*

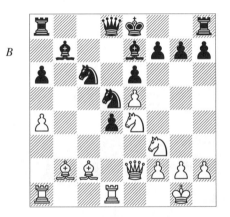

After White regains the d4-pawn, there are two ways he can play for the advantage. The first method only applies if Black has castled kingside, and is based on a direct attack on the king, aided by the two active bishops. The second plan is to exchange dark-squared bishops by ♗a3, and then plant a knight on d6.

16   ...   ♘cb4?!

Black plays to exchange off White's dangerous c2-bishop in order to reduce the pressure on his kingside. However, this costs time which White can use to regain the pawn on d4. Black should have tried one of the alternatives:

1) 16...♕c7 17 ♘xd4 ♘xe5 18 ♘b5! axb5 (18...♘f3+ 19 ♕xf3 axb5 20 ♖ac1 ♕f4 21 ♕d3 is also good for White) 19 ♗xe5 ♕xe5 20 ♕xb5+ ♔f8 21 ♕xb7 with just a faint edge for White.

2) 16...♘f4 17 ♕d2 (17 ♕e1 d3 18 ♕e3 is unclear) 17...♘g6 is simplest. Black transfers a

knight over to defend the exposed kingside, and at the same time attacks the e5-pawn. The position is equal.

17   ♖xd4

The correct capture, because with the rook in this active position it is hard for Black to castle.

17   ...   ♘xc2

17...0-0? fails to 18 ♘f6+ gxf6 (18...♔h8 19 ♖h4 gives White a decisive attack) 19 ♗xh7+ ♔xh7 20 ♖h4+ ♔g7 21 ♖g4+ ♔h7 22 exf6 ♘xf6 (22...♗xf6 23 ♕e4+ mates) 23 ♘g5+ and White wins.

18   ♕xc2   ♖c8

Black is still unable to castle: 18...0-0? 19 ♘f6+! gxf6 (19...♗xf6 20 exf6 g6 21 ♕d2 and White wins) 20 ♖g4+ ♔h8 21 exf6 ♘xf6 22 ♘g5 with a quick mate to follow.

19   ♕d3 *(D)*

Wherever he moves his queen, White can no longer prevent castling; for example, 19 ♕d2 0-0 20 ♘f6+?! gxf6 21 ♖g4+ ♔h8 22 ♕h6 ♖g8 23 exf6 ♗xf6 24 ♖xg8+ ♕xg8 25 ♗xf6+ ♘xf6 26 ♕xf6+ ♕g7 and Black is better.

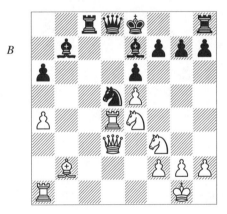

19   ...   ♕b6

Here castling does not lead to a tactical catastrophe, but rather to a positional advantage for White: 19...0-0 20 ♗a3 (20 ♘f6+ ♗xf6 21 exf6 ♕xf6 gets White nowhere) 20...f5 21 ♘d6 (21 ♗xe7 fxe4 22 ♗xd8 exd3 23 ♗g5 ♘c3 is unclear) and Black is troubled by the weak d6-square and vulnerable e6-pawn. A sample line is 21...♖c3 22 ♕d2 ♕c7 23 ♖d3 ♖c2 24 ♕d1 ♖c3 25 ♖xc3 ♕xc3 (25...♘xc3 26 ♖c1! is very good for White) 26 ♕d4 with some advantage for White.

The move played attempts to disturb White's pieces.

20   &a3

Thematically aiming for the exchange of dark-squared bishops. If Black allows a knight to settle on d6 then he will be clearly worse, so he has to continue his policy of trying to upset White's plans.

20   ...   ♘f4

21   ♘d6+!

The justification for White's previous move. He virtually forces a liquidation into an ending in which Black's king is trapped in the centre. 21 ♘f6+? gxf6 22 ♖xf4 is wrong because after 22...♖d8 Black's active b7-bishop easily compensates for the position of his king in the centre of the board.

21   ...   &xd6

Not 21...♕xd6?? 22 exd6 ♘xd3 23 d7+ winning at once.

22   ♖xd6! *(D)*

Not 22 ♖xf4?! &xa3 23 ♕xa3 &d5, followed by ...♕c5, and Black nullifies all White's pressure.

at any time he pleases, while retaining a strong grip.

2) 25...♘g6 26 f4! (threatening an immediate win with 27 f5) 26...♘xf4 27 ♖e7+ ♔d8 28 ♖xf7 ♘d5 29 ♖b1 g5 30 ♖bb7 h5 31 ♖a7 and again White will restore material equality while still exerting strong pressure on Black's position.

23   ♕e3

Black cannot afford to let White trap his king in the centre with queens still on the board, so his next move is virtually forced.

23   ...   ♕c3

23...♘g6 24 ♕a7 ♕c3 25 ♖dd1 is dead lost for Black.

24   ♕xc3

24 ♖b1 might also be good, but this gives Black several extra options and I preferred to keep it simple.

24   ...   ♘e2+

24...♖xc3 25 ♖b6 &c8 26 ♘g5, followed by ♘e4, exploits the weakness on d6 to deadly effect.

25   ♔f1   ♘xc3

26   ♖b6 *(D)*

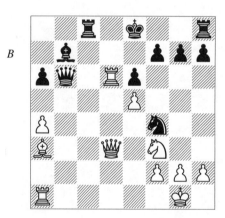

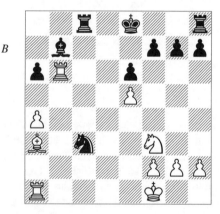

22   ...   ♕a5

The alternative was 22...♘xd3 23 ♖xb6 &xf3 24 gxf3 ♘xe5 25 ♖b7, but this ending is very unpleasant for Black despite the extra pawn(s):

1) 25...♘xf3+ 26 ♔f1 ♘d4 (26...g6 27 ♖d1 ♘xh2+ 28 ♔g2 ♘g4 29 ♖dd7 ♘e5 30 ♖e7+ ♔d8 31 &d6 ♖e8 32 ♖xe8+ ♔xe8 33 &xe5 and in this position the bishop is much stronger than the three pawns) 27 ♖e7+ ♔d8 28 ♖b1 ♖e8 29 ♖xf7 ♖g8 30 ♖bb7 ♘c6 31 ♖fd7+ ♔e8 32 ♖d6 ♘d8 33 ♖a7 a5 34 ♔g2 with a large advantage for White, since he can regain the pawn

Black's king is destined to remain in the centre until the end of the game.

26   ...   &d5

Or 26...&xf3 27 gxf3 ♖a8 28 ♖b7 ♘d5 29 f4! (preventing ...g5, which would otherwise give Black some air) 29...g6 30 ♖c1 and Black is totally tied up without even an extra pawn to show for his trouble.

27   ♖c1

Black's problems are not restricted to his poor king position since now White sets up an awkward pin along the c-file. The immediate threat is 28 ♔e1 followed by ♗b2, winning a piece.

| 27 | ... | f6 |

The only move, preparing ...♔f7 so as to defend the c8-rook and thus unpin the knight. Other moves lose quickly: 27...f5 28 ♘g5 picks up the e6-pawn, while 27...♗c4+ 28 ♔e1 ♘d5 only swaps the pin on the knight for an equally unpleasant pin on the bishop; after 29 ♖b7, followed by ♘d2, White wins material.

| 28 | ♗b2! (D) |

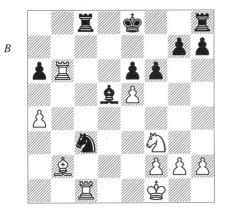

The start of a precisely calculated sequence which leads to a forced win. It doesn't matter that the bishop abandons the a3-f8 diagonal, because Black never has time to castle.

| 28 | ... | ♗c4+ |
| 29 | ♔e1 | ♘xa4 |

Forced. The knight must attack the b6-rook, or else White wins with 30 ♖xc4 followed by 31 ♖b8+. If 29...♘d5, then White wins by 30 ♖xe6+ ♔f7 31 ♖d6!.

| 30 | ♖b4 |

Forcing Black to exchange on b2.

| 30 | ... | ♘xb2 |
| 31 | ♖xb2 |

Now White is threatening to win a piece with 32 ♖bc2, so the reply is again forced. Note that the pawns on a6 and e6 prevent Black from unpinning by retreating his bishop to one of those squares.

| 31 | ... | ♔d7 |
| 32 | ♖b7+ | ♔d8 |

32...♔c6 33 ♖xg7 ♔d5 34 ♖d1+ ♔c5 (or 34...♔e4 35 ♖d4+ ♔f5 36 g4#) 35 exf6 ♖hf8 36 ♘e5 is also an easy win.

| 33 | ♖xg7 | ♗d5 |

There isn't much choice as White was threatening 34 exf6, and 33...f5 loses to 34 ♘g5.

| 34 | ♖xc8+ | ♔xc8 (D) |

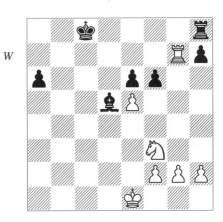

| 35 | exf6! |

The final point of the sequence started at move 28. Black cannot play 35...♗xf3 due to 36 f7. The result is that White gets his knight to e5.

35	...	♖f8
36	f7	♔d7
37	♘e5+	♔d6
38	f4

With his passed pawn secure on f7, White has an easy win.

| 38 | ... | a5 |

Black cannot even save the pawn by 38...h5 because of 39 ♘g6.

| 39 | ♖xh7 | a4 |

39...♗xg2 loses to 40 ♘g6.

| 40 | g4 |

Keeping the important g-pawn. 40 ♘g6?? is a blunder due to 40...a3 and White can no longer win, but 40 ♔f2! would have been slightly simpler, cutting out the possibility in the following note.

| 40 | ... | a3 |

40...♗g2 was the best chance, stopping the rook reaching a3, but White can still win by 41 ♔f2 a3 42 ♘g6 (42 ♘c4+ ♔e7 43 ♘xa3 ♗e4 44 ♖h5 ♖xf7 45 ♔e3 is of course also sufficient) 42...a2 43 ♘xf8 a1♕ 44 ♘g6 ♕f1+ 45 ♔g3 ♕f3+ 46 ♔h4 ♕h3+ 47 ♔g5 ♕xh7 48 f8♕+ followed by h4.

| 41 | ♖h3 | a2 |
| 42 | ♖a3 | 1-0 |

Black's pawn is stopped and White wins by simply pushing his g-pawn.

The next game was played in one of the season's critical matches – the clash of titans between Lübeck and Solingen. In the end, Lübeck emerged a narrow victor by 4½-3½, so this game, one of Lübeck's two wins in the match, played a significant role in deciding the Bundesliga. My first surprise came even before the first pawn was pushed. Most Bundesliga matches are played in pairs, with one game on Saturday and one on Sunday. This game was played on Sunday and when I entered the playing room I had to rub my eyes, because across the board from me sat Eric Lobron. He had not played for Solingen in the Saturday match, and had parachuted in as a little surprise for the Sunday game. Eric and I met across the board rather often in the 1980s (one encounter is given in *John Nunn's Best Games*), but I had not faced him for over a decade.

In the Winawer French, Black gives up his dark-squared bishop to damage White's pawn-structure. In this game, which is a Classical French, Black also gives up his dark-squared bishop, but this time without doubling White's pawns. This certainly sounds like a bad deal, and indeed I find the whole idea slightly dubious. Even though White cannot immediately exploit Black's weakened dark squares, the ever-present possibility of a dark-square bind restricts Black's options. An opposite-coloured bishop position soon results, but with White clearly better as all his pieces are more active than their enemy counterparts. Tempted by Black's time-trouble, I committed the error of trying to force matters straight away rather than increasing the pressure more slowly. Black, however, missed his best chance at move 29 and was soon in a dire situation.

Game 44
J. Nunn – E. Lobron
Bundesliga 2001/2
French Defence, Classical Variation

1	e4	e6

A second surprise. I recalled Eric's preference for the Caro-Kann and the Sicilian, and I was unable to remember any game in which he had played the French. However, in ten years it is of course possible to learn a new opening.

2	d4	d5
3	♘c3	♘f6
4	e5	♘fd7
5	f4	c5
6	♘f3	♘c6
7	♗e3	cxd4
8	♘xd4	♗c5
9	♕d2	a6

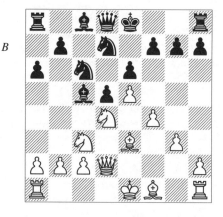

At the time, this line was quite topical, with many leading grandmasters adopting one side or the other. Theoretically speaking, White's results in the standard variations after 10 0-0-0 had not been too impressive, so I decided to play a less common idea. Since Lobron was not a regular French player, I could always hope that an unusual line might prove confusing.

10	g3 *(D)*	

Although it had been played a few times before, this move came into prominence as a result of the game Kasparov-Shirov, Astana 2001 (although the move-order was slightly different in that Black had played ...0-0 instead of ...a6). I suspected that Kasparov wouldn't be playing 10 g3 regularly, but I reasoned that even if he plays it only once, it can't be a really stupid move. The idea is to reserve the option of castling on either side, at least for the moment. The bishop may appear poorly placed on g2, since it is staring at the securely defended d5-pawn, but in any case it is not easy to find a good square for this bishop and it often ends up clumsily placed. At least on g2 it does not block the central files, which then become available for the white rooks. Despite its adoption by the World No. 1, 10 g3 has not really caught on in the years since this game. It simply isn't sharp enough to give White an advantage against accurate play.

10	**...**	**0-0**
11	**♗g2**	

White can still castle on either side, but he is more likely to castle kingside, since he has spent two tempi on g3 and ♗g2 and otherwise these moves would be wasted.

11	**...**	**♗xd4**

11...♘xd4 12 ♗xd4 b5 is the most popular line, and indeed this solid continuation looks like Black's best bet. After 13 ♘e2 ♕c7, for example, Black threatens to develop his light-squared bishop by ...b4, ...a5 and ...♗a6. White can only claim the faintest edge in this position.

The text-move is slightly more risky because, unless Black follows it up by an immediate ...♘xd4, White has the chance to retain his dark-squared bishop. Although this does not create an immediate problem for Black, in the long run there is the danger that Black will suffer from dark-square weaknesses.

12	**♗xd4** *(D)*

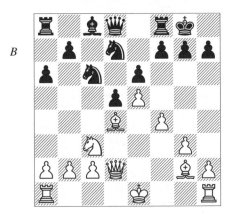

12	**...**	**b5?!**

Now White can definitely retain his dark-squared bishop. 12...♘xd4 13 ♕xd4 removes the dark-squared bishop, but then White's queen occupies an active central square. It is clear that if Black intends an eventual liquidation on d4, it is better to start with 11...♘xd4 because then

he can choose the moment for the second exchange.

12...♘b6 is probably the best continuation; after 13 b3 (13 ♗c5 ♘c4 14 ♕f2 ♖e8 gives Black active counterplay since 15 b3 can be met by 15...♕a5) 13...♘xd4 14 ♕xd4 ♗d7 Black can develop play along the c-file, which will serve to tie White down to some extent. White is still slightly better, but it will be hard to make progress.

13	**♗f2** *(D)*

Trying to punish Black for not exchanging the bishop. Now Lobron thought for quite a long time, because Black needs to generate some counterplay. In the end he decided to transfer his knight from d7 to e4, which is indeed a sensible plan. If Black doesn't act quickly, White can consolidate his position, and then the pressure he has on the dark squares will definitely give him the advantage. The game Manik-P.Balogh, Presov 2001 continued 13 0-0 b4 14 ♘e2 a5 15 ♖fe1 ♗a6 16 ♗f2, resulting in a similar type of position in which White has kept his dark-squared bishop. After the further moves 16...♕c7 17 ♘d4 ♖fc8 18 ♖ac1 ♘xd4 19 ♗xd4 ♘c5 20 ♕e3 White had retained an edge.

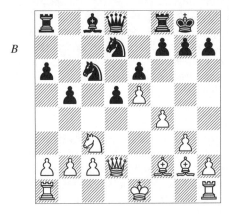

13	**...**	**♗b7**

Black decides to develop his bishop modestly. On this square the bishop will support an eventual knight transfer to c5 and e4. The alternative is to try to activate the bishop at a6. This was tested in Wittmann-Obermayr, Frohnleiten 2000, which continued 13...b4 14 ♘a4 a5 15 c4! bxc3 16 ♕xc3 ♗b7 17 0-0 ♖c8 and now 18 ♕d2 would have left White with a slight advantage.

14   0-0   ♕e7 *(D)*

Black might contemplate playing ...f6, which eliminates the cramping e5-pawn but gives White's bishops greater scope. However, in this position 14...f6 is bad due to 15 f5!? ♘dxe5 16 fxe6 d4 17 ♘d5 with some advantage for White.

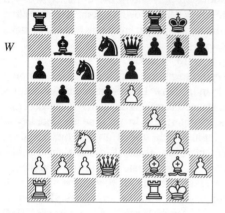

15   ♖ad1

15 a3 ♖fd8 16 ♖fe1 ♖ac8 17 b4 is a promising alternative plan designed to prevent Black's knight transfer to e4. In Gofshtein-Kern, Recklinghausen 2001 Black tried 17...♘xb4? 18 axb4 ♕xb4 but after 19 ♘e4 ♕xd2 20 ♘xd2 ♖xc2 21 ♘b3 ♖dc8 22 ♗f1 ♔f8 23 ♗d4 ♔e7 24 ♗d3 his active rook was driven back, leaving White with a large advantage. In this line we can see how White's dark-square pressure can be a long-term irritation for Black.

15   ...   ♖fd8

15...♘c5 (15...f6 fails to 16 ♘xd5) looks bad on account of 16 ♗xd5, but then 16...♖fd8 17 ♕e3 ♘a4 18 ♗xc6 ♗xc6 19 ♘xa4 bxa4 gives Black drawing chances in view of the opposite-coloured bishops and White's weak king position. In fact, White might be better off replying 16 a3, followed by b4, as in the note to White's 15th move.

The text-move is designed to rule out any tactical tricks on d5, and thus prepare the knight manoeuvre to e4. White has to consider how to react to this. I decided just to allow the knight to come to e4, playing instead to maintain control of the blockading square d4.

16   ♘e2   ♘c5
17   ♘d4   ♘e4

Both sides have executed their plans.

18   ♕e2

Just at this moment Black could have taken the dark-squared bishop, although then White would have a slight advantage thanks to his better bishop. However, having spent so much time manoeuvring his knight to e4, it is not surprisingly that Black does not want to exchange it immediately. He could have made this exchange at move 12 without any effort, and to play it now would be an admission that he had made the wrong choice earlier.

After the text-move, Black always has to take into account the possibility of White playing ♗xe4.

18   ...   b4 *(D)*

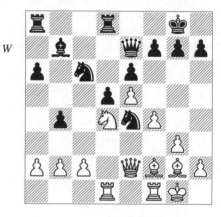

19   ♗e3?!

Once again, White plays to keep his bishop. His only real plan is at some stage to play ♗xe4, and then try to exploit the weak dark squares on Black's queenside. Of course, this plan requires a good deal of care as if it goes wrong White could easily be mated along the long light diagonal. Hence White moves the bishop to a square where it will blockade the e4-pawn if White exchanges on e4 later, and thus prevent Black from opening the long diagonal. However, this move is too cautious and wastes time. White should have preferred the immediate 19 ♗xe4 dxe4 20 ♘b3, with a slight advantage. Although his bishop isn't on e3, there isn't really much danger of White being mated on the long diagonal. After 20...♕c7 21 ♘c5 ♘e7 22 ♖d6, for example, Black is under pressure.

19   ...   ♖ac8?!

Black commits an inaccuracy in turn; the rook isn't particularly useful on c8, and the tempo spent moving it there would have been better used trying to activate Black's bishop, thereby exploiting White's loss of time on the previous move. It follows that 19...a5 is correct, with good chances for equality.

20 ♘b3

Thanks to Black's previous move, White doesn't have to take immediately on e4 and he can first improve the position of his pieces. Now the bishop's diagonal from e3 to a7 is open and, after a later ♗xe4, the knight or bishop can come to c5, or White can play ♗b6, depending on circumstances.

20 ... ♕c7 *(D)*

The best defence, preventing the bishop from going to b6. 20...a5 is no longer possible, since 21 ♗b6 ♖d7 22 ♗xe4 dxe4 23 ♖xd7 ♕xd7 24 ♖d1 ♕e7 25 ♘c5 gives White tremendous pressure.

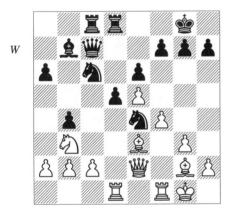

21 ♗xe4

White has no more useful preparatory moves and must take the plunge.

21 ... dxe4

22 ♕c4

White has an edge and Black must take care. A good outcome for White would be the exchange of all the major pieces. Then White would be able to attack Black's queenside pawns with his minor pieces, and bring his king to e3 to attack the e4-pawn. Despite the opposite-coloured bishops, Black would be in considerable difficulties in a pure minor-piece ending.

22 ... a5

Supporting the weak b4-pawn, but allowing White's pieces further inroads on the queenside. 22...♕b8 is bad in view of 23 ♘c5, but

perhaps Black should have activated his pieces at the cost of a pawn by 22...♖d5 23 ♖xd5 exd5 24 ♕xd5 ♘e7. After the further moves 25 ♕d6 ♘f5 26 ♕xc7 ♖xc7 27 ♗c5 a5 White would not find it easy to exploit his extra pawn.

23 ♕b5

White has a definite advantage and it is not easy for Black to find a good defensive plan. Moreover, Black had used a lot of time and now faced the likelihood of time-trouble.

23 ... ♖xd1?

Black attempts to solve his problems by tactical means, but it turns out that the liquidation of all the rooks helps White. He should have preferred 23...♖d5, which is similar to the previous note, or the more solid 23...♕b8.

24 ♖xd1 ♖d8

This is based on a tricky idea but in fact it only increases White's advantage.

25 ♖xd8+ ♕xd8 *(D)*

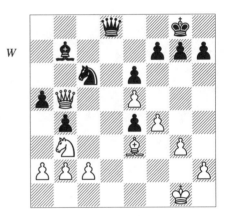

26 ♔f2!

Black had pinned his hopes on the perpetual check after 26 ♕xb7 ♕d1+, but this simple move kills Black's counterplay, leaving him in a very passive position.

26 ... ♕c8

The key line is 26...♕d1 (26...♗a8 27 ♕b6 is similar to the game) 27 ♘d2 (stopping the check on f3) 27...♕h1 (Black has to go for counterplay because otherwise he simply loses a piece; 27...♗a8 28 ♕a6 doesn't help) 28 ♘f1 ♕f3+ 29 ♔e1 and now that the fun's over, Black loses at least one piece on the queenside. After the move played, White has a large advantage because Black's queenside pawns are vulnerable and White's pieces can penetrate on the weak dark squares. There is no real danger of perpetual check.

> 27   ♘c5   ♗a8
> 28   ♕a6

An awkward move to meet.

> 28   ...   ♕d8

Lobron plays to keep the queens on. The alternative is 28...♕xa6 29 ♘xa6 ♘e7! (after 29...♔f8 30 ♗c5+ the king cannot move to e8) and Black still has some drawing chances, but clearly this is a very unpleasant position.

> 29   ♘d7?! (D)

White tries to force a decision in Black's time-trouble, but this move gives Black an unnecessary chance. The correct plan was 29 ♘b3 h5 30 ♘d2, aiming to transfer the knight to d6 without giving Black counterplay by taking the e4-pawn. After 30...♘e7 31 ♕d6 ♕e8 32 ♕b6, for example, Black is in serious trouble.

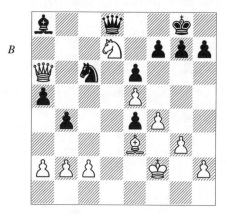

The move played is objectively inferior, but in time-trouble it would have been very hard for Black to find the only possibility to give him a chance of a draw.

> 29   ...   b3?

Black misses his opportunity. 29...h6! (not 29...♘e7 30 ♗b6 and White wins the pawn on a5) was the right idea, the point being that after 30 ♘b6 ♕d1 31 ♕xa8+? ♔h7 White cannot avoid a draw. Therefore White would have to play 31 ♕e2 ♕d8 32 ♕d2, with an ending similar to that arising in the note to Black's 28th move.

> 30   axb3   ♘b4

At the cost of a pawn, Black has activated his knight. However, White retains his powerful dark-square grip.

> 31   ♕d6

Threatening ♘f6+, so Black has no time to take the pawn on c2.

> 31   ...   ♕c8

31...♕e8 32 c3 ♘d3+ 33 ♔g1 should also win for White.

> 32   c4

This is useful because it controls the d5-square.

> 32   ...   ♘d3+ (D)

32...♗c6 33 ♘c5 ♘c2 34 ♔e2 h6 35 ♗d2 ♕a8 36 ♔d1 is also winning for White.

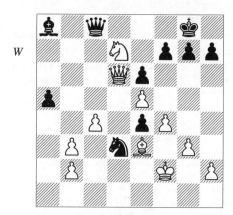

> 33   ♔g1?!

A slip which makes life harder for White. 33 ♔e2! is much simpler, since after 33...h5 (33...♗c6 34 ♘c5 ♘xc5 35 ♕xc5 ♕d8 36 ♗d4 h6 37 ♔e3 also wins for White) 34 ♘b6 ♕e8 35 ♘xa8 ♕xa8 36 f5! exf5 37 e6 fxe6 38 ♕xe6+ ♔h8 39 ♕xf5 White wins comfortably.

> 33   ...   ♗c6!

Black finds the only chance. 33...♘xb2? 34 ♘b6 ♕e8 35 ♘xa8 ♕xa8 36 c5 is an easy win, because with the king on g1 Black has no checks (this was the reason for my choice of square at move 33). White also wins after 33...h6 34 f5 exf5 35 e6 ♗c6 (35...fxe6 36 ♕xe6+ ♔h8 37 ♗d4 is decisive) 36 ♗d4.

> 34   ♘b6

The defect of having the king on g1 is that it does not control e1, and so after 34 ♘c5 ♘e1 Black's knight reaches f3, which looks as if it might provide some counterplay. However, even in this case White should win by 35 ♗d2 ♘f3+ 36 ♔f2 ♘xh2 37 ♗xa5, followed by the exchange of queens, as then White's queenside pawns would be unstoppable.

| 34 | ... | ♛e8 |
| 35 | ♕c7 (D) | |

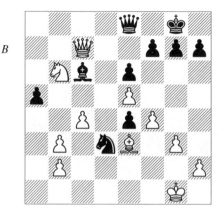

Now there is a deadly threat of ♘c8, followed either by ♘e7+ or ♕xc6, so Black doesn't have time to take the pawn on b2.

| 35 | ... | h5?? |

Black doesn't notice the threat and loses at once. 35...f5 was the only chance, threatening ...♕h5 followed by perpetual check. White

should still win, although accurate play is required: 36 exf6 gxf6 37 g4! (37 ♕d6? ♕h5 38 ♕xe6+ ♔g7 39 g4 ♕h3 leads to a draw) and now:

1) 37...♘e1 forces White to continue accurately:

1a) 38 ♘c8 ♕d7 39 ♕xd7 (39 ♕xc6? ♕d1 is a draw) 39...♗xd7 favours White but is not totally clear in view of the opposite-coloured bishops.

1b) 38 ♔f2! ♘d3+ (38...♘c2 loses to 39 ♘c8) 39 ♔g3, with an extra pawn and strong pressure for White, should win in due course.

2) 37...♘xb2 38 f5! exf5 39 ♗d4, threatening both 40 ♗xb2 and 40 ♗xf6, leaves Black without a satisfactory defence.

| 36 | ♘c8 | |

Threatening both 37 ♘e7+ and 37 ♕xc6. Material loss is inevitable.

| 36 | ... | ♕d7 |

This loses a piece, but there was no hope in any case; for example, 36...♗a8 37 ♘d6, followed by ♕xa5, is an easy win.

| 37 | ♕xc6 | 1-0 |

I ended the 2001/2 Bundesliga season with the excellent score of 9½/12 and Lübeck once again took the Championship. The 4NCL finished shortly after the Bundesliga and on the final weekend at the start of May I scored two draws and the following interesting win.

The opening of this game must set some sort of record for weird chess. After 16 moves, seven of White's pieces are on their original squares, while six of Black's are also on the back rank! Contemporary opening play involves dealing with the concrete problems of each position and rejects being bound by general principles; despite the bizarre position, both sides have played quite logically. Perhaps encouraged by the eccentric position, White decides to sacrifice a pawn for a central breakthrough. However, in view of White's lack of development this seems like a risky idea at best. White wins the exchange, but at the cost of both time and the complete disappearance of his pawn centre. Compensation which is based on both a lead in development and open lines in the centre is likely to be very dangerous, and so it proves. White's king gets trapped in the middle and is subjected to a deadly onslaught.

Game 45

P. Wells – J. Nunn

British League (4NCL) 2001/2

Trompowsky Opening

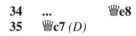

| 1 | d4 | ♘f6 |
| 2 | ♗g5 | |

Julian Hodgson has been playing the Trompowsky for as long as anyone can remember and his efforts have almost single-handedly led

to a whole generation of players adopting the opening, at least on a part-time basis. A line which was once dismissed as a harmless eccentricity is now regarded as a 'proper' opening. Not surprisingly, this has led to a considerable body of theory building up in the Trompowsky – perhaps putting off some people who were originally attracted to the opening precisely because of the lack of theory.

2   ...   ♘e4

Of course, Black can play a wide range of normal developing moves, such as 2...c5, 2...d5, 2...g6 and 2...e6, but this move, at once attacking White's bishop, is the most direct challenge to the Trompowsky.

3   ♗f4

3 ♗h4 is also playable, although in this case White must be prepared to enter the sharp line 3...c5 4 f3 g5 5 fxe4 gxh4, which current theory suggests is satisfactory for Black. Julian Hodgson has tried the eccentric 3 h4 on a few occasions, but this idea can't really be recommended. After 3...c5 4 dxc5 (4 d5 ♕b6 5 ♘d2 ♘xg5 6 hxg5 g6 7 e4 d6 also gives White no advantage) 4...♘a6 5 ♘d2 ♘axc5 6 ♘gf3 d5, followed by ...f6 and ...e5, Black achieves a pleasant position in which the move h4 looks totally out of place.

3   ...   c5 (D)

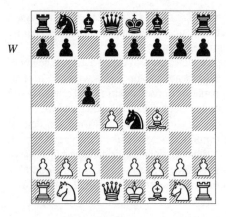

4   f3

White has an important alternative in the odd-looking 4 d5 ♕b6 5 ♗c1 (5 ♘d2 ♕xb2 6 ♘xe4 ♕b4+ 7 ♕d2 ♕xe4 gives White some play for the pawn, but not really enough), which aims to push Black's pieces back with gain of time. After 5...e6 (if Black wants to avoid transposing to the game, then he should try 5...g6 6 f3 ♘d6 with an unclear position) 6 f3 ♘f6 7 c4 we have transposed to the game, although with the move numbers differing by one.

4   ...   ♕a5+

4...♘f6 is possible, although White need not go in for 5 d5 ♕b6 since he has an interesting alternative in 5 dxc5, which offers him fair chances of an advantage.

5   c3   ♘f6 (D)

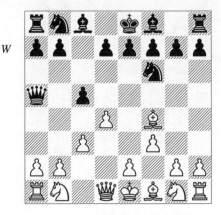

Now the way splits.

6   d5

6 ♘d2 cxd4 7 ♘b3 is an important alternative. There is quite a lot of theory on this position, but in my view Black's best line is the rarely-played 7...♕d8 8 cxd4 a5! (8...d5 is solid and reliable, but not very exciting); for example, 9 e4 (9 a4 gives away the b4-square) 9...a4 10 ♘d2 a3 11 b3 e6 12 ♗d3 ♘c6 and Black's access to b4 gives him satisfactory play.

6   ...   ♕b6

An important finesse. Just at the moment it is rather awkward for White to defend the attacked b2-pawn, so this move forces a concession.

7   ♗c1

The alternatives are:

1) 7 ♕d2? falls into a trap which has claimed several victims: after 7...♘xd5! Black wins material for insufficient compensation.

2) 7 b3 e6 8 e4 and now:

2a) 8...♗d6 is met by 9 ♗g5 (but not 9 e5? ♘xd5).

2b) 8...exd5 9 exd5 ♗d6 10 ♗g5 ♗e7 11 c4 and now the best line for Black is probably 11...♕d6! (threatening 12...♕e5+) 12 ♕e2 ♘c6! and the knight reaches d4, solving Black's main problem in this line, the development of his b8-knight.

7   ...   e6

This leads to a type of Benoni position. Black can also simply develop by 7...g6 8 e4 d6, after which the position resembles more a King's Indian.

8 c4 *(D)*

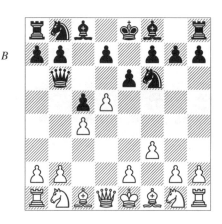

8 ... exd5

Black has several alternatives here:

1) 8...♕b4+ is risky. After 9 ♗d2!, both 9...♕xb2 10 ♘c3 and 9...♕xc4 10 e4 give White good play for the pawn.

2) 8...♗d6 9 e4 ♗e5 is a curious idea; Black intends ...♗d4 and ...e5 to develop his bad bishop outside the pawn-chain. I find this plan rather unnatural, but there isn't enough evidence to offer a firm verdict.

3) 8...g6 is a promising move. The idea is to delay the exchange on d5 so as to avoid giving White's knights access to the c4-square. After 9 e4 d6 10 ♘c3 ♗g7 Black has fair play, since he can always exchange on d5 later if he wishes.

9 cxd5 d6

9...♗d6 has also been played in this position, but here it has considerably less point since Black cannot support the bishop with ...e5 after ...♗e5-d4.

9...c4 is the most common move; Black is prepared to sacrifice a pawn in order to activate his dark-squared bishop. After 10 e3 ♗c5 11 ♔f2 0-0 12 ♗xc4 ♖e8 Black has considerable pressure for the pawn, but whether it is really sufficient is hard to say.

10 e4

We have reached a typical Benoni structure with the slightly unusual feature that Black's queen is on b6 instead of d8.

10 ... g6 *(D)*

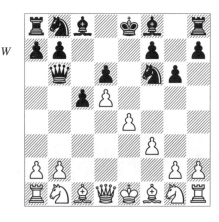

11 ♘a3!?

An interesting and original plan, trying to exploit the position of Black's queen. The main alternative is 11 ♘c3, when the position should be compared with that arising from the standard line 1 d4 ♘f6 2 c4 c5 3 d5 e6 4 ♘c3 exd5 5 cxd5 d6 6 e4 g6 7 f3. The only difference (apart from the move-number!) is that Black's queen stands on b6 rather than d8. Normally one would expect a free developing move to be an asset, but in this case matters are not so clear. The queen is not especially well placed on b6, and will probably have to retreat at some stage. Therefore the assessment is very similar to that of the analogous Benoni line, namely that White is slightly better.

11 ... ♘bd7

There isn't much choice, since the immediate 11...♗g7 fails to 12 ♘c4 followed by ♗f4, and the d6-pawn is in trouble.

12 ♘c4 ♕c7

Now Black is threatening to drive the knight away by ...b5, a move which White immediately prevents.

13 a4 ♘b6

After 13...♗g7 14 ♗f4 ♘e5 15 ♘xe5 dxe5 16 ♗e3 the pawn-structure rather favours White, who will have a ready-made attack on the queenside with ♖c1 and a later b4. Therefore Black must exchange or expel the c4-knight before playing ...♗g7.

14 ♘a3 *(D)*

This is a curious game in that both players seem determined to flout the principle that one shouldn't move the same piece twice in the

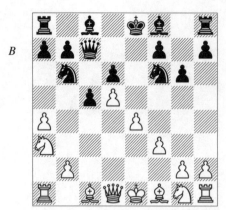

B

opening. This is the third move by White's queen's knight, to add to the three he has made with his queen's bishop (ending up on its original square!). Black also has nothing to boast about regarding his adherence to general principles, since his king's knight and queen have both moved three times. However, the fact that these moves are not in accordance with general principles does not mean that they are bad. Modern grandmasters are willing to ignore time-honoured principles if they see a good reason for doing so, and each of the moves played in the opening of this game is based on a firm logical foundation; it is only to a casual observer that they look odd. Here White retreats his knight in accordance with another principle – that the player with more space should avoid exchanges. Indeed, after 14 ♗f4 ♘xc4 15 ♗xc4 ♗g7 16 ♘e2 0-0 17 0-0 ♘d7 the exchange of knights has freed Black's position and given him a comfortable game. White therefore prefers to step backwards with his knight in order to kick the b6-knight away with a5 and then move his knight forwards again, to c4 or possibly b5.

14   ...   ♗d7

Once again Black postpones the development of his kingside. The reason is that if he has to meet a5 with ...♘bd7, then White will play ♘c4 again, restraining Black from playing ...♗g7. Nor can he play 14...♗g7 due to 15 ♘b5 followed by ♗f4, attacking the d6-pawn. The only solution is to clear c8 so that the knight can retreat there after White's a5, supporting the d6-pawn and enabling Black to play ...♗g7.

15   a5

15 ♘b5 ♕b8 will probably transpose to the game, as there is nothing better than 16 a5.

15   ...   ♘c8
16   ♘b5

The quiet 16 ♘c4 ♗g7 17 ♗d3 0-0 18 ♘e2 ♖b8, followed by ...b5, gives Black good counterplay on the queenside, so White prefers to take dynamic action.

16   ...   ♕b8 (D)

W

This position must set some sort of record. After 16 moves by both sides, White has only one piece off his back rank, while Black has just two. Indeed, White has only moved two of his pieces, occupying seven moves, while he has made nine pawn moves! Tarrasch would be turning in his grave.

17   ♗g5   ♗g7
18   e5?

White decides to sacrifice a pawn to break through in the centre. This is certainly a dangerous idea, and it leads almost by force to the win of an exchange. However, I think it is wrong as it allows Black's pieces to spring to life to such an extent that after a few moves the only question is whether White can hold the balance. Quiet play by 18 ♗d3 is more appropriate; after 18...0-0 19 ♕d2 ♗xb5 20 ♗xb5 a6 21 ♗d3 ♘d7 followed by ...b5 the position is roughly equal.

18   ...   dxe5
19   d6   0-0 (D)

The only alternative is 19...♗xb5 20 ♗xb5+ ♔f8 but after 21 d7 White's dangerous passed pawn and Black's poor king position give White tremendous play for the pawn; for example:

1) 21...♘d6 22 a6 ♕c7 23 axb7 ♘xb7 (23...♖b8 24 ♖a6! ♘xb5 25 ♖c6! is a neat variation which wins for White) 24 ♖a6 h6 25 ♗xf6 ♗xf6 26 ♘e2 ♔g7 27 ♘c3 with strong pressure for White.

2) 21...♘e7 22 a6 b6 (22...bxa6 23 ♖xa6 ♕xb5 24 d8♕+ ♖xd8 25 ♕xd8+ ♕e8 26 ♕d6 leaves Black completely tied up) 23 ♕d3 h6 24 ♖d1 ♕d8 25 ♗xf6 ♗xf6 26 ♘e2 with more than enough for the pawn.

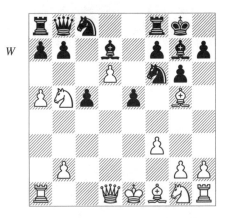

W

20 ♘c7

Forced, or else Black wins the d6-pawn by playing ...♗xb5. Now White gains the exchange, but at a heavy cost. Black will secure at least one and possibly two pawns for the exchange, and White is still three moves away from castling.

20 ... ♘e8

A difficult decision. Black's problem is that he doesn't want to leave the knight on c7 longer than necessary, as White might simply complete his development and only then take the exchange. The text-move forces the immediate capture on a8, which is to Black's benefit, but at the cost of withdrawing another piece to the back rank. 20...♖d8 was the main alternative, hoping to force ♘xa8 without losing time retreating the knight. In my view both lines lead to an advantage for Black, but the text-move is more forcing and clear-cut.

21 ♘xa8 ♘exd6 (D)

Black is of course happy to see the advanced d-pawn disappear, but it will now take him another move to capture the trapped a8-knight. White can use this time either to catch up with his development or to win the c5-pawn.

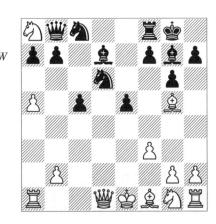

W

However, White faces a fundamental problem to which there isn't really a solution. If he plays to develop his pieces, then Black will consolidate his position and have two pawns for the exchange. Since, in addition, the position is one which favours minor pieces rather than rooks (there is only one open file, and this is easily blocked by a piece occupying the outpost on d4, for example by ...♘f5-d4), Black would then have the advantage on purely positional grounds. However, if White goes for the c5-pawn, then he remains far behind in development, and when Black opens the e-file with ...e4 White will be subjected to a dangerous attack. Neither option is very tempting, and White soon ends up with a clear disadvantage.

22 ♘e2

White decides to play for development. The following lines, while not exhaustive, give some idea of the problems White faces if he adopts the other plan:

1) 22 ♖c1 ♕xa8 23 ♖xc5 ♗c6 and the coming ...e4 will be very dangerous for White; for example, 24 ♕d2 e4 25 ♗e2 ♖e8 26 ♔f1 ♘f5 27 fxe4 ♘d4 with a strong attack for Black.

2) 22 ♕c1 ♕xa8 23 ♕xc5 e4! (D) (playing for the attack is correct; it is wrong to continue 23...♘f5 24 ♗d3 ♘d4 25 ♘e2! ♘b3 26 ♕c7 ♘xa1 27 ♕xd7, when Black has regained the exchange but at a heavy cost – after 27...♘b3 28 ♕d5 ♘d4 29 ♘xd4 exd4 30 0-0 White's two bishops and active pieces give him more than enough play for the pawn) and now:

2a) 24 ♕c7 ♗c6 and then:

2a1) 25 ♖d1 ♗e5 26 f4 ♗xb2 27 ♖xd6 ♘xd6 28 ♕xd6 ♗c3+ 29 ♔f2 e3+ 30 ♔xe3

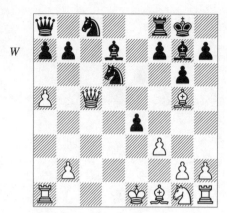

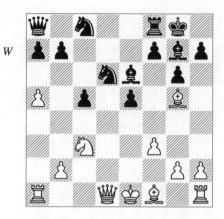

♖e8+ 31 ♗e7 (31 ♔f2 ♗e1#) 31...b5 with a winning attack.

2a2) 25 0-0-0 b6 26 ♗e2 (26 ♖xd6? ♘xd6 27 ♕xd6 exf3 wins for Black) 26...h6 27 ♗f4 ♘b5 28 ♕b8 ♕xb8 29 ♗xb8 ♘d4 is clearly better for Black.

2b) 24 ♖d1 b6 25 ♕c7 (both 25 ♕a3 ♖e8 26 ♔f2 ♖e5 27 ♗d2 ♖d5 and 25 axb6 axb6 26 ♕a3 ♕c6 27 ♖c1 ♕d5 28 ♗f4 ♖e8 give Black a clear advantage) 25...♗c6 26 ♗e2 ♖e8 27 ♔f1 (27 ♔f2? loses to 27...♗e5!) 27...♘b5 28 ♕f4 ♘d4 with a strong initiative for Black.

22   ...   ♗e6

Black wisely delays capturing the trapped knight because 22...♕xa8 23 ♗e7! ♘xe7 24 ♕xd6 ♕e8 25 ♕xc5 gives White more defensive chances thanks to the exchange of minor pieces (although even here Black has an edge after 25...♘c6). However, 22...♗c6 was a good alternative to the text-move, aiming for ...e4 at some stage.

23   ♘c3   ♕xa8 (D)

Now Black has two pawns for the exchange and if he is allowed to consolidate then he will be up on both material and position. Therefore, White tries to disturb Black's position, although this is rather a forlorn hope given White's poor development.

24   ♗e3

After 24 ♘d5 ♕b8 (24...b5 is also promising) 25 ♘f6+ (after 25 ♖c1 f6 26 ♗e3 b6, followed by ...♖d8 and ...♘f5, Black is clearly better) 25...♔h8 26 h4 e4! 27 fxe4 (27 f4 ♘e8! 28 ♘xe4 f6 29 ♘xc5 ♗f5 traps the g5-bishop) 27...♘e8 28 ♕f3 ♕e5 29 ♘xe8 ♖xe8 30 ♗e2 ♘d6 Black will end up with two pawns and an active position for the exchange.

24   ...   c4

Saving the c4-pawn. Since Black now has two pawns for the exchange, he need only bring his queen back into play by ...♕b8-c7 to claim a large advantage.

25   ♗c5

White tries to make something of the pin on the d6-knight before Black can consolidate. This plan doesn't meet with success, but it is hard to suggest a better alternative.

25   ...   ♕b8

26   ♘e4 (D)

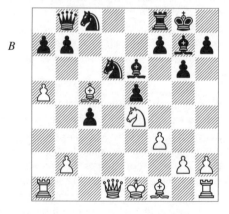

26   ...   ♘xe4!

The simple 26...♖d8 27 ♕d2 b6 28 axb6 axb6 29 ♗b4 ♕c7 30 ♖d1 ♘b7 is also very good for Black, but the text-move is more energetic. Black offers a second exchange to step up his initiative.

27   fxe4

Wisely, White declines. After 27 ♗xf8 ♗xf8 28 fxe4 ♗b4+ 29 ♔f2 ♘d6 30 ♕c2 ♕d8 Black's minor pieces are extremely strong and

White's king is doomed by the dark-square weaknesses.

27 ... ☖e8?!

Black suddenly suffers from an unnecessary outbreak of caution. The text-move proves good enough, but the simple 27...♕c7! 28 ♗xf8 ♗xf8 would have given Black a deadly attack; for example, 29 ♗e2 (29 ☖a4 ♘d6 does not help White) 29...♗b4+ 30 ♔f1 ♘d6 31 ♗f3 c3 and wins.

28 ♕a4

28 ♗xc4 ♗xc4 29 ♕a4 fails to 29...b5 30 axb6 ♘xb6 31 ♗xb6 ☖c8 32 ♕xa7 ♕d6 33 b3 (or 33 ♔f2 ♕d2+ 34 ♔g1 ♗h6, followed by ...♗d3, with a winning attack) 33...♗b5 34 ☖f1 ♕c6 35 ♔f2 ♗xf1 36 ♔xf1 ♕xe4 and the extra pawn is enough to win.

28 ... ☖d8

29 ♗xc4

Otherwise ...♘d6 consolidates.

29 ... ♕c7! *(D)*

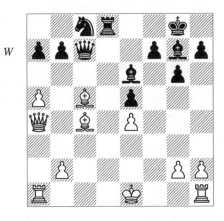

The key point. Black's queen returns to the game and skewers the white bishops.

30 ♗xe6

Forced.

30 ... ♕xc5

31 ♗d5

Trying to block the d-file, but Black breaks through in any case. The alternative was 31 ♗xf7+ ♔xf7 32 ♕b3+ ♔e7 33 ☖f1 (after 33 ♕xb7+ ☖d7 34 ♕b3 ♕d4 35 ♕c2 ♘d6 Black wins easily), but after 33...♘d6 34 a6 b5 Black not only consolidates his extra material but even takes over the initiative himself.

31 ... ♕e3+

32 ♔f1

32 ♔d1 ♘e7 is even worse.

32 ... ♘e7 *(D)*

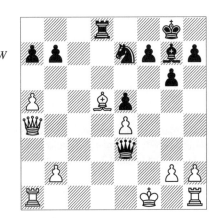

White's situation is hopeless, as his king is trapped in the centre and both rooks are still on their original squares. The immediate threat is 33...♘xd5 34 exd5 ☖d6.

33 ♕a3

The alternatives also lose:

1) 33 ☖d1 ♘xd5 34 ☖xd5 (or 34 exd5 ☖d6) 34...☖c8 (Black has an overwhelming attack) 35 ☖d1 ♗f8 followed by ...♗c5 winning easily.

2) 33 ♕c2 ♘xd5 34 exd5 ☖xd5 35 ☖e1 ♕f4+ 36 ♕f2 ♕b4 also gives White no hope of survival.

33 ... ♘xd5

34 exd5 ♕f4+

35 ♔e2

35 ♕f3 ♕c4+ 36 ♔e2 ♕xd5 is hopeless as Black's attack gathers strength after ...☖d6 or ...e4.

35 ... ♕e4+

35...☖c8 is even simpler, as Black wins after 36 ♕d3 e4 or 36 ♕b3 ☖c4.

36 ♔f2

White tries to keep his rooks connected. After 36 ♔f1 ♕c4+ 37 ♔f2 ♕c2+ 38 ♔f1 e4 the end is not far off.

36 ... ☖c8

Now the black rook enters the attack. By this point Black has several routes to victory; for example, 36...♕c2+ transposing to the previous note.

37 ♕f3

37 ☖ac1 loses to 37...☖xc1 38 ☖xc1 ♕f4+, so this is forced.

37	...	♛d4+
38	♔g3	

Or 38 ♔e1 ♖c2 39 ♖d1 ♛b4+ 40 ♔f1 e4 41 ♛e3 ♛c4+ 42 ♔g1 ♗h6 and Black wins.

| 38 | ... | e4 |

Now the black bishop joins in with gain of tempo.

39	♛e2 *(D)*	
39	...	♖c2!
	0-1	

A neat finish. After 40 ♛xc2 (40 ♛e1 ♛d3+ also mates in a few moves), Black mates by 40...♛e3+ 41 ♔g4 h5+ 42 ♔h4 ♗f6#.

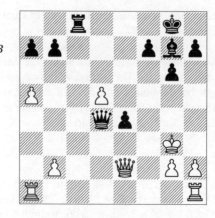

My score of 5/7 in the 4NCL was also very satisfactory and Beeson Gregory took the title for the second year in a row. Unfortunately, this was to be my last appearance in the 4NCL. The Beeson Gregory team lost its sponsorship and most of its top players, so there seemed little point in taking part the following season. Thus for the 2002/3 season my chess was virtually reduced to playing in the Bundesliga. My only other chess was the traditional visit to Bunratty in February 2003, where I shared in a large tie for first place on 4½/6.

Lübeck, having taken the Bundesliga title the previous two seasons, were looking for a hat-trick. The Lübeck team was remarkable because it almost looked like the English national squad, with Adams, Speelman, Hodgson, Conquest and myself all playing regularly. There were no German players in the team, a fact which caused some controversy and led to calls for a restriction on foreign participation in the Bundesliga.

The following game was important in deciding the Bundesliga. This year the contest was basically between Porz and Lübeck. Earlier in the season, Lübeck beat Porz in their individual match by 5-3; after this, Porz could only hope that Lübeck would slip up and indeed this almost happened when Lübeck played Baden Oos. A loss in this match would have let Porz draw level with Lübeck. Shirov, playing for Lübeck, lost to Dautov, while six games were drawn. However, the following game enabled Lübeck to draw the match and so maintain a one-point lead over Porz, which they kept until the end of the season.

In this game White's opening play is inconsistent: he cannot decide whether to attack or to play positionally. The consequence is that Black emerges from the opening with a comfortable position. However, encouraged by a small slip from Black, White regains the thread of the game and starts to develop slight pressure. The crucial phase occurs at moves 27-31. In this minor-piece ending, Black's repeated reluctance to play the move ...f5 costs him dearly. Pushing the f-pawn looks ugly because it both blocks in Black's bishop and cedes White a potential outside passed pawn. However, sometimes one must probe deeper into a position and not be guided by what 'looks' right. If concrete calculation shows that the visually repugnant move is correct, then play it! When White threatens to create an outside passed pawn on the queenside as well, it is all over.

Game 46
J. Nunn – L. Keitlinghaus
Bundesliga 2002/3
Scandinavian Defence

1	e4	d5		3	♘c3	♛a5
2	exd5	♛xd5		4	d4	c6

5   &c4   &f5
6   &d2

The main point of delaying ♘f3 is to be able to play g4 in some circumstances. Even though White did not make the most of his chances in this game, I feel this is quite a promising plan.

6   ...   e6

After 6...♘f6 7 ♘d5 ♕d8 8 ♘xf6+ gxf6 9 c3 e6, White can exploit the delayed development of his king's knight to play 10 ♘e2 followed by ♘g3, which is slightly awkward for Black.

7   g4

The other way to give this line independent significance is to play 7 d5 cxd5 8 ♘xd5 ♕d8 9 ♕e2, with interesting complications which might be quite favourable for White.

7   ...   &g6 (D)

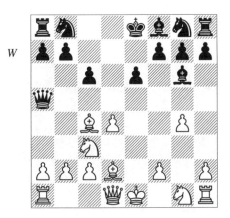

8   ♕e2

There is quite a range of interesting options for White here. 8 h4, 8 ♘ge2 and 8 d5 are all playable, but perhaps the most dangerous alternative is 8 ♘h3!?, intending to play the knight to f4.

8   ...   &b4

This is the best move since 8...♘f6 (8...&xc2 is risky as 9 d5 gives White a very strong attack) 9 f4 &e7 10 f5 exf5 11 g5 ♘h5 (after 11...&h5 12 ♘f3 ♘fd7 13 ♘b5! White has a dangerous attack) 12 0-0-0 is very unpleasant for Black – his king is trapped in the centre and his pieces lack coordination.

9   f4

This seems to me the most logical follow-up to White's previous move. 9 0-0-0 is playable and might transpose into the game after 9...♘e7 10 f4. I also considered 9 ♘h3, which was

played in a game Baklan-Sjödahl, Bundesliga 1999/00, where White gained the advantage after 9...♘e7 10 ♘f4 ♘d7 11 0-0-0 0-0-0 12 h4 h5 13 g5. However, it seemed to me that Black might be able to play ...&xc2 at move 9 or 10, and therefore I cautiously decided on a line which did not allow ...&xc2.

9   ...   ♘e7

9...&xc2 is not possible here due to 10 ♖c1 &a4 11 f5 with a massive attack.

10   0-0-0   ♘d7 (D)

With White's kingside pawns already on the move, the natural place for Black's king is on the queenside. As an example of how easily Black can go wrong here, suppose Black plays 10...♕c7?!. Then 11 f5! exf5 12 gxf5 &xc3 (12...&xf5 13 &xf7+ ♔xf7 14 ♕c4+ leads to a position with equal material but with Black's king stuck in the centre) 13 &xc3 &xf5 14 ♘f3 gives White a crushing attack; Black can't even play 14...0-0 due to 15 &b4 ♖e8 16 ♖he1 winning material.

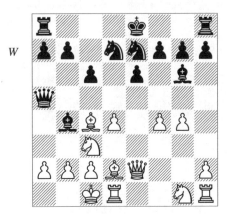

11   ♘f3?

Having started off aggressively with moves such as g4 and f4, White suddenly suffers from an attack of timidity and decides simply to complete his development. The result of this inconsistent play is that Black more or less equalizes within a few moves. 11 a3 is more natural; after 11...&xc3 (11...&xa3 12 f5 exf5 13 ♘a2 is good for White as Black doesn't get enough compensation for the piece) 12 &xc3 ♕c7 13 f5 exf5 White can try:

1) 14 gxf5 &xf5! (after 14...♕f4+? 15 ♔b1 ♕xf5 16 ♖e1 White had a massive attack for the pawn in Perez-Vazquez, Havana 1999 and

went on to win quickly) 15 ♖e1 ♘b6 16 ♗b4 ♘xc4 17 ♕xe7+ ♕xe7 18 ♖xe7+ ♔d8 and here a draw was agreed in Alvim-Dijksman, IECC e-mail 1999, but Black may even be slightly better.

2) 14 ♖e1! and now:

2a) 14...♘f6 15 gxf5 ♗xf5 16 ♗b4 ♗e4 (16...♕f4+ 17 ♔b1 0-0-0 18 ♗xe7 ♖xd4 19 ♖f1 ♕e4 20 ♗xf7! favours White as 20...♕xh1 loses to 21 ♗xf6 gxf6 22 ♘f3 and the queen is trapped) 17 ♗xe7 ♔xe7 (17...♕xe7 18 ♗d3 and White wins a piece) 18 ♕f3 ♔f8 19 ♖xe4 ♘xe4 20 ♕xe4 with a large advantage to White.

2b) 14...♕f4+ 15 ♔b1 ♗e4 16 gxf5 (White's attack persists into the endgame) 16...♕xe2 17 ♘xe2 ♘xf5 (17...♗xf5 18 ♘f4 is even worse) 18 ♘g3+ ♔d8 19 ♘xf5 ♗xf5 20 ♖hf1 g6 21 ♗xf7 with an unpleasant position for Black in view of White's two bishops and lead in development.

2c) 14...♘b6! (the best defence) 15 ♗b3 (15 ♗b4 0-0-0 16 ♗xe7 ♖xd4 is unclear) 15...fxg4 16 ♗b4 ♘bc8 17 ♕xg4 0-0 18 h4 and White has a dangerous attack in return for the pawn.

11   ...   ♕c7 (D)

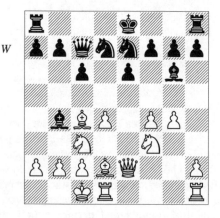

12   ♘e5

This rather uninspiring move is clearly not going to give White much, but after his error on the previous move he cannot hope for a great deal. Perhaps the best line is 12 f5 exf5 (12...♗xc3 13 ♗xc3 exf5 14 ♖he1 is very good for White) 13 gxf5 ♗h5 (13...♗xf5 14 ♗xf7+ ♔xf7 15 ♕c4+ is excellent for White) 14 ♘e4 ♗xd2+ 15 ♖xd2 (15 ♘exd2 tries to prevent castling, but after 15...♘b6 16 ♖he1

♘xc4 17 ♕xc4 ♗xf3 18 ♘xf3 0-0 White has only an edge) 15...0-0-0 16 ♘g3 ♗xf3 17 ♕xf3, but even here White has only a slight advantage; for example, 17...♖hf8 18 ♕g4 g6 19 ♖e1 ♘f6 20 ♕h4 ♘ed5 and Black's position is solid.

12   ...   0-0-0

Black's king reaches safety.

13   a3   ♘xe5

13...♗a5 was also good, keeping White guessing about the exchange on e5.

14   dxe5   ♗a5

The opening is over. Black has managed to develop all his minor pieces, and the open d-file indicates that major-piece exchanges are not far off. White's only remaining hope lies with his space advantage on the kingside and the slight weakness of the d6-square.

15   ♕f2 (D)

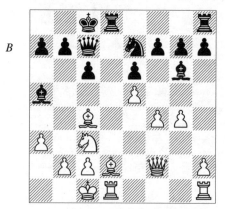

After a lacklustre opening, White tries to make the most of his remaining faint edge.

15   ...   ♗b6?!

The attack on the a7-pawn is more awkward than it might appear, but here Black could have equalized by playing 15...♔b8! 16 ♗e3 b5 (16...a6 is impossible due to 17 b4) 17 ♗c5 ♔a8! (17...♗xc3? 18 ♗d6 ♖xd6 19 exd6 ♕a5 20 dxe7 bxc4 21 ♕f3! wins for White) 18 ♗b3 (18 ♗d6 ♕b7 does not help White) 18...♗xc3 19 bxc3 h5 20 h3 ♗e4 and White has no advantage.

16   ♗e3

Now White can claim an edge.

16   ...   ♖xd1+

It is hard to put one's finger on a single mistake by Black, but he gradually drifts into an inferior ending. I think that at some stage (here, for example) he should have played ...h5 as after White's h3 the exchange of h-pawns would reduce the impact of White's kingside space advantage.

17	♖xd1	♖d8
18	♖xd8+	♕xd8 *(D)*

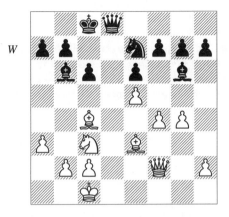

Now Black is ready for ...♗xe3+ followed by ...♕b6, with a likely draw.

19   ♗c5!

In my book *Secrets of Practical Chess*, I introduced the term 'collinear move' to describe a move such as this, in which two opposing pieces face each other, and one slides along the line of attack without capturing the enemy piece. For some reason such moves are very easy to overlook.

19   ...   ♗xc5

Black thought for a long time, but eventually decided to go into an inferior ending. It is true that otherwise he has trouble finding a constructive move; for example, 19...♘d5? is met by 20 ♗xd5 cxd5 21 ♘b5 with a large advantage for White. If Black just waits, White can improve his position with moves such as b4 and possibly ♘a4.

20   ♕xc5   b6?!

20...♔b8 followed by ...♘c8 may look passive but is better than the faulty text-move.

21   ♕f2?!

Missing a good chance to secure a clear advantage. 21 ♗a6+! was stronger since after 21...♔b8 (forced, as 21...♔d7? 22 ♕d6+ ♔e8 23 ♗b7 c5 24 ♘b5 and 21...♔c7? 22 ♘b5+ ♔b8 23 ♕d6+ ♕xd6 24 exd6 both win for White) 22 ♕d6+ ♔c7 (22...♕xd6 23 exd6 ♘d5

24 ♘xd5 cxd5 25 ♔d2 is promising for White as Black's king is sealed out of the game) 23 ♘e2 ♗e4 24 ♘d4 White has strong pressure.

21   ...   b5

Black aims to force the exchange of queens, but at the cost of a slight weakening of his queenside pawn-structure. It might have been better for Black to have taken his last chance to play ...h5 since White's reply prevents this move.

22	♗e2	♕b6
23	♕xb6	axb6 *(D)*

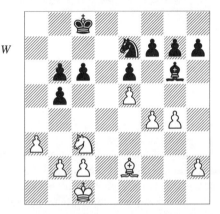

This ending differs from the one Black was aiming for at move 18 in one small but important detail – his pawn is on b5 rather than b7. This has a number of undesirable effects. Firstly, Black's queenside pawn-mass is immobilized so long as any white piece is attacking b5; secondly, the c6-pawn is weak and can be put under pressure by ♗f3; finally, White has the long-term possibility of making an outside passed pawn on the queenside (for example by c4, forcing ...bxc4, and then a4 and b4). However, despite all these potential slight advantages, the position remains drawish and there is no question that with accurate play Black should hold the game.

24   ♔d2

24 h4 h6 would lead to play similar to the game.

24	...	♔d7
25	♗f3	f6

A good move. Black must try to weaken White's grip.

26   exf6

A tough decision, as 26 h4 also looked promising. However, after 26...h6 27 h5 ♗h7 28

♘e2 fxe5 29 fxe5 c5 I don't see a way forward for White so the move played appears more accurate.

| 26 | ... | gxf6 |
| 27 | h4 (D) | |

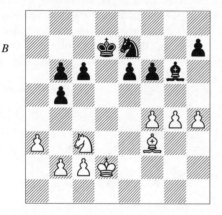

The possibility of an outside passed pawn on the kingside looms nearer.

| 27 | ... | h6 |

Black seeks to prevent h5 followed by g5. In a position such as this, mistakes often take the form of incorrect plans rather than isolated wrong moves. Such incorrect plans are often the result of a player not appreciating some important nuance in the position. Here the key point is that if White is allowed time to improve his position then Black will eventually fall into serious difficulties. Black must therefore take action, even if this involves playing a move which at first sight appears anti-positional. White's main asset is his kingside pawn-formation, and Black should have taken steps to break it up by playing ...f5. This move appears ugly because it puts a pawn on a light square and blocks in Black's bishop, but it was essential to secure squares for Black's pieces. Of course, ...f5 seriously weakens e5, but White's knight is far away from this square and therefore Black will have time to force through ...e5 and liquidate the weakness. Black could have played ...f5 at virtually any point over the next few moves, and it is his reluctance to play this move which is the real problem, rather than an individual move to which one can assign a question mark. The immediate 27...f5 is perfectly good; after 28 h5 (28 g5 ♚d6 is similar) 28...♗f7 29 g5 (29 ♚e3 fxg4 30 ♗xg4 ♘f5+ is safe for Black)

29...e5! 30 ♚e3 ♚d6 it is hard to see any way for White to make progress.

| 28 | h5 | ♗h7 |
| 29 | ♗e4 | |

Aiming to drive away Black's bishop, and so free the white king to advance to e3. White certainly has an advantage, but with correct play Black could still have held on.

| 29 | ... | ♗g8 |

But now Black is flirting with danger. It wasn't necessary to bury his bishop on g8, because he could have continued 29...f5! (not 29...♗xe4? 30 ♘xe4 e5 31 fxe5 fxe5 32 g5 and the outside passed pawn gives White a large advantage) 30 ♗d3 e5! 31 ♚e3 (31 fxe5 ♚e6 32 ♘e2 ♚xe5 33 c3 c5 is safe for Black, while 31 g5 hxg5 32 fxg5 ♚e6 leads to a position similar to that in the note to Black's 30th move) 31...e4 32 ♗e2 ♚e6 and White cannot make progress.

| 30 | ♗d3 (D) | |

Black was certainly threatening 30...f5, so White steps back with his bishop.

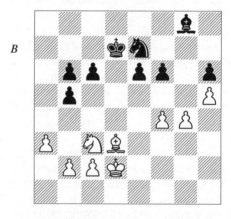

| 30 | ... | ♚e8?! |

Black decides to transfer his king to the kingside in case White creates a passed pawn there, but this plan leaves his queenside pawns weak. Black cannot exchange knights; for example, 30...♘d5 31 ♘xd5 exd5 32 ♚e3 ♚e6 33 g5 hxg5 34 fxg5 fxg5 35 h6 ♚e5 36 ♚f3 with a winning position for White, since if Black counterattacks with his king, then White plays his king to g7 and makes a whole queen. However, 30...f5! was still the correct defence. After 31 g5 hxg5 32 fxg5 e5 33 ♚e3 ♚e6 White's pawns are 'outside' and more advanced than Black's, but still it is hard to see how to make any progress. Without the support of White's minor pieces, his pawns cannot force their way through.

31   ♘e4 (D)

Objectively speaking, this move, played in Black's time-trouble, was probably the best chance to win. The alternative was 31 ♔e3 but even here 31...f5! 32 g5 hxg5 33 fxg5 e5, followed by playing the king back to e6, should be enough to draw.

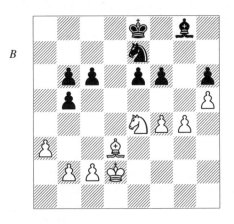

31   ...   ♔f7?

After this mistake it's all over. 31...♘d5! was correct, when after 32 g5 Black may try:

1) 32...f5 is possible but double-edged. The main line runs 33 gxh6 fxe4 34 ♗xe4 ♘f6 35 ♗xc6+ ♔f7 36 ♗xb5 (36 ♔c3? ♗h7 37 ♔b4 ♗xc2 38 ♔xb5 ♘d5 is risky only for White) 36...♗h7 37 a4 ♘xh5 38 b4 ♘xf4 39 a5 bxa5 40 bxa5 and Black still needs to take care, although it must be a draw with good defence.

2) 32...♔e7! is safest, when 33 ♘xf6 (33 gxh6 ♘xf4 is at least equal for Black) 33...♘xf6 34 gxf6+ ♔xf6 35 ♗e4 c5 leads nowhere for White.

32   ♘d6+

Black's king switch to the kingside has left his queenside too exposed.

32   ...   ♔g7
33   c4! (D)

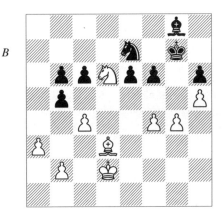

All Black's pieces are far away so White starts some queenside action. Black cannot cope with this while his pieces are so passively placed.

33   ...   bxc4
34   ♗xc4   c5?!

Black tries to give his knight a square, but simply loses a pawn. However, other moves do not help because Black's knight is immobilized and so his king cannot return to the queenside. The alternatives are:

1) 34...b5 35 ♗b3 e5 36 ♗xg8 ♔xg8 37 fxe5 fxe5 38 ♘f5 and White wins.

2) 34...♘d5 35 ♗xd5 exd5 (35...cxd5 36 ♘c8) 36 b4 b5 (36...♔f8 37 a4 ♔e7 38 ♘f5+ wins for White) 37 ♘f5+ ♔h7 38 ♘d4 and the pawns start to drop off.

35   ♘e8+   1-0

Since after 35...♔f7 36 ♘c7 Black loses his e-pawn without repairing any of the defects of his position.

My score of 11½/15 was one of my best-ever results in the Bundesliga. I was all set to play again for Lübeck in the 2003/4 season, but about a month before the first match came news that the team had lost its sponsor. The circumstances surrounding this are still not entirely clear, but it put the whole team in a very unfortunate position. They were all registered to play for Lübeck, and under Bundesliga rules this meant that they could not play for another club in the 2003/4 season. This was especially disappointing to me because it was the only chess I was playing. As my chess activities had been winding down for several years, and with my 50th birthday not far off, this seemed like a good place to retire, at least from international play.

It is perhaps worth explaining this decision in more detail, because it is true that many grandmasters continue playing in their fifties and some exceptional talents, such as Viktor Korchnoi, carry on into their seventies. My decision to retire was based on a combination of factors, of which two are most important. The first is that although it is possible to continue playing after 50, most grandmasters suffer a decline of form after this age. If you look at the results of Ribli, Timman and Andersson, for example, all of whom were at one time in the world elite, their ratings in early 2005 were 2602, 2607 and 2579. The decline of playing strength with advancing years is, I think, not to do with a decreased understanding of chess, but more to do with practical effects. It does become harder to concentrate for long periods, oversights become more frequent, and tiredness sets in more quickly. Eyesight often deteriorates, and this is made worse by all-too-common problems such as poor lighting in the tournament hall. Unfortunately, changes in the organization of tournaments have exacerbated these difficulties. Rest days have become less frequent and in many cases have disappeared completely, while time-limits have become faster. All this adds up to a good deal of disappointment for older players who see their ratings steadily decline. The second reason is frustration at the direction the chess world is taking, but for more on this, see the chapter on the state of the chess world (page 270).

In 2004 the only chess I played was at Bunratty, where I tied for second place with 4½/6, but later in the year I had a success in another field. I had long been interested in chess problem-solving and over the years I had taken part in various national and international events. At times, however, my interest in problem-solving would wane and years would go by without any events. Although I had won the British Championship three times, my highest place in the world championship had been second. I used the extra time available as a result of dropping over-the-board play to undertake some problem-solving training, ready for the world championship to be held in Greece during September 2004. This obviously worked, because I won the world championship and helped Britain gain the silver medals in the team event (unlike over-the-board play, it is a 'British' team rather than an 'English' one). In addition, I gained a grandmaster title for solving, based on the world championship and my two previous norms from 1978 and 1990. It must be unusual to gain a title based on results over as long a period as 26 years! In addition to over-the-board play and problem-solving, I believe there are two other chess grandmaster titles available, for correspondence play and for problem composition, and who knows, maybe one day I will be tempted to go for one of these!

In 2005 I played rather miserably at Bunratty, scoring 4/6, but my problem-solving activities once again provided some success. In June, Britain gained the silver medals in the inaugural European Solving Championship and I came fourth in the individual event. Later in the year the World Solving Championship took place again, and this time Britain won the gold medals, while I secured bronze medals in the individual. In addition I won the Open Solving Championship. Although I had lost the individual world championship, I was delighted at the performance of the British team (the other members were Jonathan Mestel and Michael McDowell).

It is with a distinct feeling of sadness that I conclude this final volume in my collection of best games. My 40 years of tournament play have left me with many fond memories of chess and chess-players. Although I will no longer be active on the international circuit, I am still involved in the chess world, both through my problem-solving activities and via Gambit Publications.

Studies

My interest in endgame studies was sparked at an early age when I borrowed a book from my local public library. This book was *The Tactics of End-Games* by Jeno Ban (Corvina Press, 1963), which sounds like a textbook on endgames, but is in fact an introduction to endgame studies written for the over-the-board player. I would still recommend this book to an over-the-player who is interested in endgame studies; the carefully chosen examples are sharp and to the point, and can be understood without following lengthy analysis. I was immediately captivated by the extraordinary tactical ideas to be found in endgame studies and read the book avidly. From this point on, although I was primarily interested in the over-the-board game, I would solve studies I found in magazines and would periodically try composing studies myself. This was primarily for my own entertainment; although several did eventually appear in print, many other efforts remained unpublished until now.

For this section, in addition to presenting my published studies, I have gone through my dusty old notebooks and searched out my hitherto unpublished studies. In order to be complete, I have included all my unpublished studies that are analytically sound. Some of these are perhaps not of especially high quality, especially those composed as a teenager, but they accurately reflect my tastes at the time – single, sharp lines involving mate or stalemate.

In my three volumes on 5-man endings (*Secrets of Rook Endings*, *Secrets of Pawnless Endings* and *Secrets of Minor-Piece Endings*) there are a large number of positions marked as 'Original' which arose from my work with the 5-man databases. Some of these undoubtedly qualify as excellent studies, but I have decided to exclude all of them apart from the handful which were entered in study tourneys. Anyone who takes an interest in such database-derived studies can easily find them in the above-mentioned books and therefore there seems little point in repeating them here.

The group of studies 16-19 was composed with the aid of computer databases. I sent them off to various study tourneys to see what the judges involved would make of them. In most cases they were evaluated together with the traditionally composed studies, although one judge gave a 'Special Honourable Mention' to distinguish the study from those composed without computer assistance. In the roughly 15 years since, the topic of what I will call DASC (database-assisted study composition) has become a highly controversial issue, with strong feelings being aroused. There is a wide spectrum of views on DASC, ranging from the view that DASC studies should be segregated into special events, to their full acceptance on an equal basis to traditionally composed studies.

The arguments in favour of segregation for DASC studies may be summarized as:

1) DASC is so different from traditional methods of study composition that you cannot fairly judge the products in the same category.

2) DASC is unfair in that some composers will have access to the latest databases while others will not. Relegating DASC studies to separate events at least ensures a level playing-field in non-DASC study tourneys.

However, I do not agree with these arguments and I feel that DASC and traditional studies should be judged side by side in the same tourneys. Regarding the first argument above, there is no doubt that the techniques of DASC are very different from those of traditional composing. There is a general perception that databases make study composing easy. Indeed, there are even programs which will mine databases for long series of unique moves, so some people think you just switch it on and out pop studies one after the other. However, the reality is quite different. It may be easy to create a sound study with DASC, but to create a worthwhile one is another matter altogether. Unfortunately, a number of studies have been published recently which look as if they have been taken more or less at random from databases. The solutions consist of a long series of not especially exciting moves, and the study just trails off without any particular point at the end. Another typical feature of such studies is that the moves are hard to understand and are often backed up by large quantities of complex and obscure analysis. Clearly such studies, lacking in all positive qualities except for soundness, should not be honoured by judges. However, other recent DASC studies are quite the opposite, and feature sharp, pointed solutions which are readily understood without a computer. In these cases the composer has made a valuable discovery and found a hidden gem. There seems to me no reason why such studies should not be honoured. Finding such positions is by no means easy, even with a database, but even if it is less time-consuming than traditional composition, I don't see that this matters. Surely artistic merit should be measured not in man-hours but in the impact of the final work.

The 'level playing-field' argument also seems to me to carry little weight. Computers are helpful in study composition not only because they provide access to databases. Playing programs such as *Fritz*, when run on modern hardware, are invaluable not only for checking the soundness of studies, but also for sometimes suggesting extraordinary ideas which might form the basis of a future study. Once you have started banning things there doesn't seem any obvious place to stop. It is inevitable that those who have access to the best tools are more likely to produce a better result – it is the same in any field of human activity. To try to limit the whole study world to a kind of lowest common denominator is unwise and counter-productive.

My own view is that the process by which a study is created is immaterial to any estimation of its worth. Nobody would judge an architecture award on the basis of the type of scaffolding used; only the final product is relevant. It is better to have confidence in the ability of judges to distinguish the valuable from the worthless, rather than impose arbitrary and restrictive rules. Contemporary judges need to be aware of the special features relating to DASC, and should only honour DASC studies if the composer has found something of genuine value.

A further problem for those who wish to remove DASC studies from tourneys is that the scope of databases is steadily widening, and more and more positions will be caught by a restriction on DASC studies. Many study enthusiasts, and especially those who are over-the-board players, value studies with few pieces since lightweight compositions usually have more natural positions and are more relevant to the over-the-board game. Databases already encompass a wide range of 6-man positions, and in February 2005 the results of the first 7-man database arrived on my desk by e-mail. Many studies with 7 or 8 men depend in some measure on the evaluation of database positions. If study enthusiasts are really committed to popularizing endgame studies amongst over-the-board players, they should embrace DASC studies rather than approach them as one would a venomous spider.

In 1999 I spent some time working on king and pawn endings. The theory of these endings is quite extensive, but much of it is concentrated in certain limited areas. Positions with few pawns have of course been analysed in detail, and the theory of corresponding squares, which arises in positions with blocked pawns, has also been deeply investigated. However, there has been relatively little effort expended on game-like positions with several mobile pawns. The reason is, of course, that such positions are often very hard to analyse. The book *Secrets of Pawn Endings* by Müller and Lamprecht (Everyman, 2000) was a notable attempt to push the boundaries outward, especially in the chapter 'Complicated Cases', which tackled a number of tricky over-the-board positions.

I had access to a program written by Danish programmer Lars Rasmussen which enables one to create a database for king and pawn endings with up to (about) seven pawns, although there are some limitations. Each pawn-structure requires the construction of a separate database and the program only works for certain endings, mainly those in which there are no passed pawns and the result does not depend on a queen ending. Moreover, the results are not guaranteed, so you always have to check the analysis by hand afterwards. Despite these limitations, I discovered several interesting positions and made up a story around some of them in the hope that this would prove more interesting than a dry list of positions. This was published as the *Brains of the Earth* challenge and proved quite tricky. Garry Kasparov solved all the positions, and GM Karsten Müller made just one small slip, which he quickly corrected. You may find these positions as studies 21-25 below.

Solutions may be found on pages 246-60. One further point: for the hitherto unpublished studies, the year given is the year of composition.

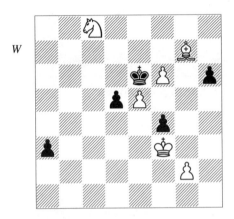

1) White to play and win
Unpublished, 1969

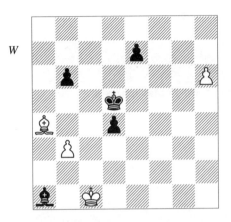

3) White to play and win
Unpublished, 1969

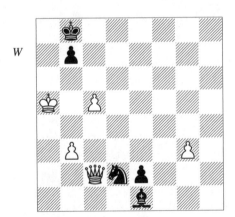

2) White to play and win
Unpublished, 1969

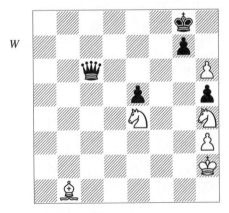

4) White to play and win
Unpublished, 1972

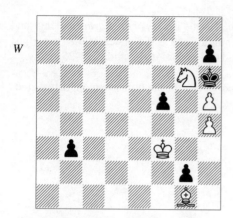

5) White to play and win
EG, 1978

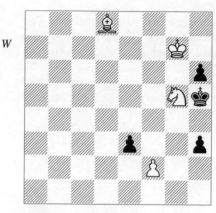

8) White to play and win
Unpublished, 1979

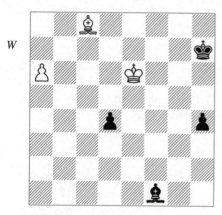

6) White to play and win
EG, 1979

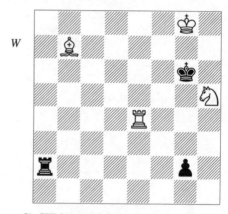

9) White to play and win
Schaakbulletin, 1982

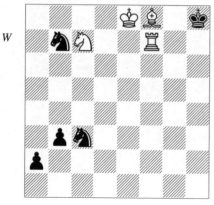

7) White to play and win
EG, 1979

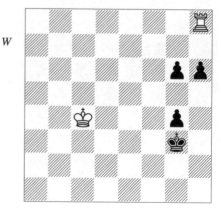

10) White to play and win
Schaakbulletin, 1982
(correction by J.Beasley, 2003)

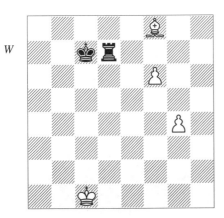

11) White to play and win
Schaakbulletin, 1983

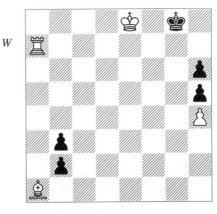

14) White to play and win
Unpublished, 1984

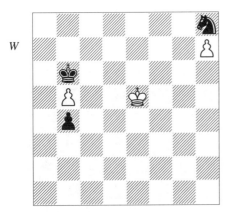

12) White to play and draw
Due Alfieri, 1983

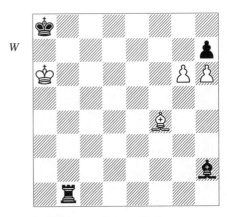

15) White to play and win
Unpublished, 1984

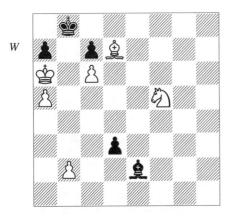

13) White to play and draw
Unpublished, 1984(?)

16) White to play and win
Commendation, *Die Schwalbe*, 1990

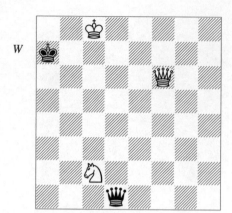

17) White to play and win
2nd Prize, *Magyar Sakkèlet*, 1991

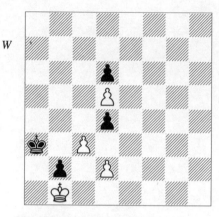

20) White to play and win
Daily Telegraph, 1994

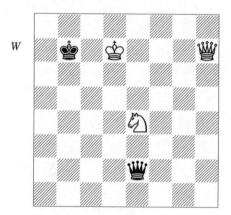

18) White to play and win
Special Honourable Mention,
Schakend Nederland, 1991

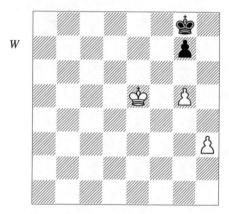

21) White to play and win
'*Brains of the Earth*', 1999

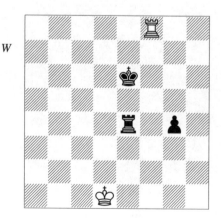

19) White to play and draw
Special Honourable Mention,
Schakend Nederland, 1992

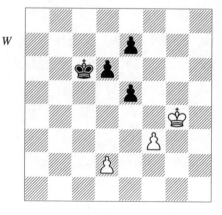

22) White to play and draw
'*Brains of the Earth*', 1999

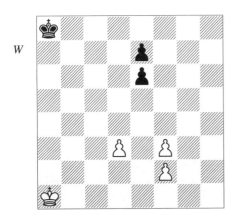

23) White to play and win
'Brains of the Earth', 1999

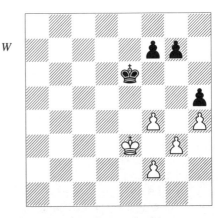

25) White to play and win
'Brains of the Earth', 1999

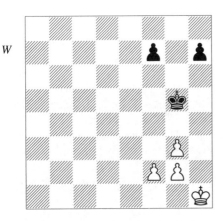

24) White to play and win
'Brains of the Earth', 1999

Solutions to Studies

1)

Here the battle rages around the long diagonal. If White can force it open then he will stop the a-pawn and win.

1 ♗h8!

The only winning move; for example:

1) 1 ♘e7? a2 2 f7 a1♕ 3 f8♕ ♕f1+ 4 ♔g4 ♕xg2+ 5 ♔xf4 ♕f2+ only leads to perpetual check.

2) 1 f7? ♔xf7 2 ♘d6+ (2 ♗h8? ♔e6 would even favour Black) 2...♔g7 3 ♘f5+ ♔g6 4 ♘d4 a2 5 ♘b3 ♔f5 6 e6 ♔xe6 7 ♔xf4 ♔f6 with an easy draw.

3) 1 ♗xh6? a2 2 f7 ♔xf7 3 e6+ ♔f6! 4 e7 a1♕ 5 e8♕ ♕f1+ 6 ♔g4 ♕xg2+ 7 ♔xf4 ♕f2+ draws.

1 ... a2

Now that White's bishop is out of range he is threatening 2 f7, so Black can only push his pawn and hope for the best.

2 f7 a1♕
3 f8♘+!

3 f8♕? loses after 3...♕f1+ 4 ♔g4 ♕xg2+ and Black either mates or wins White's queen.

3 ... ♔f5

3...♔f7 allows 4 e6+, winning the queen.

4 ♘e7+

4 ♘d6+? ♔g5 5 ♘e6+ ♔g6 6 ♘xf4+ ♔h7 7 ♗f6 is not enough to win; for example, 7...♕a3+ 8 ♔g4 d4 and the d-pawn becomes very strong.

4 ... ♔g5
5 ♘e6+ ♔h5
6 ♘xf4+

White can also play 6 g4+ fxg3 (6...♔h4 7 ♗f6+ ♔h3 8 ♘xf4+ ♔h2 9 ♘exd5 should be a win as White can escape the checks by running his king up the board; for example, 9...♕f1+ 10 ♔e3 ♕c1+ 11 ♔d4 ♕b2+ 12 ♔c5 ♕a3+ 13 ♔b6 ♕b3+ 14 ♔c7 ♕c4+ 15 ♔d8 and White is ready to push his e-pawn) and only then deliver mate by 7 ♘f4+ ♔g5 8 ♗f6# but this point does not seem of great significance.

6 ... ♔g5
7 ♗f6#

In studies it is important that the solution is essentially unique, so it is worth noting that 7 ♘h3+? ♔h5 8 ♘xd5 ♕a3+ only leads to a draw because White's pieces are not especially well coordinated.

2)

In view of the strength of Black's passed pawn, White's only winning chance is to play for a direct attack against the black king.

1 ♔b6!

1 ♕d3? fails to 1...♘xb3+ 2 ♔b5 ♗a5 3 ♕xe2 ♘d4+ 4 ♔xa5 ♘xe2 5 c6 and the result is a draw.

1 ... ♘xb3

1...♘c4+ 2 ♕xc4 ♗a5+ 3 ♔xa5 e1♕+ 4 ♔b6 ♕xg3 5 ♕f7 forces mate.

2 ♕xb3

2 ♕xe2? ♗a5+ leads to the same draw as after 1 ♕d3?.

2 ... ♗a5+
3 ♔xa5 e1♕+
4 ♔b6 ♕e8

4...♔c8 avoids mate but after 5 ♕g8+ ♔d7 6 ♕f7+ ♔d8 7 ♕c7+ ♔e8 8 ♔xb7 White has an easily winning queen-and-pawn ending.

5 ♕d5!

After 5 ♔a5? ♕e5 6 ♔b4 ♕d4+ Black draws comfortably.

5 ... ♕g6+
6 ♕d6+ ♕xd6+
7 cxd6 ♔c8
8 ♔c5

8 g4 ♔d7 9 ♔c5 is an alternative move-order.

8 ... ♔d7
9 g4

White must not delay or Black draws by pushing his b-pawn.

9 ... b5
10 g5 b4
11 g6 b3
12 g7 b2
13 g8♕ b1♕

and White mates by, for example, **14 ♕f7+**. Other checks also win; for example, White can lose time by 14 ♕g4+ ♔d8 15 ♕g8+.

3)

The first phase of the battle revolves around the diagonal a1-h8. If Black can open it so that his bishop controls h8, then Black will draw at least.

    1   **♔b1**

Gaining a tempo to transfer the king to the blockading square d3.

1	...	♗c3
2	♔c2	♗a1
3	♔d3	

3 ♗c6+? is too early since after 3...♔e6 Black can stop the h-pawn.

    3   **...**   **e5** *(D)*

W

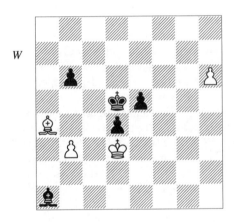

Black's only chance is to use his e-pawn to dislodge the white king from d3.

    4   **♗c6+!**

This deflection allows White to transfer his king to the more secure blockading square e4.

4	...	♔xc6
5	♔e4	

Now there is no hope of opening the long diagonal, so Black also plays to promote one of his pawns.

5	...	d3
6	h7	d2
7	h8♕	d1♕
8	♕c8+	♔b5

After other king moves Black loses his queen to a skewer.

9	♕c4+	♔a5
10	♕a4#	

4)

White's only winning chance is to play for a direct attack against Black's king.

    1   **h7+**   **♔xh7**

1...♔h8 2 ♘g5 and White wins.

2	♘f6+	♔h6
3	♘g8+	♔g5
4	♔g3	

With the deadly threat of 5 ♘f3+.

4	...	e4
5	♘f3+	exf3

King moves lose the queen to a knight fork.

    6   **h4#**

5)

White's minor pieces must struggle against Black's two dangerous passed pawns.

    1   **♗e3+**

1 ♗d4? b2 and 1 ♘f4? b2 2 ♗c5 g1♕ 3 ♗xg1 b1♕ are winning for Black.

    1   **...**   **f4!**

Or 1...♔g7 (1...♔xh5 2 ♘f4+ wins the g2-pawn with check, whereupon White's bishop can stop the b-pawn) 2 ♔xg2 hxg6 (2...b2 3 ♗d4+) 3 h6+ ♔h7 4 ♗c1 f4 5 ♔f3 ♔xh6 6 ♔g4! (not 6 ♔xf4? ♔h5 7 ♔g3 b2 8 ♗xb2 g5 drawing) 6...♔g7 7 ♔xf4 and White wins.

    2   **♘xf4**

2 ♗xf4+? ♔xh5 wins for Black.

    2   **...**   **g1♕!**

2...b2 3 ♘d3+ followed by ♘xb2 wins for White.

3	♗xg1	b2
4	♗c5 *(D)*	

B

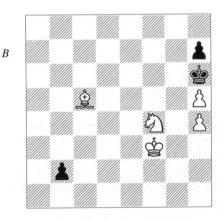

It appears to be all over for Black, but he has one trick left.

| 4 | ... | ♔g7 |

Playing for stalemate.

| 5 | ♗d4+ | ♔h6 |
| 6 | ♘e6! | |

White counters by playing for mate.

6	...	b1♕
7	♗g7+	♔xh5
8	♘f4+	♔xh4
9	♗f6#	

6)

| 1 | a7 | ♗g2 |
| 2 | ♔e5 | |

The only move. After 2 ♔f6? ♔h6 3 ♗f5 ♗a8 4 ♔e5 d3 White must even play accurately to draw: 5 ♔f4! d2 6 ♗c2.

| 2 | ... | d3 |

This offers more resistance than 2...♔g7 3 ♔xd4 ♔f6 4 ♗g4 (threatening 5 ♔e3 and 6 ♗f3) 4...♔g5 5 ♗e6 followed by ♗d5, and White wins.

| 3 | ♗f5+ | |

White must eliminate the dangerous d-pawn.

| 3 | ... | ♔g7 |

Relatively the best square for the king.

| 4 | ♗xd3 | h3 |
| 5 | ♗f1 (D) | |

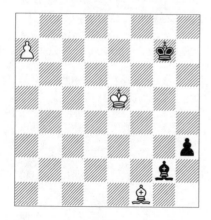

Now the bishops and pawns are mutually immobilized, so both sides are forced to manoeuvre with their kings.

| 5 | ... | ♔f7 |

With the black king on f8, g8, h8, g6, h6, g5 or h5 White wins by ♗xg2 followed by a8♕(+), so no other third move would have improved Black's chances.

| 6 | ♔d6 | |

6 ♔f4? ♔e7 draws; for example, 7 ♔g3 ♗a8 8 ♗xh3 ♔d8 9 ♗g2 ♔c7 10 ♗xa8 ♔b6 and the pawn is lost. After the text-move, Black's king is only safe on f7, g7 and h7 but sooner or later he must move outside this zone.

| 6 | ... | ♔f6 |

6...♔g7 7 ♔e7 ♔h7 8 ♔f6 ♔h6 9 ♗xg2 hxg2 10 a8♕ leads to mate.

7	♗xg2	hxg2
8	a8♕	g1♕
9	♕f8+	♔g6
10	♕g8+	

and wins Black's queen.

7)

There is an interesting story relating to this study. I was very happy with it when it was published, but soon afterwards a reader pointed out a possible drawing line for Black. At the time I was doubtful that his suggestion really did draw, but to prove a win for White seemed very difficult. Looking at it again with the aid of today's computers, I was able to prove a win so the study can once again be considered sound.

| 1 | ♘d5! | |

Threatening 2 ♘f6, mating in a few moves, or simply 2 ♗g7+. Other moves are ineffective: 1 ♗g7+? ♔g8 2 ♗xc3 ♘d6+ 3 ♔e7 ♘xf7 4 ♘d5 ♘g5 leads to a draw, while the alternatives 1 ♗e7?? ♘e4, 1 ♖f1?? b2 2 ♔f7 ♘d8+ 3 ♔g6 b1♕+ and 1 ♘e6?? a1♕ even win for Black.

| 1 | ... | ♘xd5 |

1...a1♕ loses to 2 ♗g7+ ♔h7 3 ♗xc3+ ♔g6 4 ♖f6+ followed by ♗xa1, but it is much harder to refute 1...♘e4!?, which is the reader's suggestion mentioned above. However, in the end I (with silicon assistance) found the following win: 2 ♗g7+ ♔h7 (2...♔g8 3 ♘e7+ ♔h7 4 ♗f8+ ♔h8 5 ♘g6+ ♔g8 6 ♖g7#) 3 ♔f8! (threatening 4 ♖f5 with a quick mate to follow; 3 ♘f6+? is wrong and only leads to a draw after 3...♘xf6+ 4 ♗xf6+ ♔g6 5 ♔e7 ♘d6 6 ♖g7+ ♔f5 7 ♖g5+ ♔f4 8 ♖h5 ♘e4 9 ♗b2 ♔e3 10 ♖h3+ ♔d2 11 ♖xb3 ♔c2 12 ♖b8 ♘c5) 3...♘bd6 (3...♘ec5 4 ♘f4 ♘d6 and 3...♘bc5 4 ♘f4 ♘d6 lead to the same position, in which White wins by 5 ♖c7! ♘ce4 6 ♗a1+ ♔h6 7 ♖g7 ♘f5 8 ♖g6+ ♔h7 9 ♖g2 ♘eg3 10 ♗f6) 4 ♖f4! (the immediate 4 ♖f3? is bad owing to 4...♘g5) 4...♔g6 (4...♘c5 5 ♖h4+ ♔g6 6 ♖h6+ ♔f5 7 ♘e7+ ♔e4 8 ♖xd6 and White wins) 5

♖f3! ♘f5 (now 5...♘g5 is impossible due to 6 ♖f6+, while 5...♘b7 loses to 6 ♖xb3 ♘bc5 7 ♖a3 ♘e6+ 8 ♔g8 ♘xg7 9 ♖a6+) 6 ♗a1! ♘d2 (6...♘c5 7 ♘e7+ ♘xe7 8 ♔xe7 wins for White) 7 ♖d3 winning the b3-pawn and the game.

2 ♗g7+ ♔g8

2...♔h7 3 ♗b2+ followed by ♖xb7 is winning for White.

3 ♖xb7

Black's only hope is to play for stalemate. He must sacrifice the knight before the pawns, because if he gives away a pawn first then White need not accept the knight.

3 ... ♘c7+!

4 ♖xc7 a1♕

4...b2 5 ♗xb2 a1♕ 6 ♖g7+ ♔h8 7 ♖g2+ wins for White.

5 ♗xa1 b2 *(D)*

W

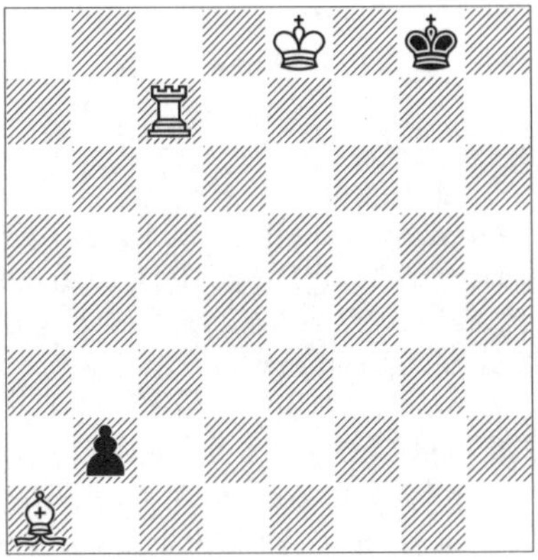

6 ♖a7!

A position of reciprocal zugzwang.

6 ... b1♕

7 ♖g7+ ♔h8

8 ♖g1+

and White wins.

8)

It isn't easy to find a good way to stop Black's pawns.

1 ♘f3!

Other moves:

1) 1 fxe3?? hxg5 2 ♗c7 ♔h4! even wins for Black.

2) 1 ♘xh3? exf2 2 ♘xf2 is stalemate.

3) 1 ♘e4? is tempting, but Black has a clever defence: 1...♔g4! (not 1...h2? 2 f3! h1♘ 3 ♘c3 forcing mate in a few moves) 2 fxe3 ♔f3 3 ♘d2+ ♔e2! 4 ♗c7 ♔xd2 5 e4 ♔d3 and White loses his pawn.

1 ... exf2

1...e2 2 ♗c7 stops the pawns.

2 ♘h2

The pawns are blockaded so Black's only hope is to play for stalemate.

2 ... f1♕

3 ♘xf1 h2

4 ♔f6!

Lifting the stalemate and so forcing Black to promote.

4 ... h1♘

Or 4...h1♕ 5 ♘g3+ and White wins.

5 ♔f5

and mate next move by ♘g3#.

9)

1 ♘g3!

Not 1 ♘f4+? ♔f5 2 ♘h3 (2 ♘e2 ♖xe2 is also a draw) 2...g1♕+ 3 ♘xg1 ♖g2+ and Black draws.

1 ... ♖a8+!

Aiming for stalemate. There are two other important defences for Black:

1) 1...g1♕ 2 ♖g4+ ♔h6 3 ♘f5+ ♔h5 4 ♖xg1 sets up a potential stalemate, but White can evade the rook checks: 4...♖a8+ 5 ♔f7! (5 ♔h7? ♖h8+ 6 ♔g7 ♖g8+ draws) 5...♖f8+ 6 ♔e6 ♖f6+ 7 ♔e5 ♖e6+ 8 ♔d4 (8 ♔f4 also wins) 8...♖e4+ 9 ♔d3 and the checks run out.

2) 1...♔g5 and now:

2a) 2 ♗c8? ♖a8 3 ♖g4+ ♔f6 4 ♘h5+ ♔e5 draws.

2b) 2 ♖e1? ♔f4! 3 ♘e4 (3 ♘h5+ ♔g5 4 ♘g7 ♔g4 and White will soon have to give up his bishop for the pawn) 3...♖e2 4 ♖g1 ♖b2 5 ♗c6 (5 ♘c5 ♔g3, 5 ♘d6 ♖xb7 6 ♘xb7 ♔g3 and 5 ♗d5 ♔e5 6 ♘c3 ♔d4 are all drawn) 5...♖c2 and White's bishop cannot escape the rook's attack.

2c) 2 ♖e7! is the way to win: 2...g1♕ (after 2...♔g4 3 ♖g7+ ♔h3 4 ♘f5 ♔h2 5 ♖h7+ ♔g1 6 ♘h4 White wins the pawn) 3 ♖g7+ and each of the black king's moves is met by a discovered attack.

2 ♗xa8 g1♕

3 ♖g4+ ♔h6

4 ♘f5+

4 ♗e4? ♕b6 and 4 ♗f3? ♕xg3 only draw.

4 ... ♔h5

5   ♖g3!

The correct square for the rook; 5 ♖g2? and 5 ♖g7? are both met by 5...♕d1 with a draw.

5   ...   ♕d1

6   ♗f3+

and White wins.

10)

1   ♔d3!

1 ♖xh6? ♔f2 2 ♖xg6 g3 and 1 ♖a8? ♔f2 draw comfortably.

1   ...   h5

The alternative 1...♔f2 also demands accurate play by White: 2 ♖f8+! ♔g2 (2...♔g3 3 ♔e2 is worse) 3 ♔e2! g3 (3...h5 4 ♖f2+ ♔g3 5 ♖f6 g5 6 ♖f5 and White wins) 4 ♖h8! h5 5 ♖h6! and the series of four 'only' moves by White has transposed back into the main line.

2   ♔e2

Not 2 ♖h6? h4 3 ♔e2 h3 4 ♔f1 ♔h2 5 ♖xg6 g3 drawing.

2   ...   ♔g2

2...h4 3 ♔f1 and White wins.

3   ♖h7!

There is a reciprocal zugzwang in the main line and White must take care that it arrives with Black to move. After 3 ♖h6? g3 it is White to play in the reciprocal zugzwang and now the position is a draw: 4 ♔e1 (4 ♔e3 ♔f1 and 4 ♖xg6 h4 5 ♔e3 h3 6 ♔f4 h2 are also drawn) 4...♔h2 5 ♖xg6 h4 6 ♔f1 h3 7 ♖g8 g2+ 8 ♔f2 g1♕+ 9 ♖xg1 stalemate.

3   ...   g3

3...♔g3 4 ♖h6 h4 5 ♖xg6 h3 6 ♔f1 wins easily, while 3...♔g1 4 ♖h6 g3 5 ♔f3 transposes to the main line.

4   ♖h6! (D)

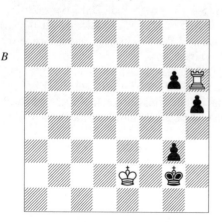

Now it is Black to play in the reciprocal zugzwang.

4   ...   ♔h2

4...♔g1 5 ♔f3 and White wins.

5   ♖xg6   h4

6   ♔f3   ♔g1

with a winning position for White; for example, 7 ♖g4 ♔f1 8 ♖a4 ♔g1 9 ♖xh4 g2 10 ♖g4 ♔h1 11 ♔f2 with a quick mate.

As originally published, White's king stood on d4, but in this case both 1 ♔d3 and 1 ♔e3 win for White. The correction was pointed out by John Beasley. This study, with its hesitating rook, is reminiscent of a famous Réti study (w♔e7, ♖d4 vs b♔e5, ♙d5, *Münchener Neueste Nachrichten*, 1928) in which White wins by 1 ♖d3! d4 2 ♖d1 or 1 ♖d2! d4 2 ♖d1, although the mechanisms involved in the two studies are quite different. My study avoids the ambiguity in the choice of squares for the rook, but has two pawns more than Réti's study.

11)

1   g5

The alternatives are inferior: 1 ♗e7? ♖xe7 2 fxe7 ♔d7, 1 ♗a3? ♖f7! 2 g5 ♔d7 3 ♗b2 ♔e6 4 g6 ♖xf6 and 1 ♗g7? ♔d6 2 g5 ♔e6 3 g6 ♔f5 4 f7 ♖d8 all lead to a draw.

1   ...   ♖f7

1...♖d5 2 g6 ♖g5 3 g7 followed by f7 wins at once, while 1...♔d8 2 g6 ♔e8 3 ♗g7 is hopeless for Black. He is restricted to moving his rook back and forth along the second rank, so White can bring his king up and win at his leisure.

2   ♗e7!

The only square to win. 2 ♗a3? ♔d7 3 ♗b2 ♔e6 draws as before, and 2 ♗g7? ♔d6 3 g6 ♖c7+ 4 ♔d2 ♔e6 (threatening ...♔f5) 5 ♗h8 ♖c8 6 ♗g7 ♔f5 is also drawn.

2   ...   ♖xe7

2...♔d7 3 g6 ♖xe7 4 g7 transposes.

3   g6

Refusing the rook.

3   ...   ♔d7

4   g7

For the second time White refuses the rook. 4 f7? ♖xf7 only draws.

4   ...   ♖e8

5   f7

White wins.

12)

White must not head for the knight immediately: 1 ♔f6? b3 2 ♗g7 b2 3 ♔xh8 b1♕ 4 ♗g7 ♕g1+ 5 ♔f7 ♕d4 6 ♔g8 ♕g4+ 7 ♔f7 ♕f5+ 8 ♔g7 ♕g5+ 9 ♔f7 ♕h6 10 ♔g8 ♕g6+ 11 ♔h8 (now Black releases the stalemate) 11...♔c5 12 b6 ♕f7 13 b7 ♕f8#.

1   ♔d4!

First of all Black must be induced to take the b5-pawn.

1   ...   ♔xb5

Black has no choice but to take the pawn, since 1...♔a5 2 ♔c4 and 1...♘f7 2 ♔c4 ♔a5 3 b6 are simple draws.

2   ♔e5!

Otherwise 2...b3 wins. White has now eliminated his own pawn on b5 which caused all the trouble after 1 ♔f6? and can now head back to h8. Even though this manoeuvre has cost White a tempo he still manages to draw.

2	...	b3
3	♔f6	b2
4	♔g7	b1♕
5	♔xh8	

followed by ♔g7/g8 and the black king will be one square outside the winning zone.

13)

The date of composition is a little uncertain as it was not given in my notebook.

The choice lies between 1 ♘g3 and 1 ♘d4. Which move is correct?

1   ♘g3!

1 ♘d4? is wrong for a rather subtle reason. After 1...♗f1 (1...d2+? 2 ♘xe2 transposes to the solution) 2 ♗g4 (2 ♘b5 d2 3 ♗g4 transposes) 2...d2+ 3 ♘b5 ♗h3 4 ♗xh3 d1♕ we reach a position in which Black can eventually force White into zugzwang and release his king from the corner, after which the win is straightforward. Play might continue 5 ♗d7 (5 ♘xa7 ♕d3+ wins the bishop) 5...♕f3 6 ♘xa7 (6 b3 ♕xb3 7 ♘xa7 ♕d3+ 8 ♘b5 ♕c4 9 ♗e8 ♔c8 and the king emerges, or 6 b4 ♕e2 7 ♗f5 ♕c4 8 ♗d7 ♕xb4 and Black rounds up the b-pawn, after which he can return to force zugzwang) 6...♕e2+ 7 ♘b5 ♕xb2 (Black's doesn't need his a-pawn in order to win) 8 ♗e6 ♕e5 9 ♗d7 ♕e2 10 ♗f5 ♕c4 11 ♗d7 (this is the key position in which Black can triangulate to give White the move) 11...♕e4 12 ♘c3 ♕d3+ 13

♘b5 ♕c4 (now White must release the king) 14 ♗e8 ♔c8 15 ♗d7+ ♔d8 and, now that White doesn't have the e8-square available for his bishop, he cannot avoid mate in a few moves.

1   ...   d2+

1...♗d1 2 b4 d2 3 ♗e6 ♗e2+ 4 ♘xe2 d1♕ 5 b5 reaches the same positional draw as in the main line.

2	♘xe2	d1♕
3	b4!	♕xe2+
4	b5	

Curiously, although White has a knight less compared to the try 1 ♘d4?, the presence of a pawn on b5 secures the draw. White just plays his bishop up and down the h3-c8 diagonal and Black cannot make progress.

14)

This is an example of a scheme for a study which never made it past the drawing-board stage.

If it were Black to play then White would win by 1...b1♕ 2 ♖g7+ ♔h8 3 ♖g1+ picking up the queen, but White has no waiting move with which he can maintain this tactic. Therefore he has to adopt a new plan.

1   ♖a2! *(D)*

A very surprising move. White needs to meet ...b1♕ with a rook check on the g-file. However, 1 ♖a5? and 1 ♖a4? don't work because g4 and g5 are covered by black pawns, and 1 ♖a6? fails because after 1...b1♕ the queen covers g6. The only viable option is to hide the rook behind the b2-pawn, waiting for Black to open it. Note that 1 ♖g7+? ♔xg7 2 ♗xb2+ ♔g6 draws easily.

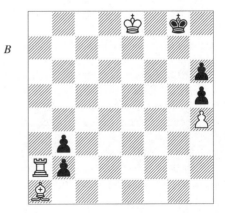

B

1	...	b1♛

After 1...bxa2 2 ♗xb2 ♚h7 3 ♚e7 (not 3 ♚f7? a1♛) 3...♚g6 4 ♚e6 White wins both black h-pawns.

2	♖g2+	♚h7
3	♖g7+	♚h8
4	♖g1+	

and wins.

Unfortunately, I was unable to find any reasonable way for the black pawns to arrive on b3 and b2 and so this idea remained just a sketch in my files.

15)

1	gxh7	

1 g7? ♖g1 2 ♗xh2 ♖g6+ 3 ♚b5 ♚b7 draws, while 1 ♗xh2? ♖b7 2 g7 ♖b6+ 3 ♚a5 ♖g6 followed by ...♚b7 leads to a similar draw.

1	...	♖b8

There is no way to stop the h-pawn, so Black plays for stalemate.

2	♗xb8	♗xb8

2...♗e5 loses to 3 ♗c7. Now promoting to queen or rook is immediate stalemate.

3	h8♘!	

3 h8♗? ♗f4! (3...♗e5? loses to 4 ♗g7) 4 h7 ♗e5 5 ♗xe5 is also stalemate.

3	...	♗f4
4	h7	♗e5

This position is a technical win, but you have to know how to do it. One line is:

5	♘g6	

5 ♘f7 also wins, but a little more slowly.

5	...	♗g7
6	♚b6	♚b8
7	♘e7	

Blocking the approach of the black king.

7	...	♗b2
8	♚c6	♗c3
9	♚d6	

Threatening 10 ♘c6+, followed by 11 ♘e5.

9	...	♗h8
10	♚e6	♚c7
11	♘g6	♗g7

The only square for the bishop, but here it provides a tempo for the white king after a later ♚f7.

12	♘f4!	

The key idea; White gets ready to transfer his knight to g7 via a tempo-gaining check on e6.

12	...	♚d8

12...♚h8 13 ♚f7 ♚d7 14 ♚g8 ♚e8 15 ♘h5 is the same.

13	♚f7	♗h8
14	♚g8	♚e8

14...♚e7 15 ♘g6+ takes the bishop with the knight.

15	♘h5	

The first key zugzwang.

15	...	♚e7
16	♘g7	

The second key zugzwang. Black's king cannot remain in contact with the f8-square, so next move White can take the bishop.

16)

1	♚d8!	

White sidesteps the dangerous queen check on g4 and puts Black into zugzwang (indeed, this is a position of reciprocal zugzwang). Other moves:

1) 1 ♚c7? (approaching the black king immediately fails to a stalemate defence) 1...♛g4 (or 1...♛e2) 2 ♛b3+ ♚a5 3 ♘c4+ ♛xc4+! 4 ♛xc4 stalemate.

2) 1 ♚d6? ♛g1! (the only move) 2 ♛b3+ ♚a5 3 ♘c4+ ♚a6 4 ♛a4+ ♚b7 5 ♘a5+ ♚b6! and White cannot make progress.

3) 1 ♛d4+? ♚b5 (1...♚a3 also draws, based on the stalemate defence 2 ♘c4+ ♚a2! and there is no mate at b2 since White's queen is pinned) 2 ♛d5+ ♚b4 draws.

1	...	♚a5

Black has few options. Most queen moves fail to 2 ♛b3+, 3 ♘c4+ and 4 ♛b6#, the exception being 1...♛g1, which runs into 2 ♛b3+ ♚a5 3 ♘c4+ ♚a6 4 ♛a4+ ♚b7 5 ♘d6+ followed by ♛b5+ and mate.

2	♚c7!	

Now that Black's king is on an inferior square White can approach with his own king. It is unusual to see a kind of triangulation in a position with heavy pieces.

2	...	♛g4

Or 2...♚a4 3 ♛d4+ ♚b5 (3...♚a3 4 ♘c4+ ♚a2 5 ♛b2#) 4 ♛c4+ ♚a5 5 ♘b3+ and White wins the queen.

3	♘b3+!	♚b4
4	♘d4+!	♚c4
5	♛b3+!	

White wins Black's queen.

17)

1 Qf2+

After 1 Qe7+? Kb6 2 Qc7+ Kb5 3 Qb7+ Kc5! 4 Qb4+ Kc6 5 Nd4+ Kd5 6 Qb5+ Ke4! 7 Qf5+ Ke3 Black manages to draw.

1 ... Ka6

2 Kc7! Qb1

The only move as 2...Kb5 costs Black his queen after 3 Qb6+.

3 Qf6+!

Not 3 Qe2+? Ka5 4 Qd2+ (4 Qe5+ Ka4 is the same) 4...Ka4 5 Qc3 Qb6+! (the only move to draw) with stalemate. The move played, returning to f6, gains an important tempo since 3...Ka7 fails to 4 Qd4+.

3 ... Ka5

4 Qc3+

4 Qc6? fails to 4...Qb8+.

4 ... Ka4 (D)

4...Ka6 5 Qc6+ Ka5 6 Qa8+ wins the queen, but after the text-move White has a position from the note to White's third move with White to play, and this gives him time to prevent the stalemate defence.

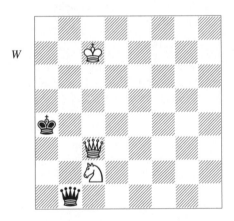

W

5 Kc8!

White can maintain the win by 5 Qa3+ or 5 Qc4+, but these moves lose time as White has to return to c3 on the following move. The position after 5 Kc8! (which returns the king to its original square) is reciprocal zugzwang.

5 ... Qb6

Forced, as 5...Qb3 6 Qa1+ loses the queen at once.

6 Qa3+ Kb5

7 Qb4+ Ka6

Or 7...Kc6 8 Nd4+.

8 Qa4+ Qa5

9 Nb4+

9 Qc6+ loses time.

9 ... Kb6

10 Qc6+ Ka7

11 Qb7#

18)

This study is fairly complicated and anyone who solved it deserved congratulations.

1 Nd6+!

1 Nc5+? Kb6! and 1 Kd6+? Ka8! only draw.

1 ... Ka6

The most resilient defence. 1...Ka7 loses to 2 Kd8 Kb6 3 Qc7+ Ka6 4 Qb7+ Ka5 5 Qb3! Ka6 6 Kc7 Qe7+ 7 Kc6, but the alternative 1...Kb6 is tougher to refute. White can win only by 2 Qf5!, which gives rise to a reciprocal zugzwang. Then 2...Ka6 (2...Ka7 3 Kc7 and 2...Qa6 3 Qf2+! Ka5 4 Qd2+ Kb6 5 Qb4+ Ka7 6 Kc7! both lead to a quick mate) 3 Kd8 and now:

1) 3...Qb2 4 Qd3+ Ka7 5 Nc8+! Kb8 (or 5...Kb7 6 Qd7+ Ka6 7 Qa7+ and White wins) 6 Qd6+ Kb7 7 Qc7+ and White wins the queen.

2) 3...Ka7 4 Kc7 Qe7+ 5 Kc6 Qg7 (5...Qe2 6 Qc5+ also mates) 6 Qa5+ mates.

3) 3...Kb6 4 Qd5 Ka6 5 Qb7+ Ka5 6 Qb3 Ka6 7 Kc7 Qe7+ 8 Kc6 also mates.

2 Qh3!

It's tempting to play 2 Qf5? but this allows Black to put White in zugzwang by 2...Kb6!; after 3 Nc8+ (3 Kd8 Kc6 escapes, while 3 Qd5 is met by 3...Qg4+) 3...Ka6 White cannot make progress.

2 ... Ka7

The toughest defence. Other moves:

1) 2...Kb6 3 Qf5! transposes to 1...Kb6 above.

2) 2...Ka5 3 Qa3+ Kb6 4 Qb4+ transposes to the main line.

3) 2...Qb2 3 Qd3+ Ka7 4 Nc8+ Kb7 5 Qd5+ Kb8 6 Qd6+ mates.

4) 2...Qe1 3 Qd3+ Ka7 4 Nc8+ also mates.

5) 2...Qd2 3 Qf1+ Ka7 4 Qb5 Qg2 5 Nc8+ and mate in two more moves.

3 Nc8+!

White wants to transfer his king to the a-file, but the immediate 3 Qa3+? Qa6 4 Qc5+ Ka8 only draws.

| 3 | ... | ♔a6 |

Other moves lead to a quick mate.

| 4 | ♕a3+ | |

4 ♘d6 maintains the win but loses time.

4	...	♔b5
5	♘d6+	♔b6
6	♕b4+	

6 ♕b3+? ♔c5 draws.

| 6 | ... | ♔a6 (D) |

A key moment. White can waste time by checking again on the a-file, but sooner or later he will have to find the far from obvious continuation...

| 7 | ♕c3! | |

This move is a big surprise, since it not only allows Black's king more freedom but also gives Black a check on g4; however, it is the only way to win. The point is to prevent Black from giving a check on the c-file after the white king moves to c7; indeed, there is an immediate threat of 8 ♔c7 ♕e7+ 9 ♔c6.

| 7 | ... | ♔b6 |

Black has nothing better than to keep the white king out. The other lines are:

1) 7...♔a7 and 7...♕f1 are both met by the threat 8 ♔c7.

2) 7...♕f2 8 ♕c4+ ♔a7 9 ♕c7+ mates.

3) 7...♕g4+ 8 ♔c7 ♕a4 9 ♕d3+ ♔a5 10 ♕d5+ ♔b4 11 ♕c4+ and White wins.

4) 7...♕h5 8 ♕a3+ ♕a5 (8...♔b6 9 ♘c4+ ♔b7 10 ♕b4+ ♔a8 11 ♘b6+ and 12 ♘c8+ mates) 9 ♕d3+ ♔a7 10 ♕d4+ ♔a6 11 ♔c6 mates.

| 8 | ♔d8! | |

Another difficult quiet move; it cuts out Black's queen check on g4 and so threatens 9

♕c7+ ♔a6 10 ♕b7+ ♔a5 11 ♕b3. Surprisingly, this is the only way to win (White can waste time but must return to this idea in the end).

| 8 | ... | ♕h5 |

The alternatives are: 8...♔a6 9 ♔c7 ♕e7+ 10 ♔c6, 8...♔a7 9 ♔c7, 8...♕g2 9 ♕b4+ ♔a6 10 ♕b5+ ♔a7 11 ♘c8+ and 8...♕f1 9 ♘c4+ ♔b7 (9...♔b5 10 ♕a5+ ♔c6 11 ♕b6+) 10 ♕b4+ ♔a7 11 ♕a5+.

| 9 | ♘c4+ | |

The vulnerable position of Black's queen allows White to launch the final assault.

| 9 | ... | ♔c6 |

9...♔a6 10 ♕a3+ ♔b7 11 ♕b4+ ♔a8 12 ♘b6+ ♔a7 13 ♘c8+ ♔a8 14 ♕a4+ ♔b7 15 ♕a7+ ♔c6 16 ♕b6+ wins the queen.

| 10 | ♘e5+ | ♔b5 |

Other moves to the b-file only lead to a quicker finish, as White can check on b4 straight away.

| 11 | ♕b3+ | ♔c5 |

Or 11...♔a6 12 ♕a4+.

12 ♕c4+ ♔b6 13 ♕b4+ ♔a6 14 ♕a4+ ♔b6 15 ♘d7+ ♔b7 16 ♕b4+ ♔c6 17 ♕b6+
White wins the queen.

19)

It is hard to believe that the only move to draw involves playing White's king away from Black's pawn, but that is indeed the case.

| 1 | ♔c2! | |

The most obvious move is 1 ♔d2? (1 ♖e8+? ♔f5 2 ♖xe4 ♔xe4 3 ♔e2 g3! wins for Black, while 1 ♖f1? ♔e5! 2 ♖e1 ♔f4 is hopeless), but then 1...♔e5! puts White in zugzwang. The variations are:

1) 2 ♔d1 g3 3 ♖f1 ♔f4 4 ♖g1 ♔f3 5 ♔e2 ♔f4 with a simple win.

2) 2 ♖f7 g3 3 ♔d3 (3 ♖f1 ♔f4 4 ♖g1 ♔f3 is similar to line '1') 3...♔g4 4 ♖e7+ ♔f6 (Black exploits the fact that White's rook has lost its checking distance) 5 ♖e1 g2 6 ♖g1 ♔g5 7 ♔e3 ♔h4 8 ♔f2 ♔h3 wins for Black.

3) 2 ♖f1 g3 3 ♔d3 ♖f4 and Black wins, as we have seen before.

4) 2 ♔d3 ♖f4 3 ♖e8+ (3 ♖g8 ♖f3+! 4 ♔e2 ♔f4 followed by ...♔g3 wins for Black) 3...♔f5 4 ♔e2 ♔g5! 5 ♖h8 (trying to stop Black's king sneaking round to g3) 5...g3 followed by ...♔g4 and Black wins.

1 ... ♔e5

Trying to cut White's king off one rank further by 1...♖d4 fails to 2 ♔c3 ♖d7 3 ♖f4! ♖g7 4 ♔d3 g3 5 ♖f1 g2 6 ♖g1 ♔f5 7 ♔e3 and the king arrives just in time.

2 ♔d2!

The crucial reciprocal zugzwang arises with Black to move.

2 ... g3

After 2...♖f4 3 ♖g8! ♔f5 (3...♔e4 4 ♔e2 draws) 4 ♔e2 ♖f3 5 ♖f8+ White can exchange rooks.

3 ♔d3 ♖g4

Or 3...♖f4 4 ♖g8 drawing.

4 ♖e8+ ♔f6
5 ♖f8+

This is the crucial difference compared to line '2' in the note to White's first move. White has an extra rank of checking distance and so he can pull the black king back to the second rank.

5 ... ♔g7
6 ♖f1 g2
7 ♖g1

followed by ♔e3 and the extra tempo allows White to draw.

20)

This was in fact the first study I ever composed, when I was just 12 years old. It finally saw the light of day in 1994, when David Norwood specially requested something simple for his chess column in the *Daily Telegraph*.

1 c4

Every other move loses.

1 ... d3

After 1...♔b4 2 d3 White wins the b2-pawn and soon the game.

2 c5 dxc5
3 d6 c4
4 d7

It's hard for White to go wrong in this phase of the study!

4 ... c3
5 dxc3 d2
6 d8♖!

and White wins on material. 6 d8♕? fails to 6...d1♕+ 7 ♕xd1 stalemate.

21)

1 ♔f4!

1 ♔f5? ♔f7 is a position of reciprocal zugzwang with White to move and is therefore a draw. The alternatives 1 ♔e6? ♔f8, 1 h4? ♔f7 and 1 ♔e4? ♔f8 also lead to a draw.

1 ... ♔f8

1...♔h7 2 ♔f5 is a simple win, while 1...♔f7 2 ♔f5! turns the reciprocal zugzwang on Black.

2 ♔g4!

Not 2 ♔g3? ♔f7 3 ♔f4 ♔e6 drawing.

2 ... ♔g8

2...g6 3 ♔f4! wins easily for White. After the text-move, White must lose a tempo to arrive at this position with Black to move. Then Black will either have to move his king to the f-file (when White plays ♔h5), move his king to the h-file (when White plays ♔f5) or push his g-pawn. In order to lose a tempo White must manoeuvre with his king.

3 ♔h5! *(D)*

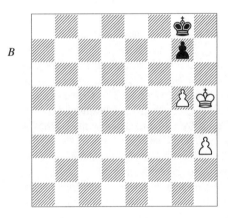

3 ... ♔h7

Or 3...♔f7 4 h4! and Black must give way, when White wins easily.

4 ♔h4

Black must meet ♔g4 by ...♔g8 and ♔h5 by ...♔h7, hence his reply is forced.

4 ... ♔h8
5 ♔g3!

White's plan is to tiptoe around the square g4 (via h4 and g3) and so threaten to come to f5 with his king. Black's king is trapped on the wrong side of the g8-square, so eventually he will be forced to play ...♔g8, but then White can reach his target position by playing ♔g4.

5 ... ♔g8

5...♔h7 6 ♔f4 ♔g8 7 ♔g4! is the same.

6 ♔g4

White has achieved his objective and Black must now make a concession.

6	...	g6

6...♔f7 is met by 7 ♔h5 and 6...♔h7 by 7 ♔f5.

7	♔f4	♔f7
8	♔e5	♔e7
9	h4	

At last White uses his reserve tempo and wins the g-pawn. It is surprising that White's king, which appeared very well placed on e5, has to move to h4 in order to secure the win.

22)

The basic principle governing this ending is that White must not allow Black to transfer his king to f8 or f7. If Black manages this, then White is gradually driven back on the kingside. Thus the white king must move up the board, to be ready to meet ...♔e8 by ♔g7. However, the route must be chosen with care as there are reciprocal zugzwangs lurking around.

1	♔g5!	

1 ♔f5? is already a fatal error, because after 1...♔d5! we have a reciprocal zugzwang with White to play: 2 ♔g6 e4 3 f4 (3 fxe4+ ♔xe4 4 ♔f7 e5 5 ♔e6 d5 is also winning for Black) 3...♔e6 4 ♔g5 d5 and Black wins. 1 ♔h5? also loses to 1...♔d5!.

1	...	♔d7

Trying to reach the kingside. 1...♔d5 2 ♔f5! is the reciprocal zugzwang with Black to play; White draws after 2...e6+ 3 ♔f6 or 2...♔d4 3 ♔e6. The alternative 1...♔c5 allows an easy draw after 2 ♔g6 ♔d4 3 ♔f7.

2	♔h6!	

It is very surprising that the king has to move away from the enemy pawns to secure the draw. The alternatives are:

1) 2 ♔f5? ♔e8! (this line illustrates what happens if Black's king is allowed to transfer to the kingside) 3 ♔e6 (3 ♔g6 ♔f8 is similar) 3...♔f8 4 ♔f5 (4 d3 ♔e8! wins for Black) 4...♔f7 5 ♔g5 e6 6 f4 exf4 7 ♔xf4 ♔f6 with an easy win.

2) 2 ♔h5? ♔e8! 3 ♔g6 ♔f8 is the same as line '1'.

3) 2 ♔g6? ♔e6! is a second reciprocal zugzwang. White to play loses after 3 d3 (or 3 ♔g5 ♔f7 4 ♔f5 e6+ 5 ♔g5 d5) 3...d5 4 ♔g5 e4 5 fxe4 dxe4 6 dxe4 ♔e5.

2	...	♔e8

After 2...♔e6 3 ♔g6! it is Black to play in the second reciprocal zugzwang. It is a draw after 3...♔d5 4 ♔f7 or 3...d5 4 d3 d4 5 ♔g5!.

3	♔g7!	

Now the position is a clear draw.

23)

It is quite hard work to exploit White's extra doubled pawn.

1	♔b2	♔b7

1...e5 2 ♔c3 ♔b7 transposes.

2	♔c3	e5

After 2...♔c6 White wins more easily: 3 ♔d4! ♔d6 4 f4! ♔c6 5 ♔e5 ♔d7 6 d4.

3	d4!	

Not 3 ♔c4? ♔c6 drawing.

3	...	♔c6

The only chance as 3...exd4+ 4 ♔xd4 ♔c6 5 ♔e5 ♔d7 6 f4 e6 7 f5 wins easily.

4	dxe5	♔d5
5	f4	♔e4
6	♔c4	♔f5

Black tries a small finesse. 6...♔xf4 7 ♔d5 transposes to the main line.

7	♔d4	

7 ♔c5 ♔xf4 (7...♔e4 8 ♔c6 ♔xf4 9 e6 also wins for White) 8 ♔d5! is just as good, transposing to the main line. However, 7 ♔d5? is wrong since 7...♔xf4 arrives at a reciprocal zugzwang with the wrong player to move; after 8 ♔e6 (8 e6 ♔f5 9 f3 ♔f6! draws) 8...♔e4! (a second reciprocal zugzwang) 9 f3+ ♔f4 White cannot win.

7	...	♔xf4
8	♔d5!	

Now it is Black to play in the reciprocal zugzwang.

8	...	♔f5

Or 8...♔f3 9 e6 and White wins.

9	f3	

Another reciprocal zugzwang.

9	...	♔g5
10	♔e4	

10 ♔c6 maintains the win, but loses time after 10...♔f5 11 ♔d5.

10	...	e6
11	♔e3!	

The last finesse. 11 f4+? ♔g4! 12 ♔e3 ♔g3! leads to a draw.

11	...	♔g6

11...♔f5 12 f4 ♔g6 13 ♔e4 is also lost.

| | 12 | f4 | ♔f5 |
| | 13 | ♔f3 | |

and White wins.

24)

In order for the solution to make sense, we must first analyse two key positions of reciprocal zugzwang.

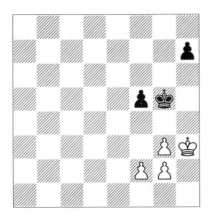

Reciprocal Z1

Black to play:

| 1 | ... | h6 |

Or:

1) 1...h5 2 f3 ♔g6 3 ♔h4 ♔h6 4 g4! hxg4 5 fxg4 fxg4 6 ♔xg4 ♔g6 7 g3 and White wins.

2) 1...♔g6 2 g4 f4 3 ♔h4 h6 4 f3 is also a win for White.

3) 1...♔h5 2 f4 is again reciprocal zugzwang, and the only reasonable move, 2...h6, then transposes to the main line.

2 f4+ ♔h5 3 g4+! fxg4+ 4 ♔g3

and White wins as Black no longer has a reserve tempo with his h-pawn.

The situation with White to play is more complex.

White to play:

| 1 | ♔h2 |

1 f3 (1 f4+ ♔h5 is now a draw as Black has the reserve tempo ...h6) 1...h5! 2 ♔h2 ♔g6 3 ♔g1 ♔f6 4 ♔f2 ♔e6! 5 ♔e2 ♔d6! (it is important to note that White cannot win with this pawn-structure unless he can gain the opposition with his king on the third rank, thereby ensuring access to f4) 6 ♔d2 ♔e6 7 ♔c3 (White

cannot hope to make progress unless he executes a by-pass at some stage) 7...♔e5 8 ♔c4 f4 and Black secures the draw.

| 1 | ... | ♔f6! |

Black must rush in order to be sure of gaining the opposition when White's king arrives on the e-file. 1...♔g6? loses to 2 ♔g1! ♔f6 3 ♔f1 ♔e5 4 ♔e1 ♔d5 5 ♔d1 ♔e5 (5...h6 deprives Black of his reserve tempo and now White can win by playing his king back to h3: 6 ♔e2 ♔e4 7 ♔f1! ♔e5 8 ♔g1 ♔f6 9 ♔h2 ♔g6 10 ♔h3 ♔g5 11 f4+ ♔h5 12 g4+! fxg4+ 13 ♔g3) 6 ♔c2 ♔e4 (6...♔d4 loses to 7 ♔d2 ♔e4 8 ♔e2 ♔d5 9 ♔f3 ♔e5 10 g4 f4 11 g3) 7 ♔c3 h6 (or else the king reaches f3) 8 ♔d2 and White wins by heading to h3 as before.

2	♔g1	♔e5
3	♔f1	♔d4
4	♔e1	

4 ♔e2 ♔e4 is similar.

| 4 | ... | ♔e5! |

Play with this pawn-structure is largely governed by the opposition. Therefore many positions with opposed kings are reciprocal zugzwang.

5 ♔d1 ♔d5! 6 ♔d2 ♔d4 7 ♔e2 ♔e4

and White cannot make progress. With the black pawns on f5 and h7 we can summarize by giving the network of corresponding squares for the kings: h3 vs g5, h2 vs f6, f1 vs d5, e1 vs e5, e2 vs e4, d1 vs d5, d2 vs d4. With White's king on g1, Black's king can be on either e6 or e5.

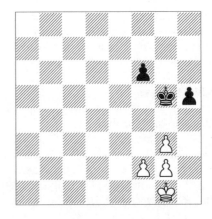

Reciprocal Z2

This is the key reciprocal zugzwang when Black arranges his pawns on f6 and h5.

Black to play:

      1 ...   **♔f5**

Or:

1) 1...♔g6 2 ♔h2 ♔f5 3 ♔h3 ♔g5 4 f4+ ♔g6 5 g4 ♔h6 6 ♔h4 hxg4 7 ♔xg4 ♔g6 8 f5+ ♔f7 9 ♔h5 ♔g7 10 g3 ♔h7 11 ♔g4! ♔h6 12 ♔f3 ♔h5 13 ♔f4 ♔h6 14 g4 ♔g7 15 ♔e4 and White wins.

2) 1...♔g4 2 ♔h2! (this position is also reciprocal zugzwang) 2...♔f5 (2...f5 3 f3+ ♔g5 4 ♔h3 ♔g6 5 ♔h4 ♔h6 6 g4) 3 ♔h3 transposes to line '1'.

      2   **f3!**

Not 2 ♔h2? ♔g4!, when the reciprocal zugzwang arises with White to play; e.g., 3 f3+ (3 ♔h1 ♔f5! is another reciprocal zugzwang) 3...♔g5! (a further reciprocal zugzwang) 4 ♔h3 (4 ♔g1 f5! 5 ♔f2 ♔f6! is a draw as White cannot gain the opposition without playing f4, but then the f4-square is not free for his king so the result is a draw in any case) 4...f5 with a fairly obvious final position of reciprocal zugzwang.

      2 ...   **♔g5**

2...♔e6 3 ♔h2! ♔f5 4 ♔h3 ♔g5 5 f4+ transposes to the analysis of 1...♔g6.

3 ♔f2 ♔f5 4 ♔e3 ♔e5 5 g4 hxg4 6 fxg4! ♔d6 7 ♔f4 ♔e6 8 g5

and White wins.

We can summarize the analysis of this position by saying that with Black's pawns on f6 and h5, play is governed by a network of corresponding squares: g1 vs g5, h1 vs f5, h2 vs g4, f1 vs f5, e2 vs e6, d2 vs d6, d1 vs d5, e1 vs e5. When the white king is on the f-file or further left, the opposition is the deciding factor, but when the king is near the h1-corner, matters are more complex.

White to play:

The play with White to move is implicit in the Black-to-move analysis.

      1   **f3**

The following lines are all in accordance with the network of corresponding squares established in the Black-to-play analysis: 1 ♔h1 ♔f5!, 1 ♔h2 ♔g4! and 1 ♔f1 ♔f5!.

      1 ...   **f5!**

This move establishes an important point. Playing f3 is ineffective if Black can set up a blockade with pawns on f5 and h5 – then White

can only win if he gains the opposition and penetrates with his king to f4. However, when his king is on g1 this is clearly impossible.

2 ♔f2 ♔f6! 3 ♔e2 ♔e6!

White cannot make progress.

We can now give the solution of the study (in the following analysis, 'Z1W', for example, means Zugzwang 1 with White to play). The position is extremely complex because the pawns are not yet fixed, and Black can still choose between various pawn arrangements. Each arrangement gives rise to a network of corresponding squares, and White is not sure which network is going to arise. This is why we started by analysing the positions in which Black has committed his pawns.

      1   **♔h2!** *(D)*

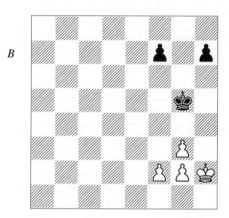

Amazing as it may seem, this is already a position of reciprocal zugzwang, although the fact that it is a draw with White to play is not relevant for the solution.

      1 ...   **f6**

This move puts up most resistance. The alternatives are:

1) 1...♔g4 2 f3+ ♔g5 3 g4! ♔h4 (3...♔f4 loses to 4 ♔h3 ♔g5 5 ♔g3) 4 ♔g1 ♔g3 5 ♔f1 and White can just wait until Black exhausts his pawn moves, and then his king will have to retreat; e.g., 5...f6 6 ♔g1! h6 7 ♔f1 ♔f4 8 ♔f2 with a simple win.

2) 1...♔f5 (1...♔g6, 1...♔f6 and 1...♔h6 lose the same way) 2 ♔h3 ♔g5 3 f4+ ♔f5 4 ♔h4 is easy.

3) 1...♔h5 2 ♔h3 (threatening g4+) 2...f5 3 f4 transposes to the Z1B analysis.

4) 1...h5 2 ♔h3 f6 (or 2...f5 3 f3) 3 f4+! transposes to the analysis of Z2B.

5) 1...h6 2 ♔h3 h5 (otherwise White wins by f4+ followed by ♔h4 or g4) 3 f4+ ♔f5 4 ♔h4 ♔g6 5 g4 hxg4 6 ♔xg4 f5+ (6...f6 is Z2B, note to Black's first move) 7 ♔f3 ♔h5 8 g3 ♔g6 9 ♔e3 and White wins.

6) 1...f5 2 ♔h3 and now 2...h6 and 2...h5 transpose into the above lines, while if the king retreats then ♔h4 followed by g4 wins. Finally, 2...♔h5 fails to 3 f4.

2 ♔h1!!

This incredible move is the only one to win. 2 ♔g1? h5! is Z2W, while 2 ♔h3? f5! is Z1W. 2 f3? f5 followed by ...h5 is a simple draw as White cannot gain the opposition on the e-file.

2 ... f5

Or:

1) 2...♔g4 3 ♔g1! h6 (3...h5 4 ♔h2! ♔f5 5 ♔h3 is the note to Black's first move in Z2B; 3...♔f5 transposes to the analysis of 2...♔g6 below; 3...f5 loses to 4 ♔f1) 4 ♔f1 and White wins.

2) 2...h5 3 ♔g1! is Z2B.

3) 2...h6 3 ♔h2 ♔g4 4 f3+ ♔g5 5 g4 and White wins comfortably.

4) 2...♔h5 3 ♔g1! ♔g5 4 ♔f1 ♔f5 5 ♔e2 (Black has no time to set up the drawn position with king on e4 and pawn on h5) 5...♔e4 6 f3+ ♔e5 7 g4 and White wins.

5) 2...♔g6 3 ♔g1 (3 g4 also wins) 3...♔f5 (3...h5 transposes into Z2B) 4 f3 h5 (or else g4+) 5 ♔f2! ♔e5 6 ♔e2 ♔d4 7 g4 hxg4 8 fxg4 ♔e4 9 g3 and Black's king is gradually driven back.

3 ♔g1! ♔f6

Black must hurry, since otherwise White's king reaches e3, with an easy win.

4 ♔f1 ♔e5

5 ♔e1!

Extreme care is necessary. 5 ♔e2? ♔e4! gives Black the opposition.

5 ... ♔d5

Black puts up the maximum resistance. We shall see later what happens if Black plays ...h6 or ...h5.

6 ♔d1!

As usual, the side with the opposition can only make progress if a by-pass is possible. Here White must choose exactly the right moment for his by-pass.

6 ... ♔e5

6...♔c5 7 ♔e2! ♔d4 8 ♔f3 ♔e5 9 g4 is a win for White.

7 ♔c2! (D)

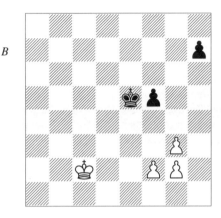

The correct moment for the by-pass.

7 ... ♔d4

7...♔e4 is met by 8 ♔c3, forcing Black to touch his h-pawn, whereupon 8...h6 9 ♔c4 h5 10 ♔c3! ♔e5 (Black has run out of reasonable pawn moves and must give way) 11 ♔d3 f4 12 gxf4+! ♔xf4 13 ♔d4 h4 14 ♔d3, gaining access to e3, gives White an easy win.

8 ♔d2 ♔e4

9 ♔e2

Now Black must move his h-pawn, or else White's king occupies f3.

9 ... h6

9...h5 10 ♔f1 also wins for White, since he has the tempo f3 in reserve to force his king to h4.

10 ♔f1!

All the manoeuvres up to now have been designed to extract the concession ...h6 from Black. Now that Black has given up his reserve tempo, White can win by playing his king to h3. We have already seen the basic winning technique in Z1B, but here it is again: **10...♔e5 11 ♔g1 ♔f6 12 ♔h2 ♔g6 13 ♔h3 ♔g5 14 f4+ ♔h5 15 g4+! fxg4+ 16 ♔g3 ♔g6 17 ♔xg4** and now White wins easily.

25)

This very natural position has a surprising solution.

1 ♔d4!

Other moves:

1) 1 ♔e4? f5+! 2 ♔d4 ♔d6 3 ♔c4 ♔c6! is a draw as Black can maintain the opposition.

2) 1 g4? and now:

2a) 1...hxg4? 2 ♔e4! g6 (2...f5+ 3 ♔d4 transposes to the main line) 3 f5+! gxf5+ (3...♔f6 4 ♔f4 wins for White) 4 ♔f4 ♔f6 5 h5 ♔g7 (5...♔e6 6 ♔g5 f4 7 ♔xf4 f5 8 ♔g5 and White wins) 6 ♔xf5 ♔h7 7 ♔xg4 ♔h6 8 f4 with an easy win for White.

2b) 1...f5!!, giving up a second pawn, secures the draw: 2 gxh5 (2 g5 ♔d5 3 ♔d3 ♔c5 draws) 2...♔d5 3 ♔d3 ♔c5 is a draw because in this position it makes no difference how many reserve tempi White has.

1 ... f6 *(D)*

The toughest defence. Other moves lose as follows:

1) 1...♔d6 2 ♔e4 ♔e6 3 f5+ ♔f6 4 ♔f4 is an easy win for White.

2) 1...g6 2 ♔c5 ♔d7 (2...♔f5 3 ♔d6 and White wins) 3 ♔d5 f6 4 ♔e4 (threatening f5) 4...f5+ (4...♔e6 loses to 5 f5+ gxf5+ 6 ♔f4) 5 ♔d5 ♔e7 6 ♔e5 ♔f7 7 ♔d6 ♔f6 8 ♔d7 ♔f7 9 f3 and the reserve tempo proves decisive.

3) 1...f5 2 ♔c5 ♔e7 3 ♔d5 ♔f6 4 ♔d6 ♔f7 5 ♔e5 g6 6 ♔d6 ♔f6 7 ♔d7 ♔f7 8 f3 and White wins.

4) 1...♔f5 2 f3! (the only move to win) 2...♔e6 3 g4! and there is no defence:

4a) 3...f5 4 gxh5 ♔d6 5 h6 gxh6 6 h5 and White wins.

4b) 3...g6 4 f5+ gxf5 5 gxh5 (5 g5 also wins) 5...♔f6 6 f4 ♔g7 7 ♔e5 ♔h6 8 ♔f6! (the f7-pawn is the important one) 8...♔xh5 9 ♔xf7 ♔xh4 10 ♔f6 ♔g4 11 ♔e5 and wins.

4c) 3...f6 4 f5+ ♔d6 5 gxh5 ♔c6 6 ♔e4 ♔d6 7 f4 ♔e7 (7...♔c5 8 ♔f3 ♔d6 9 h6 gxh6 10 ♔g4! and White wins) 8 ♔d5 ♔d7 9 h6 gxh6 10 h5 gains the opposition and wins.

2 g4!!

This move is surprising because it not only offers a pawn, but also self-destructs White's pawn-structure. However, concrete analysis always prevails over general considerations and this is indeed the only move to win. The idea is that if Black plays ...g6 White will later have the opportunity of undermining the defence of the f5-pawn by playing h5. The alternative 2 ♔c5? (2 f3? f5! is also a draw) 2...♔f5! leads to a draw:

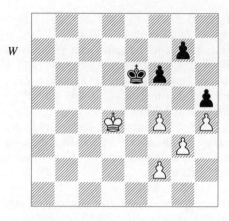

W

1) 3 f3 ♔e6! 4 ♔d4 (4 g4 g5! 5 fxg5 fxg5 6 ♔d4 draws) 4...f5! 5 ♔c5 ♔e7 6 ♔d5 ♔f6 7 ♔d6 g6 saves the game.

2) 3 ♔d6 ♔g4 4 ♔e6 transposes to line '3'.

3) 3 ♔d5 ♔g4! 4 ♔e6 (4 ♔e4 g6! 5 ♔e3 f5! 6 ♔e2 ♔h3! draws) 4...♔f3 5 ♔f7 ♔xf2 6 f5 ♔xg3 7 ♔xg7 ♔xh4 8 ♔xf6 ♔g4 and both sides promote at the same time.

2 ... hxg4

2...g6 3 f5+ gxf5 4 gxh5 ♔f7 5 ♔e3 wins for White.

3 ♔e4 f5+

The alternatives also lose:

1) 3...♔e7 4 ♔f5 ♔f7 5 ♔xg4 ♔g6 6 f5+! ♔h6 7 f3 ♔h7 8 ♔h5 and White penetrates to g6 and wins.

2) 3...g6 4 f5+! gxf5+ (4...♔f7 5 ♔f4! gxf5 6 ♔xf5 is winning for White) 5 ♔f4 is decisive. It is curious that in order to win White has to be prepared to go from being a pawn up to being a pawn down.

4 ♔d4

A position of reciprocal zugzwang.

4 ... g6

4...♔e7 5 ♔e5 g6 6 h5 mops up all Black's pawns, while after 4...♔f7 5 h5! (5 ♔e5? ♔g6! draws) 5...♔e6 6 ♔c5 ♔e7 7 ♔d5 ♔f6 8 ♔d6 White wins the vulnerable f5-pawn.

5 ♔c5

Black cannot prevent White's king from reaching e5, after which h4-h5 will break up Black's pawn-structure.

5...♔d7 6 ♔d5 ♔e7 7 ♔e5 ♔f7 8 h5! gxh5 9 ♔xf5 ♔e7 10 ♔g5 ♔e6 11 f5+! ♔e5 12 f6 ♔e6

and now White can win in various ways, such as 13 ♔g6 or 13 ♔xh5.

Problems

While chess problems make hugely entertaining puzzles, I do not think that they are very useful for improving over-the-board playing strength. However, not everything in life has to be for a strictly practical purpose (if it were, would we be playing chess at all?). From time to time I have set chess puzzle competitions using problems and studies and the response to these has always been very positive. My 2004 Christmas puzzle competition on the ChessBase website, for example, was based on the type of problem known as a 'proof game' (in which you are given the current position on the board and the move number; from this information you have to reconstruct the game). This competition attracted over 2,000 entries and a lot of enthusiastic comment. For problems to appeal to over-the-board players they must not be too complicated or esoteric, and they must only use the normal pieces, board and rules. However, within those limits people seem to be quite willing to try unfamiliar types of problem. In addition to the usual mates in n moves and studies, other types such as helpmates, selfmates, retro-analytical problems and proof games have been well received.

I support the idea of popularizing both problems and studies amongst over-the-board players. I think many players are willing to take an interest in chess composition, but the material has to be presented in a way which appeals to them. Problemists often profess to a desire to popularize their genre, but unfortunately they are sometimes their own worst enemy, since many problemists are unable to discuss problem matters without lapsing into obscure terminology. The curious thing is that although problemists use a lot of jargon, they sometimes can't agree on its precise meaning themselves and argue about whether a problem shows a particular theme or not. Players like light and natural positions, few variations, attractive mates, sacrifices, geometrical effects and paradox; they don't like ugly positions, too many variations and problems which depend on purely formal relationships between moves. They absolutely abhor jargon. At the moment there is a boom in chess problem solving competitions and I hope that these, together with other initiatives, will help chess composition become more popular amongst the wider chess fraternity.

Over the years I have composed a small number of problems, which are given below in chronological order (solutions are on pages 267-9). I am not pretending that these are of 'professional' quality and they were mostly intended for my own amusement, but some were published and a couple even won awards in problem competitions.

Readers may be unfamiliar with some of the problem types presented below, so here is a quick explanation of the terms used. In a **helpmate** both sides cooperate to help White to mate Black. Generally speaking, **Black moves first** in helpmates (in all the other problems White moves first). Thus in a helpmate in two, Black moves, White moves, Black moves and then White mates Black. However, problem number 8 is a helpmate in 3½, which means that there is an extra white move compared to a normal helpmate in 3; thus White moves first, and altogether there are 4 white moves and 3 black moves before White mates Black. Helpmates often have **twins**, in which you have to make a small change in the position and then find a new solution, or **multiple solutions**.

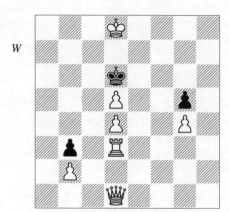

1) White to play and mate in 3
Unpublished, 1984

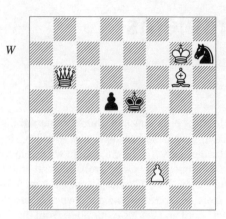

3) White to play and mate in 3
2nd Prize, *British Chess Magazine*, 1984-5

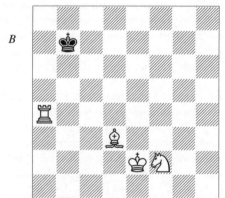

2) Helpmate in 2
Unpublished, 1984
a) Diagram
b) Move the white king to f1

4) Helpmate in 3
Unpublished, 1984
a) Diagram
b) White knight on d3

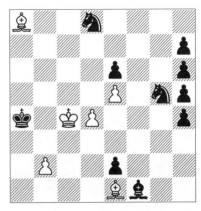

5) Helpmate in 3
British Chess Magazine, 1990
a) Diagram
b) Move the black pawn to e5
c) Move the black pawn to d4

7) White to play and mate in 24
1st Prize, Corner-to-corner Challenge, *The Problemist*, 1991

6) Helpmate in 2
British Chess Magazine, 1991
a) Diagram
b) Bishops become knights
c) Bishops become rooks

8) Helpmate in 3½
4th-6th Honourable Mention, *British Chess Magazine*, 1991
Remember that White moves first and mates Black on his fourth move, with Black's help.

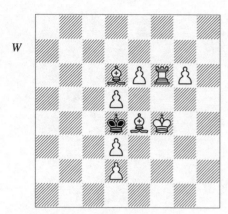

9) White to play and mate in 5
Wedding problem, 1995

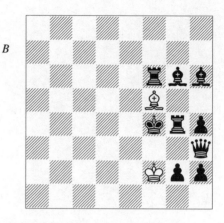

11) Helpmate in 4 (2 solutions)
50th birthday puzzles, 2004

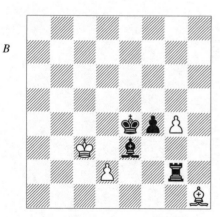

10) Helpmate in 4
British Chess Magazine, 1995

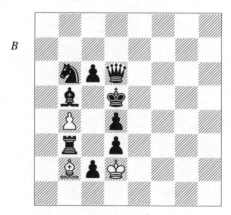

12) Helpmate in 4
50th Birthday puzzles, 2004
a) Diagram
b) Black knight on b4

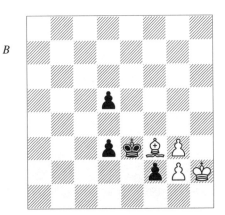

13) Helpmate in 5
The Problemist (supplement), 2005

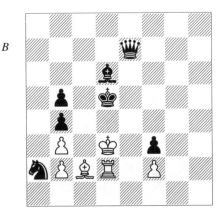

15) Helpmate in 3 (2 solutions)
The Problemist, 2005

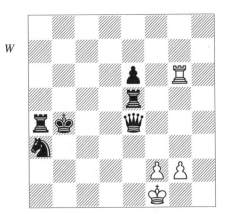

14) Helpmate in 4½
The Problemist (supplement), 2005

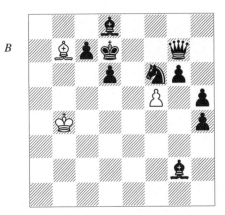

16) Helpmate in 3 (2 solutions)
British Chess Magazine, 2005

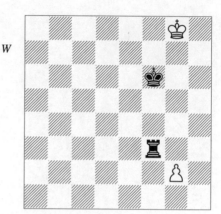

17) Helpmate in 4
The Problemist, 2005
a) Diagram
b) White rook on f5

18) Helpmate in 5½
British Chess Magazine, 2005
a) Diagram
b) Move the white pawn to f2
c) From the diagram, move the white king to h1

Remember that in each part White moves first and mates Black on his sixth move, with Black's help.

Solutions to Problems

1)

If it were Black to move first then it would be easy, because after 1...♔xd5 2 ♔d7 White forces mate: 2...♔c4 3 ♕xb3# or 2...♔e4 3 ♕f3#. However, White has no move which maintains this mate, and he can only succeed with a complete change of plan: **1 ♕c1 ♔xd5 2 ♕c8 ♔d6** (or 2...♔e4 3 ♕f5#) **3 ♕d7#**. Surprisingly, it is White's queen rather than his king which occupies d7 in the solution.

2)

Note that as helpmates generally involve Black moving first, the solution are usually written, for example, 1 B1 W1 2 B2 W2, where B1 and B2 are the black moves and W1 and W2 are the white moves. It looks odd for the move after a move number to be a black move rather than a white one, but this is a standard, albeit rather confusing, convention for writing helpmate solutions.

a) **1 ♗d5 ♖d3 2 ♔e4 ♖f3#**.
b) **1 ♖f7 ♗c3 2 ♔f3 ♗e5#**.

The main idea here is the hesitation moves by the white rook and bishop, which allow Black's king to occupy the mating square.

3)

If it were Black to move then White could mate in two more moves; for example, 1...d4 2 ♕c5+ ♔f4 (2...♔e6 3 ♗f5#) 3 ♕f5# or 1...♔f4 2 ♕e3+ ♔g4 3 ♕g3#. However, White has no waiting move to maintain these variations and so he must give up one of the mates. The solution runs **1 ♕c6** (surprisingly, White also gives the black king access to d4, but this doesn't help Black) and now 1...d4 fails as before to 2 ♕c5+ ♔f4 (2...♔e6 3 ♗f5#) 3 ♕f5#, 1...♔d4 is met by 2 ♗xh7 ♔e5 3 ♕f6# and 1...♔f4 2 ♕c3 is followed by 3 ♕g3#.

4)

Remember that the moves immediately after a move number are moves by Black.

a) **1 ♔c6 ♘g4 2 ♔d5 ♗c4+ 3 ♔e4 ♗e6#**.
b) **1 ♔c6 ♖h4 2 ♔d5 ♘g4 3 ♔e4 ♘e3#**.

In both solutions White must block his own rook to allow Black's king to advance to the fifth rank. In the first solution this is accomplished from the a-file, while in the second solution the rook must play along the whole length of the rank to be shut off from the h-file.

5)

a) **1 ♔f4 ♘e2+ 2 ♔e4 ♔b5 3 ♔d5 ♘f4#**.
b) **1 ♔e6 ♗c3 2 ♔d5 ♖xe5+ 3 ♔c4 ♖c5#**.
c) **1 d3 ♘e2 2 ♔e4 ♘c3+ 3 ♔d4 ♖e4#**.

Nothing special intended here, just some neat mates and various different ways for the black king to cross the e-file.

6)

a) **1 e1♗ ♗a4 2 ♗d2 ♗a3#**.
b) **1 e1♖ ♘d4 2 ♖d1 ♘b3#**.
c) **1 e1♘ ♖d4 2 ♘c2 ♖b1#**.

Swapping the pieces around results in three underpromotions by Black.

7)

This problem was composed specially for a tourney which asked for the maximum possible number of consecutive corner-to-corner moves by a bishop.

Both sides are very restricted in their movements. On White's side, the e1-bishop cannot move due to ...e1♕+, and the a8-bishop can only oscillate between a8 and h1 because the other squares on the long diagonal are covered by Black's pieces. Black also has few reasonable moves. He cannot play ...♗h3 because of ♗b4 followed by b3#, and ...♗g2 is met by ♗xg2 followed by ♗b4 and b3#. The d8-knight cannot move due to ♗c6#, and the g5-knight cannot move due to ♗e4 followed by ♗c2#. Thus Black is reduced to pushing his h-pawns. The solution runs **1 ♗h1 h3 2 ♗a8 h2** (Black can advance his h-pawns in various different ways, for example by 2...h4 here, but the total number of moves required for them to shuffle up the board and give themselves away on h1 is the same whichever order Black adopts) **3 ♗h1 h4 4 ♗a8 h3 5 ♗h1 h5 6 ♗a8 h4 7 ♗h1 h6 8 ♗a8 h1♕ 9 ♗xh1 h2 10 ♗a8 h3 11 ♗h1 h5 12 ♗a8 h1♕ 13 ♗xh1 h2 14 ♗a8 h4 15 ♗h1 h3 16 ♗a8 h1♕ 17 ♗xh1 h2 18 ♗a8** (Black has nearly exhausted his h-pawn tempo moves, and now his aim must be to delay mate for as long as possible; in order to do this he must jettison his pieces in the correct order) **18...♘b7 19 ♗xb7** (after 18 consecutive corner-to-corner moves, White's bishop finally visits a different square) **19...h1♕ 20 ♗xh1 ♗g2 21 ♗xg2 ♘f3** (this move forces a unique reply from White; if instead 21...♘e4, then 22 ♗b4 still works, but White can also play 22 ♗f3 or 22 ♗h1) **22 ♗b4 ♘d2+** (22...♘xd4 may be met by 23 b3+ or 23 ♗c6+, while 22...♘xe5+ 23 dxe5 e1♕ gives White a choice of 24 b3# or 24 ♗c6#) **23 ♗xd2 e1♕ 24 ♗c6#**.

8)

1...♗a1 (remember that this is a **white** move) **2 ♔e5 ♘a4+ 3 ♖d4 ♘b2 4 ♖e4 ♘d3#**. The whole solution is based on White rebuilding his bishop and knight battery one square further away so as to be able to give a double check when Black's king is on e5. Black's king needs to be temporarily shielded during this process, which forces the rook to reach e4 via d4 rather than via e1.

9)

For our wedding invitations, I composed four problems in the form of the letters 'J', 'N', 'P' and 'F'. I still suspect that GM David Norwood failed to show up at the wedding because he didn't care to admit that he couldn't solve the problems (he claimed he had suspected malaria). This is the 'F' problem, which contains a slightly unexpected underpromotion. **1 ♗c7 ♔c5 2 e7 ♔b4 3 ♖b6+ ♔a5 4 e8♖ ♔a4 5 ♖a8#**.

10)

1 ♔e5 d3 2 ♖b2 ♗a8 3 ♖b7 d4+ 4 ♔e4 ♗xb7#. This helpmate also has a corner-to-corner theme. White can't mate with d4 and ♗xg2# because the f-pawn can interpose, so the whole arrangement has to be taken apart

and reassembled in the diagonally opposite corner in order to deliver mate.

11)

I composed two helpmates for the invitations to my 50th birthday blitz tournament, in the shape of the numbers '5' and '0'. The two solutions lead to basically the same mating structure, and in both cases the white bishop must make a switchback away from the h3-c8 diagonal in order to allow Black's king to move to f5. In one solution the bishop moves g4-h5-g4 and in the other h3-g2-h3. The two solutions are:

1 ♕c3 ♗xg4 2 ♕e5 ♗h5 3 ♔f5 ♔f3 4 ♗g5 ♗g4#.

1 ♖g5 ♗xh3 2 ♖e5 ♗xg2 3 ♔f5 ♔f3 4 ♗g5 ♗h3#.

12)

In this problem there is no real link between the two solutions, except that White's bishop must manoeuvre with care in the confined space available.

a) **1 ♖xb4 ♗xd4 2 ♖b2 ♗xb2 3 ♔c5 ♔c3 4 ♕d5 ♗a3#**.

b) **1 ♔c5 ♗a1 2 ♘4d5 ♗c3 3 ♘c4+ ♔xd3 4 ♖b4 ♗xd4#**.

13)

1 f1♕ g4 2 ♕a1 g3 3 ♕e5 ♗h1 4 d4 ♔g2 5 ♔e4 ♔f2#. The bishop retreating into the corner to create a battery is a familiar idea, but here it is slightly disguised by the need to move the two white pawns first. One solver wrote "The main feature of this beautiful near-miniature is the deeply hidden ambush move to the white corner. I like also the far from trivial black play. In short: the overall effect is that of a perfect problem."

14)

1...♖h6 (a white move, remember!) **2 ♖ea5 ♖h2 3 ♕xg2+ ♔e2 4 ♕xf2+ ♔d3 5 ♕c5 ♖b2#**. This helpmate is a puzzle, pure and simple. White's rook has to undertake a mysterious manoeuvre to h2 in preparation for Black's queen to clear away the obstructing pawns. Solvers reacted positively to this problem. One commented "This is absolutely beautiful and way beyond difficult. Now I know how John Nunn's opponents must feel."

15)

The two solutions are very closely related. In each case, a white piece retreats along a battery line to make way for the white king to move off the battery line.

1 &f4 &b1 2 ♕e5 ♔c2+ 3 ♔e4 &d1#.

1 &e5 &d1 2 ♕c5 ♔d2 3 ♔d4 ♔e1#.

Solvers' comments included "A neat idea expertly executed".

16)

Another corner-related geometrical idea. The two bishops on the long diagonal move as far as they can one way or the other in order to set up the mates.

1 ♕e7 &a8 2 &b7 ♔b5 3 &c8 &c6#.

1 &h1 &g2 2 ♘e8 &h3 3 &c6 f6#.

17)

The two solutions are not that closely related, although both feature time-wasting moves by the white king. In one solution there is a neat manoeuvre by the black queen.

a) **1 ♖d5+ ♔e1 2 ♖e5 ♔d2 3 &d5 ♔e2 4 ♕d4 ♘d6#.**

b) **1 ♖f3+ ♔d2 2 ♕g1 ♔xc2 3 ♔e3 ♔c3 4 ♕f2 ♖e5#.**

18)

Three helpmates with very little material.

a) **1...g4** (this is a white move) **2 ♖h3 g5+ 3 ♔f5 g6 4 ♖h6 g7 5 ♔g6 ♔f8 6 ♔h7 g8♕#.**

b) **1...♔f8 2 ♖g3 f4 3 ♔g6 f5+ 4 ♔h7 f6 5 ♔h8 f7 6 ♖g8+ fxg8♕#.**

c) **1...g4 2 ♖f4 g5+ 3 ♔f5 g6 4 ♔g4 g7 5 ♔h3 g8♕ 6 ♖h4 ♕g2#.**

Part 'b' is similar to a previous problem composed by Ebert in 1977 (w♔c8, ♙c2; b♔c6, ♖c5 Helpmate in 5 – the solution runs 1 ♖b5 c4 2 ♔b6 c5+ 3 ♔a7 c6 4 ♔a8 c7 5 ♖b8+ cxb8♕#), although my version is half a move longer. So far as I am aware, the other two parts are original.

The State of the Chess World

I learnt to play chess when I was four years old, and took part in my first tournament when I was seven. Therefore, my tournament career extended over roughly 40 years, of which about half was as a professional player. During this time, chess has changed in many ways, and it is interesting to look back and to assess the current state of the chess world.

In 1966, the level of chess activity in the United Kingdom was probably similar to the present day. There were regular annual congresses, such as Bognor Regis, Ilford and Southend, and a good deal of club and county chess. The British Championship was won by Jonathan Penrose and the US Championship by Bobby Fischer. England finished 21st in the Havana Olympiad. Most of the top English players were either students or amateurs and professional chess activity was almost non-existent; Elo ratings and Batsford chess books still lay in the future.

Over the next several years there was a gradual increase in chess activity in England, and in many other West European countries. The Fischer-Spassky match in 1972 provided a further strong stimulus and by the late 1970s the chess scene had been totally transformed. Weekend Swiss tournaments, often with large prize funds, attracted huge turnouts and strong entries. Club and county chess continued, but the weekend circuit was the real growth area. There was also far more international chess, with Swiss tournaments such as the famous Lloyds Bank event in London providing new opportunities to gain title norms. The English national team was now sponsored and was able to field much stronger teams for events such as Olympiads and European Team Championships.

The 1980s were the golden age for international chess. I turned professional in 1981 and was fortunate to be able to enjoy the whole of this decade. New tournaments and new sponsors enlivened the chess scene and, now that I was devoting all my time to chess, my results gradually improved. There was enough money in the game to support more professional players, and as a result England became one of the leading chess countries. In 1984, 1986 and 1988 the English team finished second to the mighty Soviet Union in Olympiads, and in 1986 even came close to the gold medal. Towards the end of the decade, the GMA ran a series of World Cup tournaments. My best period was 1988-90; I briefly entered the world top ten, finished sixth in the World Cup and won the famous Wijk aan Zee tournament two years in succession.

However, in the 1990s things took a distinct turn for the worse. Firstly, the disintegration of the Soviet Union let loose a flood of strong grandmasters. The available money was suddenly harder to come by, especially as the East European grandmasters, with their low living expenses, were happy to receive fees which wouldn't keep a Western GM going for a week. Unfortunately, this increased competition arose at the same time that the chess world was suffering a general downturn. There is no clear single reason for this decline, but I believe that the Short-Kasparov breakaway in 1993 was a major factor. Up to 1990, there had always been a clear, generally recognized world championship title. The Karpov-Kasparov matches had multi-million dollar prize funds, and attracted a great deal of publicity, both in print media and on television. Kasparov later said that agreeing to the breakaway was one of the worst mistakes of his life. From 1993 up to the time of writing, the chess world has lacked a unified world championship title. Prize funds for 'world championship' matches have plummeted, since sponsors are reluctant to put up a large sum for a match which might not be recognized as a 'real' world championship. Media interest has declined and, with chess receiving less publicity in general, it is harder to attract sponsors for events of all types. Moreover, some of the top players have been unhelpful, preferring to put their own short-term interests above those of chess as a whole (and, indeed, their own long-term interests which would surely benefit if the situation in the 1980s could be restored). Thus the chaos has continued, with a slow but steady decline in top-class chess activity.

The life of the professional chess-player is in many ways quite tough. A great deal of preparation is required to maintain one's playing strength and the lengthy trips away from home are unpleasant if you have a family. Unlike many other sports, where endorsements are common, in chess little income is guaranteed and almost everything you earn depends on prize money won over-the-board. Of course, there are also advantages; you don't have a boss, you can arrange your own schedule and you usually don't have to get up early in the mornings. When you are young it is all a bit of an adventure, flying to one country after another and playing the game you love (presumably you love chess, or why would you be a professional chess-player?). However, as you get older, the negative side starts to become more significant. While you are single a modest income is enough to get by, but if you acquire a family then your finances can become stretched. You may start to wonder what will happen when, as the years go by, your playing strength starts to decline, and what you will do about a pension. The financial side of playing chess is now much less secure than it used to be, except for the absolute top players. Your financial responsibilities do not decrease with age; the uncertain income from playing chess is not a reliable way of paying for a mortgage and the expense of raising children. At one time GMs could count on a decent appearance fee for most events, but the average GM is unlikely to get one these days. Prize money, even without taking inflation into account, has declined. Round-robin events have given way to Swiss tournaments, but here there is more competition and you can be leading the whole way through, only to go home with nothing after a last-round loss. As their years advance, many players turn to chess coaching, writing or journalism, but there is insufficient demand for these activities to accommodate all ageing players. The result is that many players are obliged to continue over the board well past the time when they should have retired. This has led to some tragic cases in which grandmasters have suffered fatal heart attacks or strokes while actually at the board (Gipslis and Bagirov are examples).

My dream was always that chess would become a genuine profession, with a proper 'career path' for talented young players. Without fresh talent entering chess, it will be harder to generate publicity and sponsorship for the game, but chess has to offer a reasonable career; otherwise young players will turn to other things. Perhaps some people have the idea that chess-players are incapable of doing anything else, but this is rarely the case; indeed, grandmasters who have switched to other areas have often been very successful. Ken Rogoff became a professor of economics and worked in a senior position at the International Monetary Fund; William Watson has risen with amazing rapidity to become a partner at Slaughter & May, a leading international law firm; David Norwood is CEO of IP2IPO, a company quoted on the London stock market with a market capitalization of over £300 million; and so on. Why should a talented young player continue with chess when he could be successful in other areas? Love of the game is clearly a prerequisite, but even possessing this, few people are going to sacrifice a successful career in another area for a life of poverty in chess. Clearly one cannot expect that chess will offer as much as a high-flying career in law or business, but it seems to me that it should at least offer the prospect of a moderately successful career. Currently this is only available for the very top players, and at the time when you have to decide on a career, it is rarely possible to be sure that you are going to make it right to the top. Unfortunately, over the last decade chess seems to have moved away from being a genuine profession. Not only is there greater competition for an ever-decreasing cake, but the structure of events has changed for the worse. Increasingly, grandmasters are having to pay all their own expenses to take part in events. One example is the British Championship, in which not only do you have the prospect of working hard for two weeks and going home empty-handed but, since the event is almost always held in a busy seaside resort at the height of the holiday season, you have to pay through the nose in order even to take part.

If the current international chess climate can be described as chilly, that in Britain can be likened to an ice age. Despite isolated positive developments, such as the 4NCL, the number of top-level events has steadily declined year by year. The unfavourable chess climate has had a huge impact on

British chess. Michael Adams and Nigel Short (who lives in Greece) are still essentially full-time professionals, but after that it is hard to find a genuine professional player. Matthew Sadler now works outside the chess world, Julian Hodgson has become a successful chess teacher, I work in chess publishing and Luke McShane is a student at Oxford University. Jon Speelman and Murray Chandler play very occasionally, but spend most of their time working in chess journalism and chess publishing respectively. Further down, many players are involved in chess writing or coaching, or have jobs outside the chess world; few can afford to be chess professionals. The switch away from professional play has had a dramatic impact on team performances. The English men's team finished second in the 1984, 1986 and 1988 Olympiads and third in the 1990 Olympiad. Since then there has been a steady decline, culminating in a miserable 30th place in the 2004 Olympiad.

The near-demise of professional chess in Britain has had an impact throughout the entire system. There are currently few talented young players to take the place of the ageing older generation and those talents that do exist (or their parents!) are wisely keeping their options open as to a choice of career. Of course, one can argue that such players will do more good for the world doing something other than playing a mere game, but I will assume that we are all chess enthusiasts and would like at least some young talents to pursue a chess career and provide us with beautiful games in the future.

Why has the situation in the chess world become so negative? It is easy to say, as many chess administrators do, that the climate for sponsorship is unfavourable. While this might be a factor over short periods, the decline has being going on for so long that the basic reasons must lie elsewhere. Sad to say, I feel that the main reasons lie within the chess world itself. Responsibility for international chess lies largely with FIDE and its president Kirsan Iliumzhinov, who is also president of the republic of Kalmykia. Iliumzhinov is a controversial figure. He is a self-professed friend of Saddam Hussein and has been accused of mismanaging the finances of Kalmykia. This accusation may not be true, but it is hardly surprising that businesses have not exactly been rushing to deal with FIDE and sponsor major chess events. There are always many places a sponsor's money can go, and if there is even a hint of controversy then the money is likely to go elsewhere. Moreover, under Iliumzhinov's leadership, FIDE has made a number of poor decisions which have had a negative impact on chess. I will highlight three here.

The first bad decision was the introduction of the so-called 'FIDE time-limit', which applies to events such as Olympiads and the FIDE world championship. This time-limit involves being given 90 minutes at the start of the game, which is incremented by 30 seconds each time you make a move. The FIDE time-limit is in sharp contrast to what one might call the traditional time-limit of 2 hours for your first 40 moves, 1 hour for the next 20 moves and then half-an-hour for the remaining moves (there may or may not be an increment in this last phase). Generally speaking, games played under the FIDE time-limit last less time than those played under the traditional time-limit, which may or may not be a good thing, but the key difference is that from a certain point on, you are likely to have 30 seconds per move for the remainder of the game. This effectively makes a well-played endgame an impossibility and a quick look through the games played in events using the FIDE time-limit shows the destruction wrought on endgame play. It is indeed a pity to see grandmasters who are undoubtedly capable of playing an excellent endgame having their talents crippled by the need to make a move every 30 seconds. Had Rubinstein, Capablanca and Smyslov been forced to play so quickly, we would have been deprived of many of the endgame masterpieces which have delighted generations of chess players. The endgame is one of the most beautiful parts of chess, and to see it destroyed by FIDE, an organization supposedly devoted to supporting chess, is quite shocking. Most grandmasters dislike the FIDE time-limit and the only benefit is to arbiters, since players are obliged to keep score throughout the game. Unfortunately, arbiters are much better represented in FIDE than players (the lack of genuine representation of players within FIDE is one of the organization's main structural failings). Judging by the number of arbiters who fall asleep during the games, they are not exactly overburdened with duties, and to save themselves one of the few tasks they have to perform, they appear willing to seriously damage the game of chess.

It is quite hard to say what was in FIDE's mind when it introduced this time-limit. FIDE is not noted for giving detailed explanations for its decisions, nor does it offer any criteria which might help establish whether a particular idea has been a success or not. There only seems to have been a vague remark to the effect that a faster time-limit should stimulate media coverage. However, it is hard to see the logic behind this. Even at the FIDE time-limit, a game is likely to last about four hours, far too long for live TV coverage. If coverage has to be edited down in any case, then it doesn't really matter how long the game lasts. Moreover, by eliminating time-scrambles, the FIDE time-limit removes the only visually exciting part of the game. In any case, media coverage of the FIDE world championship has massively declined since the switch to the knock-out format (with FIDE time-limit), so logic would suggest reconsidering this decision. Unfortunately, FIDE does not like reversing a decision and thereby implicitly acknowledging that they have made a mistake.

The second major blunder by FIDE relates to the world championship. The world championship has been in chaos since the Short-Kasparov breakaway in 1993. Despite various attempts at reunification, none has so far succeeded and at time of writing the prospects for a generally recognized world championship title seem remote. The lack of a unified world championship has been hugely damaging for chess. The Karpov-Kasparov clashes which took place in the 1980s attracted a great deal of attention in the press and were well covered on television. The publicity created by these world championship matches was very helpful in raising the profile of chess generally and made it easier for other chess organizers to raise sponsorship.

Unfortunately, FIDE decided to run their world championship on a knock-out basis, with many of the matches involved being of only two games. The result has been to seriously devalue the FIDE world championship. With two-game matches, a single mistake can see a player eliminated from the event and so a large random element is introduced. The top players have by and large avoided the FIDE events, since they can see that their chances of victory are rather small, while the possible risk of an early trip home damaging their reputations is rather high. In the 2004 FIDE championship held in Tripoli, Topalov and Adams were the only players from the world top ten to take part.

The second problem with this system is that many of the matches end in a tie, necessitating a play-off. In the FIDE system, play-offs consist of a series of rapid games. If the ties continue, the games are played at a faster and faster time-limit until a decisive result is achieved. In some rounds, more than 50% of the matches have ended up in a tie-break, so that the event looks more like a rapid chess world championship than one played at a normal time-limit. Some players, believing themselves to be strong rapid players, have deliberately aimed to draw the normal time-limit games and take the match into the rapid games. This is not a recipe for thrilling chess, but one can hardly blame the players for taking advantage of a system which rewards this strategy. The effect of all this has been to produce 'world champions' such as Khalifman, Ponomariov and Kasimdzhanov, strong grandmasters all but hardly worthy successors to the likes of Lasker, Capablanca and Alekhine. Quite what FIDE was hoping to achieve with their world championship structure is far from clear, but if it was hoping that the knock-out format would attract publicity, then the plan has been an abject failure. It is not surprising that, for example, the Akopian-Khalifman 'world championship' final failed to excite people and was accorded little publicity. The FIDE world championship is now viewed as just another tournament on the calendar and its winners gain little in terms of reputation. Far more prestige is accorded to those who win traditional super-tournaments such as Wijk aan Zee and Linares, which are round-robin events played a traditional time-limit. Many players outside the world elite quite like the knock-out format, for precisely the same reasons that the very top players dislike it. Seeing the large element chance plays in the FIDE world championship, they realize that they only need to be lucky in a couple of rapid games, and they are in the big money and have a chance of winning the world title. However, the fact that the event is to a considerable extent a lottery is hardly something to boast about.

I have never been able to understand the attraction of the knock-out system for chess events. The track record of tournaments using this system is rather poor. The Interpolis Tilburg tournament was once one of the top events on the chess calendar. However, one year the organizers decided to switch to a knock-out format. Interest in the event waned, and within a couple of years it had disappeared. Wijk aan Zee toyed with the knock-out format in the 1990s, but fortunately had the good sense to realize their mistake and switch back to the traditional round-robin format. Wijk aan Zee is now regarded as one of the world's leading chess events.

In recent years, FIDE has been struggling with the problem of trying to reunify the world championship. This is admittedly a difficult matter in which one should not hope for rapid success. Moreover, some of the players involved have not been very helpful, apparently preferring the status quo to the risk of putting their reputations on the line. While this may have been the best move for them personally, the continued lack of a unified world championship has seriously damaged chess. If any reunification plan is to be a success, the top players have to be willing to make modest sacrifices for the good of the game. Unfortunately, such superb chess-players are reluctant to make any kind of sacrifice unless they can see a clear-cut payoff for them. However, despite the difficulty of the task, FIDE's behaviour has not been that of a responsible organization. One month it announces a venue and dates for a particular event, at the same time issuing a deadline for all the parties involved to sign, with various threats as to what might happen if they do not. The next month, the venue and dates have been changed, and a new deadline has been issued. The general impression is of bullying and incompetence in equal measure.

Very recently, FIDE has announced a world championship to be held in Argentina using an all-play-all format with the traditional time-limit. This shows good sense and it is to be hoped that the event is a success and helps to re-establish the credibility of the FIDE World Championship.

With the third blunder by FIDE, we move from the unfortunate to the absurd. I am referring to the matter of drug-testing. Physical sports face the problem that there are many drugs which can improve performance, and quite apart from being unfair, the use of such drugs can have a negative long-term impact on a person's health. Therefore most physical sports have a list of banned substances and a testing program, although the details may differ from sport to sport. In the late 1990s, FIDE introduced a drug-testing program for chess, despite the fact that *no drug has ever been shown to improve performance at chess*. Moreover, the list of banned substances was taken from a list for physical sports. Perhaps larger muscles might enable a player to bang the pieces down more firmly, but there is no reason why such drugs should improve mental performance. FIDE's rules for drug-testing have changed with considerable frequency; the current rules are buried in a rather obscure part of the FIDE website (http://www.fide.com/news/download/Annexes/GA2005/Annex_72a(16pages).pdf). Given the number of mix-ups which occur in other sports over drug-testing, even in sports where professional advice is available, one can only feel for the itinerant grandmaster, scraping a living by going from one tournament to another, and now expected to be an expert on pharmacology as well. At one time, FIDE's rules involved the imposition of fines of up to a quarter of a million dollars for a failed test and up to a million dollars for refusing to take a test. That's FIDE's vision for chess: a quarter of a million dollars for taking a cold remedy which can't possibly improve your play. One would have thought that national federations would have had a duty to protect their players from such blatantly unjust regulations, but in fact most of the leading federations were amazingly quiet on the subject. Fortunately, FIDE have now backed away from financial penalties, preferring instead to impose various periods of disqualification (up to a lifetime ban) for different offences. While this might be an improvement over the earlier rules, the prospect of a lifetime ban is serious enough for a professional player. Am I alone in thinking that all sense of proportion has been lost in this matter? In other professions you have to do something really serious before you are disqualified from practising; why should chess-players be disqualified for using a cold cure? Large sums of money are very rarely at stake in chess, and most grandmasters are not followed by hosts of young, adoring fans who might be tempted to indulge in cold cures if their heroes are caught in the act of so doing.

The setting-up of elaborate machinery for drug-testing seems at best to be a huge diversion from the real problems that need addressing in the chess world. At the highest level, the game is relatively 'clean', but at lower levels unethical behaviour is quite common. Players 'throw' games in return for money, ratings are manipulated and tournaments are organized with the express purpose of achieving title norms for certain players. The latest (2005) scam involves the construction of an entire non-existent tournament, together with results and games, tastelessly called the "Memorial Heroes of Chernobyl" tournament. With so many dubious activities going on, an effort to 'clean up' the game is hardly short of issues to tackle. Instead, FIDE have introduced draconian measures to deal with the one thing which isn't a genuine problem in chess: drug abuse. As usual, FIDE have never made it clear exactly what they are hoping to achieve with their drug-testing regime, which at least prevents anyone from pointing out that whatever they were hoping for has failed to materialize. However, it is generally believed that FIDE were hoping that chess might become an Olympic sport. The basis for this hope is unclear, but it seems very unlikely that it will ever come to reality. The IOC (International Olympic Committee) have made it clear that they will not increase the current total of 28 Olympic sports, and that if a new sport is admitted then a current sport must be excluded. For the 2012 Olympics, five sports are under consideration for inclusion (golf, rugby union, squash, karate and roller sports) and three (softball, baseball and modern pentathlon) face a possible axe. All the possible new entrants are physical sports, and there is no reason to suppose that this policy will change in the foreseeable future. Thus the whole drug-testing scheme seems an exercise in futility. Will FIDE change its stance? Based on past experience, not a chance.

At a national level, there may be other considerations. In some countries, government funding is available for sports, and if chess can be classified as a sport, then extra money may be available. Being classified as a sport usually involves implementing drug-testing. The problem here is that it is the federation who benefits from the extra cash, whereas it is the players who have to suffer the inconvenience of drug-testing and the potentially serious consequences if they make a mistake. Federations should therefore only go ahead with such plans after fully consulting with and obtaining the agreement of their leading players, but it seems that this is rarely, if ever, done.

FIDE uses a list of banned substances provided by WADA (World Anti-Doping Agency), but this list is largely irrelevant to chess. There seems to be a tendency for chess organizations to meekly agree to whatever list of drugs is offered, perhaps because it is not the chess administrators who will be tested, but the players. It would be more appropriate if chess organizations argued the case that the list of performance-enhancing drugs should be very different for chess than for physical sports (it might be rather short at present). This will become more important in the future with the potential development of 'cognitive enhancers', drugs designed to improve mental rather than physical performance. At the moment there are drugs which can produce some improvement in idealized memory tests, but it is unclear whether these drugs are beneficial in 'real-world' tasks, which tend to involve multiple mental functions. The question as to whether to ban them extends far beyond the boundaries of the chess world; assuming that such drugs are safe and effective, why should we not take them all the time? It is perhaps more likely that long-term use of cognitive enhancers will have deleterious side-effects, and then testing for such drugs before examinations might become routine. At the moment, however, such questions lie in the future and in any case, as I have mentioned earlier, FIDE drug-testing policy is based on a largely irrelevant list of drugs designed to improve physical performance.

In addition to FIDE, which oversees the international game, there are national chess federations which administer chess in each country. Clearly the performance of these federations is going to vary enormously from country to country, and doubtless some are effective bodies. However, the general impression is that few national federations are successfully promoting chess. National chess federations seem to fall into two main categories: the ineffective ones and those in turmoil due to internal disputes (or, if you are really unlucky, both). Of course, one must recognize that many of these bodies are purely amateur organizations, and any criticism must be tempered by the consideration that those involved are often giving up their time free of charge. However, despite this, I think it is reasonable to say that these bodies often have poor internal structures and are run by people who have little interest in the chess world outside their own federation. When I was at a dinner attended by many leading British grandmasters, one of the GMs commented that "the problem with the British Chess Federation is that it's fundamentally anti-chess", a remark which was greeted by nods of agreement virtually all round. At first I was rather shocked by this, but on thinking about it I could see how one could have this impression. It is remarkable how chess federations are so often riven by disputes; chess is, after all, not a big-money game and it is not as if huge budgets are at stake. As I write, the Indian chess federation is in chaos, while the US Chess Federation seems permanently beset by squabbles of one kind or another.

A common complaint about national chess federations is their secretive nature. This comment certainly applies to the British Chess Federation. In a recent episode, some incorrect results were submitted to FIDE by the International Rating Officer of the British Chess Federation. This affected the Elo ratings of a number of players, with some players receiving a lower rating than they should have done. Clearly this is an important matter for the players concerned, especially if they are professionals, and one would have expected a clear statement from the British Chess Federation explaining what had happened, what steps were being taken to correct the situation, and how they proposed avoiding a similar problem in the future. Instead, the British Chess Federation's main concern seemed to be to hush the whole business up – indeed, even now few players know about what happened. This secrecy is all the more remarkable in that to a large extent, the British Chess Federation is paid for by the players, via the so-called Game Fee. There have been other episodes of unnecessary secrecy over the years, in which the avoidance of embarrassment seemed to figure prominently in the BCF's considerations. One problem with brushing awkward situations under the carpet is that the underlying reasons behind them are never dealt with, which only invites further problems in the future.

The conclusion is that top-level chess is in turmoil, with no recognized world championship and a FIDE which has lost both its direction and the respect of the players. National federations are often ineffective and/or distracted by internal differences. One can only hope that the situation will improve, but at present it looks like a long road ahead.

Chess is not only world championships and grandmasters, but club and youth players as well. How is chess faring at these levels? It is, of course, harder to say, since activities at this level are less well documented, but my impression is that here the picture is altogether happier. As I write, the ChessBase website (www.chessbase.com) is featuring a story about a junior tournament in Nashville, USA, in which an amazing 5,230 players took part. These days one assumes that kids are usually glued to their computers and PlayStations and, if they are playing chess at all, it is likely to be on the Internet. However, face-to-face junior chess seems to be flourishing in many countries. Most of these kids are not hoping to become grandmasters or chess professionals (wisely so, in view of the circumstances described above); they are just playing for fun. At one time chess was considered an eccentric hobby for a child. I feel that chess is now overcoming this stereotyped image and is starting to move from 'nerdish' to 'cool'. This has clearly caught some pundits by surprise. The magazine *Computer Shopper* contains a satirical column called 'Zygote'; the author wrote recently on the subject of violent computer games: "Puzzled and bemused, Zygote turned instead to see what the best-sellers in the adult and PC market have been of late. Surely there would be buckets of gore and xenophobia there. But not a bit of it. At the time of writing, the top five consists of Aquarium Deluxe, Scrabble, Who Wants to Be a Millionaire, a flight simulator and, ahem, chess!". The German company ChessBase has had a series of hits with programs such as *Fritz* (for adults) and *Learn to Play Chess with Fritz and Chesster* (for kids). These programs often feature in general best-selling software lists. Further evidence is that just before Christmas 2004, there were stories in the press about a shortage of chess sets, with stores having to order extra to cope with unprecedented demand.

Internet chess is also a growth area. Checking just now, in the middle of a Monday (European time), which is hardly a peak period, I found 4,407 players logged onto Yahoo chess, 1,199 logged on to the Internet Chess Club and 1,665 logged on to playchess.com. That's over 7,000 people playing chess online right now, at just three of the major sites. The ease of playing chess on the Internet is a great plus for the game; you don't need a powerful PC or a broadband connection to enjoy it, so people from all over the world can participate on an equal basis.

The picture this presents could hardly be a greater contrast to the situation in top-level chess. In my view, development and growth in chess is likely to come from these lower levels. There is a large and increasing body of amateur and youth players who enjoy just playing chess, which must be good for the future of the game. It seems a pity that chess administration is in such a poor state that the professional game is unable to profit from the swell of grass-roots chess activity. In order for this to change, there would have to be sweeping changes throughout the chess world; FIDE would have to restructure and become a more responsible body, with much greater player representation. However, the leading players would also have to play a part by being more willing to make small sacrifices for the long-term future of the game. One day, perhaps, this will all come to pass, but I'm not holding my breath.

Chess Publishing and the Batsford Story

This history of chess publishing is a long one. In 1474, William Caxton published *Game and Playe of the Chesse*, one of the first books to be printed in the English language; since then, chess publishing has gone from strength to strength, at least in terms of the number of titles. It has often been said that more books have been written about chess than about any other sport or game. This might or might not be true, but certainly chess literature is very extensive. Over the last couple of decades, the number of English-language chess books published each year has steadily increased and we are now used to several new titles appearing each month. Yet this abundance is a relatively recent phenomenon. The 1966 *British Chess Magazine* listed new titles each month, and most of these were either non-English-language or simple tournament bulletins containing just games without notes. Many of the English-language titles were reprints, so the number of genuinely new titles was even less than at first sight. Pergamon was one of the few well-known publishers dabbling in chess books, and had a small chess list of about a dozen titles.

The British chess publishing scene was transformed in 1969, when a small London publishing house, B.T. Batsford, took an interest in chess. Batsford had been founded as long ago as 1843, but the revolution was triggered when Bob Wade persuaded the company to move into chess. The first Batsford chess book was *The King's Indian Defence* by Barden, Hartston and Keene, published in early 1969. This was followed later in the year by Hartston on the Benoni and O'Kelly on the Najdorf; the latter book had the odd title *The Sicilian Flank Game* – evidently 'Najdorf' was felt to be too technical to be in the title. The rate at which Batsford produced books increased from year to year and their growing list was heavily focused on openings books.

My first involvement with Batsford was when I wrote *The Pirc for the Tournament Player*, which was published in 1980. Early Batsford books had used English descriptive notation, but by this time they had switched to algebraic notation with figurines, setting a standard which is now virtually universal. Curiously, writing my first book was both easy and difficult. Easy because the amount of information available to the author was, by today's standards, very limited. I made a card index of all the worthwhile games I could collect in the Pirc, taken from *Informator*, *The Chess Player*, tournament bulletins and magazines, amounting to some 750 cards in all. I wrote comments and suggestions on these cards and sorted them according to variation. This method may sound cumbersome, but I soon became quite adept at it and produced all my opening books the same way until the advent of ChessBase computerized the whole procedure. Thanks to the limited number of games, it was possible to devote a reasonable amount of time to each one. The difficult part arose simply from the fact that there were no reasonably-priced word-processors in 1980, and I typed the whole book on a manual typewriter, a method I continued to use until the late 1980s. An author tackling the same subject today would doubtless use ChessBase, but a quick look at my main database reveals 86,005 games in the Pirc or more than 100 times the amount of material available to me in 1980. The fact that the material can be manipulated in various ways by the computer doesn't disguise the basic problem that there is rather a lot of it. Readers today quite reasonably expect more than a ChessBase printout, so authors have to add value to the raw data, which is often a formidable task. Given the heavy dependence on manual methods, it is not surprising that in 1980 there were far more misprints and other basic errors, such as missed transpositions, than there are today.

My first book also introduced me to the economics of chess publishing. It is in fact quite hard to make a profit by publishing a chess book. One of the questions that people always ask is "How many copies does a chess book sell?". It's a difficult question to answer because so many factors are involved. However, if we are talking about a book from a specialist chess publisher, then roughly speaking the publisher would probably be unhappy to sell less than 3,000 copies and happy to sell more than 5,000. Let's deal in 2005 prices and take an imaginary book that has a guide price of £17. Suppose it sells an average 4,000 copies. This gives a theoretical take of £68,000, but the largest cut of this goes to the retailer. By the time the publisher has paid for distribution, sales representation and warehousing, the amount received may be down to £28,000. From this, the publisher has to pay for editing, typesetting, proof-reading, cover design, printing, advertising, review copies and author's royalties. What's left is the profit for that title. However, the publisher will also have various other overheads, such as office and administrative expenses, which must be divided by the number of titles produced each year and subtracted from the now rather diminished profit figure for that title. This gives a more realistic profit figure for the title, but it is only part of the story. Almost all the publisher's expenses occur before the book goes on sale, while the proceeds dribble in over a period of years. Therefore one also has to take into account the lost interest on the capital that has been consumed in producing the book, which serves once again to diminish the profit. The likely result is that the publisher will be left with a profit of at most a couple of thousand pounds for the book. It is highly desirable for everyone concerned, especially the authors, that the publisher does in fact make a profit. The worst thing that can happen, from the author's point of view, is for his publisher to either go bust or pull out of chess. In the first case he may well lose not only all future royalties, but also some past royalties, since these are normally paid annually in arrears. In the second case the author's books may simply wither on the vine as the publisher loses interest in chess and turns to promoting other areas.

In view of the marginal economics, it is natural to ask how specialist chess publishers survive. The answer is that they have to keep a tight control of costs while at the same time producing a large number of books. A couple of thousand pounds profit per book starts to look healthier if you produce 20 or 30 books a year. There is also a question of critical mass. A publisher which has a high profile and produces a regular stream of new titles tends to be more successful than one which produces only a few titles per year. The new titles draw attention to the publisher's whole list, and when a retailer orders copies of a new title, he is quite likely to add in a few orders for older titles as well.

The growth of a thriving chess publishing industry had a positive effect on British chess. In the 1950s and early 1960s, opening theory in Britain consisted of reading *Modern Chess Openings*. When British players had to face East Europeans, with their trainers and thriving chess communities, it was like someone with a child's popgun facing an enemy armed with a machine-gun. By the late 1960s, British chess was already showing signs of improvement, but there is no question that progress was accelerated by the increasing availability of up-to-date opening theory. Moreover, the extra money available from chess publishing made it easier for players to turn professional, which is absolutely essential if one wishes to compete at a high level.

Returning to my dealings with Batsford, *The Pirc for the Tournament Player* was followed by other titles at intervals of between one and two years. As I mentioned, chess publishing is not exactly a pot of gold, but even taking this into account, Batsford were hardly generous with their terms. I quickly discovered how deceptive publisher's contracts can be for a naïve author. My second book was *The Benoni for the Tournament Player*, published in 1982. At that time, author's royalties were generally calculated as a percentage of the retail price and in the case of this book the figure was 10% (these days contracts more often specify the royalty as a percentage of the publisher's receipts). However, the contract for *Benoni* contained the clause "...against a royalty of 10% of the published price on all copies sold at a discount no higher than 50%; on copies sold at a higher discount the royalty will be 10% of the Publisher's proceeds". To someone with little experience of publishing, this doesn't sound too dangerous. At the time it was explained to me that if books were sold to, for example, a book club then they would be sold at a large discount, but the numbers involved would be quite high so I would still receive a reasonable amount. However, on my first royalty statement I was amazed to see the item "USA Bulk – 1524 copies – nett sales value £3048 – royalty £228.60", implying that for these copies I had received just 15p per copy. Since the retail price of the book was £6.95, this meant that my royalty rate was just over 2% for the 1524 copies. When I had been discussing the contract with Batsford, bulk sales to the US at a massive discount had never been mentioned, but it soon became clear that rather than being an exceptional occurrence, such sales were the norm. The reason for these sales was that Batsford had an agreement with a co-publisher in the US to send a large initial shipment in return for a lump sum (rather than a royalty). The co-publisher was taking on a risk, since he had to pay the money whether or not the books were eventually sold, so the sale had to be for a knock-down rate. This was a commercial decision by Batsford to recoup quickly some of the capital costs of producing a book and thereby help their cash-flow, but the effect from the author's point of view was that sales in the US, the world's largest market, provided very little in the way of royalties. As the years went by, the terms of these bulk sales became less and less favourable for authors. The figures for *Beating the Sicilian* (1984) were 1300 books sold for £1976, giving a royalty of £197.60 or 15p per book. For *Secrets of Grandmaster Play* (1987), Batsford sold 2997 books to the US for £4255.74, giving a royalty of £531.97 or 17.7p per book, just under 2% of the UK retail price of the book. A further unfortunate effect of this policy arose because the US retail price for Batsford books was often considerably lower than the UK retail price. This made it worthwhile for dealers to import US books back into the UK and sell them instead of genuine UK copies. The result was that sales on which the author received a derisory royalty were substituted for sales on which the author would have received a standard royalty.

The practical effect of all this was to significantly reduce the amount authors received in royalties to the point where writing a chess book was hardly worthwhile. On top of this, dealing with Batsford became troublesome for other reasons. Initially, production standards at Batsford were acceptable. However, as their output increased and they tried to cut costs, these standards started to slip. A common misconception about Batsford is that they had an extensive 'chess department'. In fact, the chess was always handled by just one person; for many years this was Paul Lamford, who was followed by Ian Kingston, Andrew Kinsman, Graham Burgess, David Cummings and finally Nigel Davies. As Batsford starting producing more and more books, the workload became greater and the 'department' became stretched.

One of the main problems with producing a chess book is finding a typesetter capable of doing the job. Many Batsford chess books were typeset by Graham Hillyard and on one occasion in the 1980s I visited his operation to see what was involved in chess typesetting. By today's standards, it was all amazingly primitive. True, you did type the text at a keyboard and see it on a screen, but there was no WYSIWYG (What You See Is What You Get). Any formatting codes, such as those for bold, italic or change of font, had to be laboriously entered at the keyboard. What you saw on the screen was a stream of text intermingled with a large number of formatting codes. Visualizing what this would all look like on the finished page was a skilled job. Output involved an optical device in which the characters of each font were arranged on a disc through which light shone onto photographic paper. When the operation had been completed, the paper could be developed like a film using chemicals, after which it could be hung up to dry before being sliced into individual pages. From this description, I am sure nobody will be surprised if I comment that typesetting errors were rather common. Nevertheless, Graham Hillyard was definitely one of the best typesetters employed by Batsford. Jon Speelman was unfortunate with his *Analysing the Endgame* (1981), as the typesetter made quite a mess of the diagrams. Jon laboriously wrote the corrections on the proofs, but apparently the typesetter couldn't be bothered to make the changes and so the book appeared with, amongst other horrors, White's entire queenside missing on page 118. On another occasion, a typesetter 'helpfully' ran the text through his spell-checker before starting work; unfortunately, this removed all repeated words, including cases such as '0-0 0-0' and 'exd5 exd5'.

By the late 1980s, I was becoming more and more disillusioned with Batsford. Not only were the financial terms deteriorating, but two episodes in particular caused me to desert Batsford and seek another publisher. The first involved *Najdorf for the Tournament Player* (1989). By now I had acquired a word-processor, which made it far easier to include recent material and I had made a big effort to hand in a book which was really up-to-date. I suggested handing the book in on disc rather than paper, which I believed would save time because the typesetter wouldn't have to type the text in again. However, Batsford refused this offer and I delivered the book on paper. Time passed and, despite frequent enquiries, I didn't hear anything about my book. Finally, a year after I had handed in my up-to-date book, I received the proofs with the comment "It's a bit out-of-date now, so would you mind updating it for us". Actually, I did mind and refused to do anything other than correct errors. Despite this, the book was moderately successful. However, the real horror came with *The Complete Pirc* (1989). For this book, Batsford used a typesetter who apparently knew nothing whatsoever about chess. The result was that the proofs were in a dreadful state, with numerous errors on every page. I eventually counted over 2,000 errors introduced by the typesetter. What was ridiculous about this was that even someone who knows nothing about chess should have realized that a chessboard is square rather than 7x8, as many of the diagrams on the proofs were. This and *The Marshall Attack* (1989, typeset by the same company as *The Complete Pirc*) have more errors than any of my other books. When there are thousands of errors you are bound to miss some, and in making the corrections the typesetter introduced some new errors which I didn't see until the book was printed.

The upshot was that I decided not to write any further books for Batsford, at least for the time being. Seeing Batsford's output of chess books, several other publishers had concluded that there must be money in chess and started up their own chess lists. Therefore it was not hard to make a move away from Batsford, and I signed up my next couple of titles with George Allen & Unwin, a larger publisher. This change had advantages and disadvantages. George Allen & Unwin had higher production standards than Batsford, and my books were properly edited and typeset. Moreover, George Allen & Unwin were able to secure better terms for foreign-language deals than Batsford. However, the fact that nobody at the company knew anything about chess was a bit of a problem. After I had delivered one book, I received a call explaining that it was awkward having the 'boards' (i.e., diagrams) mixed up with the text, and asking whether it would be possible to put them all at the end of the book. The publishers who were attracted to chess at this time probably didn't realize that Batsford were only making a profit from their chess books by cutting quite a lot of corners and by having a large output. When it became obvious that it was hard to make money out of chess books, these other publishers lost interest. In particular, George Allen & Unwin decided not to commission any more chess titles and their chess list was eventually sold to Batsford. As mentioned earlier, a chess list cannot be viable unless the publisher continues to promote it and support it with new titles, so once a publisher loses interest, selling the list to another publisher may be the best solution.

At this time all roads in British chess publishing seemed to lead to Batsford, but changes were afoot which would eventually lead to a more competitive environment. Pergamon were the only other significant chess publisher, but this company had a poor reputation for dealing with authors. In 1991 the head of Pergamon, Robert Maxwell, died in peculiar circumstances. Afterwards it was discovered that he had been illegally raiding his companies' pension funds to support his own lavish lifestyle and give the appearance that his businesses were still in a healthy state. Maxwell's companies collapsed and the assets of Pergamon were sold off. The chess list was bought by a small publisher called Cadogan. Buying a chess list from a bankrupt company can be very profitable. Instead of painfully building up a list over a period of several years, you can obtain the stock and rights to a large number of titles at a stroke. Such assets can often be bought at a knock-down price and, of course, the buyer has avoided paying the bills for actually producing the books. Old debts, such as unpaid royalties, are not passed on to the buyer, who is at most liable to pay royalties on books sold after the transfer. After a series of restructurings, the chess division of Cadogan became what is now Everyman Chess, a major chess publisher best known for Kasparov's *My Great Predecessors* series.

However, in 1992 Batsford were still the dominant force, but in view of the problems I had experienced before I was reluctant to return to them. I was particularly concerned with their typesetting, which had led to so much trouble before. While I had been with George Allen & Unwin, Batsford had changed their typesetting arrangements and now most of their books were being typeset by 'B.B.Enterprises', which turned out to be Byron Jacobs. The fact that Batsford's books were being typeset by a chess-player was certainly a positive step, but unfortunately Byron's system, based on an Atari ST, was rather primitive and the resulting books were quite ugly. The solution which occurred to me was to do my own typesetting. Investigation showed that a reasonably sophisticated system could be set up for a moderate cost in hardware and software. Since by this time the professional chess world was starting to decline, I was happy to create a second source of income by typesetting some Batsford books. The first book I typeset was my own *Secrets of Rook Endings* (1992) and within a couple of years I was quite busy typesetting a fair proportion of Batsford books. When Petra moved to England to live with me in 1994, she quickly picked up typesetting skills, and was soon typesetting Cadogan books under the name 'Chessetter'.

The typesetting business was welcome, and for a time everything ran smoothly. However, Batsford had for several years suffered from financial problems, but now these problems were becoming more serious. Batsford were publishing about 120 books per year, of which 20 were chess books. The chess division was moderately profitable, but some of the other divisions were not. The Batsford management was replaced, and the new management sold the property Batsford owned in London's West End and the company moved to rented premises in Fulham. They also sought to increase their output of chess books, since these were one of the profitable parts of the business. The number of chess books per year climbed towards 30 and the system was starting to show to strain. The 'chess department' still consisted of just one person, at this time Graham Burgess, and he was responsible for general administration, commissioning, editing and proof-reading the vast majority of these titles. My wife and I handled most of the typesetting, but this work was steadily becoming more unpleasant. Not only were Batsford becoming slower and slower to pay for work done but, in their eagerness to recoup money invested in each title, they were insisting on schedules which were tighter and tighter. The result was that a number of all-night sessions became necessary to meet Batsford's deadlines for the handing in of typeset books (irritatingly, the books often then sat on somebody's desk for weeks before moving on to the next stage). Under these circumstances, it is not surprising that very occasional mistakes started to creep in. Batsford's quality control in other areas, such as printing, was also on the way down. Moreover, a number of new bureaucratic demands took up an increasing amount of time. I was dismayed at the way standards were declining, but having no direct say in Batsford's operations I could do no more than express my unhappiness.

The climax came when Raymond Keene proposed to write a series of 12 beginners' books for Batsford, an idea to which the Batsford management was favourably disposed. Graham Burgess, as the Batsford chess editor, was strongly opposed to this plan but apparently this made little difference. I also voiced my opposition, and the result was that a kind of 'dirty war' erupted within Batsford, in which Graham Burgess and I were the main targets. Graham was becoming increasingly disenchanted with his job and it is curious that Batsford went to such lengths to alienate the two people who, by working very long hours for rather modest pay, were keeping the Batsford chess list afloat.

This was the situation when Graham Burgess approached me with the idea of leaving Batsford and setting up a new chess publishing company which would be committed to the high production standards which had become impossible at Batsford. It didn't take long to make my decision. Neither of us had any experience of running a business, so I approached Murray Chandler, who at the time was owner and managing director of the *British Chess Magazine*, to sound him out about the new venture. Murray was enthusiastic, and so in late November 1996 Graham handed in his notice at Batsford. Perhaps belatedly realizing how valuable he was, Batsford started hinting about an improved offer, but to no avail and in February 1997 Gambit Publications was born.

The skills of the three founders proved a good combination. Murray's long experience with running small businesses enabled Gambit to avoid many of the mistakes which often endanger start-up companies, Graham was able to transfer his commissioning and editorial skills from Batsford to Gambit, while I took charge of production and was able to help deal with the technical side of publishing. One of the problems with starting a new publishing company is that it's a long time before any money comes in. It helps if you can buy the stock of a bankrupt publisher, but Gambit has never done this. First of all, you have to commission the books, the authors have to write them, you have to produce and distribute them and finally you might receive some money. This process can take years, which is tough on the cash-flow. Gambit chose a different route to maintain itself while the Gambit chess list was being built up – we started working for other chess publishers. First of all, Gambit offered to manage the production of some Batsford books, from the point at which the author delivered the book to the point at which the typeset book was ready for the printers. All other aspects of book production would remain in Batsford's hands. Perhaps by this stage Batsford were missing Graham's capacity for working long hours – even with the production outsourced, they found it necessary to employ one and a half people to take over his workload. Graham's immediate replacement was David Cummings, who did a good job given the difficult circumstances at Batsford. However, the old Batsford talent for focusing on the really unimportant matters was still evident. On one occasion I was hauled to the Batsford offices to inspect an alleged defect in my diagrams, namely that they were too light. A few months earlier I had received a complaint from someone else at Batsford that the diagrams were too dark, but I had ignored this and left the diagrams exactly as they were. Now the exact opposite was being claimed. While I was thinking that it was hard to please some people, David Cummings proudly gave me a copy of a book I had edited, *Richard Réti's Best Games* (by Harry Golombek), which had just arrived from the printer. I pointed out that they had spelt the author's name 'Harry Golmbek' on the front cover. David Cummings, who did not come from a publishing background, had assumed that if you hand a cover designer a disc containing the cover text, it will come out correctly. Needless to say, the books went out with 'Golmbek' on the cover.

Batsford's financial woes continued. Gambit had more and more difficulty getting paid for the work done under the outsourcing arrangement, and Gambit had to threaten to sue Batsford. In view of these problems, Gambit stopped doing work for Batsford, which turned out to be a very good move. The authors were not so lucky; despite the increasingly ominous signs from Batsford, there was nothing they could do other than hope for the best. The authors' royalties, which had been paid later and later each year, stopped completely in 1998. I sent a series of increasingly irritated letters to Batsford, starting in late 1998 and running into 1999, concerning royalties unpaid from 1st January 1998. Advances and foreign-rights payments had also ceased. Occasionally, Batsford would pay some small item, but far more slowly than new unpaid royalties mounted up. In the summer of 1999, Graham Burgess and I went to a lawyer to see what could be done about recovering the unpaid sums. It immediately became obvious that this would not be a straightforward matter under English law. If someone owes you £1,000, then you just go to court and sue him for the £1,000; the problem in our case was that the amount Batsford owed in royalties was unknown. It wasn't that Batsford had sent royalty statements but no money; they simply hadn't sent any royalty statements at all. Therefore the effort had to be a two-stage process; first force Batsford to hand over the information enabling the royalties to be calculated, and then, when the figures were known, try to get the money. Batsford claimed that they did not have the figures enabling the royalties to be calculated. A meeting was arranged at Batsford on July 26, 1999, attended by Graham and myself, to try to make progress in resolving the issue. It soon became apparent that Batsford's records were in a mess. Their distributors, Bailey's, had recently installed a new computer system which had suffered from a number of glitches. The result was that the sales information supplied by Bailey's to Batsford was rather chaotic and some parts were missing entirely. Batsford had made little or no attempt to resolve these problems and obtain accurate sales data, thereby providing themselves with a ready-made excuse for not calculating or paying the royalties. Records of advances were available on one computer but not another, while the foreign rights sales for 1998 had apparently vanished into a black hole. Eventually, Batsford agreed to pay a limited amount, which appeared to be progress. The only problem was that the cheque had to be signed by the Chairman, Gerry Mizrahi, and he was not present (at least this was a better excuse than a previous one offered by Batsford, that they had simply run out of cheques). Graham and I hung around the Batsford offices for a time, waiting for the appearance of Mr Mizrahi, but in the end we gave up. Indeed, Mr Mizrahi probably had other matters on his mind because shortly after, with the cheque still unpaid, Batsford went into receivership.

This had a considerable impact on Batsford's chess authors, who were owed about 18 months of royalties, advances and foreign rights sales. The receiver (an official who administers insolvent companies) produced a statement showing that Batsford's debts exceeded three million pounds, while their assets amounted to only about a quarter of a million. Ironically, the printing company that actually put Batsford into receivership ended up with nothing, because in a receivership the taxman and the banks get the first bite at the assets; after they had eaten their fill there was nothing left, either for the printers or the authors. In absolute terms, I probably lost more from the collapse than any other Batsford chess author, because I had so many books in print with them; the total was undoubtedly several thousand pounds, although owing to the messy records I never knew the exact figure. However, I at least had other sources of income and could withstand the shock; some of the other authors were more seriously affected. The receiver very quickly sold the stock and rights of the Batsford chess list to Chrysalis, a large media company which had a book publishing arm. Chrysalis had no obligation to pay the missing royalties to the authors and they did not do so, although to be fair Chrysalis have paid royalties for all copies sold after they acquired the stock from the receiver. Chrysalis retained the Batsford name, and have continued to run the Batsford chess list right up to the present day. Many people have contacted me about my Batsford chess books since 1999, and have been surprised when I directed them to Chrysalis; apparently the story of the Batsford insolvency is not widely known. It was an inglorious end to more than a century and a half of publishing history, and thirty years of chess publishing.

In the meantime, Gambit had entered into an arrangement with Cadogan similar to, but more extensive than, its earlier arrangement with Batsford. This involved commissioning books for Cadogan and taking them all the way through to printed copies. However, this arrangement lasted only for a relatively short time and since 2000 Gambit has focused solely on its own books. The situation in British chess publishing has remained the same for the last few years; there are three major publishers, Gambit, Everyman and Chrysalis/Batsford, with occasional chess books being produced by publishers outside the big three.

That brings us up to date and I would like to end by answering a couple of common questions regarding chess books. I am often asked 'Why are chess books so expensive?'. But are they? I have explained earlier how most chess books offer only marginal profitability. Occasionally there is a best-seller, which certainly helps, but I doubt if any chess publisher is making excessive profits. As Pergamon and Batsford authors will testify, it doesn't help anybody if a publisher goes bankrupt. If chess books don't offer a decent return on the capital invested, the publisher will either run into financial difficulties or simply stop producing chess books; either situation is very bad for the authors. Chess is a specialized area and the sales of chess books don't justify bargain-basement prices. It is perhaps interesting to compare the price of chess books with that of another specialized area I am slightly familiar with, undergraduate mathematics textbooks. When I was an undergraduate I used *Lebesgue Integration & Measure* by Weir (Cambridge University Press, 1973). This is a pretty good book on Lebesgue integration and is still used today; it costs £23.99 (all prices taken from amazon.co.uk) for 293 pages which are a tiny bit larger than Gambit's A5 size. Gambit's *Nimzo-Indian: 4 e3* by Carsten Hansen is 320 pages and so has roughly the same text area as Weir's book; it costs £12.81 on Amazon. An old classic such as Hardy and Wright's

An Introduction to the Theory of Numbers (Oxford University Press, 1938; revised in 1979) is £28.50 for 452 pages. *Fundamental Chess Endings* by Müller and Lamprecht, with 384 rather larger pages, is £13.99. Some of my old textbooks are still available, but only on a 'print-on-demand' basis. These have much higher prices; for example, *Topics In Algebra* by Herstein (originally Blaisdell, 1964; the currently available edition is from John Wiley & Sons, 1975) is £68.50 for 400 pages. Moreover, mathematics at the undergraduate level is fairly static, so books such as Weir's can go on selling for decades with only the most minor changes. Chess books, especially openings books, have a limited lifetime and the publisher must recover his costs within that period. Comparing the potential market between chess and undergraduate mathematics is of course very difficult, but my basic point is that chess books do not appear expensive when compared to other specialized areas.

Another common question is 'If the books were cheaper, wouldn't you sell more copies?'. Of course, this applies to any item, not only chess books, but not surprisingly few things are given away almost for free. Setting a price for a chess book is a tricky business and there is a certain amount of guesswork involved. Publishers are generally quite keen to keep prices as low as possible, but of course they expect to make a profit out of each book, so there is a limit to how far prices can be reduced. In the extreme case, if the publisher's revenue per copy was below the cost of production (and remember that the publisher's revenue is less than half the retail price), selling more copies would only result in increased losses! There are economies of scale if you have larger print-runs, but these economies are less than one might expect. It is also very risky to have a large initial print-run, because if demand is less than expected you can easily make a huge loss. Even large publishers can get this type of decision spectacularly wrong. In 1999, the well-known publisher Dorling Kindersley (often known as just 'DK') printed 13 million *Star Wars* books, but only sold 3 million of them. The unsold books caused a £3 million loss on operations and a £14 million write-off against the unsold stock. The *Star Wars* fiasco so weakened DK that it had to offer itself for sale, and in 2000 it was bought by Pearson. A small specialist chess publisher can't afford to make large losses on a title and is likely to exercise caution regarding print-run decisions.

I hope that this short chapter has given readers some insight into the ups and downs of chess publishing. I find the world of chess books quite interesting and now that I have retired from over-the-board play, I am happy to have found work which keeps me in contact with the wonderful game of chess.

Index of Nunn's Opponents

Numbers refer to pages. When a page number appears in **bold**, it indicates that Nunn had White in that game.

Index of Openings

Other books from Grandmaster John Nunn

Understanding Chess Move by Move
The classic bestseller – 30 top-level games are dissected, with every move explained.
240 pages, 248 mm x 172 mm
$19.95/£14.99

John Nunn's Chess Puzzle Book
For players looking to test themselves to the limit – probably the toughest chess puzzle book on the planet.
208 pages, 210 mm by 145 mm
$19.95/£13.99

Endgame Challenge
Magic, mystery, and truly amazing chess studies – admire the solutions or try to solve them if you dare!
256 pages, 248 mm by 172 mm
$24.95/£17.99

Secrets of Pawnless Endings
Summarises the correct strategy for all important endgames where no pawns remain on the board.
384 pages, 210 mm by 145 mm
$19.95/£14.99

Secrets of Practical Chess
This acclaimed guide may be the most important book a competitive player will ever read. Discover how to make the most of your own talents!
176 pages, 210 mm by 145 mm
$19.95/£14.99

101 Brilliant Chess Miniatures
Games of stunning quality, won or lost between top players in 25 moves or fewer.
176 pages, 210 mm by 145 mm
$19.95/£13.99

Secrets of Rook Endings
Rook endings occur frequently – be prepared! The definitive coverage of the endgame rook vs rook & pawn.
352 pages, 210 mm by 145 mm
$19.95/£14.99

Solving in Style
The beauty and ingenuity of chess problems can help you to find startling tactical solutions in your own games.
248 pages, 210 mm by 145 mm
$17.95/£12.99

Learn Chess
This lucid guide assumes no prior knowledge of chess, and will take a complete beginner to club-player level.
192 pages, 198 mm by 130 mm
$9.95/£7.99

Learn Chess Tactics
If you are good at tactics, you will win more chess games. Here Nunn teaches all the standard tactical motifs that masters use.
160 pages, 248 mm by 172 mm
$19.95/£12.99

About the Publisher – Gambit's mission is simple: to publish great chess books, which can be enjoyed and understood by players of all levels. Our company is 100% owned and run by expert chessplayers. Our reputation for originality and unrivalled editorial standards is important to us. If we get a great manuscript by a little-known author, we will publish it. If we get a great manuscript by a famous author, well, we celebrate! Chess is our passion.

 **www.gambitbooks.com**